D1927894

Tolley's Charity Administration Handbook

Second Edition

by

Don Bawtree
and
Kate Kirkland
of
BDO Stoy Hayward

Tolley Publishing

Published by
Butterworths Tolley
2 Addiscombe Road
Croydon Surrey CR9 5AF England
020-8686 9141

Typeset in Great Britain by
Tradespools Limited
Frome, Somerset

Printed in Great Britain by
Butler & Tanner Ltd, Frome and London

ISBN 0 75450 268-6

About the authors

Don Bawtree

Don Bawtree qualified as a chartered accountant in 1983. He joined BDO Stoy Hayward in April 1996 as a specialist charity audit and accounting partner within the Charities Unit. He has acted for a wide range of charity clients.

Don lectures on charity accounting issues and is a regular contributor for the press. He is the author of the NGO Finance SORP Compliance Checklist. He is regularly involved with the Charity Commission on auditing and accounting issues, and has provided training for them. He is trustee and treasurer of several local charities.

Don is Chair of the Institute of Chartered Accountants' (ICA) Charity courses, and a Technical referee for ICA sponsored charity research. He was also a Member of a Home Office practitioners' working party implementing *Charities Act 1993 Part VI.*

Kate Kirkland

Kate Kirkland joined BDO Stoy Hayward as Director — Charity Unit in April 1995. She was formerly head of the Trustee Services Unit at the National Council for Voluntary Organisations where she earned a reputation as a leading authority on charity governance. Kate edited *The Good Trustee Guide*, a major reference work, and co-authored *Building on Trust: A Study of Charity Trustees* with Professor Naomi Sargent. She has also provided advice and trustee training for a large number of organisations. She was a member of the Charity Commission's Advisory Group on Trusteeship and she continues to maintain close links with the Charity Commission.

Kate has an honours degree in economics and operational research and a diploma in the management of voluntary organisations. Her previous work experience spans local government, charity fund-raising, further education and business management. Since joining BDO Stoy Hayward her clients have included Guide Dogs for the Blind Association, NCH Action for Children, the Sue Ryder Foundation, Save the Children, the Gardeners' Royal Benevolent Society and the Royal Agricultural Benevolent Institution.

Kate was a trustee of Oxfam for nine years and is currently a trustee of the Family Welfare Association and the Ashoka Trust.

About this book

Background

Running a charity is very like running a growing business. Each leap forward means having to take on board more legislation or regulations. Ignorance is no defence but how is the busy manager to know that their new idea has legal or fiscal implications?

Many charity administrators bring business skills into their first voluntary sector job. They understand accounts, VAT and human resource management. But what happens if they fail to appreciate that charities operate in a different regulatory framework to businesses, or that that framework has itself changed radically in the last few years?

The administration of charities is becoming more and more complicated. The voluntary sector environment has become more competitive, more charities are chasing less money, with fewer staff and volunteers. There are more sources of funding with the creation of the National Lottery, new European programmes, and a greater commitment from the commercial sector to community involvement. There is more information to access, be it on line, from independent magazines, umbrella bodies or regulators.

This book provides a first point of reference for the charity administrator, especially in relation to finance and charity administration matters. It covers a wide range of topics from accounts to the new regulations for commercial participators, from PAYE administration to uniform business rates. The second edition includes updated sections on the revised SORP, the new Getting Britain Giving proposals and the *Human Rights Act 1998*. To some questions it will give the complete answer, to others it will act as a signpost pointing you in the right direction where you can obtain the information that you need.

Inevitably there will be some who think some sections are too brief, and others who feel that some sections are too long or irrelevant. We hope that where a section is not directly relevant to your situation you may still find the information useful in broadening your understanding of issues faced by others in the sector. Either way any comments or suggestions for improving on the coverage or content would be taken in the spirit in which they are intended!

It is worth noting that Scottish charities are subject to their own regime and the Charity Commission applies to England and Wales only. However, it would have been tedious to the reader if we had made this point every time we referred to the Charity Commission. Generally the information covered is similar for Scottish charities but it is worth referring to Chapter 101 on Scotland.

At BDO Stoy Hayward we aim to take a holistic approach to our clients, to understand their activities as widely as we can, and help them achieve their mission. This requires our team to have a wide understanding of many issues, and so we are grateful to many members of the charity unit for their help and advice in putting this book together. Special thanks must go to Tony Austin for the tax chapters. Others who made a contribution include Edward Finch, Tim Buss from our VAT department, Peter Robinson and Barbara Gourley from our Business Systems Advice team, Peter Copp from Business Recovery Services and Geoff Smith from our RSL team. We must also thank Charity Appointments and our indefatigable assistants Ian Allsop and Catherine Bourg for their contribution to research, typing and re-typing!

Don Bawtree and Kate Kirkland

Contents

Contents

Table of Statutes

Table of Statutes

Table of Statutory Instruments

1947/2662	House to House Collections Regulations	88.1, 88.4
	reg 6	
	(1)(13)	88.7
1974/140	Charitable Collections (Transitional Provisions) Order	88.2
1981/1794	Transfer of Undertakings (Protection of Employees) Regulations	39.20, 39.22, 39.23, 39.47, 81.18, 109.12
1984/565	Public Charitable Collections (Scotland) Regulations	68.15, 101.28
1985/1204	Betting, Gaming, Lotteries and Amusements (Northern Ireland) Order	
	arts 133, 155	28.4
1991/2825	Food Premises (Registration) Regulations	5.12
1992/3004	Workplace (Health, Safety and Welfare) Regulations	105.11
1992/2165	Charities Accounts (Scotland) Regulations	101.14, 101.17, 101.19, 116.13
1992/2335	Charities (Receiver and Manager) Regulations	70.19
1992/2355	Charities (Misleading Names) Regulations	94.7
1992/2980	Charities (Quantity Surveyors' Reports) Regulations	6.18
1992/3288	Package Travel, Package Holidays and Package Tours Regulations	50.29
1993/1624	Charities (Exemption from Accounting Requirements) (Scotland) Regulations	101.20
1993/2254	Public Trusts (Reorganisation) (Scotland) (No 2) Regulations	4.19, 35.7, 35.8
1993/2774	Charities (Designated Religious Bodies) (Scotland) Order	15.15, 44.10, 101.13
1993/3222	Exempt Entertainments (Variation of Monetary Limit) Order	79.7
1994/3024	Charitable Institutions (Fundraising) Regulations	108.10
1995/2056	Charities (Dormant Accounts) (Scotland) Regulations	101.11
1995/2092	Companies (Summary Financial Statement) Regulations	3.4
1995/2724	Charities (Accounts and Reports) Regulations	1.11, 2.2, 9.2, 115.1
	reg 5	1.4
	Pt III	107.8
1996/180	Charities (Exemption from Registration) Regulations	44.5, 95.5
1998/1833	Working Time Regulations	39.28
1999/1925	Collective Redundancies and Transfer of Undertakings (Protection of Employment) (Amendment) Regulations	39.47
1999/3242	Management of Health and Safety at Work Regulations	109.13
1999/3312	Maternity and Parental Leave etc Regulations	39.29
2000/1551	Part-time Workers (Prevention of Less Favourable Treatment) Regulations	39.36
1999/740	Industrial and Provident Societies (Fees) Regulations	62.3
1999/2093	Telecommunications (Data Protection and Privacy) Regulations	30.22, 30.25
1998/3170	Telecommunications (Data Protection and Privacy) (Direct Marketing) Regulations	30.1
1999/1994	VAT (Sports, Sports Competitions and Physical Education) Order	46.42
2000/2868	Charities (Accounts and Reports) Regulations	2.2, 2.15, 2.17, 2.18

Table of Cases

Useful Addresses

Action with Communities in Rural England (ACRE)
Somerford Court
Somerford Road
Cirencester
Gloucestershire
GL7 1TW
tel: (01285) 653477
fax: (01285) 654537
www.acreciro.demon.co.uk

Advisory, Conciliation and Arbitration Service (ACAS)
Head Office
Brandon House
180 Borough High Street
London
SE1 1LW
tel: (020) 7210 3613
fax: (020) 7210 3645
www.acas.org.uk

Almshouse Association (The)
Billingbear Lodge
Carters Hill
Wokingham
Berkshire
RG40 5RU
tel: (01344) 452922
fax: (01344) 862062
www.almshouses.org

Arts Council of England
14 Great Peter Street
London
SW1P 3NQ
tel: (020) 7312 0123
fax: (020) 7973 6590
www.artscouncil.org.uk

Arts Council of Northern Ireland
77 Malone Road
Belfast
BT9 6AQ
tel: (028) 90 667 000
www.artscouncil-ni.org

Useful Addresses

Arts Council of Wales
Holst House
9 Museum Place
Cardiff
CF1 3NX
tel: (029) 20 376 500
www.ccc-acw.org.uk

Association of Charitable Foundations (ACF)
2 Plough Yard
London
EC2 3LP
tel: (020) 7422 8600
www.acf.org.uk

Association of Charitable Officers
Beechwood House
Willyotts Close
Potters Bar
Herts
EN6 2HN
tel: (01707) 651777
fax: (01707) 660477

Association of Chief Executives of Voluntary Organisations (ACEVO)
Middlesex House
130 College Road
Harrow
Middlesex
HA1 1BQ
tel: (020) 8424 2334
fax: (020) 8426 0055
www.acevo.org.uk

British Quality Foundation (The)
32–34 Great Peter Street
London SW1P 2QX
tel: (020) 7654 5000
fax: (020) 7654 5001
www.quality-foundation.co.uk

British Standards Institution
389 Chiswick High Road
London W4 AL
tel: (020) 8996 7327
fax: (020) 8996 7400
www.bsi.org.uk

Business in the Community
44 Baker Street
London
W1M 1DH
tel: 0870 600 2482
fax: (020) 7486 1700
www.bitc.org.uk

Charities Advisory Trust
Radius Works
Back Lane
Hampstead
London
NW3 1HL
tel: (020) 7435 6523
fax: (020) 7431 3739

Charities Aid Foundation (CAF)
Kings Hill
West Malling
Kent
ME19 4TA
tel: (01732) 520 000
fax: (01732) 520 001
www.cafonline.org

Charities Evaluation Services
4 Coldbath Square
London
EC1R 5HL
tel: (020) 7713 5722
fax: (020) 7713 5692

Charities Tax Reform Group (CTRG)
12 Little College Street
London
SW1P 3SH
tel: (020) 7222 1265
fax: (020) 7222 1250

Charity Commission for England and Wales
Harmsworth House
13–15 Bouverie Street
London
EC4Y 8DP
tel: 0870 333 0123
fax: (020) 7674 2300
www.charity-commission.gov.uk

Second Floor
20 Kings Parade
Queens Dock
Liverpool
L3 4DQ
tel: 0870 333 0123
fax: (0151) 703 1555
www.charity-commission.gov.uk

Woodfield House
Tangier
Taunton
Somerset
TA1 4BL
tel: 0870 333 0123
fax: (01823) 345003
www.charity-commission.gov.uk

Charity Finance Directors Group
Camelford House
87–89 Albert Embankment
London
SE1 7TP
tel: (020) 7793 1400
fax: (020) 7793 1600
www.cfdg.org.uk

Charity Law Association
c/o Speechly Beecham
6 St Andrew's Street
London
EC4A 3LX
tel: (020) 7353 3290

Commission for Racial Equality
Elliot House
10–12 Allington Street
London
SW1E 5EH
tel: (020) 7828 7022
fax: (020) 7630 7605
www.cre.gov.uk

Community Foundation Network
2 Plough Yard
London
EC2 3LP
tel: (020) 7422 8611
fax: (020) 7422 8616

Community Matters
8–9 Upper Street
London
N1 0PQ
tel: (020) 7226 0189
fax: (020) 7354 9570
www.communitymatters.org.uk

Community Network
2nd Floor
50 Studd Street
London
N1 0QP
tel: (020) 7359 4594
fax: (020) 7704 6471
www.community-network.org

Companies House (Registrar of Companies)
Crown Way
Cardiff
CF4 3UZ
tel: (01222) 388588
fax: (01222) 380900
www.companieshouse.gov.uk

Directory of Social Change
24 Stephenson Way
London
NW1 2DP
tel: (020) 7209 4949
fax: (020) 7209 4130
www.dsc.org.uk

Disability Rights Commission
Freepost MID 02164
Stratford-upon-Avon
CV37 9BR
tel: 08457 622 633
fax: (08457) 778 878
www.drc-gb.org

English Sports Council
PO Box 649
London
WC1H 0QP
tel: 0345 649649
www.english.sports.gov.uk

Equal Opportunities Commission
Arndale House
Arndale Centre
Manchester
M4 3EQ
tel: (0161) 833 9244
fax: (0161) 835 8312
www.eoc.org.uk

Ethical Investment Research Service (EIRIS)
80–84 Bondway
London
SW8 1SF
tel: (020) 7840 5700
www.eiris.org.uk

Useful Addresses

Heritage Lottery Fund
7 Holbein Place
London
SW1W 8NR
tel: (020) 7591 6000
www.hlf.org.uk

Housing Corporation (The)
London
W1P 0BN
tel: (020) 7393 2000
fax: (020) 7393 2111
www.housingcorp.gov.uk

Independent Complaints Reviewer to the Charity Commission
Newspaper House
8–16 Great New Street
New Street Square
London
EC4A 3EU
tel: (020) 7583 1172
fax: (020) 7583 1173
www.icrev.demon.co.uk/lcrbook.htm

Industrial Common Ownership Movement (ICOM)
115 Hamstead Road
Birmingham
B20 2BT
tel: (0121) 523 6886
fax: (0121) 554 7117
www.icof.co.uk

Inland Revenue Charities

England, Wales and Northern Ireland

St John's House
Merton Road
Bootle
Merseyside
L69 9BB
tel: (0151) 472 6000
fax: (0151) 472 6004
www.inlandrevenue.gov.uk

Scotland

Trinity Park House
South Trinity Road
Edinburgh
EH5 3SD
tel: (0131) 551 8217
fax: (0131) 552 0746
www.inlandrevenue.gov.uk

Institute of Charity Fundraising Managers (ICFM)
208 Market Towers
Nine Elms Lane
London
SW8 5NQ
tel: (020) 7627 3436
fax: (020) 7627 3508
www.icfm.org.uk

Institute of Chartered Accountants in England & Wales
Moorgate Place
London
EC2 2BJ
tel: (020) 7920 8100
fax: (020) 7920 0547
www.icaew.org.uk

Institute of Chartered Accountants of Scotland
21 Haymarket Yards
Edinburgh
EH12 5BH
tel: (0131) 347 0100
fax: (0131) 347 0105
www.icas.org.uk

InterChange Legal Advisory Service
InterChange Studios
Dalby Street
London
NW5 3NQ
tel: (020) 7284 0530
fax: (020) 7482 5292
www.interchange.org.uk

Investors in People UK
4th Floor
7–10 Chandos Street
London W1M 9DE
tel: (020) 7467 1900
fax: (020) 7636 2386
www.IIPuk.co.uk

Law Society of Scotland
26 Drumsheugh Gardens
Edinburgh
EH3 7YR
tel: (0131) 226 7411
fax: (0131) 225 2934
www.lawscot.org.uk

Useful Addresses

Legislation Monitoring Service for Charities
12 Little College Street
London
SW1P 3SH
tel: (020) 7222 1265
fax: (020) 7222 1250
www.charitynet.org/~lmsc

Millennium Commission
Portland House
Stag Place
London
SW1E 5EZ
tel: (020) 7880 2030
www.culture.gov.uk

National Association of Councils for Voluntary Service (NACVS)
3rd Floor
Arundel Court
177 Arundel Street
Sheffield
S1 2NU
tel: (0114) 278 6636
fax: (0114) 278 7004
www.nacvs.org.uk

National Association of Volunteer Bureaux
New Oxford House
16 Waterloo Street
Birmingham
B2 5UG
tel: (0121) 633 4555
fax: (0121) 633 4043
www.navb.org.uk

National Centre for Volunteering
Regent's Wharf
8 All Saints Street
London
N1 9RL
tel: (020) 7520 8900
fax: (020) 7520 8910
www.volunteering.org.uk

National Council for Voluntary Organisations (NCVO)
Regent's Wharf
8 All Saints Street
London
N1 9RL
tel: (020) 7713 6161
fax: (020) 7713 6300
www.ncvo-vol.org.uk

National Housing Federation (NHF)
175 Gray's Inn Road
London
WC1X 8UP
tel: (020) 7278 6571
fax: (020) 7833 8323
www.housing.org.uk

National Lottery Charities Board (NLCB)
St Vincent House
Suffolk Street
London
SW1Y 4NL
tel: (020) 7747 5300
www.nlcb.org.uk

New Opportunities Fund
Heron House
322 High Holborn
London
WC1V 7PW
tel: 0845 0000 121
www.nof.org.uk

Northern Ireland Council for Voluntary Action
61 Duncalm Gardens
Belfast
BT15 2GB
tel: (028) 9087 7777
fax: (028) 9087 7799
www.nicva.org

Official Custodian for Charities
Office of the Parliamentary Commissioner for Administration
Millbank Tower
London
SW1P 4QP
tel: 0845 015 4033
fax: (020) 7217 4160

Registry of Friendly Societies
Victory House
30–34 Kingsway
London
WC2B 6ES
tel: (020) 7663 5276
fax: (020) 7269 9806
www.companies-house.gov.uk/notes/friendly_socs

Scottish Arts Council
12 Manor Place
Edinburgh
EH3 7DD
tel: (0131) 240 2443
www.sac.org.uk

Useful Addresses

Scottish Charities Office
25 Chambers Street
Edinburgh
EH1 1LA
tel: (0131) 226 2626
fax: (0131) 226 691

Scottish Council for Voluntary Organisations (SCVO)
18–19 Claremont Crescent
Edinburgh
EH7 4QD
tel: (0131) 556 3882
fax: (0131) 556 0279
www.scvo.org.uk

Scottish Homes
Thistle House
91 Haymarket Terrace
Edinburgh
Midlothian
EH12 5HE
tel: (0131) 313 0044
www.scot-homes.gov.uk

Scottish Sports Council
Caledonia House
South Gyle
Edinburgh
EH12 9DQ
tel: (0131) 339 9000

Sports Council for Wales
Sophia Gardens
Cardiff
CF1 9SW
tel: (029) 20 300 500
www.sports-council-wales.co.uk

Sports Council of Northern Ireland
House of Sport
2a Upper Malone Road
Belfast
BT9 5LA
tel: (028) 90 381 222
www.sportni.org

Tai Cwmru/Housing for Wales
25–30 Lambourne Crescent
Llanishen
Cardiff
CF4 5ZJ
tel: (029) 20 825 111
fax: (029) 20 826 989
www.tc-hfw.gov.uk

United Kingdom Accreditation Service
21–47 High Street
Feltham
Middlesex TW13 4UN
tel: (020) 8917 8400
fax: (020) 8917 8500
www.ukas.com

Wales Council for Voluntary Action
Llys Hor
Crescent Road
Caerphilly
Mid Glamorgan
CF8 1XL
tel: (029) 20 855 100
fax: (029) 20 855 101
www.wcva.org.uk

Other Useful Websites

Local Government Information Unit
www.lgiu.gov.uk

Scottish Local Government Information Unit
www.slgiu.gov.uk

HM Customs & Excise
www.hmce.gov.uk

HM Treasury
www.hm-treasury.gov.uk

Open Government Charities
www.open.gov.uk/index/t_charities.htm

UK Fundraising Information for Charities
www.fundraising.co.uk/index.html

Abbreviations

CDF	Common Deposit Fund
CIF	Common Investment Fund
DDA 1995	Disability Discrimination Act 1995
DfEE	Department for Education and Employment
DTI	Department of Trade and Industry
ELM	External Lottery Manager
ESF	European Social Fund
FICO	Financial and Intermediaries Claims Office
FRS	Financial Reporting Standard
HAG	Housing Association Grant
ICTA 1988	Income and Corporation Tax Act 1988
IMRO	Investment Management Regulatory Office
IPS	Industrial and Provident Society
LRMPSA 1990	Law Reform (Miscellaneous Provisions) (Scotland) Act 1990
NDPB	Non-departmental Public Body
OMVEU-RHA	Open Market Value for Existing Use by Registered Housing Association
PAYE	Pay As You Earn
RSL	Registered Social Landlord
SOFA	Statement of Financial Activities
SORP	Statement of Recommended Practice
SSAP	Statement of Standard Accounting Practice
TEC	Training and Enterprise
TUPE	Transfer of Undertakings (Protection of Employment)
VATA 1994	Value Added Tax Act 1994

1 Accounting Reference Dates and Periods

1.1 Accounts for all charities, except those too small to be registered, have to be prepared in line with a timetable determined by law. The relevant legislation varies, however, according to the charity's legal structure, whether or not it is registered, the registering or regulating body and its location.

1.2 The *Charities Act 1992* introduced the concept of a financial year for unincorporated registered charities (the parts relating to accounts are now consolidated into the *Charities Act 1993*). Prior to the passing of the Act those charities were required to prepare accounts for consecutive periods not exceeding fifteen months.

1.3 A charity's financial year-end is known as its Accounting Reference Date (ARD), and the financial period running up to that date is known as the Accounting Reference Period (ARP).

Unincorporated registered charities

1.4 *Paragraph 5* of the *Charities (Accounts and Reports) Regulations 1995* sets out how a charity's first financial year should be determined.

- *Unincorporated registered charities formed on or after 1 March 1996*

  The first financial 'year' of an unincorporated charity (such as a trust or association) formed on or after 1 March 1996 runs from the date of the charity's formation to a date, chosen by the trustees as the Accounting Reference Date, or a date within seven days either side of the Accounting Reference Date. The Accounting Reference Date is determined by the trustees and must be at least six, but no more than eighteen months after the date the charity was established. There is no requirement to file a separate form recording this date with the Charity Commission (for English and Welsh charities) or the Inland Revenue (for Scottish charities).

- *Unincorporated registered charities formed before 1 March 1996*

  The first financial 'year' of an unincorporated charity formed before 1 March 1996, is generally the accounting period starting on the day immediately following the end of the period for which the charity was required to prepare accounts under previous legislation and ending on its Accounting Reference Date, or a date within seven days either side of the Accounting Reference Date. The Accounting Reference Date for the first financial year must be not less than six months nor more than eighteen months after the date on which the financial year began.

1.5 Subsequent financial years of a charity begin with the day immediately following the end of the charity's previous financial year and end on its Accounting Reference Date, or a date determined by the trustees within seven days either side of the Accounting Reference Date.

Charitable companies registered with the Charity Commission

1.6 Companies automatically have their first year-end, i.e. their Accounting Reference Date, as the last day of the month which is twelve months from their incorporation date. This may be altered by the directors (i.e. the charity trustees) selecting another date, and filing the relevant form (form 225) with Companies House.

1.7 The permitted duration of accounting periods, and rules governing their changes, are the same as for unincorporated charities, although the legislation is set out in the *Companies Act 1985 ss 224* and *225*. One important difference, however, is that the *Companies Act 1985* permits the lengthening or shortening of the accounting period during the original period. The *Charities Act 1993* is silent on this matter.

Other types of charity

Excepted charities

1.8 Excepted charities should comply with the Regulations for registered charities unless other legislation applies.

Exempt charities

1.9 Unless other legislation or other legal obligation exists, exempt charities are required to make up consecutive statements of account relating to a period of not more than fifteen months. [*Charities Act 1993 s 46*].

Industrial and Provident Societies

1.10 All industrial and provident societies must choose a year-end between 31 August and 31 January, unless the Registrar of Friendly Societies has granted permission for the use of another date. [*Industrial and Provident Societies Act 1965 s 39*].

Amending the Accounting Reference Date

1.11 Accounts can always be made up to a date within seven days either side of the Accounting Reference Date in order to facilitate the production of accounts based on a 52 week year, rather than on a calendar year. References to 'year' and 'twelve months' in the *Charities (Accounts and Reports) Regulations 1995* allow for this minor variation, as do the *Companies Act 1985* and the *Law Reform (Miscellaneous Provisions) (Scotland) Act 1990 s 15 (LRMPSA 1990)*.

1.12 After the Accounting Reference Date has been set for the first financial year, the trustees of unincorporated charities can choose to amend it to a date between six and eighteen months of the previous Accounting Reference Date if there are exceptional reasons. The regulations only permit such a change of year-end if the previous two accounting periods were for twelve months. The reasons for a change in the Accounting Reference Date will need to be disclosed in the accounts of any charity required to prepare accruals accounts.

1.13 *Section 225* of the *Companies Act 1985* contains similar provisions for amending the Accounting Reference Date. However, although the maximum length of an extended accounting period is the same, i.e. eighteen months, the *Companies Act 1985* does not specify a minimum length of time for shortened accounting periods. Also, the minimum length of time which must pass before a company's Accounting Reference Date can subsequently be altered is five years, in contrast to the two permitted for unincorporated charities, although exceptions are permitted to bring subsidiary company year-ends into line with those of their parent undertaking.

2 Accounts: General Requirements

Charities Act Regulations

2.1 There has long been a general requirement for all charities based in the United Kingdom to maintain accounting records and to produce sets of accounts on a regular basis. However, in order to improve the quality of charity accounts and to establish procedures for charities to report to the Charity Commission on a regular basis, allowing the Commission to exercise its duty to monitor charities, a new accounting and reporting regime for charities came into effect on 1 March 1996.

2.2 The regime implemented the changes introduced in the *Charities Act 1992* (now consolidated into *Charities Act 1993*) requiring most charities to send annual accounts, an annual report and an annual return to the Charity Commission and to have their accounts scrutinised by a registered auditor or an independent examiner. Under the Act trustees were also obliged to supply copies of the charity's accounts to the public upon request. The *Charities (Accounts and Reports) Regulations 1995 (SI 1995 No 2724)* and *2000 (SI 2000 No 2868)* set out the requirements for the form and content of a charity's accounts and annual report, the duties of the auditor or independent examiner and the form of the auditor's or independent examiner's report.

2.3 Unincorporated registered charities are obliged to comply with the Regulations in relation to the format of their accounts. Charitable companies should seek to comply with the Regulations as far as is practicable. In some instances, however, the format of their annual accounts will be prescribed by other recommendations or requirements.

SORP

2.4 In addition to these changes the Statement of Recommended Practice on Accounting by Charities (SORP) was issued in 1995 and updated in 2000. It applies to all charities in the United Kingdom regardless of whether they are incorporated or unincorporated, unless another SORP, such as the one for housing associations, applies. Although there is no statutory requirement for charities to comply with the SORP, the Charity Commission expects charities to model their accounts on it and would require a charity to justify the reasons for any non-compliance. The Regulations which are obligatory for unincorporated charities, draw heavily upon the SORP and in a limited number of instances make direct reference to the SORP.

Scotland

2.5 Most Scottish charities have to follow regulations set out in the *LRMPSA 1990*, as well as the SORP.

Allowance for size

2.6 An accounting regime suitable for large charities would be inappropriate for many others — 67 per cent of charities have an annual income of less than £10,000. Therefore the detailed requirements of the new regime are graduated according to the size of the charity, as shown in Table 1. Charitable companies must produce annual reports and accounts and send them to the Charity Commission, together with an annual return, and must follow the requirements set out in the *Companies Act 1985* for the form of the report and accounts and the type of scrutiny required.

2.6 Accounts: General Requirements

Table 1 *Charities Act 1993* **requirements for unincorporated charities**

Size	**Type of Accounts**	**Annual Report**	**Scrutiny**	**Annual Report and Accounts**	**Charity Commission Annual Return**
Up to **£10k** annual income or expenditure	Receipts and Payments or Accruals accounts	Simplified	None routinely required	Charity Commission may request	Simple
More than **£10k** income or expenditure but not more than **£100k** income	Receipts and Payments (plus Statement of Assets and Liabilities) or Accruals accounts	Simplified	Independent examination or audit	Must be sent to the Charity Commission	Full
More than **£100k** income but not more than **£250k** income or expenditure in the current year or in either of the preceding two years	Accruals accounts	Simplified	Independent examination or audit	Must be sent to the Charity Commission	Full
More than **£250k** income or expenditure in the current year or in either of the two preceding years	Accruals accounts	Full	Audit	Must be sent to the Charity Commission	Full

Filing with the Charity Commission

2.7 Trustees of registered charities in England and Wales with income or expenditure in excess of £10,000 must file the charity's statutory annual accounts and annual report with the Charity Commission within ten months of the charity's financial year-end. [*Charities Act 1993 s 45*]. If the charity's income and expenditure is below £10,000 the annual report and accounts need only to be filed on request. [*Charities Act 1993 s 45(3A)*].

Standard of record keeping

2.8 The standards to which the books of account should be maintained is defined by law, although the sort of accounting records (i.e. cash books or computerised records) is not legally defined. *Charities Act 1993 s 41* requires trustees of unincorporated charities to keep accounting records which:

- can disclose at any time, with reasonable accuracy, the charity's financial position;
- will enable the trustees to prepare accounts which comply with the annual charity accounting requirements;
- are sufficient to show and explain all the charity's financial transactions; and
- record the charity's assets and liabilities.

2.9 The requirements for charities regulated by the *Companies Act 1985*, the *Industrial and Provident Societies Act 1968* or the *LRMPSA 1990* are not significantly different.

2.10 The accounting records should contain entries from day to day showing income and expenditure and recording the acquisition of assets and liabilities. This does not mean that the accounting records have to be written up on a daily basis. A sensible target is to produce a trial balance once a month. It will not always be practicable to include accounting data from diverse operations, such as local volunteer groups, on such a regular basis.

Retention of records

2.11 *Section 41* of the *Charities Act 1993* requires unincorporated charities to keep accounting records for at least six years from the end of the financial year in which they are made (i.e. for seven years). This requirement differs from requirements of *s 222* of the *Companies Act 1985* which stipulate that records of private companies must be retained for three years (charitable companies are private, rather than public, companies). However, as the Inland Revenue can make adjustments to PAYE deductions going back six years and VAT inquiries may also go back six years, all charities would be well advised to keep financial records for at least seven years.

2.12 Financial records include:

- books of account;
- minutes of meetings authorising expenditure;
- other authorisations of expenditure;
- documentation relating to the verification of the receipt of income;
- documentation relating to the verification of expenditure;
- bank statements; and
- records of assets and liabilities.

2.13 Accounts: General Requirements

2.13 Claims under the *Consumer Protection Act 1987* can go back ten years, so it is advisable to keep records of the purchase or sale of major goods for at least that length of time.

Accruals or receipts and payments accounts

2.14 Depending on their size, or the requirements of their governing document or funders, some charities are required to prepare accounts on an accruals basis. Those that are not required to do so may choose between preparing them on an accruals basis or a receipts and payments basis.

2.15 Accrual accounts give a true and fair view of an organisation's financial affairs as they show all transactions affecting the accounting period, whether or not they are represented as a cash transaction, i.e. monthly accounts would show an amount equivalent to one-twelfth of, for example, an annual payment for rent. Charities preparing accounts on an accruals basis should follow the format recommended by the

Table 2 Accounts requirements

Type of Charity	Accounts requirement
Charitable company registered in UK	*Companies Act 1985* layout, amended for the Charities SORP
Unincorporated charities registered in England or Wales with income over £100,000	*Charities Act 1993 s 42* and *Charities (Accounts and Reports) Regulations 2000*, broadly requiring compliance with the Charities SORP
Unincorporated charities registered in England or Wales with income equal to or less than £100,000	*Charities Act 1993 s 42* permits receipts and payments accounts to be prepared, otherwise accruals accounts in accordance with the Charities SORP
Industrial and provident societies	Revenue account and balance sheet required under the *Industrial and Provident Societies Act 1965 s 39*
Other exempt charities	*Charities Act 1993 s 46(1)* requires an income and expenditure account and a balance sheet in the absence of any other requirement, complying with the Charities SORP
Scottish unincorporated charities with gross receipts over £25,000	*LRMPSA 1990* and regulations, broadly requiring compliance with the SORP
Scottish unincorporated charities with gross receipts of not more than £25,000	*LRMPSA 1990* permits receipts and payments accounts to be prepared

Statement of Recommended Practice on Accounting for Charities (SORP) unless another SORP applies.

2.16 Receipts and payment accounts are a factual record summarising all the cash transactions made during the relevant period and listing the charity's remaining cash and non-cash assets and its liabilities. Accounting standards do not generally apply to such accounts, because they do not purport to give a true and fair view of either the financial activities for the year or the state of affairs at the year-end. The Charity Commission has issued a guide, 'Accounting for the Smaller Charity' for charities preparing annual accounts on the receipts and payment basis.

2.17 Table 2 on page 6 sets out the main accounts requirements for different types of charity.

2.18 The audit requirement also affects the presentation of year-end accounts. Audited accounts must show a true and fair view of the state of the charity's financial affairs. Therefore, most charities seek to comply with the SORP as a matter of best practice and as a means of ensuring compliance with the *Charities (Accounts and Reports) Regulations 2000.*

2.19 The formats for the accounts of some charities are not governed, however, by the charities SORP but by recommendations or regulations that are more specific to a particular type of organisation, as shown in Table 3.

Table 3 Accounts requirements for particular types of charity

Type of charity	Requirement
Housing associations/Registered Social Landlords (RSLs)	Accounts prepared in accordance with the Accounting Requirements for Registered Social Landlords General Determination 1997 & 1998 and the SORP for RSLs, issued in March 1999
Universities	Accruals accounts prepared under the Higher Education SORP
Common Investment Funds/Common Deposit Funds	Accruals accounts prepared in accordance with *Charities Act 1993 Accounting Regulations 2 Sch* and the SORP for Unit Trusts
Non-departmental public bodies	Accounts prepared in accordance with HM Treasury guidance, supplemented by Charities SORP

2.20 Accounts: General Requirements

2.20 In addition excepted charities, especially denominational churches, have modified accounting requirements under their own rules. These broadly follow the requirements of the Charities SORP but reference should be made to each particular set of rules.

Audit requirement

2.21 Most charities will be required to have their annual accounts audited or otherwise subjected to some form of external scrutiny. For unincorporated charities this scrutiny will be in the form of an independent examination or an audit, whereas charitable and other limited companies will be required to have an audit or an exemption report. Industrial and provident societies have similar audit requirements to limited companies under *Industrial and Provident Societies Act 1968 s 3*.

2.22 The Charity Commissioners have powers under *ss 43 (4)–(6)* of the *Charities Act 1993* to make an order requiring the audit of accounts, e.g. if audited accounts have not been produced within ten months of the end of the relevant financial year or if the Commissioners consider it desirable to have a full audit of accounts that have been independently examined. In certain circumstances the trustees can be jointly and severally liable for the cost of such an audit.

Public right to see accounts

2.23 The *Charities Act 1993* requires the trustees of all charities in England and Wales to send a copy of the charity's most recent accounts to any member of the public who requests a copy in writing, within two months of the request. [*Charities Act 1993 s 47 (2)*]. Failure to do so may result, on conviction, in a fine. The trustees may charge a reasonable fee in respect of the cost of complying with such a request. [*Charities Act 1993 s 47(2)(b)*].

3 Accounts: Summary Financial Information

Summary accounts

3.1 The Charities SORP refers to summary accounts as 'statements which summarise financial information based on the full financial statements'. The SORP encompasses a wide range of summary information and creates a two-tier approach, depending on the exact nature and content of the summary.

3.2 Confusion abounds regarding summary accounts, for a number of reasons. Firstly terminology is muddled, secondly the relevant legislation is in different places, thirdly no one document provides all the answers, and fourthly no one seems to mind if mistakes are made!

Terminology

3.3 Statutory accounts are well defined by the SORP, legislation and accounting standards. Management accounts are not governed by any regulatory framework, as they are produced for internal use by management and trustees. Summary accounts are rarely produced for public consumption, except by charities and public companies.

3.4 The *Companies Act 1985* distinguishes between summary accounts and non-statutory accounts. The legislation relating to summary accounts is contained in *SI 1995 No 2092*, a section that relates only to public companies and thus does not apply to charitable companies. However, the sections relating to non-statutory accounts apply to all companies including charitable companies. This distinction between summary accounts and non-statutory accounts is probably more helpful than the terminology used by the SORP. Charities sometimes include their full (or almost full) annual accounts in a document, before they have been audited and approved by the trustees. The SORP usually refers to such accounts as summary financial statements, as opposed to summary financial information.

Legislation applying to unincorporated charities in England and Wales

3.5 Whenever the full audited accounts are provided, the auditor's report and the annual report should also be attached.

3.6 Whenever accounts contain less information than the full audited statutory accounts the trustees must decide whether they form a summarised financial statement or summary financial information. Summarised financial statements are usually closer to the full accounts than is summary financial information. Although it is impossible to provide a precise distinction, Table 4 sets out some of the characteristics of summarised financial statements and summary financial information, based on the SORP and the Companies Act. In many cases it will be a matter of judgement as to which term is correct.

3.7 Accounts: Summary Financial Information

Table 4 Characteristics indicating the status of accounts

Characteristics of summarised financial statements	**Characteristics of summary financial information**
Derived from a set of full (annual) accounts, whether or not audited/ examined	May be based on mid-year or early draft figures
Includes information on the SOFA and the balance sheet	May refer only to parts of either the SOFA or the balance sheet
Represents an account in any form purporting to be a balance sheet or SOFA	Makes no reference to the balance sheet or SOFA
May represent all the charity, or just a branch	Represents just part of the activities of the charity.

3.7 If trustees are still not sure whether the information represents a summarised financial statement or summary financial information, then a good test is to ask whether or not the information is intended as a substitute for the full accounts (i.e. do you expect members to vote on the annual accounts relying more on the summary information than the full accounts, as often happens?).

3.8 Once the status of the information has been determined the trustees must append the appropriate signed statement to the accounts, encompassing the SORP's requirements. A summarised financial statement would be accompanied by the following statement with the words in italics being amended as necessary:

> 'These summary financial statements are not the statutory accounts, but a summary relating to both the Statement of Financial Activities and the balance sheet. The full financial statements, from which the summary is derived have/*have not* been audited. The audit report was unqualified/*qualified/contained an emphasis of matter—further details are provided in the summary statements. This summary is for the branch only, and has been extracted from the full accounts of ''name of main charity''*. The full accounts, annual report and auditor's report may be obtained from (insert address). The annual report and accounts, which were approved on (insert date), have/*have not* been filed with the Charity Commission.
>
> Signed on behalf of the trustees...'

3.9 References to 'audit' should be amended to 'examination' or 'independent examination' as necessary. Only registered charities need to refer to the filing requirement.

3.10 Summarised financial information should be accompanied by a statement such as

> 'This summarised information is provided in order to (state purpose, e.g. assist readers' understanding of the costs incurred in running the project). This information is/*is not* derived from the charity's full accounts, *which have/have*

not been audited. The most recent full accounts, annual report and auditor's report may be obtained from (insert address).

Signed on behalf of the trustees...'

3.11 If the full accounts have been audited or examined then the auditor or examiner should attach a statement to summary financial statements giving an opinion as to whether or not the summary financial statements are consistent with the full annual accounts.

Auditor's/Examiner's statement

3.12 The auditors' statement for unincorporated charities is prescribed in the Audit Practice Board's Note 11. It sets out the addressee, the respective responsibilities of the trustees and auditors, the basis of the opinion and the opinion itself which should state whether or not the summary accounts are consistent with the annual accounts. If they are inconsistent, then such inconsistencies must be set out and explained.

3.13 No such specimen wording has been issued in respect of independent examiners or reporting accountants. However, the SORP requires that their report should follow the same principles as the auditor's statement, including an opinion as to the consistency of the figures.

3.14 Unless agreed as a special assignment, auditors would not report on summary information and any further allusion to the audit report may attract deeper credibility to the information than is, in fact, justified.

Charitable companies

3.15 Charitable companies should follow the above principles but, in addition, the *Companies Act 1985* requires them to state whether or not the relevant statutory accounts have been filed with the Registrar of Companies.

3.16 The *Companies Act 1985* specifically prohibits publication of an audit report or reporting accountant's report with non-statutory accounts.

3.17 Although the SORP states that charitable companies can produce summary financial statements without the backing of an audit report, Practice Note 11 states that 'where auditors are requested to report on additional summary financial statements published by a charitable company, they should take account of the guidance set out in relation ... to unincorporated charities and the requirements of the Companies Act.' In other words, there is no legal requirement to follow the SORP's recommendations, but it is good practice to do so.

Industrial and Provident Societies

3.18 There is no specific reference in the legislation to summary information, and so the SORP guidance should be followed.

Scottish charities

3.19 Scottish charities should follow all of the above except for the references to the Charity Commission.

3.20 Accounts: Summary Financial Information

Inconsistencies

3.20 If the auditors consider that there are inconsistencies, then they will refer to this matter in their report to the trustees. If the auditors are not satisfied with the nature of the trustees' statement they will not permit any report they have produced for the trustees to be published.

3.21 The summarised accounts should be consistent with the full accounts. This means that information has been accurately extracted from the full accounts and has been summarised in a way that is not unduly selective. Other information which may be necessary to ensure consistency (for instance a post-balance sheet event) or which is fundamental to understanding the figures should also be included.

Communicating financial information with graphics

3.22 When producing summary accounts many charities make the information more accessible by presenting it in diagrammatic form. The key advantages of using graphics to portray financial information are as follows:

- assessment of the financial position is easier;
- relationships between sets of data are portrayed more effectively;
- essential elements are communicated faster;
- the presentation has visual appeal.

3.23 However, certain factors can make diagrammatic presentations worse than useless: mismatched scales, poor selection of data, and lack of accompanying narrative can all create a misleading impression.

3.24 Graphs, bar charts, and scatter or radar diagrams, can be used to depict relationships and trends. Pie charts are best for illustrating the breakdown of a constituent whole but less suitable for illustrating absolute growth or decline. They cannot reflect the components of, for instance, a balance sheet which includes negative items. In this instance either a vertical or horizontal bar chart would be more effective. Bar charts can also be used to reflect key ratios, such as the proportion of expenditure going on direct charitable support in comparison with total expenditure.

4 Advertising

4.1 Charities advertise in a variety of circumstances, such as:

- fund-raising;
- campaigning;
- publicising a Charity Commission Scheme;
- recruiting staff, volunteers or trustees; and
- communicating other needs, e.g. raising profile or letting premises.

In some cases it will be necessary to obtain specialist advice as the amount of legislation governing the topic is substantial and complex.

4.2 Advertisements may be promoted through different media i.e.:

- newspapers and magazines;
- posters and flyers;
- radio and television;
- products, such as carrier bags, tee shirts, etc.; and
- the internet.

Codes of practice

4.3 The Advertising Standards Authority (ASA), which supervises the advertising industry's system of self regulation, produces the British Codes of Advertising and Sales Promotion, which apply to all advertisements on non-broadcast media including those in newspapers, magazines, posters on the Internet, CD-ROM, computer and video games. Charities advertising in any of these media should therefore apply the standards set out in these Codes.

4.4 These Codes state that advertisements should be legal, decent, honest and truthful, and be prepared responsibly. They also refer to the principles of fair competition in business, which is of less relevance to charities. Copies of the Codes are available from the Advertising Standards Association and are published on the ASA website, together with details of the Authority's recent adjudications. Investigated complaints about advertisements are widely publicised, and often make headline news: the greatest risk to an organisation which infringes the Code is therefore the loss of public goodwill, although in extreme cases a complaint can result in a court injunction.

4.5 Advertisements broadcast on radio or television should comply with the Radio Authority Code of Advertising Standards and Practice or the Independent Television Commission's Code of Advertising Standards and Practice. These Codes are augmented by a ten point charter published by the Broadcast Appeals Consortium, and endorsed by the major TV and radio companies. Special rules also apply to publicity produced by voluntary organisations with local authority funding: more information can be obtained from the Local Government Information Unit.

4.6 Advertising

Requirement to state registered status

4.6 A registered charity, if its gross income in its last financial year exceeded £10,000 (formerly £5,000), is required under the *Charities Act 1993 s 5* to state in English (or Welsh in the case of a Welsh charity) the fact that it is a registered charity in all advertisements, notices, and other documents issued by or on behalf of the charity and soliciting money or other property for the benefit of the charity. This applies whether the solicitation is express or implied, and whether the money or other property is to be given for any consideration or not. The charity's registered number does not need to be stated, though it is common practice to do so. Any trustee or staff member who authorises such an advertisement which fails to state that the charity is a registered charity is guilty of an offence and liable on summary conviction to a fine. In practice it is prudent for any registered charity, notwithstanding its current level of income, to comply with this requirement. Excepted charities that are not voluntarily registered must not state that they are a (registered) charity. Exempt charities may state that they are a charity exempt from registration and give their Inland Revenue number. Note that this legislation does not apply to Scottish charities.

4.7 The use of the internet, home pages and web sites is largely unregulated at the time of writing. Charities should seek to apply the same standards when using this medium as they would using any other.

VAT on advertising

4.8 Charities both provide and purchase advertising. The VAT treatment of advertisements is different in each circumstance.

Advertising provided by a charity

4.9 The selling of advertising space to commercial organisations is always regarded as a business activity. Normally any advertising would be regarded as a standard-rated taxable supply by the charity. As a concession, where at least half of the total number of advertisements in each publication is clearly from private individuals, then all the advertisement income can be treated as donations, and is therefore outside the scope of VAT. Customs, in their guidance, quote the example of a private advertisement being 'Good wishes from John and Susan Smith', which is contrasted with a business advert including as the same wording from 'John and Susan Smith, Grocers, 49 High Street'. Should the number of private advertisements amount to less than half the total, then all the income is regarded as consideration for a supply. The standard rate of VAT will apply except where the supply is made:

- to another charity and is eligible for zero rating (see 4.10);
- in connection with an exempt fund-raising activity;
- to a person who does not 'belong' in the EU; or
- to a person who 'belongs' in a different EU Member State in connection with the business activity.

Advertising purchased by a charity

4.10 Prior to 1 April 2000, advertising purchased by charities qualified for zero rating only if it was for fund-raising purposes or for making known the objects, or reasons for the objects, of the charity. [*VAT Act 1994 8 Sch Group 15 item 8*]. However, from 1 April 2000 all types of advertising purchased by a charity qualify for zero rating, including advertisements on television, cinema, billboards, buses, in newspapers, programmes, annuals, leaflets and other publications, and on Internet sites belonging to third parties.

4.11 Marketing and advertising of items to targeted individuals or groups are excluded from zero-rate relief. Customs state this exclusion includes telesales and direct mail by post or e-mail. However, certain items addressed to targeted individuals or groups will be zero-rated because of the relief granted to pre-printed fund-raising appeals and by the general relief available on certain items of printed matter.

4.12 Relief is also extended, by concession, to goods used by charities in connection with collecting monetary donations. There are three specific goods that qualify:

- certain printed stationery;
- collection boxes; and
- lapel stickers and similar tokens.

4.13 Pre-printed appeal letters, return envelopes and collecting envelopes continue to qualify for zero rating. The concession also applies to all kinds of collecting boxes and receptacles used for collecting money. The relief for lapel stickers and similar tokens extends to small items designed to be worn on clothing, such as paper stickers, ribbons, metal pins and badges, that are given freely in acknowlegment of a donation. It does not extend to clothing (of any material), mugs or similar commemorative items, Christmas cards or calendars.

4.14 Where an advertisement is carried by television, radio or cinema, the zero rate applies only to the cost of the broadcasting or screening of the advertisement, not to the cost of making it. This is in contrast to advertisements in printed media where design and preparation costs for artwork, typesetting, etc., that are closely linked to the production of a qualifying printed media advertisement are zero-rated.

4.15 To obtain zero rating, the charity will need to give the supplier a declaration in the approved format. If this has been overlooked, it is possible to correct the position subsequently.

4.16 In addition to the specific reliefs listed above, zero rating also applies to printed matter generally: therefore it will sometimes be possible for charities to obtain VAT relief on non-qualifying advertisements through an alternative route, perhaps as a leaflet, pamphlet or brochure. Zero rating is considered in more detail in Chapter 121.

Tax on income from advertising

4.17 Since the sale of goods or services constitutes a trade, it follows that the provision of advertising by a charity will also constitute a trade, and one which is almost certainly taxable unless part of a wider activity, such as publishing. The sale of advertising in a charity's publication about its own activities, or in a journal on a subject which a charitable institution or association promotes, will be part of that trade. If the production of the publication is a primary purpose of the charity, its advertising revenue forms part of the income of that trade and is usually exempt from tax.

4.18 The Inland Revenue draw a clear distinction between advertising and sponsorship. Where references to a sponsor amount to no more than an acknowledgement of the sponsor's contribution, then that sponsorship will not be regarded as trading income. However, the Inland Revenue will regard a reference to a sponsor that incorporates either the sponsor's logo, or the sponsor's corporate colours, or a mention of the sponsor's products or services as supplying advertising. Such an advertisement will normally be regarded as taxable unless it relates to a primary purpose trade, such as a theatrical entertainment, or to an exhibition or show held by an agricultural society.

Advertising schemes and alterations to trusts

4.19 There are special rules allowing smaller registered and excepted charities (but not charitable companies) that can no longer easily meet their objectives to spend their capital, or to transfer their assets to another charity or to alter their trusts. As part of the required procedures, the charity must notify as many people as possible in its area of benefit. A standard form of notice for English and Welsh charities is available from the Charity Commission. The extent of the publicity is for the trustees to decide. It may amount to using local noticeboards, or it may be appropriate to make use of newspapers covering the area of benefit. Trustees should confirm to the Charity Commission that the area covered by the selected newspaper does in fact fairly cover the charity's area of benefit. If a larger charity requires the Charity Commission to make a scheme, then it will be appropriate for the charity to advertise in a newspaper with larger, or national coverage. Scottish charities must comply with the *Public Trusts (Reorganisation) (Scotland) (No 2) Regulations 1993*.

5 Alcohol

5.1 Charities often want to sell or provide alcohol, or allow others to do so on their premises, to refresh the public who have come to take part in or enjoy their services or events, or as a way of fund-raising. However, the sale of alcohol is a complex subject and professional advice is likely to be required to ensure that the law is not broken and that all the tax and VAT implications have been taken into account. Charities considering providing alcohol must ensure that they comply with:

- their governing document;
- the terms of their lease or freehold title;
- charity law;
- tax and VAT legislation;
- the licensing laws.

Governing document

5.2 Some charities have a governing document that forbids or restricts the sale or consumption of alcohol. If there is such a restriction, the charity has either to abide by it or to apply to the Charity Commission for a scheme to amend or remove the restriction. (Scottish charities will have to apply to Inland Revenue Charities (Scotland) (formerly FICO).) The Commission will only make such a scheme if the charity can demonstrate that the removal of the restriction will enable it to pursue its charitable objects more effectively.

Lease

5.3 A lease or freehold title deed may contain a covenant forbidding the sale of alcohol, usually to prevent disturbance to neighbouring properties or for moral or religious reasons. The Charity Commission has no power to amend these types of restrictions. If the charity wishes to amend them, it would need to come to an arrangement with the person or people who have the benefit of the covenant. In most instances this will be the landlord or other landowners. If it proves extremely difficult to trace the covenant beneficiary, the charity could apply to the Land Tribunal to have the covenant released, though this is usually a lengthy process.

Charitable activity or trading?

5.4 Providing a pub or social club type service is not a charitable purpose, even under the *Recreational Charities Act 1958*, so organisations whose main or sole purpose is to provide such services cannot be registered as charities. However, charities may engage in a trade that is 'ancillary' to their main purpose or covered by certain concessions. 'Ancillary' activities are those that are not part of the charity's main purpose, but which are undertaken as an integral part of providing or meeting the charity's primary purpose. An example of a charity selling alcohol as an ancillary trade is a charitable theatre which provides a bar or restaurant for its patrons. Charities are also permitted to sell alcohol at small, one-off fund-raising events.

5.5 Alcohol can only be supplied on charity premises if, in addition to its provision being ancillary to the charity's purpose:

- it is not prohibited by the charity's governing document or any covenants relating to the charity's property;
- the accommodation of the bar does not hinder the use of the premises for the charity's charitable purposes;
- the bar is only open at times when the charity's premises are being used for charitable purposes;
- the use of the bar is limited to those participating in, watching or using the charity's services.

5.6 Providing that the running of the bar meets the conditions outlined above, the Charity Commission does not place any restrictions on the turnover or size of the bar, or the opening times, though these will have to comply with the Licensing Laws.

Tax

5.7 If a charity is supplying alcohol as a trade, any profits will be liable to tax unless the activity is ancillary or covered by the Inland Revenue's extra-statutory concession or the turnover is within the limits for the exemption for small trades, which applies from April 2000. If profits are liable for tax, the trustees should remember their duty to minimise the charity's tax liabilities. They should operate the bar through a subsidiary trading company that donates its profits to the charity by Gift Aid. If they fail to do this the trustees may be personally liable to repay to the charity any tax incurred unnecessarily.

5.8 Charities selling alcohol should display a notice setting out the conditions for use of the bar. The Charity Commission and Inland Revenue stress that if they find a blind eye being turned to non-patrons using the bar, the charity will risk having all their bar profits assessed for tax.

Social clubs

5.9 Trading activities unconnected with a charity's main purpose, for example, undertaken purely to raise funds, are not regarded as being ancillary to a primary purpose and therefore should not be carried out by a charity. If the trustees want to raise money from the sale of alcohol, or from permitting others to hire the charity's premises for events at which alcohol will be supplied, then they will usually have to set up a trading subsidiary and trade through this. If the trustees want to provide a social club, they should form an independent club. Charity law would not permit trustees to run a bar as a separate section of the charity, nor would it agree that the degree of separation was sufficient if the bar were overseen by a sub-committee of the charity. If trustees decide to set up an independent club then it will be the responsibility of those managing the club to ensure that it is properly constituted and has the necessary authority to sell alcohol. Clubs can either have a justice's on-licence or a club registration certificate.

5.10 The bar or social club could be located on the charity's premises, but the charity would need to have a formal agreement, such as an occupational licence or lease, in place between itself and the bar. If the charity owns the premises the trustees would need to check that their governing document included a power allowing the charity to let or sub-let the charity's property. The trustees will also need to check if their title deeds or land certificates allow them to let or sub-let to a non-charitable company. If the charity leases the premises in which it proposes to provide alcohol, the trustees will have to check that the terms of the lease give them power to sub-let to a non-charitable organisation. If it does not, they will have to enter into negotiations with their landlord to amend the terms of the lease.

5.11 The terms on which the charity permits another organisation to run a bar on its premises must not involve any subsidy from the charity to the separate body, even if that body is wholly owned by the charity. The bar must pay for its share of the cost of floorspace, heating, lighting, maintenance, business rates, etc. The part of the premises no longer used for charitable purposes will not be entitled to any relief from business rates.

Other considerations

5.12 If a charity is considering selling alcohol on its premises, or allowing another organisation to sell alcohol from the charity's premises, in addition to the points already covered above it must also take into account the following:

- How will the sale or storage of alcohol affect the charity's insurance?
- Will the sale of alcohol require an application to the local authority for planning permission for change of use?
- Will the toilet facilities be adequate? Will any necessary structural alterations to the bar area or toilet facilities require building regulations or Fire Authority approval?
- What arrangements will have to be made to ensure that children under the age of 14 are not allowed access to the bar area or that no one under the age of 18 can purchase or consume alcohol on the premises?
- Will anyone be prepared to take on the responsibility for becoming the licensee, given that breaches of the *Licensing Act 1964* could result in the licensee facing criminal prosecution?
- Will food be provided? If so, will the premises also have to be registered with the local authority under the *Food Premises (Registration) Regulations 1991*?
- Do the charity's users, supporters, funders or donors have any religious or moral beliefs that would make the supply of alcohol ill advised?

Licensing

5.13 The *Licensing Act 1964* (as amended) and the *Licensing (Occasional Permissions) Act 1983* strictly control the provision of alcohol to the public. These Acts do not prevent alcohol from being given away, free of charge, to the public on charity premises, provided that the cost is not included in any admission fee or indirect charges, but they require anyone selling alcohol to be licensed. Licences can be granted by:

- the local licensing justices;
- a committee for dealing with liquor licensing matters drawn from local magistrates;
- the magistrates' court.

5.14 There are various types of licence that can be granted and the choice will depend on the circumstances for which it is needed. A justice's on-licence is the most suitable for the regular sale of alcohol. The licence is granted to an individual who has to demonstrate a reasonable knowledge of the licensing laws to the licensing justices. The licensee could be a trustee or a member of the charity's staff. An on-licence specifies the premises from which alcohol can be supplied and the hours during which it can be supplied. The justices can attach conditions to the licence, such as prohibiting the consumption of alcohol off the licensed premises. An on-licence has to be renewed every three years.

5.15 If a charity wants to sell alcohol occasionally on its premises, for example at a fund-raising dinner, then an occasional licence granted under the *Licensing Act 1964* is probably the most suitable. This type of licence is usually granted to someone who already holds an on-licence, such as a publican, and allows them to sell alcohol at premises other than those specified in their on-licence or at times outside those specified.

5.16 If the charity cannot find an on-licence holder willing to sell alcohol at an event held on the charity's premises it could arrange for a representative of the charity or the organisation holding the event to be granted an occasional permission to sell alcohol under the *Licensing (Occasional Permissions) Act 1983*. Each permission runs for a 24-hour period and no more than twelve will be granted in any twelve-month period. In addition to specifying the premises and hours for the sale of alcohol, the occasional permission also specifies the type of alcohol that can be sold, so, for example, spirits could be excluded. An occasional permission cannot overrule the Welsh Sunday Closing laws.

5.17 Certain charities qualify for a theatre licence under the *Theatres Act 1968*. This licence allows them to sell alcohol, subject to the conditions specified in the *Licensing Act 1964*, without having to obtain a separate liquor licence provided that the bar is open only during and immediately before performances and that these times are within normal licensing hours. The clerk to the licensing justices must be informed in writing that the theatre intends to sell alcohol.

Scottish charities

5.18 Scottish charities have to comply with the tax and VAT legislation outlined above and with any covenants or other conditions set out in their governing document or other documentation relating to lease or ownership of property. Otherwise they should follow Scottish legislation and local regulations concerning liquor sales and licensing.

Further information

5.19 Further details and guidance about providing alcohol on charity premises are contained in the Charity Commission's booklet CC27 'Providing Alcohol on Charity Premises'.

6 Almshouses

6.1 There is an historic tradition in the UK dating back to 990 of providing almshouses for elderly people or disadvantaged people with low incomes. Many older almshouses are of historic interest or architectural merit. Almshouses include three main categories of housing which are as follows:

- Flats, cottages or bungalows specially designed for the elderly, usually with no communal facilities or warden, but often linked by an alarm system to a control centre.
- 'Sheltered Housing' usually with some communal rooms where residents can mix socially, guest rooms and facilities such as laundry or hairdressing. There is almost always a resident warden to provide security and discreet help enabling residents to maintain as much independence as possible.
- 'Very Sheltered Housing' or 'Extra Care Schemes' for frailer or more dependent people, allowing them independence and privacy yet at the same time providing the extra help they need.

6.2 Each Almshouse Charity is independent and run by trustees in accordance with its Governing Instrument. This specifies the area of benefit and the qualification of beneficiaries. Most Almshouse Charities are for older people but some provide homes for people with mental illness or learning difficulties, and there are some with no age restriction.

Primary purpose trading

6.3 The provision of housing or sheltered housing by a charity whose objects include the relief of poverty, or something similar such as the provision of housing for the needy, in return for payment, constitutes primary purpose trading. Therefore almshouse charities can charge residents for the services they provide and do not need to structure payments through a subsidiary trading company.

6.4 Almshouse residents do not pay rent. They occupy the premises under licence and make a Weekly Maintenance Contribution (WMC) which should be set at a level that covers all outgoings, including maintenance and repairs. The WMC should not normally exceed the Rent Officer's informal assessment of equivalent fair rent (where applicable) and should never be greater than the maximum Housing Benefit payable for each unit.

6.5 Until the passing of the *Charities Act 1992* almshouse trustees had to obtain the Charity Commission's consent for any changes in the WMC. However, *s 50* of the *Charities Act 1992* abolished the requirement for WMCs to be authorised or approved by the Commission.

6.6 The trustees now have sole responsibility for ensuring that the WMC together with any other income (e.g. investment income) produces sufficient, but no more than sufficient, income to cover the cost of maintaining the almshouses and any essential services provided in them including insurance, repairs, internal and external redecoration, and any other estimated future expenditure (e.g. for updating or refurbishment) highlighted in quinquennial inspection reports.

6.7 Almshouses

6.7 The WMC should not cause hardship to individual residents. Trustees should ensure that residents are receiving their due entitlement to assistance from statutory sources.

Council Tax

6.8 Council Tax is usually paid by individual residents and trustees should ensure that residents claim any Council Tax Benefit to which they are entitled.

Assistance must relieve people, not the State

6.9 Almshouse charities, like other charities for the relief of the poor, must take care not to use the charity's funds in a way that replaces assistance that people could obtain from the State, as this would be relieving the State, rather than a poor person. When assessing whether or not the WMC will cause hardship, the charity should count as part of a person's income any State benefit which that person is entitled to receive, even if the person concerned has not claimed the benefit, or refuses to claim the benefit. However, it is legitimate for trustees to use the charity's funds to relieve temporary need resulting from a delay in the payment of State benefits.

Standards

6.10 Almshouses can provide shelter and services to meet people's needs, but they should not provide a standard of housing or services that more than meets people's needs. Trustees and staff should, however, remember that being 'poor' or 'needy' is not the same as being 'destitute'. 'Poor' refers to not having the things in life that most people take for granted and what constitutes this will change with time. For example, indoor sanitation was far from universally available 100 years ago and a television set, regarded today almost as a necessity, was regarded as a luxury only 40 years ago. Someone who normally has an adequate standard of living could also qualify as a beneficiary if they are suffering temporary hardship, perhaps as a result of sickness, an accident or redundancy.

Legislation

6.11 Almshouse charities in England and Wales are governed by trust law and the *Charities Acts 1992* and *1993*. Almshouse charities in Scotland are subject to Scottish charity law and, if they are also registered social landlords, to regulations made by Scottish Homes.

Registration

6.12 Almshouse charities in England and Wales must be registered with the Charity Commission. English almshouse charities registered with the Housing Corporation as social landlords must also comply with the Housing Corporation's regulations. These include provision for internal audit and controls and require larger almshouse charities to have an Internal Audit Sub-Committee. As required by the *Housing Act 1996*, the Housing Corporation has published criteria for the deregistration of landlords. These state that only those landlords providing 50 dwellings or less will be considered for deregistration.

6.13 Welsh almshouse charities registered with Tai Cwmru/Housing for Wales as social landlords are subject to regulations made by Tai Cwmru/Housing for Wales.

Change of purpose

6.14 Unless the governing document contains a power of amendment, the trustees cannot alter it. However, they have a duty under *s 13(5)* of the *Charities Act 1993* to apply to the Charity Commission for directions if the purpose of the charity can no longer be carried out.

Housing Act 1996

6.15 Except in the case of a company incorporated under the *Companies Act 1985*, the *Housing Act 1996* requires that the consent of the Charity Commission is obtained to any variation of the objects of a registered housing association (now known as a registered social landlord) which is also a registered charity even if it has power in its governing instrument to make the amendment. However, before giving their consent the Commissioners must consult the Housing Corporation. The Commissioners also consult the Housing Corporation about changes to the objects of registered social landlords which are registered charities, where the Commissioners propose to make a Scheme to change the objects.

Mortgaging land

6.16 Trustees may wish to mortgage the charity's land in order to raise money to build new almshouses or carry out major repairs. Future income will be used to repay the sum borrowed and the interest charged. There are three possible situations:

(i) The charity is a registered social landlord. In this instance, the consent of the Housing Corporation is required.

(ii) The charity is not a registered social landlord. In such cases the new procedure under *s 38(2)* of the *Charities Act 1993* applies, and the trustees — before committing the charity to the transaction — must obtain advice, from a person they reasonably believe to have sufficient ability and experience in financial matters to advise them, and who has no personal interest in the making of the loan, confirming that:

- the loan is necessary to finance the proposed expenditure;
- the terms are reasonable;
- the charity can afford the repayment terms.

The documentation must comply with the formalities prescribed under *s 39* of the *Charities Act 1993*.

(iii) The charity is not a registered social landlord and the trustees cannot comply with the procedures under *s 38(2)* of the *Charities Act 1993*, then under *s 38(1)* an Order of the Court or of the Charity Commissioners will be required.

Sale or lease of land

6.17 Trustees may wish to dispose of land belonging to a charity which is held either as investment property, or as functional property for a number of reasons:

- The land may have become surplus to requirements.
- It may be in the interests of the beneficiaries to relocate the almshouse to another site.
- The sale may increase investment income.

6.18 Almshouses

6.18 Again there are a number of situations which require different treatment:

(*a*) The charity is a registered social landlord, or the land has been grant-aided by the Housing Corporation. In this instance the consent of the Housing Corporation is required.

(*b*) The charity is not in category (*a*) and either there is no power in its governing document to dispose of land or the trustees are unable to follow the procedure set out in (*c*) below, the consent of the Charity Commission under *s 36(1)* of the *Charities Act 1993* may be required. If so the formalities prescribed under *s 37* must be observed.

(*c*) The charity is not in category (*a*) and the trustees have an express or implied power to dispose of land, and the land is not held on trust for use for charitable purposes. Before committing themselves to the transaction, the trustees are obliged by *s 36(2)* of the *Charities Act 1993* to:

- obtain a written report from a qualified surveyor covering all matters set out in the *Charities (Quantity Surveyors' Reports) Regulations 1992*;
- advertise the land for sale as advised by the surveyor (unless the surveyor advises positively against this); and
- reach a decision that the terms of the proposed transaction are the best reasonably obtainable for the charity.

The formalities prescribed under *s 37* must then be observed.

(*d*) The charity is not in category (*a*) and the land is held on trust for use for charitable purposes, but there is a power to sell or lease it, the procedure set out in (*b*) above must be followed, but in addition trustees must normally publish notices inviting members of the public to make representations to them about the proposed sale or lease, and must take account of any representations received before deciding whether or not to proceed. Again, the documentation must comply with the prescribed formalities.

6.19 The *Trusts of Land and Appointment of Trustees Act 1996* gives trustees a general statutory power to sell, or to grant a lease over, land owned by a charity. However, this power can only be exercised in furtherance of the objects of the charity. It may be necessary for the Charity Commission to make a Scheme to authorise the disposal of any land which is held on trusts which provide for the land to be used as an almshouse.

Connected persons

6.20 Any disposal of land by a charity, which is not in category (*a*), to a connected person or to a trustee or nominee of a connected person, will require the consent of the Charity Commission under *s 36(1)* of the *Charities Act 1993*. 'Connected person' is defined in *Sch 5* to that Act and includes:

- a charity trustee or trustee for the charity;
- a person who is a donor of any land to the charity;
- a child (including step-child or illegitimate child), parent, grandchild, grand-parent, brother or sister of any trustee or donor of land;
- an officer, agent or employee of the charity;
- the spouse (or a person living with another as that person's husband or wife) of any of the above people;

- an institution which is controlled by any of the above people; or
- a body corporate in which any of the above people have a substantial interest.

Sex Discrimination Act 1975

6.21 If the governing document of an almshouse charity requires the benefits to be conferred only on people of a particular sex, the trustees are exempt from the *Sex Discrimination Act 1975* and it is permissible for them to advertise for residents inviting applications only from people of that sex.

Race Relations Act 1976

6.22 The Housing Corporation likes all registered social landlords to have an equal opportunities policy along the lines of 'the charity is committed to the principles of equal opportunities and observes the letter and spirit of current legislation as far as the governing document allows'. If the governing document restricts beneficiaries to one particular racial group (this must be defined not by colour but by reference to race, nationality or ethnic or national origins) then the trustees are exempt from prosecution under the *Race Relations Act 1976* if they advertise for residents from that racial group.

Investments

6.23 Unless the governing document contains specific investment powers, the trustees will be confined to those contained in the *Trustee Investments Act 1961* (see Chapter 71).

Maintenance

6.24 Under the *Defective Premises Act 1972* trustees have a duty to keep gas, electrical, water and heating installations in proper working order and to replace or repair them when necessary as a result of fair wear and tear.

Accounts

6.25 Generally speaking, charitable almshouses have to comply with the accounting regulations for charities. If they are registered with the Housing Corporation, they are required to comply with *The Accounting Requirements for Registered Social Landlords General Determination 1997* which was announced in the Housing Corporation Circular R2 12/97. For accounting periods commencing on or after 1 April 1997, they must also comply with *The Accounting Requirements for Registered Social Landlords (Amending) Determination 1998*. The *Housing Act 1996* requires them to submit accounts, audited by a qualified auditor in the specified form, to the Housing Corporation within six months of the end of the accounting period. They should also comply with the Statement of Recommended Practice (SORP), 'Accounting by Registered Social Landlords'.

6.26 Statements of accounts of all 'local charities for the relief of poverty' (which includes most almshouse charities) should be sent to the appropriate local authority in whose area the charity operates. Until statements of accounts are sent to the appropriate local authority, trustees must make the statements of account available for public inspection and provide copies of the statements to the public at a reasonable cost.

6.27 Almshouses

Financial control

6.27 An annual budget of estimated income and expenditure will be needed in order to calculate the WMC.

6.28 It is advisable to set up an extraordinary repair fund to provide for major repairs such as re-roofing and a cyclical maintenance fund to provide for regular maintenance such as redecoration.

6.29 Trustees should be provided with financial reports on a monthly basis or at least for every trustees' meeting and given any training they might need to interpret them.

Residents

Filling vacancies

6.30 The Charity Commission normally permits vacancies to be filled from a waiting list for up to twelve months, after which vacancies must be advertised.

6.31 Some local authorities have the right to nominate people to fill vacancies in almshouses, particularly ones that have been built or improved with Housing Association Grant (HAG) now known as Social Housing Grant. In such instances, those nominated must fulfil the criteria contained in the governing document, i.e. the same criteria as any other applicant. Trustees have the right to turn down any person they believe would be unsuitable, explaining their reasons to the nominating body.

6.32 Applicants should be visited by a trustee or member of staff to find out if they are sufficiently independent to care for themselves in an almshouse and to explain to the applicant what moving to the almshouse would entail, including details of the WMC, the role of the Warden (if applicable), the circumstances in which they would be asked to leave, the policy on pets, upkeep of gardens, laundry, etc.

6.33 New residents should be made welcome and given a letter of appointment setting out the terms of the appointment, level of WMC and arrangements for notifying changes. It is good practice to provide them with a resident's handbook, which includes details of how they can obtain domiciliary support, how residents are consulted about any major changes, the Resident's Committees (if applicable), the complaints procedure, arrangements for visitors etc.

Maintaining effectiveness

6.34 If the trustees believe that there are insufficient needy people in their area of benefit and they have taken steps to search out potential beneficiaries without success, then they should consider approaching the Charity Commission for a scheme to do one or more of the following:

- extend the area of benefit;
- amend the purposes of the charity, so the almshouses can be sold and the resources used in some other way to support poor people;
- give the charity's assets to another charity providing shelter for a disadvantaged group of people.

6.35 The Charity Commission has power under the *Charities Act 1993* to transfer to the Official Custodian for Charities land or other assets belonging to a charity that they consider to be at risk.

Further advice

6.36 Further information and advice can be obtained from the Almshouse Association, the Housing Corporation, Tai Cwmru/Housing for Wales and Scottish Homes.

The Almshouse Association
Billingbear Lodge
Carters Hill
Wokingham
Berkshire
RG40 5RU
Tel: 01344 452 922
Fax: 01344 862 062
Email: funds@almshouse.org
www.almshouses.org

The Housing Corporation
London
W1P 0BN
Tel: 020 7393 2000
Fax: 020 7393 2111
Email: enquiries@housingcorp.gov.uk
www.housingcorp.gov.uk

Scottish Homes
Thistle House
91 Haymarket Terrace
Edinburgh
Midlothian
EH12 5HE
Tel: 0131 313 0044
www.scot-homes.gov.uk

Tai Cwmru/Housing for Wales
25-30 Lambourne Crescent
Llanishen
Cardiff
CF4 5ZJ
Tel: 029 20 825 111
Fax: 029 20 826 989
Email: info@tc-hfw.gov.uk
www.tc-hfw.gov.uk

7 Annual Return

Charity Commission

7.1 In order to keep the Charity Commission's register of charities up to date and allow the Commission to discharge its monitoring responsibilities, all registered charities whose gross annual income or total expenditure is in excess of £10,000 are required by *s 48* of the *Charities Act 1993* to prepare an annual return and send it to the Charity Commission within ten months of the end of the financial year to which the return relates. This annual return is in addition to the annual report required by *s 45*.

7.2 Charities with gross annual income and total expenditure of less than £10,000 are sent a simplified version of the annual return form.

7.3 The return should be signed by a trustee. Any amendments to the charity's governing document, objects, area of benefit, or a change of bank account that have not already been reported to the Charity Commission should be noted on the return or, where this is not possible, set out in a covering letter and sent to the Commission with the completed annual return.

7.4 Persistent failure to submit an annual return without a reasonable excuse is an offence punishable by a fine. *Section 48(3)*, however, gives the Commissioners power to waive the requirement to produce an annual return for a particular charity or class of charities.

Companies House

7.5 Charitable companies are also required by *s 363* of the *Companies Act 1985* to submit an annual return each year (form 363A which is blank or form 363S which is already filled in) in order to keep the register of companies up to date. The form must be signed by a director or the company secretary and returned within 28 days of the return date together with a filing fee. Failure to file the return within the prescribed time period results in a fine.

Registrar of Friendly Societies

7.6 Charities that are industrial and provident societies are required by *s 39* of the *Industrial and Provident Societies Act 1965* to submit an annual return (form AR15) to the Registrar of Friendly Societies within seven months of the end of the financial year to which the return relates.

Scotland

7.7 There is no equivalent to the Charity Commission's annual return in Scotland. The Inland Revenue Index is not systematically updated. Scottish charities should inform the Inland Revenue of any changes in a charity's circumstances that would affect the Index as and when they arise.

8 Associations

8.1 An association is formed when two or more people come together to do something lawful for the purpose of benefiting themselves or others, but which is not intended to make a profit for themselves or others. To be an association the parties should also have an intention to create a legal relationship between themselves, though this does not need to be explicitly stated. This is what differentiates an association from a group of friends, even though the founding members of an association may be a group of friends.

Unincorporated associations

8.2 An unincorporated charitable association is an association whose objects are charitable in law and which is not registered as a company or an industrial and provident society, and is not incorporated under statute or royal charter. An unincorporated charity does not need to be called an association to have that legal structure; it may well be known as a society, club, campaign or even as a trust. The unincorporated association is the most common constitutional form adopted by charities in Scotland.

Governing document

8.3 The governing document of an unincorporated charitable association is its constitution or rules. It sets out the purpose, or objects, of the association, who can become a member, and the procedural rules for holding meetings, deciding policy and action, electing the governing body, etc. The procedure for amending the governing document will depend on whether it contains a power of amendment. Even if there is a power of amendment, changes to the objects clause on the Trustees' powers will usually require authorisation by the Charity Commission.

8.4 English and Welsh charities can obtain a model governing document from the Charity Commission and Scottish charities can obtain a model governing document from the Scottish Council for Voluntary Organisations. The model documents can be adapted to suit a particular charity's needs.

Advantages

8.5 The unincorporated association structure is particularly suitable for membership organisations where it is important that the people ultimately in control of the organisation are democratically elected from amongst the membership by the membership. It has the advantage of being simple and flexible and unincorporated associations can be set up or wound up easily and cheaply.

Disadvantages

8.6 The main disadvantage of using the unincorporated organisation structure is that the charity itself has no legal identity so the members of the governing body can be held personally liable for the charity's debts and for other claims. The charity cannot enter into contracts or agreements in its own name. Land, property and other assets have to be held by the trustees individually, or by holding trustees, or a custodian trustee. All contracts have to be entered into by individuals, such as the trustees, a sub-group of the trustees, or holding or custodian trustees. The signatories and/or the governing body could be held personally liable for a breach of contract. Similarly if someone wants to take legal action against the charity, the lawsuit would be against the individuals who comprise the governing body or individuals who authorised the action in question. If a charity wanted to take legal action against another party, it would have to do so in the name of an individual or individuals.

European associations

8.7 No other European country has a body equivalent to the Charity Commission. For regulatory purposes, charities are grouped with mutual societies in many other European countries. The different approaches to charity law, tax reliefs and other concessions give rise to problems for charities trying to work throughout Europe. Proposals have therefore been put forward to operate a new legal entity, a European association. This would be an incorporated body operating in several European countries and would have a different legal structure to the English association.

9 Audit

Financial audit

9.1 Audit is often equated with the phrase 'external scrutiny of the accounts'. An external auditor's role is to opine as to whether or not the accounts give a true and fair view of the charity's financial affairs. The way in which statutory audits are conducted is specified by law, in statements of auditing standards (SASs), and in Practice Notes.

9.2 The statutory rules regarding the auditing of charity accounts are set out in *Charities Act 1993* and the *Charities (Accounts and Reports) Regulations 1995* for unincorporated charities, in the *Companies Act 1985* for charities that are limited companies and in further legislation for Scottish charities and Industrial and Provident Societies. Although the group turnover limit for audit exemption has recently been raised to £1 million, there have been no revisions in respect of charities. As Table 5 illustrates, they also vary according to the charity's income, expenditure and assets.

Table 5 Audit requirements

Charity's legal status	Income/expenditure threshold	Minimum level of scrutiny required
Registered, unincorporated charities in England and Wales	Up to £10k gross annual income or expenditure	No external scrutiny required
	Exceeding £10k but not exceeding £250k gross annual income or total expenditure in year accounts are prepared or either of the two previous years	Independent examination
	Exceeding £250k gross annual income or total expenditure in the year accounts are prepared or either of the two previous years	Audit
Registered charitable company	Not exceeding £90k gross annual income, not part of a group and if defined as small by *Companies Act 1985 s 249B(1)(c)*	No external scrutiny required

9.2 Audit

Table 5 Audit requirements *continued*

Charity's legal status	Income/expenditure threshold	Minimum level of scrutiny required
Charitable company	Exceeding £90k but not exceeding £250k gross annual income, not part of a group and if defined as small by *Companies Act 1985 s 249B(1)(c)*	Report of reporting accountant as defined by *Companies Act 1985 s 249D*
	Exceeding £250k gross annual income	Audit
Charitable industrial and provident society	Turnover below £90k	No external scrutiny required
	Turnover below £250k, and total assets below £1.4m	Reporting accountant
	Turnover of £250k or more, or total assets of £1.4m or more	Audit
Other exempt charities	All sizes	No specific audit requirement but may have to comply with other statutory regimes
Excepted charity, registered on a voluntary basis, unincorporated Scottish charities	Up to £100k gross annual income or expenditure in year accounts are prepared or either of the two previous years	Independent examination
	Exceeding £100k gross annual income or expenditure in the year accounts are prepared or either of the two previous years	Audit

9.3 In some instances there will also be audit requirements set out in the charity's governing document or by a funder. Where these are more stringent than the statutory requirements the charity must abide by the higher requirement. It may be possible to alter a constitutional requirement if a power of amendment exists in the governing document, but such an alteration would be subject to the consent of the members under the relevant legislation and may require the Charity Commission to make a Scheme.

Choice of scrutiny

9.4 Where a choice of type of external scrutiny exists, an organisation cannot cherry-pick elements of both regimes: for instance a small unincorporated charity must have either an examination or an audit, not a mixture of the two. The decision as to which type of scrutiny will be chosen has to be formalised in different ways.

- Unincorporated charities decide through the trustees, and no formal documentation is required, other than a trustee minute.
- For limited companies the decision is made by the directors, and ratified by the members. Even if the directors elect not to have an audit, one will still be required if at least 10% of the members (or if limited by shares, a member or members holding not less than 10% of the shares) deposit a notice in writing at least one month before the end of the relevant accounting period requesting an audit.
- Certain industrial and provident societies cannot exempt themselves from audit, most notably housing associations and those with a subsidiary. Those that have a choice must have the approval of 90% of the society's members with voting rights and the resolution must be approved by at least 80% of the votes actually cast.

Auditors' duties

9.5 Often the audit is seen as a year-end accounting exercise so that at least once a year a reliable set of accounts is produced. This should not be the case. The auditor should issue his client with a letter of engagement which clearly sets out what is expected of both the charity and of the auditor. This should make it clear that the auditor's duty is to report on the accounts prepared by the charity, and these accounts are the responsibility of the trustees, and not of the auditors. However, it is common for the auditor to be involved to some extent in the preparation of the accounts, especially in the final drafting of the statutory formats. Whilst this is permitted, the charity should be clear that this is not actually part of the auditor's statutory duty, and does not absolve the trustees of responsibility for their accounts. Any such work should be the subject of a separate section of the engagement letter.

Other types of audit

9.6 Apart from the statutory annual audit requirement, other audits exist which relate to both financial and non-financial areas. The annual audit may also be extended to cover governance (for example compliance with a code of good practice), and other financial audits may be carried out at the same time as the year end exercise: for instance, funders may require a separate report on the use of their funds. The terms of such work should again be clearly defined and agreed in advance: the audit practice note governing charities points out that it is the trustees' responsibility to identify any such extra audit requirement, not the auditors'.

9.7 Audit

9.7 Internal audit is not geared towards expressing an opinion on the accounts, but is instead part of the internal control and risk management mechanism. Increasingly audit is also being applied to non-financial measurement as well, whether in the context of benchmarking an organisation's achievements and efficiency, or through other areas such as environmental or social audit.

Social auditing

9.8 Social auditing is a way of measuring the social and ethical performance of an organisation and has become topical in the light of the debate about corporate social responsibility, and the social and ethical standards expected of businesses in present day society. A social audit looks at the objectives of an organisation and compares its performance in certain areas with them. It will also survey the opinions of various stakeholders. For a voluntary organisation, the stakeholders will typically include staff, service users, beneficiaries, communities, funders, suppliers, and regulatory bodies – in other words anyone affected by, or who can affect, an organisation. Social auditing is a form of evaluation in that it encompasses the assessment of a situation or process, but it goes further as it can be used as a development tool, as it allows a charity to recognise and respond to the views of its stakeholders. Although the idea of social auditing dates back to the 1950s it has provoked fresh interest recently with the New Economics Foundation carrying out social audits for Traidcraft Exchange and for the Body Shop.

Social auditing in the voluntary sector

9.9 A charity's accounts say little about how far a charity is going in fulfilling its mission statement, so the advantages of undertaking a social audit to assess the effectiveness of an organisation's activities are clear. It is not only appropriate to those voluntary organisations whose social impact is easy to measure. Whatever the future of the voluntary sector, there is a growing belief that organisations that can assess their impact in relation to their goals, and demonstrate a more open form of accountability, will be ones that survive.

How a social audit is conducted

9.10 First the organisation has to agree that carrying out a social audit would be advantageous and identify what it is already doing in the way of social audit, perhaps without describing the process as such. For example, it may be monitoring its employment statistics to assess the impact of its equal opportunities policy.

9.11 The charity may well need to clarify what its social objectives are, what it has stated that it is aiming to achieve, and the steps it is already taking to achieve its objectives.

9.12 The next step is to agree who the charity's stakeholders are, what the issues are that concern them, and how the charity will go about consulting its stakeholders.

9.13 At this stage an independent auditor can select a series of key external benchmarks that can be used to assess performance and compare it with that of similar organisations and sector norms. Under the guidance of the auditor the charity then sets up a 'social bookkeeping system' to record the data collected, both quantitative and qualitative.

9.14 At the year-end a social statement should be prepared by analysing and interpreting the social accounting information collected. The statement and accounts are then examined by the auditor and an audit review panel usually drawn from the charity's staff and trustees. This panel will draw up recommendations based on the results and develop an action plan in order to ensure that the lessons learnt are incorporated into the charity's planning and management and the process of social auditing itself improved. Finally, the social accounts are published so that stakeholders can compare the rhetoric with the reality and hold the trustees to account.

9.15 Even if the social accounts show that an organisation is falling short of its aims, the exercise should strengthen the charity in the longer term by focusing the trustees attention on the areas in most need of improvement. Hopefully, the social accounts for subsequent years will show improving trends. Where they do not it may be appropriate for funders to withdraw their support.

Advantages of social auditing

9.16 There are many advantages to be gained by charities carrying out a form of social auditing. An independent assessment of social impact can aid strategic planning and development in that it provides trustees and staff with direction. It can give an organisation credibility and because the results of the audit are made public, enhance public confidence. It provides a form of accountability though it should be stressed that the primary function of the audit is to provide an opportunity to improve an organisation's social performance and not as an attack or critique. It encompasses many perspectives from different stakeholders but can also give a common sense of purpose amongst them. It is comprehensive, maybe not initially, but over time. Lastly it is comparative and enables an organisation to judge its performance against others in the sector.

Disadvantages of social auditing

9.17 The disadvantages are that a social audit may be disheartening if it shows that an organisation is falling short in terms of its desired social impact. The process may be too expensive for charities to undertake annually. However, over time, as processes are in place, it does become cheaper.

10 Auditors

10.1 'Auditor' is often a generic title used to apply to the person carrying out the external scrutiny of the accounts at the year end. In fact only a minority of charities require an audit in the true sense (see Chapter 9). This chapter only applies to auditors in the strictest legal sense, although some of the principles may be usefully applied in other cases.

Appointment

10.2 The first auditors of a charitable company are elected by the company directors/ trustees, and thereafter auditors are appointed or re-appointed at the annual general meeting. [*Companies Act 1985 s 385* and *385(a)*]. Unincorporated charities often apply the same regime either from custom, or because of the requirements of the constitution. If the governing document is silent on powers of appointment, the trustees must appoint. The *Charities Act 1993* is silent on this matter. Similar regulations for Scotland are silent on the appointment of the first auditor but annual appointment is covered in *LRMPSA Reg 7(2)*.

10.3 A charitable company can elect to dispense with the need to reappoint auditors annually, as an administrative convenience, by passing an elective resolution. [*Companies Act 1985 s 386*]. An auditor of an industrial and provident society continues in office automatically unless he resigns, becomes otherwise ineligible, or is removed by resolution.

10.4 The Charity Commission can order a charity to be audited and, in certain circumstances, can also appoint the auditor. In such a case the costs of the audit are recoverable from the trustees or, if the Commission think this impractical, from the funds of the charity.

Removal and resignation

10.5 There is a statutory procedure under the *Companies Act ss 391* and *393* for the removal of auditors. However, this is rarely used as it requires a general meeting of the members. Therefore in practice the procedure for removing auditors for charities of all legal structures tends to be the same, namely that the incumbent is asked to resign his office, thereby creating a casual vacancy, which the directors or trustees then fill by their chosen appointment. This appointment is then formally ratified in general meeting, usually the annual general meeting. The governing documents of unincorporated charities usually provide the trustees with the power to fill such casual vacancies.

10.6 Increasingly such changes in appointment only occur after discussions with the incumbent auditor and a tender process including written and verbal presentations. It is therefore rare for the auditor to be unaware of a forthcoming change and to be unprepared for resignation.

10.7 Both the *Companies Act 1985*, the *Charities Act 1993* and Scottish Regulations have procedures to follow on a change of auditors, in addition to the protocols which accountancy firms follow on a change of professional appointment.

10.8 The auditor of an unincorporated charity is required under the *Charities Act 1993*

Regulations and the Scottish Regulations to inform the trustees in writing if there are any circumstances connected with his ceasing to hold office which ought to be brought to their attention, or, if there are no such circumstances, to issue a statement to that effect. If there are any relevant circumstances to report, then a copy of this letter should be sent by the auditor to the Charity Commission. In Scotland, if the auditor so requests, a statement has to be included in the trustees' report.

10.9 Similarly, under the *Companies Act 1985 s 392*, an outgoing auditor of a limited company must deposit at the registered office of the company a similar statement of matters which should be brought to the attention of the members or creditors of the company. If there are any such circumstances then the statement must be filed with the Registrar of Companies within 28 days. Whether or not such circumstances exist, the company must file a copy of the resignation with the Registrar within 14 days of receipt.

Qualifications

10.10 An auditor of a registered charity, whether a limited company or unincorporated, must be eligible under the *Companies Act 1985 s 25*, which requires the auditor to be a member of a recognised supervisory body, and eligible under those rules. The recognised bodies are:

- The Institute of Chartered Accountants in England and Wales,
- The Institute of Chartered Accountants in Scotland,
- The Institute of Chartered Accountants in Ireland,
- The Association of Authorised Public Accountants, and
- The Association of Chartered Certified Accountants.

10.11 The appointment can be in respect of a firm or an individual, although in all cases the auditor should be independent of the charity. Members of the Association of International Auditors are also eligible to carry out these audits under the supervision of one of the above bodies.

10.12 The same rules broadly apply to industrial and provident societies.

Powers

10.13 The auditors or examiners of an unincorporated charity have rights. They have a right of access to any books, documents and other records (however kept) which relate to the charity concerned and which the auditor or examiner considers necessary to inspect. They are also entitled to require such information and explanations from past or present officers or employees of the charity as they consider necessary.

10.14 The rights of company auditors are slightly different. The right of access in this instance pertains to the company's books, accounts and vouchers, and the auditor has a right to require information from the company's officers, defined as the directors and the company secretary. Company auditors are also entitled to notice of general meetings, to attend, and also to be heard in respect of any business which concerns them. [*Companies Act 1985 s 389*].

10.15 The rights of the auditor of an industrial and provident society are very similar to the rights of a company auditor.

10.16 Auditors

10.16 The main difference between the rights of a company auditor and the rights of an auditor of an unincorporated charity is the wider ranging right of the charity examiner or auditor to require information from not just present officers of the company, as the *Companies Act 1985* prescribes, but also past officers and employees. Under the *Companies Act 1985* an officer is guilty of an offence if he misleads the auditor. The comparable situation for unincorporated charities is dealt with by the whistleblowing rules of the *Charities Act 1993*. There is no equivalent of the whistleblowing rules, however, for Scottish charities.

Duties

10.17 All auditors have a statutory duty to report in the prescribed form on the accounts. The style of this report is highly stylised, and is set out in standards issued by the Auditing Practices Board.

10.18 The *Companies Act 1985*, the *Charities Act 1993*, and the Scottish *Charity Accounting Regulations* all require the auditor to consider the following areas in his report:

- whether the accounts have been prepared in accordance with the relevant legislation and show a true and fair view;
- whether the directors report/annual report is consistent with the accounts;
- whether proper accounting records have been kept and whether the accounts agree with those records; and
- whether all information and explanations to which he is entitled have been given.

10.19 Of the above only the first area is usually included in the report of the auditor. The other areas are included only if the auditor has formed a negative opinion in respect of them. Additionally, company auditors are required to report by exception if proper returns have not been received from branches not visited by them, or if a company has claimed exemption from the requirement to prepare group accounts to which it was not entitled. Company auditors are also required to make good any omission from the accounts of disclosures of emoluments received by directors. [*Companies Act 1985 6 Sch*].

Charities receiving substantial public funds

10.20 Some charities, including charities in the NHS, receive substantial public funds and have their accounts audited by the Comptroller and Auditor General or by auditors from the Audit Commission. The Charity Commission has powers to disapply the audit and independent examination provisions of *Part VI* of the *Charities Act 1993* in instances where a charity's accounts are scrutinised by these bodies.

11 Borrowings

11.1 All types of charity may borrow, provided that their governing document contains a clause permitting them to do so. This clause is usually incorporated into most governing documents at the charity's formation. However, trustees should be aware of any potential limitation in their powers which may exist, for example restricting a charity from borrowing at over a certain rate of interest, or from offering certain types of security.

11.2 Whatever the powers of the trustees, they should never act imprudently. This responsibility can impose a greater burden on those with a financial background, who may need to guide their colleagues on the full implications of larger borrowing decisions. Where the sum is substantial a smaller finance group can be established to consider the impact of a loan, to examine budgets and cash flow forecasts, and most importantly to confirm that the charity not only needs the borrowing, but has the ability to service and repay the loan. Professional advice may be needed.

11.3 Charities must keep a record of any loans. Details will be needed to ensure that the routine payments and accounting are accurate both in respect of capital repayment and any interest due. Sometimes confusion arises over whether an amount was intended as a loan or as a gift. Where supposed donors request their money back on the basis that it was intended as a loan it will be particularly useful for an organisation to demonstrate that it has operational procedures in place for recording all loans, whether interest bearing or not.

Types of borrowing

11.4 The range of loan finance available to a charity is as great as the range available to individuals or commercial organisations. Some commercial lending is designed to be tax efficient in the hands of a commercial company, or is preferred because it enables a business to present its accounts in a certain way. These advantages, which are not attractive to charitable organisations, may make these forms of lending less competitive as a result. Trustees should not assume that the same considerations which inform their judgements in commerce automatically apply in the charity context.

11.5 Loans from banks or other financial institutions will usually require some form of security. If this is to be land, then the *Charities Act 1993 s 38* procedures must be followed. These require the trustees to obtain an Order of the Court or of the Charity Commissioners, or written professional advice (this can be from an external source or from a suitably qualified trustee or member of staff) about whether or not the loan is necessary, whether the terms of the loan are reasonable, and whether the charity has the ability to repay the loan on those terms. Other security, such as a floating charge over book debts, may be granted without the need for statutory procedures, although again the governing document should be consulted. It is possible for individuals to guarantee loans instead of the charity granting security. Banks are accustomed to this approach in the context of small businesses, but any guarantor needs to be aware that the commitment is not merely a cosmetic exercise to enable a charity to obtain a loan. Banks can and do call in guaranteed loans, and do go to the guarantor for any losses realised, even though this process may sometimes extend over several years.

11.6 Charities also have access to sources of lending which are not available to other organisations. These include benefactors and trustees, other charities, and specialist lending institutions. Benefactors and trustees are often prepared to make interest free loans, and these can be easier to appeal for than outright donations. Once the money has been passed over there is always the hope that it will be converted into a donation subsequently. Where individuals make substantial loans interest free it should be clear that the lender has no control over the application of any investment income arising, to avoid personal tax complications for the lender. [*ICTA 1988 s 660*].

11.7 Often trustees may wish to support their own charity through loans. Where they are interest bearing, the interest received will comprise a benefit to the trustee and would therefore be in breach of trust unless specifically authorised by the governing document. Where such loans are made interest free, the charity should be conscious of the possibility of a conflict of interest arising between the future needs of the charity and the trustee personally. Obvious problems may arise if a trustee has committed a significant sum to the charity, which then begins to get into financial difficulties. Similarly over-dependence on one source of finance, be it loan or donation, can impair the trustees' ability to act objectively in the best interests of the charity.

Interest

11.8 If any interest is paid to the lender, and if the interest is intended or capable of running for more than a year, then the interest should be paid to the lender net of basic rate tax, and the tax deducted accounted for to the Inland Revenue.

Loan to or from trading subsidiaries

11.9 The relationship between the charity and its trading subsidiary is discussed in Chapter 112. Usually it is the charity that lends money to its subsidiary, but occasionally a subsidiary is in a position to lend money to the charity and, as the subsidiary is usually under the control of the charity trustees, this is a readily available source of finance for the charity. The directors of the trading subsidiary should be prepared to resist such requests for finance if it is not in the best interests of the company. The directors of the trading subsidiary need to act responsibly towards that entity in isolation, and should not jeopardise its solvency out of a desire to help out the parent body.

Other sources of finance

11.10 On a more commercial basis, there are also organisations which lend on formal terms to charities. Some of these are special interest charities supporting particular types of charitable endeavour (for instance, the Architectural Heritage Fund), others are charities supporting the sector more widely, such as Charities Aid Foundation's loan services. Beyond the charitable sector organisations like Industrial Common Ownership Finance Ltd and social banks will lend to charities on more advantageous terms than a charity could obtain elsewhere.

11.11 Loan or deposit covenants are another form of financial support. Although many charities account for these as gifts in the year of receipt, they are loans and should be regarded as such on the face of the charity's balance sheet, showing a release into income over the life of the agreement. Although this accounting procedure is often ignored, the auditors accept the situation only on the grounds of immateriality.

11.12 Finally, charities should not always assume that loans are to be avoided. Sometimes the trustees should actively consider whether taking out a loan could be the best means of achieving the charity's objects: for instance, where an immediate need requires cash, where fund-raising pledges are still being honoured, or as an alternative to holding surplus cash in reserves. In this situation a charity may accept that it can afford to operate without a large working capital reserve if it has security available, for instance, in the form of property, against which it can borrow in an emergency.

12 Branches

12.1 The precise status of any form of branch network can have far-reaching consequences. It is important therefore to ensure that this status is clear to everybody concerned before taking actions which may have repercussions for either the main charity or the other groups.

12.2 Branches are defined in the SORP as 'entities or administrative bodies set up, for example, to conduct a particular aspect of the business of the . . . charity, or to conduct the business of the . . . charity in a particular way'.

Definitions

12.3 Branches may be called by many names: the following list is not exhaustive, but is set out to help the reader consider to what extent any internal arrangement may in fact fall within the definition. Branches are variously called: branch, group, region, area, Friends, supporters, league, chapter and project. The branch may or may not be formally constituted. It may operate at a considerable distance from the parent organisation, and it may or may not hold itself accountable to the parent charity. None of these factors are of fundamental importance to the status of a branch, although together they may begin to indicate more clearly the legal position.

12.4 The key issue is one of autonomy, or control. Who does, or should, exercise control over the affairs of the branch? This should be answered not on the basis of the current relationship with the branch, but on the underlying facts. Reference should be made to the constitutional position and the administrative arrangements. The SORP lists some characteristics of a non-autonomous branch as follows:

- it uses the name of the reporting (i.e. main) charity within its title;
- it exclusively raises funds for the main charity and/or for its own local activities;
- it uses the main charity's registration number to receive tax relief on its activities;
- it is perceived by the public to be the main charity's local representative, or its representative for a particular purpose;
- it receives support from the main charity through advice, publicity materials, etc.;
- it receives finance towards the main charity's primary purpose activities;
- it is staffed by employees of the main charity;
- its funds are the legal property of the main charity, whether or not a local bank account is operated.

12.5 A branch may therefore be simply part of the administrative machinery of the main charity, or a separate legal entity. Constitutional arrangements such as power of appointment, removal and veto must be examined. Where the status is still unclear following the applications of the various tests listed, then legal advice may be needed, or advice should be sought from the Charity Commission. Informal fund-raising groups are not charities.

Friends

12.6 Several charities have organisations linked to them known as 'Friends'. Usually

Friends are a means of involving a wide circle of people who wish to support the charity without becoming legally responsible for it. Sometimes the reason for setting up a group of Friends is because some supporters are willing to raise funds for the charity but wish to control where the funds are applied by imposing some form of restriction on the transfer of the funds. Whether or not the Friends organisation is a separate registered charity, it may be necessary for the accounts to be consolidated into the main charity's accounts. Determination of the precise status of 'the Friends' will be vital here.

Clarification important

12.7 The reasons for determining the status of branches include identifying all the risks that the main charity bears, which may be increased by a lack of central control. For instance, a contractual liability in a branch may follow through to the main charity, but may be the type of liability that the trustees of the main charity would never have accepted in their own right.

12.8 Charities with branches or dispersed operations therefore need to clarify their own legal structures, and then ensure that systems operate which maximise the efficiency of the organisation, minimise the risk, and also preserve the goodwill and co-operation of the local staff and volunteers at branch level. The systems in operation will need to cover a wide range of topics, but especially they will need to cover accounting and tax matters, and the use of delegated authorities.

Operational authority

12.9 The authorities within which a local branch can operate should be clearly set out in a standard form used by the main charity with all its branch operations. These agreements may take several different forms, and will depend on the exact nature of the relationship. However, they typically fall into certain categories:

- a full branch constitution incorporating the relationship with the main charity;
- a separate agreement covering specific areas; and
- a franchise agreement.

12.10 In all cases, it is important for the main charity to have confidence in certain key areas, namely:

- the delegated authority for the local committee to enter into contractual agreements, and operate local bank accounts;
- the terms of reference of local committees;
- the geographical area, or other important limitation, on the branch's activity;
- the adoption of policies and safeguards instituted by the centre;
- the terms and conditions of local employment arrangements;
- the approach to fund-raising, and the use of the national charity's name; and
- the operation of a sound system of internal controls.

12.11 Many of these issues will be addressed when the branch is first formed, but thereafter it is important for the trustees to be able to monitor the activities of the local branch. This will require some form of reporting back to the centre, a need which may be underlined by year end accounting needs, and tax factors.

12.12 Branches

12.12 A charity whose branches are not autonomous should include the financial performance of branches within its annual accounts, consolidated on a line by line basis gross, not net. Where branches hold general purpose funds it is common for the annual accounts to highlight these in the reserves analysis, perhaps even as designated funds. The requirement for trustees to report on branch activities in the main charity's accounts underlines the need for them to exercise a proper level of management control during the year.

Financial reporting

12.13 Where a branch network is seen as being a part of the main organisation, then it is possible for the combined activities of the branches to create a tax liability. This liability can be caused either by the branches undertaking transactions and activities which were not approved by the centre, or simply by the scale of the activities which, when combined, trigger either a requirement to be registered for VAT, or become sufficiently large for the Revenue to regard the scale of activity as taxable. For this reason many organisations run centralized functions for branches providing not only accounting but also other administrative support.

12.14 Where branches do their own accounting it is important for the centre to receive regular financial reports from the branches, in a format that allows the central finance department to collate and review them within a meaningful timeframe. In some cases, depending on the structure adopted, it may be necessary for the local branch to be reporting on two entities, the charitable activity, and the trading subsidiary.

12.15 Whatever the regularity of the financial reporting, the annual accounts will certainly need to incorporate the material results of non-autonomous branches. It will therefore be necessary in these circumstances to plan the year-end accounting work, and the audit, much further ahead than would be necessary for a stand-alone entity. The likely programme is as follows.

Table 6 Typical audit schedule for charity with branches

Timescale	Work
3–6 months before the year-end	Agree a format for the year-end accounts package with main charity finance department, local branch accountants and auditors
Just before the year-end	Issue accounts pack to branches and explain the reason for any changes from previous years. Notify them of any changes in the audit arrangements
1–2 months after the year-end	Collect accounts from branches, review and query as appropriate
Later	Audit of local results if carried out centrally, and feedback to branches on results of consolidation exercise

12.16 Although financial information may be returned from branches throughout the year, often the annual exercise is the most detailed and the most complete. Advantage should be taken of the information presented at this stage to gain a thorough understanding of local operations.

Audit

12.17 Whether or not an audit is required at local level will be a matter for individual consideration in each case. However, the following factors will need to be taken into consideration by both the main charity's auditor and the finance department.

- Does the national or local constitution require some form of audit or examination?
- Do any local funding arrangements require audit/examination?
- Can the main auditor express an opinion on the accounts of the whole organisation based on records available at the centre?
- Can the main auditor report on individual branches from the centre, or does a local auditor need to be involved?
- Who should bear the cost of local audit work?
- Can the work of internal audit be relied on in this area?

12.18 The auditors of charitable companies have a duty under the *Companies Act 1985* to state if proper returns adequate for their audit have not been received from branches not visited by them. The *Companies Act 1985* includes no definition of branch, although there is some discussion in the context of overseas companies in the DTI July 1992 Consultative Document on the *EC 11th Company Law Directive*.

VAT

12.19 Where the branch organisation also forms part of the VAT registration, then the branches will need to submit quarterly returns in line with the main charity. As an administrative convenience the centre may structure its affairs so that no money is passed either way at this stage, but all transactions are handled on a 'current account' maintained between the branch and the centre, with any cash balance being settled up later.

Trading subsidiaries

12.20 If a trading subsidiary is operated by the main charity, then a branch may also operate as a branch of the subsidiary. This will require a second set of books to be maintained by branches, which may be undesirable. Added complications such as this are particularly unwelcome where the branch is operated by volunteers, whose goodwill (and patience) is important to the success of the local operation.

Practical approaches

12.21 To reduce the complexity of administering branch structures, the following approaches are often applied.

12.22 Branches

- A tiered organisation is set up, with more complex or larger branches being entitled to undertake a wider range of activities than smaller or simpler branches.
- Branches are allocated to groupings, usually geographic regions, and intervening layers of management and support are used.
- An internal audit function is developed which also has a support role to the branches.
- Branches are restricted in the range of activity which they can undertake, with the centre taking the view that, for instance, fund-raising opportunities foregone are less of a cost than the administration of small sums, with the concomitant risk.
- The organisation is set up under a franchise agreement.
- Detailed system manuals and procedures, possibly involving some sort of centralised banking arrangements, are imposed from the centre.
- All trading activities are undertaken by the centre, with branches acting as agent.

Banking

12.22 Banking arrangements can also be used both to help and control local branches. The exact needs of the charity will determine the bank selected, but where branches are involved, often the need for easy local banking, overnight clearing to a central account, and the operation of a local account as part of the main account will be additional factors to take into account when selecting a bank. Where branches are mainly fund-raising groups, then the nature of the money being banked may also affect the choice of banker. For example, some banks are more geared up than others to receive and handle large volumes of coinage.

Overseas branches

12.23 Branches do not operate in the UK alone. It has been a common misconception that once a charity has passed money over to its overseas operations its trust obligations have been discharged. The definition of the autonomy of an overseas branch is essentially the same as the definition for a branch in the UK, with some obvious exceptions. Therefore, where an overseas branch is operating as part of the UK charity, then it is fully accountable to the trustees in the UK.

12.24 This aspect of overseas branch operations is emphasised by *ICTA 1988 s 506* which states that an application of funds overseas is not qualifying expenditure unless the charity has taken reasonable steps when making the transfer to ensure that it is applied for charitable purposes.

12.25 In some cases the treatment of overseas activities may be slightly different in practice compared with the comparable treatment of a similar situation in the UK. For instance, equipment sent to a branch in the UK will continue to be recorded as an asset of the charity, but may be written out of the books if despatched to an overseas project as it would not be cost-effective to recover it. Such policies do not alter the trustees' underlying duty to protect the assets, however. For instance, it would probably still be appropriate to obtain adequate insurance cover for the equipment.

Other branch relationships

12.26 Some organisations describe themselves as having branches when the relationship does not fit into the definition for non-autonomous branches described above. For instance, umbrella bodies and connected charities fall outside the 'branch' definition, as do relationships such as that between an Anglican diocese and parochial church councils.

13 Budgets

General considerations

13.1 A budget is the financial representation of the organisation's plans for a future period. Many of the aspects of budgeting are the same for a charity as they are for a commercial enterprise, or indeed for an individual. There are, however, certain features of a charity's affairs which make the budget process more fraught than in these other situations. One of these is the frequency with which volunteer treasurers, with little formal training in the subject, are put in the position of having to produce budgets (or accounts) and explain them. Some general principles are therefore set out below, followed by points of more detailed application to charities below.

Why budget?

13.2 A budget provides an element of internal control for a charity. It sets out the income the organisation intends to generate and how it intends to apply its resources, and enables the trustees to monitor the financial progress against that plan. Without the budget, the actual results noted during and after the year are only of limited value. Figures can only be compared with those of previous years', which may have been subject to all sorts of distortions.

Budget bases

13.3 Because a budget is looking ahead it has to be based on certain assumptions, both in the detail and in the overall plan of the charity. It is important that these are clearly understood by the users of the budget if it is to be of any use. Normally budgets end up as tough but realistic estimates; tough enough to make the organisation seek to be efficient and dynamic, but realistic enough not to lure the trustees into dangerous over- or underspending.

13.4 Most organisations will base next year's figures on a mixture of what happened last year and expectations for next year, together with external factors such as changes in tax recoveries, inflation and so on. It follows that those preparing the budget need access to information. Alternative approaches include zero based budgets (similar to priority based budgets) where the budget is drawn up starting from scratch, and every line of income and expenditure is challenged. This can be a very time consuming exercise but it is useful to adopt this approach occasionally as it helps to identify priorities. Outcome focused managers often prefer activity based budgeting which groups costs according to specific outcomes or activities, rather than by departments or units.

13.5 An 'ideal' budget is a budget that sets out the results if everything was perfect. It has the two great disadvantages, first of deluding the reader into thinking that it will happen, and therefore taking decisions accordingly, and second also of only ever reporting negative variances (i.e. bad news) from then on. However, where a budget is presented which includes some sensitivity analysis, an optimistic version as well as a likely version could be presented to show the organisation what might be achievable.

13.6 A budget should not just concentrate on income and expenditure, any more than should the management accounts. Unless a balance sheet is also presented, it is difficult to be certain that the overall impact of a course of action has been understood. For instance, an increase in income applied totally to purchasing an asset, such as a property, could lead to financial difficulties, even though total income exceeded total expenditure. For the same reason, a cash flow statement should also be produced, although sometimes this may be derived from the balance sheet and the Statement of Financial Activities (SOFA).

Setting the budget

13.7 The budget should not drive the charity. The charity should have its own strategic or operational plan from which the budget is derived. The effect of preparing the budget may lead to some plans being curtailed, or funds identified that are available to spend. For these reasons, the budget setting process should be an inclusive one, working both top down and bottom up. The overall budget parameters, such as the proportion of income to be allocated to particular services, should be determined by the trustees, the team leaders can then develop their plans and budgets in this context and feed them back up for consolidation and review. The consolidated budget is then reviewed, negotiated and amended until it is accepted by the trustees. In larger organisations this process may take several months. It may be necessary to be preparing next year's budgets before the previous year's accounts are finalised. Ideally, the budget for the next period will be part of a longer cycle, say a three-year plan, which will therefore be continuously updated.

The view of the Charity Commission

13.8 The Charity Commission have increasingly laid greater emphasis on the need for budgeting procedures in charities. They have drawn attention to them in a number of leaflets described below.

Internal Financial Controls

13.9 CC8 'Internal Financial Controls for Charities' states that proper and realistic estimates of expected income and expenditure should be made in order to have full control over the charity's finances. The budgets and accounts should only be approved by the trustees after discussion, and only if the trustees understand the financial information.

Charities and trading

13.10 When establishing a trading subsidiary the Charity Commission advises the trustees to take certain budgetary considerations into account (see CC35 'Charities and Trading'). The subsidiary should be financially viable as soon as possible. Normally it is expected that this will be within the first five years of its operation, although in practice many smaller charities would be expecting viability within twelve months. Other factors include how any inter-entity debts are to be settled, the timing of Gift Aid payments, and the return to be achieved on any initial investment.

Charities' reserves

13.11 Charities should realistically assess their reserves needs as 'an essential part of good financial management practice', advises the Charity Commission in CC19 'Charities' Reserves'. The reserves policy should be informed by income and expenditure forecasts, and an analysis of future needs, opportunities, risks and contingencies.

13.12 Budgets

Charity v commercial budgeting

13.12 The following additional complexities must be taken into account when producing a charity's budget. These are unlikely to be relevant in comparably sized commercial enterprises. Many of these factors are as relevant to the production of management accounts as they are to the production of budgets.

Outcomes

13.13 The budget is not the ultimate determinant of the projected success or otherwise of the organisation, in the same way that the accounts are not primarily concerned with surplus or deficit. The budget should be driven by the plan to achieve the outcomes specified in the plan. The budget should therefore put any surplus or deficit into the context of other factors.

Branches

13.14 Branch results should be planned, either in summary in the centre, or from detailed budgets submitted by them individually. This lengthens the budgeting process.

Investments

13.15 The total return on investments, both capital and income, should be forecast; this can be based on the investment manager's own predictions, and the required returns to which the manager operates.

Gifts in kind/donated facilities

13.16 Often these are omitted from the budget. If they are central to the charity then they should be included as part of the fundamental measurement of the operation. Even where they are less important, their inclusion will reduce variances requiring explanations on management accounts, and in some cases will ensure that performance ratios are more accurately anticipated. Where overheads are allocated out to projects and departments, then the exclusion of donated facilities can seriously distort the assessment of the costs of individual units.

Funds

13.17 Funds need separate presentation. Designated funds might be grouped together with general funds, or treated as a memorandum, depending on their significance. Restricted funds should be presented separately from the general fund, although it is likely that the level of detail will be less than on the general fund as income and expenditure will often comprise grants, discrete items, or allocations from general fund items.

14 Capital Gains Tax

Definition

14.1 A capital gain arises when an asset which has increased in value is given away, sold, exchanged or disposed of in any other way, other than in the course of trade. Tax is charged on the increase in value with an allowance made for the length of time the asset has been owned. This allowance takes the form of an indexation allowance based on the Retail Price Index and applies to individuals and trusts up to 5 April 1998 and to companies. From 6 April 1998, individuals and trusts are entitled to taper relief, which reduces the gain by a percentage. This percentage varies according to the length of time the asset has been owned since April 1998 and whether or not it is a business asset. Companies, industrial and provident societies, and unincorporated associations do not pay capital gains tax as such; they pay corporation tax on their profits which will include any capital gains. However, trusts do pay capital gains tax on any non-exempt capital gains.

14.2 Most capital gains made by charities are exempt from tax provided that the gain is used for charitable purposes. This exemption from capital gains tax can be lost, however, where the charity has incurred non-qualifying expenditure, i.e. expenditure for non-charitable purposes, such as funding a trading subsidiary. The exemption is not lost, however, if the proceeds of the sale of an asset, excluding the gain, are spent on a non-charitable purpose. [*Taxation of Chargeable Gains Act 1992 s 256*]. When an asset forms part of a charity's permanent endowment, the terms of the endowment may require gains made from the sale of the asset to be re-invested in similar assets. Where this is the case the gain will be exempt from capital gains tax.

Gains

14.3 A chargeable gain on which capital gains tax is payable can arise on the disposal of an asset by sale or gift. Where the disposal is not at arm's length e.g. in the case of a gift, the market value of the asset is normally substituted for any proceeds. Allowable deductions in arriving at the chargeable gain are the cost of the asset, expenditure on improvement or enhancement of the asset, the incidental costs of acquisition and disposal and any available indexation allowance or taper relief.

Losses

14.4 Capital losses occurring in the same or an earlier period may be deducted from chargeable gains in calculating the liability to capital gains tax. Losses are calculated in the same way as gains, except that indexation allowance and taper relief do not apply. The legislation makes no reference to capital losses made by charities and it is arguable whether it must be implied from the legislation that because a gain is not a chargeable gain, a loss is not allowable. This point is only relevant where a charity has at some time made capital losses and is subject to tax on its chargeable gains because, for example, it has incurred non-qualifying expenditure. Where a charity has a loss of tax exemption because of the rules relating to non-qualifying expenditure, it can choose by election what income or gains are taxed. A charity may elect to pay tax on its chargeable gains and seek to argue that capital losses are deductible.

14.5 Capital Gains Tax

Loss of charitable status

14.5 In a body set up as a trust the trustees are liable for the trust's taxes and can be held personally liable if the trust cannot pay its taxes. Where a charitable trust is wound up, or its objects cease to be charitable, there is a deemed disposal of all the trust's assets at their market value and any gain arising will be subject to capital gains tax unless they are passed to another charity to be applied for charitable purposes. Where there is a non-exempt capital gain and the assets held were acquired using the proceeds from the disposal of other assets with an exempt gain accrued at the time, that original gain also becomes taxable. The gain is assessed on individuals who are trustees at the time when the disposals were made. Therefore, if it is likely that a trust will cease to be charitable at some future date, trustees should be aware of these provisions and should seek an indemnity on retirement as gains made when they were trustees could become subject to tax at a much later date.

Gifts to charity

14.6 When a donor wishes to give an asset to a charity, or sell it to the charity at less than its market value, its value is assumed to be an amount that does not give rise to a gain or a loss, so the donor does not have to pay capital gains tax. [*Taxation of Chargeable Gains Act 1992 ss 257, 258*]. Similar rules apply to gifts and sales below market value to institutions listed in the *Inheritance Tax Act 1984*, such as universities, museums and art galleries. If the sale of an asset would make a loss the donor may wish to consider selling the asset to a third party, offsetting the loss against any capital gains they have made in order to reduce their overall liability for capital gains tax, and donating the proceeds of the sale to a charity under Gift Aid, thus increasing the value of the gift to the charity. From April 2000 individuals and companies can also get tax relief for the value of gifts of quoted securities, unit trusts and certain other investments when calculating their income or profits for tax purposes.

Trading companies

14.7 A charity's subsidiary trading company is fully liable for tax on any capital gains it makes from the sale or disposal of assets. The tax liability can be avoided, however, by using Gift Aid to pass the profits to the charity.

14.8 It may be advisable for the charity, rather than the trading subsidiary, to own assets which could give rise to capital gains. Professional advice should be sought.

15 Charitable Purposes

What is a charity?

15.1 There is no comprehensive definition of charity in English law. The modern concept of charity has evolved from the preamble to the *Charitable Uses Act 1601* (since repealed), popularly known as the Statute of Elizabeth I, which listed the following as being regarded as charitable:

- relief of aged, impotent (weak or powerless) and poor people;
- maintenance of sick and maimed soldiers and mariners;
- maintenance of schools of learning, free schools, and scholars in universities;
- repair of bridges, ports, havens, causeways, churches, sea banks and highways;
- education and preferment (advancement) of orphans;
- relief, stock or maintenance of houses of correction;
- marriages of poor maids;
- supportation, aid and help of young tradesmen, handicraftsmen and persons decayed (fallen into misfortune);
- relief or redemption of prisoners or captives; and
- aid or ease of any poor inhabitants concerning payment of fifteens (a tax on movable property), setting out soldiers (a tax to equip soldiers), and other taxes.

15.2 Since then decisions on what is, or is not, regarded as charitable have evolved from these by analogy. This allows purposes that could not have been imagined in 1601, to become charitable today. So, for example, 'the preferment of orphans' is analogous to 'the provision of orphanages' which is analogous to 'caring for disadvantaged children', which is analogous to 'caring for children suffering from sexual abuse'. Therefore an organisation such as Childline can be registered as a charity.

15.3 In 1891 in a landmark case, which subsequently has become known as the *Pemsel* case, the judge, Lord MacNaghten, drew on the *1601 Act* and an 1804 definition of charitable objects to group charitable purposes into four 'heads' or categories (*Income Tax Special Purpose Commissioners v Pemsel 1891 AC 531*). These are:

- the relief of poverty;
- the advancement of education;
- the advancement of religion; and
- other purposes beneficial to the community in a way recognised as charitable.

Perhaps surprisingly these four heads are still in use today and although derived from English case law, they are also used in Scotland by the Inland Revenue.

15.4 Although the Courts still refer to the Elizabethan preamble and the Pemsel classification they have developed charity law so that the law's view of what is charitable has kept in step with changing social needs and conditions. Public opinion is very much taken into account when the Courts are determining the current interpretation of the law. Therefore although public opinion does not determine what is legally charitable, the Courts and the Charity Commission know that their interpretation of public benefit will be supported by most people and will reflect people's ethical views about what should be regarded as beneficial. Examples of new purposes that have been accepted as charitable in recent years included the promotion of racial harmony and the preservation of the environment.

The review of the register

15.5 At the time of writing the Charity Commission is carrying out a thorough review of its register of charities. The Commission considers that as the understanding of what is legally charitable evolves over time, and because it is now 35 years since the register was established, there are likely to be organisations listed on the register that the public would no longer regard as deserving charitable status and organisations not on it that the public see as being charitable.

15.6 The review is not seeking to change the law, but it is looking to see if there is scope for the Charity Commission to further extend the boundaries of charitable status using its powers to apply and interpret the law. Since the review commenced organisations established for the relief of unemployment and organisations established for the promotion of urban and rural regeneration have been recognised as being charitable (see Chapter 21 and Chapter 18).

Relief of poverty

15.7 Although MacNaghten's first head of charity only refers to poverty, the *1601 Act* referred to the aged, impotent and poor. The meaning of 'poverty' can also be interpreted in a broad sense. Therefore 'poor' includes not only those who qualify for State means-tested benefits, but also those who have fallen on hard times relative to their usual standard of living. It can also be interpreted to include people who are ill, or suffering from some form of mental or physical impairment, regardless of their financial status.

15.8 Charities whose purposes fall under the relief of poverty can have a small group of beneficiaries, for example, the ex-employees of a firm that has gone bankrupt, unlike charities coming under the other three heads which must be established for public benefit.

15.9 As well as dealing with the effects of poverty, organisations can tackle the root causes of poverty, providing they do not overstep the Charity Commission's guidance on political activities, if they are registered in England or Wales. The Inland Revenue, which 'recognises' charities in Scotland, could refuse recognition on similar grounds.

15.10 For more information see Chapter 19.

Advancement of education

15.11 As with poverty, there is no set definition of education. A wide interpretation is used that includes more than just academic teaching. Universities, schools that have opted out of local authority control, private schools operating on a not-for-profit basis, nurseries, museums, art galleries, theatres and concert halls, youth clubs, schools of needlework and craft centres are all examples of organisations that have registered under this head. Business education is also included, as long as it is not bespoke advice or consultancy.

15.12 The promotion of physical education and the provision of sports equipment and facilities is regarded as charitable, but sports clubs and the promotion of sport are not.

15.13 For more information about educational charities see Chapter 38. Chapter 93 provides more information about recreational charities.

Advancement of religion

15.14 The main considerations for a charity to be registered under the third head are that the religion is of a kind accepted by the court. Therefore it does not necessarily have to be Christian. One definition used for religion has been 'faith in a God and worship of that God' (South Place Ethical Society 1980), although a wider definition is accepted whereby mainstream religions that do not conform to this definition, such as Hinduism and Buddhism, are included.

15.15 The *Charities (Designated Religious Bodies) (Scotland) Order 1993* lists Scottish religious bodies that are exempt from certain provisions of the *Law Reform (Miscellaneous Provisions) (Scotland) Act 1990*, including the accounting provisions.

15.16 More information about religious charities is contained in Chapter 95.

Other purposes beneficial to the community

15.17 The fourth head is the broadest one. It is under this that many new charities register by analogy with the *1601 Act* although it is by no means a loophole through which all good causes can be registered, as there must be evidence of public benefit to a substantial part of the community and the activity must be recognised as charitable. It is under this head that racial harmony and sexual equality, environmental protection, provision of public amenities, promotion of public safety and the promotion of industry, the arts and commerce fall. (See Chapter 17.)

15.18 Animal welfare also comes under this head, though animal charities are only registered providing that their main purpose is to benefit humanity, for example 'upholding human dignity by the prevention of cruelty to animals'.

15.19 The provision of village halls and community centres, as referred to in the *Recreational Charities Act 1958*, is also covered under this head, but such provision is only deemed charitable if the facilities are provided in the interest of social welfare.

Public benefit

15.20 There is no clear definition as to what exactly constitutes a 'substantial' part of the community, as required for a purpose to be charitable under all but the relief of poverty head. It very much depends on the context. Clubs that restrict membership on other than functional (for example, the promotion of lace-making) or geographic grounds (for example, the residents of Charity Village) are unlikely to be regarded as charitable. However, an organisation established to support people suffering from a rare disease would be considered charitable even if there were only ten potential beneficiaries, provided that membership was open to all those affected by the disease.

Catch-all objects

15.21 When drafting a charity's objects it is possible to make them very wide, e.g. 'to relieve poverty, advance education, promote religion anywhere in the world and do all such other things that may benefit the community in a way recognised as charitable', and then go on to add more specific clauses indicating the type of work and areas in which the charity will initially operate.

16 Charitable Status

16.1 Organisations in England and Wales operating on a not-for-profit basis will be charities by definition if their objects or purposes are wholly and exclusively charitable (see Chapter 15) and, if apart from those for the relief of poverty, they also provide a public benefit.

Charitable status independent of registration

16.2 Most charities are required by *s 3(2)* of the *Charities Act 1993* to register with the Charity Commission (see Chapter 94) but it is not this registration that grants them charitable status, it is meeting the criteria for a charity outlined above.

Charitable status not dependent on legal structure

16.3 An organisation's status as a charity is a completely separate matter from the legal structure it chooses to use. Thus a benevolent society that adopts the legal structure of a company or an industrial and provident society will be charitable provided that:

- its objects are wholly and exclusively charitable;
- it provides a public benefit; and
- it operates on a not-for-profit basis.

Advantages of charitable status

16.4 Having charitable status brings and confers a number of tax and other advantages.

- Being a charity attracts funding and other support from the general public as, on the whole, the British public regard charities as 'a good thing'.
- Some funding bodies can give grants only to charitable organisations.
- Charities are entitled to 80% business rate relief, with a further 20% at the discretion of the local authority (see Chapter 90).
- Charities enjoy a number of tax reliefs (see Chapter 111).
- Charities are entitled to call on the Charity Commission for support and guidance and the Commission's role as a regulator enhances public confidence in charities by detecting and detering abuse.

Disadvantages of charitable status

16.5 There are, however, some disadvantages attached to being a charity including the following.

- Some needy people have a negative attitude to receiving 'charity' and therefore will not seek help.
- Charities have to comply with charity law and regulation in addition to legislation relating to their legal structure. This can restrict their political and campaigning activities and means they have to structure certain trading activities

through subsidiary trading companies which may, in turn, add to their operating costs.

- With some exceptions, members of the governing body cannot be paid. This can result in their not giving sufficient time to their duties.
- In some instances charity trustees can be held personally liable for their actions and this can deter some people from being willing to act as trustees.
- Charity trustees have to act in the best interests of the charity, with prudence and within the law and the charity's governing document. This may produce a conflict with their personal code of ethics, e.g. they may be unable to exclude certain investments from the charity's portfolio which they themselves would not wish to hold.

Declaration of charitable status

16.6 *Section 5* of *Charities Act 1993* requires all registered charitable trusts and associations with an annual income of more than £10,000 to include a statement of charitable status on the following documents:

- all notices, advertisements and other documents soliciting money or other property for the benefit of the charity,
- cheques, bills of exchange, promissory notes and orders for money or goods, and
- bills, invoices, receipts and letters of credit.

Welsh charities may use 'elusen cafrestredig' on documents wholly in Welsh.

16.7 *Section 68* of the *Charities Act 1993* requires charitable companies whose name does not include the words 'charity' or 'charitable' to include a statement indicating their charitable status on a similar range of documents and also on:

- all business letters;
- all notices and other official publications; and
- all conveyances purporting to be executed by the company

16.8 While there is no statute or case law yet on whether these requirements apply to e-mails or to information on websites, the general consensus is that they do.

17 Charities for Other Purposes Beneficial to the Community

17.1 Organisations that are not established to relieve poverty, advance education or religion but which are of benefit to the community may qualify for charitable status under the 'fourth head' of charity defined by Lord MacNaghten in the *Pemsel* case in 1891 (*Income Tax Special Purpose Commissioners v Pemsel, 1891 AC 531*). By analogy organisations engaged in activities undreamed of when the *Charitable Uses Act 1601* was drafted can be registered as charities.

17.2 Charities for other purposes beneficial to the community must, like all charities be for purposes that are wholly and exclusively charitable, and must be for public benefit. Examples of 'fourth head' charities include those:

- providing relief for the elderly, sick or disabled where there is no financial need;
- promoting racial harmony;
- promoting sexual equality;
- providing resettlement and rehabilitation for offenders or substance abusers;
- providing help for victims of natural disasters;
- providing recreational facilities open to everyone, or to people from a disadvantaged group such as the elderly or people with disabilities;
- promoting industry, the arts and commerce for the public benefit;
- engaged in conservation or protection of the environment;
- promoting public safety.

17.3 Animal welfare is not of itself a charitable activity. However, animal charities whose main purpose is to benefit humanity can be registered in this category. Preventing humans being cruel to animals or enabling them to care for animals is seen as upholding human dignity.

17.4 Sports clubs set up to benefit their members only cannot be charitable. Neither are organisations to promote political or propagandist purposes or to promote a particular point of view. The Thatcher Foundation is an example of such an organisation that was refused charitable status. Town twinning organisations and other organisations designed to promote international friendship do not qualify for charitable status.

18 Charities for the Promotion of Urban and Rural Regeneration

18.1 Following public consultation, the Charity Commissioners have recently recognised the Promotion of Urban and Rural Regeneration for public benefit in areas of social and economic deprivation as a charitable purpose in its own right.

18.2 In its leaflet RR 2 — *Promotion of Urban and Rural Regeneration* the Charity Commission cite as a possible object that would be acceptable 'The promotion for the public benefit of urban or rural regeneration in areas of social and economic deprivation (and in particular [specify area]) by all or any of the following means: [specify activities]'.

Criteria for charitable status

18.3 For a regeneration organisation to be granted charitable status it would need to show that:

- it has effective criteria for determining whether or not an area is in need of regeneration;
- its activities will cover a broad spectrum of regeneration work including at least three of the activities listed in 18.8 below;
- the public benefit arising will outweigh any private benefit which may be conferred on individuals or companies in the area and that the organisation has clear criteria by which this can be determined;
- its objects are exclusively charitable.

Public v private benefit

18.4 Most tangible benefits of regeneration appear to go to individuals, for example in the form of increased property prices, or to companies rather than to the wider public. For an organisation to be charitable its purpose and activities must be restricted to public benefit and any private benefit that does arise should do so only as a side effect of the achievement of the charitable purpose. Therefore a regeneration organisation applying for charitable status will need to demonstrate that its activities will not result in an unacceptable level of private benefit.

18.5 Therefore, if the main problems in an area are poor housing and high crime, but unemployment is low, charitable status would not be granted to a regeneration organisation that intends to focus on activities to regenerate the area by further reducing the level of unemployment as this would have only a marginal effect on deprivation in the area. The private benefit accruing to local employers would be likely to be greater than the public benefit.

18.6 Criteria that might be used to weigh up the balance between public and private benefit include:

- the increase in the number of homes for sale and house prices;
- the change in the waiting list for social housing;
- the change in the rate of participation of local people in community events;

- the increase in public amenities;
- the change in the health of the local population;
- the reduction in unemployment;
- the reduction in unemployment benefit compared with the amount that the charity would have to pay an employer to take on unemployed people;
- the change in the crime rate.

18.7 In assessing whether an organisation is set up for public or private benefit the Charity Commission will take into account the support and participation of a large part of the community in developing the regeneration plans, the impact of the organisation's activities on the local community and the composition of the trustee body. This should be independent of companies or funding bodies that stand to gain from the regeneration activities. If some of the trustees are likely to gain personally from the regeneration the charity's governing document must contain provision for the declaration of interests. Trustees with an interest should absent themselves from discussions in which they may have a conflict of interest and may not vote on them. The charity's promoters should be able to demonstrate that having an individual with a private interest as a trustee is to the benefit of the charity, notwithstanding the potential conflict.

Regeneration activities

18.8 The types of activities that an urban or rural regeneration charity might carry out include:

- providing, maintaining and improving public amenities;
- providing, maintaining and improving recreational facilities;
- preserving buildings in the area that are of historic or architectural interest;
- conserving, maintaining or improving environmental features such as docks, canals, public footpaths, etc.;
- providing, maintaining and improving roads and accessibility to main transport routes;
- providing public healthcare facilities;
- providing childcare facilities;
- promoting public safety and the prevention of crime.

18.9 They can also carry out activities that would also qualify as charitable under the heads of the relief of poverty or the advancement of education or that could be done by a charity established for the relief of unemployment, such as:

- providing financial assistance to people in need;
- providing housing for those in need;
- improving housing standards generally in a area of deprivation;
- helping unemployed people to find employment;
- providing education, training, work experience and advice to unemployed people with the aim of helping them gain employment;
- providing financial or technical assistance to new businesses;

- providing financial or technical assistance to existing businesses where it would enable them to employ and train unemployed people;
- providing land or buildings to businesses on favourable terms in order to create training and employment opportunities for unemployed people.

Accounting requirements

18.10 These may well be complex depending on the activities carried out and the way in which the charity works i.e. as a front-line operation or as a co-ordinating body sub-contracting some of the work to other charitable or non-charitable organisations. Specialist advice will be needed.

18.11 If a regeneration charity owns land or property the trustees will have to decide whether it should be accounted for as functional property or investment property, particularly where the property has been used for both purposes. As with charities for the relief of unemployment if the charity provides land or property to a business start-up on favourable terms the trustees will similarly have to decide whether it should be accounted for as functional property or investment property. Again, as with charities for the relief of unemployment, where payment is made to a commercial company to take on unemployed people the charity will need to agree with the company the economic cost of employing and training such staff. The charity should not pay an amount in excess of the economic cost.

19 Charities for the Relief of Poverty

19.1 The relief of poverty was one of the four 'heads' of charity defined by Lord MacNaghten in the *Pemsel* case in 1891 (*Income Tax Special Purpose Commissioners v Pemsel 1891 AC 531*). 'Poverty' is a relative term. People living in poverty in the UK today have possessions, such as televisions and refrigerators, that were regarded as luxuries only 50 years ago. In comparison with many people living in the Third World, poor people in the UK are relatively rich. Charities for the relief of poverty often define their beneficiary group as 'people who cannot afford the normal things in life that most people take for granted'.

19.2 The relief of poverty or financial hardship also includes giving help to people in financial need who are suffering from the effects of old age, sickness or a disability. To qualify for help a person's hardship does not have to be long-term. They may qualify for help because their circumstances have changed suddenly perhaps due to job loss, bereavement or sickness.

19.3 People may qualify for help from a charity regardless of whether or not they are entitled to State benefits. Some people in receipt of a number of State benefits may need additional help and people who do not qualify for State benefits may need help in particular circumstances.

19.4 Depending on the wording of a charity's governing document there may be a number of ways in which they can relieve poverty:

- Gifts of money. These could be in the form of a one-off grant, for example to purchase furniture or clothing, pay utility bills or towards funeral expenses; a regular weekly allowance to supplement a person's income or a regular payment to purchase a particular item or service such as a television licence or telephone line rental; payments to cover travelling expenses to hospitals, children's homes or prisons where more frequent visits than public funds provide for are desirable.

- Provision of goods, such as radio and television sets, washing machines, furniture, bedding, clothing, food, fuel, heating appliances, prams, used cars, etc.

- Payment for services such as laundry, home insulation, decorating and repairs, meals on wheels, child-minding, respite care, and holidays.

- Provision of facilities such as essential tools or books, lessons or equipment for children with particular talent in music, sport, ballet, art, etc., travelling expenses to enable someone to earn their living, training to enable someone to gain employment or enhance the quality of their life.

19.5 Charities for the relief of poverty often give extra help to those who are both poor and sick. They can provide grants towards the cost of special diets, adapting a home to meet the needs of someone with a physical disability, or convalescent care. They can provide medical equipment such as a wheelchair, either outright or on loan. They can provide services such as personal or nursing care, physiotherapy or chiropody in the home, respite care, shopping, gardening, exchange of library books, counselling, befriending, etc.

19.6 Some charities also seek to relieve poverty by campaigning against the root causes of poverty and for changes in State benefits, others by making grants to other charities for projects designed to relieve poverty.

State benefits

19.7 Charities must take care that the assistance they provide is not replacing any State benefit that the recipient is entitled to, as the recipient would be no better off and the charity's funds would be merely relieving the State. Charities can, however, make grants or loans to relieve immediate need when there is a delay in the receipt of State benefits. Charities should encourage their beneficiaries to claim any State benefits to which they are entitled. When assessing a person's need for assistance the trustees should take into account all the State benefits a person should be claiming, even if they are unwilling to claim them.

Social Fund

19.8 The Social Fund is intended to help people meet exceptional expenses from their regular income. It provides help in the form of grants and interest free loans. People do not have a statutory right to assistance from the Social Fund and many applicants are turned away as the grants budget has been exhausted and the applicant has no means of repaying a loan. Social Fund officials are in some circumstances obliged by law to consider if an applicant could get help from another source such as a charity. Therefore trustees of charities that give help to needy people should establish good contacts with the local Benefits Agency so that the Agency has a good understanding of the circumstances in which the charity can offer assistance. If trustees believe that the Agency is using the charity in order to avoid Social Fund expenditure they should take the matter up with the official concerned or at a higher level.

19.9 If a person has been promised a Social Fund loan a charity can still assist them if:

- they are in urgent need and there is a delay in the receipt of the money;
- the person would clearly not be able to repay the loan in the time specified (this is an exception to the general principle that charitable funds should not be used to replace State funding);
- the Social Fund loan promised is insufficient to meet the person's need.

Charities relieving hardship that are not for the public benefit

19.10 Organisations established to assist a particular named person or a specific group of individuals cannot usually be granted charitable status as they do not exist for the public benefit. Charities relieving hardship are an exception to this general principle, as they can be established to assist a specific group of individuals such as those working for the same employer. Benevolent Funds are examples of charities that are not established for the public benefit.

20 Charities for the Relief of Sickness

20.1 Although very many charities exist to help the sick and ill, the relief of sickness itself is not listed as one of the four heads of charity. It can be interpreted either as falling within the first head 'the relief of poverty', or the fourth 'other purposes beneficial to the community', which in turn are both derived from the preamble to the *Elizabethan Charitable Uses Act 1601* examples of charitable activity which included the relief of aged, impotent and poor people.

Beneficiaries

20.2 The definition of who qualifies as 'sick' is also now established as a wide one, and includes the mentally ill, the disabled, the infirm and convalescent, and those suffering from an addiction. The governing document should always be consulted to ensure that potential beneficiaries qualify and that the objects are not too narrowly drawn, for instance beneficiaries have to be both 'sick' and 'poor'. Again before giving assistance trustees need to be sure that:

- the person has a clear need for assistance;
- the benefits or assistance proposed are related to that need;
- the benefits or assistance proposed are not available from other non-charitable sources.

20.3 The activities undertaken by charities involved in the relief of sickness are widespread and include direct provision to the sick in hospitals, homes and day centres, through visiting, full-time or respite care, support to providers of health services through training, education and campaigning, and research carried out in-house, or commissioned or funded through fellowships and academic appointments. Help may be provided by the charity directly, or by the charity giving money or vouchers to the beneficiaries to enable them to pay for help themselves, or by the charity arranging for another organisation to provide the assistance required, in return for the charity giving the provider a fee, subscription or donation.

Items and services charities can provide

20.4 In its publication CC6 — *Charities for the Relief of Sickness* the Charity Commission lists the following items and services as those which it may be appropriate for a charity, established for the relief of sickness, to provide. The list is not intended to be exhaustive.

Items that may be given or loaned include:

- bedding
- clothing
- food for special diets
- fuel or the equivalent in savings stamps or pre-charged keys
- heating appliances
- medical or other equipment
- wheelchairs

- televisions or TV licences
- radios
- washing machines
- telephones
- prescription 'season tickets'.

Services that could be provided include:

- bathing
- foot care
- hair washing
- shaving
- help in the home
- adaptations to the homes of disabled people
- laundering
- meals on wheels
- nursing aid
- physiotherapy in the home
- gardening
- reading
- exchange of library books
- shopping
- sitting-in
- tape-recording books and newspapers
- child minding
- outings and entertainments
- travelling companions
- counselling.

20.5 Other special arrangements may be made, such as periods of rest or change of environment, treatment at convalescent homes or health clinics, temporary relief for those having the care of a sick or a person with a disability, help for relatives and friends to visit or care for patients, and transport.

VAT

20.6 Often the provision of services by a charity involved in health care will be under a contract, either with a statutory provider or with an individual. Such a supply is therefore a business supply but it will normally be exempt from VAT if it constitutes a welfare service. Where such welfare services are provided consistently below cost they may be outside the scope of VAT (see Chapter 46).

20.7 Charities for the Relief of Sickness

Contracts

20.7 As charities have increasingly been drawn into the contract culture, so there has been a growing need for them to understand the implications of entering into such arrangements. The position is complicated by the lack of distinction between grants, contracts, and such things as 'service level agreements'. In practice every such arrangement will be either a contract or a grant, and its exact nature needs to be identified as it may have consequences for the trustees.

20.8 A contract is a trading obligation which creates rights and expectations between the parties. In a contract, there will be an exchange for value. In this context a charity will provide a service usually on behalf of the health authority or local authority in exchange for an agreed fee. The contractual risk is therefore with the charity to perform its part of the agreement. If it fails, then the other party can take legal action against the charity or, if the charity is unincorporated, against the trustees personally as in this instance it is the trustees who are party to the contract. Although such a contractual arrangement is by definition trading, it is usually primary purpose trading.

20.9 Where the charity is receiving a grant to help it provide a service, then no such contractual exchange is taking place. However, the charity will still need to account for the use of the grant monies, if only through the statutory accounts. Any unspent grant income should be repaid to the grantor, whereas any profit on a contract, subject to any dispute over performance or costed services, can be kept by the charity and used for any charitable purpose.

Relationships with statutory providers

20.10 A charity should not use its funds to pay for or provide services that a public body is legally required to provide at public expense. This means that it is permissible for a charity to provide additional services, or to provide a qualitatively better service, as in both of these cases this extra element can be paid for from the charity's own funds.

20.11 A health authority, for instance, may contract with a charity to provide services on its behalf. The contract price should not be subsidised by the charity either financially or by the provision of other services or volunteer time. Where additional features are to be provided these must be in addition to the basic service provided by the authority, albeit through the medium of a contract at a proper price with a charity. This means that in the case of a service which should be provided by the public sector, using public funds, then although there may be a competitive tendering process the charity should only offer to provide the service at the full economic cost.

20.12 It is not always easy to identify what the contracting party is legally obliged to provide out of public funds, and for this reason charities which are new to such arrangements should be extremely careful, obtaining evidence of the public body's responsibilities before entering into the contract. Local authorities often have discretion about the exact nature of provision to be made, and in this case it will be necessary to consider what the pattern of the service has been in the past, to ensure that the voluntary sector is not simply being seen as a cheap, alternative source of provision.

20.13 It is not uncommon for a representative of the public body to act as a trustee of the charity, either because the charity needs the expertise, or because the public body wishes to have some influence over the relationship. This is an area for potential conflict of interest and should, if possible, be avoided. There is no reason why the representative cannot attend trustee meetings for some or all of the agenda, and simply have observer or adviser status. If the individual is a trustee, it may be necessary for that person not to be involved with any discussion or decision relating to the relationship between the public body and the charity, or for the Charity Commission to be asked to give their specific approval to certain transactions and arrangements.

Gifts to hospitals and doctors' surgeries

20.14 Subject to the condition that a charity should not use its funds to pay for statutory services, a charity can make a gift to a hospital provided that the hospital concerned cares for sick people primarily from the charity's area of benefit and that the people will benefit directly from the gift. A charity may also loan equipment to a hospital on terms agreed between them and the hospital which should include details of who is responsible for the cost of maintaining the equipment. Once the equipment is no longer needed it should be returned to the charity.

20.15 Similarly, a charity can also give, loan or provide a grant to purchase equipment for a doctor's surgery, provided that the trustees are satisfied that the equipment is needed, cannot be provided by the doctor out of the practice's funds, and will be used to benefit patients living within the charity's area of benefit.

21 Charities for the Relief of Unemployment

21.1 Until recently charities were not permitted to have an express object of helping unemployed people. Charities helped unemployed people under the charitable heads of the relief of poverty and advancing education. They could provide training so that a person could gain skills and hopefully find employment but they could not provide employment as such. However, the Courts have now recognised that securing gainful employment for unemployed people is charitable in its own right.

21.2 In its leaflet RR3 — *Charities for the Relief of Unemployment* the Charity Commission cite as a possible object that would be acceptable 'the relief of unemployment for the public benefit in such ways as may be thought fit, including assistance to find employment'.

Criteria for charitable status

21.3 In order to gain charitable status an organisation established for the relief of unemployment will need to show that:

- it is set up for the primary purpose of relieving unemployment for the public benefit;
- its activities are designed to relieve unemployment generally or to relieve unemployment in a significant section of the community;
- any benefit accruing to private interests must be strictly incidental to the charity's primary purpose.

21.4 Assistance to unemployed people should be directed to the relief of a charitable need and the level of assistance provided should be commensurate to that need. In practice this means that to qualify for charitable status an organisation must be set up for the benefit of people seeking employment but who are unable to find work because of their lack of skills, youth, age, infirmity or disablement, poverty, social or economic circumstances. Organisations established to help employed people become self-employed will not normally qualify for charitable status.

Activities to relieve unemployment

21.5 The following are examples of the type of activities a charity established for the relief of unemployment may engage in:

- providing advice and training to unemployed people about employment, self-employment and the establishment of co-operatives;
- providing assistance with preparation of CV's and job search;
- providing a job club;
- providing practical support, such as accommodation, child-care facilities and assistance with travelling expenses;
- providing land or premises at below market rents to businesses starting up;
- providing capital grants to new businesses;
- paying a commercial business to take on unemployed people.

Accounting requirements

21.6 Where land or property are provided to a business start-up the trustees will have to decide whether it should be accounted for as functional property or investment property. Specialist advice is likely to be needed particularly where the property has been used for both purposes.

21.7 Where payment is made to a commercial company to take on unemployed people the charity will need to agree with the company the economic cost of employing and training such staff. The charity should not pay an amount in excess of the economic cost.

22 Charity Commission: Structure and Administration

Introduction

22.1 The Charity Commission is a non-ministerial government department, accountable to Parliament and the courts for promoting the effective use of charitable resources, giving information and advice to charities, investigating misconduct and abuse, and maintaining a public register of all charities with the exception of those that are exempted or excepted from registration. Its remit extends to England and Wales only, although the Commission has some supervisory powers over Scottish charities that are controlled from England or Wales. Scottish charities are regulated by the Scottish Charities Office and charities in Northern Ireland by the Department of Health and Social Services.

The Charity Commissioners

22.2 *Paragraph 1* of *Sch 1* to the *Charities Act 1993* lays down that there must be a Chief Charity Commissioner (currently John Stoker) and two other Commissioners appointed by the Secretary of State. At least two of them must be legally qualified. It also gives the Secretary of State authority to appoint not more than two additional Commissioners. Currently there are four full or part-time Commissioners, Michael Carpenter and Jean Warburton who are legally qualified and two lay Commissioners, Julia Unwin and David Taylor. The Commisioners are salaried civil servants.

22.3 The Chief Commissioner has the power to appoint assistant commissioners, officers and employees to discharge the functions of the Commission. The Commission has a staff of about 550, based in offices in London, Liverpool and Taunton and a budget of £21 million per year.

Commission's Role

22.4 The *Charities Act 1992* gave the Charity Commission a more proactive role in monitoring charities, supported by a new accounting and reporting regime. It also strengthened the powers of the Charity Commission to investigate and deal with abuse and mismanagement and to protect charity property. These parts of the Act are consolidated into the *Charities Act 1993. Section 29* of the *1993 Act* gives the Commission a specific power to advise trustees on any matter concerning their duties. Charity trustees can protect themselves from committing a breach of trust by seeking advice in writing from the Commission, referring to *s 29*. If they provide, to the best of their knowledge, the full facts of the situation and act on the Commission's advice they will be deemed to have acted in accordance with the charity's trusts.

22.5 The Charity Commission has a dual role as the regulator and friend of the charitable sector. As regulator, it monitors charities, investigates complaints and can bring legal proceedings against a charity or individuals associated with it. As friend, it provides advice and support by means of publications, workshops, conferences, a newsletter and an internet site, as well as dealing with written and telephone requests for advice. Its specific functions include the following.

- Determining whether or not an organisation is a charity within the meaning of *s 96(1)* and *s 97(1)* of the *Charities Act 1993* and can be entered on the register. Also determining, under *s 3(4)* whether or not an institution can remain on the register or should be removed because it no longer appears to be a charity because of a change in its activities, or because it has ceased to operate, or ceased to exist.

- Receiving and monitoring charities' accounts and trustees' reports and making them available to the public.
- Making Orders or Schemes allowing trustees to do something in the interests of the charity but which is outside their powers.
- Authorising actions which need consent, such as a change in the objects of a charitable company or certain land transactions.
- With the consent of the Director of Public Prosecutions, instituting proceedings against anyone acting as a trustee while disqualified.
- Keeping a register of all individuals who have been removed from office by the Commissioners, or by the High Court after *s 45(1)* of the *Charities Act 1992* came into force, and making it available to the public.
- In certain circumstances, granting waivers from disqualification from trusteeship, under *s 72(4)* of the *Charities Act 1993*.
- If there is reason to suspect a serious problem in connection with the affairs of a charity, unless it is exempt, instituting a *s 8* inquiry under the *Charities Act 1993* and calling for evidence (see Chapter 70).
- If as a result of a *s 8* inquiry the Commissioners are satisfied that there has been misconduct or mismanagement or that a charity's property needs protection, they can use powers in *s 18* to suspend any trustee, official or employee of the charity, appoint additional trustees, vest the charity's property in the official custodian, or appoint a receiver and manager.
- Requiring a charity to change its name in certain circumstances.
- Ordering an audit of a charity's accounts in certain circumstances.
- Authorising *ex gratia* payments.
- Giving directions about dormant charity bank accounts.
- Ordering taxation of a solicitor's bill.
- Making Schemes to establish common investment funds and common deposit funds for charities.

No power to manage

22.6 *Section 1(4)* of the *Charities Act 1993* expressly prohibits the Charity Commission from taking part in, or taking over, the management of a charity. However, *s 18* of the Act gives the Commission power to appoint a Receiver and Manager if it finds, in the course of a *s 8* inquiry, that there has been misconduct or mismanagement, or that the charity's assets need protecting (see Chapter 70).

Complaints about standards of service

22.7 The Charity Commission has established a procedure for dealing with complaints about the standards of its service. Any person or organisation affected by the actions of the Charity Commission may make a complaint by telephoning and asking to speak to the Customer Complaints Manager or by writing to them. Complaints should be made within three months of the date of the subject of the complaint.

22.8 The Customer Complaints Manager will investigate the complaint and normally reply within ten working days. If this is not possible the Customer Complaints Manager will write explaining the reasons for the delay, the actions the Commission are taking and indicating by when a response can be expected.

22.9 If the Customer Complaints Manager is unable to resolve matters to the complainant's satisfaction the complainant can then ask the Regional Operational Manager to look into the complaint. This must be done within one month of the date of the letter from the Customer Complaints Manager.

22.10 If matters remain unresolved the complainant can then approach the Charity Commission's Independent Complaints Reviewer, Mrs Jodi Berg, at Newspaper House (First Floor), 8 – 16 Great New Street, New Street Square, London EC4A 3EU. This must be done within three months of the Commission completing its own investigations and offering a final response. The Independent Complaints Reviewer can only investigate complaints about the standards of service. She cannot review decisions taken by the Charity Commissioners.

22.11 If the complainant is still dissatisfied, their final recourse is to ask their MP to take the matter up with the Parliamentary Ombudsman.

Complaints about Commissioners' decisions

22.12 If a person or organisation is unhappy about a decision taken by the Charity Commission they should initially write to the Customer Complaints Manager setting out the reasons why they believe the decision to be wrong. This must be done within three months of the date of the relevant decision. The Customer Complaints Manager will arrange for the case to be reviewed by a senior member of staff who was not involved in the original decision. A full response will normally be given within ten working days. If this is not possible the Customer Complaints Manager will write explaining the reasons for the delay, the actions the Commission are taking and indicating by when a response can be expected.

22.13 If the complainant is not satisfied they can ask the Regional Operations Manager to consider their request for a review. This must be done within one month of the date of the letter explaining the outcome of the review.

22.14 If the complainant is still not satisfied their next step is to ask for the Board of Commissioners to consider the case again. This must be done within three months of the date of the letter from the Regional Operations Manager.

22.15 If the Charity Commission refuses to register an organisation as a charity, and the Board of Commissioners refuses to overturn its decision, the Attorney-General and the organisation's trustees, or people claiming to be its trustees, can appeal to the High Court. In order to do this, the organisation must not be exempt from registration or come within the categories listed in *s 3(5)* of the *Charities Act 1993* as being not required to register.

22.16 *Section 4* of the *Charities Act 1993* permits anyone who is, or who may be, affected by the registration of a charity to appeal against the Commission's decision to register the organisation. Most appeals of this type have been brought by the Inland Revenue.

22.17 The public can appeal to the High Court against an Order or Scheme made by the Commissioners within three months of the order or scheme coming into force.

22.18 If the Charity Commission finds trustees guilty of a breach of trust or a breach of duty, the trustees can appeal to the Attorney-General or the High Court.

Official custodian

22.19 The Official Custodian for Charities is an employee of the Charity Commission who has powers under *s 21* of the *Charities Act 1993* to hold land on behalf of charities. Using the Official Custodian to hold land saves unincorporated charities from going to the trouble and expense of transferring title to land every time a trustee ceases to hold office, or from having to appoint holding trustees.

22.20 Responsibility for managing charity land held by the Official Custodian remains with the charity trustees and they can do the same sort of things with it that they could if ownership were vested in them. The charity trustees, not the Official Custodian, are deemed to be the landlord for the purpose of the *Landlord and Tenant Act 1927*.

22.21 If the Charity Commission has instituted an inquiry under *s 18(1)* of the *Charities Act 1993* and found misconduct of management, or found that a charity's assets needed protection, they can make an order requiring the charity's property to be transferred to the Official Custodian, though in practice this happens only on rare occasions.

22.22 In the past the Official Custodian of Charities also held investments on behalf of some charities. However, *s 23* of the *Charities Act 1993* required the Official Custodian to divest herself of all property except land, making charity trustees take greater responsibility for the management of charity investments.

23 Commercial Participators

23.1 The *Charities Act 1992* was intended to promote public giving to charity by increasing public confidence in them. One of the ways in which it sought to do this was by giving the public clearer information about just how much a charity would receive when a commercial venture claimed to be giving a proportion of their profits, or a certain amount per item sold, to a charity.

23.2 In 1988 the Woodfield Report recommended that whenever goods or services were offered for sale with the indication that some part of the proceeds was to be donated to charity, the public should be given information about which charity, or charities, were to benefit (and, if more than one, in what proportion) and the manner in which the amount the charities would receive would be calculated. Doubts were expressed about the practicality of Woodfield's suggestions, but, not withstanding these, the *1992 Charities Act* contained sections that deal with relationships between charities and commercial ventures, known as commercial participators.

Definition

23.3 *Section 58(1)* of the *Charities Act 1992* defines a commercial participator as:

'In relation to any charitable institution. . .any person who

- carries on for gain a business other than a fund-raising business, but
- in the course of that business, engages in any promotional venture in the course of which it is represented that charitable contributions are to be given to or applied for the benefit of the institution'.

23.4 A charity's own trading company could be argued to come within that definition, but the *Deregulation and Contracting Out Act 1994 s 25* clarified that a trading company owned by a charitable institution is not a commercial participator.

Examples of commercial participators

23.5 Some companies encourage the public to buy their brand of a particular product, for example tea, by advertising that for every packet sold they will donate 20p to a named charity.

23.6 Some banks and financial institutions enter into joint promotional ventures with charities that bear the name and/or logo of a charity, sometimes together with an illustration of its work. The arrangement benefits both parties. In return for being given access to the names and addresses of those on the charity's donor/supporter database, the bank agrees to give the charity a fee for each card issued, and a small percentage of the expenditure on the card.

23.7 When there is a disaster, for example an earthquake or the loss of a lifeboat, some businesses will decide to donate a proportion of their sales or profits to a named charity helping the victims. Even when they have no formal agreement with the charity concerned, if they advertise what they are doing in advance, they become commercial participators and must comply with the Act. However, if they advertise after the event then it is not a solicitation and therefore may not be a commercial participation.

How the public will be reassured

23.8 The legislation will open arrangements between commercial participators and charities to public scrutiny in two ways:

- any commercial participator who claims to be assisting a charity will have to have an agreement with the charity and make its claims only in accordance with that agreement; or
- any representations made by the commercial participator must be accompanied by a statement which clarifies specified matters relating to those representations, such as the proportion of the proceeds the charity will receive.

The agreement between the charity and the commercial participator

23.9 *Section 59(2)* of the *Charities Act 1992* requires there to be an agreement between any commercial participator who represents that part of the proceeds will be donated to charity, and the charity concerned. The agreement must be in writing and must be signed by or on behalf of the charitable institution and the commercial participator. The agreement must specify:

- the name and address of each of the parties;
- the date on which the agreement was signed;
- the duration of the agreement;
- any terms relating to the early termination of the agreement;
- any terms relating to the variation of the agreement during that period.

23.10 In addition the agreement must also contain the following:

- A statement of its principal objectives and the methods to be used in pursuit of those objectives. For each method specified there should be a description of the types of charitable contributions which are to be donated and of the circumstances in which they are to be given.
- Provision as to the manner in which the parties will determine:
  - — if there is more than one charitable institution party to the agreement, the proportion in which the institutions which are so party are respectively to benefit under the agreement; and
  - — the proportion of the consideration given for goods or services sold or supplied by the commercial participator, or of any other proceeds of a promotional venture undertaken by him, which is to be given to or applied for the benefit of the charitable institution; or
  - — the sums by way of donations by the commercial participator in connection with the sale or supply of any goods or services sold or supplied by him which are to be so given or applied.
- Provision as to any amount by way of remuneration or expenses which the commercial participator is to be entitled to receive in respect of things done by him in pursuance of the agreement and the manner in which any such amount is to be determined.

23.11 The regulations require that monies should be paid over by the commercial participator to the charitable institution within 28 days of receipt, unless other arrangements are specified in the agreement.

23.12 Commercial Participators

Tripartite agreements

23.12 The regulations are written in a way that pre-supposes that the agreement is made between a charity and a commercial participator. However, the involvement of a commercial participator often means that some type of trading is taking place. Unless the trading activity is part of the charity's primary purpose, it will be carried out by the charity's trading subsidiary, therefore the commercial participator will need to contract with the charity's trading company, rather than with the charity. The charity could sign an agreement with the commercial participator if it was a principal in the arrangement, and the charity's trading company was merely acting as the charity's agent. However, it is most important that the charity is not a principal, because to be so would mean that the charity was engaging in non-primary purpose trading activity, which would be a breach of charity law. The charity would also be receiving income that would not be covered by one of the exemptions from income tax set out in the *Income and Corporation Taxes Act 1988 s 505*, and as a result would have to pay income tax on the income it received from the deal with the commercial participator.

23.13 Ventures involving commercial participators will therefore require an agreement between the commercial participator and the charity's trading company and, in order to comply with the *Charities Act 1992 s 59(2)*, an agreement between the charity and the commercial participator.

23.14 Given that the commercial exploitation of a charity's name, logo and goodwill is not primary purpose trading, many charities will have appointed their trading companies as licensees to exploit these on their behalf, thus avoiding a breach of charity law and any possible tax liability that could arise if a charity raised money in this way. However, the *Charities Act 1992 s 59(2)* makes it absolutely clear that any agreement allowing a commercial participator to exploit the name of a charitable institution has to be between the institution and the commercial participator. It cannot be between a charitable institution's trading company and a commercial participator.

23.15 The Home Office, who are responsible for the regulations, suggest that the obvious answer is to set up tripartite agreements between the charity, its trading company and the commercial participator. The solution is not, however, as straightforward as it first appears. In drawing up such an agreement it is important to show that the charity is not a principal in the arrangement; rather, the charity's sole purpose in entering into the agreement must be to demonstrate that it has no objection to the agreement between its trading company and the commercial participator. The charity must not take any role in the agreement that suggests that the charity itself is trading with the commercial participator, or that suggests that the charity was supplying a service to the trading company, as this could render ineffective the covenanted payment of profits from the trading company to the charity, because it could then be argued that the trading company was making covenanted payment in return for the services supplied.

23.16 Great care must be taken in drafting tripartite agreements and structuring the ways the charity receives money from the commercial participator if any liability for tax is to be minimised. As well as considering how income from the deal may be taxed, the VAT implications of the deal must also be considered. Customs and Excise have confirmed that arrangements between charitable institutions and commercial participators for the licensing of the charity's name will attract VAT.

23.17 In relation to Affinity Card Schemes, where the contractual arrangements allow a clear separation between payments for promotional services, and contributions for which the charity is not obliged to do anything in return, only the initial payment (typically one-fifth) will attract VAT. Also, following a Court of Appeal decision (*Customs & Excise Comrs v Civil Service Motoring Association [1988] STC 111*), in some cases payments may be treated as exempt from VAT. This is an area which needs to be assessed on a case by case basis.

Transitional provisions

23.18 The Act and regulations do not contain any transitional provisions for agreements entered into prior to 1 March 1995. So if a charity's trading company is party to an existing agreement with a commercial participator that commenced before 1 March 1995 but which is still extant, then the charity will have to enter into a supplemental agreement with the commercial participator in order to conform with the Act.

Retailer as a commercial participator

23.19 If, for example, a tea company agrees to give a named charity 5p for every packet of tea sold that carries printed details of the promotion, the tea company is clearly a commercial participator. But if the tea is sold in a supermarket, is the supermarket also a commercial participator? By displaying the tea on their shelves the supermarket is clearly promoting it for sale, so it could be argued that it is a commercial participator and should have an agreement with the charity concerned. However, this clearly was not the intention of the Act.

Christmas cards

23.20 Many charities sell Christmas cards using a commercial participator. In recent years there has been considerable media interest highlighting the extent to which charities actually benefit from these arrangements. The Charity Commission and the Advertising Standards Authority believe it is important that the public does not get the impression that charities benefit more from such arrangements than is actually the case. The Commission suggests that any statement on the packaging of the cards should inform the public what the net donation to the charity will be after all expenses have been paid. Many of the public are not aware that in most instances charities make much more profit per card from cards sold through the charity's own mail order catalogues or in their charity shops than when cards supporting the charity are sold in supermarkets and chain stores.

Enforceability

23.21 Breaching the requirements for *s 59* agreements is a criminal offence giving rise to a maximum fine of £500. The court may also grant an injunction to a charity if the commercial participator solicits money for the charity without an agreement.

23.22 Penalties for failing to comply with *s 59* requirements for agreements attach to the commercial participator, not the charity. It will be in a charity's long-term interest to make a potential commercial participator aware of this legislation, though doing so may not be the most positive way to commence negotiations and might even deter some companies from entering into such arrangements.

23.23 If a charity has entered into an agreement that is defective, then it can only be enforced by the commercial participator by an order of the court. There may be some circumstances in which a commercial participator wishes to enforce an agreement, for example because the charity is not making an agreed payment for goods the commercial participator has agreed to provide at a heavily discounted price as part of the agreement. However, it is much more likely that a charity would wish to enforce an agreement, for example because the commercial participator is holding on to the proceeds and not passing them onto the charity within the agreed timescale.

23.24 The legislation requires the commercial participator to pay sums due to the charity within 28 days of receipt or such other period as may be agreed. If the commercial participator pays the money to the charity's trading company, which then keeps it until the end of its financial year, when it covenants its profits to the charity, then the commercial participator may be guilty of a criminal offence!

Commercial participators statement

23.25 The Home Office guidelines recommend that the statement should be along the lines of 'a minimum of X% of the purchase price of £X per item sold will be paid to Charity Y'. It will be easy to comply with this if the deal is a simple one, for example, allowing the commercial participator to use the charity's name in return for 10p per item sold. However, most deals will be more complex and will involve the charity's trading company. If this is the case it may not be possible to know in advance how much the charity will receive, because the trading company will have to deduct a proportion of its fixed costs from the money received. The more successful the promotion, the smaller will be the amount per item sold needed to cover the trading company's fixed costs. The solution here will be a statement along the lines of 'X% of each item sold will be paid to XYZ Ltd, a company that covenants all its profits to charity Y', though strictly speaking the contract will then be between the commercial participator and the trading company and therefore may be outside the Act. This wording links the commercial participator with the Charity even though the commercial participator cannot legally say that they are making a donation to the charity.

23.26 Agreements are only needed if the commercial participator makes a 'representation'. However, *s 58(6)(a)* of the Act defines a representation very widely:

> ' "represent" and "solicit" mean respectively represent and solicit in any manner whatever, whether expressly or impliedly and whether done:
>
> - by speaking directly to the person or persons to whom the representation or solicitation is addressed (whether when in his or their presence or not); or
> - by means of a statement published in any newspaper, film or radio or television programme...'

23.27 If a spokesperson for a commercial participator is giving a television interview and mentions their company's support for a charity it would obviously not be practical for them to give all the details that must be specified in the statement. Similarly, if a shop assistant wears a charity's T-shirt of their own choosing it would be ridiculous to suggest that the shop should put up a sign saying that X% of the sales of all items in the shop will be donated to T-shirt charity. However, if the shop had a policy requiring all their assistants to wear one particular charity's T-shirts, then this could be interpreted as the shop supporting a particular charity and therefore a representation was being made.

23.28 Failure to make the statement required by the *Charities Act 1992 s 59* is a criminal offence carrying a maximum penalty of £5,000. [*Charities Act 1992, s 60(7)*]. The penalty can be imposed for each offence, i.e. for each item sold without the required statement being made, so selling 100 items at £1 each without the required statement could cost a commercial participator £500,000. The risk involved in the agreement not fully satisfying the regulations, and the commercial participator being found guilty of a criminal offence and fined as a result, may be sufficient to deter potential commercial participators from considering such deals. Charities themselves may become less willing to suggest them, fearing the bad publicity that would result from their involvement in a deal that lead to a company being fined as a result of breaching charity law.

Limitations of the controls on commercial participation

23.29 The *Charities Act 1992* contains no controls over commercial participators who seek to raise money for general charitable purposes, such as 'the homeless 'rather than for particular charities. The unscrupulous may use this to exploit the public's willingness to give to charity but any scandals will undermine the Act's attempts to increase public confidence in charities.

23.30 Most deals require such complex, and therefore costly, agreements between a charity, its trading company, and a commercial participator that many potential commercial participators may believe the risks associated with entering into such arrangements will surpass the benefits they are likely to gain.

24 Common Investment Funds and Common Deposit Funds

Common investment funds

24.1 Common investment funds (CIFs), and the closely related common deposit funds (CDFs) are means by which charities can pool the funds they have available for investment and obtain certain advantages that are not available to them through conventional investment products. CIFs are similar to unit trusts and are charities in their own right, established and registered by the Charity Commission. They are controlled by *s 24* of the *Charities Act 1993*, and have a separate set of accounting regulations.

24.2 Any charity in England and Wales may participate in a CIF unless its constitution specifically prohibits it, or the terms of the CIF specifically disqualify it. However, CIFs are not available to Scottish charities, and therefore for this type of investment Scottish charities have to look to unit trusts.

24.3 CIFs are administered by professional fund managers and operate like unit trusts. A charity's money is thus being spread over a wider range of investments than would otherwise be possible for a portfolio of this size. This has the advantage of reducing overall risk to each participating charity. The charity gains in other ways too: individual dealing fees are reduced and all income is paid gross, reducing paperwork for the charity administrator and improving cash flow. A CIF is a special range investment, and as such does not have to be split between narrower and wider range investments where the *Trustee Investments Act 1961* applies, and does not have to be included in the initial division of funds.

24.4 Commonly a CIF has two pools of funds: income units and accumulation units. Income units pay a regular income stream, whereas accumulation units are rolled into the value of the fund and its income reinvested to increase its value.

Powers and policy

24.5 Each CIF has its own powers and policies which are available from the fund on request. Charities considering investing in a CIF should obtain this information first and review it before making a decision to invest. Issues to consider will include the cost structure, the fund manager, and the fund's performance.

Charges

24.6 Management and administration charges typically range between 0.15% to 1.00%, although initial charges or a minimum fee may also apply. Most distribute income quarterly.

Performance

24.7 Because CIFs invest in a range of investments, their performance can be expected to be predictable and broadly in line with market conditions. The WM company publishes regular reports of common investment fund performance.

Common Investment Funds for Charities

Name of Fund	Provider
CAF Balance Growth Fund	CAF/Deutsche Asset Management
CAF Income Fund	CAF/Deutsche Asset Management
Charibond	M & G
Charifund	M & G
Chariguard Overseas Equity Fund	Dresdner RCM Global Investors (UK) Ltd
Chariguard Fixed Interest Fund	Dresdner RCM Global Investors (UK) Ltd
Chariguard UK Equity Fund	Dresdner RCM Global Investors (UK) Ltd
Charinco	Mercury Asset Management
Charishare	Mercury Asset Management
Charishare Tobacco Restricted*	Mercury Asset Management
ChariTrak	Barclays Global Investors Ltd
Charity Equity Fund	Schroder Investment Management Limited
Charity Fixed Interest Fund	Schroder Investment Management Limited
COIF Charities Fixed Interest Fund	CCLA Investment Management Ltd
COIF Charities Investment Fund	CCLA Investment Management Ltd
Common Fund for Growth	HSBC Investment Bank
Common Fund for Income	HSBC Investment Bank
Diversified Charity Fund	Lazard Asset Management
Fledgeling Bond Fund	Fleming Asset Management
Fledgeling UK Equity Fund	Fleming Asset Management
Growth Trust for Charities	Cazenove Fund Management
Income Plus Fund	Baring Asset Management
Income Trust for Charities	Cazenove Fund Management
National Association of Almshouses Common Investment Fund (NAACIF)	M & G
UK Growth & Income Fund	Baring Asset Management

*Limited to NHS Charitable Funds and certain other health related charities

Ethical CIFs

24.8 Charities are only allowed to adopt ethical investment policies in particular circumstances (see 71.15). Trustees may therefore only place funds in an ethical CIF if the CIF excludes investments that the charity would be permitted to exclude. At present there is only one ethical CIF, the Charishare Tobacco Restricted Fund.

24.9 Common Investment Funds and Common Deposit Funds

Investment portfolios

24.9 Occasionally charities set up a fund that they refer to as a common investment fund. Unless this is established as a CIF by the Court or by a Scheme of the Charity Commission, then this term is a misnomer, and should be avoided. It is more likely to be simply an investment portfolio which has been combined as the result of the common accounting for a number of restricted funds or subsidiary trusts. Occasionally charities operate informal investment schemes together with other charities. This is likely to constitute a breach of trust by the charities, and should be formalised with the Charity Commission.

24.10 Where a charity has established a single charity CIF, this is more commonly known as a 'pooling scheme'. Pooling schemes are not limited to single charities and their special trusts and can include commonly controlled charities. Pooling schemes are also established by a Scheme.

Common deposit funds

24.11 Common deposit funds (CDFs) are used to pool cash deposits from several charities and are themselves charities. Like CIFs, CDFs can only be created by the Court or by a Scheme of the Charity Commission and are not available to Scottish charities. Charities can deposit money directly into a CDF where it is then managed by duly appointed trustees. Deposits are repayable, with interest, at a rate determined under the scheme.

Advantages

24.12 The cash deposited in a CDF is pooled and invested in the money market – sterling deposits with banks, building societies and local and central government. Because the money is pooled, larger sums are available for investment and interest rates are generally higher than a charity could obtain on its own from an individual bank or building society deposit. There are few account charges and interest is paid gross. A CDF may therefore be particularly suitable for charities depositing smaller sums. They also have the advantage of spreading the risk if any one deposit taker should fail.

24.13 CDFs are useful for short-term investment, for example investing income being held pending expenditure on the purposes of the charity. However, they are not considered suitable for longer term investment as there is no protection against inflation. The benefits of CDFs are as follows:

- charities obtain money market rates of interest;
- the account is in the name of the charity, therefore there is no need to change the names of the account holders if trustees change;
- interest is paid gross;
- easy access to funds;
- regular statements.

24.14 As with common investment funds, an investment in a CDF cannot be assigned or sold.

24.15 It is not uncommon for charities to establish informal common deposit funds, whereby they seek to obtain higher interest rate returns by combining cash balances. These may constitute unauthorised common deposit funds, which would again represent a breach of trust by all the trustees. There is also the risk of the charity operating the scheme contravening the banking regulations.

Future developments

24.16 The Treasury has expressed concern that many trustees of common investment funds are not trained investment experts and therefore charity funds might not be properly safeguarded. In November 1996 the Charity Commission issued a consultation document on the structure and regulation of common investment funds. This proposed that trustees of CIFs established in the future should be authorised under the *Financial Services Act 1986* (most trustees would not have the time to become authorised), or the trusteeship of the funds should be given to corporate trustees, such as banks.

25 Companies

25.1 There are three legal structures commonly adopted by charities: a company limited by guarantee or shares, a trust or an unincorporated association. Most larger charities are set up as companies limited by guarantee. These are always private companies, not public ones.

Limited companies

25.2 Charities use the structure of a limited company for two different purposes: to conduct their own affairs, or as a vehicle for conducting non-charitable activities, such as trading. Where a limited company is used to carry out the charity's objects, the constitution may be either that of a guarantee company or a company limited by shares. Subsidiary trading companies are usually companies limited by shares, with the charity owning all the shares.

25.3 A company limited by guarantee is an incorporated organisation i.e. it has a legal personality of its own, separate from its members, so it can take action and enter into legal agreements in its own name. Other types of incorporated organisations include industrial and provident societies, companies with a share capital, and bodies set up under Royal Charter or by Act of Parliament.

25.4 A registered charity which is also a guarantee company is subject to the same regime as any other limited company, with one or two minor exceptions. As a result it has to consider two major pieces of legislation in all its transactions: the *Companies Act 1985* and, for charities in England and Wales, the *Charities Act 1993* or, in Scotland, the *Law Reform (Miscellaneous Provisions) (Scotland) Act 1990*.

Advantages of incorporation

25.5 There are a number of reasons for incorporation as a company. The primary motive for incorporation as a limited company is usually the desire to limit the liability of trustees in the event of a claim against the charity, however arising. The effectiveness of this protection is dependent on the circumstances and directors should not assume blanket immunity. Generally where the directors have acted in good faith, and the claim arises through normal business operations, or a contractual claim, then the protection is effective, but reference should be made to Chapter 76.

25.6 Secondly, a body corporate, such as a company, is a legal person in its own right. This means that it can enter into contracts and own assets such as investments or properties. There is no need for such items to be held by individuals acting on behalf of the charity.

25.7 Thirdly, a company has perpetual succession. This means that there is no need to transfer contracts, leases, title deeds, etc. to new signatories whenever the persons who originally signed them cease to be directors.

25.8 Incorporated organisations also have the advantage of permanence. They continue to exist until they are formally dissolved and cannot merely 'fade away'.

25.9 A possible additional advantage of being a company is that structure's comparative familiarity overseas, especially within Europe. Although there are proposals for the formation of a new type of incorporated charitable entity which would be recognised throughout Europe, in the meantime the limited company structure is probably the most familiar, and the one with which funders or others entering into contracts feel most comfortable.

Disadvantages of incorporation

25.10 Incorporation brings with it additional paper work and costs, such as filing fees and the staff costs of complying with company legislation. Audit fees may also be higher.

25.11 Companies have to make the names of their directors publicly available. In certain circumstances this might prevent people from being willing to act as trustees.

Companies limited by guarantee

25.12 The advantages for a charity in being formed as a guarantee company are that, in certain circumstances, the liability of the members of the company for the debts of the company in the event of the company being unable to meet its own debts is limited to the amount of their guarantee — usually a nominal sum such as £10, and there is no necessity to issue share certificates. In contrast the trustees of an unincorporated organisation, such as a trust or an association, are personally liable for the debts of the organisation if it is unable to pay them.

25.13 A company limited by guarantee is generally recommended as the most suitable structure for a charity that employs staff, owns property or investments, or is involved in contracts or other operations which involve risk.

25.14 The governing document of a company guarantee is its memorandum and articles of association, see Chapter 80. In all cases a company has two important tiers in its governing structure: the members and the directors.

Members and directors

25.15 The members of a company limited by guarantee are those people who, having agreed to become members, have their names entered on the register of members. Because the company has no shares, no certificate is issued to the member. However, it is prudent for a new member to confirm willingness to be a member in writing as a formal record. Members have the same rights as do shareholders in companies with a share capital, except that they have no right to a dividend or to participate in the assets of the company on its winding up. The directors are those people elected by the members to govern the company. Directors are usually, but not necessarily, members.

25.16 Under company legislation a company need only have one member and it can also have only one director. However, in the case of a charitable company the Charity Commissioners would usually require there to be a minimum of three directors.

25.17 The members of the company are not necessarily the same as the people commonly referred to as the 'members' of a charitable organisation. Often the 'membership' is a much looser grouping of supporters, or interested people, who in return for a subscription, have certain rights of information and who may even elect committee members. They are not automatically the same as the members recognised under the *Companies Act 1985*. It is important to maintain a proper register of the legal membership, as the company needs to obtain the sanction of its members for certain transactions.

25.18 Companies

Charitable companies limited by shares

25.18 While it is more usual for charities to adopt the format of being limited by guarantee rather than by shares, some charities do choose to have shareholders in much the same way as a commercial limited company, except that no profit can accrue to the shareholders of a charitable company. Although similar to other limited companies, special rules apply to charitable companies, whatever their form or constitution.

Company law requirements

25.19 The formalities of the *Companies Act 1985* apply to guarantee companies throughout the UK. In particular this means that any changes in directors, the company secretary and the registered office need to be filed with Companies House. In addition an annual return, which is a shuttle document, needs to be completed each year and filed, as well as the annual return made to the Charity Commission.

25.20 Guarantee companies have broadly the same accounting and audit rules as other limited companies. However, there are two main differences:

- Guarantee companies must file their full memorandum and articles with the Registrar of Companies on incorporation. Companies limited by shares must register a memorandum but may adopt model articles set out in Table A accompanying the *Companies Act 1985*. Insofar as no articles are registered, or those registered do not contradict or exclude Table A, the provisions of that Table will be deemed to apply.
- Charitable guarantee companies are entitled to drop the word 'limited' from their title. Where this is done, then letters and orders must refer to the fact that the charity is a limited company. These disclosure requirements are additional to those required for unincorporated charities by the *Charities Act 1993*. To obtain the exemption the charity must submit a statutory declaration to the Registrar of Companies.

Procedures

25.21 The Charity Commission have the power to petition the High Court for the winding up of a charitable company if they have opened an inquiry under the *Charities Act 1993 s 8*, and are satisfied that they should exercise their powers for the protection of the charity. A *section 8* inquiry cannot be undertaken on an exempt charity.

25.22 The *Companies Act 1985* lays down procedures for the alteration of a company's memorandum and articles of association. Where such changes relate to a company's objects, its memorandum, or to a clause in its articles concerning how property can be applied, then the written consent of the Charity Commission is required in advance, and that consent must be copied to the Registrar of Companies with the company's own filing. [*Companies Act 1985 ss 4, 9, 17*; *Charities Act 1993 s 64(2)*].

25.23 A charity, whether a company or not, should not act in breach of its own constitution or in breach of trust. Companies have a power (*Companies Act 1985 s 35*) to ratify constitutional breaches in certain circumstances. However, this power is specifically limited for charitable companies, so that such an act can only be ratified if the incident in question was a commercial transaction, and the other party did not know that the transaction was beyond the powers of the company. [*Charities Act 1993 s 65*].

25.24 Certain other transactions that are permitted by the *Companies Act 1985* need the prior written consent of the Charity Commissioners if they are to be carried out by charitable companies. They all relate to transactions, either directly or indirectly, with directors or connected parties. Also, although a charitable guarantee company does not need to publicise its name under the *Companies Act 1985*, it is required to do so by the *Charities Act 1993*.

Directors

25.25 The trustees of an incorporated charity are the directors of a charitable company. Often charities have senior executives whose job title includes the word 'director', for instance,'Director of Resources'. Unless formally appointed to the board, this staff member is not a director in terms of the *Companies Act 1985*. Two situations need care. First, the trustees need to be aware of their responsibilities both as charity trustees and as company directors, and to understand that they have responsibilities under both charity and company law. Second, the senior executive staff should avoid acting in the capacity of directors, or else they risk becoming a shadow director i.e. a person with no formal voting rights, but someone in accordance with whose directions or instructions the directors of the company are accustomed to act. [*Companies Act 1985 s 741(2)*]. Company law treats shadow directors in the same way as other directors.

Company secretary

25.26 In addition to members and directors, a limited company is also required to appoint a company secretary. The company secretary cannot be the same person as a sole director, but could be another director. The role of the company secretary in a private limited company is typically either a nominal one, mainly confined to signing statutory returns, or is developed to a wider role as 'the chief administrative officer of the company'. In either case, the company secretary is an officer of the company and liable as such in certain circumstances.

Registers

25.27 Limited companies are obliged to maintain certain registers, either at their principal place of business or at their registered office. These registers include registers of members, directors and secretaries, directors' interests, charges, interests in shares, and debenture holders. Often these registers are maintained in one bound volume and can easily become out of date. This can present difficulties if problems arise, as the definitive proof of a claim is the entry on the register.

Accounting and audit requirements

25.28 Limited companies are not subject to the accounting and auditing requirements of the *Charities Act 1993*. They are, however, subject to the *Companies Act 1985* which requires all companies (except public limited companies) to file accounts and a directors' report with the Registrar of Companies within ten months of the year end. The accounts must comply with the prescribed format and other disclosure requirements of the *Companies Act 1985*, but in practice this allows charities to adopt the SORP in full, since certain sections of the prescribed formats may be amended by the company.

25.29 Not all companies are required by company law to have a full audit. A charitable company with income of between £90,000 and £250,000, and total assets of less than £1.4 million can elect to have a compilation report instead, prepared by a reporting accountant. Charitable companies with an income of less than £90,000 and total assets of less than £1.4 million require no external check on their accounts. The thresholds for commercial companies are higher than those for charitable companies.

25.30 Where a company is part of a group, for instance a charitable company with a trading subsidiary, then a full audit is automatically required unless the group itself is eligible and qualifies as a small group.

Requirement to state name

25.31 Companies must state their full name on all business letters, notices, official publications, cheques, orders, invoices, receipts and similar documents. On all business letters and orders it must also state the company's country of registration and registration number, and the address of the registered office.

Members rights

25.32 The members have statutory rights under the *Companies Act 1985*, including:

- the right to receive the accounts 21 days before the AGM;
- the right for two or more members, if at least 5% of the membership, to call a general meeting;
- the right for any member, or groups of members, if at least 5% of the membership, to circulate a resolution for such a meeting;
- the right to remove the directors;
- the right to remove the auditors.

Forms

25.33 Many of the transactions carried out by a company need to be supported by forms filed with Companies House (either Companies House, Crown Way, Cardiff, CF4 3UZ, or for companies registered in Scotland, Companies House, 37 Castle Terrace, Edinburgh, EH1 2EB). These forms are often subject to minor amendment and it is always worth checking that the charity is using the current version. The list shown in Table 7 is not exhaustive, as many of the forms relate to transactions in which charitable companies are most unlikely to participate. These are not listed here, and neither are those forms specifically needed only on incorporation.

25.34 Forms marked * are posted on Companies House's website. They can be printed off, completed, signed and returned to Companies House. At the time of writing they cannot be filed electronically as the law requires them to be personally signed.

25.35 Limited companies are subject to corporation tax on their income. However, most charitable companies will avoid corporation tax by operating within the exemptions available to them, and trading companies will avoid corporation tax by donating their profits to their parent charity using a deed of covenant or Gift Aid.

Dormant companies

25.36 A charitable company is said to be dormant if during a financial year there is no significant financial activity. A dormant company must comply with all parts of the *Companies Act 1985* regarding the preparation and submission of annual reports and accounts, as well as director's reports but because it has not undertaken any financial transactions, it is exempted from the requirement to have an audit.

25.37 The *Companies Act 1985 ss 249A–249E* excepts companies with a total turnover or income of under £90,000 and assets or funds of under £1.4 million from having its accounts audited. This includes charitable companies unless their memorandum and articles of association state otherwise. This has removed the need for many small charitable companies to go into dormancy in order to avoid audit fees. However, a

Table 7 Companies House forms commonly used by charities

Form number	Subject matter
6	Cancellation or alteration to objects
30(5)(a) to (c)	Omitting the word 'limited' from company name
88(2)	Return of allotment of shares
225*	Notice of accounting reference date (for a newly incorporated company)
225(1)*	Notice of accounting reference date given during the course of an accounting reference period
225(2)*	Notice of accounting reference date given after the end of an accounting reference period by a parent or subsidiary undertaking
287*	Change in situation of registered office
288a*	Appointment of director or secretary
288b*	Resignation of director or secretary
288c*	Change of particulars for director or secretary
353	Register of members
363a	Annual return
391	Notice of resolution removing auditor
652(a)	Application for striking off

dormant charitable company needs to pass an elective resolution to gain exemption from the audit requirements of the *Companies Act 1985*.

Review of company law

25.38 In March 2000 the Department of Trade & Industry issued a consultative document containing proposals on corporate governance, large company reporting, private companies, charitable companies, corporate information issues and restoration to the register. Issues which may affect charities include:

- widening the definition of shadow directorship;
- restating directors' duties;
- reducing the filing date for small companies to five months;
- reducing accounts detail.

25.39 In addition it is proposed that there should be a new, separate form of incorporation for charities to address the conflicts between charity regulation and the *Companies Act*.

26 Contracts

Legal contracts

26.1 Contracts are agreements that are legally enforceable by the courts. Contracts usually take the form of signed documents, but a written contract is not essential for the vast majority of legally enforceable contracts. A legally enforceable contract can exist without it being in writing except in certain situations.

26.2 For a contract to be valid a number of conditions have to be met.

- There must be at least two parties with the capacity to enter into a contract. If charities wish to enter into contracts, the corporate body in the case of an incorporated charity or the governing body in the case of an unincorporated charity must have the power to enter into contracts, the contracts must be within the charity's objects, and those signing the contract must be authorised to do so.
- An offer must be made and must be accepted clearly and without qualification. Although the acceptance of the offer must be unconditional, the offer can stipulate that the contract comes into being only if certain conditions are met.
- An offer and an acceptance form a contract only if there is sufficient certainty as to what has been agreed.
- There must be consideration, i.e. something of material value must be given in exchange for what is offered, either at the time the contract is entered into or within some agreed time period in the future. For a contract to exist, the amount of the consideration does not have to reflect the value of what is offered, e.g. a peppercorn or £1 could be exchanged for a year's lease on a prime office building.
- The parties to the contract must intend to create a legally binding agreement. The courts almost always find that arrangements of a business nature where one party is paid to provide goods or services for another are intended to be legally binding agreements.

Joint or joint and several liability

26.3 If two or more charities agree to provide a service under a contract, for example, to run a day centre for a local authority, their liability could be joint, or joint and several. All parties to the contract should be clear what liability they are taking on and if it is joint and several (i.e. each party is potentially liable to provide the full amount or service even if they have only agreed to provide a small proportion) this should be an explicit part of the agreement. This is because the potential consequences of joint and several liability are likely to be very different from joint liability, where each party to the contract is only liable for the share it has contracted to provide.

Service agreements

26.4 The term 'service agreement' is frequently used for internal agreements between parts of a charity, such as the headquarters, branches, projects, departments, units, etc. Such agreements cannot be contracts, because there is only one party, the charity, and it could not enforce a contract against itself, so it is preferable that they are known by another term. However, the terms 'service agreement' and 'service level agreement' are also used in numerous other ways by voluntary organisations although they have no meaning in law. Therefore whenever such terms are used it is important to realise that one may or may not be referring to a legally enforceable contract.

Contract culture

26.5 The term 'contract culture' is used to refer to the way in which the state has changed from being a direct provider of goods and services to an enabler, ensuring that certain levels of provision of health, education and community services are provided by continuing to finance them, but contracting out their delivery to a wide range of private and voluntary agencies, particularly since the passing of the *Local Government Act 1988* and the *NHS and Community Care Act 1990*.

26.6 Charities can provide services that a public body is legally required to provide, but only if they do so at the public expense and the service falls within their charitable objects. The public body must enter into a contract with the charity and pay the charity a fee that covers the full cost of providing the service. The full cost will include staff costs, such as salaries, pensions, recruitment and training, accommodation, materials, utilities and the costs of tendering for the contract, monitoring it, attending meetings with the public body, accountancy and audit costs attributable to the contracted activities. In addition a sum should be included as a contribution to the overall governance and management costs of the charity.

26.7 Trustees cannot use the charity's funds to subsidise the service, though they can use the charity's funds to provide a higher quality of service than the public body is required to provide.

26.8 In many instances the public body has a good deal of discretion over the level of care it has to provide and there are considerable differences in different parts of the country. This can make it extremely difficult for a charity to decide if it is crossing the boundary between supplementing state provision or relieving it.

26.9 Providing services for public bodies under contract is primary purpose trading (see Chapter 48). Income generated will not be subject to tax, providing that any profit is applied for charitable purposes (see Chapter 111). Premises used to provide the service will qualify for business rate relief (see Chapter 90). However, charities get no special treatment in respect of VAT on their business activities.

26.10 Where a charitable company carries out more than 50% of its business with a public body, or where the public body is represented on the trustee board, the charity could be regarded as a 'regulated' company under local government law.

Contract risk

26.11 Charities should be aware that if they are entering into contracts with local authorities they will increase their exposure to contractual risks. In addition, if they are dependent on contracts for a high level of their income they will inevitably face uncertainty in financial planning and may compromise their independence.

26.12 Charities should not enter into contracts unless they are reasonably certain they have enough liquid assets (e.g. cash) to meet their liabilities. The contractual terms should always be studied carefully. Many charities wishing to return leased office equipment, such as photocopiers, have found to their cost that early termination of the lease triggers large penalty payments.

26.13 Contracts

26.13 Unincorporated charities entering into contracts should consider whether or not it would be prudent to become incorporated in order to reduce the trustees' risk of personal liability for contracts.

26.14 Charities carrying out services under contract are likely to need public liability insurance, indemnity insurance and commercial insurances such as fire, theft, vehicle and employer/occupier liability insurance.

Contractual rights for third parties

26.15 Charities and their trading subsidiaries enter into a large number of legal contracts many of which involve third parties. *The Contracts (Rights of Third Parties) Act 1999* came into force on 11 May 2000, bringing about a fundamental change to the law of contract, by giving third parties contractual rights in certain circumstances.

26.16 *Section 1* of the Act gives a third party the right to enforce a contractual term in circumstances where the contract expressly provides for it, or the contractual term purports to confer a benefit on the third party. To qualify for the right to enforce the third party must be identified in the contract by name, class or description.

26.17 Qualifying third parties have the right to enforce any contractual term that confers a benefit on the third party, including terms that exclude or limit a third party's liability. Any rights that the third party acquire under the Act are in addition to those already available under existing law. The Act only passes the benefits of contracts, not their burdens. So if charity A and charity B agree that charity C will make a payment this cannot be enforced unless charity C expressly joins into the contract.

26.18 A contracting party faced with a third party claim will have the same rights as if the claim had been brought by the other contracting party. The contracting party can also take advantage of any express contractual provisions which limit the third party's rights and which would have been available if the third party had been the contracting party. Conversely, the contract may expressly limit the rights of a contacting party faced with a third party claim.

26.19 The Act contains provisions to avoid a contracting party being liable to another party to the contract and to a third party for the same loss. Any award to the third party will be reduced to the extent that any loss in respect of the term relied upon has already been recovered by another party to the contract.

26.20 The following types of contracts are excluded from the Act:

- employment contracts;
- contracts under bills of exchange, promissory notes or other negotiable instruments;
- contracts for carriage of goods that are subject to the rules of the appropriate international transport convention.

26.21 Charities will need to review their standard forms and contractual documents to see if the Act applies and what amendments, if any, are necessary or appropriate. This will be particularly important in the case of contracts which the charity is accustomed to renew annually, such as commercial participator or professional fundraiser agreements. If the Act applies the charity has three main options:

- To preserve the current position and exclude the operation of the Act (the Act is not retrospective)

- To allow third party rights, but retain the option of subsequently amending the contract to vary those rights
- To give third parties enforceable rights and restrict their own ability to amend the contract in certain circumstances.

27 Corporate Governance

27.1 There have been a number of major reports on corporate governance published in the last ten years including the Cadbury Committee's report *The Financial Aspects of Corporate Governance* published in 1992, the Greenbury Report on *Directors' Remuneration* published in 1995, and the Hampel Committee (the successor to Cadbury) Report in January 1998. Subsequently in June 1998 the Hampel Committee published its 'Combined Code' which was derived from its own final report and those of the Cadbury and Greenbury Committees. The Combined Code requires directors to report on all internal controls, not just internal financial controls. A working party, established by the Institute of Chartered Accountants in England and Wales, developed guidance for directors on risk, internal control and governance and their report (the Turnbull Report) was published in September 1999.

27.2 Corporate governance is not the same as charity governance in that charity trustees do not 'own' the charity in the way that shareholders own a company. However, the trustees do have to act in the interests of the present and future beneficiaries, so to an extent the analogy is legitimate. In other respects the role directors play in the strategic leadership, direction and monitoring of a company is very similar to the role trustees play in governing a charity. While the reports listed above focus on improving standards of governance of commercial companies, many of their recommendations are just as applicable to the governance of charities. Similarly the Report of the Committee into Standards in Public Life (the Nolan Report) and the National Housing Federation's report 'Competence and Accountability on Housing Association Governance' contain recommendations that are applicable to a wide range of charities.

Cadbury Committee

27.3 The Cadbury Committee's report covered the control and reporting functions of boards and the role of auditors. The Committee developed a Code of Best Practice to be adopted by listed companies and reported upon in their annual report and accounts. The code is based on principles of openness, integrity and accountability, all of which find a ready echo in the voluntary sector.

27.4 The Cadbury code recommends the following.

- **The Board of Directors** The code requires all directors to meet regularly in order to retain full and proper control over the entity. There should be clear lines of delegated authority and divisions of responsibility.
- **Non-Executive Directors** Non-executive directors should be independent in every way and appointed for a specific period.
- **Executive Directors** Contracts should not exceed three years. There should be a separate remuneration committee made up of non-executive directors to determine executive directors' remuneration.
- **Reporting and Controls** The board should ensure that an objective and professional relationship is maintained with auditors. The board should establish an audit committee comprising at least three non-executive directors with written terms of reference dealing clearly with its authority and duties. The directors should report on their responsibilities for the accounts, the effectiveness of the system of internal control, and whether the business is a going concern, with supporting assumptions or qualifications as necessary.

Audit committees

27.5 Cadbury lists the following advantages of establishing an audit committee. An audit committee can help to:

- improve the quality of financial reporting by reviewing the financial statements on behalf of the board;
- create a climate of discipline and control which will reduce the opportunity for fraud;
- enable the non-executive directors to contribute an independent judgement and play a positive role;
- help the finance director by providing a forum in which he can raise issues of concern and which he can use to get things done which might otherwise be difficult;
- strengthen the position of the external auditor, by providing a channel of communication and forum for issues of concern;
- provide a framework within which the external auditor can assert his independence in the event of a dispute with management;
- strengthen the position of the internal audit function; and
- increase public confidence in the accounts.

Specimen terms of reference are suggested by Cadbury. These cover constitution, membership, attendance at meetings, frequency of meetings (at least twice a year), authority, duties and reporting procedures.

Greenbury Committee

27.6 The Greenbury Committee's report focused on directors' remuneration. As directors of charitable companies are, in the main, unpaid this report has little relevance for the voluntary sector at present. However, as the Charity Commission shows an increasing willingness to permit charities to have a power to remunerate trustees it may become more relevant in the future. A general principle stated in the Greenbury report that does have relevance for the voluntary sector was the need for companies to establish a remuneration committee made up of non-executive directors, to set and review the remuneration of directors. Setting and reviewing the remuneration of the Chief Executive Officer is a responsibility that many charities do not currently discharge effectively and yet it is a subject that chief executives are naturally reluctant to raise. If this responsibility is not carried out by the board acting as a whole, the trustees should establish a remuneration sub-committee to set and review the chief executive's remuneration.

Hampel Committee

27.7 Like the Cadbury Committee's recommendations, the Hampel Committee's recommendations also have relevance for the voluntary sector. Hampel extended Cadbury's work to include the need for directors to be accountable for the internal control and risk management of all aspects of the governance and management of companies, not just financial governance and management. Hampel recommended that the board should maintain a sound internal control system and that the directors, at least annually, should review the system's effectiveness and report to shareholders that they have done so. Where no internal audit function exists the Hampel Committee recommended that the board should consider whether or not such a function was needed.

Turnbull Committee

27.8 The Turnbull Committee Report was published in September 1999 and sets out the need for companies to establish good internal control and risk management systems. Principle D.2 of the Turnbull Combined Code states: 'The board should maintain a sound system of internal control to safeguard shareholders' investment and the company's assets'. Provision D.2.1 of the code states that: 'The board should, at least annually, conduct a review of the effectiveness of the group's system of internal control and should report to shareholders that they have done so. The review should cover all controls including financial, operational and compliance controls and risk management'. Provision D.2.2 'Companies that do not have an internal audit system should from time to time review the need for one'.

27.9 The Combined Code does not suggest increased regulation for regulation's sake. Rather it recognises the need to ensure that there is a risk-based approach to developing sound business practices in order to protect the shareholders' interests. It states that all companies need clear systems of internal controls that are part of the normal management and governance processes of the organisation, embedded within the organisation's operations, and not seen treated as a separate exercise undertaken to meet regulatory requirements. The guidance also recommends that companies should be able to respond promptly to risks arising from both within and outside the company.

27.10 Although the Turnbull Report recommendations apply at the moment only to listed companies, they are likely in time to have a significant effect on charities. More and more charities will establish an internal audit function, carried out by the charity's own staff, or by an external firm of auditors, or by consortia arrangements in which a number of charities combine resources to provide a shared internal audit function.

27.11 Categories of significant risk to be assessed include organisational, operational, financial and compliance risks. For a charity these might include risks arising from bad publicity or restructuring the management structure, inappropriate treatment of beneficiaries or the introduction of new services, misallocation of restricted funding or a declining trend in income from a particular source, and failure to comply with the charity's ethical investment policy or to account correctly for VAT.

27.12 The Board should take responsibility for deciding the acceptable level of risk, the threat of risks crystallising, the charity's ability to contain the impact of risks crystallising and the cost to benefit ratio of operating internal controls. It will need to consider how to evaluate and manage key risks, how to effectively control areas of known weakness, how to monitor the implementation of measures to eliminate or control risk, and whether more assessment and monitoring are needed.

27.13 Periodically the Board will need to consider any changes to significant, known risk factors, the organisation's ability to respond quickly and effectively to changes in its operating environment, the quality of its control monitoring, any incidents of major control failures and the effectiveness of its year-ending reporting process.

Nolan Committee

27.14 The Nolan Committee Report looked at good governance for public spending bodies and set out seven principles to govern the conduct for those in public life. The principles have relevance for the governance of most charities, and particularly those that are non-departmental public bodies and those that derive the majority of their income from public funds. The seven principles are:

- Selflessness
- Integrity
- Objectivity
- Accountability
- Openness
- Honesty
- Leadership.

27.15 NCVO has produced a Model Code of Conduct for Voluntary Sector Boards based on the seven Nolan principles. It suggests that the model code be used as a guide to good practice, rather than as a definitive code. In summary the code sets out that trustees should behave with:

- Selflessness: acting in the best interests of the charity as a whole, and not seeking to gain financial or other material benefits for themselves, their families, their friends or the organisation they work for or represent.
- Integrity: not placing themselves under financial or other obligations to individuals or organisations that might seek to influence them; not only avoiding impropriety but avoiding situations that might lead to suggestions of impropriety; and not accepting gifts and hospitality that could been seen as influencing their judgement.
- Objectivity: making sure that all their actions and decisions are made solely on merit.
- Accountability: acting in ways that preserve public confidence in the charity and being prepared to give account to all the charity's stakeholders for all their actions and decisions.
- Openness: handling all confidential material with due care, but otherwise being as open as possible about the trustees actions and decisions, and the reasons for them.
- Honesty: declaring any conflicts of interest and resolving them in the interests of the charity.
- Leadership: setting a good example of corporate leadership and developing a good, constructive working relationship with the staff.

National Housing Federation

27.16 The National Housing Federation (formerly known as the National Federation of Housing Associations) held an Inquiry into Housing Association Governance in 1995. Its report, 'Competence and Accountability' (the Hancock Report), contained a draft Code of Governance, designed to improve the competence and accountability of housing associations (now known as registered social landlords), but much of which is relevant to many other types of voluntary organisation.

27.17 Corporate Governance

27.17 Amongst the Code's recommendations are the following:

- the Board should be given a clear statement of their role, with the emphasis of this role being on directing rather than managing;
- the Board should be given a clear statement of the role of Board members, the Chair, the Treasurer and any other honorary officers and the Chief Executive;
- the maximum size of the Board should be 15;
- there should be formal, published and open selection procedures for Board members and comprehensive induction arrangements; and
- there shoud be regular assessment of Board members' performance.

28 Corporation Tax

28.1 Charities that are companies, industrial and provident societies, or unincorporated associations are within the scope of corporation tax. Corporation tax is payable on taxable profits in an accounting period, which is normally their financial year. Profits include both income and capital gains though in the case of most charities these will be exempt from tax.

Self assessment

28.2 Where a charity or its subsidiary trading company has taxable income or gains, it is required to notify the Inland Revenue within twelve months from the end of its accounting period, unless it has made a corporation tax return in respect of that period. Where the Inland Revenue know that an entity may be liable to corporation tax, it will issue it with a notice to file a corporation tax return. The return must be submitted within twelve months of the year-end. Under the self assessment provisions, an entity is also required to make payment of corporation tax according to its calculation of tax payable. No assessments are made but the Inland Revenue have until 12 months after the tax return filing date to raise any queries by starting an enquiry. Companies and charities that come within the scope of corporation tax are liable to penalties for failing to notify the Inland Revenue that they are liable to corporation tax, or for failing to submit a corporation tax return on time, and interest is charged on any corporation tax paid late.

Exemption

28.3 The rules of corporation tax are the same for charities as they are for commercial companies except that charities are exempt from corporation tax on certain classes of income and gains.

Section 505 exemptions

28.4 The main exemptions from corporation tax on income are to be found in *s 505* of *Income and Corporation Taxes Act 1988*. This section provides exemption from tax on:

- profits or gains arising in respect of rent or other receipts from land, wherever situated, provided that the land is vested in the company for charitable purposes and the income is only applied to charitable purposes;
- interest, annuities, annual payments, dividends etc. arising in the UK or overseas where the income in question forms part of the income of a charity or is, according to rules and regulations established by Act of Parliament, Charter, Decree, Deed of Trust or Will, applicable to charitable purposes only, so far as any of this income is applied to charitable purposes only;
- certain public revenue dividends to the extent that they are applicable and applied only for the repair of any cathedral, college, church, chapel or building used only for divine worship;
- the profits of a trade carried on by a charity if the profits are applied solely for the purposes of the charity and either the trade is exercised in the course of the actual carrying out of a primary purpose of the charity or the work in connection with the trade is mainly carried on by beneficiaries of the charity; and

- profits accruing to a charity from a lottery if the lottery is promoted and conducted in accordance with the *Lotteries and Amusements Act 1976 ss 3* or *5* or *Articles 133* and *155* of the *Betting, Gaming, Lotteries and Amusements (Northern Ireland) Order 1985* and the profits are applied solely to the charity's purposes.

Exemption for small trading and other income

28.5 From April 2000, there is a new tax exemption for the profits of small trading activities. This applies to trading profits and other casual profits, such as sponsorship and some royalties, provided that the total turnover from all the activities is within certain limits. It also applies if, at the beginning of the period, there was a reasonable expectation that turnover would be within those limits, even if they are later exceeded. The Revenue may ask for evidence to support any argument that the turnover was greater than originally expected. The annual turnover limit is £5,000 or, if greater, 25% of the charity's total income from all sources but is subject to an overall limit of £50,000.

Other exemptions

28.6 There are a number of provisions charging tax on certain types of income or gains where a specific exemption is made for charities.

- Charities are exempt from the special charges relating to Certificates of Deposit if the profits or gains are applied to charitable purposes only.

- Charities are exempt from the offshore funds legislation if the gains are applicable and applied for charitable purposes.

- Charities are exempt from the accrued income scheme which applies on a transfer of certain interest bearing securities where the interest is applied for charitable purposes only.

- The charge to tax where a pension fund surplus is repaid to an employer does not apply where the employer is a charity.

- Charities do not have to pay corporation tax on capital gains if they are applied for charitable purposes.

Conditions

28.7 Most of the above exemptions require that the income or gains are applied only for charitable purposes. There are therefore three requirements: first that the money is applied, second that it is for charitable purposes and third that it is not also for any other purpose. Strictly, because corporation tax is an annual tax, the income or gains should be applied in the same year in which they arise. In practice, the Inland Revenue do not appear to insist on this, subject to the rules for qualifying expenditure. If a charity applies its income in any matter permitted by its governing document then it should be arguable that the income is applied for charitable purposes only. Application includes spending the money on legitimate administration expenses of the charity, investing in funds held for charitable purposes or applying it according to an order or advice given by the Charity Commission. Where, however, income is left uninvested or applied for non-charitable purposes, the charity is probably acting in breach of its governing document and the income or gains are taxable.

Trading

28.8 Where a charity is carrying on trading activities, there are additional conditions which must be satisfied for the trading profits to be exempt from tax. Normally, a trade involves the sale of goods or services as part of a commercial enterprise but for tax purposes, a single or occasional venture may also be treated as a trade where there is an intention of making a profit. The fact that the profits are a form of fund raising for the charity is irrelevant in deciding whether or not a trading activity exists. Unless within the small trading exemption, the two additional conditions which must be satisfied if trading profits are to be exempt from tax are that the trade must be exercised in the course of the actual carrying out of a primary purpose of the charity or the work in connection with the trade must be mainly carried out by beneficiaries of the charity.

Primary purpose trading

28.9 Examples of primary purpose trades are:

- the provision of educational services by a charitable school;
- the holding of an exhibition by a charitable art gallery or museum;
- the sale of tickets for a theatrical production staged by a charitable theatre company;
- the provision of health care services or residential accommodation by a care charity;
- the sale of certain educational goods by a charitable art gallery or museum.

Ancillary trading

28.10 Additionally, the exemption from tax on trading profits extends to activities which are ancillary to the carrying out of a primary purpose. Examples of ancillary trading are:

- the renting of accommodation to students by a university or college;
- sales of goods or services for the benefits of students, or the provision of a crèche for the children of students, by a school or college;
- the sale of food and drink to patrons of a charitable art gallery, museum or theatre;
- the sale of confectionery, toiletries and flowers to patients and their visitors by a League of Friends hospital shop.

28.11 The above activities cannot be extended without putting the tax exemption under *s 505* at risk. For example, if a museum sells a range of goods some of which are not educational, or a college rents accommodation for tourists during the holiday periods, or a theatre restaurant or bar is open to members of the general public the whole of the exemption for all primary purpose trading activities is lost, unless the amounts involved are small in themselves and the turnover of that part of the trade is less than 10% of the total turnover.

Concession for fund raising

28.12 By concession, the Inland Revenue do not seek to tax the profits of some small scale events arranged to raise funds for charity, but the organisation must comply fully with the terms of the concession. This concession applies to 'bazaars, jumble sales, gymkhanas, carnivals, fireworks displays and similar activities arranged by voluntary organisations or charities for the purposes of raising funds for charity'. The following conditions must, however, also be satisfied:

- the activities are supported substantially because the public are aware that any profits will be devoted to charity;
- no more than 15 events of the same kind at the same location may be held in any year, unless the weekly gross takings do not exceed £1,000;
- the profits are transferred to charities or are otherwise applied for charitable purposes.

28.13 The list of events quoted is not exhaustive and the concession will often apply to other similar events such as fêtes, concerts, dinners, dances and sports matches.

Donated goods

28.14 A number of charities raise funds by selling donated goods either as a regular activity in charity shops or as an occasional activity at e.g. a jumble sale or fête. Provided that the goods are not subjected to significant refurbishment, or used or processed to make other goods, e.g. cloth being made up into garments, such sales are not a trading activity. The sales are simply the realisation of the value of the donated goods. This is so even where the donated goods are sorted, cleaned and minor repairs are made.

Sponsorship

28.15 Business sponsorship is also a common method used by charities to raise funds but it can easily amount to a trading activity, either as a separate trade or as part of another trade. If the sponsorship payments are not made in return for goods or services provided by the charity, they will normally be classed as charitable donations and, therefore, not taxable. However, where the charity agrees to provide some goods or services, including publicity, advertising or entertaining, in return for the sponsorship payments, the arrangement may be treated as trading.

28.16 Unless it amounts to advertising, merely acknowledging a sponsor's contribution will not normally make sponsorship a trading activity. The Inland Revenue regard a reference to a sponsor as an advertisement if it incorporates either the sponsor's logo, the sponsor's corporate colours or mention of the sponsor's products or services. Similarly, the Inland Revenue will normally treat sponsorship payments as trading income if the sponsor is allowed use of the charity's mailing list or logo; or if the charity endorses the sponsor's products or services; or the charity grants the sponsor exclusive rights to sell its goods or services on the charity's premises. Nevertheless, if the sponsorship income forms part of another trade, rather than a trade in itself, and that trade is a primary purpose trade then the profits will be exempt from tax. An example of this would be where a business sponsors a charitable theatre's stage production.

Affinity credit cards

28.17 The fees received by a charity from the issue or use of credit cards bearing the name of the charity is trading income, which is not from a primary purpose or ancillary trade and is therefore taxable. It may be possible to arrange for series of payments to be made for the use of the charity's logo by separate agreement, in which the charity is not obliged to do anything in return. The payments should be exempt from tax as annual payments. A separate agreement would be needed for the use of the charity's mailing list and promotional activities as fees received for these services would be taxable. If the arrangement is structured through a charity's trading subsidiary, care is needed over the agreement between the charity and its subsidiary for the use of the charity's name.

Royalties

28.18 The taxation treatment of royalties depends on their nature and what the charity does or has done in return. In most cases they will be taxable, either as trading income or under Schedule D Case VI, for which there is no specific exemption outside the exemption for small trading and other income. In some cases where the charity has done nothing to earn the royalty, the royalty fees could be treated as an annual payment, which would be exempt from corporation tax.

Calculation of profit

28.19 Having established that a charity is carrying on a trade which is not for a primary purpose or within the concessions, the actual profit of the trade must be calculated in order to arrive at any tax liability. In arriving at these profits, the charity will be able to deduct not only the direct expenditure of the trade but also a proportion of other indirect overheads which may be partly attributable, such as the running costs of the premises, salaries and administration costs. It may also be possible to organise events that amount to trading activities so as to minimise the profit. This can be achieved by the charity setting a minimum charge and inviting an additional voluntary donation. However, promotional material and tickets must clearly state that:

- only the minimum charge need be paid;
- further contributions are entirely discretionary;
- no additional benefit is secured by making an additional payment.

Costs can be deducted from this in order to arrive at the taxable profit. If this is done then only the minimum charge qualifies as taxable income.

28.20 If a charity makes a loss from a trading activity, the loss will be regarded as charitable expenditure if the activities are within the charity's objects. If they are not, the loss may be regarded as non-charitable expenditure, which can result in a general loss of the charity's exemption from corporation tax.

Loss of exemptions

28.21 There is a complex set of rules which restricts the amount of a charity's income which is exempt from tax. This restriction depends upon the amount of a charity's qualifying expenditure and relevant income and gains. Qualifying expenditure is expenditure incurred for charitable purposes only. Relevant income and gains are any income or gains which are taxable or which would be taxable without the main exemptions provided by the *Taxes Act*. In this context, expenditure includes any money spent by the charity in the year for whatever purpose and, as stated above, can include certain trading losses. Tax exemptions are lost when a charity's income and gains are £10,000 or more, its relevant income and gains exceed its qualifying expenditure and the charity has incurred non-qualifying expenditure. Examples of non-qualifying expenditure would be losses from a trade which was not a primary purpose trade or a loan which broadly is not made for charitable purposes by way of investment or for the benefit of the charity.

Net relevant income

28.22 The first stage in assessing whether or not the charity's income is exempt from tax is to ascertain whether the relevant income of the year exceeds the qualifying expenditure of that year. If it does not, the rules do not apply.

Non-qualifying expenditure

28.23 The next stage is to ascertain whether or not there is non-qualifying expenditure for that year. Where there is both non-qualifying expenditure and a shortfall of qualifying expenditure over relevant income and gains, then there is a loss of tax exemption. The non-qualifying expenditure gives rise to a loss of exemption but it is restricted in that year to the shortfall of qualifying expenditure. See the following example.

Relevant income	£100,000
Qualifying expenditure	£75,000
Non-qualifying expenditure	£120,000
Loss of exemption	£100,000 – £75,000 = £25,000

28.24 If, as in the above example, the non-qualifying expenditure for the year exceeds the shortfall of qualifying expenditure, the charity is retrospectively deemed to have incurred non-qualifying expenditure in the previous year. The amount being equal to the surplus non-qualifying expenditure. In the above example this would be £95,000 i.e. £120,000 – £25,000. The calculations must then be repeated for the previous year to see if, retrospectively, tax exemption is also lost in that year. As long as there is a surplus of non-qualifying expenditure, the charity must carry it back for up to six years. Surpluses of non-qualifying expenditure do not, however, have to be carried forward.

28.25 There is one limitation on the carry-back principle. Expenditure is not carried back if the charity can show that it represents expenditure of non-taxable sums i.e. sums which were not taxable in any event, with or without exemption, such as donations and legacies. In these circumstances, the amount of non-qualifying expenditure which would otherwise be carried back is compared with the non-taxable sums received, so that only the excess, if any, is carried back. If in the above example, the charity had received donations in the year of £80,000, the amount carried back to the earlier year would only have been the additional £15,000.

28.26 The limit of £10,000 on a charity's income and gains after which tax exemptions are lost was set in 1986 when this legislation was introduced. It has not been increased since that date and therefore, in real terms, it is of much less benefit than it originally was.

29 Custodian Trustee

29.1 A custodian trustee is a corporate body, commonly a bank, insurance company or local authority, which holds investments or land on behalf of a charity and is empowered to act in accordance with rules set out in the *Public Trustee Act 1906 s 14*. The Charity Commission will permit a charity to have all its investments and land held by just one custodian trustee.

Method of appointment

29.2 A custodian trustee can be appointed under *s 4(1)* of the *Public Trustee Act 1906* in any of the following ways:

- by the governing document of the charity when it is first established;
- by the person or persons with power to appoint trustees;
- by an Order or Scheme of the Court.

The Charity Commission can also appoint a custodian trustee by an Order or Scheme under *s 16* of the *Charities Act 1993*.

Responsibilities

29.3 The activities of custodian trustees are limited to holding legal title to investments or land, receiving income from these assets and remitting income to the charity. They play no further part in the management of the charity or its assets. They cannot act on behalf of the managing trustees, even if there are none.

29.4 Custodian trustees must act on the instructions of the charity trustees unless doing so would be unlawful or a breach of trust. If a custodian trustee acts unlawfully or commits a breach of trust while acting on the instructions of the charity trustees, legal liability rests with the charity trustees. However, if custodian trustees commit a breach of trust by acting outside the terms of their agreement with the charity whose assets they hold, the custodian trustees will be legally liable.

Advantages of having a custodian trustee

29.5 Unincorporated charities often choose to use a custodian trustee, or a group of holding trustees (see Chapter 56) to hold title to their land or investments. This is because unincorporated charities cannot hold their investments or land in the name of the charity, as an unincorporated body has no legal personality of its own. If the trustees hold legal title, expense is incurred every time there is a change in the governing body and legal title has to be transferred to the new body of trustees.

Fees

29.6 Custodian trustees usually charge a fee for their services. Under general law all charity trustees have the power to appoint a custodian trustee, but they may not remunerate a custodian trustee unless the charity's governing document contains a clear power permitting such a payment or if, more rarely, the Commissioners have made an Order or Scheme allowing the trustees to remunerate a custodian trustee.

29.7 Custodian Trustee

29.7 Some corporate bodies, including charities, local authorities and trust corporations set up to serve religious denominations, such as the Church of England's Diocesan Boards of Finance, are willing to act as custodian trustees without remuneration.

Termination

29.8 If a charity wishes to dispense with the services of its custodian trustee, the trusteeship must be terminated by an order of the court or the Charity Commission acting under the *Public Trustee Act 1906 s 4(1)(a)*.

30 Data Protection

30.1 The *Data Protection Act 1998* came into force on 1 March 2000 and substantially altered previous data protection laws. It applies to any organisation that collects or uses information about recognisable living individuals and will have a particular impact on charity fund-raisers. In addition the *Telecommunications (Direct Marketing and Privacy) Regulations 1999* impose additional requirements for direct marketing to organisations and individuals by phone and fax.

30.2 The *Data Protection Act 1998* applies to both personal data held on computers (automated data) and on paper (manual records) providing that the manual records are structured by reference to an individual and data are easily accessible. Examples of manual records are card indexes, filing systems structured by an individual's name, correspondence files cross-referenced with automated files, personal notes cross-referenced with automated files and documents scanned by document image processing techniques.

30.3 The Act gives rights to individuals (data subjects) and imposes duties on the collecting organisation (the data controller) and its employees who hold and process personal data. Charities should consider giving one member of staff overall responsibility for ensuring that all the charity's data processing complies with the legislation and ensure that all staff, particularly those in fund-raising, supporter management and operational departments, are aware of the legislation and know who to contact for detailed advice.

Data subjects

30.4 A data subject is any individual whose personal data are obtained, held, used and otherwise processed by an organisation within the meaning of the data protection legislation. Examples of the types of individuals charities hold data on are current and former employees, job applicants, current and former beneficiaries and potential beneficiaries, contacts, suppliers, etc.

Data controllers

30.5 A data controller is an individual or organisation that determines the purposes for which and the manner in which personal data are processed.

Personal data

30.6 Personal data is any information that relates to a living individual. It can be as little as name, address, telephone number and e-mail address, or it may include, for example, information about a person's state of health, educational qualifications or financial circumstances. Information about an individual working for another charity in the same field would be personal data, whereas information about the charity they worked for is not personal data.

Sensitive personal data

30.7 Because of their sensitive nature some types of personal data have been defined as 'sensitive personal data' by the Act and are subject to a stricter data protection regime. These are:

- Racial or ethnic origin;
- Political opinions;
- Religious and similar beliefs;
- Membership of a trade union;
- Physical or mental health or condition;
- Sexual life;
- Committed or alleged offences.

30.8 Sensitive personal data cannot be processed unless one of a number of criteria are satisfied. The two most significant of these criteria are processing with explicit consent of the data subject and processing by an employer for the purposes of compliance with employment legislation.

Processing

30.9 Processing includes virtually anything that can be done with data, including typing data into a computer, storing it on a hard drive, copying it onto a disk, or reading it from a computer screen. Processing also includes collecting, recording, holding, retrieval, consultation, use, disclosure, combining, blocking and destruction of data.

30.10 All organisations, including charities, must comply with data protection rules when:

- asking for personal information on questionnaires or application forms;
- active or passive collection or dissemination of personal data on the Internet or the organisation's intranet or Extranet;
- sending personal data within or outside the organisation by e-mail or telephone;
- direct marketing;
- compiling and using mailing lists;
- compiling personal data for inclusion in directories or publications;
- using existing personal data for new purposes;
- using third parties to carry out any processing;
- dealing with employment issues;
- monitoring employees' use of the telephone, computer, Internet and e-mail.

Notification

30.11 The old registration procedure has been replaced by a simplified notification system. A charity that is a data controller has a duty to notify the Data Protection Commissioner about its processing operations with personal data. It must provide the Commissioner with information about:

- the personal data processed by the charity;
- the categories of individuals whose data are processed;
- the purposes for which data are processed;
- to whom the data are disclosed;

- the countries outside the European Economic Area to which data are transferred. (The export of personal data to non-EEA countries is now illegal unless the data controller can show that the country of the transferee is 'safe' for data protection purposes or one of the exemptions in the Act applies.);
- the data security measures employed.

30.12 Notification has to be renewed every year. The fee for and renewal is £35.

Data protection principles

30.13 The *Data Protection Act 1998* sets out eight data protection principles that must be observed by all employees of charities that are data controllers. They are:

(i) Personal data must be processed fairly and lawfully;

(ii) Personal data shall be obtained for one or more specified and lawful purposes and not further processed in any manner incompatible with such purpose(s);

(iii) Personal data must be adequate, relevant and not excessive in relation to the purpose(s) for which they are processed;

(iv) Personal data must be accurate and kept up to date;

(v) Personal data shall not be kept longer than is necessary for the purpose(s) for which they have been processed;

(vi) Personal data must be processed in accordance with the rights of data subjects;

(vii) Personal data must be protected by appropriate data security measures;

(viii) Personal data shall be adequately protected when transferred outside the European Economic Area.

30.14 Breaches of the principles may result in a complaint by the individual concerned, a claim for compensation by the individual concerned, or possible enforcement action by the Data Protection Commissioner.

Data subjects' rights

30.15 Any data subject may demand to see and/or have a copy of all personal data held and processed about him.

30.16 They have a right to object to the processing of their personal data where such processing may cause substantial and unwarranted damage or distress. This right applies in relation to perfectly lawful processing that is unwanted by the data subject for a specified and justifiable reason because it is causing or likely to cause them damage or distress.

30.17 Data subjects have the right to request that an organisation corrects, blocks, erases or destroys any personal data that is incorrect or misleading or that contains information and/or opinions that are based on inaccurate data.

30.18 Every individual has the right to request that organisations, including charities, stop or do not begin processing their personal data for the purpose of direct marketing.

30.19 Data Protection

30.19 Individuals have rights in relation to decisions that significantly affect them that are made using solely automated means i.e. with no human involvement. Where decisions are taken in this manner the data subject should be informed. Within 21 days of the data subject being informed of the decision, they have the right to ask for the decision to be reconsidered and for information about the basis on which the decision was made. The data collector should respond within 21 days.

30.20 Finally any data subject can claim compensation through the Courts for any damage, or damage and distress suffered as a result of a breach of the Act.

Obtaining data subjects' consent

30.21 When collecting personal data charities must provide data subjects with the following:

- The name of the organisation or individual that will be processing the data, for example the charity, its trading company, or both;
- The primary purpose of the processing e.g. to record a donation, send a publication, provide services;
- Details of any other purposes that the data will be used for, e.g. information or mail order catalogues;
- Details of any third parties to whom the data may be disclosed;
- Details of how the data subject can opt-out of having their data used for anything other than the primary purpose.

Telecommunications (Data Protection and Privacy) Regulations 1999

30.22 The *Telecommunications (Data Protection and Privacy) Regulations 1999* came into force on 1 March 2000. They introduce stricter requirements for direct marketing to organisations and individuals by phone and fax only. The Data Protection Act, however, covers all direct marketing methods.

30.23 The regulations apply to both organisation to organisation marketing and organisation to consumer marketing. Charities will need to obtain prior consent (opt-in) from individuals or businesses for conducting marketing by automated-calling systems and sending unsolicited marketing faxes to individuals. Charities may only make marketing calls to individuals or unsolicited marketing faxes to organisations where those concerned have not objected (opted-out) to such use of their data.

30.24 The Regulations require that organisations check with the Telephone Preference Service and the Fax Preference Service to find out if individuals or organisations have registered to opt-out from receiving direct marketing by telephone or fax.

Data Protection Commissioner

30.25 The Data Protection Commissioner is responsible for enforcing both the *Data Protection Act 1998* and the *Telecommunications (Data Protection and Privacy) Regulations 1999*. The Commissioner can:

- hear complaints from individuals;
- enter a data controller's premises and carry out an inspection, if there is a suspected breach or offence;

- serve an information notice requesting information about a suspected breach of data protection principles;
- serve an enforcement notice for breaches of data protection principles;
- prosecute the data controller or its employees for specific breaches of the Act.

Breach of provisions

30.26 Failure to notify with the Data Protection Commission and unlawfully obtaining, processing, selling or disclosing personal data without authorisation are criminal offences giving rise to fines of up to £5,000 in a Magistrates' Court. The organisation or an employee can be prosecuted. The Act provides for separate personal liability for any officers, directors or trustees of companies that have breached the Act.

31 Devolution and Regionalisation

31.1 The devolution of political power to Scotland, Wales and Northern Ireland and to the English regions has had an impact on many charities, particularly charities based in England but working UK-wide. Devolution has an impact on how charities need to position themselves in order to gain credibility with funding bodies, how they deliver services, how they exercise their political leverage and how they hold themselves accountable.

31.2 Charities need to question the impact of devolution on their overall strategy, decision-making, structure, governance, service delivery, campaigning, and fundraising, financial and human resource strategies. The also need to consider if they need to build new relationships with potential and existing funders and new alliances with other voluntary organisations. In some instances devolution has led to charities restructuring, transforming their national branches into autonomous organisations or adopting a federal structure, in order to take advantage of the opportunities presented by devolution.

Scottish Parliament

31.3 The *Scotland Act 1998* laid out the legislative details of the Scottish Parliament which took up its full powers in July 1999. It is written in terms of reserved powers, prescribing everything over which the Westminster Parliament retains control. The UK Parliament retains powers over:

- UK foreign policy, including European Union policy;
- UK defence and national security;
- UK fiscal, economic and monetary system;
- Common markets for UK goods and services;
- The constitution;
- Social security;
- Employment legislation;
- Transport safety and regulation;
- Company law;
- Certain other matters presently subject to UK or GB regulation, including the National Lottery and equality rights legislation.

31.4 All remaining areas are automatically devolved to the Scottish Parliament including:;

- Health;
- Education;
- Social welfare;
- Economic development;
- Environment;
- Transport;

- Responsibility for local authorities and non-departmental government bodies.

31.5 The Scottish Parliament can introduce new legislation and amend or repeal existing legislation in these areas. Committees and individual Members of the Scottish Parliament can introduce legislation and the Parliament can consider legislation promoted by an external body, such as a Scottish charity. Charities operating in Scotland can therefore influence policy and provide information and expertise on a wide range of issues being debated by the Parliament. Committees of the Scottish Parliament seek evidence on a regular basis from voluntary organisations on a broad range of policy issues.

Relationship to Westminster

31.6 The UK Parliament remains sovereign but Westminster MPs can no longer debate or question Ministers on devolved matters. A Secretary of State for Scotland remains in the UK Cabinet and represents the interests of Scotland in the UK Parliament. MPs from Scotland continue to sit at Westminster.

31.7 Most of the funding for Scotland's public expenditure programme continues to be met through the 'Block' and formula process under which the UK government previously transferred money to the Scottish Office.

Scottish Civic Forum

31.8 The Scottish Civic Forum was launched in March 1999. Membership includes over 600 organisations including voluntary organisations, charities, churches, trade unions, and business and professional associations. The Forum's purpose is to enable civic society to engage more actively in the policy development process and to complement and add value to the existing mechanisms for consultation.

Wales

31.9 The *Government of Wales Act 1998* laid out the legislative details of the National Assembly for Wales which also took up its full powers in July 1999. The Westminster Parliament retains responsibility for all primary legislation affecting Wales and the Assembly is responsible for putting it into practice through regulations, orders and guidance. The Assembly is also responsible for:

- input into UK policy, focusing on the implications for Wales;
- input into European policies for Wales;
- formulating secondary legislation;
- setting standards and targets for public bodies, monitoring their progress and dealing with any shortcomings;
- allocating its budget which is determined by Westminster;
- the annual assessment and allocation of funding for local authorities;
- policy development and implementation regarding agriculture and fisheries, arts and culture, economic development, education and training, environment, health, housing, local government, planning, social services, sport and recreation, tourism, transport and highways, Welsh language.

31.10 Devolution and Regionalisation

Relationship to Westminster

31.10 Westminster retains responsibility for criminal justice, immigration, taxation, defence, foreign affairs, social security, the employment service and broadcasting. In areas where power has been devolved the Assembly is responsible for drawing up the secondary or subordinate legislation needed to put the laws into effect.

The Voluntary Sector Scheme

31.11 The Welsh Office and the voluntary and community sector in Wales have agreed a Compact establishing the framework for future working relationships between government and the sector in Wales. The Voluntary Sector Scheme will be based on the Compact and will set out the practical arrangements to enable voluntary and community organisations to engage with Assembly Secretaries and committees. These will include:

- A National Assembly-Voluntary Sector Forum made up of members of the Assembly and elected representatives of the sector to oversee the implementation of the Voluntary Sector Scheme;
- Meetings between each Assembly Secretary and Subject committee with relevant voluntary sector networks in order to plan co-operation;
- Panels of voluntary sector advisors who can be called on to serve on Assembly working groups and give advice to committees.

Northern Ireland Assembly

31.12 The Northern Ireland Assembly took up its power in December 1999, following the Belfast (Good Friday) Agreement. It was suspended in February 2000 but recommenced its work in May 2000. It has full legislative and executive authority to make laws and take decisions on all the functions of the Northern Ireland Departments. Unlike the Welsh Assembly, the Northern Ireland Assembly can enact primary legislation and unlike the Scottish Parliament, it has responsibility for energy.

31.13 The Secretary of State for Northern Ireland remains responsible for matters not devolved to the Assembly including policing, security policy, prisons, criminal justice, international relations, taxation, national insurance, regulation of financial services and regulation of broadcasting.

Regionalisation

31.14 There are nine English regions:

- East of England;
- East Midlands;
- London;
- North East;
- North West;
- South East;
- South West;
- West Midlands;

- Yorkshire and the Humber.

With the exception of London, all have broadly similar infrastructures.

31.15 Government Offices for the Regions (GORs) were established in 1994, bringing together the existing regional government offices dealing with transport, the environment, education and trade and industry. Their remit is to promote competitiveness, prosperity and quality of life in their region through business enterprise, sustainability and regeneration. They also have a role in identifying issues specific to their region and ensuring that these are fed into the national policy making-process.

31.16 The GORs act as the government sponsoring unit for the Regional Development Agencies (RDAs) which were established in 1999 under the *Regional Development Agencies Act 1998* in each of the English regions except London. GORs provide advice to RDAs about government policies and programmes and guidance relating to the operation of the RDAs. The GORs are responsible for administering the grant-in-aid paid to the RDAs and for other funding streams such as the European Social Fund and New Deal for Communities.

31.17 Each RDA is managed by a RDA Board, the majority of whose members come from business. Their purpose is to promote the economic, social and physical regeneration of their region. All are required to produce a Regional Economic Strategy that should include input from the voluntary sector and identify key partners, including voluntary organisations, to help implement the strategy.

31.18 RDAs are responsible for administering the Single Regeneration Budget (SRB) for the regions, which is used primarily to support excluded communities, often using voluntary organisations as delivery agents.

London

31.19 London differs from the other regions in that it is the only one to have democratic representation. The first elections for the London Mayor and Greater London Assembly, which together form the Greater London Authority (GLA), were held in May 2000. The RDA for London is known as the London Development Agency. It has broadly similar responsibilities and functions as the other RDAs, though slightly wider as responsibilities for transport and policing are also devolved to the GLA, unlike other RDAs. The LDA came into being in July 2000 and is accountable to the GLA.

Regional Voluntary Sector Networks

31.20 In response to regionalisation Regional Voluntary Sector Networks (RVSNs) have been established in all the regions providing a link between regional and local bodies. In addition some regional interest groups have been established to deal with issues facing particular communities, such as black and minority ethnic groups, at a regional level.

The Compact

31.21 The relationship between central government and the voluntary sector is set out in the Compact (*Compact on Relations between Government and the Voluntary and Community Sector in England*, The Home Office, 2000). The principles set out in the Compact relate to GORs as well as RDAs. The Compact outlines a new approach to partnership between the Government and the voluntary sector in England based on shared values. It has been drawn up following extensive consultation with the voluntary and community sector and Government departments. The underlying philosophy is that voluntary and community activity is fundamental to the development of a democratic, socially inclusive society. It sets out a list of shared principles and undertakings by the Government on issues such as independence of the sector, funding, policy development, and better government and by the voluntary sector on funding and accountability, policy development and consultation, and good practice. Copies are available from the Home Office Voluntary and Community Unit.

32 Directors

Director

32.1 The word 'director' is used in the voluntary sector in a number of different contexts. The trustees of a charitable company may be referred to as the (company) directors, as may the directors of industrial and provident societies. The most senior member of staff may also be referred to as 'the Director', or others as 'the Director of Operations', 'the Director of Finance', 'the Director of Fund-raising'. Some of these 'directorships' are of no statutory significance, though in some circumstances staff could be judged to be acting in a statutory capacity as shadow directors.

Shadow director

32.2 A shadow director is defined by the *Companies Act 1985* as being someone in accordance with whose directions or instructions the directors of the company are accustomed to act. Merely providing trustees with information, as a chief executive might do, or advising them, as an accountant or solicitor might do, does not amount to acting as a shadow director. A chief executive who dominated the board of trustees and controlled almost all of the charity's activities could, on the other hand, be regarded as a shadow director.

32.3 Although the *Companies Act 1985* recognises the existence of shadow directors, in practice it is rare for an individual to be held to be a shadow director. Where someone does act as a shadow director then they become liable to incur penalties personally if the company is in default of its obligations under the *1985* and *1989 Companies Acts* or the *Insolvency Act 1986*.

32.4 In the remainder of this chapter the term 'director' is used to refer to a charitable company's directors (i.e. the trustees).

Appointment

32.5 The first directors are appointed in the company formation process and subsequent directors are appointed in accordance with the company's articles. In practice, when a new commercial company is set up, it is often acquired from formation agents who set up 'off-the-shelf' companies with their own staff as the first directors. These directors then appoint the purchaser's nominees as directors and resign themselves.

32.6 On appointment new directors record their consent to act by signing form 288a which is then dated and countersigned by the company secretary or another trustee. The Secretary sends the form to Companies House, and the directors' details are entered in the register of directors in the charity's statutory books. Members of the public can gain access to the names of directors of a charitable company by contacting Companies House.

32.7 Limited companies, other than public limited companies, sometimes have only one director, but then that person cannot also be the company secretary. A body corporate, e.g. another limited company, can be a company director, in which case an individual will be appointed by the body corporate to act on its behalf. Frequently, the articles of the company will stipulate that there must be a minimum number of directors greater than one.

32.8 Directors

Qualifications

32.8 Any adult person who is not disqualified by law, or prohibited by the charity's articles of association, may become a director of a charitable company.

Disqualification under the Charities Act 1993

32.9 *Section 72* of *Charities Act 1993* disqualifies people from becoming directors (trustees) of a charitable company if they:

- have unspent convictions for offences involving deception or dishonesty;
- are undischarged bankrupts;
- have been at any time removed from trusteeship of a charity by the Charity Commission or the Court in England, Wales or Scotland, because of misconduct;
- are disqualified from being company directors under the *Company Directors Disqualification Act 1986*;
- have failed to make payments under county court administration orders; or
- have made compositions (i.e. come to an arrangement) with their creditors and have not been discharged.

32.10 As soon as someone comes within *s 72*, i.e. the day they are convicted of an offence involving dishonesty, they are automatically disqualified from acting as a trustee. It is a criminal offence to act as a charity trustee while disqualified.

Waiver from disqualification

32.11 The Charity Commission can grant a waiver from disqualification, however, under *s 72(4)* of *Charities Act 1993* either generally or in relation to a charity or a specific class of charities. For example, waivers may be given to ex-offenders so that they can serve on the boards of charities working with offenders. Anyone convicted of a relevant offence or who becomes bankrupt and who wishes to remain eligible to be a charity trustee may apply to the Commission for a waiver.

Disqualification under the Company Directors Disqualification Act 1986

32.12 Under the *Company Directors Disqualification Act 1986* the court may disqualify people:

- who have been convicted of criminal offences relating to the promotion, formation, management or liquidation of a company;
- who have been persistently in default of company legislation for filing accounts and other documents;
- who have been found guilty of fraudulent trading or fraud; or
- whose conduct as a director has made them unfit to be involved in the management of a company.

Duties

32.13 All company directors have a fiduciary duty and a duty of care, in addition to other duties under charity law described in Chapter 108. Breach of these duties exposes the director to action from the body corporate or its members. The fiduciary duty means that company directors must act in the best interests of the organisation as a whole, avoid conflicts of interest and notify the charity if one occurs, and not misuse information for personal gain even after they have left the company, or in the case of directors of charitable companies have ceased to be members of the charity's board. Directors of limited companies also have a duty with regard to the employees' interests. [*Companies Act 1985 s 309*].

Directors' meetings

32.14 In order to manage the affairs of the company, the directors need to meet as a group. The frequency of these meetings, what they consider, and how they are transacted will depend on the nature of the company's activities and the internal rules set out within the articles of association or in standing orders. In CC3 'Responsibilities of Charity Trustees' the Charity Commission reminds trustees that trusteeship requires 'time, understanding and effort'. Trustees must be 'prepared to take an active part in the running of the charity'. They should 'meet regularly if they are to administer their charity properly. How often that needs to be will depend on the size and nature of the charity'.

32.15 Company directors need to meet at least annually in order to transact the formal business of the year in relation to the annual accounts and appointment and remuneration of officers. There are no formal procedures prescribed for the calling of directors' meetings, or the notice period, unless these are specified in the articles. Directors should take their responsibilities seriously. It will be appropriate for them to receive regular progress reports, management accounts and be informed of major developments, and they should consider any recommendations arising from the audit and the auditor's management letter.

Trading subsidiaries

32.16 Where a charity operates a trading subsidiary the directors of the trading subsidiary should meet independently of the charity trustees, and transact business in their capacity as that company's directors.

Personal liabilities

32.17 Although an advantage of incorporation is the limitation of liability, directors of companies can still incur personal liabilities, some of which cannot be covered by insurance. The two most clear cut situations are where a person acts as a director when disqualified, when a director may be held liable for all of the company's debts incurred whilst he was a director (*Company Directors Disqualification Act 1986 s 15*) or when a company, or industrial and provident society, is insolvent. The risks and effect of insolvency are covered in Chapter 65. Directors should be alert not only to actual insolvency, but also to situations where they ought to have known that insolvency was inevitable.

Office holders

32.18 A company director is an office holder, i.e. the role of the director is defined not by an employment contract, but by virtue of the office itself. Sometimes this distinction is not just academic, for example, if someone is both an office holder and an employee they could be removed from office as a director under the provisions of the *Companies Act 1985*, but may still have a claim against the company under their rights as an employee.

32.19 Directors

Payment of directors

32.19 Directors of a charitable company cannot be paid, or otherwise benefit from their office, unless the governing document expressly permits this. Similarly, a director of a subsidiary trading company who is a trustee of the holding charity cannot be paid for acting as a director of the subsidiary company, unless the governing document of the charity specifically provides for this. However, staff of the charity can be paid for acting as directors of the charity's wholly owned trading subsidiary.

32.20 The Charity Commission has stated that wherever trustees act as directors of a trading subsidiary, two points need to be borne in mind:

- the potential for conflict of interest; and
- that the appointment of trustees as directors cannot be used as a method of paying trustees 'by the back door'.

Disclosure

32.21 There is no requirement to list all the names of a charity's directors on its stationery. However, if one director is named, other than within the text or as a signatory, then **all** directors must be named. Sometimes a charitable company lists the names of its patrons. 'Patron' is not a legally recognised title, but if any patron is also a director then if this person's name is listed it will be necessary to list all the directors' names as well.

32.22 There is a general trend for companies not to disclose directors' names because of the need to reprint stationery every time there is a change of directors. It may be helpful for parties with whom an organisation is dealing to understand the status of the people who make up the charity's board, so this trend is not necessarily a welcome one. The use of laser printers to customise letterheads may allow greater flexibility in the future.

32.23 The names of directors must be set out in the annual report. The SORP requires charities to list the names of all the trustees on the date the report was approved (or at least 50 if there are more than 50 trustees), and also to list the names of all trustees who served during the year. The *Companies Act 1985 s 234* requires companies to list all the names of directors who served during the year (even if there are more than 50), but there is no requirement to list the names of directors at the date of signing. As the annual report requirement applies to incorporated charities only subsidiary trading companies can omit to list the names of directors at the date of signing.

Removal from office

32.24 Directors may cease to hold their office in a number of ways, the most common being resignation or retirement at the end of an agreed term of office. Notice of a director ceasing to hold office should be filed at Companies House. The notice does not need to be signed by the director resigning, but needs to be signed by another director or by the company secretary.

32.25 Occasionally a director may cease to hold office for more dramatic reasons, for example, as a result of being removed by the Charity Commission, or through failure to comply with the terms of appointment. Often the governing document will set out certain qualifications upon which a director holds office. The most common are some sort of role definition (a member of the local authority) or attendance at a predetermined number of meetings. This latter route has even been used by private companies as an attempt to force out directors, by calling meetings at short notice in impossible locations. Where a director is also a member of the company, ceasing to hold office as a director has no effect on that person's entitlement or rights as a member.

32.26 Directors of charitable companies may be removed by the members in a general meeting, as long as 28 days notice of the resolution is provided. The director has a right to defend himself or herself in writing or at the meeting. [*Companies Act 1985 s 304*].

Company law review

32.27 As a result of the continuing company law review directors may be affected by a possible widening of the definition of shadow director to include persons with whose instructions any one or more directors are accustomed to act, rather than the board as a whole. The duties of directors may be restated under the general headings of:

- compliance and loyalty;
- independence of judgement;
- conflict of interest;
- fairness;
- care, skill and diligence.

Industrial and provident societies

32.28 An industrial and provident society is governed by the members of the board, or committee. These members act as trustees and their names must be recorded in the register of officers. Their election will be in accordance with the rules of the industrial and provident society.

33 Disability Discrimination

Disability Discrimination Act 1995

33.1 The *Disability Discrimination Act 1995 (DDA 1995)* introduced new measures aimed at ending the discrimination faced by many people with disabilities. It gave disabled people new rights in the areas of:

- employment;
- access to goods and services;
- the management, buying, or renting of land or property.

33.2 In addition the Act:

- required schools, colleges and universities to provide information for disabled people;
- allowed the Government to set minimum standards to assist disabled people to use public transport;
- set up the National Disability Council to advise Government on eliminating discrimination against disabled people.

33.3 The new employment rights came into force in England, Wales, Scotland and Northern Ireland on 2 December 1996. Some of the rights relating to goods and services came into force on 1 October 1999, and other rights will be introduced over time.

33.4 Disability is defined in the Act as 'a physical or mental impairment which has a substantial and long-term adverse affect on his ability to carry out normal day-to-day activities'. [*DDA 1995 s 1*]. Examples of physical impairment are blindness, deafness, heart disease, arthritis, diabetes, epilepsy, and chronic fatigue syndrome. Mental impairments include conditions usually referred to as learning disabilities but a mental illness is only classified as an impairment if it is a clinically well-recognised mental illness that has lasted, or could be expected to last, at least twelve months. The regulations exclude some conditions, for example addiction to alcohol, drugs or nicotine and seasonal conditions such as hay fever. People who are HIV positive do not come within the definition until they have an impairment that has some effect on their ability to carry out normal day-to-day activities (*1 Sch 8*).

33.5 The Act abolished the registration scheme that was created under the *Disabled Persons (Employment) Act 1944*, but anyone who was registered as a disabled person under that Act continues to qualify as a disabled person, irrespective of whether or not they meet the definition of disabled in *s 1* of the *DDA 1995*.

33.6 Any employer with 15 or more workers, including casuals, agency workers and freelancers, as well as employees, is required by the Act to make reasonable adjustments to physical features of their premises and work practices, so that employees, or potential employees with a disability, are not placed at a substantial disadvantage. The Disability Rights Task Force has recommended that the DDA should apply to all employers with two or more employees.

33.7 It is also unlawful for organisations providing goods or services to the public, whether paid for or free, to treat a person with disabilities less favourably for a reason related to their disability, without justification, by refusing to provide the goods or service, by providing on less favourable terms or by treating the person with a disability in a different manner. Service providers must take reasonable steps to:

- change the way in which services are provided if existing practices make it impossible or unreasonably difficult for people with disabilities to use the services;
- provide equipment or support to enable people with disabilities to use the service;
- deliver the services by alternative methods where physical barriers prevent people with disabilities from accessing them.

33.8 The above applies to all charities, not just those providing social care for people with disabilities. The provision of education and the use of any means of transport are, however, excluded from this part of the Act. From 2004 service providers will also have to take reasonable steps to alter their premises or other physical features that make it impossible or unreasonably difficult for people with disabilities to use a service.

33.9 'Justification' has different meanings in relation to employment or to access to goods and services. In relation to employment discrimination is justifiable if the reason for it is both material and substantial. For example, a charity leasing offices on the third floor of an old building without a lift would not be expected to install a lift in order to employ someone who used a wheelchair (although the charity would be expected to have looked into the feasibility and cost of making alterations even if it later decided that they were unreasonable). However, if a potential employee needed a braille keyboard, the employer would be expected to provide one. In one case that has come before a tribunal (*Tarling* v *Wisdom Toothbrushes Ltd*) the tribunal held that an employee had been dismissed because of a disability and that it was not reasonable for the employer to ignore advice to buy a special chair costing about £1,000 (but which would have cost the employer £200 to buy given the assistance available) that would have enabled the employee to perform her duties satisfactorily.

33.10 In relation to the provision of goods and services discrimination is justifiable if providing an inferior service to the disabled person is necessary in order for the service provider to be able to provide the service to the disabled person or other members of the public. Similarly the service provider can justify not providing a service to a disabled person if they would otherwise be unable to provide the service at all. A service provider is justified in refusing to enter into a contract with a disabled person if that person is unable to understand the nature of the agreement or to give informed consent. The Act does not require service providers to do anything that would endanger the health and safety of any person, including the disabled person in question, or anything that would fundamentally alter the nature of the service, professional or business.

Disability Rights Commission

33.11 The *Disability Rights Commission Act 1999* established the Disability Rights Commission (DRC) which opened for business on 25 April 2000. The DRC is an independent body set up by the Government to help secure civil rights for disabled people. Its statutory duties are to:

- work to eliminate discrimination against disabled people;

- promote equal opportunities for disabled people;
- encourage good practice in the treatment of disabled people;
- advise the Government on the working of disability legislation (the *Disability Discrimination Act (DDA) 1995* and the *Disability Rights Commission Act 1999*).

33.12 In order to carry out these duties, the DRC has a number of specific functions:

- Assisting disabled people to secure their rights, and arranging for legal advice and help where appropriate.
- Providing information and advice to disabled people and to employers and service providers about their rights and duties under the DDA.
- Preparing and reviewing statutory codes of practice, which provide practical guidance to employers and service providers on meeting their obligations under the DDA and on good practice.
- Providing an independent conciliation service in the event of disputes between disabled people and service providers over access to goods and services, and monitoring the performance of the conciliation service.
- Undertaking formal investigations into how disabled people are treated in a particular organisation or sector, and into unlawful acts by particular organisations.
- Carrying out research to inform discussion and policy-making and to ascertain how well the law affecting the rights of disabled people is working.

33.13 The *Disability Rights Commission Act 1999* defines the powers of the Disability Rights Commission (DRC). The DRC is as much concerned with educating public opinion and promoting good practice as with enforcement. Wherever possible, the Commission aims to work in partnership with employers and service providers, adopting a non-confrontational approach. As well as its advisory and educative role, the Commission has enforcement powers to enable it to fulfil its task of securing civil rights for disabled people. These powers include:

Power to conduct formal investigations

- The Commission may decide to conduct a formal investigation for any purpose connected with the performance of its duties.
- The Commission has power to require any person to give written or oral information for the purposes of a formal investigation.

Power to serve non-discrimination notices

- If through a formal investigation the Commission is satisfied that a person has committed or is committing an unlawful act, it may serve him or her with a non-discrimination notice.
- A non-discrimination notice gives details of the unlawful act and requires him or her not to commit any further unlawful acts of the same kind.
- The notice may also require the person to produce an action plan to ensure compliance with the law. If the Commission considers that an action plan is inadequate it may apply to a county court (or in Scotland to the sheriff) for an order.

Power to enter into an agreement

- As an alternative to taking enforcement action against a person whom it believes has committed an unlawful act, the Commission may enter into a written agreement with them.
- Under such an agreement, the person concerned agrees not to commit any further unlawful acts of the same kind (and to take any other action as may be specified in the agreement), while the Commission agrees not to take any relevant enforcement action.
- If, however, the other party to an agreement fails to comply with their undertakings, the Commission may apply to a county court (or in Scotland to the sheriff) for an order.

Power to act over persistent discrimination

- If a person has been served with a non-discrimination notice or has been found to have committed an act of unlawful discrimination, and is, in the view of the Commission, likely to commit further such acts, it can apply to the county court for an injunction (or in Scotland to the sheriff for an interdict).

Power to provide assistance

- The Commission may grant assistance to an individual who is bringing proceedings in connection with unlawful discrimination. This is a matter for the discretion of the Commission, which will take into account whether the case raises a matter of principle, and whether it is unreasonable to expect the applicant to deal with the case unaided.
- If given, assistance may take the form of legal advice and/or representation, efforts to settle the dispute, or any other assistance which the DRC thinks appropriate.

Power to issue Codes of Practice

- The Commission may prepare and issue Codes of Practice, giving practical guidance to employers, service providers and others concerned with promoting equal opportunities for disabled people and encouraging good practice. Such Codes of Practice must be approved by the Secretary of State and laid before Parliament.
- Failure to observe any provision of a Code of Practice does **not** make a person liable to proceedings, but a court or tribunal must take into account any provision of a Code that it considers relevant to any proceedings.

Power for conciliation of disputes

- Although no member or employee of the Commission may provide conciliation services in relation to disputes arising under Part III of the *Disability Discrimination Act (DDA) 1995* concerning access to goods and services, the Commission may make arrangements for the provision of conciliation services by another person or persons.

33.14 Disability Discrimination

Making a complaint

33.14 A person with a disability who believes that they have been discriminated against can seek advice from the DRC. If they wish to pursue a claim that they have been unlawfully treated by an employer or potential employer they must bring their complaint to an Employment Tribunal. The complaint must usually be made within three months of the alleged discrimination. A person who believes that a service provider has discriminated against him or her may bring civil proceedings in the County Court (Sheriff's Court in Scotland). Court action must be brought within six months of the alleged discrimination. Industrial tribunals and courts can award compensation for financial loss and for injury to feelings.

Good practice

33.15 Charity trustees and senior managers should ensure that the charity has a positive policy to ensure inclusion of disabled people and the policy should be communicated to all staff. All staff should be aware that it is illegal to discriminate against disabled people and staff dealing with employment matters, or the provision of services, may need to be given additional training so that they are fully aware of the charity's policy, its legal obligations and the duty of reasonable adjustments.

33.16 The implementation and effectiveness of the charity's policy should be regularly monitored and reviewed. Any acts of discrimination committed by staff or volunteers should be addressed through the charity's disciplinary rules and procedures.

33.17 Charities should consult from time to time with the DRC and disabled people to ensure that their needs are being met and should establish a feedback and complaints procedure that is easy for people with disabilities to use.

33.18 In some instances long-term sickness could be classified as a disability so it is important that charities have good sickness and absence management policies, and take legal advice if considering dismissing someone on grounds connected to sickness or disability. The one-year qualifying period does not apply to persons claiming unfair dismissal on the grounds of disability.

33.19 Employers can apply for a job introductory subsidy (£75 a week) for a six-week trial period to assess a disabled person's suitability for a particular job. People with disabilities are also entitled to financial assistance from the Access to Work Scheme to cover the cost of, for example, special equipment, adaptations to premises and travel costs.

33.20 In the first year since the Act came into force over 500 cases were heard by industrial tribunals, though awards have been made in only a handful of cases. However, the number of cases is expected to rise dramatically as more employees become aware of the Act and organisations supporting disabled people provide free legal advice to those seeking to make claims. Charities should take steps to ensure that they are complying with the Act and not open themselves up to possible actions which, even if they are successfully defended, are costly in staff time and money.

Positive discrimination

33.21 Charities set up to help people with certain kinds of disabilities are permitted to discriminate in their favour and similarly charities providing supported employment may treat one group of severely disabled people more favourably than other people.

Further information

The Disability Discrimination Act 1995: A good practice guide for managers and employers. HMSO 1999.

www.disability.gov.uk
www.drc-gb.org

34 Disaster Appeals

34.1 When a disaster happens there is usually an immediate public response, often before any formal appeal has been launched. This was certainly the case in 1997 following the death of Diana, Princess of Wales. In some instances, such as the Ethiopian Famine, the money raised was not sufficient to meet the needs of all the potential beneficiaries, despite the public's generosity. However, in others too much money is raised and those affected may end up being accused of profiteering from their tragedy. This can happen when the horror of a disaster attracts widespread media coverage and a generous public response, but the need for financial assistance is not great, as only a small number of breadwinners have been lost or those killed were children.

34.2 The Attorney-General has drawn up guidelines, which are issued in the Charity Commission's series of leaflets (CC40 'Disaster Appeals: Attorney-General's Guidelines'), to remove doubts about the precise status of such appeals, to reassure the public that their money will go to the purpose they intended and to ensure that appeals are set up in the most appropriate manner, taking advantage of any tax concessions that might be applicable. These guidelines are merely advisory in Scotland.

34.3 Whenever there is a disaster in England or Wales the Charity Commission will respond with urgency to requests for advice and if a charitable appeal is to be launched they will speed up the normal registration procedures. The Red Cross also operates a disaster appeal scheme with a 24-hour helpline (0800 777100) to assist with the setting up of disaster appeals.

Charitable or non-charitable appeal

34.4 One of the first decisions that has to be made is whether the appeal should be charitable or not. The main advantage of such an appeal being charitable is that donations can attract tax relief, which acts as an incentive to donors and makes the value of donations to the appeal greater. The main disadvantages are that:

- individual beneficiaries cannot be named;
- the amount that can be given to any one affected individual is limited to that appropriate to their needs, with the surplus going to other appropriate charitable purposes; and
- charitable trusts in England and Wales are subject to the regulatory requirements of the Charity Commission.

34.5 A non-charitable trust has the following advantages:

- the money raised can be for a named individual or individuals;
- no limit is imposed on the amount that can be given to any one affected individual, unless one has been imposed by the terms of the appeal;
- the court acting on behalf of the beneficiaries has ultimate control over the trust.

However, a non-charitable trust has the disadvantage of not attracting any tax reliefs or concessions.

Wording

34.6 If the appeal is to be charitable it must be worded in a way that does not jeopardise an application for charitable status. Even if the appeal is to be non-charitable, care must be taken with the terms so that the public is clear about who will benefit whether or not all the money raised will go to the beneficiaries and, if not, what will happen to any surplus.

34.7 Where an appeal is for a specific purpose and more money is raised than is needed for that purpose the surplus will belong to the donors. The organisers would then be left with the expensive and arguably pointless exercise of trying to return it to them. For this reason organisers are advised to state what will happen to the surplus if the appeal is over-subscribed or at least state that any surplus will be applied for charitable purposes at the trustees' discretion.

34.8 If a gift is sent before the publication of an appeal the trust will have to write to the donor asking for their permission to add the gift to the appeal fund. Where too many gifts are received to make this practicable, the published appeal should state that all donations already received will be added to the appeal fund unless the donors notify the organisers within, say, ten days, or by a specific date, that this is not their wish.

35 Dissolution

35.1 There are a number of reasons for a charity ceasing to exist including:

- the achievement of its charitable objects;
- insolvency;
- inability to raise supporters;
- inability to raise funds;
- objects are out of date; and
- service provided is no longer required.

Disposal of remaining assets

35.2 Most charities have a clause in their governing document enabling them to be wound up and stating what should be done with any remaining assets once all the charity's financial obligations have been met. Commonly such clauses state that the surplus should be given to a charity with similar charitable objects, but sometimes a specific charity is named or the trustees are given complete discretion to exercise in this event.

Process of closing down

35.3 The process of dissolution, the ending or closing down of an organisation, will depend on whether it is solvent or insolvent and its legal status i.e. whether it is incorporated or unincorporated.

Insolvent charities

35.4 Incorporated organisations that are insolvent will go into insolvent liquidation, a process governed by the *Insolvency Act 1986* in which any remaining assets are disposed of and outstanding liabilities are met insofar as they can be. If an unincorporated organisation becomes insolvent it does not have to go through the formal process of liquidation, as the trustees will be personally liable to meet any financial obligations still outstanding when all the charity's assets have been realised and used to pay outstanding debts. The trustees of unincorporated charities should take all possible steps to reduce their liabilities, such as giving precautionary notice of redundancy to staff, once they suspect that the charity may become insolvent.

Solvent charities

35.5 If a solvent incorporated organisation wishes to wind up it will normally go through a formal liquidation which is also governed by the *Insolvency Act 1986*. Solvent Industrial and Provident Societies may be wound up by an instrument of dissolution signed by at least three-quarters of its members. Solvent unincorporated organisations wind up in accordance with procedures set out in their governing document. If they have permanent endowment unincorporated charities cannot generally be wound up. The Charity Commission will usually direct the charity to amalgamate with another charity with the same or similar objects.

35.6 If the governing document of an unincorporated charitable association or a charitable trust does not contain a winding up clause the charity can use all its assets for charitable purposes or give them to another charity or charities to use for purposes within the donor charity's objects. Whatever the governing document says, assets in restricted funds can only be used to discharge liabilities relating to those funds; they cannot be used to pay off general creditors.

Very small charities

35.7 *Section 75* of the *Charities Act 1993* does, however, enable very small registered charities i.e. those with income in the last financial year of less than £1,000 to spend their endowment and wind themselves up if their endowment does not include land and the trustees believe the income from the assets is too small to achieve any useful purpose and transferring the assets to another charity is not practical. The decision to spend permanent endowment must be ratified by at least two-thirds of the governing body, publicised and the Charity Commission notified. Small Scottish charities can wind themselves up in a similar manner under *Public Trusts (Reorganisation) (Scotland) (No 2) Regulations 1993 (SI 1993 No 2254).*

Small charities

35.8 *Section 74* of the *Charities Act 1993* enables the trustees of small registered charities to transfer their assets to one or more charities with similar objects by passing a resolution by a two-thirds majority provided that:

- the charity's income from all sources was less than £5,000 in the last financial year;
- the charity does not hold land on trusts which stipulate that the land can be used only for the purposes of the charity; and
- the trustees of the recipient charity or charities have indicated that they are willing to accept the assets.

Again, in Scotland, *Public Trusts (Reorganisation) (Scotland) (No 2) Regulations 1993 (SI 1993 No 2254)* applies.

Removal from register

35.9 Charitable companies and industrial and provident societies come into existence when they are entered on the register of companies or friendly societies and similarly cease to exist when they are removed from the relevant register. If unincorporated charitable trusts and associations use the powers in their governing documents to dissolve themselves they must inform the Charity Commission if they are registered in England and Wales. [*Charities Act 1993 s 3(7)(b)*]. The Commission will want copies of the final accounts and a certified copy of the resolution to dissolve.

35.10 If a charity's assets include payments under deeds of covenant or GAYE these will need to be formally assigned to another charity and the donors and Inland Revenue notified.

36 Dividends

36.1 Charities may receive dividends from the investment of their funds or from a subsidiary, which may have been set up to carry out a trading activity. Dividends from UK companies are received with a tax credit attached. This tax credit can be set against the liability of the recipient to UK tax on the dividend or, if the recipient is not liable to UK tax, the tax credit may be reclaimed. The gross amount on which tax, if any, is to be paid is the aggregate of the dividend and the tax credit.

36.2 Charities are exempt from UK income tax or corporation tax where the dividend income in question forms part of the income of the charity or by Act of Parliament, Charter Decree, Deed of Trust or Will is applicable for charitable purposes only. The amount is only exempt, however, in so far as it is applied for charitable purposes only. Dividends received by charities from foreign companies are also exempt from income tax and corporation tax, provided that the same conditions apply. In the case of foreign dividends there will usually be an amount of foreign tax paid according to the tax legislation of the country concerned and the provisions of a Double Tax Treaty with the UK. Charities cannot reclaim any foreign tax properly suffered in these circumstances.

36.3 Charities cannot reclaim the UK tax credit on dividends received following changes which took effect from 6 April 1999. Recognising the special position of charities there is a compensation scheme to cushion the impact of the changes. This compensation takes the form of a payment to a charity of a percentage of the dividends it receives on a sliding scale over five years from 6 April 1999, as shown in Table 8.

Table 8 Compensatory payments

Year	%
2000/2001	17
2001/2002	13
2002/2003	8
2003/2004	4

37 Donations

Introduction

37.1 Donations are an important source of many charities' income, along with legacies, grants, fees, and income from investments and trading activities. They present a range of administrative and management issues. For example, estimating donated income is difficult because it is usually the most volatile source of income and more sophisticated budgeting techniques are required to avoid expenditure plans being hit by a shortfall in donated income. The rules for Gift Aid (see Chapter 110) must be understood and applied, as must the rules for annualising reciprocal benefits, and the regulations controlling fund-raising activities such as street collections (see Chapter 50) and sponsorship (see Chapter 108). Some donations will give rise to trust obligations and these must be recognised and complied with. Charities need to have good internal control systems to ensure that all incoming income, particularly cash, is recorded (see Chapter 68).

37.2 Donations are gifts which may have conditions attached to their use (requiring them to be classified as restricted income) but not conditions that create a contractual obligation between the donor and the recipient. The distinction is important when considering their tax treatment, their presentation in the accounts, and in identifying whether or not there is any liability for repayment on non-performance. Donations therefore exclude amounts received under 'service agreements' where those agreements amount to contracts, but include restricted fund income. 'Sponsorship' may be a donation or it may be a contractual trading agreement. The determining factor will be reciprocity, that is what the sponsor will receive in return for their sponsorship payment.

Cash donations

37.3 Cash donations are probably the most potentially volatile element of a charity's income stream, especially where the method of collection relies on major events such as flag days which can be affected by factors beyond anyone's control. This volatility should be factored into the planning process and the control system by rigorous interrogation of the premises for predicting this level of income, a budget where the basis for the predicted income figure is clearly understood, and explanations of the final receipts analysed against other known data and comparatives.

37.4 All income received should be subject to a system of internal control. Donations are particularly vulnerable to the risk of theft or diversion since they are one-sided transactions: the donation comes in, and nothing comparable to a purchase order or invoice comes into or out of the charity to identify the event. As trustees are responsible for establishing controls, they should therefore pay close attention to donated income. The SORP has drawn attention to the need for charities to account for all resources accruing to the charity, either on the face of the accounts or within the annual report. Whilst cash donations are easily fitted into the internal financial control systems, charities should also consider the implications of other types of donations.

Donated assets

37.5 Traditionally donations are assumed to equate to cash, but in fact charities receive a wide variety of gifted income: assets (gifts in kind), facilities, services, publicity and time. As trustees must always act in the best interests of the charity they should normally accept all donations offered. However, there may be exceptional circumstances when the trustees feel that accepting a donation would be inappropriate, for instance if the source of the donation is an organisation whose aims are directly opposed to the charity's, or where there is a suspicion that the funds are the product of an illegal activity, e.g. money laundering, or where the costs of converting a donated property would exceed the cost of leasing or building a new development.

37.6 Accounting for donated assets will depend on their nature:

- a functional asset, e.g. a minibus to be used by the charity;
- an investment asset, e.g. a valuable picture to be retained for sale in the future;
- goods for resale, e.g. bric-à-brac to a charity shop;
- goods for distribution, e.g. damaged stock for beneficiaries.

37.7 Assets given for retention by a charity should be shown as income in the period in which they are receivable and taken to the balance sheet. Whatever systems of internal control charities operate should also be applied as far as possible to gifts. In particular, correspondence files should be maintained and any policy on acknowledging gifts adhered to.

37.8 The value attributed to the asset should be the gross value to the charity, not the donor's valuation. Sometimes these values may differ widely. If the item is likely to show up in the accounts or the annual report at an embarassingly different amount, then appropriate diplomatic wording may be required.

37.9 Goods for resale and for distribution are also valued at the value to the charity, but they are only recognised as income when they are disposed of, either by sale or by distribution. The effect of this, in respect of goods for sale, is that only the sale proceeds are shown in the accounts. There will be no stock adjustment. The trustees should not forget that the underlying assets still exist even if a figure representing them does not appear in the accounts. The trustees are still responsible for protecting the assets and insuring them pending disposal.

Intangibles

37.10 The SORP requires intangible assets (e.g. donated facilities, beneficial loans, donated services, some volunteer time) to be valued in the accounts if the charity would have otherwise had to purchase them and the benefit is quantifiable and material. The value to be included should be the cost to the donor. The logic of this disclosure requirement is that the charity reflects the total resource made available to it, and can account for its stewardship of those resources. However, there are problems connected with this accounting and issues for organisations to consider as a result of the new presentation.

37.11 Donated facilities are only recognised when they are used, and so whenever an item of income is recorded, an equal and matching item of expenditure will be required. This therefore has no net effect on any surplus or deficit for the year, and consequently the recording of intangibles tends to be the sort of adjustment which is processed at the year end, when the audited accounts are being prepared. Sometimes this is the only practicable approach, especially in the case of occasional donations, but where the donated facility is fundamental to the operation of the charity, then the income and expenditure should form part of the budgeting process and the regular management accounting. There are two reasons for this. First, by building the income and expenditure into the budgets, the trustees and staff are fully aware of the total costs of running the operation, and can assess the importance of the intangible income stream. Second, the fewer the changes between the management accounts and the annual accounts, the more confidence the trustees and senior executive staff can have in the financial reporting.

37.12 Trustees should consider the significance of intangible income and ensure that the financial reporting is in line with its significance to the organisation. Often, in larger charities, this income stream is not material and is therefore not reported in the accounts. There is, however, a danger of this policy being self-fulfilling: they are not reported because they are small, and they must be small, because otherwise they would have been reported in the past. Although it is difficult to quantify such intangibles, especially in branch operations, it is not impossible.

38 Educational Charities

Definition of charitable purposes

38.1 The MacNaghten classification includes the advancement of education in its four heads of charity (see Chapter 15). The definition is wider than the provision of academic education and has been applied to a surprisingly wide variety of objects. These have included:

- the provision of holiday camps for Boy Scouts (*Re Alexander [1932] The Times 30 June*);
- to 'encourage, exercise and maintain standards of crafts both ancient and modern' (*CIR v White and Others (re Clerkenwell Association of Craftsmen) [1980] Ch D 55 TC 651*);
- the advancement of the knowledge of dowsing (Charity Commissioners' Annual Report 1966 Appendix A, p 31, The British Society of Dowsers);
- diffusion of knowledge of Egyptology (*Re British School of Egyptian Archaeology, Murray v Public Trustee [1954] 1 WLR 546*).

38.2 It is difficult to be precise as to where the line is drawn between the advancement of education and a non-charitable purpose. Examples of failed educational charitable purposes have included the Margaret Thatcher Foundation (too political), specific training for members of a profession (too much private advantage), and a library of pornography (anti-social). It is clear that the definition of education is wide, and this was emphasised by Lord Hailsham in 1980 when he drew attention to the need for the definition to take account of social developments, which may lead to new areas of education being charitable in line with social values.

Organisations involved in education

38.3 If the range of activities which are classified as charitable is wide, then so are the variety of organisations involved in education, and their charitable status. Excluding the purely state sector, the following are some of the more significant categories or organisations which may be charitable and in some way, advance or provide education:

- universities: mainly exempt charities under the *Charities Act 1993, 2 Sch*;
- other higher education institutes (HEIs) and further education institutes (FEIs) which may or may not be charitable;
- voluntary schools: may be charitable, often depending on governing body composition;
- independent schools: often established as registered charities or linked to a charitable foundation;
- student unions: can be registered charities in their own right, but usually operate within the framework of the university;
- learned societies: registered charities, often established under royal charter;
- pre-school playgroups: may be independent registered charities, or members of the Pre-school Learning Alliance, the umbrella body for England (there are sister organisations in Wales and Scotland);

- Training and Enterprise Councils (TECs) (Local Enterprise Companies in Scotland): Oldham TEC applied for charitable status but its application was rejected (*IRC v Oldham Training and Enterprise Council [1996] STC 1218*);
- voluntary organisations with educational objects which target specific beneficiary groups, e.g. Workers Educational Association, NACRO.

38.4 Educational charities derive income from many sources. Many charge fees for provision of services which may be funded through private or state sources. Higher and Further Education provision is funded at arm's length by Central Government through their respective funding councils or National Assemblies. Many voluntary organisations receive government funding indirectly through sub-contracting to provide specific education 'content' to TECs or fully accredited HEIs and FEIs.

38.5 Charities involved in education may do so by the direct provision of educational services (as do many independent schools) or by the promoting of education either by grants and scholarships, or in a less direct way. Educational charities apply their funds in three main ways:

- providing for the education of individuals;
- giving special benefits for schools and other educational establishments;
- making grants to other educational charities.

38.6 Educational charities should not use their funds to subsidise mandatory provision.

Accounting for educational activities

38.7 There are various accounting requirements which apply to the variety of educational charities already discussed. In general, registered educational charities will comply with the Charities SORP. Other educational charities will have their own accounting requirements stipulated by a government department or will have a separate SORP.

38.8 Universities have their own SORP, Accounting in Higher Education Institutions, 1994, issued by the Committee of Vice-Chancellors and Principals (currently due for revision). A draft revised SORP incorporating the requirements for both HEIs and FEIs has been issued and a final version is expected by the end of 2000.

38.9 Separate guidance has also been produced for independent schools, in conjunction with the Charity Commission and ISIS (The Independent Schools Information Service) (SCIS in Scotland). The guidance follows the Charities SORP, but presents the accounts in a way more attractive to this sector by, for instance, suggesting that unrestricted funds can be analysed on the face of the SOFA between core/school activities and other activities.

38.10 In most respects accounting for schools is similar to accounting for other charities. Schools will often have a number of immaterial restricted funds formed for funding scholarships or prizes, and may also have substantial functional fixed assets in property. Guidance from the Charity Finance Directors' Group in conjunction with NCVO on the presentation of this element of the accounts suggests that it may be useful to categorise these assets in a 'capital reserve' to distinguish them from reserves that are more accurately described as 'free'. Neither SCVO or the Scottish Charity Finance Directors' Group have issued guidance for Scottish charities.

38.11 Educational Charities

Educational costs

38.11 Many charities not directly involved in education may still incur educational costs. Charities involved in campaigning about health care, for instance, may spend money on educating the public about a particular issue. Sometimes activities may be dual purpose. Advertisements promoting the needs of the homeless, for instance, may be promoting both a campaign for change in government policy with regard to the homeless and the financial needs of a charity for the homeless.

38.12 The presentation of such costs in the statutory accounts needs careful consideration. The suggested headings within which to categorise expenditure on the SOFA include 'Publicity and Fund raising' (or 'cost of generating funds' as it is described in the new SORP). Costs included here should relate only to fund-raising related activities: where the publicity relates to campaigns to change opinions or policies etc., it should be presented as part of charitable expenditure. Sometimes a split of the cost may be appropriate.

Education and tax

38.13 The supply of educational services for a fee will not be taxable if the income falls within the main exemptions for direct tax. Although a school's fee income derives from trading, it is primary purpose trading and hence the income from it is not taxable. Schools and colleges in particular need to beware of other income generating activities which fall outside their primary purposes, but which seem to fit naturally alongside the school's other operations. Second-hand uniform shops, second-hand book shops and conference facilities are common examples of fund-raising which should be handled through a separate trading subsidiary. An alternative structure is for all trading, including the provision of education, to be structured through a non-charitable trading company owned and managed by a charitable foundation.

38.14 Educational services are exempt for VAT purposes if provided by eligible bodies. These are schools and universities, but will also include registered charities if surpluses arising from educational activities are reapplied to the further provision of education (see 117.8).

38.15 Trading businesses who give used plant or machines, such as second-hand computers, or their own trading stock to schools and colleges do not have to bring market value into account when calculating their profits for tax purposes and therefore do not get taxed on the value of their gift.

39 Employment

39.1 An employee is an individual who has entered into a contract of service. [*Employment Protection (Consolidation) Act 1978 s 153*]. All employees have a contract once an offer has been made and accepted. The contract does not have to be in writing to be legally binding — it can be an oral agreement. However, under the *Employment Rights Act 1996* virtually all new employees must be given a written statement of employment particulars describing the major terms of their employment, such as:

- names of employer and employee;
- job title;
- date employment began;
- rate of pay;
- pay period;
- hours of work;
- holiday entitlement and pay;
- sick pay arrangements;
- pension arrangements;
- amount of notice required of employee and employer; and
- arrangements for grievance, appeals, disciplinary rules (where there are 20 or more employees) and information on how disciplinary matters are dealt with.

Although not a legal requirement, many charities also include the following in a contract of employment:

- maternity and paternity leave;
- dependency and compassionate leave;
- time off for public duties;
- allowable expenses; and
- redundancy notice and pay.

39.2 Where an employer/employee relationship exists both the employer and the employees have duties to each other, some of which are implied by the nature of the contract, some imposed by statute and some that may be written into an agreement. In this respect, charities are no different from any other employer. A charity may, however, have volunteers and a higher than average number of casual workers and persons providing some form of consultancy service. In these cases, an employer/employee relationship does not always exist. It is important, however, for a charity to know whether it is legally an individual's employer or if the individual is self-employed, a contractor, a secondee or a volunteer so that it can ensure that it is fulfilling all its obligations.

Obligations of employment

39.3 An employer has a duty to provide work when available, to pay the employee and to provide an itemised pay statement, to reimburse certain expenses, to provide a safe working environment as required by *Health and Safety at Work Act 1994*, not to order the employee to do anything dangerous or illegal, and to behave in a reasonable and fair manner. In return, the employee has a duty to behave loyally, reasonably and honestly, to provide services personally, to carry out reasonable instructions and generally co-operate to carry out the work in a competent manner, to adapt to new ways of work, if necessary after training, to pass to the employer copyright for work done in the course of employment, to volunteer relevant information that comes into the employee's possession and to treat confidential information accordingly.

39.4 Additionally, an employee has statutory rights not to be discriminated against on the grounds of race, gender, disability or marital status unless there is a lawful reason, not to be unfairly dismissed, to receive a minimum period of notice, to belong, or to not belong, to a trade union, to take reasonable time off for public duties (with or without pay), to receive statutory sick pay, and, where appropriate, maternity pay and maternity leave and parental leave. Some of these rights, however, may only apply after a minimum period of employment has been completed.

39.5 There is also a legal requirement for an employer to operate PAYE for the deduction of tax and national insurance contributions from an employee's pay and to provide the employee and the Inland Revenue with certain end of year tax information.

Volunteers

39.6 Volunteers will not normally be regarded as employees for the purposes of employment law provided that they receive no payment other than reimbursement of genuine out-of-pocket expenses. If they receive more than this, however, they may be treated as employees both for the purposes of employment rights and for tax and national insurance purposes. The Inland Revenue accept that unpaid volunteers may be reimbursed certain expenses free of tax. These are:

- travel expenses, including travel from home to the usual place of work;
- the cost of specialist clothing;
- the cost of meals taken where the voluntary work occupies more than four hours a day or because it has to be carried out at mealtimes; and
- the actual cost of childcare incurred for the person to be available to do the voluntary work.

39.7 Where volunteers use their own cars for travelling, the expenses reimbursed must not be greater than the Inland Revenue agreed mileage rates. Any expenses reimbursed in excess of the above are taxable and the Inland Revenue may consider that they constitute pay and should be subject to tax under PAYE. Where a charity has a large number of volunteers they may be able to agree with the Inland Revenue a flat rate expense allowance, provided that they can show that there is unlikely to be any profit element as far as the volunteer is concerned. However, in a 1997 employment tribunal the payment of a fixed rate of expenses was deemed to be employment. Charities should keep careful records of all expenses reimbursed to volunteers, who should provide evidence of the cost incurred in support of their claim. If the charity does not have such records, the Inland Revenue may, in the absence of evidence to the contrary, consider these amounts to be pay.

39.8 Other forms of payment to volunteers, such as honoraria, may result in the 'volunteer' being regarded as an employee for tax and national insurance purposes.

39.9 Paid volunteers may only be reimbursed expenses tax free if the expenditure was necessarily incurred in carrying out the work. This usually limits expenses to the cost of travelling while actually carrying out the work and any expenditure incurred, for example, for materials etc., while doing so. Reimbursement of the cost of travel from home to the normal place of work and meals taken while at work will be taxable. These costs are not related to the job itself but to the circumstances of the employee.

Employment status

39.10 Employment status can be much more difficult to establish in the case of casual, part-time or temporary workers and those on a fixed term contract. This is an area which is always considered by the Inland Revenue when carrying out a PAYE compliance audit and which frequently results in additional sums having to be paid to the Inland Revenue, going back for a number of years, for failing to deduct tax under PAYE.

Deciding factors

39.11 A person's employment status depends upon the contract or arrangement with the charity. It does not necessarily depend upon the hours worked, the frequency of the work or whether the person may be self-employed in respect of other work carried out, although these factors must be considered.

39.12 The following are the six main relevant factors, which have been laid down by the courts, to be used in determining whether a person is employed or self-employed but the emphasis to be placed upon any of these factors will depend on the circumstances and it is a question of weighing up all the relevant facts of the case.

- The degree of control exercised by the employer over the employee in terms of responsibility for the work, working hours and how and where the work is carried out. A person in a senior position or carrying out specialist work may be an employee, but will not have a great deal of supervision. He may have authority over other employees, which a self-employed person probably would not. An employee would also be expected to conform with the normal working hours and practices of the employer, whereas a self-employed person carrying out services for an organisation would generally have more freedom provided the necessary tasks were satisfactorily completed.

- A person is more likely to be an employee if the work they are carrying out is being done by other employees, as opposed to being a specialist service which that particular person has been brought in to provide. Casual and temporary employees often fall into this category as they are brought in during busy periods or for seasonal events and work alongside other employees doing the same tasks.

- An employee is not normally expected to have his or her own equipment or to use it in the employment, except in certain trades where it is normal practice for a person to have their own tools. It would be unusual for a self-employed person to require the charity to provide an office, computer and telephone when the work could be carried out just as easily at the person's own office or home. In some cases, however, the work carried out is such that it would not be normal to provide your own equipment whether you were an employee or self-employed. This was the main argument put by the Inland Revenue against a video engineer who worked on equipment provided by the TV or film company for whom he was working. The courts held that he was self-employed because he was not in the business of providing his own equipment. The equipment used was not of that nature.

39.13 Employment

- With a contract of service there is a mutual obligation by the employer to provide work and by the employee to carry it out. A person who is self-employed is under no such obligation to take on work offered until they have contracted to do so and then the contract would normally only be for a specific task or tasks. An employee can normally be asked to carry out a number of tasks during normal working hours and within a general job description.
- Whether the parties treat their relationship as employer/employee, with all the duties this implies, including being personally involved in providing a service to the employer. A self-employed person will not necessarily be expected to undertake the work himself/herself but may sub-contract it or use one of his or her own employees. On the other hand, a person may not have any employees or anyone to whom they can sub-contract the work and it may require their specialist skills or knowledge but the terms of contract can still be that of a self-employed person.
- Whether the person carrying out the work can really be said to be in business on their own account. This is increasingly becoming the most important test. Persons who are self-employed will normally be responsible for their own work and liable for anything that goes wrong as a result. They will also be expected to correct any errors or make good any deficiencies in their own time and at their own expense. Employers are generally liable for the actions of their employees. A self-employed person is more likely to charge a fee for the services carried out. While this may be charged at an hourly rate, they will not normally be paid for turning up at work. When entering into contracts for the services of a self-employed person, the Inland Revenue will look to see how that person is remunerated. A charity will have a stronger argument that the person is self-employed if they pay a fee for a job, however it may be calculated, rather than paying the person an hourly rate for a number of hours worked, since this is generally a sign of casual employment. A person carrying on business on their own account will also normally have other clients and will fit their work in to suit their clients' needs and not work exclusively for one client at a time, as in the case of an employee. It is not, however, sufficient for a person to be taxed as self-employed with regard to other work carried out and charities should not be misled into believing that because a person is treated by the Inland Revenue as self-employed in one respect, they will not be treated as an employee in another. For example, doctors with their own practice will normally be self-employed but may well also have contracts with hospitals as employed consultants.

Agreeing status with tax authorities

39.13 Each Inland Revenue tax district has at least one inspector who will deal with enquiries about the status of employees. If they are provided with all the relevant facts they will make a decision as to whether a person is employed or self-employed on behalf of an employer and, based on the facts given, this will be binding on both the Inland Revenue and the Contributions Agency for the purposes of national insurance. The Contributions Agency will also deal with these enquiries. Where a charity is in doubt as to status, it should contact its PAYE tax district or the local Contributions Agency office. In making such an enquiry it is important that the charity considers all the relevant factors and bases its argument thereon. It is also much more helpful if there is a written contract or letter of engagement between the parties setting out all the terms of the agreement including those matters referred to above. It is the employer's duty to ensure that PAYE is operated, where necessary, but it is up to individuals to agree their final tax liabilities with the Inland Revenue. The PAYE system does not necessarily collect the correct amount of tax due and if individuals feel they have been incorrectly treated as employees they can themselves take the matter up with the Inland Revenue and appeal to the Commissioners. It must be said, however, that if an employer operates PAYE the Inland Revenue consider that this is evidence that the employer considered a contract of employment existed. On the other hand, the fact that a contract states that it is not to be a contract of employment and that the individual is responsible for their own tax liability cannot alter the real nature of the contract if the terms are such that it is a contract of service rather than a contract for services.

Office holders

39.14 In addition to employees, there are office holders, whose rights and duties are determined by the position they hold, as opposed to a contract of employment. Typically, the office holders for a charity will be the company directors, honorary officers and the company secretary. If these persons are paid for their duties then, for tax purposes, they are treated in the same way as employees.

Agency staff

39.15 Temporary staff employed through an agency are treated as employees of the agency as long as the employer pays the agency for their services. The agency is therefore required to operate PAYE and not the organisation which is using the temporary staff.

Equal opportunities in employment

39.16 The *Sex Discrimination Act 1975*, the *Race Relations Act 1976* and the *Disability Discrimination Act 1995* prohibit various forms of discrimination and the *Equal Pay Act 1970* ensures that men and women's pay and conditions are the same for like work. Many charities have equal opportunities policies that go beyond the legislation, prohibiting forms of discrimination that are not unlawful, and doing more than is required of them in an attempt to treat fairly all potential employees, service users, members, etc.

Religion

39.17 Discrimination on the grounds of religion is unlawful in Northern Ireland but not in the rest of the UK. However, some religious groups, e.g. Sikhs and Jews, come within the definition of 'ethnic group' for the purposes of the *Race Relations Act 1976*, so discrimination against them would be unlawful. Roman Catholics and Muslims do not come within the definition of an ethnic group.

Age

39.18 Using age as the basis for selecting employees for redundancy is unlawful. [*Employment Protection (Consolidation) Act 1978*].

People with criminal records

39.19 The *Rehabilitation of Offenders Act 1974* gives ex-offenders the right to withhold information about 'spent' convictions and makes it unlawful for an employer to dismiss an employee or refuse to employ someone because they have a spent conviction. There are exceptions in the case of those working with children or vulnerable people.

39.20 Employment

Transfer of Undertakings Regulations (TUPE)

39.20 Many charities have recently been taking on work previously done by a local authority or are considering merging with another charity. Where this is the case, or in any other situation where a charity takes on workers previously employed by another employer, they will be affected by the *Transfer of Undertakings (Protection of Employment) Regulations 1981 (TUPE)*. The main implications are that the charity will have to provide their new employees with their existing terms and conditions, with the exception of their occupational pension scheme. The charity is not obliged to give their new employees rights to a comparable occupational pension scheme.

39.21 Before agreeing to such a transfer, a charity should therefore ask for a list of the current employees and their terms and conditions of employment, together with details of self-employed persons, casual workers, contractors and consultants who might claim they were employees. They should also obtain details of any policies or schemes such as holiday pay schemes or permanent health insurance or profit-sharing or bonus schemes. The charity should also ask for information about any current or pending employment disputes.

39.22 *TUPE* also imposes an obligation on a charity to consult with employee representatives about employees likely to be affected by a transfer. This applies not just to employees who are being transferred, but to the charity's existing employees who will be affected by the arrival of new colleagues.

39.23 *TUPE* is a complex and changing area of legislation. Charity administrators who believe they may be affected should seek professional advice.

Minimum wage

39.24 On 1 October 2000 the national minimum wage for workers increased to £3.70 per hour. For workers aged 18 to 21 the national minimum wage increased to £3.20 per hour from June 2000. At the time of writing there is no national minimum wage for workers aged under 18.

39.25 The national minimum wage applies to virtually all workers, including seasonals, part-timers, casuals, etc. It does not apply to people running their own business on a self-employed basis or to volunteers who receive only reimbursement of genuine out-of-pocket expenses and no benefits other than the training necessary for them to carry out their volunteer work. It also does not apply to resident members of charitable religious communities (unless they run a school, further or higher education institute), volunteers who receive a payment towards subsistence and who are working for a charity, voluntary organisation, associated fund-raising body or statutory body and who have been placed with that body by a charity acting in pursuance of its charitable objects (for example volunteers in Emmaus Communities) and volunteers who receive accommodation or meals because it is necessary for them to carry out their work.

39.26 The national minimum wage does apply, however, to volunteers who receive payment above genuine reimbursement of expenses, lump sum expenses, or an honorarium, or training beyond what is needed for them to carry out their volunteer work, or other benefits such as free or discounted admission to fund-raising events, or shop discounts.

39.27 Employers must keep adequate records to show that the national minimum wage is being paid.

Working Time Regulations

39.28 The *Working Time Regulations 1998* make it unlawful for employers to require employees to work more than 48 hours per week, averaged over a 17 week period unless the employee agrees otherwise in writing, or unless the employee can determine their working hours themselves (e.g. senior managers), or workers choose to work longer hours on a voluntary basis. The Regulations give virtually all workers, including part-timers, freelance workers, agency workers and casuals, the right to:

- four weeks paid annual leave after 13 weeks of continuous service;
- a 20 minute rest break if the working day is longer than six hours (workers between the school leaving age and 18 are entitled to 30 minutes if the working day is longer than 4.5 hours);
- a rest period of 11 consecutive hours every 24 hours (48 hours for workers between the school leaving age and 18);
- a weekly rest period of at least 24 hours;
- a maximum of eight hours work per 24 hours for night workers;
- health assessments for night workers.

Family friendly legislation

39.29 The *Maternity and Parental Leave etc Regulations 1999* introduced new statutory provisions relating to maternity and parental leave and to time off for dependants.

Maternity leave

39.30 From 30 April 2000 ordinary (previously known as basic') paid maternity leave was extended to 18 weeks. Additional (previously known as 'longer') maternity leave (11 weeks before the expected week of childbirth plus 28 weeks after the week of the birth) can be taken by women after a qualifying period of 12 months continuous employment. Most contractual rights continue during maternity leave, apart from the right to remuneration. After ordinary maternity leave a woman has the right to return to the same job on the same pay and conditions. After additional maternity leave a woman has the right to return to the same or another suitable job, unless the employer has fewer than six employees just before the woman's maternity leave ends and the employer does not have the same or another suitable job available.

Parental leave

39.31 Parents who have one year's service with an employer are entitled to 13 weeks unpaid parental leave for each child born or adopted after 15 December 1999. This is in addition to statutory maternity leave. The leave must be taken before the child's 5th birthday, or 18th birthday if the child is disabled, or within five years of the child's placement for adoption with the family.

39.32 The leave must be taken in blocks of no shorter than one week and no more than four weeks may be taken in any one year. The period can be extended by individual, workforce or collective agreements.

39.33 The employee is normally required to give the employer 21 days' notice of his/her intention to take parental leave. The employer may, on proper notice, delay the leave for up to six months if the business would be disrupted if parental leave were granted. The employer must, however, offer an alternative time when the leave can be taken.

Paternity leave

39.34 Fathers wanting to take time off at the time of a birth should give 21 days' notice of the expected week of childbirth and state how long they wish to take off. The father then has the right to take time off when the birth actually occurs and the employer has no right to postpone the leave.

Leave for dependent emergencies

39.35 All employees have the right to reasonable unpaid time off to deal with unexpected or sudden emergencies relating to dependants, including sons, daughters, spouses, parents or anyone else who lives with the employee as a member of their family, or even a distant relative or neighbour who is dependent on the employee. The right is intended to cover unexpected situations, so the worker could take a few days off to arrange care for a dependant who has suddenly become ill, but could not take a month off to care for the dependant.

Part-timers' rights

39.36 Part-time workers have enjoyed the same statutory rights (pro rata) as full-time workers doing comparable jobs for the same employer for some time. The *Part-time Workers (Prevention of Less Favourable Treatment) Regulations 2000* came into force on 1 July 2000, ensuring that part-time workers can now enjoy the same contractual rights as full-time workers, and must now be treated no less favourably than full-time workers. The Regulations encourage employers to adopt a flexible approach to allowing full-time workers to work part-time following a period of absence or a variation of their contract of employment if they wish to do so.

39.37 The Regulations apply to agency workers, homeworkers, casuals and freelance workers as well as employees but not to those who are genuinely self-employed. Part-time workers now have the right:

- to the same hourly rate of pay;
- to the same rate of overtime pay;
- not to be treated less favourably in relation to contractual sick pay, contractual maternity pay, contractual annual leave and other leave, access to occupational pensions and other benefits;
- not to be denied access to training because they are part-time;
- not to be treated less favourably in selection for redundancy.

Fixed term contracts

39.38 From 25 October 1999 workers on fixed contracts of at least one year are no longer able to waive the right to claim unfair dismissal if the contract is not renewed when it ends. Dismissal at the end of the contract must be for a fair reason, such as redundancy. Workers on fixed-term contracts of two years or more can still waive their right to claim redundancy pay. However, even when they have waived this right workers are still entitled to all other redundancy rights such as the right to be offered suitable alternative employment.

Trades union recognition

39.39 The sections of the *Employment Relations Act 1999* relating to the recognition of trades unions came into force on 6 June 2000. Unions can request recognition if an employer employs at least 21 workers, or an average of 21 workers in the previous 13 weeks. Requests must:

- be in writing;
- identify the Union(s) and the bargaining unit;
- state that the request is made under *Schedule A1* to the *Trade Union and Labour Relations (Consolidation) Act 1992*;
- be accompanied by a certificate that the Union is independent.

39.40 The employer has ten working days within which to agree a bargaining unit and that the Union is to be recognised, or inform the Union that the request has not been accepted, but indicate a willingness to negotiate, in which case an extension of at least 20 working days will be granted.

39.41 If an employer fails to respond, or rejects the application and is unwilling to negotiate, or if no agreement is reached within the extension period, the Union may apply to the Central Arbitration Committee (CAC) for a determination as to whether the proposed bargaining unit is appropriate and whether the Union has the support of a majority of the workers constituting the bargaining unit.

39.42 If, within ten working days of indicating a willingness to negotiate, the employer proposes that ACAS be requested to assist in the negotiations and the Union rejects the proposal, or fails to accept the proposal within ten working days, the Union will lose its right to refer the matter to the CAC.

39.43 Once the bargaining unit has been settled, the CAC will issue a declaration that the Union is recognised providing that:

- the employer accepts that the Union enjoys the support of a majority of the workforce;
- the CAC is satisfied that more than 50% of the bargaining unit are members of the Union seeking recognition;
- following a secret ballot, a majority of the bargaining unit who voted and 40% of those eligible to vote within the bargaining unit have supported recognition.

39.44 If the Union is unsuccessful the CAC will not entertain another application for three years. Equally derecognition cannot take place until after a period of three years.

39.45 Once a Union is recognised the employer and the Union must try to reach a procedural agreement for the conduct of collective bargaining, failing which the Union may apply to the CAC to have the default procedure implemented. The recognition procedure is legally binding and both the employer and the Union can apply to the Court if there is a breach. For breaches of non-binding agreements either party can apply to the CAC.

Qualifying period for unfair dismissal

39.46 The qualifying period for unfair dismissal was reduced from two years to one for all dismissals on or after 1 June 1999. For some dismissals, e.g. those relating to pregnancy, sex or racial discrimination, or unjustifiable disability discrimination there is no qualifying period.

39.47 Employment

Consultation on collective redundancies

39.47 The *Collective Redundancies and Transfer of Undertakings (Protection of Employment) (Amendment) Regulations 1999* came into force on 28 July 1999. The Regulations amend the *Trade Union and Labour Relations (Consolidation) Act 1992* and the *Transfer of Undertakings (Protection of Employment) Regulations 1981 (SI 1981 No 1794)* insofar as they relate to information and consultation. There is a statutory requirement to consult when 20 or more redundancies are proposed. The Regulations require that:

- where an employer recognises a union they must negotiate with that union;
- consultation in relation to redundancies must include all employers who might be affected, not just those who may be dismissed;
- employers must comply with requirements in relation to the election of employee representatives, including making suitable arrangements for the election to take place, ensuring that all affected employees may vote and that the voting is conducted in secret.

Right to be accompanied in disciplinary and grievance proceeding

39.48 From 4 September 2000 employees and other workers such as casuals, agency workers and freelancers have the right to be accompanied by a trade union official or fellow worker in formal disciplinary or grievance proceedings. The companion will be able to address the hearing, but will have no right to answer questions or speak on behalf of the worker. The right to be accompanied will apply where a disciplinary proceeding could lead to a formal warning or where a grievance relates to the employer's performance of a statutory, contractual or other duty towards the worker.

References

39.49 There is no obligation on an employer to provide a reference. Where references are provided:

- they must be factually accurate, but do not have to be comprehensive;
- they must not be misleading;
- they must be reasonable and fair to both the employee and the person to whom the reference is supplied;
- they must not breach the employer's implied duty of trust and confidence;
- any inaccuracies must not be due to negligence or maliciousness.

Whistle blowing

39.50 The *Public Interest Disclosure Act 1998* promotes accountability in the public, private and voluntary sectors, by offering employees who whistle blow on their employers' malpractice protection, in certain circumstances, against dismissal and discrimination. The type of disclosures that qualify are those relating to:

- Miscarriage of justice;
- A criminal offence;
- Risk to the health and safety of an individual;

- Risk of damage to the environment;
- Concealment of any of the above.

39.51 The Act permits disclosures where an employee has a reasonable belief that one of the events listed above has occurred, is occurring, or is likely to occur. Complaints are intended to be made to the employer in the first instance or to a prescribed person, such as the Commissioners of the Inland Revenue or the Director of General Water Services.

39.52 In certain circumstances an employee will be protected even if they make a complaint in the first instance to the media, the police or their MP. To be protected they would need to show that they had acted in good faith, believe that the complaint is substantially true and not act out of personal gain. They must also believe that they would suffer a detriment if they complained to their employer in the first instance, or that the evidence would be destroyed if they went to their employer, or that they have previously made substantially the same complaint before and it has not been acted upon.

40 Entertainment

40.1 Charities get involved in entertaining for a number of reasons, perhaps the most common being fund-raising when events such as concerts and firework displays are organised. However, they may entertain guests on a more private basis, such as to build relationships with potential donors, they may provide public entertainment as part of their primary purposes, and they may run events for social, or semi-social purposes. All these activities are affected differently by tax law, VAT, licensing arrangements and commercial considerations. In addition, many events will be put on with sponsorship from a commercial business which may thereby become a commercial participator under the *Charities Act 1992 s 58*.

Primary purpose activities

40.2 Some organisations undertake to provide entertainment as part of their primary purpose; for example a theatre may run a dramatic production, an orchestra perform a concert, a museum run an exhibition or a special needs group put on a display, etc. Where such events are primary purpose trading there will be no direct tax implication. Furthermore, the exemption from tax for primary purpose trades extends to ancillary activities, so a charity can sell food and drink to visitors attending a play or concert or visiting an art exhibition.

40.3 Where sponsorship is intended to fund a trading activity of the charity, then the sponsorship payments will normally be regarded as part of the income of that trade. Where a charitable theatre receives business sponsorship towards the cost of a production, then that sponsorship income will be regarded as trading income, but it will not be taxable if it is treated as exempt along with the income arising from the trade.

Fund-raising activities

40.4 Where a charity puts on an entertainment event in order to raise funds then it needs to consider the following. Can the event be undertaken by the charity? Is it taxable? Is it subject to VAT? What other licences may be needed? Is it commercially justifiable?

Can the event be undertaken by the charity?

40.5 The constraints on whether the event can be undertaken by the charity or if it needs to be put through a non-charitable company are the governing document of the charity and the tax position. Most governing documents include a power such as 'to raise funds. . .provided that in raising funds the trustees shall not undertake any substantial permanent trading activity and shall comply with any relevant statutory regulations'. Where this, or a similar clause, is present then the charity should be able to set up a fund-raising event. However, the administrator should check with the governing document for any specific exclusions or terms of trust which may impinge on the planned event.

Is the event taxable?

40.6 The principles of trading and the approach of the Inland Revenue are set out in Chapter 112. However, it is common for charities to assume that events such as a sponsored premier, or a dinner dance, are simply not a taxable activity. Since many commercial operations provide similar entertainment on a profit-making basis, then this is clearly a misconception and any entertainment run as a fund-raising event should be seriously considered for operation through a trading subsidiary.

40.7 If the event is taxable, then profits will be calculated in the usual way. As with all trading events, overheads can be apportioned, and some goods and services provided at undervalue can be treated as a deduction at full commercial value. This method of calculating the profit should not be relied upon to eliminate all profits on an event where, for instance, celebrities have provided substantial, and therefore expensive, time free of charge. It is intended to apply to small notional costs only.

40.8 Where an entertainment, or indeed any other fund-raising event, is to be run by a charity, the amount of tax payable may be minimised by making a minimum charge and inviting those attending to make an additional voluntary contribution. The Inland Revenue have stated that such donations will not be taxable as long as all the following conditions are satisfied.

- It is clearly stated on all publicity material, including tickets, that anyone paying only the minimum charge will be admitted without further payment.
- The additional payment does not secure any particular benefit (for example, admission to a better seat in the auditorium).
- The extent of further contributions is ultimately left to ticket holders to decide (even if the organiser indicates a desired level of donation).
- For film or theatre performances, concerts, sporting fixtures and similar events the minimum charge is not less than the usual price for the particular seats at a normal commercial event of the same type.
- For dances, dinners and similar functions the sum of the basic minimum charges is not less than the total costs incurred in arranging the event.

Concessions for small scale fund-raising activities

40.9 Income from entertainment will not be regarded as taxable, even if the entertainment is not primary purpose, if it is covered by the concessions relating to small scale fund-raising activities. These activities include fetes, balls, bazaars, gala shows, performances or similar events that do not form part of a series of similar events. A charity can run up to 15 events of any of these types in a year without having to pay tax on the income generated and they will be exempt for VAT purposes. Furthermore a charity can run any number of small scale events (e.g. coffee mornings) if the income from such events is under £1,000 a week.

Is it subject to VAT?

40.10 Many events run as entertainment will constitute a business activity and are therefore subject to VAT. The admission to premises for a charge is always regarded as a business supply, and charities should not assume that because the event does no more than cover its cost, or is only a one-off event, they do not have to charge VAT.

40.11 Following the *Finance Act 2000*, events of the type described in 40.9 above will be accorded the same treatment for both VAT and direct tax, thus removing a long standing source of irritation for charity administrators who previously had to interpret and apply two sets of rules.

40.12 The location of an event can affect its eligibility for the exemption. The determining factor will again be the likelihood of it distorting competition. An event does not qualify for exemption if the event is likely to place a commercial enterprise at a disadvantage.

40.13 An event does not qualify for VAT exemption where accommodation is provided by the charity organising the event, unless the accommodation does not exceed two nights in total and does not fall within a special scheme known as the tour operators' margin scheme.

40.14 Where an event is organised on behalf of a charity by a club or a business as agent, then the income passed to the charity is covered by the exemption. As with the direct tax, it is open to an organisation to charge a minimum fee and invite those attending to make an additional donation. These donations will be outside the scope of VAT on the same criteria as those set out above in relation to direct tax.

40.15 In some cases admission charges by an eligible body will also be exempt, if they relate to a museum, gallery, art exhibition, zoo, or a theatrical, musical or choreographic performance of a cultural nature. An eligible body is non-profit making, essentially managed and administered on a voluntary basis, and applies any profits made by the events to the improvement or continuance of the relevant facilities.

40.16 If a charity concludes that the planned event does not fall within the exemption, then the supply of the service is liable to VAT at the standard rate, assuming that the registration threshold is breached. It may or may not be an advantage for the event to be exempt. If it is not exempt, on the one hand VAT will either have to be deducted from ticket prices, reducing the profit or ticket prices will have to be increased, which could affect the number sold. However, on the other hand, if it is not exempt it will be possible to recover VAT charged on costs incurred in running the event. Assuming the event operates at a profit then the exemption should be beneficial, but only a detailed individual analysis of the event will determine the full impact of its VAT status.

What other licences may be needed?

40.17 Charities today are taking on an ever broadening range of fund-raising activities, ranging from trout fishing to ballooning, from barn dances to beach barbecues, from challenge holidays to golf days. This book can only give an indication of the type of events that will require licences or that are subject to other regulations. Detailed advice should be taken before proceeding with any new type of event.

40.18 Stage plays may require licences under the *Theatres Act 1968*, film shows under the *Cinemas Act 1985*, and a licence is normally required for public dancing, music or other public entertainment. Licences may also be required for sporting events where spectators are invited, and for public music entertainments in the open air, even on private land. There are exemptions for lower key events such as garden fêtes and religious services, and fees are not always payable with other applications.

40.19 Where copyright music is to be played, another range of licences and consents will be required, and a broader range of activity than just public performance – for instance, a dancing club – would require such a licence. A Performing Right licence may cover a variety of situations where music is reproduced, but for live performances permission will need to be sought from the copyright owner. Separate licences are needed in respect of recorded material, and can be obtained from Phonographic Performance Limited or Video Performance Limited. If the event is to be recorded then a licence should be obtained from the Mechanical Copyright Protection Society.

40.20 The provision of alcohol is subject to strict regulation (see Chapter 5). Similarly, food provided at an event is also subject to regulations issued under the *Food Safety Act 1990*. These apply even to food prepared at home for sale at a charity event.

40.21 Where groups of people attend a public event they may represent a public meeting, an assembly, or a procession. These terms have legal connotations which require separate consideration, as each is governed by different legislation, including the *Public Meeting Act 1908*, *Representation of the People Act 1983*, *Public Order Act 1986*, the *Criminal Justice and Public Order Act 1994*, and even the *Control of Pollution Act 1974* in respect of the use of loudspeakers.

40.22 Finally, charities should ensure that in running any entertainment they comply with local bye laws. The detailed nature of these requirements suggests that charities should be obtaining professional legal advice before embarking on any event which may require external sanction.

Commercial justification

40.23 It is by no means uncommon for enthusiastic fund-raisers, or groups, to create grand entertainments on a lavish scale for fund-raising purposes. The events are always apparently exciting and dynamic, and promise substantial returns to the charity if all goes well. Very often the timing of such events is such that urgent decisions need to be made if the event is to go ahead, and opportunities not to be missed. In such situations the prudent trustee would do well to remind him or herself of the statutory complications and licensing requirements before allowing the organisation to commit itself to holding an event that has not been thoroughly planned.

40.24 A detailed financial plan should be prepared for any event which is likely to involve the commitment of the charity's resources. The detail should encompass itemised cash flows, on a frequency to match the event: possibly even daily in some cases. The income and expenditure should be properly timed, in order to identify any possibility of the charity being required to provide temporary finance, and the expenditure in particular should be estimated in meticulous detail to ensure that not only have all costs been taken into consideration, but all contingencies have been catered for, such as all insurances including cancellation insurance due to weather or other events, or costs for taxis home late at night.

40.25 The assumptions underlying these forecasts should be rigorously challenged. What is the basis for expecting the suggested numbers? Are any celebrities committed to attending? Are their fees already known? Has the site been 'walked' to assess the equipment needs? These and many other questions need to be asked.

40.26 Before committing to an event, the trustees should be content that the potential reward is sufficient to justify the investment of time and money and the risk to the charity's good name. There is no arithmetic answer to this question, but again there are certain key questions. Has some simple sensitivity analysis been done to indicate the effect of lower than expected numbers on expected income? What is the break-even point? On this basis, is the risk still worthwhile given the impact on the general resources of the charity? If the event fails completely, who can or will underwrite the financial loss, and what will be the effect on future voluntary income and support? Even if the event succeeds, is it of a quality and ethos which supports the overall mission of the charity?

40.27 Even where all these questions are satisfactorily answered, it is wise for the trustees to make a point of keeping in touch with the developments of major events and ensure that information provided to them is factual, and not wishful thinking on behalf of the event organiser. It can be very difficult for such a person to have to admit to impending failure, especially when there is still a hope for success, however slim. The ultimate decision to cancel should be in the hands of the trustees, not the event organiser.

Private entertaining

40.28 Trustees and executive staff sometimes incur expenditure in the provision of entertaining. Where the amounts or nature become either material or beyond what is strictly required in the best interests of the charity, then the expense may represent a taxable benefit on the individual, be a breach of trust, or could amount to a personal benefit to a trustee that requires repayment.

40.29 It is unlikely that individual sums involved would be material, but the accumulation of such amounts over a period of years can quickly amount to several thousand pounds, and even where this is still not significant to a charity, the profile of the organisation can be damaged by, for instance, imbalanced media coverage. Therefore, a charity should establish clear guidance as to what is an acceptable level of such expenditure, and the circumstances when such expenditure is justified, and then ensure that the guidelines are being followed.

40.30 Such entertaining expenditure is not an allowable deduction in the tax computations of a trading company. It will therefore create a difference between the profits in a trading subsidiary shown in the accounts, and the profits to be taxed, which will be higher. If a covenant payment is set up based on all the profits chargeable to tax, the effect will be to leave the company with a loss, making it insolvent if the share capital is only of minimal value. This situation is hard to correct without some tax becoming payable, and therefore, wherever possible, such entertainment costs should be limited to a bare minimum, and care taken as to whether they rightly sit in the company or the charity.

Semi-social entertaining

40.31 In some charities the members themselves meet in the furtherance of the charitable objectives, and in the course of these activities begin to operate more on a social level than a charitable one. For instance, local branch volunteers may use the same facilities to hold a training event and to hold a Christmas dinner. Alternatively, an institution or learned society may follow a meeting of its members with a dinner dance.

40.32 Apart from all the other considerations already set out above, this type of activity needs assessing to judge whether or not it ought to be carried out by the charity. The implications may be wide-ranging. Not only is there the potential for charitable property to be misapplied, but events which run at a loss, and claims arising from accidents and other damage may rest incorrectly with the charity.

40.33 Charities should establish what can and cannot be undertaken using charitable resources. For instance, the Christmas dinner should either be a mechanism for thanking and motivating volunteers, or it should be undertaken entirely separately from the charity's affairs. Where any benefit is provided to volunteers, the tax treatment will need separate consideration.

40.34 Although it is customary for some charity members to meet at dinner dance type events, charities can only jusitfy running dinner dances if they are organised as fund-raising events, which the members attend with a view to raising funds and not having a subsidised evening out. If there is any doubt, such events are better organised by a separate committee that subsequently transfers any 'profit' to the charity.

40.35 Entertaining staff and even trustees may also create tax liabilities for the individuals. For instance the provision of a sandwich lunch to trustees (directors) of a charitable company is, strictly speaking, an assessable benefit which should be declared on their P11Ds.

41 European Community Legislation and Funding

41.1 For most charities the European dimension is relevant to them for two reasons, the legal and tax background, and the availability of funds from central budgets. The largest single impact in the first category has probably been the introduction of VAT, a tax originally introduced in 1973 as both simple to understand and to operate. It is now estimated that charities lose approximately £450 million a year through irrecoverable VAT.

41.2 The range of activities of charities is also ever increasing, as many have been formed from previously public sector bodies, or act as service providers funded under contracts from central or local government. In these areas the importance of European developments or financing initiatives often assumes great significance.

Information on Europe

41.3 As the influence of European affairs intensifies, the European Commission has tried to make access to information on Europe easier. In the UK this policy is being carried out by a national network of local outlets including:

- European Public Information Centres (EPIC);
- European Documentation Centres (EDCs);
- European Information Centres (EICs);
- Rural Carrefours;
- European Resource Centres for Schools and Colleges;
- European Reference Centres;
- Innovation Relay Centres.

41.4 There are also a number of national independent organisations which can provide sector specific information. The voluntary sector will naturally turn to the National Council for Voluntary Organisations (or in Scotland to the Scottish Council for Voluntary Organisations, or in Wales to the Welsh Council for Voluntary Action), especially in respect of funding under Objective 3 of the European Social Fund. Other organisations include the AIRE Centre (Advice for Individuals Rights in Europe), who can advise on working abroad, pension transfers, human rights, asylum and immigration. The Trade Union Congress (TUC) has a European Information Service which services TUC staff and affiliated unions.

41.5 Further information can be obtained either from the European Commission Representation in the United Kingdom, 8 Storey's Gate, London, or from separate offices in Cardiff, Edinburgh or Belfast. Alternatively information in respect of a specific Member State can be obtained from that country's embassy.

Legal background

41.6 European law is effected in the UK in different ways. A regulation is a law immediately binding on each and every Member State. A decision is equally binding, but differs from a regulation in not applying to all States, but just to one specific State or element of that State, such as a company. Finally, directives are issued to instruct Member States to bring into force a European law within a certain timetable.

41.7 Certain proposals in the future development of European legislation involve charities, in particular the proposals for the harmonisation of VAT throughout Europe, and, in tandem with that development, the creation of a new legal entity for charities to adopt, the European Association (see Chapter 8). Neither of these developments is moving ahead rapidly. Harmonisation of VAT may result in the loss of zero rating reliefs in the UK, and other countries too have their own sectors to safeguard. The development of the European Association was started seriously in 1991 with the publication of a draft regulation, but the finalisation of this process still seems some way off. The Charity Commission tracks progress on this matter regularly in its annual report.

Funding

41.8 Revenue in the EC's general budget is made up of VAT, customs duties, agricultural levies, sugar and isoglucose levies and a proportion of Member States' GNP. These resources are distributed through funds and budget lines.

41.9 There are four main structural funds across the European Union established to:

- reduce unemployment;
- improve and develop the skills of employed people;
- invest in rural or industrial areas in decline;
- invest in areas with low economic development.

41.10 The four funds are:

- the European Social Fund (ESF);
- the European Regional Development Fund (ERDF);
- the European Agricultural Guidance and Guarantee Fund (EAGGF);
- the Financial Instrument for Fisheries Guidance (FIFG).

Charities tend to be involved mainly with the first two funds, the ESF and ERDF, described in more detail below.

41.11 In 1999, the EU completed the second reform of the Structural Funds, and the priority Objectives were redefined and reduced from the six established in 1993 to the following three for the 2000–2006 period:

Objective 1: Promoting the development and structural adjustment of regions whose development is lagging behind.

Objective 2: Supporting the economic and social conversion of areas facing structural difficulties.

Objective 3: Supporting the adaptation and modernisation of education, training and employment policies and systems.

41.12 The interaction between the EU and Great Britain is now on a regional basis — in 1999 nine new Regional Development Agencies came into formal existence in England. For further information on the activities of the EU in a region the local office should be contacted. The regions are:

South East
South West
London
Eastern
East Midlands
West Midlands
Yorkshire and the Humber
North West
North East
Scotland
Northern Ireland
Wales

The European Social Fund

41.13 Money is disbursed in line with the three Objectives and one new Community Initiative, and in line with the annual National Action Plan for Employment. The Community Initiative is called EQUAL and aims to tackle discrimination and inequality in the labour market across the EU.

41.14 Any legally constituted organisation can apply for funds under a competitive bidding process for projects under these objectives, although clearly some are more likely to appeal to certain types of charity than others. Projects are usually supported for up to two years, and the current programme period runs from 2000–2006.

41.15 Although the timing of receipts of ESF funds has been a source of problems for charities, the principles are quite clear. In general ESF will pay about 45% of a project's costs (those which are eligible). 30% of the first year's approved spend can be paid in advance, and thereafter regular claims are paid subject to a final retention pending final approval of the project.

41.16 Further information about the ESF, and how to apply for funds, can be obtained from the ESF website (www.esfnews.gov.uk), the ESF unit within the DfEE, your local government office or, in Scotland, the Scottish Executive.

The European Regional Development Fund

41.17 The ERDF is another structural fund, which co-finances actions to reduce the gaps in socio-economic development with areas of the European Union. Funds are targeted at improving infrastructure, productive investment, local development, human resources and the environment.

41.18 As with the ESF, the programme period runs from 2000–2006, and again concentrates on the three priority Objectives. The first two objectives are based on specific designated areas, the third is EU wide.

41.19 Information on the programmes run on a regional basis within Objectives 1 and 2 and the Community initiatives Interreg III and Urban is available directly from the regional offices or the ERDF website (www.inforegio.org).

42 *Ex Gratia* Payments

Definition

42.1 An *ex gratia* payment is one which an organisation feels morally obliged to make, even though it is not under any legal obligation to make the payment, it has no power under the charity's governing document to make the payment and the trustees cannot justify the payment as being in the best interests of the organisation. Most *ex gratia* payments made by charities are generally either in the context of an individual leaving the charity's employment, or where a charity receives a legacy due to technical error in drafting a will, though the legacy was clearly intended for another beneficiary. In principle no charitable organisation can ordinarily make such a payment, as by definition it is outside its governing rules. The position is stricter for charities than it is for other commercial organisations.

Principles

42.2 These are provided for under the *Charities Act 1993 s 27*, which gives the Charity Commission the power to authorise an *ex gratia* payment, by issuing an order. Such a payment may represent an application of the charity's assets, or a waiver of entitlement to receiving something.

42.3 Further guidance is provided in leaflet CC7 '*Ex Gratia* Payments by Charities' which generally expands on *s 27*. In particular, it highlights the distinction between the situation where to refuse payment would be morally wrong, and where to do so would simply create bitter disappointment. The example used is of a legacy where the amount received by the charity was much greater than the testator had intended, to such an extent that an honourable man would conclude that part of the estate received was really intended for someone else. This is a different position to one in which potential beneficiaries are upset because they have not received as much as they had hoped for from the estate, because the testator consciously decided to give elsewhere. Such a distinction is helpful in weighing up whether the charity should approach the Charity Commission for a suitable order.

42.4 If an *ex gratia* payment has been made without obtaining the consent of the Charity Commission, then the position should be rectified by informing the Commission and obtaining its advice. This is especially important as such payments fall within the broad responsibilities of the auditor in reporting matters to the Charity Commission under the whistle-blowing requirement. Such matters are therefore likely to be raised during the audit, and the charity would be acting prudently to regularise matters before they involve further professional time and money.

42.5 There is no concept of materiality in this context. Although minor payments which are effectively *ex gratia* may seem unimportant, neither the legislation nor Charity Commission guidance refer to any *de minimis* levels.

Accounting treatment

42.6 The Charities SORP requires additional disclosure in the accounts of any *ex gratia* payment, whether the value is represented by payment, non-monetary benefit, or waiver of rights to which the charity is entitled, and where the payment is not made as an application of funds or property for charitable purposes but in fulfilment of a compelling moral obligation. The same note should also disclose the nature and date of the authority for such a payment. The authority will be by the court, the Attorney-General or the Charity Commission. This disclosure is not a requirement of the accounts regulations, and therefore can be omitted whilst the accounts still comply with the requirements of the *Charities Act 1993*. In practice, and in some circumstances, such an omission of disclosure may call into question the integrity of the trustees.

42.7 The revised SORP clarifies the position regarding redundancy payments. If trustees believe that offering redundancy payments that are in excess of the statutory minimum level helps to motivate and retain staff, and thus benefits the charity, then such redundancy payments will not be regarded as *ex gratia* payments.

Industrial and Provident Societies

42.8 The prohibition on making *ex gratia* payments is not dissimilar to that for registered charities. They can be made if they are genuine, reasonably incidental to the business, and made for the benefit and prosperity of the organisation (*Parke v Daily News [1962] 2 All ER 929*).

Non-charitable companies

42.9 These companies can make payments on the same basis as an industrial and provident society, but can also make an *ex gratia* payment to current or past employees if the company has ceased operation or is being transferred to another company. [*Companies Act 1985 s 719*].

Scottish charities

42.10 Scottish legislation has no comparable power in *LRMPSA 1990* for the authorisation of *ex gratia* payments.

Taxation

42.11 *Ex gratia* payments will not necessarily qualify for tax relief in non-charitable companies. A normal business case for the allowability of the expenditure will be needed. In the unusual instance of substantial payments being made from a charity which were not in fulfilment of the charitable objectives, the tax status of the charity itself may be called into question.

42.12 *Ex gratia* payments may be taxable upon individuals, depending upon their circumstances. It used to be the case that up to £30,000 could be given to an ex-employee *ex gratia* and free of tax. Where such payments are now paid on retirement, the Inland Revenue regard them as relevant benefits under an unapproved retirement benefits scheme (*ICTA 1988 s 612*) and therefore taxable in full. Theoretically, such payments can still be made in the case of redundancy or compensation for loss of office, although any payment which flows from the terms of the contract of employment may still be taxable.

Honoraria

42.13 Honoraria are often *ex gratia*: they are payments made to individuals in return for services rendered to the charity, usually in an administrative capacity, but the amount paid is not intended to reflect the commercial value of the service rendered. Although this can be an effective means of a charity obtaining services at a low cost, honoraria should always be considered carefully before being approved by trustees.

42.14 An honorarium is not usually regarded by trustees as a contractual arrangement, giving the individual employment rights or making that person subject to PAYE. This may not be correct. An honorarium is also sometimes wrongly adopted as a means of paying a trustee who perhaps contributes more in time and resources than do other trustees. Somehow naming a payment to a trustee as an honorarium seems to change the trustee's perception. This is an illusion. The rules about payments to trustees apply irrespective of the amount paid or services provided.

42.15 Where a charity has a subsidiary, this should not be used to camouflage such payments. The trustees effectively control the company's assets as well as the charity's and the effect of paying an honorarium through the company is therefore nullified. Where it is appropriate for a company to pay an honorarium in its own right, then it may of course do so.

42.16 Trustees should realistically assess how necessary it is to make such a payment, and ensure that the payment is the best use of its resources. Honoraria should not be used as a means by which a charity can support a 'deserving individual' unless that individual fits in to the general charitable purposes of the charity, in which case support may be better provided through some form of direct charitable expenditure.

Other payments needing authority or advice

42.17 In addition to *ex gratia* payments there are other types of payment that may require consent or advice from the Charity Commission. For example, there are payments which the trustees have no legal obligation or power to make, but which they believe to be in the best interest of the charity. If the trustees can satisfy the Charity Commission that making such a payment will benefit the charity, the Commissioners can authorise the payment by making an Order under *s 26* of the *Charities Act 1993*. Similarly there may be instances where the trustees are unsure about the correctness of making a payment, perhaps because of a lack of clarity in the wording of their governing document. In these situations the trustees can seek advice from the Charity Commission on an informal basis or in more complex cases under *s 29* of the *Charities Act 1993*. Where trustees have sought the Charity Commission's advice they are protected by law from personal liability for breach of trust.

43 Examination of Accounts

43.1 Unincorporated charities with a total annual income of less than £250,000 are permitted under the *Charities Act 1993 s 43* to have their accounts examined by an independent examiner who is reasonably believed by the trustees to have the requisite ability and practical experience to carry out a competent examination of the accounts. Charities who fall within the light touch regime (see Chapter 77) need have no external scrutiny of their accounts at all. Scottish charities have a similar but not identical regime. The directions described below do not apply outside England and Wales, but may still usefully inform examiners working in Scotland.

43.2 Because *ss 41–43* of the *Charities Act 1993* do not apply to limited companies, then an examination is not available as an option to charities that are limited companies, and company law applies instead. Friendly societies and industrial and provident societies are required to appoint auditors under the *Industrial and Provident Societies Act 1968*, unless they are very small.

43.3 A charity may also have an audit requirement as a result of obligations existing outside the statutory framework, such as a requirement within its governing document, another statutory regime, or at the insistence of a donor or financier.

43.4 There are no formal procedures required in opting for an examination, except the normal routines for trustees' decisions. However, the Charity Commission has issued Guidance Notes on the selection of examiners, and Directions on the carrying out of an independent examination. These documents support the summary requirements set out in the accounting regulations.

43.5 An independent examination provides some degree of assurance about the annual accounts, but trustees and charity administrators must understand that the examiner is not required to form an opinion as to whether or not the accounts show a true and fair view. The examiner's report will merely indicate whether or not the accounts are in agreement with the underlying accounting records and comply with relevant legislation.

Examiner's report

43.6 The regulations stipulate the nature of the report which the examiner must give, and the powers and rights of the examiner. The report should be addressed, and signed and dated by the examiner, state that it is a report under *s 43*, and specifically cover the matters set out below either by negative assurance, or by a specific statement.

- Negative assurance:
  - — whether accounting records have been kept in accordance with the *Charities Act 1993*;
  - — whether the accounts accord with those records;
  - — whether the accounts comply with the accounting regulations, if full accrual accounts have been prepared.
- Specific statement:
  - — whether or not any matter has come to the examiner's attention in connection with the examination to which attention should be drawn in order for the reader to reach a proper understanding of the accounts.

- If the circumstance exists, a statement explaining:
  - any material breach of trust;
  - that information or explanations have been withheld;
  - any inconsistencies between the accounts, if prepared on an accruals basis, and the annual report.

Examiner's rights

43.7 The examiner has a statutory right of access to any books, documents and other records, however kept, which relate to the charity concerned. The examiner also has the right to obtain information from past or present trustees, officers and employees. Note that this right extends beyond that conferred on company auditors under the *Companies Act 1985 s 389*, which relates only to current officers of the company.

Independence

43.8 The examiner must be an independent person. The following would normally be considered to be connected and therefore not acceptable as an examiner: a charity trustee or anyone else closely involved with the charity's administration, a major donor to the charity, a major beneficiary of the charity, or a close relative, business partner or employee of any of these.

Qualifications

43.9 The Charity Commission recommends that where a charity has gross assets in excess of £1,000,000, or gross income of more than £100,000, then the examiner chosen should be a qualified accountant. If the accounts are prepared on an accruals basis, complying in full with the SORP, then the examiner should have a commensurate understanding of the issues involved. Any prospective examiner should be aware of and consider the examination guidelines prior to accepting the appointment.

43.10 If a charity wishes to appoint a firm to undertake an examination, then the appointment should be with an individual in that firm, in which case the name of the firm or company can be added to the report. In all cases a formal letter of engagement between the examiner and the charity should be prepared. This does not need to be re-issued each year.

43.11 When choosing an examiner the trustees should have regard to the guidance issued by the Commission. This states that where trustees are unable to obtain the services of a competent examiner on a voluntary basis, then they are not only entitled, but should be prepared, to pay a fee, and regard it as a proper expense of the charity.

Examiner's duties

43.12 Anyone acting as an independent examiner is under a duty of care and must act reasonably and responsibly. If the examiner is a professional accountant a higher duty of care will be expected of him/her.

43.13 The examiner's work should be in accordance with the twelve directions issued by the Charity Commission. In summary the examiner is required to:

- check that the charity is entitled to have an examination, rather than an audit, and that it is entitled to prepare receipts and payments accounts, if applicable;

- obtain an understanding of the charity's structure and financial activities in order to plan the specific procedures;
- record any procedures carried out, and any matters which are important to support eventual conclusions;
- compare the accounts with the accounting records;
- review the accounting records in order to provide a reasonable likelihood of identifying any material failure to maintain them; and
- carry out analytical procedures to identify unusual items or disclosures, and obtain suitable explanations.

Where the accounts are prepared on an accruals basis:

- decide whether the accounts comply with the Regulations;
- consider the accounting policies, and material judgments;
- enquire of the trustees about material events after the year end which may affect the accounts; and
- compare the accounts with the annual report, and consider any inconsistencies.

In all cases:

- review and assess all conclusions and evidence, in the light of the required examiner's report set out above; and
- inform the Charity Commission in writing if, whilst acting in the capacity as examiner, information or evidence is obtained which gives the examiner reasonable cause to believe that any one or more of the charity trustees has been responsible for deliberate or reckless misconduct in the administration of the charity.

43.14 The above work is not an audit, and although it may involve test checks of the accounting records it will often not be necessary for source documentation to be inspected by the examiner. If, after carrying out the above procedures, the examiner suspects that the accounts may be materially mis-stated then additional verification work may be undertaken.

44 Excepted Charities

44.1 Most charities have to register with the Charity Commission, but the Charity Commission can issue Orders, and the National Heritage Secretary can issue regulations, excepting some charities from the need to register with the Commission. Excepted charities in England and Wales may register voluntarily if they wish, provided the Charity Commission agrees that there is a public interest in their registration. If they do so they will be given a charity number. An excepted charity that registers voluntarily may ask to be removed from the Charity Commission's register at any time. There are estimated to be over 100,000 charities in England and Wales that are excepted from compulsory registration.

Charities registered with other bodies

44.2 Some charities are excepted from registering with the Charity Commission because they are registered with another body. Examples include:

- some Scout and Guide groups;
- some voluntary state schools, provided they hold no property apart from school premises;
- some religious charities; and
- about 25,000 armed forces charities wholly or mainly concerned with the promotion of the efficiency of the armed forces.

Small charities

44.3 Very small charities, i.e. any charity whose income from all sources does not in aggregate amount to more than £1,000 per year and which has neither any permanent endowment, nor the use or occupation of any land or buildings, are excepted from the requirement to register, as they are felt to be too small to merit the degree of scrutiny that registration brings. [*Charities Act 1993 s 3(5)(c)*].

Places of worship

44.4 Places of worship registered under the *Places of Worship Registration Act 1855* are also excepted from registering. The exception in respect of registered places of worship should not be misunderstood. All churches are not automatically excepted because of this section: certain properties are registered under the *Places of Worship Registration Act 1855*, but the exception, and rate relief, attaches only to the property (and related buildings) itself, and not to activities undertaken within the property. The Registrar General maintains a list of relevant places of worship and this is open to public inspection. [*Charities Act 1993 s 3(5)(14)*].

Religious charities

44.5 The organisations listed below were excepted from registration by the *Charities (Exemption from Registration) Regulations 1996 (SI 1996 No 180)*. These Regulations are due to expire on 1 March 2001. The exception extends to a charity wholly or mainly concerned with the advancement of religion, being a charity connected with a body named in the list below and either:

- having as a trustee a trust corporation connected with that body;
- established wholly or mainly to make provision for public religious worship; or
- in respect of which accounts are sent annually to the Methodist Conference, a Methodist Synod or any committee or department appointed or established by the Methodist Conference.

The bodies referred to are:

- a church within the meaning of the *Baptists and Congregational Trust Act 1951 s 2*;
- a church which is affiliated to the Fellowship of Independent Evangelical Churches;
- a church which is a member of the General Assembly of Unitarian and Free Christian Churches;
- the Calvinistic Methodist or Presbyterian Church of Wales;
- the Church of England;
- the Church in Wales;
- the Methodist Church;
- the Religious Society of Friends; and
- the United Reform Church.

44.6 A charity is permanently excepted where it exists for the advancement of religion, and the application of its income in a particular manner is conditional upon a grave, tomb or personal monument being kept in good order; and the income of the charity does not amount to more than £1,000 a year.

Regulation

44.7 An excepted charity is under a very similar regime as any registered charity. The general trust and stewardship obligations apply, they can seek advice and support from the Charity Commission and are subject to its powers of investigation. They are bound by the same rules on fund-raising and public collections. They are subject to the same rules for the preparation and scrutiny of accounts and the same tax rules apply. There are, however, a few key differences. Firstly, by definition, excepted charities will not have a registered charity number (unless they are voluntarily registered). Where it is necessary to produce evidence of charitable status, it is generally acceptable to quote an Inland Revenue reference, making clear that this is an Inland Revenue reference, and not a registered charity number.

44.8 Secondly, an excepted charity does not have to file its annual accounts and report with the Charity Commission, although the Charity Commission has the power to ask for them. Most excepted charities will have their own internal guidance on accounting and audit, which will often be more stringent than the *Charities Act 1993* requirements. For instance, the Church of England rules for Parochial Church Councils (PCCs) do not recognise the light touch regime. They require all PCCs to be examined or audited.

Operation of other charities

44.9 Excepted charities may also operate other charities. If these are separately constituted or are outside the objects of the excepted charity, then they should not automatically be assumed to fall within the exception. A separate charity operated by an excepted charity may need to be registered in its own right and accounts and audit procedures complied with individually.

Scotland

44.10 There are equivalent Scottish provisions for excepted charities in the *Charities (Designated Religious Bodies) (Scotland) Order 1993 (SI 1993 No 2774)*, which lists a number of both Protestant and Catholic church bodies.

Possible developments

44.11 At the time of writing the Charity Commission and the Home Office are conducting a public consultation exercise, seeking views on when registration as a charity should be voluntary. The reason for this is that the purpose of registration has changed considerably since the register was established in 1960 so the current arrangements are out of date and often lead to confusion and misunderstandings.

44.12 There are no plans to remove the option of voluntary registration for very small charities, though the threshold defining a charity as small may be raised.

44.13 It would be possible to extend voluntary registration if the purpose of registration can be achieved in some other way. This has led to a proposal to make registration voluntary for charities that are supervised by a relevant umbrella body, referred to in the consultation document as a 'Responsible Body'. Responsible bodies would have to meet certain criteria laid down by the Charity Commission and would be monitored by it. They would not take over the Commission's legal responsibility for unregistered charities. They would remain within the Commission's jurisdiction and subject to the full range of its powers.

44.14 A decision on the future of voluntary registration is likely to be made towards the end of 2000.

45 Exempt Charities

45.1 Exempt charities are bodies that are established for charitable purposes, but that are excluded from the supervisory and monitoring powers of the Charity Commission because they are subject to their own statutory provisions. They cannot register with the Charity Commission. Exempt charities include:

- charitable friendly societies, which must comply with the *Friendly and Industrial and Provident Societies Acts 1965 and 1968* and *Friendly Societies Acts 1974* and *1992*;
- charitable industrial and provident societies, which must comply with the *Friendly and Industrial and Provident Societies Acts 1965 and 1968* and the *Industrial and Provident Societies Act 1978*;
- higher education corporations, which must comply with the *Education Reform Act 1988*, as amended.

A full list is given in *Sch 2* to the *Charities Act 1993* and includes a number of specifically named national museums, universities and medical schools.

45.2 The Charity Commission has only limited powers in connection with the administration of exempt charities as they are subject to the jurisdiction of another supervisory body. Exempt charities do not have to comply with the *Charities Act 1993* requirements on the sale, leasing, disposal and mortgaging of land, and do not have to comply with the *Charities Act 1993* requirements relating to the form and content of accounts, audit and annual report. However, they are subject to the more general provisions of the Act. For instance, they are required to keep proper accounting records, and prepare accounts for periods of up to 15 months. The accounting requirements of their particular supervisory body are likely to be similar to those of the Charity Commission.

45.3 The Charity Commission cannot exercise its powers under *s 8* of the *Charities Act 1993* to institute an inquiry into the affairs of an exempt charity, nor can it act to protect the charity's interests under *s 18* or to require it to change its name under *s 6*. It does, however, have other powers which it may use on application of either the exempt charity itself, or the Court. Under *s 16* of the *Charities Act 1993* the Charity Commission can make Schemes for the application of property *cy-près* and for the administration of an exempt charity. It can make Orders to vest land in the Official Custodian for Charities (*ss 16* and *21*) and to sanction actions that are in the interests of an exempt charity but not within the trustees' existing powers (*s 26*). The Commission can authorise *ex gratia* payments under *s 27*, accept documents for safekeeping under *s 30*, and waive the disqualification of a trustee under *s 72*. The Commission can also make Schemes under *s 17* to establish common investment funds for exempt charities and under *s 24* to establish common deposit funds.

45.4 As with any charity, the trustees (or a trustee) of an exempt charity may write to the Charity Commission for formal advice about a proposed course of action, and in following that advice the trustees will be deemed to have acted in accordance with their trusts. [*Charities Act 1993 s 29*]. This is always subject to the trustees not having reasonable cause to suspect that:

- the advice was given in ignorance of material facts, or
- material facts have changed since the advice was given, or

- a court decision has also been obtained, or
- there are proceedings in hand to obtain a court decision.

45.5 Trustees of exempt charities may be incorporated under the *Charities Act 1993 s 50*, in the same way as those of a registered charity and the Charity Commission can amend, enforce or dissolve their certificates of incorporation (*ss 56, 58* and *61*).

45.6 Exempt charities are subject to the same tax regime as registered charities and the provisions in *Part II* of the *Charities Act 1992* relating to fund-raising also apply to them.

45.7 Although exempt charities are not closely controlled by the Charity Commission, trustees of exempt charities need to be aware of their own constitutional requirements, and the principles of charity and trust law generally. In particular, the Charities SORP does not apply only to registered charities, and so an exempt charity should follow it unless another, more specific SORP must be followed. In the context of charitable status, the term 'exempt' has no relevance to the type of supply for VAT purposes.

46 Exemptions from VAT

Background

46.1 *Article 13* of the *EC Sixth Directive* provides the basis for exemptions from VAT in the areas of social welfare and property. These reliefs are enacted in UK law by the *Value Added Tax Act (VATA) 1994 9 Sch.* Charities are most likely to find the following relevant:

- Group 1 Land and Buildings
- Group 6 Education
- Group 7 Health and welfare
- Group 9 Trade Unions and Professional Bodies
- Group 10 Sporting services provided by Non-profit Making Bodies
- Group 12 Fund-raising
- Group 13 Cultural services.

46.2 The advantage of an exempt supply is that it is not subject to VAT and charities whose supplies fall within this category may therefore benefit. However, there is essentially no relief for input tax on supplies of goods and services made to the charity that relate to exempt supplies. This therefore distinguishes the VAT position from those of zero-rated supplies. VAT incurred in making exempt supplies may only be recovered if the total exempt input tax is de minimis, i.e. the exempt input tax of the business in any quarter does not exceed £625 per month on average and 50% of total input tax. A charity making only exempt supplies cannot normally register for VAT.

46.3 The Customs and Excise Notices mentioned in this chapter are available from the local VAT office. The information contained in these Notices and in this section is for general guidance only, and can never be a substitute for detailed professional guidance.

Land and buildings: *Group 1*

46.4 Charities may buy, sell, lease or rent out properties and may also carry out major refurbishments to such properties. Each of these transactions have VAT implications and, although the legislation in this area is somewhat of a minefield, with careful professional guidance a charity may be able to make significant VAT savings.

46.5 *VATA 1994 9 Sch Group 1* sets out the general rule that a lease of land, a right over land or licence to occupy land is exempt. The 'election to waive exemption' (more frequently known as the 'option to tax') allows a person (including a charity) to tax certain supplies of property. It can be exercised by a person making what would otherwise be an exempt supply in relation to a building or undeveloped land.

Supplies not affected by the option to tax

46.6 Certain supplies remain exempt even though the option to tax has been exercised on the property in question. These are very important for charities and include the following.

- A building or part of a building intended for use as a dwelling or number of dwellings or solely for a relevant residential purpose (see Chapter 121). An exception to this relates to supplies made on or after 19 March 1997 and an option to tax can still have effect where:
  - — at or before the time of the grant/sale both the parties agree in writing to the vendor exercising the option to tax; and
  - — at the time the supply is made, the purchaser intends to use the property for the purpose of making a zero-rated supply under *VATA 1994 8 Sch Group 5 Item 1(b)*, i.e. for conversion into one or more dwellings, or for use solely for a relevant residential purpose (e.g. care home, hospice, student residence etc.).
- A building or part of a building intended for use solely for a relevant charitable purpose (see Chapter 121), other than as an office.
- A supply of land to a registered housing association which certifies to the supplier that the land is to be used for the construction of dwellings or buildings solely for a relevant residential purpose other than as an office.

46.7 The complex anti-avoidance provisions introduced by the *Finance Act 1997* disapplying the option to tax in specified circumstances are outside the scope of this book, though they are considered in the chapter 'Land and Buildings' in *Tolley's VAT Planning*.

Exercising the option to tax

46.8 The option will have no effect unless written notification of it is given to the local VAT office within 30 days of it having been made or such longer period allowed by Customs. The written notification must state unambiguously which property is involved and the date from which the option has effect. *VATA 1994 10 Sch Item 2* sets out the general requirements.

46.9 A person wishing to exercise an option to tax land or property from which they have already received exempt income must usually first obtain written permission from Customs. Also, an option cannot be made retrospectively, although Customs will usually accept a belated notification of an option, e.g. where VAT has been charged on rents but not notified to them.

Effect of opting to tax

46.10 The option is generally a relieving measure which allows a landlord to recover VAT incurred on, for example, the construction, refurbishment or management of a property. Once a charity has exercised the option for any property, it must charge VAT on all future supplies in relation to that property which would otherwise be exempt. For example, it is not possible to exercise the option in order to tax rents, but then to sell on an exempt basis the freehold of a property in future. The option remains effective even if the property is sold and re-acquired.

46.11 Unless the lease specifically provides otherwise, a landlord has a right to add VAT to the rent agreed under the lease following an option to tax — there is nothing in the legislation requiring him to consult his tenant before opting. Tenants that are exempt or partly exempt will suffer irrecoverable input tax if their landlord exercises the option to tax. If partly-exempt, the tenant will be unable to recover all their input tax under the partial exemption rules, unless it falls within the de minimis limit. Where the exempt input tax of a tenant does not amount to more than £625 per month on average and 50% of total input tax, all such input tax is treated as attributable to taxable supplies and therefore recoverable in full subject to the normal rules.

Revoking the option to tax

46.12 An option to tax can be revoked within three months from the date on which it is made, provided it has not been put into practical effect through the charging of VAT or the recovery of input tax, and provided that the property in question has not been purchased as a VAT free transfer of a going concern. This, therefore, has little practical benefit. Revocation is also allowed 20 or more years after the election has had effect. In all cases, the person exercising the option to tax must obtain the written consent of Customs to the revocation.

Restrictions on use by a charity

46.13 Customs take the view that a tenant intending to use a building (or part of one) for a relevant charitable purpose is not required by law to issue a qualifying use certificate to the landlord. This could put the landlord at risk, since he is unable to opt to tax, but there is no onus on the tenant to prove his user status. Landlords who have opted, or who intend to opt, and who receive claims that a building is being used, or is intended for use, for a qualifying purpose, may seek to obtain suitable indemnities from the tenant.

Other supplies of interests in land

46.14 These include the following:

- Payments made to a landlord to surrender a lease or vary the terms of a lease are exempt from VAT, unless the landlord has opted to tax.
- Reverse surrender payments, i.e. where the landlord pays the tenant to surrender his lease, are exempt unless the tenant has exercised the option.
- Inducement payments such as reverse premiums are standard rated for VAT purposes. However, there have been a number of successful appeals in the Courts on this point, and it should be closely monitored.
- Grants of licences to occupy land where the land is unspecified, so that the tenant has unspecified use, are standard-rated for VAT.
- Dilapidation payments made to a landlord to cover wear and tear on vacation of a property are outside the scope for VAT.

46.15 In general, the area of land and property VAT is highly complex and professional advice should be sought.

Education: *Group 6*

46.16 The supply of education, research or vocational training by a charity will generally be exempt if it is made for consideration. If the charity is not a school, university or other similarly approved institution, exemption will only apply if it falls within the definition in *VATA 1994 9 Sch Group 6 note 1(f)*, i.e. 'any other body which is precluded from distributing and does not distribute the profit it makes and which applies those profits to the continuance or improvement of such supplies'. It is therefore important to ensure that, although a charitable organisation may overall be non-profit making, if exemption is desired, then any surplus created by a particular activity should be put back into the same project rather than applied elsewhere. The supply of any goods or services (other than examinations services) which are closely connected to the supply of education, research or vocational training are also exempt provided that they are for the direct use of the pupil, student or trainee. Examples include accommodation, catering, transport and school trips.

46.17 When a charity purchases supplies of education or training, they will be exempt from VAT if supplied by an eligible body such as a university. In the case of research, the supply will be exempt if made by one eligible body to another. However, supplies of research by an eligible body to an ineligible one, e.g. medical research supplied to a commercial enterprise such as a pharmaceutical company, will be taxable at the standard rate.

46.18 Charities should note that, in some cases, it may be beneficial to ensure that VAT is charged on educational services, e.g. where the supply is to a body such as an NHS Trust or a local authority that can generally recover the VAT charged. In that instance, the use of a trading subsidiary structure should be considered.

46.19 The Customs and Excise Notice 'Education' (Notice 701/30/95 dated 1 August 1995) sets out detailed guidance on this area. The Notice gives examples of what constitutes 'education', 'research' and 'vocational training'.

Health and welfare: *Group 7*

Welfare

46.20 Welfare services and related goods supplied by charities may qualify for exemption if certain conditions are fulfilled. *VATA 1994 9 Sch Group 7 items 9* and *10* exempt:

- *Item 9*: the supply, otherwise than for profit, by a charity or public body of welfare services and of goods supplied in connection therewith.
- *Item 10*: the supply, otherwise than for profit, of goods and services incidental to the provision of spiritual welfare by a religious community to a resident member of that community in return for a subscription or other consideration paid as a condition of membership.

46.21 Welfare services are defined as financial and other assistance given to people in need, and are directly connected with:

- the provision of care, treatment or instruction designed to promote the physical or mental welfare of elderly, sick, distressed or disabled persons;
- the protection of children and young persons; or
- the provision of spiritual welfare by a religious institution as part of a course of instruction or a retreat, not being a course or a retreat designed primarily to provide recreation or a holiday.

46.22 The three main strands of any welfare services are as follows:

- They will be of help and benefit to the recipient.
- They will be given rather than sold — although Customs accept that a nominal charge can be made.
- They will be provided to people in need.

46.23 'Care' means some form of continuing personal contact in looking after, helping or supervising people.

46.24 The exemption does not include the supply of accommodation or catering except where it is ancillary to the provision of care, treatment or instruction.

'Otherwise than for profit'

46.25 This phrase was considered by the Court of Appeal in *Bell Concord Educational Trust Ltd v Customs & Excise Comrs [1989] STC 264*, in the context of education provided by a charity. It was held that the making of a surplus was not an object of the company and that it did not systematically aim to make a profit. The Trust's memorandum and articles provided that no distributions could be made to members and, since the only activity of the charity was the provision of education, it was decided that supplies were made otherwise than for profit. Customs have interpreted this case as allowing charities to budget for a surplus in setting fees, provided that the surplus is ploughed back directly into the activity in question. Where the charity intends to use the surplus as a subsidy for different activities it is seen as operating for a profit and its activities do not qualify for exemption, even where the subsidised activities are charitable in their own right.

Supplies of welfare services 'at below cost'

46.26 By concession the supply of welfare services and related goods made by charities consistently 'below cost' to people for the relief of distress are non-business supplies and therefore outside the scope of VAT. 'Below cost' means the cost of providing the welfare is subsidised by at least 15% from the charity's own funds. Customs will need to be satisfied that the subsidised services are available equally to all distressed persons. The service subsidy must be available not only to those people who cannot afford to pay the full rate but also to those who can afford it. Further, it must not be applied conditionally e.g. only during spells of very cold weather or only to persons living in a certain area or of a certain age. Any services provided for people who are not distressed could attract VAT.

Meals on wheels and catering

46.27 This service is often run by a charity on behalf of a local authority. Any charge made to the recipient for the meals is not consideration paid to the charity but is part of the local authority's non-business income. If the charity makes a charge to the local authority for providing the service, this is a taxable supply of a delivery service and not a welfare supply by the charity. The local authorities can recover the VAT charged.

46.28 Supplies of food and drink by charities from trolleys, canteens or shops are business but exempt when connected with the welfare of those in hospital or prison, or those visiting them (Customs and Excise Notice 701/1/95 'Charities').

The 'protection of children and young persons'

46.29 This exemption is not limited to protection from harm but also includes:

- services designed to improve the well-being of the young; and
- the protection of the young from malign influences.

An example of a welfare service falling within this category is the provision of accommodation in a children's home.

46.30 Exemptions from VAT

'Spiritual welfare'

46.30 In determining whether a supply qualifies as spiritual welfare Customs look to the intention behind the supply. Useful indicators include the way in which the supply is advertised and the objects and purpose of the organisation making the supply. A meeting of persons who have suffered a bereavement would qualify where the purpose of the meeting is held out as the provision of spiritual succour. On the other hand, conferences, courses of instruction or retreats cannot be treated as exempt when the spiritual welfare element is an incidental benefit and not the main purpose of the supply. For example, a course in theology is not the provision of spiritual welfare but an educational process. The charity could instead consider whether this supply falls within the education exemption (see 46.16). As with welfare, the recipient of spiritual welfare must be a person in need of such and not someone who merely wishes to expand their knowledge of spiritual matters.

46.31 Exemption is afforded to the supply of goods only when they are provided by a charity in connection with a welfare service.

Health

46.32 The provision of medical services for a consideration is generally exempt from VAT. The services of most qualified medical professionals are exempted under *items 1, 2, 3* and *5* of *Group 7*. This exemption extends to the services of unqualified staff who are supervised by registered staff e.g. a qualified nurse supervising an unqualified care assistant. Broadly, the services exempted cover most medical and paramedical professionals including doctors, dentists, nurses, ophthalmic opticians, chiropodists and physiotherapists. They do not cover the services of paramedics not listed in the register kept under the *Professions Supplementary to Medicine Act 1960* such as acupuncturists.

46.33 The exemption in *Group 4* is a wide exemption to cover the provision of care or medical or surgical treatment in an approved hospital or other institution. This would cover a private hospital, authorised hospices, etc. The exemption does not extend to veterinary hospitals or practices.

Trade Unions and Professional Bodies: *Group 9*

46.34 *VATA 1994 9 Sch Group 9* allows for the provision of facilities and advantages to members of clubs, associations and other such organisations, by certain non-profit making bodies, to be treated as VAT exempt. The non-profit making bodies falling into this category would be trade unions, or similar organisations whose main objective is to negotiate the terms and conditions of employment of its members, professional associations whereby membership is restricted to individuals seeking or holding an appropriate qualification, learned or representational associations, and other similar organisations.

46.35 The exemption covers the provision of services and related goods by the qualifying body to its members, provided that they are made available without payment (other than a membership subscription) and provided they relate to the aims of the organisation.

46.36 Exemption does not apply to:

- supplies that do not relate to the body's aims as set out in its rules or constitution;

- the supply of any right of admission to any premises, event, or performance, to which non-members are admitted for a consideration;
- any supplies which are not provided automatically as a result of membership and for which an additional sum is charged; and
- supplies to non-members.

46.37 Where clearly identifiable zero-rated benefits (i.e. a yearbook) are provided in return for membership subscriptions, the subscription (or a proportion) may be treated as zero-rated.

Sporting services provided by non-profit making bodies: *Group 10*

46.38 An exemption from VAT for sporting and physical education services supplied by non-profit making bodies to individual sporting participants came into effect on 1 April 1994. It exempts services closely linked with and essential to sport or physical recreation supplied to individuals taking part in the activity where the supplies are made by:

- a 'non-profit making body' having members, to those of its members who are granted membership for a period of three months or more; and
- a 'non-profit making body' which does not run a membership scheme (e.g. a charity).

46.39 The supply of any services of residential accommodation, catering, bar facilities or transport as well as supplies by local authorities, government departments and non-departmental public bodies such as Sports Councils are specifically excluded.

46.40 A 'non-profit making body' is one whose constitution or articles of association preclude it from distributing surpluses of income over expenditure to its members, shareholders or any other party. However, sporting services will not be excluded from exemption simply because profits on certain activities are used to subsidise other activities (e.g. profits on the bar are used to subsidise subscriptions).

46.41 Customs recently issued the following clarification of the applicability of the exemption to sports centres operated by charitable trusts and like bodies:

> 'Where a sports centre operated by a charitable trust or similar non-profit making body makes supplies of sporting and physical education services of a type which would normally qualify for exemption from VAT and does not operate a full membership scheme (for example, where members do not have voting rights or any form of control over the management of the centre), such services will be exempt from VAT. This relates only to supplies to individuals using the centre and applies irrespective of whether users are called 'members' for the purposes of obtaining a discount on use of the facilities.
>
> Where such a sports centre operates a full membership scheme and limits its application to selected activities or locations, exemption of qualifying services will be limited to supplies to members, even if an activity is not used by members. For example, where a centre provides a swimming pool and squash courts and the membership scheme is only for squash players, supplies to all users of the swimming pool, other than squash members, will continue to be standard rated.'

46.42 Exemptions from VAT

46.42 After several attempts, changes to *Group 10* were introduced by the *VAT (Sports, Sports Competitions and Physical Education) Order SI 1999 No 1994* with effect from 1 January 2000. The changes are aimed to prevent VAT avoidance by proprietary clubs and to restrict the exemption to genuine non-profit-making sports clubs.

46.43 Further details of the exemption are contained in Customs and Excise Notice 701/45/94 'Sports and physical education'.

Relief for importation

46.44 Charities are entitled to special reliefs from VAT on certain imports of goods from a place outside the Member States of the EU. These are not exemptions within *Sch 9* of *VATA 1994*, but are contained in EC law and in UK statutory instruments and statements of practice. They include the following.

- Basic necessities (i.e. food, medicines, clothing, blankets, orthopaedic equipment and crutches, required to meet a person's immediate needs) obtained without charge for distribution free of charge to the needy by a 'relevant organisation'. Excluded are alcoholic beverages, tobacco products, coffee, tea and motor vehicles other than ambulances.
- Goods donated by a person established outside the Member States to a 'relevant organisation' for use to raise funds at occasional charity events for the benefit of the needy also qualify for relief. There must be no commercial intent on the part of the donor. Alcoholic beverages etc. are excluded as above.
- Goods imported by a 'relevant organisation' for distribution or loan, free of charge, to victims of, or for meeting its operating needs in the relief of, a disaster affecting the territory of one or more Member States. This relief applies only if the EC Commission has authorised the importation of the goods.
- Articles donated to or imported by an approved organisation principally engaged in the education of, or the provision of assistance to, blind or handicapped persons for loan, hire or transfer on a non-profit making basis where those goods are specially designed for the education or employment.

46.45 'Relevant organisation' means a State organisation or other approved charitable or philanthropic organisation.

46.46 The above reliefs are conditional on:

- the goods being put to the use or purpose specified; and
- unless specifically allowed, the goods not being lent, hired out or transferred unless to an organisation which would itself be entitled to the relief if importing the goods on that date. In the latter case, prior notification in writing must be received from Customs and the goods must be used solely in accordance with the relieving provisions.

46.47 Full details of all the goods which qualify for relief are contained in Customs and Excise Notice 317 'Imports by Charities'.

Fund-raising: *Group 12*

46.48 In the case of charity fund-raising events, it is important that the planning of such events extends to ensuring that they fall within the scope of the VAT exemption where this is advantageous, as will usually be the case. *VATA 1994 9 Sch Group 12 items 1* and *2* exempt:

- 'The supply of goods and services by a charity in connection with a fund-raising event organised for charitable purposes by a charity or jointly by more than one charity'; and

- 'The supply of goods and services by a qualifying body in connection with a fund-raising event organised exclusively for its own benefit.'

46.49 Prior to 1 April 2000 a fund-raising event was defined as a fête, ball, bazaar, gala show, performance or similar event which is separate from, and not forming any part of, a series of regularly run or similar events. With effect from 1 April 2000, all fund-raising events including participatory, Internet and 'virtual' events are exempt, subject to the conditions on the number of events described in paragraph 46.50 below. Goods and services connected with a fund-raising event and within the scope of the exemption include admission charges, sponsorship income directly connected to the fund-raising event, sales of advertising space in commemorative brochures and merchandising income. In relation to merchandising income, if the licence to market items connected with the event is granted to third parties, the licence fee will be exempt, but the merchandise sold by third parties will be taxable.

46.50 The exemption used to be limited to one-off events. However, with effect from 1 April 2000, a charity can now conduct up to 15 fund-raising events of any one type in any one location in any one year. In addition an unlimited number of small-scale events, such as coffee mornings, where gross takings do not exceed £1,000, can now be held and treated as exempt.

46.51 The exemption will not now apply to events which are likely to create a distortion of 'competition'. Customs have not at the time of writing issued any guidance on what they will regard as distortion. This could lead to confusion and uncertainty and is not satisfactory. It is hoped that some guidance will be issued by Customs.

46.52 The EC legislation does not specify that fund-raising must be the main purpose of the event. Accordingly, in the case of *Newsvendors Benevolent Institution, Lon/96/567, July 1996 (14343)* the tribunal found that a charity which raised funds through holding a festival dinner and carol concert came within the exemption even though the events served other purposes, i.e. the dinner dance was originally organised to thank contributors and to enable the outgoing festival chairman to hand over to his successor, and the carol concert was a religious service. However, if the raising of funds is merely an incidental purpose, the event will not qualify for VAT exemption. For example, events organised by a rugby club which included stag nights, annual dinners, annual general meetings, barbecues, and end of season and New Year parties did not qualify as fund-raising events (*Blaydon Rugby Football Club [1996] VATTR1, Manchester February 1996 (13656)*). An important change introduced from 1 April 2000 is that, in order to qualify for the exemption, the event must be promoted as a fund-raising event. Customs have advised that this means publicity material, tickets and other items should clearly refer to the fund-raising purpose of the event.

46.53 For the purpose of this exemption, 'charity' includes a body corporate which is wholly owned by a charity and whose profits, from whatever source, are payable to a charity by virtue of a deed of covenant or trust or otherwise.

46.54 A qualifying body can only benefit from the exemption in *item 2* in connection with a fund-raising event which has been organised exclusively for its own benefit. Qualifying bodies are those with aims and objectives of a political, religious, philanthropic, philosophical or patriotic nature. [*VATA 1994 s 94(3)*]. They include those bodies in *item 1 Group 9* and cover trade unions, professional associations, learned societies, pressure groups, and any non-profit making body which is established for the principal purpose of providing facilities for participating in sport or physical education. Also included is any body which is an eligible body for the purpose of *item 2* of the *Group 13* cultural services exemption (see 46.57).

Alternative structures for fund-raising events

46.55 When a fund-raising event does not qualify for exempt treatment, it is still open to a charity or any other body to set a basic minimum charge which will be standard-rated, and to invite those attending the event to supplement this with a voluntary donation. The extra contributions will be outside the scope of VAT if all the following conditions are met:

- it is clearly stated on all publicity material, including tickets, that anyone paying only the minimum charge will be admitted without a further payment;
- the extra payment does not give any particular benefit (for example admission to a better position in the stadium or auditorium);
- the extent of further contributions is ultimately left to ticket holders to decide, even if the organiser indicates a desired level of donation;
- for film or theatre performances, concerts, sporting fixtures, etc. the minimum charge is not less than the usual price of the particular seats at a normal commercial event of the same type;
- for dances, dinners and similar functions, the minimum total sum upon which the organisers will be liable to account for VAT will not be less than their total costs incurred in arranging the event.

46.56 If the publicity material for a fund-raising event suggests that those paying a recommended extra amount are more likely to be admitted than those paying merely the basic ticket price, then the extra amount becomes part of the consideration for a supply of services, rather than a pure donation, and as such the full payment is subject to VAT at the standard rate.

Cultural services: *Group 13*

46.57 *VATA 1994 13 Sch Group 13* provides an exemption from VAT since 1 June 1996 (but backdated to 1 January 1990) for admission charges to certain cultural places and events. In particular, it exempts the supply by a public body or an eligible body of a right of admission to:

- a museum, gallery, art exhibition or zoo; or
- a theatrical, musical or choreographic performance of a cultural nature.

A charity may fall within the definition of 'eligible body' where it:

- is precluded from distributing, and does not distribute, any profit it makes;
- applies any profits made from the above-mentioned supplies to the continuance or improvement of the facilities made available by means of the supplies.

46.58 However, the exemption only applies where the body is managed and administered on a voluntary basis by persons who have no direct or indirect financial interest in its activities. The scope of the exemption is therefore much more limited than might appear on first sight, although Customs permit technical staff, such as back stage staff, to be remunerated without prejudicing the exemption.

46.59 These two conditions were considered in the case of *Glastonbury Abbey, LON/95/2909, November 1996 (14579)*. The Chairman said that it would be a question of fact and degree whether a body was administered on an 'essentially' voluntary basis, this being the condition which may be imposed by the UK under the EC law. She had regard to the number of people involved (14 trustees and 101 voluntary workers compared with the small number of paid workers) and the amounts paid in salaries as compared with annual turnover. The tribunal concluded that the appellant was managed and administered on an essentially voluntary basis. Turning to the second condition, the tribunal held that neither the custodian nor the deputy custodian (who were both paid a salary) had any direct or indirect interest in the results of the activities, which the tribunal held to be references to the sharing of profits or gains of the organisation and not the receipt of a salary. Thus the Abbey's activities were found to be exempt from VAT.

46.60 The decision in the *Glastonbury Abbey* case means that a number of cultural bodies who employ limited managerial staff or sub-contractors may be able to claim that they are within the scope of the exemption for cultural services. Nevertheless, the exemption is strictly drawn and in practice is limited to small enterprises e.g. museums staffed by volunteers or amateur dramatic groups who would in any case often fall below the turnover threshold. Further detail on the exemption may be found in Customs and Excise Notice 701/47 'Cultural Services'.

47 Expenses

47.1 Payments by a charity to volunteers, including members of the governing body, or members of staff are either remuneration or reimbursement of out-of-pocket expenses. It is important to distinguish between these types of payment and ascertain whether the recipient is a volunteer or staff member for a number of legal reasons and because the tax treatment of the payment may vary as a result.

47.2 'Out-of-pocket' expenses are necessary costs genuinely incurred by staff or volunteers in the nature of the work they do for an organisation. Examples are the cost of any necessary travel, other than the cost of travelling between home and the usual place of work, postage, stationery, telephone calls, cleaning materials for the charity's premises, hotel accommodation if the person is required to be away from home overnight and the cost of providing care for a dependant. It is good practice to issue guidance about the maximum amount that can be claimed for such things as meals, hotels and dependant care.

47.3 Charities should require any person claiming out-of-pocket expenses to produce a receipt for the expenditure unless it is genuinely impossible to do so, e.g. fees for cloakrooms or parking meters. Receipts should be kept by the person responsible for producing the charity's accounts for audit purposes and in case the Charity Commission, the Scottish Charities Office, the Inland Revenue or the Benefits Agency asks to see them. Charities should have an appropriate system for authorising claims for expenses.

Tax

47.4 Income tax does not have to be paid on genuine expenses allowed by the Inland Revenue, and receipt of such expenses does not affect a person's entitlement to benefits. However, if the charity reimburses expenses to paid staff which the Inland Revenue does not allow for employees, such as the cost of travel between home and the usual place of work, these will be subject to tax and national insurance.

47.5 Different tax rules apply to unpaid volunteers. Unpaid volunteers may be reimbursed tax-free for travel expenses between home and the usual place of volunteering, for the actual cost of meals taken because of voluntary work for more than four hours in any one day, or because the voluntary work must be carried out at meal times, and for the cost of dependant care necessary to allow the volunteer to be available for voluntary work.

47.6 Charities have to declare reimbursed expenses on the Inland Revenue form P11D or P9D unless the charity has a dispensation. Dispensations are granted to organisations whose only entries on P11D and/or P9D forms would relate to the reimbursement of expenses genuinely incurred wholly in the course of business or to benefits in kind such as accommodation. If the charity does not have a dispensation the recipients must declare their reimbursed expenses on their income tax self-assessment forms. Therefore good record-keeping is essential.

Right to be reimbursed

47.7 Employers have a statutory duty under the *Employment Rights Act 1996* to reimburse their employees for expenses incurred in carrying out their employer's requirements.

Under the *Trustee Act 1925 s 30(2)* trustees of charitable trusts and associations, including holding and custodian trustees, have a statutory right to be reimbursed for any expense incurred in their service as a trustee. Members of charitable associations who are not trustees do not have a statutory right to have their expenses reimbursed. However, they can be reimbursed if this is not prohibited by the charity's governing document. Trustees of charitable companies do not have a statutory right to have their expenses reimbursed. This can only be done if the governing document contains an explicit clause permitting the payment of trustees' expenses or if the members have approved payment. Trustees of charitable industrial and provident societies can have their expenses reimbursed provided that their rules contain a clause explicitly permitting this.

47.8 Expenses reimbursed to trustees must be disclosed in the charity's annual accounts.

Expenses or remuneration?

47.9 Salaries and wages are clearly remuneration. However, some other payments or benefits commonly referred to as 'expenses' may in fact amount to remuneration and therefore be forbidden by law or the charities governing document. Such payments may also be subject to income tax or could affect the State benefits a person is receiving. Examples of payments to volunteers that are often described as 'expenses' but which are really remuneration include:

- honoraria;
- per diem expenses that are paid regardless of the amount actually spent;
- payments to compensate for loss of earnings;
- payments that the claimant would have incurred anyway, e.g. home telephone line rental; and
- mileage rates above those set by the Inland Revenue.

47.10 All payments that are in reality remuneration should be paid as such. Paid volunteers should be treated the same way as employees for tax purposes. If the volunteer is being paid above the tax threshold, income tax should be deducted through PAYE. If the volunteer is self-employed, he or she should pay any tax due.

Payments to trustees

47.11 Particular care must be taken with payments to trustees. It is a basic principle of trust law that trustees must not benefit from their trust unless the governing document contains an express power permitting payment, or payment has been authorised by the Charity Commission or the Court. Reimbursing genuine expenses does not produce a benefit for the trustee, it merely prevents them from being worse off as a result of their trusteeship. However, any form of remuneration is a benefit and is therefore a breach of trust unless explicitly authorised by the governing document, the Charity Commission or the Court. If a trustee has received an improper payment or benefit they can be required to repay the amount received to the charity or, if the benefit was in goods or kind, a sum equivalent to the value of the benefit received.

47.12 Some governing documents permit trustees from certain professions, such as solicitors or accountants, to be paid for providing professional services to the charity. In some instances the Charity Commission will authorise payments to trustees for professional services when this is not explicitly allowed in the governing document. The services rendered must be of a professional nature and not just assistance with the general administration of the charity. If a trustee is to benefit in this way the other trustees should consider whether or not it is truly in the best interests of the charity to use that particular person or firm. The discussion should be minuted and the minute should make it clear that the person concerned was not present for that part of the meeting and, if required to do so, had declared their interest.

47.13 The restrictions on paying trustees apply not just to individuals but also to businesses which the trustee owns, or in which the trustee is a partner or has a substantial share holding, or of which the trustee is the managing director. Many governing documents include a clause which prohibits the charity from entering into contracts with a company in which a trustee owns shares amounting to 1% or more of the voting rights.

47.14 Trustees of charitable trusts and associations who are solicitors may ask their partners to undertake paid professional work for the charity, however it must be clear that it is the partner or partners personally that are being hired and not the firm. It is likely that the firm's own governing document will not permit any partner to receive a personal benefit from work undertaken in the firm's time and using its facilities.

47.15 Trustees of charitable companies are under a statutory obligation to disclose their interest in any contract or piece of work from which they might profit. [*Companies Act 1985 s 317*]. The governing documents or codes of practice of some unincorporated charities also require trustees to disclose any conflicts of interest. If the governing document of a charitable company permits trustees to be paid, either for their work as directors of a charitable company or for work that they do for the charity, a copy of their service contract or a memorandum setting out the terms of their remuneration must be kept and must be available to company members. Any form of remuneration paid to trustees must be disclosed in the charity's annual accounts.

47.16 Trustees who receive a fee for acting on the board of directors of their charity's wholly owned, non-charitable, trading subsidiary may keep the fee if the governing document of the charity explicitly allows this, or if they have applied to the Charity Commission and been granted authority to keep the fee. Otherwise they must pay the fee to the charity.

Payments to members

47.17 Members of charities who are not trustees may receive remuneration provided this is not prohibited by the governing document.

48 Fees

Trading

48.1 Charities can trade, charging fees for goods or services, provided that this is part of their primary purpose or ancillary to their primary purpose. For example, a charitable theatre company can charge admission to its shows and it could also sell refreshments to patrons attending shows. Similarly, a charity training people with learning disabilities to garden could charge a fee if the beneficiaries provided a gardening service. Profits from primary purpose trading or ancillary trading will be free from corporation tax, but in some circumstances the charity will have to charge VAT on the goods or services it provides.

Paid to employees

48.2 As a matter of good practice contracts of employment should specify whether any remuneration an employee receives for work undertaken on behalf of the employer, either in the employer's time or in the employee's time, or arising out directly from the employment, for example, a fee for writing an article or taking part in a televised discussion, can be retained by the employee or must be given to the employer.

Setting up a charity

48.3 Neither the Charity Commission nor the Inland Revenue currently charge a fee for registering or recognising a charity, though the *Charities Act 1993 s 85* gives the Charity Commission power to charge a fee. However, solicitors' fees for drafting the governing document could well amount to several hundred pounds. If the charity is incorporated a registration fee will have to be paid to Companies House or the Registrar of Friendly Societies (about £900). The registration fee for an industrial and provident society will be lower if model rules from a promoting body, for example, the National Housing Federation, are used (around £100 if no amendments are made or around £300 if up to six minor amendments are made).

49 Friendly Societies

49.1 A minority of charities are formed as friendly societies. These are often confused with industrial and provident societies, which have similar rules. Both are represented in the *Friendly and Industrial and Provident Societies Act 1968*. However, friendly societies have distinct legislation which is generally unfamiliar because of the relatively small number of charitable friendly societies — in 1996 there were only 72 benevolent friendly societies in existence. This unfamiliarity has been exacerbated by the changes brought about by the *Friendly Societies Act 1992* which ended the formation of new charitable friendly societies, and by the general trend for charities who wish to be incorporated to set themselves up as limited companies.

Registration and regulation

49.2 There are two registration areas: Scotland, and the rest of the UK, known as the central registration area. The administration and registration functions of the Registrar are carried out in London and Edinburgh.

49.3 *The Financial Services and Markets Act 2000* disbanded the Friendly Societies Commission and gave its regulatory powers to the Financial Services Authority. The Authority protects friendly societies and their funds and ensures that they comply with the *Friendly Societies Act 1992* provisions.

Types of friendly society

49.4 Since February 1993, friendly societies can only be incorporated under the *Friendly Societies Act 1992* for purposes defined in *Sch 2*. These purposes are not charitable, comprising mainly long-term insurance business and general insurance business. However, before that date friendly societies could be established for other purposes:

- genuine friendly or mutual assurance societies;
- cattle insurance societies;
- benevolent societies established for benevolent or charitable purposes;
- working men's clubs;
- specially authorised societies approved by the Treasury which undertake activities such as the promotion of science, literature and fine arts;
- old people's home societies.

49.5 Some benevolent friendly societies, old people's home societies and specially authorised societies will be charitable. Those that are classified as exempt charities cannot register with the Charity Commission, though, prior to 1 February 1993, they could register voluntarily. As exempt charities the parts of the *Charities Act 1993* relating to accounts, audit and property transactions are broadly disapplied. However, the fund-raising provisions under the *Charities Act 1992* apply fully to benevolent societies. Benevolent friendly societies are eligible for all the tax reliefs and other benefits of charitable status if their purpose is wholly charitable and they are for public benefit. Their status is usually a matter for negotiation with the Inland Revenue. Specially authorised societies, of which there were 131 in 1996, may exist for charitable or non-charitable purposes.

Constitution

49.6 A benevolent friendly society has to have certain rules which are prescribed by legislation, setting out its name, registered office, its objects, meeting and voting procedures, how the committee of management (the trustee body) is appointed and removed, investment powers, accounting and audit arrangements, how the books may be inspected, dispute procedures and how the rules may be amended. A general meeting must be held at least every fifteen months. The committee must comprise at least two members, and the act stipulates provisions for the age of members, appointment, co-option and retirement. There must also be a chief executive and a secretary, though the roles can be fulfilled by one person. The chief executive should have the requisite knowledge and experience to discharge his duties, and any changes in this appointment should be notified to the Registrar within 28 days.

49.7 A friendly society may have trustees appointed to hold property and to act in other situations where an unincorporated body cannot reasonably act. This is not the same as taking responsibility for the management and administration of the charity.

49.8 Branches have particular significance in friendly societies, which may be registered as such, or may have instead to register as a separate society.

Finances

49.9 Friendly societies have to keep accounting records and maintain an internal control system. The accounting record requirements are very similar to those which apply to charitable limited companies. Auditors must be appointed with similar duties to those set out in the *Companies Act 1985*.

50 Fund-Raising

50.1 Charities depend on a variety of sources for the funding to do their work. The main ones are:

- endowments;
- legacies;
- public donations;
- public appeals;
- grants from trusts, local authorities or The National Lottery;
- contracts with statutory and other bodies;
- fees for services;
- special events e.g. coffee mornings, jumble sales, concerts, gala balls;
- raffles and lotteries;
- direct mail;
- sponsorship; and
- primary purpose and ancillary trading.

50.2 In addition to these, charities may also obtain funding by recovering income or corporation tax paid on donations, from the profits of their trading subsidiaries, and from investment income.

50.3 While the public may regard all the above means of income generation as forms of fund-raising, the law draws a distinction between fund-raising and trading. Sometimes the distinction is hard to make, but it is important that the charity administrator does so, or seeks advice, because of the charity law and tax implications.

Fund-raising or trading?

50.4 Fund-raising is defined as raising money for charity in a manner that does not amount to trading. Trading is defined fully in a separate section (see Chapter 112), but in summary, for an activity to be considered as trading it must meet at least one of the main 'badges' of trade.

- There must be repetition.
- There must be a profit motive.
- There must be an identifiable selling organisation or mechanism (e.g. a catalogue).
- Items are acquired for the purpose of being re-sold e.g. Christmas cards, pens, mugs, etc.

50.5 The following examples illustrate the difference between fund-raising and trading.

- The sale of tickets to an annual fireworks party is fund-raising, provided the event is not held by the same charity more than three times a year in the same locality, even though the event is held regularly and there is a profit motive.

- The sale of Christmas cards is trading because:
  - there is repetition — the cards are sold over a period of weeks;
  - there is a profit motive;
  - there is a selling organisation — the cards are sold by charity shops and commercial retailers, at Christmas fairs and through catalogues; and
  - the cards are purchased with the intention of selling them.
- The sale of tickets for concerts put on by a charitable school to raise money for the school building fund is fund-raising if the concerts are held occasionally, but trading if they are held more than three times a year.
- The sale of tickets for a play performed by a charitable theatre company is primary purpose trading. Primary purpose, because the charity exists to educate the public by the performance of plays and trading because:
  - there is repetition;
  - there is a selling organisation;
  - the service is of a commercial nature (people do not attend largely in order to support the charity); and
  - there may be a profit motive, though it would not be necessary to prove this as there are already sufficient grounds to classify the activity as trading.

Regulation of fund-raising

50.6 Every charity fund-raising scandal has an impact on the public's willingness to support charities. Regulation is therefore an important way of ensuring that the public is confident that money given to charity will reach its intended destination. When John Major introduced the *1992 Charities Act* he commented that one of the Act's main aims was to open wider the floodgates of giving by ensuring even greater public confidence in charities. *Part II* of the *1992 Act* deals with the control of fund-raising and *Part III* with public charitable collections. Both *Part II* and *Part III* apply to all registered charities, to exempt and excepted charities and to charitable institutions, i.e. institutions established for charitable, benevolent or philanthropic purposes. An institution established under the laws of another country could qualify as long as its objects were charitable in English law.

50.7 *Sections 58–64* of the Act deal with professional fund-raisers in order to protect both charities and the public from unscrupulous fund-raisers, and with commercial participators, so that when the public is encouraged to buy a certain product or service on the grounds that the purchase will benefit a charity, they are given access to certain basic information about by how much the charity will actually benefit (see Chapter 23 for more information about commercial participators). *Sections 65–71* deal with public charitable collections. It was the then Government's intention to introduce new regulations controlling public collections, such as house-to-house collections and street collections but at the time of writing no new regulations have yet been introduced. For more information about public charitable collections see Chapter 88.

Professional fund-raisers

50.8 *Section 58* of the *Charities Act 1992* defines professional fund-raisers as 'any person. . .who carries on a fund-raising business' or 'any other person. . .who for reward solicits money or other property for the benefit of a charitable institution'. At first sight a charity's own subsidiary trading company could be said to come within this definition. However, trading subsidiaries wholly owned by charities are exempted from the regulations. Examples of professional fund-raisers would be:

- persons who agree to raise money for an appeal for an arts centre in return for a fixed percentage of the sum raised;
- someone who agrees to organise a fund-raising pop concert in return for an agreed fee;
- covenant renewal agencies; or
- telephone appeal companies.

50.9 The regulations require there to be a written agreement between a professional fund-raiser and a charity containing the following:

- the name and address of the parties to the agreement;
- the date on which the agreement was signed by each of those parties;
- the period or duration of the agreement; and
- any terms enabling the agreement to be brought to an end prematurely or altered during the period of the agreement.

50.10 In addition, the agreement must contain the following.

- A statement of the principal objectives for the fund-raising and the methods to be used in the pursuit of those objectives.
- If more than one charitable institution is party to the agreement, the proportions in which each charitable institution is respectively to benefit under the agreement.
- Details of the amount and the methods of calculation of expenses and remuneration to be paid to the professional fund-raiser under the terms of the agreement.

Exemptions

50.11 As mentioned above, a charity's own charity subsidiary is exempted from the definition of a professional fund-raiser and there are also exemptions for:

- charitable institutions e.g. Children in Need;
- companies connected with charitable institutions e.g. Cards for Christmas, a charitable institution that co-ordinates the sale of Christmas cards for a number of charities;
- low paid workers e.g. someone paid a nominal sum of £5 a day, plus expenses, or less than £500 per year for 'rattling' a collecting tin in the street or organising a fund-raising event;
- collectors e.g. collectors or agents paid by professional fund-raisers to solicit funds do not themselves become professional fund-raisers;
- celebrities e.g. well-known people who make an appeal on behalf of a charitable institution on television, radio or in the cinema, even if they receive a fee from the charity or a professional fund-raiser.

Using a professional fund-raiser

50.12 Employing a professional fund-raiser can be the most cost-effective way of raising funds. However, trustees should think carefully before engaging a professional fund-raiser, because the public can be hostile to the idea of someone making a profit from fund-raising. They need to check whether or not:

- employing a professional fund-raiser is essential to achieve their aims;
- all other feasible and less expensive methods of fund-raising have been explored; and
- using the charity's own staff or volunteers would be more effective.

50.13 If the services of a professional fund-raiser are considered necessary then the charity administrator should:

- take advice from the Institute of Charity Fundraising Managers;
- put the assignment out to tender;
- prepare a proper form of agreement under the regulations;
- be clear about all the terms in the agreement; and
- look at proper security arrangements to make sure that the risk of wrongdoing such as fraud are minimised.

Breaches of the regulations

50.14 If a professional fund-raiser solicits money for the benefit of a charitable institution without a written agreement, the court may, at the request of the charitable institution, grant an injunction. Agreements that do not comply with the *s 59* requirements are enforceable only to the extent as may be provided by a court order.

50.15 Professional fund-raisers who breach the *Charities Act 1992 s 60* by failing to indicate one of the following are committing a criminal offence and can be subject to a fine of up to £5,000:

- which charities will benefit;
- how the fund-raisers remuneration will be determined;
- that donors who give more than £50 in response to a telephone appeal must be given notice that they have a right to cancel the donation within seven days of receiving the notification of the right to cancel;
- that donors who give more than £50 in response to a radio or TV appeal by credit or debit card have a right to a refund if they give written notice within seven days of the broadcast.

Fund-raising appeals

50.16 When a charity appeals for money the purpose of the appeal should be clearly stated. If the appeal is for general funds then it should be clear to the reader that any specific project described in the appeal literature is only an example of the type of work carried out by the charity. If the appeal is for a specific project then the appeal literature must make clear what will happen to any surplus funds raised or what will happen to money raised if, after a considerable period of time, insufficient funds have been raised to undertake the particular project, for example to repair a church spire. If this is not done then in the event of an insufficient amount of money being raised the trustees must return money given by identifiable donors. Money put into collection boxes or raised at jumble sales or by competitions can be regarded as given by unidentifiable donors. If an appeal raises more money than is required and the appeal did not specify what would happen to any surplus funds then the trustees must write to the Charity Commission for advice on whether a Scheme will be needed to enable the money to be spent on other charitable purposes.

50.17 Funds raised for a special appeal should be accounted for separately as a restricted fund.

Fund-raising for other charities

50.18 If a local charity raises funds for another charity by acting as a fund-raising agent any literature should make clear which charity the funds raised will benefit. The collecting charity must be certain that the beneficiary organisation is a registered charity before making any claims to that effect. Failure to do so could be an offence under *section 63* of the *Charities Act 1992*.

50.19 The collecting charity will only be able to contribute to the costs of fund-raising if the purpose for which funds are being raised comes within the collecting charity's charitable objects. For example, a local breast cancer charity could use some of its funds to raise funds for a national breast cancer charity but could not use its funds to raise funds for a local environmental charity.

50.20 The collecting charity should seek the beneficiary charity's prior consent to the use of its name and should allow the beneficiary charity to approve any fund-raising method or literature that will be used. Funds raised will belong to the beneficiary charity, not the collecting charity.

Fund-raising for health service bodies or local authorities

50.21 If a charity agrees to raise funds for capital equipment or buildings the appeal will have fulfilled its charitable objects once the equipment or buildings have been provided. Donors will then have no control of the future use or sale of the equipment or buildings. Therefore to protect the intentions of the donors and their own integrity charities should consider having a legal agreement drawn up that specifies the terms on which the appeal funds will be transferred and places restrictions on the future use of the equipment or buildings for which they have raised funds.

Broadcast appeals

50.22 The Broadcast Appeals Consortium has issued a code of conduct and general guidance for charities and broadcasters. Broadcast appeals should not be misleading in any way about a charity's activities or how the money being appealed for will be used. They must deal with the topic sensitively, respecting the dignity of the potential beneficiaries, and not exaggerate the degree of need. Comparisons with other charities should not be made and fund-raising messages should not be addressed specifically to children.

Chain letters

50.23 These are not prohibited by law, although the Charity Commission has expressed concern about charities using chain letters as a method of fund-raising (Report of the Charity Commissioners 1991 and 1993). Once started they are difficult to stop and if they reach their target the charity could then be in the position of misleading the public. The Institute of Charity Fundraising Managers also advises against the use of chain letters. If a chain letter is used to raise money for a charity the letter must state the name of the charity. If the charity is registered and has an income of over £10,000 a year, the fact that the charity is registered must be on every copy of the letter.

Competitions

50.24 A competition must involve skill that is not at so low a level that almost every entrant could win, i.e. a competition is not the same as a lottery. Competitions are not subject to any specific legislation, but must comply with the British Codes of Advertising and Sales Promotion. Entry fees for competitors may be subject to VAT and the proceeds to corporation tax.

Direct mail

50.25 If a charity raises funds through direct mail and keeps information about donors on computer it must register under the *Data Protection Act 1984*. All direct mailings should comply with the rules on list and database practice issued by the Advertising Standards Authority and, if appropriate, the rules on distance selling.

Telephone fund-raising

50.26 If a commercial company undertakes telephone fund-raising for a charity it will be acting as a professional fund-raiser and must therefore have a written agreement with the charity in accordance with *Part II* of the *Charities Act 1992*.

50.27 Telephone fund-raising is an increasingly common and successful means of raising money, but can provoke strong negative reactions in some members of the public. The Institute of Charity Fundraising Managers have produced a code of good practice for telephone fund-raising, for use by charities and professional telephone fund-raising agencies in an attempt to ensure that the method does not fall into disrepute and become illegal. The Code recommends that:

- calls should not be made after 9 pm;
- calls should not be made to people under the age of 16;
- calls should not be made to numbers randomly generated by computers;
- callers should be pleasant and honest and accept termination of the call without argument;
- callers must give their name and the name of the charity on whose behalf they are calling;
- callers must state that the purpose of the call is to raise support; and
- if asked, callers who are deemed to be acting for professional fund-raisers should supply the name of the professional fund-raising agency and the cost to the charity of each call.

Challenge events

50.28 Overseas adventure treks and bike rides in which participants have to raise a minimum amount of sponsorship have become a popular way of raising funds in the last few years, particularly as they also generate publicity for the charity and often lead to long-term relationships between the charity and participants. They are also challenging for fund-raising departments for a number of reasons:

- they are not package tours but package tour regulations may apply;
- participants are volunteers, but depending on the cost of the challenge, the professional fundraiser regulations may apply; and
- money raised is a donation, but because participants get something in return there are tax and VAT implications.

Professional advice is likely to be needed by any charity organising such an event for the first time.

50.29 The Department of Trade and Industry (DTI) takes the view that if transport and accommodation are provided for participants a challenge event falls within the scope of the *Package Travel, Package Holidays and Package Tours Regulations 1992 (SI 1992 No 3288)*. These regulations set out requirements that will need to be followed when drawing up contracts between the charity and the participants, when designing brochures and when giving information before travel.

50.30 The Civil Aviation Authority (CAA) takes the view that if flights are provided, the flight arrangements must by protected by an Air Travel Organiser's Licence (ATOL bond). The licence holder must lodge bond money with the CAA, so in the event of the airline becoming insolvent, the bond can be used to reimburse anyone unable to travel because of the organiser's failure and to repatriate anyone overseas at the time of the failure.

50.31 Therefore charities or their trading subsidiaries must either have an ATOL bond or must act as the agent for an ATOL holder.

50.32 The Inland Revenue may regard any fee paid by participants and the sponsorship donations they collect as trading income because the participant gets a benefit from taking part in the event. The scale of most challenge events is such that they do not qualify for the tax concessions that apply to small-scale fund-raising events. If an outside organiser runs the challenge event and contracts to give the charity a donation no liability to tax on the amount raised arises. However, in most instances the organiser will want to use the charity's name and logo in promoting the event so the Inland Revenue will treat the donation as taxable income. Therefore most charities structure challenge events through their trading subsidiary.

50.33 Charities also have to consider if their challenge events fall within the Tour Operators Margin Scheme (TOMS) for VAT purposes. TOMS applies to anyone who buys in and sells travel facilities for the direct benefit of the traveller. TOMS means that a charity will have to relate all the direct purchases relating to the event (travel, accommodation, tour guides, etc.) to the sums received in order to calculate the gross profit margin. No VAT can be recovered on the direct purchases. However, events outside the EU are zero-rated so VAT paid on indirect purchases can be recovered.

Face-to-face donor recruitment

50.34 Face-to-face donor recruitment, in which teams of paid, usually young, fund-raisers, clipboard in hand, approach people in the street and talk to them about the charity they are recruiting for, is another fund-raising method that has become popular in recent years. Like telephone fund-raising, it is unpopular with many people but is very successful at recruiting people under 40 who are not already supporting a charity. The Institute of Charity Fundraising Managers has issued a code of practice on what is referred to as 'personal solicitation for committed gifts'. It has also drawn up a draft donors' rights charter and an accompanying complaints procedure.

Fund-raising events

50.35 Charities organise a wide variety of fund-raising events from gala balls to bingo nights, sponsored walks to bungee jumps, teddy bears picnics to hunger lunches. No matter how worthy the cause these events must comply with relevant legislation. Organisations may need to seek advice on the following.

- Is consent required from the police or local authority?
- If food is to be served, what food hygiene regulations will apply?
- If alcohol is to be served, what are the licensing arrangements?
- Is the charity's insurance adequate to cover any liabilities arising from accidents, cancellations by celebrities, rain, etc.?
- If there is to be a raffle does it need to be registered with the local authority or the Gaming Board?
- What are the tax and VAT implications?
- Can sponsorship be obtained to cover the costs?
- Have the local media been informed, particularly the local newspapers?

Further information

50.36 Fund-raising is a complex area as charity administrators have to take into account not just charity law, but a wide range of other legislation and there are often complex tax and VAT issues that require professional advice if the charity is to take maximum advantage of the various concessions. Information on the direct tax and VAT implications of fund-raising are given in Chapters 28, 46, 108, 117 and 121. Further advice can be obtained from the Institute of Charity Fundraising Managers and there are a number of excellent books on the subject including Tolley's Fund-Raising for Charities.

51 Funds

51.1 The funds of a charity are not simply its cash balances, nor are they necessarily limited to those funds managed by investment or fund managers. The funds are the unexpended balances that represent the wealth of the organisation, including investments and cash, less its liabilities. The funds may be analysed into differing types, as described below, and comprise individual funds or trusts. Certain types of funds retained by a charity or its subsidiary are subject to trust law, which is a complex area often requiring legal advice.

51.2 In day-to-day terms it is important to understand the types of fund operated by a charity in order to understand what resources are available to spend, and for what purpose they may be expended. The definition of the funds therefore has implications for the whole financial management of the charity and will also have bearing on matters such as the internal control procedures and any computerised accounting system selected. Before considering these implications it is important to clarify the types of fund a charity may have.

Types of fund

Restricted funds

51.3 Restricted funds are funds which are subject to specific trusts, either declared by the donor when making the donation or accepted by the donor in responding to a specific appeal, for example to restore or repair a church spire or to help people in the aftermath of a natural disaster. Restricted funds may be restricted income funds, which are expendable at the discretion of the trustees in line with the nature of the fund, or restricted capital funds, where the fund has to be retained either permanently or for some fixed period of time or until some specific event occurs. In practice the terms 'restricted income fund' and 'restricted capital fund' are little used. Restricted income funds tend to be known simply as 'restricted funds', and restricted capital funds as 'endowment funds'. This convention is followed hereafter in this chapter.

51.4 A restricted fund exists to be applied for a particular purpose, usually defined either by a function or a geographical factor. A gift given to be used in a specified period of time is not a restricted fund on the basis of the time restriction alone. If the charity can legally use the funds immediately on whatever it chooses then the income is simply unrestricted. If the income cannot be used immediately it is deferred as a liability until the relevant future period.

51.5 The latest SORP clarifies that where funds are provided for fixed assets, the trustees' obligations, and the accounting treatment, will vary. Sometimes the trustees may be required to hold the asset on trust for a specific purpose, on other occasions trustees may have discharged their obligations simply by acquiring the asset. By extension, a gift of a fixed asset is accorded the same treatment as a gift of money to acquire an asset.

51.6 If a restricted fund represents an asset that will be retained for some time by the charity it is logical to reflect the using up of that asset by amortising the restricted fund value over the expected life of the asset, or even the donor's own expectations of how long the asset can reasonably be regarded as restricted.

51.7 Money given to a charity on condition that, for example, the charity raises matching funds or that someone visits a certain country, is not restricted as such conditions do not create a trust obligation.

51.8 Where restricted funds are held, there is an expectation that they will be applied within a reasonable period. If the fund is not applied reasonably quickly, then it should be invested in order to maintain the fund's value pending application and hopefully add to the fund. In some cases, for instance over the life of a major appeal, it may be appropriate for a separate bank account or investment account to be set up to identify the return earned. There is, however, no requirement to operate a separate new bank account for a restricted fund. The notional interest earned can be calculated and credited to the fund.

51.9 If a charity receives a restricted gift for a purpose which it is unable to meet, either for practical reasons or because using assets in this way would constitute a breach of the charity's governing document, then the fund is not restricted. The gift will need to be returned and the donation becomes a liability pending its repayment.

Endowment funds

51.10 Restricted capital funds or endowment funds, fall into two further categories, permanent endowment and expendable endowment.

Permanent endowment

51.11 A permanent endowment fund is a capital fund where the trustees have no power to convert the capital into income. The fund has to be maintained at its value indefinitely, although the individual assets making up that fund may in some cases be exchanged. For instance, if a portfolio of shares is left to a charity to generate income for supporting the general purposes of the charity then shares making up the portfolio could, in the absence of any express provision to the contrary, be traded to maximise the investment return. On the other hand, an art collection given to a charity as permanent endowment would have to be preserved largely intact. Items within the collection could be loaned, or even swapped or sold provided the purpose was to enhance the collection. The charity could not sell part of the collection merely to raise income.

Expendable endowment

51.12 An expendable endowment fund is a form of capital fund. The trustees are not obliged to spend the fund until it is converted into income. Usually there is a condition attached to the receipt of the fund stating that the trustees cannot initially convert the capital into income, but may do so at some time in the future, perhaps on the happening of a certain event, or after a fixed period of time.

Unrestricted funds

51.13 If no specific terms of trust govern funds they are unrestricted and can be used for any purpose within the objects of the charity, subject to any power of accumulation within the governing document. If they are left as free funds they are usually referred to as the general fund, or accumulated funds. However, if the trustees decide to set aside amounts for particular purposes these funds are known as designated funds.

51.14 Funds

Designated funds

51.14 Designated funds should represent the trustees' genuine intentions. Although the trustees remain free to remove the designation, this should only be done if there was a change in a charity's circumstances, e.g. if a planned new building was no longer required. Funds should not be designated merely to reduce the apparent level of a charity's free reserves.

51.15 If a designation is revoked funds shown as designated in one set of accounts, may be released to general funds in the next set. The SORP permits designated funds to be presented as a separate column on the face of the SOFA, although more usually movements on designated funds are shown exclusively in a note to the accounts.

51.16 In assessing the reasonableness of a charity's reserves levels, funders will take note of the level of designated funds. Assuming that they are reasonable both in nature and in quantum, they will reflect prudent management by the charity. For instance, it would be prudent to set aside income to fund future capital expenditure or to meet redundancy liabilities in local authority funded project-based charities. Although designated funds are easy to create and subsequently remove, it would be imprudent for a charity to use designated funds in order to camouflage excess balances. Unconvincing reasons for setting up designated funds, or transfers and releases of such funds year on year for little apparent purpose, serve only to undermine the credibility of the charity's financial reporting.

Financial management

Internal controls

51.17 A charity which has a surplus on its restricted funds but a deficit on its unrestricted funds is prima facie insolvent. Since the SORP was introduced and charities are presenting their balance sheets according to type of fund, it has become apparent that quite a number are technically insolvent. As charities can only use funds within the attached terms of trust, it is increasingly important for the internal financial controls to distinguish between types of fund received and to record income properly as soon as possible. This means recording receipts according to the type of appeal, and checking accompanying correspondence to ensure that gifts are not simply assumed to be for general purposes.

51.18 Whenever fund-raising literature is being prepared or despatched, then the finance department should be informed. In this way the nature of incoming funds can be understood and properly accounted for. Early discussion may also make it possible to avoid the accidental creation of restricted funds by making it clear that funds received may be used for wider purposes than is the main subject of the appeal. Such additional wording may also be important where an appeal either raises too much money or fails to reach its target. In both cases some money may need to be repaid to the donors.

Management accounting

51.19 Although few charities produce management information in SORP format, much of the information presented in a full set of accounts should be capable of extraction directly from the accounting system. This is because the annual accounts are merely a stylised presentation of matters under the control of the charity's trustees throughout the year. Indeed management accounts will be more detailed in places, for instance most charities do not disclose all their fund analysis by every individual fund due to immateriality, whereas these will all need accounting for within the management information system.

51.20 As a result the management accounting system for charities must accommodate not only the traditional nominal ledger expense analysis (natural costs), and probably cost centre and/or project or departmental analysis, but also fund analysis. This extra dimension to the accounting analysis may need to be done on spreadsheets, as the degree of analysis of each figure may be too time consuming to handle when allocating individual items within the main accounts system itself.

51.21 Whatever system is used, the accounting should also routinely reflect any allocation of income to the funds and also the deduction of any administration costs relating to the fund. If this element of the accounting is not incorporated into the accounting function then the figures presented in the year end accounts, especially on the general funds, may be substantially different to expectations.

51.22 Charities differ in their approach to cost allocation by fund. The need for more or less sophisticated methods will depend on both the nature and volume of the individual restricted funds.

51.23 When restricted funds are represented by grants, it may sometimes be possible for a proportion of administration costs to be charged to each fund on an 'arithmetic' basis. These costs could include management and administration, and the costs associated with obtaining the grant. In other cases it may be more appropriate to operate each fund as a separate entity, with the actual costs associated with each fund deducted from that fund.

Revaluation reserves

51.24 Revalution reserves arise when a fixed asset is valued upwards. They represent the difference between the original cost and the current accounts valuation (carrying value). They are of little significance to trustees except as a means of remembering the historical composition of reserves. However, the *Companies Act 1985* requires them to be separately distinguished in the accounts.

Endowment income and expenditure

51.25 In the past trustees have had to credit endowment funds with capital returns, whilst the income return has been available for the general purposes for which the fund was established. The Charity Commission has recognised that changes in taxation and reward schemes have resulted in investment returns arising in a growing variety of ways that are no longer in line with trust law. As a result of these developments a consultation launched in August 2000 is considering three ways forward:

- the continuation of the current arrangements for the treatment of investment returns from capital funds;
- complete liberalisation so that charities are free to spend or save any of their capital or income;
- a middle way called 'total return' that lumps together all forms of return on investments to produce a 'total return'. Some of this can be used to meet the needs of present beneficiaries while the remainder is added to capital to help meet the needs of future beneficiaries.

51.26 Expenses incurred in the administration, protection or enhancement of an endowment should normally be charged to it, as should any related depreciation or improvement.

52 Governance

52.1 Governing a voluntary organisation is never straightforward. In *Towards Voluntary Sector Codes of Practice* Julian Ashby wrote 'It (governance) is undertaken by volunteers with limited time but all the responsibilities of company directors. It also has to balance the requirements of different stakeholders and maintain an appropriate relationship with staff. It is a role that is not always well understood or carried out effectively'. Other observers of charity boards might be more inclined to write that it is a role that is frequently misunderstood or carried out ineffectively, or in a manner that causes friction with those employed to help, by people with limited time, and in some instances limited competence, some of whom see their role as being to represent the interests of one particular group of stakeholders.

52.2 Most charities are formed by a small group of individuals who see a need in society and decide to do something about it. In the start-up phase of the organisation, this group will do everything from developing the charity's mission and strategy to stuffing envelopes and washing tea towels. They are unlikely to distinguish between governance and management (see Fig 1).

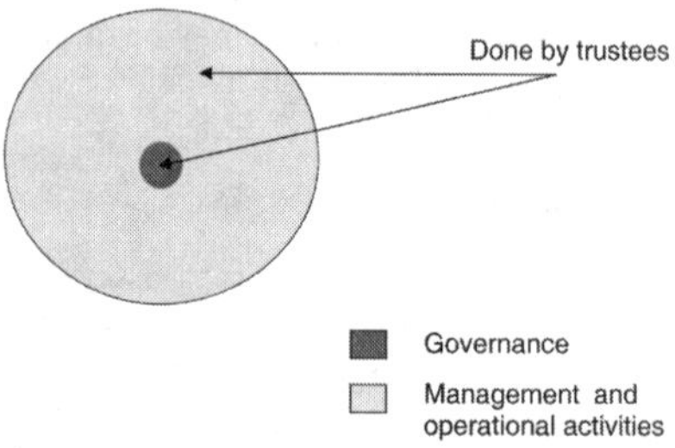

Fig 1: Emerging organisation

52.3 If the charity grows, it is likely to attract more volunteers and eventually start to employ paid staff. At this stage the trustees begin to delegate some of the charity's work and there is a separation of the governance and management roles (see Fig 2).

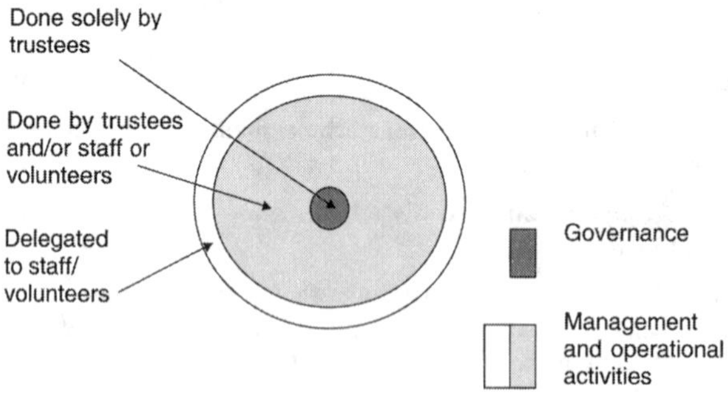

Fig 2: Small to medium-sized organisations

52.4 Finally, in large, professionally staffed organisations, the roles of staff and trustees become largely discrete, with the trustees' role being to govern the charity and the staffs' to implement the trustees' policies and strategy and manage the organisation on a day to day basis as shown in Fig 3.

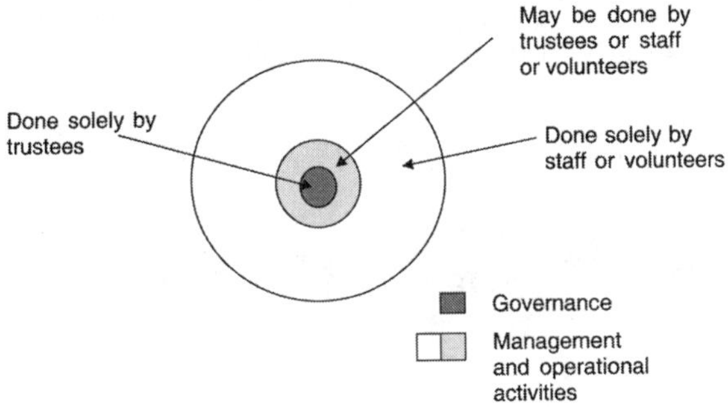

Fig 3: Large organisations with professional staff

52.5 However, the picture presented by some commentators of a complete division between governance and management is oversimplified. They confuse governance with strategic management and limit management to operational management. 'Governance' is not the same as 'management', but neither is it totally discrete. Governance is an integral part of the system by which organisations are managed and controlled. It is too complicated and too dynamic to be reduced to a simple division of labour with trustees 'governing' and staff taking responsibility for day-to-day operational management. Trustees should quite rightly focus most of their attention on issues of governance, such as setting long-term strategy and policy, but from time to time they will have to carry out management tasks, such as appointing, appraising or dismissing members of staff. Similarly, operational matters will be the main focus of the staff's work, but at times they will have a most valuable input into strategic issues. For example staff input will be essential in the strategic planning process.

52.6 There will always be some degree of overlap between governance and management and the key to the successful running of an organisation is how well this overlap is managed by the staff and trustees.

52.7 The Cadbury Committee on corporate governance defined the roles of directors as:

- setting strategic aims;
- providing leadership to put them into effect;
- supervising the management of the business; and
- reporting to the shareholders.

Charity governance is not dissimilar. Trustees must:

- ensure that the charity has purpose and direction;
- ensure that the charity's work has the desired impact on its beneficiaries;
- provide leadership and direct the staff; and
- be accountable to multiple stakeholders.

52.8 Governance

52.8 The key difference, however, between charity and corporate governance is that unlike company directors whose objective it is to bring the greatest benefit to shareholders and who personally benefit from their role, charity trustees, with some exceptions, do not benefit personally from their trusteeship and must always act as stewards for the greater good. They must always act in the best interests of the charity's present and future beneficiaries and must set aside their own personal interests and even their personal ethics, for example in avoiding investments in companies producing or selling certain products, unless such restrictions would further the charity's objects.

53 Governing Document

53.1 The document that sets out the purpose for which a charity is established and how it is to be operated is known as the 'governing document' or the 'governing instrument'. The format of this document will vary according to the legal status of the charity, the most usual being:

- the memorandum and articles of association, if the charity is a company;
- a trust deed, a declaration of trust, or a will, if the charity is a trust;
- a constitution or rules, if the charity is an unincorporated association; or
- rules, if the charity is an industrial and provident society.

In addition to the above, some charities will have been set up by Royal Charter or Act of Parliament.

53.2 Trustees and senior staff should know and understand their governing document because it is arguably the charity's most important document, setting out its aims or charitable objects, its rules and the trustees' powers. All trustees should be given a copy of the charity's governing document as soon as they are elected or appointed, as they have a legal obligation to ensure that everything the organisation does complies with it and it provides the framework for everything the charity does. If the governing document is written in language that is difficult to understand, the trustees should also be given a 'plain English' version.

53.3 A charity's governing document sets out the terms of the trust between the charity's donors/funders, the trustees and the beneficiaries. For charitable unincorporated associations, companies and industrial and provident societies the governing document is a type of contract, enforceable in the courts.

53.4 Professional advice is usually needed in drafting a governing document. However, both the Charity Commission and the Charity Law Association have produced model governing documents for English and Welsh charities and the Scottish Council for Voluntary Organisations has produced model documents for Scottish charities. These can be adapted to meet the requirements of particular charities, thus saving the expense of drafting a document from scratch.

53.5 A good governing document will be drafted in such a way that the objects are sufficiently broad to encompass not only what the charity does at present but also what it might expand to do in the future. It should be written in plain English and be reasonably comprehensive, setting out the rules and procedures that are likely to be needed. It is advisable to include a power of amendment.

53.6 While the format of the governing document varies according to an organisation's legal status, most will include details of the charity's:

- name and location;
- objects;
- powers, including any powers to amend the governing document;
- membership;
- governing body, including method of appointment and indemnification;
- meetings, including quorum, procedures, minutes;

- audit requirements;
- use of the seal;
- dissolution.

Powers

53.7 Charities are strictly speaking only allowed to engage in activities that are directly related to their objects. So a charity established to provide a helpline for people suffering from bereavement can operate a telephone helpline, but may not be able to employ staff, open a bank account, lease premises, etc., as these activities do not directly relieve the suffering of the bereaved, but are merely a means to that end. Charities need powers to undertake these 'means' activities. Some powers will be given by statute or implied, others will be express powers or included in a general catch-all power.

Statutory powers

53.8 Statutory powers are those given under statute, such as the powers charities are given to undertake certain property transactions in the *Charities Act 1993*. Other statutory powers are given to a type of organisation, and therefore apply to all organisations of that type, charitable or otherwise. For example, charitable companies do not need an explicit power of amendment in their governing document because all companies have been granted this power under the *Companies Act 1985 ss 4, 9, 17*. A charity's governing document can extend a statutory power, for example, to give a charity wider powers of investment than it would otherwise have, or it may restrict a statutory power, for example, narrowing a charitable company's power to amend its governing document.

Implied powers

53.9 Implied powers are those a court would find necessary for an organisation to have in order for it to achieve its charitable objects, such as the power to open a bank account. They can be exercised even when they are not explicit in statute, or in the charity's governing document.

Express powers

53.10 Express powers are those explicitly stated in the charity's governing document because they do not exist under statute and are not so intrinsic to the achievement of the charity's objects that they can be implied. Examples are powers allowing charitable funds to be used to purchase trustee indemnity insurance, and powers to delegate investment fund management.

General powers

53.11 Most governing documents will also include a general, catch-all power, such as 'the power to take any action that the trustees see fit to achieve the charity's charitable objects'. This will enable the organisation to develop its work in the future without having frequently to redraft its governing document or go to the Charity Commission for a Scheme. However, the proposed action must be:

- lawful;
- not one for which an explicit power is needed;
- not explicitly prohibited by the governing document; and
- one which comes within the wording of the general power.

53.12 It is possible for trustees to unintentially commit a breach of trust by assuming that their catch-all clause allows anything lawful. For example, some trustees have invested all their assets in equities, assuming that the catch-all clause in their governing document allows them to do so. However, if they do not have explicit wider powers of investment in their governing document they are constrained by the *Trustee Investment Act 1961* which stipulates that no more than 75% of the portfolio can be invested in equities.

Powers relating to money

53.13 Most governing documents will include the power to raise funds and to invite and receive contributions. If this power is not explicit it could be included under a general power or implied. Some governing documents will prohibit the charity from engaging in substantial non-primary purpose trading. Again, most governing documents will include the power to operate a bank account and carry out financial transactions, though this power could be implied if it is not explicit. Raising money through loans or other forms of borrowing requires an explicit power, as does using charitable funds to pay for trustee indemnity insurance. Where there is a statutory obligation to do something, such as to take out employers' liability insurance, the charity does not require a specific power.

Powers relating to property

53.14 If a charity is ever likely to occupy premises, its governing document should contain clauses allowing the trustees powers to buy, sell, let, exchange, mortgage, build, etc.

Powers relating to employment

53.15 Companies and industrial and provident societies have an implied power to employ staff. This implied power does not extend to unincorporated charities, though it may be covered by a general power if it is not included as a specific power.

Other powers

53.16 Many charities will have specific powers permitting them to carry out activities that are not directly in furtherance of their objects, but are closely related to them. For example they may have powers to conduct and publish research, hold conferences or public meetings, advise other charities or public bodies, or undertake joint activities with other organisations whose objects are included in their own.

Conflict of interest

53.17 Some governing documents contain clauses relating to potential conflicts of interest. For example, they may include a clause excluding people from becoming trustees if they have certain types of relationship with a member or members of the charity's staff, or they may explicitly allow users of the charity's services to become trustees subject to certain conditions.

Membership

53.18 If the charity has a membership the governing document will usually describe the various classes of membership, eligibility for membership, rights, responsibilities and benefits of membership, the rights of members to resign and the rights of the charity to terminate an individual's membership.

53.19 If the governing document merely states that these matters can be determined by the members at a general meeting or by the trustees, these decisions become known as the charity's 'rules' or 'standing orders'.

Meetings

53.20 Membership charities will have clauses in their governing document relating to the requirements for annual general meetings, including the notice which must be given, the quorum, the business which must be conducted, how voting will take place, the majority required to pass a resolution, etc. The governing document will also contain the procedures for holding general, special or extraordinary meetings.

Governing body

53.21 The governing document usually sets out:

- the names of the first members of the governing body;
- the maximum and minimum of people who can form the governing body;
- criteria of eligibility for membership of the governing body;
- the method of selection, election or appointment;
- the length of term of appointment;
- any limits placed on the number of consecutive terms that can be served;
- procedures for resignation;
- how casual vacancies are filled;
- the powers of the governing body, including powers of delegation;
- the frequency at which the governing body meets;
- the quorum and procedures for meetings.

53.22 It may also specify that honorary officers should be appointed or elected. These will normally be a chairperson, vice-chairperson and honorary treasurer but in some instances there will also be an honorary secretary.

53.23 If the governing document gives the trustees powers to delegate to sub-committees it will often include details of how the sub-committees are to be composed, i.e. exclusively of trustees, or by a mixture of trustee and non-trustee members.

The seal

53.24 The governing documents of many incorporated charities and of some unincorporated charities that have an incorporated trustee board include directions on reporting the use of the seal. The seal is a stamping device used to show that an incorporated body has entered into a legally binding agreement. Industrial and provident societies are required to have a seal. Companies and incorporated trustee bodies are no longer required to have a seal, but may continue to use one if they so wish.

Bank accounts

53.25 Some governing documents include clauses setting out:

- that all bank accounts in which the charity's money is lodged must be in the name of the charity;
- which bank the charity is to bank with;
- how many signatories there must be to the charity's account;
- how many signatures are required for each transaction; and
- who the signatories can be, e.g. at least one must be a trustee.

Audit and accounts

53.26 The governing document may stipulate:

- the types of financial records that must be kept;
- the types of accounts that must be prepared; and
- the way in which the accounts must be audited.

Frequently the governing document will contain a requirement for a full audit even though this may not be required by statute.

Property and insurance

53.27 Provisions relating to the use, upkeep and insurance of property and other assets are frequently contained in a charity's governing document.

Indemnification

53.28 The governing document should include a clause to the effect that if trustees act prudently, lawfully and in accordance with their governing document then any liabilities they incur as trustees can be met from the charity's resources. It may also add that trustees will not be held responsible for the wrongful actions of staff or agents provided that they have exercised proper care in their appointment and supervision.

Branches

53.29 Where a charity has a branch structure the governing document often includes the rules governing relationships between the main charity and its branches. The governing document should make it clear whether the branches are autonomous or controlled by, and part of, the main charity.

Amendment

53.30 Charitable companies frequently do not have an explicit power of amendment in the governing document, because they have this power under company law. An Industrial and Provident Society's rules must include provision for amendment under the *Industrial and Provident Societies Act 1965 1 Sch 5*. It is an advantage for trusts and unincorporated associations to include a power of amendment in their governing document, as it will save them from having to apply to the Charity Commission for a Scheme should they wish to amend their governing document or to Inland Revenue Charities (Scotland) (formerly FICO) in the case of Scottish charities. All charities, even those with statutory powers of amendment, are required to obtain the Charity Commission's consent to amendments to their governing document relating to the charity's objects, powers of amendment and dissolution. Unincorporated charities may have a power to sell or mortgage property, but in some circumstances will also require the Charity Commission's consent before doing so.

Small charities — alteration of trusts

53.31 *Section 74* of the *Charities Act 1993* enables some small charities to alter their trusts so that they can use their income and capital in more appropriate or effective ways. *Section 74* applies to charities that are neither exempt from registration with the Charity Commission nor charitable companies and that:

- do not have gross income of more than £5,000 in their last financial year;
- do not hold any land on trust that require the land to be used for any particular purpose, or purposes, of the charity.

Dissolution

53.32 The governing document should specify what happens to any remaining assets if the charity is wound up or dissolved and has met all its financial obligations.

Standard governing documents

53.33 The Charity Commission recommends that standard governing documents should only be used by branches of, or organisations affiliated to, certain bodies, namely:

- Age Concern
- Amateur Dramatic Societies
- Arts Associations (Arts Council models)
- Assemblies of God
- Boys Clubs
- Childminding Association
- Choirs
- Church Preservation Trusts
- Citizens Advice Bureaux
- Civic Amenity Societies
- Community associations (suitable for community centres)
- Councils for Voluntary Service
- Crossroads Care Attendant Schemes
- Gateways
- Homestart
- Hospital League of Friends
- Independent School Trusts
- Inner Wheel Club Benevolent Funds
- Institute of Advanced Motorists (Local Groups)

- Interchange
- Lions Club Charity Trust Fund
- Local Building Preservation Trusts
- Masonic Lodge Benevolent Funds
- Mind
- National Playing Fields Association
- NCVO
- Out of School Schemes
- Parent Teacher Associations: Area Confederations, C of E Voluntary Aided Schools, Girls Public Day School Trusts
- Pre-School Playgroup
- Relate
- Rotary Club Trust Funds
- Round Table Charitable Funds
- Royal Antediluvian Order of Buffaloes: Minor Lodge Benevolent Funds, Provincial Grand Lodge Benevolent Fund
- Rural Community Councils (County or District)
- School Fund (NAHT)
- School Funds (Secondary Heads Association)
- Scope (Affiliated Groups)
- Scouts
- Third Age Trust
- Toy Library: General, Handicapped Children
- United Trusts Services
- Victim Support Schemes
- Village Hall (ACRE)
- Women's Institutes
- YMCA
- Young Farmers' Clubs
- Youth Clubs
- Youth Hostel Association

54 Grant Making

Gifts not contracts

54.1 A grant is essentially a gift. The donor has no right to receive anything in return from the charity except perhaps a simple acknowledgement. If a recipient has to provide the donor with something in exchange for the 'grant', the donor is contracting with the recipient, not giving a grant. As the giving of a grant does not create a contract, the recipient's right to a grant cannot be enforced in the courts. The donor can, however, attach terms and conditions to a grant, for example stipulating what it must be spent on, though usually this is specified by the potential recipient in their grant application. No matter who sets the terms and conditions, grants can only be used for the purpose for which they were given. If they are spent in any other way the donor can require the grant to be repaid, or take action for breach of trust.

54.2 Grants are discretionary payments, so they can be withdrawn or changed by the donor at any time and the recipient has no recourse in law. However, as a matter of good practice a grant-making organisation should not agree to give a grant without being sure that it has the resources to honour its promise and if a recipient fails to satisfy the conditions of a grant those making the grant should attempt to find out why this has happened before they cut off further funding.

Tax treatment

54.3 One-off payments by charities to individuals, for example to purchase essential clothing or a cooker, are treated as donations and there are no tax consequences for the individual or the charity. Regular payments, such as a pension from a charitable benevolent fund, are treated as income and the recipient may have to pay income tax if their total income exceeds their personal allowance. Scholarships are an exception to this rule as they are not generally taxed as income. [*Income and Corporation Taxes Act 1988 s 331*]. However, if a company sets up an educational trust to provide scholarships for the children of its employees, the scholarships will be regarded as a benefit for employees and the employees will be taxed on it.

54.4 If the recipient of a regular payment made by a charity is receiving income related welfare benefits, extra care should be taken to ensure that the charity's funds are actually benefiting the recipient, and do not merely result in the recipient's benefits being cut. Usually a person can receive up to £20 a week as a charitable payment before their benefit is affected.

54.5 Grants made by a charity to another organisation are usually outside the scope of tax provided that the grant is to be used for a charitable purpose.

Grant-making trusts

54.6 Grant-making trusts are a distinct and important part of the voluntary sector. They disburse funds usually to other charities or to non-charitable, philanthropic organisations to spend on charitable activities. They vary tremendously in size from multi-million pound foundations, such as the Wellcome Trust, to very small trusts set up by individuals. The latter are sometimes referred to as 'private', 'family' or 'personal' trusts, but these terms can be misleading. If a trust is a registered charity it is publicly accountable. The trustees as a body, not the settlor (i.e. the person who provides the capital sum to establish the trust fund), are responsible for making decisions about grants. In practice, however, if the settlor is a trustee their opinion will carry a lot of weight.

54.7 Most grant-making charities require applicants to make a good case for funding. The applicant will be expected to demonstrate that they will use the grant to good effect, producing the desired outcome in a cost-effective manner. They will also need to demonstrate that they have a prudent level of reserves, enough to ensure their future viability but not so much that they are well able themselves to finance the work for which they are seeking funding.

Good practice in making grants

54.8 Unsuitable applications waste the time and resources of both the party making the application and the grant-making trusts that receive them. This can be minimised if grant-making trusts establish clear guidelines about the type of projects they will and will not fund and make this information readily available, together with details of the typical size of grants made, perhaps maximum and minimum and average size, and their application procedure. This information can be sent directly to organisations that the grant-making trust knows it would be interested in funding and/or supplied to the publishers of directories of grant-making trusts.

54.9 Similarly a grant-making trust should establish clear procedures for processing applications and make the details available to potential applicants. They should:

- give applicants their timetable and procedures for processing grants;
- ask applicants for, and check, their:
  - experience of doing similar work;
  - expected outcomes of the work to be funded;
  - financial competence;
  - current financial position; and
  - names of senior staff/trustees.

54.10 Decision-making procedures should be established taking into account the following points.

- Will any delegated authority be given to staff? If so, what level and what criteria will be used for approving applications?
- What will be the trust's policy for dealing with any conflicts of interest, i.e. funding work of an organisation that employs a trustee of the grant-making trust?
- Notification — how quickly will applicants be told of decisions.

54.11 Giving applicants the reasons why an application has been turned down consumes resources but is helpful to the applicant and can be cost-effective for a grant-making trust in the long run if it serves to educate applicants and deter unsuitable applications in the future.

54.12 When selecting from applications, trustees and staff should judge on substance rather than presentation, except to the extent that the presentation is material. They should also take into consideration whether or not the project needs a variety of funders to ensure its long-term stability and the organisation's demonstrable commitment to equal opportunities in the selection of its staff and beneficiaries.

54.13 Grant Making

54.13 Grant-making trusts should confirm grant offers in writing giving details of:

- the amount of the grant;
- the purpose of the grant;
- the duration of the grant;
- any conditions attached;
- the arrangements for payment;
- monitoring and evaluation arrangements; and
- details of circumstances in which the grant might be terminated.

54.14 Grant-makers should check the effectiveness of their funding, if only to guide them in making future funding decisions. Therefore, they should establish monitoring and evaluation procedures. It is best for the grantee and grantor to agree how effectiveness will be measured at the outset. They will need to agree the frequency with which various parameters such as performance measures/outputs/outcomes will be monitored. If the project is jointly-funded the funders should consider co-operating with the other funders on methods of monitoring and/or evaluation.

Dissemination

54.15 It is good practice for funders to encourage organisations that they have funded to disseminate the results of their work, and give details of innovative approaches, etc. to others. If necessary the funder should be prepared to fund the costs of dissemination. Similarly, funders should be prepared to disseminate the results of any evaluations they carry out.

55 Groups

55.1 A group structure exists when one legal entity has control over another. The key element in deciding whether or not several entities legally form a group is therefore 'control'. If a group exists, then the responsibilities of the holding entity's trustees may need reassessing, and relationships redefining as the holding entity's trustees will be accountable for the activities of the group. It follows from this that the issue is not one of accounting significance only. If the trustees of the holding charity are supposed to be in control of a group of subsidiary operations, then it is legitimate to ensure that the actual degree of control mirrors the accounting treatment, presenting the group's financial activities in one consolidated statement.

55.2 The most common type of group to exist is the charity that operates a trading subsidiary. In this case usually the shares in the subsidiary are owned either by the charity in its own name, or by some individuals on the charity's behalf. The subsidiary exists usually to carry out an aspect of trading which the charity either cannot, or prefers not to, operate itself. The reasons are usually tax driven, either direct tax or VAT, but may also include the need to limit contractual risk, or to conduct an activity not within the objects of the charity.

VAT considerations

55.3 It should be noted that whilst it is necessary to meet an 'under common control' condition to achieve a 'VAT Group' it is also necessary to obtain Customs' approval in advance. A VAT group is VAT registered as a single 'person' with all members using the same VAT registration number. The benefits of a VAT group may be a simplification of VAT reporting obligations or the removal of an obligation to charge VAT on transactions between VAT group members. It is, however, an area in which professional advice is usually appropriate because of the range of complex issues to be considered.

What is control?

55.4 In the past commercial organisations have used strict accounting definitions of control to manipulate their accountability. By buying or selling one share, a majority shareholding could become a minority shareholding, thus altering the presentation dramatically. Control is therefore now defined in wider terms. The *Companies Act 1985* defines a group as to include any corporate body (i.e. not just limited companies), with control over a subsidiary undertaking, which includes unincorporated bodies. [*Companies Act 1985 s 734*]. The Charities SORP adopts a similar definition, but does not restrict groups to being corporate bodies. For a company the hallmarks of control are if the holding entity:

- holds a majority of the voting rights of another undertaking;
- is a member (i.e. shareholder) of another undertaking and has the right to appoint or remove a majority of its board;
- is a member (i.e. shareholder) of another undertaking and has an agreement with the other members (i.e. shareholders) so that it has control over the voting rights; or
- has the right to exercise a dominant control over another undertaking because of a control contract or provisions contained in the governing document of the subsidiary.

55.5 Control may also exist if the parent entity holds a participating interest (20% or more) and either exercises a dominant influence over the undertaking, or they are managed on a unified basis.

55.6 The SORP applies similar rules to charities that are not company subsidiaries, setting out the following situations:

- parent charity trustees and/or members or employees can appoint or remove most of the subsidiary's trustees;
- the subsidiary's constitution gives the parent's trustees powers to direct the subsidiary trustees;
- the subsidiary's objects are substantially confined to the benefit of the parent.

Other indicators of control include where the subsidiary's operating and financial policies are in accordance with the main charities or where, whatever the activities of the subsidiary, all the risks and rewards lie with the main charity.

Branches

55.7 Normally the consideration of branches is a different matter to that of groups. A branch is usually either independent, or a part of the main organisation with no separate legal persona. The question of control is still an important one, but in a different context. As far as the accounting treatment is concerned, branches which are not legally autonomous are treated as though they are an integral part of the charity.

The uses of types of groups

55.8 The simplest and most common type of group is described above at 55.2. However, it is one of a number of options, and charities will adopt differing structures depending upon their needs. Some structures are set out in Table 9 below, in approximate order of their greatest frequency.

Group structure

55.9 The simplest way of forming a group is for the shares in the subsidiary company (which should therefore be limited by shares, not by guarantee) to be owned by the holding charity directly or, if the charity is unincorporated, by holding trustees on behalf of the charity. Appropriate documentation should be put in place to ensure that those named on the share certificates hold the shares on trust for the charity, and do not legally hold the beneficial ownership of the company themselves.

55.10 In this way the subsidiary is completely controlled by the charity, and a group automatically exists. The shareholders have the right to remove directors, but in practice, once the first directors are appointed, then board membership issues are usually dealt with by the directors themselves.

55.11 The directors of the subsidiary company will have a duty to act in the best interest of that company. Therefore care must be taken to avoid conflicts of interest with the charity. The Charity Commission recommends that this is best achieved by at least one director not being a trustee, and one trustee not being a director.

55.12 In many groups there will be a sharing of office facilities and equipment. This is especially true where a charity fund-raising department operates in the charity's own

Table 9

Holding entity	**Subsidiaries**	**Logic**
Charity	Trading company	To carry out non-primary purpose and non-ancillary trading, or fund-raising activities where a trading subsidiary can be used to minimise VAT or limit risk, or both
Charity	Several commercial trading companies	To carry out different trades, perhaps subject to differing contractual risk, or to separate commercial activities from other activities that are not profit-making but which may not be exclusively charitable, e.g. campaigning, holding title, etc.
Charity	Charitable subsidiary	To undertake charitable work subject to contractual risk, or a specific project
Non-charitable organisation	Charity	To carry out the charitable activities of an organisation that is not itself exclusively charitable

premises but is attracting income streams such as sponsorships, which may need to be put through the subsidiary trading company.

55.13 In this instance the charity should ensure that there is no hidden subsidy for the subsidiary by way of the free provision of services and facilities. This would represent a non-charitable application of the charity's assets, and would therefore not only be a breach of trust, but could also lead to a tax charge on the charity, reduced rates of VAT recovery, and limit business rate relief.

55.14 Two specific types of intra-group supply may need further consideration. First, if a registered charity is making land available to the subsidiary, then a lease or licence may be required. Because the disposition is to a connected person, an order from the Charity Commission authorising such a transaction will also be required. Second, the Charity Commission requires that equipment which is to be used exclusively by the subsidiary should be purchased by the subsidiary. This will affect the ability of the subsidiary to pass all of its profits to the charity under a profit stripping Gift Aid payment due to the differences between the accounting and tax treatment of fixed asset depreciation. The ramifications of acquiring such equipment should therefore be considered before the purchase is made.

Financing the subsidiary

55.15 New companies usually need some initial finance to start them off. Unfortunately it is not always easy for the charity to provide this finance, either because applying funds to a small trading operation may constitute non-qualifying expenditure for tax purposes, or because the application represents a breach of the trustees' investment powers. Although many charities regard these handicaps as anachronistic, they serve to focus trustees' attention on the commercial and whole business rationale for setting up a subsidiary.

55.16 There are a number of means of providing a subsidiary company with its initial working capital. These are shown in Table 10.

55.17 The clear recommendation of the Charity Commission is that subsidiaries should be funded by long-term secured loans with clear repayment terms and interest which is paid, rather than simply recorded as a book entry. The principles underlying this recommendation apply equally to all charities, not just those that are registered.

Accounting for subsidiaries

55.18 The revised SORP introduced a new set of rules for consolidation in the accounts. A parent charity should prepare consolidated accounts including all its subsidiary undertakings except where any of the following apply:

- the gross income of the group is no more than the *Charities Act 1993* audit threshold;
- the subsidiary undertakings/results are immaterial to the group;
- the accounts have to be aggregated under liquidation.

55.19 Whilst under the *Companies Act 1985* not all groups have to produce consolidated accounts, previously the SORP made this an automatic requirement for all groups, whatever their size. Consolidated accounts are accounts that reflect the transactions and balance sheet of the combined entities, as though they are one.

55.20 The broad requirements are as follows:

- that the SOFA should be consolidated;
- the balance sheet should be presented for the group and the charity;
- a cash flow statement is only required, if relevant, for the group;
- if a separate income and expenditure account is presented, it should be for the group only;
- a note should set out the profit and loss accounts of any subsidiaries; and
- notes to the balance sheet should separate out charity and group items.

55.21 Although much of this is cumbersome and of only limited relevance to most readers, it is not particularly complex. Strictly speaking a separate SOFA is required for the charity as well as the group. However, the Charity Commission will normally accept just the group SOFA if the assets and liabilities of the parent are distinguishable and the results of any subsidiary clearly stated.

55.22 When consolidating accounts, each income and expenditure item is individually consolidated, after adjusting out any inter-entity charges. For instance a management

Table 10 Methods of financing a trading subsidiary

Method	Advantages	Disadvantages
Share capital	Makes the subsidiary company solvent, as share capital is not re-payable except in a winding up situation	Ties up charity money long-term May not be a qualifying investment Is unsecured if the subsidiary company is wound up Cannot usually be repaid unless the subsidiary company is wound up
Interest bearing, secured long-term loan from charity	Is repayable but committed long-term. Lender receives interest	Ties up charity money long-term May not be a qualifying investment
Mezzanine finance	Cheap, long-term and flexible for the subsidiary company	Too risky with no prudent gain for the charity
Trading balance from charity	Simple and flexible	May not provide enough resource for the subsidiary company May be a slippery slope leading to charity money being tied up long-term
Commercial loan from a bank, for example	Simplest, and justifies commercial rationale of subsidiary	Probably more expensive than internal sources of capital Charity cannot guarantee or underwrite finance
Commercial equity	Long-term and third party	Dilutes control and can be difficult to obtain unless an exit route can be created
External gift or loan	Inexpensive	Difficult to persuade a donor to give to a commercial operation Charities have limited ability to divert gifts to their trading subsidiaries
Charity gift or grants	Creates a one-off non-taxable surplus in the subsidiary	Only possible if the subsidiary is in some way fulfilling the charity's objects. Should be discussed with the Charity Commission first (Inland Revenue Charities in Scotland)

charge from the charity to the subsidiary would not show as income and cost on the consolidated accounts.

55.23 Where the subsidiary is carrying out non-primary purpose activities, i.e. commercial trading, then previously only the net income of the trading had to be shown, subject to certain provisos, namely that the trading activity itself was not material, was not derived from the charitable activity, and that the full results were shown in the notes. This treatment is no longer permitted under the revised SORP.

55.24 It should be noted that the statutory whistleblowing requirement under the accounts *Reg 6(5)* relates not only to charities, but also to any institution or body corporate connected with the charity. This would naturally extend to the group, although where the charity is a limited company then the requirement would primarily be a public interest duty.

55.25 Because a limited company can have wide commercial objects and can also ratify some *ultra vires* acts in retrospect, the Charity Commission is uneasy about the degree to which activities which could otherwise be undertaken by the charity are being undertaken by a trading company in its stead. There are also other problems. There is always a danger of a charity, having established a group structure, losing sight of the purpose for which it was formed, and the wrong drivers leading to an activity being operated in the wrong entity. For instance the success of the fund-raising department's trading operations may lead to an expansion of its activities to such an extent that rate relief becomes jeopardised. The risk of costs being misallocated and incurring VAT or direct tax penalties has already been referred to. Employment matters can also become blurred, and the true employer not clearly identified. The underlying principle is to regard the subsidiary as a separate commercial operation, with the relationship maintained at arm's length wherever practicable. Issues such as licensing agreements, employment contracts, shared facilities should always be considered not only from the group's perspective, but also from the charity's.

56 Holding Trustees

56.1 A holding trustee is an individual or a corporate body that is not a trust corporation, that holds investments and/or land on behalf of a charity, but who, unlike a custodian trustee, does not have to act in accordance with the rules set out in the *Public Trustee Act 1906*.

56.2 Holding trustees have to act on the instructions of the charity trustees (or 'managing' trustees as charity trustees of charities with holding trustees are sometimes called in order to help distinguish between the roles) unless doing so would be unlawful or a breach of trust. If a holding trustee commits a breach of trust by acting outside the terms of their agreement with the charity, the holding trustee will be legally liable. Unlike custodian trustees, holding trustees are also liable for breaches of trust carried out on the instructions of the charity trustees. Holding trustees should refuse to carry out instructions that would lead to a breach of trust and therefore it is very important for them to have full details of the purposes for which property is held and any conditions attached.

56.3 Unincorporated charities cannot hold assets in the charity's name as they have no legal personality of their own. Therefore they often prefer to use a small group of holding trustees to hold title to their investments or land, rather than all their trustees, as this avoids the expense of having to transfer legal title to a new body of trustees every time there is a change on the governing body. If a charity has holding trustees the Charity Commission generally requires there to be a minimum of three, but does not stipulate a maximum number.

56.4 Holding trustees hold legal title to investments. They also hold legal title to land if they are individuals, or, if the holding trustee is a corporate body, to land that is not registered with the Land Registry. Holding trustees hold land as joint tenants, so legal advice should be sought before appointing holding trustees to hold land. Holding trustees do not usually have any powers of management.

56.5 Sometimes a charity's governing document will specify who the holding trustees are to be. If not, the charity trustees can appoint suitable individuals or corporate bodies. Unless excluded by the governing document, there is no reason why a charity trustee could not also be a holding trustee of the same charity.

Vesting

56.6 Vesting is the name of the process by which legal ownership of investments or land is passed to holding or custodian trustees. Vesting has to take place whenever a new holding or custodian trustee is appointed.

56.7 Other physical assets, for example, computers or cars, can be held by the trustees of an unincorporated charity without being formally vested in them. The trustees can transfer them simply by handing them over.

57 Honorary Officers

57.1 Most charities find they need to allocate specific responsibilities to certain trustees, usually known as the 'officers' or the 'honorary officers'. Almost all will have a chairperson and a treasurer, as these roles are particularly important. Many will also have a vice-chair and secretary. The honorary officers may have specific roles, functions and responsibilities set out in the charity's governing document, which may also contain procedures for their appointment.

57.2 In additional to their specific functions it is useful to have a small group of trustees who can:

- deal with urgent matters requiring attention between board meetings;
- take the lead in deciding which matters should be brought to the board;
- act as spokespersons for the charity and represent it at public gatherings;
- assist with the recruitment of senior staff;
- act as a link between the trustees and the charity's staff;
- sit on grievance and disciplinary panels.

57.3 The honorary officers should remember that they are 'first amongst equals'. They are agents of the board and should only act on its behalf where they have delegated authority so to do. The full board should be kept regularly informed of any decisions or activities the honorary officers undertake on its behalf. The honorary officers may play a leading role on the board, but must remember that it is the whole board who are responsible for governing the charity and each member has joint liability for the board's decisions. If the honorary officers take too strong a lead, or form a powerful inner cabal, they risk abusing their power. Other trustees may feel that their contribution is not required, and so the charity loses the skills, experience and commitment these trustees have to offer.

57.4 It is good practice to develop job descriptions and person specifications for the honorary officers and to allow the board of trustees to elect their honorary officers from candidates who meet the criteria. Trusteeship is a group activity and groups usually perform best when their leaders have the support of the majority of team members.

The chairperson

57.5 The role of the chairperson extends well beyond chairing the meetings of the board of trustees. The chairperson has to act as the leader of the board, making sure it fulfils its responsibilities for the governance of the charity and is focused on achieving the charity's mission. Vision and leadership are essential qualities for a good chairperson, together with good people skills and the ability to act with fairness and impartiality. The chairperson must work closely with the chief executive, helping to establish a mutually supportive relationship between the trustees and the staff.

57.6 The chairperson, together with the chief executive and sometimes the other honorary officers, will usually plan and draw up the agendas for board meetings. It is normally the chairperson's responsibility to supervise and appraise the work of the chief executive. The chairperson may also be called upon to act as a spokesperson for the charity and represent it at functions, meetings and in the press and broadcasting media. Other tasks may include authorising action to be taken between meetings of the full board, signing cheques for amounts above those for which authority has been delegated to staff and signing legal documents.

The vice-chairperson

57.7 The vice-chairperson acts for the chairperson when he or she is not available and undertakes assignments at the request of the chairperson.

The secretary

57.8 The secretary is responsible for the smooth running of the board of trustees and its committees, including overseeing the preparation and circulation of board papers and agendas, minute taking (this is a particularly important task as these form the legal record of the board's decisions), checking that a quorum is present, booking the meeting room, organising refreshments, etc. The secretary is also responsible for communicating with the members, organising the annual general meeting and any special or extraordinary meetings. Charitable companies have to appoint a company secretary, whose duties are to ensure that the charity complies with the requirements of company law as set out in the *Companies Act 1985*, including keeping the Register of Members, Register of Directors and Register of Charges up to date and notifying Companies House of any changes in trustees, preparing and filing the annual return and making sure that the company documents are kept safely. The company secretary does not need to be a director of the company and can therefore be a member of staff.

57.9 Because of the wide-ranging, responsible and continuous nature of the secretary's duties, most organisations large enough to employ staff will assign the secretary's duties to a paid member of staff rather than to a trustee. In many medium to larger sized organisations most of the secretary's duties will be carried out by the chief executive's assistant. In the largest charities the company secretary's role may be split between a number of people including the Head of Finance and the Head of Human Resources.

57.10 Some charities have both an honorary officer known as the 'secretary' or 'honorary secretary' and a company secretary. If this is the case it is important to distinguish between the role of the honorary secretary and that of the company secretary as each has different legal liabilities. The honorary secretary's role will normally be confined to taking minutes of meetings from which all staff are excluded, acting as an additional member of the small group who may be authorised to take certain actions between meetings, or nominated as the one whom the chairperson is required to consult about certain matters. The honorary secretary would have the same legal liability as any other trustee and would not, for example, be personally liable for failing to submit formal returns, for example to Companies House. The company secretary of a charitable company is an officer of the company by virtue of the *Companies Act 1985* and could be liable to prosecution if he breached the requirements of company law. If found guilty he could be fined or in exceptional circumstances imprisoned.

The treasurer

57.11 The role of the treasurer is to take the lead in helping the trustees discharge their financial responsibilities, by making sure that they understand the charity's business plan and budget, the financial implications of their decisions and that they do not expose the charity to undue financial risk. The treasurer should also ensure that the board receives timely, accurate financial reports which present the information trustees require in an 'easy to understand' format, and help the board by interpreting and explaining such matters as charity accounting requirements and the difference between statutory and management accounts. The treasurer will also play a lead role in appointing, monitoring and liaising with the auditors and other professional advisers, such as tax advisers or investment managers, that the board wishes to employ.

57.12 The precise tasks of a treasurer will depend on the size of the charity and the skills of the staff it employs. In any charity duties are likely to include:

- presenting financial reports to the board and the AGM;
- keeping the board aware of its financial responsibilities;
- ensuring that the charity's accounts are prepared in a suitable format;
- ensuring that the accounts and financial systems are examined or audited in accordance with legislation and the charity's governing document;
- liaising with the auditors and any other financial advisers.

In smaller charities the treasurer may personally maintain the financial records, prepare and monitor budgets and prepare and present financial reports.

57.13 The treasurer need not be a professionally qualified accountant, but should have a sufficient level of commercial and financial acumen to guide the financial affairs of the charity and command the respect of trustees, staff and other key stakeholders, such as major funders. To be effective, the treasurer will need to have a thorough understanding of the nature of the charity's work. Detailed knowledge of charity accounting regulations is less necessary than a willingness to acquire it, or knowing when to seek professional advice.

Job descriptions for honorary officers

57.14 The following specimen job descriptions are typical of those in current use.

Job description for a chairperson/vice-chairperson

The role of the chairperson is to lead the board of trustees, ensuring that it fulfils its responsibilities for the governance of the charity; to work in partnership with the chief executive, helping him or her achieve the aims of the charity; and to optimise the relationship between the board of trustees and the staff/volunteers.

The responsibilities of the chairperson will include:

- providing leadership for the board of trustees;
- planning an annual cycle of board meetings;
- setting agendas for the board meetings;
- chairing board meetings;
- ensuring that actions agreed at board meetings have been taken;
- liaising with the chief executive to keep an overview of the charity's affairs and to provide any necessary support;
- appraising the performance of the chief executive;

- sitting on appointment and disciplinary panels; and
- representing the charity at functions, meetings and acting as a spokesperson as appropriate.

Person specification for a chairperson/vice-chairperson

In addition to the qualities needed by all trustees, the chairperson/vice-chairperson should also possess the following:

- leadership skills;
- experience of committee work;
- tact and diplomacy;
- good 'people' skills; and
- impartiality, fairness and the ability to respect confidences.

In most circumstances the chairperson/vice-chairperson should have knowledge of, or involvement with, the type of work undertaken by the charity, the voluntary sector or other relevant networks.

Job description for a secretary

The role of the secretary is to support the chairperson by ensuring the smooth functioning of the board. The responsibilities of the secretary will include either doing the following tasks or delegating them to a member of staff and ensuring that they have been carried out:

- preparing agendas with the chairperson and chief executive;
- making the arrangements for meetings (booking the room, arranging for equipment and refreshments, organising facilities for those with special needs, etc.);
- minuting board meetings;
- ensuring that the minutes are signed by the chairperson once they have been approved;
- checking that a quorum is present at board meetings;
- circulating agendas, papers and minutes;
- receiving agenda items from other trustees/staff;
- checking that trustees and staff have carried out action agreed at a previous meeting;
- circulating members with agendas and minutes of the annual general meeting and any special or extraordinary general meetings;
- acting as company secretary where this role is not delegated to a member of staff; and
- sitting on appraisal, recruitment and disciplinary panels as required.

Person specification for a secretary

In addition to the qualities needed by all trustees, the secretary should also possess the following:

- organisational ability;

- knowledge or experience of business and committee procedures; and
- minute-taking experience, if this is not being delegated to staff.

Job description for a treasurer

The overall role of a treasurer is to maintain an overview of a charity's affairs, ensuring its financial viability and that proper financial records and procedures are maintained. The responsibilities of the treasurer will include:

- overseeing, approving and presenting budgets, accounts and financial statements;
- being assured that the financial resources of the charity meet its present and future needs;
- the preparation and presentation of financial reports to the board;
- ensuring that appropriate accounting procedures and controls are in place;
- liaising with paid staff and volunteers about financial matters;
- advising on the financial implications of the charity's strategic plans;
- ensuring that financial investments are consistent with the aims and objects of the charity;
- monitoring the charity's investment activity and ensuring its consistency with the charity's policies and legal responsibilities;
- ensuring that the accounts are prepared in the form required by law, included in the annual report and submitted to the relevant statutory bodies, e.g. the Charity Commission, the Registrar of Companies, Inland Revenue etc.;
- ensuring that the accounts are audited in the manner required by law and the charity's governing documents, and that any recommendations made by the auditors are implemented;
- keeping the board informed about its financial duties and responsibilities;
- contributing to the fund-raising strategy of the charity;
- making a formal presentation of the accounts at the annual general meeting and drawing attention to important points in a coherent and easy to understand manner; and
- sitting on appraisal, recruitment and disciplinary panels as required.

In addition to the qualities needed by all trustees, the treasurer should also possess the following:

- financial knowledge and experience;
- a willingness to be available to staff for advice and enquiries on an ad hoc basis;
- some experience of charity finance, fund-raising and pension schemes;
- the skills to analyse proposals and examine their financial consequences;
- a preparedness to make unpopular recommendations to the board.

58 Housing Associations/Registered Social Landlords

Constitution

58.1 The *Housing Act 1996* established the new concept of 'Registered Social Landlord' (RSL) to supersede that of 'Registered Housing Association'. The definition of a housing association is contained in the *Housing Associations Act 1985* and remains unchanged. To be 'registered' means inclusion on the Housing Corporation register of social landlords.

58.2 The Housing Corporation is a public body sponsored by the Department of the Environment, Transport and the Regions and its role is to fund and regulate RSLs in England. Scottish Homes, The National Assembly for Wales and the Northern Ireland Housing Executive perform the equivalent role in other parts of the UK.

58.3 There are three types of body eligible for registration:

- a registered charity that is a housing association;
- an industrial and provident society (provided it fulfils certain conditions);
- a company (also subject to conditions).

The principal condition referred to above is that the body is non-profit making. This is defined as not trading for profit or having a constitution that prohibits the issuing of capital with interest or dividend exceeding a rate determined by the Treasury. The other conditions, set out in *s 2(2)(4)* and *(5)* of the *1996 Act*, concern the objects of the social landlord.

Charitable status

58.4 A registered social landlord can be charitable or non-charitable depending upon its objects. An RSL may have charitable status if its objects are restricted to measures for the relief of poverty and the objects of many refer to housing being provided for persons in 'necessitous circumstances'. However, there is no statutory definition of 'necessitous circumstances' and in practice this is usually taken to mean those on less than average incomes or those in receipt of benefit.

58.5 Charitable industrial and provident societies may not register with the Charity Commission as they are deemed to be 'exempt charities' (see Chapter 45). Other charitable social landlords must be registered with the Charity Commission.

58.6 Specific tax exemptions are available to charities but charitable status does not give a blanket exemption from tax. Confirmation of exemption should be sought from the Inland Revenue.

Funding

58.7 The *Housing Act 1996* replaced Housing Association Grant with Social Housing Grant which may be paid by the Housing Corporation to RSLs to assist with their expenditure on housing activities. The Corporation lays down certain principles about how social housing grant can be applied for, the types of housing activities it will cover, how it will be calculated, and how it will be paid. It will also attach conditions to the receipt of grant and these apply to the RSL to which it is paid and to any other RSL that subsequently comes into possession of the property funded by grant.

58.8 Housing Associations/Registered Social Landlords

Accounting requirements

58.8 The *Housing Act 1996* gives the Housing Corporation the power to lay down accounting requirements for RSLs. The current accounting requirements are set out in The Accounting Requirements for Registered Social Landlords General Determination 1997 and The Accounting Requirements for Registered Social Landlords (Amending) Determination 1998. These requirements are based on the *Companies Act 1985* with such additional information that the Housing Corporation considers necessary to monitor a registered social landlord. These requirements do not conflict with those of the Registrar of Friendly Societies (industrial and provident societies) or the Charity Commission. In some cases an RSL may have to supply further additional information to satisfy the requirements of another body with which it is registered.

58.9 The Housing Corporation is currently considering responses to its consultation on the Accounting Determination 2000 which will replace the 1997 and 1998 Determinations and is expected to become effective for periods ending on or after 31 March 2001.

58.10 The Statement of Recommended Practice: 'Accounting by Registered Social Landlords' was published jointly in March 1999 by the National Housing Federation, the Welsh Federation of Housing Associations and the Scottish Federation of Housing Associations and is effective for accounting periods ending on or after 31 March 2000. The SORP outlines the requirements for the primary financial statements. It also outlines other disclosures to be given in the notes to the accounts. Illustrative examples are provided in the appendices.

58.11 This SORP requires housing properties to be shown either at historical cost net of Social Housing Grant or at valuation. If properties are shown at cost, only costs that are directly attributable to bringing the properties into working condition for their intended use should be included. Any property valuation should use the existing use value for social housing (EUV-SH) as defined in the SORP.

58.12 Other important features are that:

- Social Housing Grant and other government grants should be deducted from the cost of fixed assets where they contribute towards capital expenditure or they should be credited to the income and expenditure account as part of turnover where they contribute to revenue expenditure.
- Works to existing housing properties that result in an enhancement of economic benefits of the asset are deemed to be improvements and should be capitalised.
- Properties should not be shown at an amount exceeding their recoverable amount.
- The depreciable amount of housing properties should be allocated on a systematic basis over the useful economic life of the properties and recognised as an expense in the income and expenditure account. The only grounds for not charging depreciation are that the depreciation charge and accumulated depreciation are immaterial.

59 Human Rights Act 1998

59.1 The *Human Rights Act 1998* came fully into force on 2 October 2000 and effectively incorporated most of the European Convention on Human Rights into UK law. Human rights cases can now be brought in UK Courts, rather than just in the European Court of Human Rights in Strasbourg. It will affect all public authorities in the UK (including the Charity Commission) and all private and voluntary bodies carrying out public functions.

59.2 The *Human Rights Act* gives every citizen statutory rights based on the European Convention on Human Rights that can be enforced against public authorities and private bodies carrying out public functions. The Act:

- obliges UK Courts and Tribunals to take into account (but not necessarily follow) the decisions and opinions of the European Court of Human Rights;
- requires that all legislation is interpreted in a way compatible with the Convention;
- makes it unlawful for a 'public authority' to act, or fail to act, in a way that is incompatible with the Convention. Where a public authority breaches this requirement the Act allows a person affected (a 'victim') to bring proceedings against that public authority;
- the Act permits a victim to rely on the Convention in any legal proceedings involving a public authority.

59.3 There are a number of rights and freedoms listed in the European Convention on Human Rights. They are:

- The right to life (Article 2)
- Freedom from torture and inhuman or degrading treatment or punishment (Article 3)
- Freedom from slavery and enforced or compulsory labour (Article 4)
- The right to liberty and security of person (subject to a derogation applicable to Northern Ireland) (Article 5)
- The right to a fair and public trial within a reasonable time (Article 6)
- The freedom from retrospective criminal law and no punishment within law (Article 7)
- The right to respect for private and family life, home and correspondence (Article 8)
- The freedom of thought, conscience and religion (Article 9)
- The freedom of expression (Article 10)
- The freedom of assembly and association (Article 11)
- The right to marry and found a family (Article 12)
- The prohibition of discrimination and the enjoyment of the Convention rights (Article 14)

- The right to peaceful enjoyment of possessions and protection of property (Article 1 of Protocol 1)
- The right to education (subject to a UK reserve) (Article 2 of Protocol 1)
- The right to free elections (Article 3 of Protocol 1)
- The right not to be subject to use of the death penalty (Articles 1 and 2 of Protocol 6).

Interference with a person's human rights

59.4 Some human rights are absolute (for example the prohibition on slavery), some are limited i.e. the Convention provides explicit and finite circumstances in which the general right can be interfered with (for example the right to liberty) and some are qualified. If there is to be an interference with a qualified right, any interference:

- can only be 'prescribed by' or 'in accordance with' the law (in other words there must be clear legal rules which apply and which justify the interference);
- must have a legitimate aim;
- must be 'necessary in a democratic society' (this implies that any interference must be as small and as reasonable as possible).

What is meant by 'public authority'?

59.5 The meaning of 'public authority' or 'public function' is deliberately not defined in the *Human Rights Act*. It will be left to the Courts to interpret. The Houses of Parliament are specifically excluded from the definition, apart from the House of Lords when it is sitting as a Court.

59.6 Although the term 'public authority' is not defined, there are three broad categories of public authorities:

- Public authorities whose functions are all public, such as Government Departments, Agencies (including the Charity Commission), local authorities, health authorities and trusts, the armed forces, the police, prison and immigration authorities, Courts and tribunals.
- Persons or organisations that carry out a mixture of public and private functions, such as Railtrack, and the privatised utility companies.
- Private organisations, including charities, that carry out functions that central or local government would otherwise have to undertake.

59.7 Many charities believe they are unaffected by the Act as they do not regard themselves to be public authorities. However, many charities will be considered as public authorities for the purposes of the Act, particularly those that have been given a statutory authority to carry out work on behalf of a local authority.

59.8 Indeed, all charities should have procedures in place to alert them to breaches of the Act. Even if a charity does not fall under the definition of 'public authority', the Courts do. Therefore, any action before them has to be considered in light of the Act. Any charity facing Court action must ensure compliance, as any breach of the Convention will damage their public image.

Private bodies with public functions

59.9 Examples of private bodies with public functions are:

- privatised utilities that exercise public functions;
- regulatory bodies;
- professional bodies in their regulatory capacities;
- charities and voluntary organisations that carry out public functions for central or local authorities, such as running a residential home;
- private or independent schools;
- private companies managing contracted out prisons;
- bodies that are legally public corporations.

Key characteristics of a public authority

59.10 In some cases it may be difficult to decide whether or not an organisation is a public authority. Organisations may need to take legal advice to clarify this, but the characteristics of a public authority would include:

- the body performs or operates in the public domain as an integral part of a statutory system that performs public law duties;
- the duty performed is of public significance;
- the rights or obligations of individuals may be affected in performance of the duty;
- an individual may be deprived of some legitimate expectation in performance of the duty;
- the body is non-statutory but is established under the authority of a national or local government body;
- the body's work is supported by statutory powers and penalties;
- the body's work involves regulating the activities of the public or section of the public;
- the body performs functions that national or local government bodies or a health authority would otherwise perform;
- the body is under a duty to act judicially in exercising what amounts to public powers.

59.11 Charities should carefully consider whether or not their functions, i.e. their legal powers and duties, render them likely to be considered as a public authority for the purposes of the *Human Rights Act*. They should look carefully at each of the Convention rights and freedoms and consider whether what they do is likely to affect those rights. If so, they should ensure that their procedures and policies are compatible with the Convention.

Charities with public and private functions

59.12 Charities will be carrying out a public function if they are doing work that would normally be the responsibility of central government or a local or health authority. Therefore charities contracting to do statutory work for local or health authorities will fall within the scope of the *Human Rights Act*.

59.13 Examples of charities with public functions might include:

- residential homes;
- hospices;
- healthcare and advice centres;
- child care agencies;
- housing associations;
- family planning and abortion advice centres.

However, when these charities are raising funds or recruiting staff they are acting privately.

Taking action under the Act

59.14 Only someone who is, or would be, a victim of an action by a public authority can take action under the Act. A victim can be an individual, a company or other organisation. An indirect victim, for example a spouse, can bring a human rights challenge if the victim is dead or unable to bring proceedings themselves. The Act aims to prevent public authorities from acting in ways that are incompatible with a Convention right, but it is possible that parties in private law actions may be able to use the Act in their proceedings.

59.15 Victims of an infringement of their rights or freedoms under the Convention can take the public authority concerned to Court for breaching their rights, or rely on Convention rights in the course of any other Court proceedings involving a public authority. Victims will still be free to take their case to the European Court of Human Rights but only after they have exhausted all domestic remedies.

59.16 Victims must bring proceedings under the Act within one year of the act complained of, although the Courts can extend this period under certain circumstances.

59.17 The Courts can grant a wide range of remedies including damages, declarations, quashing, mandatory and prohibitive orders and, in certain circumstances, injunctions.

Implications for charities that fall within the scope of the Human Rights Act

59.18 The *Human Rights Act* makes it unlawful for any organisation to carry out a public function in a way that is incompatible with the rights and freedoms guaranteed by the European Convention on Human Rights. The Act does not create any new offences. To act unlawfully under the *Human Rights Act* does not mean that a charity (or its trustees) will have committed a criminal offence. Charities do not risk prosecution if they have acted unlawfully under the Act unless they have at the same time breached the existing criminal law.

59.19 However, if a charity does breach the *Human Rights Act* it would be liable to the remedies available to the Courts. For example, if someone brings a case against a charity under the *Human Rights Act* they could apply to the Courts for damages against it. There is also the possibility that a claim that a charity has acted unlawfully under the *Human Rights Act* could arise during the course of other litigation against the charity. For example, if a charity were facing an action for negligence there is a likelihood that the prosecution could claim that the charity had also breached the *Human Rights Act*.

59.20 Damages are restricted to civil proceedings as criminal courts do not have the power to award damages or compensation in respect of Convention violations. However there are other remedies open to criminal courts to grant, such as staying proceedings, quashing indictments and excluding evidence.

59.21 Before damages are awarded the court must be satisfied that the award is necessary to afford just satisfaction to the person in whose favour it is made (*s 8(3)(4)*). As often happens with decisions of the Court of Human Rights a simple finding that an unlawful act has occurred may be considered a sufficient remedy in all the circumstances. The level of damages awarded by UK courts must be commensurate with the level of damages awarded by the Court of Human Rights. Such awards usually range between £5,000–£15,000.

59.22 The *Human Rights Act* would not apply if the charity could not have acted differently because of existing primary legislation.

Convention rights most likely to affect charities

59.23 Some Convention rights are likely to have more impact on charities and voluntary organisations than others do. Examples of those that are likely to affect such organisations are:

- Article 3 — Right not to be subjected to torture or inhuman treatment. This includes the right not to be subjected to degrading treatment and so could apply to organisations providing care, such as hospitals, residential homes etc.
- Article 6 — Right to a fair trial. This right might affect procedures for case reviews, complaints hearings, tribunals and appeals conducted by charities.
- Article 8 — Right to respect for private and family life. This has relevance for organisations providing care homes or domiciliary care and to any organisation with a public function that holds personal information.
- Article 9 — Freedom of thought, conscience and religion. This might affect, for example a charity running a care home where one of the patients is Muslim and wishes to wear the chadoor. The home may find this inconvenient and contrary to its policies but it could not force compliance with the policy because under Article 9 the patient has a right to manifest her religion.
- Article 2 of the First Protocol — Right to education. This may be relevant for issues involving special educational needs provision, access to, or expulsion or exclusion of children from, schools, and (when taken together with Article 14: Prohibition of discrimination) the provision of education which is discriminatory between sexes, races or other categories (although this is only likely to be an issue where adequate educational provision is not available elsewhere locally for children excluded from schools that do discriminate, such as single sex schools).

59.24 Some rights are not absolute and they can come into conflict with other rights in the Act or be subject to limitations at law. In such cases it is for the Courts to decide how the competing rights were to be balanced.

59.25 If a charity's trustees think some of its procedures are in conflict with human rights they may wish to consider seeking legal advice.

Benefits for charities of the Human Rights Act

59.26 The implementation of the *Human Rights Act* will bring new responsibilities for some charities, but it will also bring opportunities. Charities will be able to take advantage of the Act to challenge the activities of others where the rights of their organisation are being infringed. For example charities will be able to take action against public authorities, including the Charity Commission, where they believe that a public body has infringed their rights, for example under Article 9 (freedom of thought, conscience and religion), Article 10 (freedom of expression) or Article 1 of the First Protocol (protection of property).

59.27 Charities can also use the Act as an opportunity to build the principles of human rights into their policies and procedures to help develop and implement good practice and improve attitudes and behaviour towards people that they help and work with.

Further information

59.28 There are a number of websites and helplines that provide information about the *Human Rights Act*. These include:

The Home Office Human Rights Unit: *http://www.homeoffice.gov.uk/hract*

The Home Office Human Rights Helpline: Telephone: 020 7273 2166

The Council of Europe, Human Rights Directorate: *http://www.dhdirhr.coe.fr*
This site contains details of the Council's work in the human rights field.

The European Court of Human Rights: *http://www.dhcour.coe.fr*
This site contains details of the Strasbourg Court's judgments.

60 Income Tax

Tax on charitable income

60.1 As most charities are corporate bodies or unincorporated associations they are liable to corporation tax on their income subject to specific exemptions. Charitable trusts, however, are subject to income tax at the basic rate on their income unless a tax exemption or extra-statutory concession applies and the income that would otherwise be taxable is used only for charitable purposes.

60.2 Charitable trusts enjoy the same exemptions from tax on their income as do charities subject to corporation tax and the same rules for non-qualifying payments apply for income tax purposes as they do for corporation tax (see Chapter 28). Charitable trusts must make a return of any taxable income and account for any tax payable under the procedures for self assessment and must notify the Revenue of liability to tax within 6 months of the end of the year of assessment (i.e. by 5 October) if no tax return has been received. In most instances a tax return will be unnecessary as no tax will be payable and the Revenue will not normally issue a tax return.

Reclaiming tax paid

60.3 Charities, whether trusts or companies, will receive income net of tax deducted at source from payments made under Gift Aid. Tax should not be deducted at source, however, from interest on bank or building society deposits or government securities (gilts). Assuming the charity qualifies for tax exemption on its income, any income tax suffered by deduction at source can then be reclaimed.

Deducting income tax

60.4 A company which borrows money, other than from a UK bank, on a loan which lasts or is intended to last for not less than a year, is required to deduct tax at source from any interest paid to the lender. The tax so deducted must be accounted for to the Inland Revenue on a quarterly basis using form CT61. The form, together with the payment, should be sent to the Collector of Taxes within 14 days of the end of each calendar quarter and, if different, 14 days from the company's year-end. The Inland Revenue will charge interest on any tax not paid by the due date. The lender will be treated as having received income net of UK tax and the company should be able to obtain a deduction for the gross interest paid. These provisions can apply to the trading subsidiaries of charities who have had to borrow funds to finance their operations. The rules do not apply to overdrafts or loans that are to be repaid within a year.

60.5 Charities are also, of course, required to deduct income tax from payments to individuals in return for work under the Inland Revenue's Pay As You Earn (PAYE) scheme. Employers have a duty to register for PAYE, operate it by sending tax and national insurance payments to the collector of taxes on a monthly basis. Charities are required by law to keep PAYE records. Failure to do this can result in the employer being held liable for all tax and national insurance payments that should have been deducted and paid to the collector of taxes, plus interest for late payment, plus penalties.

61 Incorporation of Trustees

Advantages of incorporating the trustee body

61.1 Trustees of unincorporated charitable trusts or associations usually have to enter into legal agreements in their individual names, or in the names of holding or custodian trustees, because the charity has no legal personality of its own. Trustee incorporation is a process by which the charity trustees of an unincorporated trust or association can incorporate themselves as a body. The charity can then vest its property in the name of the incorporated body. This avoids the need to execute deeds transferring land or investments every time new trustees are appointed to an unincorporated charity. Incorporation of the trustee body also allows trustees to enter into contracts and sue, or be sued, in the name of the incorporated body.

61.2 The *Charitable Trustees Incorporation Act 1872* enabled the trustees of charities established for religious, educational, literary, scientific or public charitable purposes to apply to the Charity Commission for a certificate of incorporation. The *1872 Act* was substantially amended by the *Charities Act 1992* and the provisions are now contained in *Part VII* of the *Charities Act 1993*.

61.3 *Section 50* of the *Charities Act 1993* gives the Charity Commission power to grant a certificate of incorporation provided that the Commissioners consider that incorporation of the trustees would be in the interests of the charity. It allows the Commissioners to include any conditions or directions they judge to be desirable in the certificate. They cannot issue a certificate of incorporation to a charity that is required to be registered under *s 3* of the *Charities Act 1993* but is not so registered.

Impact on trustee liability

61.4 Incorporation of the trustees gives the governing body, not the charity, legal personality, permanent succession, and the right to own property, enter into legal agreements and take legal action in the name of the governing body. However, it does not limit the liability of members and trustees in the way that the incorporation of the charity would, so they continue to remain liable to the same extent as if they had not incorporated.

61.5 If a charity's trustees do not consider that they need the additional protection that incorporating as a charitable company or industrial and provident society would bring, but do own property and/or investments or enter into leases and/or contracts, trustee incorporation could be an appropriate and cost-saving option.

Procedure

61.6 Trustees of registered charities and charities that are exempt or excepted from registration with the Charity Commission can apply to the Commissioners for a certificate of incorporation. An application pack CHY–1093 is available from the Commission. They will need to send the following with their application:

- a copy of the governing document, if the Charity Commission does not already have a copy;
- a list of the charity's property or any property held in trust for the charity;
- the names of the current trustees, and evidence of their appointment in legal terms;

- the proposed name with which the trustees wish to be incorporated;
- a statement of why the trustees consider that incorporation of the trustees would be in the best interests of the charity.

Naming the incorporated body

61.7 The Charity Commission advises that the name of the incorporated body should contain either the word 'trustees' or some similar word such as 'governors'. It should not contain the word 'registered', as this could lead the public to believe that the charity is registered under the *Companies Acts*. Suggested forms are 'The Trustees of the Charity, The XYZ Association' and 'The Incorporated Trustees of the Charity of A N Other'.

Transferring property to the incorporated body

61.8 Once granted, the certificate of incorporation automatically vests all the property of the charity in the incorporated body, with the exception of any property vested in the Official Custodian. Land vested in the Official Custodian can remain so, but may be transferred by a Charity Commission Order to the incorporated body at the trustees' request. If individuals, such as holding trustees, hold equities, bonds, etc. in trust for the charity they must transfer them into the name of the incorporated body.

Seal

61.9 Trustees incorporated under the *Charities Act 1993 s 50* are no longer required to have a common seal. If they choose to have a common seal, documents must be executed using the seal. The trustees must ensure that:

- the design of the common seal includes the name of the incorporated body;
- they have agreed proper measures for the seal's safe keeping; and
- they have agreed regulations for the use of the seal.

If an incorporated body of trustees does not choose to have a common seal, perhaps because of the associated costs, they can execute documents by either:

- having them signed by a majority of the trustees and thereby expressed as being executed by the incorporated body; or
- using an authority granted by the trustees, which should be in writing or by resolution of the trustees, that allows for documents to be executed by two or more trustees in the name of, and on behalf of, the incorporated body.

Amendment

61.10 The trustees cannot amend the certificate of incorporation. However, the Charity Commission has powers, under *s 56* of the *Charities Act 1993* to amend a certificate of incorporation in response to a request from the incorporated body or, on rare occasions, because the Commission believes the conditions in the certificate need amendment. Amendments are made by making an Order or by issuing a new certificate of incorporation.

61.11 Incorporation of Trustees

Dissolution

61.11 Similarly under *s 61* of the *Charities Act 1993* the Commission has power to make an Order for dissolution of an incorporated body either at the trustees request or because the Commission believes that the incorporated body has no assets and does not operate, or because the charity's objects have been achieved or are incapable of being achieved, or because the charity has either ceased to exist or was not a charity at the time of incorporation. If the trustees wish the incorporated body dissolved they must demonstrate to the Charity Commission that this is in the best interests of the charity. Unless the trustees can do this the Commission cannot make an order dissolving the incorporated body.

Gifts

61.12 Gifts made around the time of incorporation of a trustee body are treated as if they had been given to the incorporated body, even if they were actually given to the charity or for the purposes of the charity. [*Charities Act 1993 s 59*].

62 Industrial and Provident Societies

62.1 Most industrial and provident societies are not charities. However, many housing associations/Registered Social Landlords (of which many will be charities) and a small number of other charities use this legal structure. In total, 10,125 industrial and provident societies (excluding credit unions) held assets worth £37.5 billion at the end of 1995: the largest grouping was the 4,041 housing associations holding assets of £18 billion. The housing associations may also be registered with the Housing Corporation, Scottish Homes, or Tai Cymru under the *Housing Acts*. They are primarily affected by two pieces of legislation, the *Industrial and Provident Societies Act 1965*, and the *Friendly and Industrial and Provident Societies Act 1968*. The *1965 Act* contains general provisions about industrial and provident societies, whereas the *1968 Act* is mainly concerned with accounting and audit. Industrial and provident societies are regulated through the Registrar of Friendly Societies, based in London.

Registration

62.2 Industrial and provident societies adopt a set of rules, which are then submitted to the Registrar of Friendly Societies for registration. These rules have to include 14 matters set out in *1 Sch* to the *1965 Act*, including matters such as name, objects, meetings, shareholdings, provision for audit and borrowing and investment powers. The rules also set out the powers of remuneration in respect of the committee and officers: this takes into account a clear authority for members of the committee to be paid expenses, without which such payments would be *ultra vires*.

62.3 The *Industrial and Provident Societies (Fees) Regulations 1999* set out the scale of fees for registration and other matters. The fee for registering a new society is £900, although this is reduced to £90 if model rules are used without amendment. Making more than ten amendments to the model rules increases the fee to £800. The fee for registering amendments to existing rules is £725 if there are more than ten amendments.

62.4 Charitable industrial and provident societies are exempt charities under the *Charities Act 1993 s 46*. This means that they cannot be registered with the Charity Commission, or quote a charity number. If they need to obtain the tax benefits of being wholly charitable, then they apply direct to the Inland Revenue and will be given a Revenue Reference number which they can use on their stationery. In Scotland industrial and provident societies must be recognised by the Inland Revenue Charities (Scotland).

Structure

62.5 A society may be registered as an industrial and provident society if it is carrying on any industry, business or trade, and is either a co-operative society, or is conducting its business for the benefit of the community and there are special reasons why the society should be registered as an industrial and provident society rather than a limited company. The term 'business' is not a strictly defined one in this context, and charities will often be able to fit within its scope. Once registered, an industrial and provident society does have similarities to a company: it is a body corporate, with perpetual succession and limited liability. Unlike a company the legislation governing an industrial and provident society is not as detailed, nor often as irrelevant, although the registration process can be cumbersome, and the structure of management may also be unfamiliar to those involved. It must be democratically controlled by its members.

62.6 Although an industrial and provident society is similar in its democratic structure to a charitable association, it differs in being a body corporate: it has a share capital, and all members have to hold at least one share, which must be recorded in the register of members.

62.7 An industrial and provident society is not a common form of structure for a charity to adopt, partly because the structure came into existence to serve a particular, not exclusively charitable, purpose, and partly because often a company limited by guarantee can achieve the same ends, in which case the Registrar of Friendly Societies would require the organisation to adopt that alternative constitution. The *Industrial and Provident Societies Act 1965* includes detailed provisions setting out how a company might convert itself into an industrial and provident society, or vice versa.

Registers

62.8 Every registered society must keep at its registered office a register recording:

- the names and addresses of members;
- the number of shares per member;
- a statement of other property in the society held by each member;
- the date at which a person started or ceased to be a member;
- the names and addresses of the officers of the society, noting the office and the date of appointment.

Accounts

62.9 The *Charities Act 1993* requires exempt charities to prepare accounts at least every fifteen months, unless other legislation includes another requirement. A trustees' or auditors' report is not required by the *Charities Act 1993*, but accounts must be made available to the public, for a reasonable fee if necessary, within two months of being requested.

62.10 Industrial and provident societies, as exempt charities, have their own legislation governing accounts and audit. All industrial and provident societies have year-ends of 31 August or 31 December, unless otherwise agreed with the Registrar. Every society must keep proper books of account, and establish and maintain a satisfactory system of financial control. Annual accounts have to include revenue accounts dealing with one or more aspects of the society's business, and a balance sheet, duly audited and signed by the secretary of the society and two members of the committee, acting on behalf of the committee. Because the specification of the accounts is so brief, charitable industrial and provident societies are able to comply with the charities SORP in full: the distinction between a revenue account and the SOFA is carried through into the SORP in the consideration of FRS 3 and the need for a summary income and expenditure account where appropriate. The audit requirement is set out separately, and the duly audited accounts have to be filed as part of the annual return, with the Registrar by 31 March.

62.11 Every registered society must keep a copy of the latest balance sheet, together with its audit report, hung in a conspicuous position at the registered office of the society at all times.

Annual return

62.12 All industrial and provident societies have to submit an annual return, including the accounts. These then go on public record and are open to inspection.

Audit report

62.13 The audit report is an opinion as to the truth and fairness of the accounts, confirming compliance with the accounting requirements of the 1968 Act. The auditor has also to consider whether proper books of account have been kept, whether a satisfactory internal control system is in place, and whether the accounts agree to the records. Only if the society has failed in any material respect would this be reported in the audit report itself. Similarly, if the auditors fail to obtain necessary information or explanations this will be disclosed.

Auditor

62.14 Industrial and provident societies are not required to re-appoint their auditors annually (see 10.3).

63 Inheritance Tax

63.1 Inheritance tax is chargeable on the value of a person's estate at the day of their death, plus the value of gifts made by them during the previous seven years. Legacies, bequests and lifetime gifts to charities are exempt from inheritance tax. [*Inheritance Tax Act 1984*].

Qualifications of exemption

63.2 To qualify for exemption from inheritance tax the gift must be irrevocable and used only for charitable purposes.

63.3 The charity exemption applies to transfers of value attributable to property which is given to a charity. It is essential that the gift becomes the property of a charity or is held on trust for charitable purposes only. No relief is available, however, if the property or any part of it may become applicable for non-charitable purposes, so that a gift to a temporary charity would not qualify. Relief is also not available if the property is not immediately vested in the charity. Therefore, a gift in a settlement where an individual has a life interest is not exempt from inheritance tax.

63.4 There is no general restriction on the charity exemption under the reservation of benefit rules where the donor retains some benefit. However, if the property given is land and the donor, their spouse or a person connected with the donor is entitled to possession or occupation of the land rent free, or at a rent below the full market rent, then the charity exemption will not apply.

Deed of Variation

63.5 It is possible for the beneficiaries of a person's estate to enter into a Deed of Variation and to elect that for inheritance tax purposes the variation shall have effect as if the provisions of the Deed were included in the will. The beneficiaries can also transfer part of the estate to a charity and qualify for the charity exemption, even through there is no such provision in the original will. As the variation applies only for inheritance tax and capital gains tax purposes, the gift is treated for all other purposes as if it had been made by the beneficiary.

63.6 There have been cases where the beneficiary has then applied the provisions of the Gift Aid scheme so that the charity receives a further repayment of income tax and the beneficiary receives relief from income tax at the higher rate on the gross amount. This arrangement has been successfully challenged by the Inland Revenue in a case taken to the Special Commissioners who decided that the Gift Aid rules could not apply because the beneficiary had received a benefit. The benefit in question was the saving in inheritance tax, thus increasing the value of the estate (before the charitable donation) which passed to him (*St Dunstan's v Major* [*1997*] *STC (SCD) 212*).

63.7 As the Inland Revenue are challenging these arrangements any person considering entering into them may have to take the case to appeal before the courts and should therefore take professional advice.

64 Inland Revenue

Claims Administration

64.1 The Inland Revenue has a specialist office responsible for the tax affairs of charities, including their subsidiaries. Formerly this was part of the Financial Intermediaries and Claims Office (FICO) but is now known as Inland Revenue Charities. The office will provide help and information to charities and their advisers on taxation matters and these should be addressed to:

For England, Wales and Northern Ireland

Inland Revenue Charities
St John's House
Merton Road
Bootle
Merseyside
L69 9BB

For Scotland

Inland Revenue Charities
(Scotland)
Trinity Park House
South Trinity Road
Edinburgh
EH5 3SD

64.2 Inland Revenue Charities deals with claims for exemption by charities and their repayment claims. It also examines the accounts of charities and also those of their trading subsidiaries whose files have now been, or are being transferred to Inland Revenue Charities from the local districts. In examining claims by charities, Inland Revenue Charities has a continuous programme of on-site inspection visits to check on the charity's compliance with the requirements of the tax legislation.

Investigations

Special Compliance Office

64.3 Investigations by the Inland Revenue are broadly dealt with at two levels. The Special Compliance Office concentrates on uncovering tax evasion, dealing mainly with the larger more serious cases. The Office is divided into units which deal with serious cases of fraud relating to business accounts, suspected criminal offences in other areas, particularly in connection with fraud relating to the construction industry, Pay As You Earn (PAYE), Gift Aid, special offices handling highly technical areas and covering particular industries and PAYE audit and special trade investigation units. It is outside the scope of this book to deal with the handling of investigations by a Special Compliance Office. At any sign of their involvement, professional advice should be sought immediately, preferably from an accountant or lawyer familiar with dealing with these matters. Investigations by Special Compliance Office can lead to criminal proceedings as well as very severe financial penalties.

Inland Revenue Charities

64.4 More routine investigations are carried out at district level. For charities, this will involve Inland Revenue Charities, except in relation to PAYE and related matters in connection with employees, which are dealt with by the PAYE district concerned. These offices have a continuous programme of on-site inspection visits, where they will examine the charity's or the company's records to ensure proper compliance with the legislation, regulations and procedures.

64.5 Inland Revenue

Records

64.5 In carrying out a PAYE investigation or compliance audit, the Inland Revenue will ask to see all of the charity's or the company's books and records and not merely the payroll calculations. This is because their enquires will include looking at payments to individuals who may be employees but who have not been treated as such and reimbursed expenses and payments relating to employees that may give rise to taxable benefits. It is important that a note is kept of questions asked, replies given and any matters that the Inland Revenue consider give rise to additional tax.

Settlements

64.6 Where benefits have been provided to employees that have not been included on forms P11D, the Inland Revenue will often seek a global settlement from the organisation rather than make an assessment on each individual employee. Such a settlement may well cover all of the previous six years. In these circumstances the tax will normally be collected on a grossed up basis i.e. the payment in respect of the employee is treated as a net sum but a penalty will not normally be included. It is often possible to negotiate the amount of such a settlement with the Inland Revenue, so it is important to consider what the Inland Revenue say at the initial stage and then seek professional advice before agreeing a settlement. An employer is required to make full disclosure to the Inland Revenue but is not required to reach agreement on every point at the time the investigation takes place. Any contentious matters can be the subject of further correspondence.

Penalties

64.7 A penalty, if charged, will be calculated as a percentage of the tax and NIC underpaid as a result of fraud or neglect. The maximum penalty of 100% of the tax is only ever charged in the most extreme cases and it is normally a lot less. The amount of the reduction depends upon the extent to which all details were disclosed to the Inland Revenue, the extent to which the employer co-operated with the inspection and the gravity of the offence. The Inland Revenue have produced a leaflet on this subject (IR109) which is normally sent to employers before an inspection takes place.

64.8 Interest will also be charged on any tax which the employer has failed to deduct. This will include cases where a person was treated as self-employed but it is later established that the individual concerned should have been treated as an employee. In these circumstances, there is a liability to both tax and National Insurance Contributions (NIC) (employee's and employer's contributions). The Inland Revenue do not normally treat payments as being net of deductions. This is not the case, however, where it was clearly the understanding of both parties that PAYE was to have been operated and the employee believed that a net sum was being paid.

Professional advice essential

64.9 The issues involved in these investigations are not always clear and the Inland Revenue's view is open to challenge. Professional advice should therefore be taken at an early stage. Because the Inland Revenue will normally look back over a number of years, substantial amounts can often be involved.

65 Insolvency

Insolvency

65.1 'Insolvent' is the technical term for what the layman may describe as bankrupt, bust or broke. It has a specific meaning in legislation, and is important to identify when a charity has become insolvent. Failure to do so can lead to increased financial losses, and the exposure of trustees to personal financial risk and possible criminal penalties. There are two main tests to assess solvency, one is a more practical, cash flow test, and the other an arithmetic, balance sheet test. Depending on the outcome of such tests, and the nature of the charity's constitution, the trustees will need to act accordingly. These tests are enshrined in the principal legislation governing insolvency, the *Insolvency Act 1986*, which partly applies to unincorporated organisations. Because of the extremely complex situations that can arise during an insolvency, and the risks involved, organisations and their trustees should take appropriate professional advice as soon as possible if they think that their organisation might be insolvent.

Cash flow test

65.2 An organisation is insolvent if it cannot pay its debts as they fall due, or if this situation is likely to arise in the foreseeable future, usually the next twelve months. The *Insolvency Act 1986 s 123*, specifically in the context of companies and Industrial and Provident Societies, states that this situation arises where:

- a creditor for over £750 has demanded the amount due, and within three weeks the organisation has neither paid nor made satisfactory arrangements to pay, or
- the organisation has not paid a creditor after being ordered by a court to do so, or
- the High Court is satisfied that the organisation is unable to pay its debts.

Financial administrators of companies should be alert to creditors pressurising companies to pay debts by presenting a winding up petition on the basis that the company has failed to pay a debt within 21 days of a demand being made. This may result in compulsory liquidation. Although it is a valid defence that the amount in question is subject to dispute, this explanation must be put to the court before it agrees to appoint a liquidator, usually the Official Receiver.

Balance sheet test

65.3 Where a charity has passed the cash flow test (which is also a test applied by the auditors in reporting on all charity financial statements), it may yet fail another test based on the organisation's current balance sheet. The *Insolvency Act 1986* states that an organisation is insolvent if its total assets are less than its total liabilities, including contingent liabilities and prospective liabilities. This is an extremely tough definition, because of its inclusion of prospective and contingent liabilities. A contingent liability is one which potentially exists now, but the circumstances which may trigger the payment have not yet occurred: for instance, a claim for unfair dismissal being heard by a tribunal, where the verdict is still unsure. A prospective liability is a liability which the organisation knows it will have in the future. This category is so wide as to make every organisation potentially insolvent on this test, as most will have some long-term financial commitments that are certain, whereas raising a matching amount of income is not certain. This is as true for organisations that trade, as it is for those which rely exclusively on voluntary income. This is a situation where the strict definitions above begin to get blurred, and one in which many organisations find themselves before it is clear that they are genuinely and thoroughly insolvent.

Implications

65.4 The implications of insolvency are obvious: the organisation will be unable to continue to operate for want of funds. The nature of the process of closing down the insolvent organisation will depend on its legal structure.

Limited companies and industrial and provident societies

65.5 A charitable company will eventually go into liquidation. This is a process in which a liquidator is appointed to take control of the affairs of the charity and wind it up. In the meantime, the key considerations in the minds of the trustees will be twofold: to reduce the risk of loss to the creditors, and to preserve the work of the charity.

65.6 A company or industrial and provident society is obliged, when insolvent, to act in the best interests of its creditors. This duty does not seem to be the most appropriate for a charity, and is not an obligation which exists in many other countries where the first duty may be to the members, or even the beneficiaries. However, in the UK directors and trustees have to look after the creditors first. This means that from the moment that the trustees are aware of the insolvent position they must collect all possible sums owing, should not incur any expenditure, and should not pay off any creditor in preference to another. This latter point means that money may not be paid into an account in overdraft: a separate, credit only account at a separate bank should be opened.

65.7 There are alternatives to liquidation for insolvent companies, whereby the company can enter into an arrangement with the creditors. This is best administered formally by an insolvency practitioner under the *Insolvency Act 1986*, but can be operated informally. The High Court can alternatively make an Administration Order by which the appointee, with the sanction of the creditors, seeks to rescue the failing company. The final alternative for a company, and the only option for an industrial and provident society, is the appointment of a liquidator to wind up the entity: such an appointment is made by the creditors at a special meeting convened for the purpose, and follows on from a members meeting where the liquidator may be nominated by the members. Wherever insolvency is apparently inevitable, or even possible, an insolvency practitioner should be consulted as soon as possible. Insolvency practitioners are used to acting quickly and at very short notice, and will be prepared to advise an organisation initially on a free basis. They would hope that if a liquidator is to be appointed that they would be the nominee, but a reputable practitioner will not simply suggest that liquidation is necessary due to their own vested interest.

65.8 Assuming that the directors/trustees have not been guilty of trading whilst insolvent, or preferring one creditor to another, then they should be able to rely on the protection afforded to them by incorporation. This means that any debts which remain unpaid when all the assets are exhausted simply remain unpaid, and the company is eventually struck off. This protection is important as usually not all creditors are paid in full. This is because there are strict priorities to the order in which creditors may be paid, the value realised by assets during a liquidation is substantially less than would normally be obtained, and the liquidator himself will be charging fees which rank high in the order of preference. An initial assessment by the finance staff, based on accounts values, that the liquidator should just meet all the liabilities is usually likely to be completely wrong.

65.9 Assets held by a charitable company are not part of the company's corperate property if held within permanent endowment or restricted income funds. These assets cannot be distributed to the company's creditors, and if they were so applied then the directors could be liable to make good the loss.

Company Directors Disqualification Act 1986

65.10 The *Company Directors Disqualification Act 1986* only applies to limited companies, and only to directors who are guilty of wrongful trading (i.e. they continued to trade when they knew, or ought to have known, that there was no reasonable prospect of the charity avoiding going into insolvent liquidation). A person will be disqualified as a company director if that person was a director of an insolvent company, and that person's conduct as a director makes them unfit to be involved in managing a company. A report is made to the DTI by the liquidator as a basis for a decision to be reached by the Courts.

Unincorporated organisations

65.11 These organisations do not have limited liability, and therefore the trustees are personally liable for the outstanding debts of the charity. The constitution may govern what happens in such a situation, but again professional advice should be sought as soon as possible, as procedures are not specified to the same extent as they are in the case of limited companies and industrial and provident societies. The order of preference for the payment of creditors is also not defined in the same way.

65.12 In this situation, because each trustee is personally liable, it would be appropriate for trustees also to take personal advice on their own position. The trustees would normally fund this themselves, rather than look to the charity to pay for the advice. The charity can pay for advice on the position of the charity and the trustees as a whole. In certain circumstances it will be appropriate or necessary for a trustee to enter into an action against a fellow trustee. By this stage the charity is likely either to have a receiver and manager appointed by the Charity Commission, or to have ceased operations.

Insolvency indicators

Going concern

65.13 Accounts will indicate an insolvent position where the balance sheet as a whole is negative, or where the balance sheet remains positive only by virtue of assets such as functional land or buildings that cannot readily be used to pay debts. Often in this situation it may be possible to borrow commercially against the assets, thus repaying short-term debts with longer term borrowing. This will not alter the total balance sheet position, but will enable the organisation to meet its debts and reschedule its financial position.

Cash strains

65.14 The presence of high cash balances does not always indicate a high degree of solvency, again for two reasons. Many organisations receive income in advance, especially subscription-based charities where members will pay a proportion of next year's dues before the current year-end. In this case the income is treated as deferred income, that is, a liability. The difficulty with this sort of liability is that in day-to-day terms it never needs repayment and no apparent cost has to be incurred to meet any obligation against it. Trustees should be very aware that this is a perception and not reality: the receipt of deferred income, even subscriptions, involves some future cost against that same income. Organisations that do not take this into account are 'robbing Peter to pay Paul' and may need, at some stage, to catch up.

65.15 High cash balances can also camouflage insolvency where the fund analysis is incomplete. It is possible for a restricted fund to be in deficit, if expenditure has been incurred in advance of anticipated funding. In general, though, restricted funds will be in credit, with balances pending their application. These positive fund balances can appear to offset negative balances on general funds. The charity has a positive balance sheet, but in reality may be insolvent because its positive fund balances can only be spent on the purposes for which they were given.

65.16 In both these cases there may be no apparent cash strain in the organisation, and the accounts may only indicate insolvency in apparently the harshest interpretation of the word. However, the reality of the situation is that the charity is operating whilst insolvent, and the trustees are exposing themselves to personal loss.

65.17 Often the reality of insolvency is only starkly apparent when the auditors report on the year end accounts. Whatever the state of a charity's own financial reports, there are usually other signs of an insolvent situation developing, and these should be regarded seriously. Typical indicators are an inability to operate within agreed borrowing facilities, pressure from creditors, failure to observe credit limits or terms, and having to reschedule or cancel payments. These pressures are more than the routine of financial management, and indicate either insolvency or poor cash management. To assess whether the organisation is genuinely facing insolvency the trustees should immediately investigate whether, for example, there are assets not being properly employed, or debts or grants uncollected, or whether the apparent strains stem from an administrative disaster, that requires equally immediate attention.

Forecasts

65.18 All charities should be operating to budgets. A forecast has a slightly different function in that it predicts the most likely out turn over a period of time, whereas the budget is usually the target result. At the start of a financial period the budget and the forecast for the period will be very similar, or the same: as time progresses the forecast results will identify likely future variances from budget.

65.19 Where an organisation is potentially facing insolvency the need for sensible forecasts is enhanced, and these forecasts must particularly take into consideration the effect of variations in income streams. Traditionally voluntary income has been seen to be difficult to predict, on the basis that it is by definition not contractual and therefore must be uncertain. In fact this is not generally true: various strands of income have established patterns, and the risk to the going concern of the organisation is the sensitivity of a few percentage points down turn. Where this degree of sensitivity is likely to lead to potential insolvency, then the risks should be carefully evaluated.

Avoiding insolvency

65.20 Insolvency is usually apparent when debts are unpaid due to a lack of cash, and so struggling organisations need to concentrate especially on their cash management. Sometimes this is beyond their power, and there is no easy answer to those which are dependent on the annual grant receivable in April, or European funding which is delayed. However, charities should ensure that funding problems are not exacerbated by poor management. Options to improve the cash position include:

- renegotiation of timing of grant receipts;
- using supplier credit terms;
- making regular claims for income tax recoveries;
- attracting interest free loans from supporters;
- obtaining security from third parties for financing the charity.

65.21 Insolvency may alternatively result from lack of income or over-expenditure. If possible, steps must be taken to resolve the situation, however unpalatable they appear to trustees. It may be wise to consult the Charity Commission in advance, especially if these measures are likely to generate complaints or adverse publicity, such as the closing of an entire operation.

65.22 Finally, the lack of cash may represent lack of support which cannot be managed because the charity simply no longer has an important function to fulfil, either because it has achieved its purpose, or because its objects are out of date. When a fund-raising strategy cannot revitalise the organisation then insolvency may be unavoidable unless there is an opportunity to merge with, or be taken over by, another charity with appropriate objects.

Receivers

65.23 Confusion can exist because an insolvent charity may encounter this term in three differing contexts. For the sake of clarification these are set out below.

Administrative receiver

65.24 An administrative receiver is an insolvency practitioner who may be appointed under a debenture for the debenture holder to recover his loan from assets secured under a charge. Normally the lender is a bank, and such a power of appointment is a part of the finance agreement. Charities should be aware of any such powers which exist in their finance arrangements.

Official Receiver

65.25 The Official Receiver is a court official dealing with insolvencies and personal bankruptcies. The Court may appoint the Official Receiver who may sub-contract the work to an insolvency practitioner.

Receiver and manager

65.26 A receiver and manager is a person appointed by the Charity Commission under *s 18* of the *Charities Act 1993*, to take over some or all of the duties of the trustees if the Commission is satisfied that there has been misconduct or mismanagement, or that the charity's assets are in need of protection, or a *s 8* inquiry has been instituted. The receiver and manager acts to protect the assets of the charity, and eventually either closes it down or improves the charity's financial affairs so it can continue to operate.

Dissolution

65.27 When a registered charity ceases to operate the Charity Commission removes it from the register using its powers under *s 3(4)* of the *Charities Act 1993*. In addition to removal from the register a charitable company would also be dissolved under the *Companies Act*. (See Chapter 35.)

66 Insurance

66.1 Charity trustees have a duty to safeguard the assets of the charity and any trading companies it may own, both tangible and intangible, and a responsibility towards any staff or volunteers who work for the charity. Cover may be required for a wide range of items, including the property of the charity (such as land, buildings, plant, furniture, vehicles, equipment and computers); its liabilities to employees, volunteers and the public; accidents, sickness and costs arising from staff taking maternity leave; cash on the premises or in transit; motor insurance; insurance for fund-raising or special events; and loss of key people. An up to date inventory of all property, furniture and equipment must be kept for insurance and other purposes.

66.2 In some instances there will be a statutory duty to take out insurance, but in others it will be a matter for discretion, balancing risk against the cost of insurance.

Insuring property

66.3 If a charity owns the freehold of the premises it occupies it will be solely responsible for insuring them against the main material damage risks of fire, explosion, aircraft, lightning, storm and tempest. The Charity Commission recommends that trustees should insure buildings for their full reinstatement value, even if the governing document does not require reinstatement. They should take professional advice about this amount, which may need to include any necessary:

- demolition work;
- site clearance;
- architects, surveyors and other professional fees;
- costs associated with compliance with planning requirements and building regulations;
- rebuilding.

66.4 The buildings insurance should be regularly reviewed to check that cover is adequate and has kept apace with fluctuations in property prices and the cost of building materials. The amount of cover should take into account the fact that a building could be burnt down on the last day before renewal. Therefore, it needs to be sufficient to cover the cost of replacement at that time, if this is likely to be greater than the cost at the start of the insured period. If a claim is made and the charity is found to be under-insured, the trustees could be personally liable to make up the shortfall.

66.5 If a charity's premises are leased, then the lease should specify whether the landlord or the lessee, i.e. the charity, is responsible for insuring the property and/or the contents. If a charity is a landlord then the trustees should consider who will be responsible for insuring the building when they draw up a lease. It may well be in the charity's best interest to retain responsibility for insuring the building, but if this is the case then it should be reflected in the rents charged. If the charity passes responsibility to the lessee or lessees then it must monitor closely that adequate insurance cover has been taken out.

Contents

66.6 Insurance should be taken out against physical damage to the contents arising from fire, flood or explosion, theft, and 'all risks' e.g. loss or damage caused by war, nuclear contamination, riot and civil commotion. Lessees are usually responsible for insuring the contents of the part of the building which they occupy. An 'all risks' policy will generally cover damage to contents from most events, but the trustees may need to consider whether the insurance should:

- be on a 'new for old' basis;
- be index linked;
- cover losses from theft;
- cover accidental damage;
- cover goods or cash in transit;
- cover specified high-value items such as computers.

66.7 In some instances charities will be unable to afford the cost of insurance. This could well be the case for a charitable art gallery or museum. Where this is so, trustees should seek advice from the Charity Commission. This could protect them from being found guilty of a breach of trust should under-insured items go missing. Computer insurance is an area where a charity can easily find itself over-insured, as costs are declining. The cost of replacing a two-year old computer would be much less than the computer's cost at the time of purchase.

Business interruption/Additional cost of working

66.8 Cover for consequential loss that indemnifies an organisation against loss of income or profit will often be inappropriate for a charity. However, cover against the additional cost of working, such as the cost of renting alternative premises if the charity's premises are unusable as the result of any of the material damage risks listed at 66.3 and hiring equipment whilst awaiting repairs or replacements, is often more appropriate and may be advisable for some charities.

Employers' liability insurance

66.9 Charities employing staff are required under the *Employers' Liability (Compulsory Insurance) Act 1969* to take out employers' liability insurance to insure against any liability for personal injury, illness or disease sustained or contracted by their employees as a result of their employment. Most insurance companies will offer cover of £10 million. All individuals who have a contract of employment with the charity must be covered. Some volunteers, for example, those in receipt of honoraria, may be regarded as employees for the purposes of this Act. A copy of the certificate of insurance must be displayed at all premises where employees are based. Failure to take out employers' liability insurance or to display the certificate showing that a valid policy is in force will be subject to a heavy fine.

Employers' legal expenses

66.10 Employers' legal expenses insurance is not compulsory. It provides cover against losses related to employment matters, such as legal expenses and compensation arising from industrial tribunal awards. This is probably the most useful form of cover for potential legal liabilities that a charity needs.

66.11 Insurance

Public liability insurance/product liability insurance

66.11 There is no statutory requirement for charities to take out public liability insurance or product liability insurance. However, it is prudent for every charity that occupies premises, holds public events or sells or distributes products to have these types of insurance. If they do not, the trustees could be found to have breached their duty of trust.

66.12 Public liability insurance protects charities from claims arising from members of the public for any death, injury, illness, and/or loss of, or damage to, property incurred as the result of negligence on the part of the charity or one of its employees or volunteers whilst on the charity's premises or as a result of the charity's activities. It is generally linked to premises or to fund-raising events. It does not cover liabilities arising from the charity's work, for example, liabilities arising as the result of being given incorrect information, or to products manufactured or supplied by the charity.

66.13 'Members of the public' normally includes the charity's volunteers (including the trustees), users and beneficiaries, but policies should be checked to make sure this is in fact the case. This is particularly important if volunteers, including trustees, are not explicitly included in the employers' liability insurance. Volunteers should be informed about the extent of cover provided for them by the charity and made aware of any exclusions, and of any alternative arrangements the charity has made to protect them. For example, some policies exclude cover for volunteers over the age of 70 working in charity shops.

66.14 *Section 2(2)* of the *Unfair Contract Terms Act 1977* means that positioning a disclaimer notice, such as those frequently seen in car parks and cloakrooms, may not be an effective way of restricting the charity's liability for loss or damage resulting from negligence except in so far as the notice satisfies the requirement of reasonableness, while *s 2(1)* of the Act states that disclaimer notices cannot exclude or restrict liability for death or personal injury resulting from negligence.

66.15 Product liability insurance will be needed by charities that sell products to the public to protect them from liabilities arising under the *Consumer Protection Act 1987*, the *Sale of Goods Act 1979* or under Common Rules of Negligence. For example, a consumer who sustains serious injuries from using an item purchased from a charity's trading company's mail order catalogue could sue the trading company. Without adequate product liability insurance such a claim could result in the trading company becoming insolvent, and the trustees having to write off the charity's investment in the trading company.

Motor insurance

66.16 If a charity owns or operates vehicles it must comply with the *Road Traffic Act 1988* which stipulates third party insurance as a minimum requirement. If volunteers drive their own vehicles in the course of their volunteering work, the charity must ensure that the volunteers have suitable insurance. If a volunteer's insurance provider levies a higher premium as a result of the car being used for the charity's business, the volunteer can be reimbursed from charity funds for the additional premium.

Fidelity guarantee insurance

66.17 If employees or volunteers handle large amounts of cash, the charity should consider taking out fidelity insurance to protect against any possible fraud or dishonesty. The insurer will usually insist on background checks with the police. If this is the case the trustees will have to put their duty to protect the charity's property before any personal distaste at appearing not to trust staff and volunteers. Fidelity guarantee insurance also protects against theft of money by a forged signature on a cheque or the fraudulent use of computer equipment.

Professional indemnity insurance/errors and omissions

66.18 Professional indemnity/errors and omissions insurance protects against claims arising from a charity's work. The use of 'Professional' in this instance can be misleading as this insurance applies not only to true professionals e.g. lawyers, accountants, etc., but also to care workers, carpenters, gardeners etc. This type of insurance would, for example, protect the charity against a claim for a loss, injury or damage suffered by an individual or an organisation as the result of following incorrect advice given by an employee or volunteer of the charity. This type of insurance is particularly useful for charities providing professional services or complex, and potentially contentious, advice.

Trustee indemnity insurance/directors' and officers' insurance

66.19 For details of this see Chapter 114.

Other types of insurance

66.20 It is possible for a charity to insure against any risk providing that no illegality is involved, an insurer is willing to cover the risk and that the charity can justify that the degree of risk or potential consequences for the charity are such as to warrant the expenditure on the premium. Risks that charities have insured against include:

- staff sickness, to cover the cost of paying sick pay;
- pregnancy, to cover the cost of maternity pay and temporary replacement staffing;
- rain/bad weather, to cover loss of income from a fund-raising event;
- personal accident or assault, to protect employees and volunteers from claims made against them by members of the public for personal injury or assault in the course of their duties;
- the life of a key person;
- loss of computer data;
- non-appearance, to protect against the withdrawal of a celebrity from a fund-raising event;
- glass, to cover breakage of charity shop windows;
- goods in transit;
- travel insurance for personnel travelling abroad against medical expenses, repatriation costs and detention;
- defamation in a charity's publications;
- medical malpractice, to cover risks faced by those in the healthcare sector over and above those covered by professional indemnity insurance.

66.21 Insurance

Obtaining insurance cover

66.21 Insurance cover can be obtained directly from an insurance company or from an intermediary, such as a broker. If an intermediary is approached, care should be taken to ensure that they are offering independent advice and are not tied to a particular insurance company. It is good practice to obtain up to three comparable quotes from insurers or brokers.

66.22 When choosing a policy charities should look at their past claims record in order to decide the most appropriate excess, which is in effect a partial retention of risk. The trustees' duty to act prudently makes them risk averse and prone to choose low excess levels, with correspondingly high premiums. However, examining the history of losses may indicate that they are quite steady from year to year and it may be better for the charity to accept the cost of covering some losses themselves rather than insure against them. By opting for a higher excess, the charity can reduce costs of its insurance premiums. The overall level of risk to the charity remains unchanged.

Fulfilling conditions

66.23 It is essential that the person responsible for the charity's insurance understands any conditions stipulated in the insurance policies and ensures that they are fulfilled. Failure to do so can be costly. Consequential loss insurance, for example, may be dependent on your charity taking proper precautions against loss. For example, the reimbursement for damage to information held on computer is often conditional on the maintenance of regular back-ups, which the fire insurance may in turn require to be stored at different premises. Some computer policies exclude damage to computers from water, so it will be important to ensure computers are not located under sprinklers installed to limit fire damage.

67 Internal Audit

67.1 Internal audit is an extension of the internal controls operated by the trustees. The internal audit team appraises, monitors and reviews the accounting and internal control systems and reports directly to the trustees. Internal audit does not replace the function or need for external statutory audit, but may usefully supplement it.

67.2 The relevant Auditing Standard, published by the Auditing Practices Board, states that generally internal audit will undertake the following:

- reviews of accounting and internal control systems, often including a review of the design of systems, monitoring their operation and recommending improvements;
- examination of financial and operating information — this may include a review of the means used to identify, measure, classify and report such information, supported by detailed testing of transactions, balances and procedures;
- reviews of the economy, efficiency, and effectiveness of operations including non-financial controls of an organisation;
- reviews of compliance with laws, regulations and other external requirements, and with internal policies and procedures; and
- special investigations, such as a fraud enquiry.

Why have internal audit?

External requirement

67.3 In some circumstances an organisation is automatically required by external factors to operate an internal audit function, either because of the type of organisation it is, or because of an external funder's specific requirement. Frequently, organisations set up internal audit functions voluntarily, before any of the external factors come into play. The following circumstances all have a bearing in deciding whether or not an internal audit function is either useful or necessary.

67.4 When a charity's affairs become of a scale or degree of complexity that the trustees or the finance department, conclude that a failure to comply with laid down procedures would be difficult to identify in a timely manner through routine controls, then the need for an internal audit function is indicated. It will allow the charity to devote more attention to the effectiveness of the control procedures themselves, rather than rely on detection of errors or non-compliance well after the event.

67.5 Often a charity will be operating through locations remote from head office control. These local operations may be in the form of non-autonomous branches, shops, or projects, and may be in the UK or overseas. In these situations it may be difficult for the finance department to confirm that procedures which appear to be operating properly are in fact doing so: the additional resource of internal audit can help in these circumstances.

67.6 Some charities regularly find themselves in need of additional finance related services, such as creating new systems for new projects, updating procedures manuals, and carrying out routine procedures such as stock counts and ad hoc investigations, including fraud enquiries or efficiency reviews. There comes a point when the number of such occasional pieces of work becomes disruptive to the normal pattern of work for the finance department, or the costs of outsourcing such work become prohibitive. At this point the formalisation of the role into some form of internal audit function becomes desirable.

67.7 As is the case in many situations, charities will often consider implementing an internal audit function before a comparably sized commercial operation would. The reasons for this are partly to do with the factors already listed: charities become more complex, specialist and diversified before most similarly sized commercial organisations. However, other factors may also encourage charities to consider internal audit sooner, rather than later. Internal audit can play a valuable role in providing support to staff and volunteers who are struggling with understanding financial matters, or with the internal procedures and reporting requirements of the charity as a whole. Not all local staff will have the degree of training necessary for them to be ideally qualified for their job and many charities will use volunteers in administrative capacities, typically in running charity shops, or acting as branch treasurers.

67.8 Internal audit staff can visit these staff and volunteers, and not only carry out the traditional functions of that department, but also provide guidance and on the spot training on relevant issues. In this way the overall operation of the charity is strengthened, and internal audit is not seen as merely a policing function, which in turn helps the internal auditor in his or her role. With each such visit the amount of knowledge within the internal audit department develops, allowing procedures to be modified and targeted more effectively in future.

Creating an internal audit function

67.9 As with any department or function, clear terms of reference and guidelines need to be established in advance. Normally an internal audit team should have direct access to the trustees or to the audit sub-committee and be able to report independently of the finance function if necessary. The definition of the internal auditor's role becomes even more important where it is envisaged that the support element will be an intrinsic part of the job: there is a real danger that the internal auditor may subconsciously 'change sides' unless the brief is very well defined. Internal audit can be carried out either in-house or using an external provider i.e. 'outsourcing'.

In-house internal audit

67.10 Charities operating full-time internal audit functions are unusual, simply because the costs of maintaining them often outweigh the benefits. However, for larger and more complex organisations this may be possible, with full-time qualified staff. More often it will be appropriate for costs to be contained either by using part-time staff, or by the use of volunteers.

67.11 Volunteer internal audit functions are rarely formally set up. It is not uncommon, however, for charities to ask a suitably qualified individual to carry out occasional pieces of review work and where this is the case, such individuals can be considered as acting as internal auditors.

67.12 All internal auditors should have job descriptions, suitable training, adequate direction, a reporting format and a programme of work designed to cover the essential areas normally over a three to five year cycle. With volunteers even more care will be needed in ensuring that those involved are indeed adequately qualified and suitably motivated for the task.

Outsourced internal audit

67.13 Internal audit services can be purchased from accountancy practices or other firms offering these services. Usually a programme of work is agreed and a certain number of days work is purchased at an agreed fee. Internal audit differs markedly from external audit and it should not be assumed that all firms offering external audit services can automatically conduct efficient internal audit.

67.14 It is generally recommended that the same firm should not carry out external and internal audit work. There is, however, no legal constraint on the provision of such services by the external auditor and provided the function can be operated sufficiently independently of the external audit, there are some advantages to using the same firm, in terms of shared knowledge and more effective co-operation. Operating the two functions independently means at least involving another partner from the firm, and preferably a separate department or office.

67.15 Several consortia of charities operate systems where the costs of an internal audit team are shared between a number of participating organisations. This can provide the benefits of cost control, with the advantages of developing a stronger relationship more often associated with an in-house team.

Internal and external audits

67.16 The two types of audit are fundamentally different. Internal audit is a continuous process to do with procedures, transactions, systems and effectiveness. External audit is a statutory requirement designed to express an extremely stylised opinion on the accuracy of the financial accounts once a year. The two types of audit may or may not be interested in the same areas.

67.17 Most external audits of charities will not concentrate on detailed assessments of internal control systems, but will rely on a blend of some such assessment, along with testing of closing figures and analytical review. In larger organisations, systems become more important to the external auditor and there may be greater overlap. As a result, internal audit should not be seen as a substitute for external audit. However, it will certainly complement it and the two sorts of auditor should work together. For instance, the external auditor should plan his work having regard to the internal auditor's work programme and work performed. The external auditor should review the internal audit papers where relevant, and be involved in the implementation of any recommendations which have a bearing on his/her function. Conversely, the internal auditor should be aware of the external auditor's programme, simply for administrative convenience, and may expect feedback out of the external audit on the efficacy of the internal audit function.

67.18 The external auditor may (in certain circumstances) rely on the work of the internal audit department and this may lead to some savings in professional fees. This should not, however, be seen as the prime reason for establishing an internal audit function.

67.19 The external auditors should obtain a sufficient understanding of internal audit activities to assist in planning the audit and developing an effective audit approach. Where much of internal audit is geared towards the support role, or concentrating on immaterial areas, then the external audit procedures may be unaffected. Nevertheless, the external auditor may find it helpful to be aware of any conclusions drawn by the internal audit team.

67.20 During the course of their planning the external auditors should assess the internal audit function to see if it is either possible or desirable to rely on it. Important criteria for the auditor are as follows.

- The department's organisational status. Can the department report direct to the trustees, or audit committee, and the external auditors? Does it have any other operating responsibility which might impair its independence?

- The nature and extent of the assignments carried out. The nature of the assignments carried out is self-explanatory, and the extent is usually a matter of ensuring not a broad coverage of issues, but proper coverage of a selected area. This can be particularly frustrating for the external auditor, where there may have been useful work done on, for instance, branch activities. However, the reliance on the work done is reduced simply by the number of branches visited or by the failure to address a key aspect relevant to the auditors.

- The technical competence of the personnel. This will depend on the nature of the work being performed. Certainly one would expect any internal auditor operating in a charity not only to have the necessary finance and audit skills, but also to have an understanding of charities' regulatory framework generally, and the specific framework, including the governing document, applicable to the charity in question.

- Whether the internal audit work is done properly: that is, the work is planned, supervised, reviewed and documented. Whether or not the work is done properly is often a matter of communication between the two sets of auditors, as this is often an issue of quality control rather than the quality of the work itself. The introduction of some simple procedures may enable the external auditor to place more reliance on the internal auditor's work.

67.21 Once the audit is past the planning stage, then the two sets of auditors should meet to co-ordinate their work and exchange information where appropriate. If the internal audit work is to be relied upon, then it should be treated in a very similar way to work carried out by the external auditor's own staff: for instance, it should be subject to proper supervision and review, be supported by sufficient appropriate evidence, with appropriate conclusions drawn. Sometimes the internal audit work itself will need testing to confirm its adequacy.

67.22 The external auditor should also seek to comment on the efficacy of the internal audit function to the charity, especially where they have sought to rely on it. In this way weaknesses in this aspect of the internal controls of the charity can be identified and improvements suggested.

Risk management

67.23 As charities become increasingly complex and face an increasing number of changes each year in areas such as governance, controls assurance and fund-raising demands, this in turn focuses attention on risk and the need to ensure that the link between risk management and control is kept under review. As a result, charities have an increasing need to focus attention on their internal audit functions and, in particular, the quality of the resources available.

A new definition

67.24 In the light of this, the Institute of Internal Auditors has approved a new definition of internal auditing. This will be the umbrella under which the framework of ethics, standards and guidance is developed and will be the driving force behind many of the Institute's new initiatives:

> 'Internal auditing is an independent, objective, assurance and consulting activity designed to add value and improve an organisation's operations. It helps an organisation accomplish its objectives by bringing a systematic, disciplined approach to evaluate and improve the effectiveness of risk management, control and governance processes.'

67.25 The new definition recognises the significance of corporate governance and the need to manage risk with appropriate controls. The internal audit function becomes a process by which a charity can gain assurance that the risks it faces are understood and adequately managed in the context of dynamic change.

Monitoring control effectiveness

67.26 An integrated risk management and internal audit process will ensure that the senior management team identify risks to charity objectives and assess the controls in place to manage them, however, this will not work without monitoring control effectiveness. Once risks and appropriate controls have been identified, an effective monitoring process will check to see that those controls actually work. Charities may rely entirely on the site visits by the internal auditors to fulfil this role but this may provide little indication as to whether controls are working in the time between site visits, especially if only addressed say once in a three year cycle.

68 Internal Financial Controls

68.1 An effective internal control system is an essential part of the efficient management of a company, according to both the Cadbury and Hampel Committees. In a charity context, trustees should establish a system of controls that help to manage risk and control the economy, efficiency and effectiveness of the charity. Such a system will protect the property of the charity and ensure that it is applied only towards its objects. The operation of the control system will often be a matter for the executive staff, but this does not absolve the trustees of ultimate responsibility.

68.2 Internal controls generally cover a wide range of topics, including personnel and administration matters. Additionally, it may be important to have control systems in place for activities carried out to fulfill the charity's purpose (for example, residential care standards) and for the use of the charity's name and/or logo. There should also be procedures for dealing with the media and crisis management. Internal financial controls are therefore just one part of the overall internal control system and are concerned with safeguarding assets and ensuring that financial procedures, including transactions and reporting, are reliable. They are as relevant to the smaller charity as they are to the larger one, but naturally their nature and sophistication will be different.

68.3 In smaller charities much of the day-to-day administration may be undertaken by the trustees themselves. In these instances trustees should divide responsibility for functions so that no one trustee has too much authority, or has the ability to conceal or misrepresent transactions.

68.4 An internal financial control system needs to be clearly documented, communicated and maintained. It should also be monitored for compliance. The external audit is not necessarily designed to ensure that all internal control procedures are adhered to and therefore trustees may wish to create their own procedures for ensuring compliance. In larger charities this may take the form of an internal audit function, but in smaller ones it may take the form of occasional reviews carried out by disinterested parties. Where a finance or audit committee exists, this can be a suitable forum for reviewing such matters.

68.5 All internal financial control systems should identify the charity's structure, show who is responsible for what and the reporting lines. Where authority is delegated within the structure, then all such delegation should be formally recorded by the trustees and regularly reviewed. Often the extent of such delegated authority will be included in a job description and can be updated at staff reviews. All delegated authority must always be within the scope of the governing document.

Segregation of duties

68.6 Wherever possible different people should be responsible for different aspects of an operation, so they can serve as a cross-check on each other. For instance, a trainer should not arrange a course, take bookings, dispatch invoices and bank payments for the event. The administration of the event may be carried out by the trainer, but the cash bankings should be controlled by the accounts staff. In this way, and subsequently, numbers attending and monies received can be separately compared and verified.

Competence

68.7 Staff and trustees should have the degree of competence necessary to undertake their respective roles. In growing charities the level of competence needed is likely to increase as activities become more complex. Staff will need training if they are to keep abreast of developments or new staff with appropriate qualifications and experience will have to be recruited. Frequently, charities outgrow their people as the complexities of the systems become too great for the original staff and trustees. Typical areas that can lead to breakdowns are the diversification of activities into potentially taxable areas and transactions involving other legislation, such as licences, property transactions and investments. Trustees and staff should be conscious of the dangers of getting out of their depth and take future developments into consideration when appointing new trustees, staff or advisers.

Budgets

68.8 Where realistic budgets are prepared before an accounting period they provide an easy means by which the charity can be managed and help the charity in planning to use its resources in fulfilment of its charitable objectives. Most budgets are based on a realistic estimate of what may be achieved in the coming period and will incorporate certain key targets. Commonly, the crucial target will be levels of voluntary income. Results should be reported to the trustees regularly, ideally monthly, but at least quarterly, and the reports should focus on the key areas of the operation drawing attention to the achievement or otherwise of the targets.

68.9 Budgets only operate effectively as a control tool where the trustees understand the numbers and the underlying assumptions, and can then challenge the variances between the actual results and the budgets.

Systems

68.10 The system of internal financial controls should accommodate the following key areas: income, expenditure and assets. The Charity Commission's leaflet CC8 'Internal Financial Controls for Charities' sets out the basic requirements. It includes a self-checklist that a charity can use to assess its degree of compliance and identify areas where it should re-assess its procedures.

Income

68.11 Trustees should consider the nature of the charity's income and ensure that controls are appropriate. Souces of income may include:

- grants;
- contract income;
- donations;
- legacies;
- trading income and fees;
- investment income.

68.12 Probably the most difficult area to control adequately is the complete recording of unsolicited donations received through the post. All incoming money and cheques should be recorded at the time of opening of the post with two responsible people present whenever possible. Where the size of the organisation prevents this, the charity may consider publicising a policy of acknowledging donations as a further deterrent to misappropriation at this first stage of the cycle. In larger organisations closed circuit television cameras may be installed in a room specifically designated for cash and post handling. All of these procedures should also ensure the safe custody of the unopened post. All moneys received should be banked promptly, on the same day. Records of the postal receipts should be reviewed and the nature of the item also recorded and reviewed. In this way a pattern can be established and unexplained fluctuations identified. The initial recording of the cash receipts is designed to trap the information at the earliest opportunity, so that subsequent transactions or losses can be investigated. It follows that the record is only of any real value if it is used subsequently on either a regular or occasional basis to validate subsequent bankings.

68.13 Other types of income may be received which are not unsolicited. These may include fees, responses to grant applications and investment income. In all cases a register should be established against which any subsequent receipts can be checked. Amounts received can thereby be verified for accuracy and the supporting records can also be reviewed for omissions.

68.14 A register is particularly desirable for monitoring planned giving schemes. This is because a register not only helps income to be properly controlled, but it also enables the charity to submit accurate tax reclaims reducing the risk of an overclaim, which might only be detected after a visit from the Inland Revenue.

Public collections

68.15 These are currently controlled by under a variety of legislation, principally the *House to House Collections Act 1939* for English and Welsh charities and for Scottish charities the *Civic Government (Scotland) Act 1982* and the *Public Charitable Collections (Scotland) Regulations 1984* as amended. *Part III* of the *Charities Act 1992* sets out a new framework for public charitable collections, but no regulations have to date been issued, and this part of the Act is not yet in force.

68.16 Similar controls to those recommended for unsolicited donations should be operated for the opening of collecting boxes, or envelopes. In addition, however, there should be controls over the number, location and opening of the boxes. For instance, each receptacle should have a unique number and its location recorded. Boxes should be emptied regularly and agents should report to the charity on their collecting cycle.

Trading and service income

68.17 Income is usually easier to record and control where a service or goods are being exchanged. This is for two reasons. Firstly, because it is possible to identify the costs of provision and look for a matching source of income (for instance, the revenue generated by the theatre seat) and secondly, the purchasers will often require proof of purchase for their own reasons. This means that it will be possible to use pre-numbering systems which can be reviewed subsequently for omissions.

68.18 Some trading income can also be effectively recorded as soon as it is received by the use of tills that can analyse sales by item and provide a ready source of information to compare with bankings.

Recording of income

68.19 Following the implementation of the SORP, it has become increasingly important for charities to identify any terms of trust which may attach to income received. This is because the trustees may be in breach of trust if the money is misapplied, and because the final statutory accounts will have to disclose the various types of fund. Those receiving and recording income should therefore be alert to the nature of the income received and record it accordingly.

Expenditure

68.20 Whether expenditure is to acquire an asset or to meet a revenue cost, the process should be subject to authorisation and control. The same principles of documentary evidence and custody apply as they do to income. Where supporting documentation is required, these should always be originals and not photocopies.

68.21 The Charity Commission guidelines are helpfully brief.

- All expenditure and investment should be authorised against supporting documentation.
- Cheque books should be kept in safe custody with limited access.
- The preparation of documentation for authorisation should be undertaken by someone other than the persons authorising the payment.
- There should be clear written procedures setting out who is authorised to incur expenditure.

68.22 In some smaller organisations having detailed written procedures and separation of duties may be impractical, if not impossible. In these instances alternative controls may be applied, such as lists of payments being authorised by the trustees as a body, or even by the charity obtaining all cheques back from the bank for subsequent review.

68.23 Expenditure from cash should be restricted as much as is practicable. Cash raised from events or donations should not be used to subsidise petty cash expenses. This is to ensure that expenditure authorisation procedures cannot be bypassed and because gross accounting gives a more accurate picture of the relevant items.

68.24 Controls over expenditure are only of any value if there are equivalent controls over the ability of the charity to incur liabilities. Authorisation levels for the placing of orders should be documented, and suppliers can be notified that invoices will only be paid if raised against purchase orders in an approved format.

68.25 In larger charities a high level of control needs to be delegated to the executive staff operating these expenditure procedures. Sometimes this may extend to the trustees not being represented on the bank mandate at all. This is an undesirable extreme, as it makes it even more important that no two individuals are capable, through collaboration, of misapplying funds. If trustees are not represented on the bank mandates, then details of larger transactions should be reported regularly to them, and the treasurer could augment this with a closer review of all transactions.

68.26 In no cases should blank cheques be used. However rarely or exceptionally this practice may occur, it offers an unparalleled opportunity for easy fraud, and it can become a habit in an organisation simply to avoid inconvenience, for example, when one cheque signatory has to travel some distance to sign cheques. In leaflet CC8, the Charity Commission have stated that 'the practice of signing blank cheques would be regarded as neglecting the duty of care owed by trustees'.

68.27 Payments to employees and volunteers should follow similar procedures, with adequate personnel records maintained for all staff. This should include records of rates of pay and expenses arrangements. Such records should also ensure that staff are properly identified as self-employed or employees.

68.28 Expenses should only be paid against supporting documents, in the same way as any other expense item. Wherever possible round sum allowances should be avoided since they are more likely to be regarded as taxable, and subject to deduction for national insurance. They are also less susceptible to monitoring and control.

68.29 Records of expenses need to be maintained as employees require details in order to complete their own tax returns under the self-assessment regime. It is also a requirement of the SORP for the annual accounts to disclose the amounts of expenses paid to charity trustees, including a nil return.

68.30 Payments by other methods, e.g. BACS, direct debit, etc. should be authorised in the same way as other payments. Where regular payments are established, and the transaction is only authorised on inception, the signatory should take particular note of the termination date for the arrangement. Where a number of payments are authorised in a batch, as with BACS, each item should be within the relevant signatory's powers.

Assets

68.31 Certain assets require particular forms of control. Fixed assets (cars, equipment, buildings, etc.) should be listed, checked and adequately insured. To record these assets adequately it will often be necessary to assign a unique number to the item and record it in a fixed asset register. Often the fixed asset register is the supporting evidence to the cost figure in the annual accounts. Sometimes, however, an accounting policy may require certain items to be written off and never capitalised, although they still have a value to the charity and should still be subject to recording and control.

Investments

68.32 Investments should be safeguarded by the charity and full records kept of any holdings. Where a substantial sum is held in investments then an independent investment manager should be appointed provided that the trustees have the appropriate powers of delegation. If they do not, they should approach the Commission to ascertain whether or not their powers of delegation can be widened. The investment manager should be regulated under the *Financial Services Act 1986*.

68.33 Reporting on investments held and their performance should be an intrinsic part of the management reporting of the charity. Further consideration of the role of investments in a charity is set out separately in Chapter 71. However, the basic controls that should always operate include:

- taking professional advice before selecting or disposing of investments;
- ensuring that all dividends or interest payments are received; and
- portfolio diversification to prevent one major failure seriously impacting on the charity.

Reporting

68.34 Internal financial controls require documenting, updating and monitoring. The management accounts will provide evidence of the effectiveness of the control system, as will an internal audit function. The external auditors should also submit a management letter addressed to the trustees that draws attention to any shortcomings in the system of internal financial controls. Whilst the auditor's comments will never be comprehensive, any matters arising should be brought to the attention of all the trustees as a body and the trustees should respond formally to them.

69 Internet

Background

69.1 The Internet is a loose association of thousands of networks and millions of computers across the world that all work together to share information. The Internet '*information superhighway*' is like a road system. There are a number of major routes that meet at particular points. Lots of smaller roads spread out across the countryside and feed the major routes. On the Net, the main lines carry the bulk of the traffic and are collectively known as the *Internet backbone*. The backbone is formed by the biggest networks in the system, owned by major Internet service providers (*ISP*s) such as *GTE*, *MCI*, *Sprint*, *UUNet*, and America Online's *ANS*. The backbone has so many intersecting points that if one part fails or slows down; data can be quickly re-routed over another part. This is known as *redundancy*. In some countries, the network may have less redundancy and so be more vulnerable to slowdowns or breakdowns.

69.2 The Internet's ability to handle an enormous amount of data every day trades flexibility for speed. Everyone who uses the Net shares 'bandwidth', the data carrying capacity of a network. Every time you send an email or download a file, you're contributing to the load. Web pages can take up a lot of bandwidth given the quantity of graphics and animations they may contain.

E-commerce

69.3 E-commerce is normally divided up as follows:

- business to consumer (b2c);
- business to business (b2b);
- consumer to consumer (c2c).

69.4 The b2c segment gets the most publicity but the fastest growing area is b2b. Business to business is all about electronic transactions between business, email, purchasing, invoicing and payments.

The Internet and not-for-profit organisations

69.5 The Internet can offer important opportunities to charities, but can also create a variety of problems for the unwary. As with the introduction of any other business tool, the business case for exploiting the potential of the Internet should be considered and endorsed at a senior level as part of the normal business planning process.

69.6 The implementation of an Internet strategy comprises two parts:

- eVision;
- delivery.

The first stage deals with the ebusiness concept; evaluating its potential and feasibility, how this fits in with and complements the 'business' plan, and assessing the real value of the opportunities. If this is acceptable, it will be necessary to refine the proposed strategy, identify the enabling technologies and solutions required, and ensure that approval for any necessary funding is put in place.

69.7 The delivery phase is concerned with ensuring that the vision is realised. This will involve:

- Scope and definition phase: defining in detail the scope and objectives of the ebusiness delivery stage(s), identifying the detailed requirements, costs and plans;
- Develop and Implement phase: building and delivering each of the requirements set out in the delivery stages;
- Operate and enhance phase: managing the running of the business environment and planning for the next phase of enhancement or additional solution.

Email

69.8 Email offers significant benefits:

- You can prepare and send emails for less money than either letters or faxes;
- Emails are faster than a letter and sometimes faster than fax;
- Provided precautions are taken, email can be a secure communications medium;
- It is unimportant where the recipient is physically located and, unlike a telephone call, does not need to be available to receive a message;
- Email attachments ensure:
  - the recipient gets documents *exactly* as they were sent without any corruption or degradation;
  - one can work on documents with other people in ways that are simply not possible with other media.

69.9 Email is, however, different from other forms of communication and some of the issues it raises are not immediately apparent. Bad use of email can irritate colleagues, clients, customers and suppliers.

69.10 One should not use email alone for any document that has a contractual implication. Emails, in common with faxes, have dubious value in court because they are so easy to forge. Drafts and copies of contractual documents may be sent by email, but the final version should always be sent as a printed document.

Security and the Internet

69.11 There is much talk of the Internet's security problems. To a certain extent, the sheer volume of traffic travelling over the Internet reduces the risk that someone will pick on a specific message, intercept it and understand enough about its contents to use it maliciously. The risk, however, exists. For a high profile charity or not-for-profit organisation, the risk is increased where those with malevolent intent may be specifically targeting the organisation.

69.12 To secure documents, encryption is one of the most popular techniques used. This involves encoding the file using a protocol that is agreed in advance between the sender and the recipient.

69.13 There are two simple ways to encrypt documents:

- many programs, such as Word and Excel, have options on their 'Save as . . .' panel to enter a password to save the document in encrypted form;
- the 'Zip' utility encrypts documents as they are being compressed.

69.14 Internet

Viruses

69.14 Some of the most infectious viruses are transmitted by email. They can be embedded in attachments so that just opening a Word document or an Excel spreadsheet, for example, infects a PC. Worse, some viruses spread themselves by identifying people in address books and sending them emails containing the virus.

69.15 The only guaranteed way to completely protect against viruses transmitted by email, is to stop using email altogether. Fortunately there are some less draconian measures that can provide reasonable protection:

- Install virus-checking software. Some products will check emails as they are received.
- Keep virus-checking software up to date. One should expect to have to load updates at least monthly.
- Be wary of unsolicited programs and documents. Even if the email comes from someone trustworthy, do not open any attached documents if the covering note appears strange or uncharacteristic (it might have been sent by a virus on that person's computer). Suspicious emails should be checked before use or deleted.
- Any unfamiliar messages passing through outboxes or appearing as sent items that did not arise from known users should be treated with caution.

'Signatures' and Disclaimers

69.16 It is important to recognize that emails are considered to be 'published' company documents. Thus, when an email is sent, it is considered to be from the originating organisation. In these circumstances it is important that the email should carry a signature identifying the sender to comply with the *Company Names Act 1985* and *Business Names Act 1985*. The signature may simply be text added either to the top or bottom of a mail message, giving the company name, registered office and company number.

69.17 It is also regarded as good practice to include a disclaimer to remind the reader that the mail may be confidential and privileged (this is particularly important as emails can be easily forwarded) and can help reduce liability. It is very important to seek the appropriate legal advice to formulate a disclaimer to meet the needs of your particular organisation. However an indication of a typical disclaimer (for a company 'ABC Limited') follows:

> 'This email is confidential and may be privileged; it is for use of the named recipient(s) only. If you have received it in error, please notify us immediately; please do not copy or disclose its contents to any person or body, and delete it from your computer systems. ABC Limited does not guarantee the security of any information electronically transmitted. ABC Limited is not liable for the proper and complete transmission of the information contained in this communication, nor for any delay in its receipt. THE USE OF EMAIL FOR ANY ILLEGAL PURPOSE OR FOR ANY PURPOSE OTHER THAN AS PERMITTED BY ABC Limited IS STRICTLY PROHIBITED. ABC Limited Registered Office 123 Acacia Avenue. Register Company Number: 123456'

69.18 In certain circumstances special signatures or disclaimers should be added for particular departments or people within the organisation. For example, the Human Resources department may wish to explain the data protection policy or a department that sells financial services may want to stipulate its accreditation with the relevant statutory bodies.

Acceptable use policy

69.19 There may be occasions when it is necessary to view a colleague's mailbox, for example if they are unavailable or if there is a suspicion of email malpractice of some kind. In these circumstances it is not advisable to view the mailbox unless the employee has been told that this may be done and that the organisation reserves the right to inspect mailboxes at any time. Otherwise, opening someone's emails may constitute an infringement of their rights under the *Data Protection Act 1998*.

69.20 It is best practice to set up the correct framework at the outset, with a policy such as an Acceptable Use Policy (AUP). Such a policy stipulates the terms and conditions on which email is granted to an employee and is agreed by an employee before they are granted email access. Typically, a policy covers at least three areas.

- It should contain a core definition which scopes the systems covered and the basic policy tenants (e.g. protection from illegal and immoral use).
- It should define the ownership of the IT systems, stating that use of the systems is a privilege and they are wholly owned by the organisation.
- It should include specific details and prohibitions, for example stating that junk email should not be propagated, or that non-work related internet access should only be used outside working hours.

69.21 The construction of a policy requires expertise. It is important that if that expertise is not available in-house, external assistance should be sought.

70 Investigations: Malpractice and Abuse

Charity Commission powers

70.1 The statutory power for the Charity Commission to investigate a charity is found in the *Charities Act 1993 s 8*. 'The Commissioners may from time to time institute inquiries with regard to charities or a particular charity or class of charities, either generally or for particular purposes, but no such power shall extend to any exempt charity'. The power therefore extends to excepted charities and also to any Scottish charity which is largely controlled from within England and Wales.

70.2 The Commission's powers in relation to such an inquiry are not open ended but well defined. They may demand accounts and written explanations relating to the matter in question, if necessary by statutory declaration, and copies of any relevant documents held. They may also require people to attend at a stipulated place and give evidence, some of which may be required to be under oath. The power does not extend merely to trustees or employees of a charity. Any person with information relevant to the inquiry can be asked for information and copy documents, unless they relate solely to an exempt charity.

70.3 The Commission does not have the power to investigate criminal matters. If an inquiry uncovers a possible criminal offence, such as fraud or child abuse, the Commission will notify the police.

70.4 Other public bodies (including local authorities) may pass information to the Commission, including Customs and Excise, the Inland Revenue and the Department of Trade and Industry. They may inform the Commission of the charity's name and address, its objectives if this is relevant to determining its charitable status, and of any activities undertaken by a charity already registered, but which appear to be non-charitable. The Commission has a reciprocal right to inform other authorities of relevant matters. This right extends to authorities in other countries.

70.5 Anyone who, knowingly or recklessly, provides misleading information to the Commission in the context of these powers is guilty of an offence punishable by either a fine or up to two years imprisonment, or both.

70.6 Having instituted an enquiry under *s 8*, the Commission has further powers to act for the protection of charities (other than exempt charities). It first has to satisfy itself that there has either been misconduct or mismanagement in the administration of the charity, or that it needs to act to safeguard the property and assets of the charity, or the proper application of existing or future property. Once this is established then the Commission can independently do one or more of the following by Order.

(*a*) Suspend any trustee, officer, agent or employee of the charity, pending consideration of his removal, for up to twelve months. Any such suspension must be preceded by written notice;

(*b*) appoint new or additional trustees;

(*c*) transfer property to the Official Custodian;

(*d*) forbid the disposal of charity property without the Commission's consent;

(*e*) forbid debtors making payments to the charity without the Commission's consent;

(*f*) restrict the charity's transactions; and

(*g*) appoint a receiver and manager.

70.7 If an inquiry has been instituted and both conditions referred to above apply (misconduct or mismanagement, and the need to protect property) then the Commission may remove those individuals listed at (*a*) above, and may establish a Scheme for the better administration of the charity.

70.8 The exact nature of misconduct and mismanagement has been the subject of some attention over the years, as it covers the largest numbers of cases where the Charity Commission, having instituted an inquiry has identified a cause for concern. Although there are many instances which could appear under this heading, the legislation specifically refers to only one situation: excessive payments for administrative purposes.

70.9 There are other particular instances where the Charity Commission may remove or appoint a trustee, irrespective of an inquiry being conducted. Trustees may be removed where a trustee has been bankrupt within the last five years, is a corporation in liquidation, or is incapable of acting due to mental disorder. All of these cases are rare, but two other instances are more probable: where a trustee has not acted and will not declare whether he is prepared to act or not, and where a trustee is absent, maybe outside England and Wales, and thus impeding the efficient functioning of the charity.

70.10 The Charity Commission has powers to replace a trustee, or to appoint additional trustees, if it considers this to be in the interests of the charity.

Process: What initiates an inquiry?

70.11 An inquiry is usually initiated either as a result of the Charity Commission's internal monitoring procedure or as a result of external comment. Matters requiring investigation may emerge from internal monitoring of annual returns, reviews of annual reports and accounts, or from routine visits to charities. External comments come from a variety of sources but most frequently from press comment and from individuals, many of whom have mixed motives for referring the matter to the Commission. Where charities are competing for funds, it is not unknown for one to report another to the Charity Commission in the hope that its funding application may thereby be jeopardised. The advent of the whistleblowing regime for auditors may also be expected to contribute to the initiation of enquiries.

70.12 All complaints are first screened by an evaluation officer who takes a view on whether or not:

- the complaint is groundless;
- the problem is minor and can be put right by the Commission giving the charity some advice;
- the problem is more serious, but can best be dealt with by staff in the Commission's Charity Support Division providing the charity with substantial help;
- from the evidence to date the matter is sufficiently serious to warrant the launch of a formal section 8 inquiry.

70.13 The Commission has repeatedly made it clear that it will not get involved in matters relating to the internal administration of a charity, where the matter is simply one of internal politics. The introduction to its leaflet CC47 'Investigating Charities' says,

70.14 Investigations: Malpractice and Abuse

'The Commission cannot act in the administration of a charity, nor can we interfere in its affairs, where the trustees have acted properly. We will not mount an investigation without establishing that there is good reason to do so'. The good reasons are set out most fully in a supplementary leaflet. They include:

- a lack of proper prudence, conduct or control in the administration of a charity's affairs such that funds or other assets of the charity are at risk;
- incompetent management;
- disclosure of activities which would be likely to damage the reputation of charities generally;
- misuse or misapplication of the assets or the funds of the charity;
- failure to operate within the charity's constitution or the law;
- provision of false information to the Commission, or misleading the public and others with an interest in the charity (e.g. beneficiaries or employees) in a material way;
- remuneration of the trustees where there is no power to pay them or receipt of benefits by trustees when this is not explicitly permitted by the governing document;
- significant non-compliance with the accounting requirements of the *Charities Act 1993* or with any other statutory responsibilities of charity trustees;
- actual or incipient insolvency;
- a large charity revenue accumulation or a large and increasing revenue deficit;
- any other matters arising from examination of a charity's accounts which give cause for concern;
- breach of obligations imposed on trustees by the general law, for example, trustees buying property from, or selling their own property to, their trust, or exploiting for their own benefit opportunities which have arisen to them in their capacity as trustees, or any dealing between a charity and one or more of its trustees which has not been conducted at arms' length, without proper authority;
- unacceptably high administration or fund-raising costs;
- excessive payments to any trustee or employee, or for any services rendered to the charity; and
- improper political activities.

70.14 If a charity is subject to an inquiry the trustees will be informed of its terms of reference and the name of the relevant case officer. Sometimes professionals external to the Charity Commission will also be employed. In all cases further guidance notes expanding on the Commission's leaflet CC47 'Investigating Charities' will be provided to the trustees.

70.15 The person conducting the inquiry will act impartially, in the best interests of the charity. As their inquiry progresses other matters may come to their attention which merit further investigation, and these too will be looked at.

70.16 At the end of the inquiry a report will be prepared. Usually anybody likely to be strongly criticised will be given the opportunity to respond to those criticisms, although the Commission is not obliged to accept or note any of the comments made. Where action is to be taken then the charity will be informed in writing of the proposed action. The results of inquiries may be disclosed under the Code of Open Government, or under freedom of information legislation. Results may be used in court proceedings and those of particular public interest will be published.

70.17 The results of some investigations are published in the Commission's annual report, where the underlying causes of the problem are also discussed. Each year the report also provides statistics on the numbers of investigations and the protective powers exercised. These protective powers tend to fall into two categories, firstly the powers used to assess the position and stabilise it and secondly, powers to sort out the longer term problem. Figures 1, 2 and 3 illustrate some of these statistics.

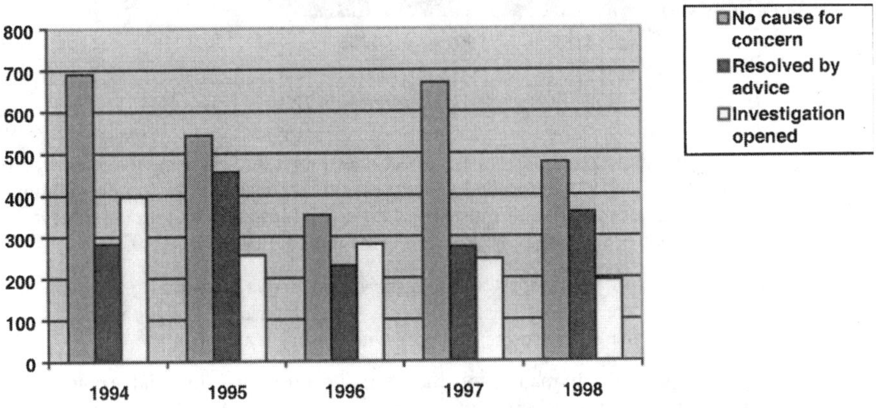

Fig 1: Evaluations to establish whether an inquiry should be opened

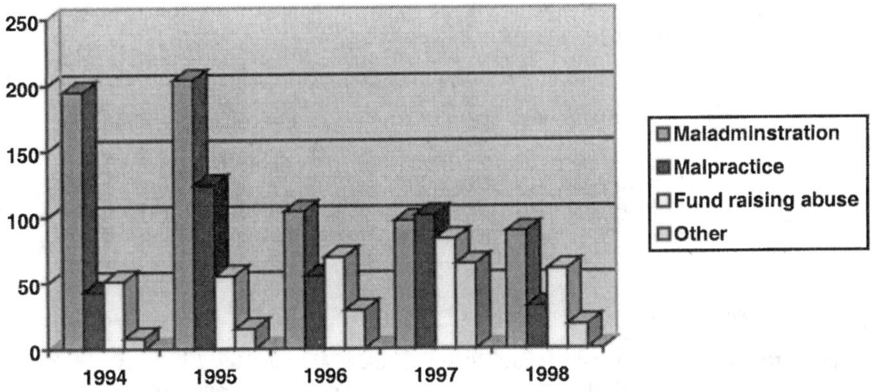

Fig 2: Inquiries substantiated

70.18 It is apparent from these figures that only a tiny minority of charities each year are subjected to the regulatory powers of the Charity Commission. The matters reported are instructive as to which matters have created the most concern. Four particular issues which are referred to in the context of recurring themes.

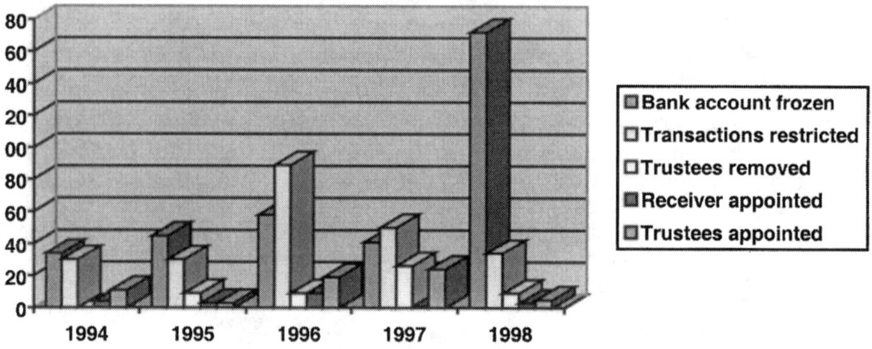

Fig 3: Protective powers exercised, excluding Orders

- The dominant founder/administrator: 'It is essential that each and every trustee is aware that they are individually and collectively responsible for the administration of their charity and must insist on full information and an equal say and involvement in the policy and activities of the charity'.
- Lack of control by the trustee body: the report draws attention to the case of a trust, where 'the founder trustee effectively ran the affairs of the charity without reference to the other trustees, two of whom were resident in the USA'.
- Rapid expansion: 'In many cases the internal controls and financial arrangements are not sufficient to cope with this change. Eventually the administration of the charity breaks down resulting in loss of funds or failure to achieve the purposes of the organisation'.
- Disaster relief efforts: 'Where an organisation launches into a small relief programme without having prepared the ground, or without any practical experience of what is required, the result can be disastrous. It is not uncommon for the following problems to be encountered:
  - — loss of funds or goods resulting from inadequate organisation or controls
  - — ineffective control over the activities of the volunteers while abroad
  - — unnecessary risk to the employees and volunteers abroad, and
  - — loss of confidence by the local communities in aid organisations generally which can undermine the patient planning of the larger or more skilled charities'.

Receiver and manager appointments

70.19 A receiver and manager appointed under the *Charities Act 1993* has a different function to one appointed under the terms of a debenture in an insolvency case. An appointment is only usually made where there is evidence that the administration of a charity has completely broken down, or if assets or income are at risk. The role and function of the receiver is determined in part by *The Charities (Receiver and Manager) Regulations 1992* and partly by the Order appointing the receiver. He or she acts under the supervision of the Charity Commission.

70.20 The regulations authorise the Charity Commission to seek security from the receiver, and to determine fees. Within three months after appointment the receiver must report to the Charity Commission setting out the asset value of the charity on appointment, the strategy for discharging their duties as set out in the Order, and other relevant matters.

70.21 In practice the receiver takes responsibility for running the charity with the usual powers in place of the trustees. This may involve putting it on to a sounder financial or administrative base, or it may be a matter of working alongside existing and new trustees and assisting them in the better performance of their duties.

Scotland

70.22 The *Law Reform (Miscellaneous Provisions) (Scotland) Act 1990* empowers the Lord Advocate to investigate any Scottish charity if it appears that any mismanagement or misconduct has taken place in the running of its affairs. The Scottish Charities Office was set up within the Crown Office to undertake this function on behalf of the Lord Advocate. The Lord Advocate may suspend anyone concerned in the 'management or control' of a charity for up to 28 days. The Court of Session has the power to stop an organisation representing itself as a charity; to suspend individuals permanently from a position of 'management or control' and to appoint a *judicial factor* (official administrator) to take care of the charity's affairs and, if necessary, wind up the charity and transfer its assets.

70.23 Just as the Charity Commission have power to investigate a Scottish charity controlled from England and Wales, so there is a similar power allowing the Scottish authorities to investigate English or Welsh charities mainly controlled from Scotland. [*LRMPSA 1990*].

71 Investments

Investment powers

71.1 Charities, with the exception of charitable common investment or common deposit funds, are not established for investment purposes. Therefore most charities can only invest funds if their investment activities are ancillary to achieving their charitable objects and their governing document contains investment powers.

71.2 There are legal restrictions on the ways in which charity funds can be invested. These can vary from one charity to another, so it is important that the trustees and charity administrators know exactly what their investment powers are, and make sure that their professional advisors are aware of them.

Trustee Investments Act 1961

71.3 At the time of writing the trustees of all charities currently have statutory powers of investment conferred by the *Trustee Investments Act 1961* (as amended). However, when the *Trustee Bill 2000* is enacted the provisions of the *Trustee Investments Act 1961* described below will be repealed. The *Trustee Investments Act 1961* requires trustees to:

- diversify their investments portfolio to reduce the risk of loss should one investment fail;
- consider the suitability of all investments for the charity's needs (i.e. long-term capital growth or income generation); and
- consider the suitability of particular investments.

71.4 The *Trustee Investments Act 1961* also places restrictions on the types of investment that can be purchased, unless the charity's governing document specifies investment powers that are wider. The Act lists permitted investments dividing them into 'narrower' range and 'wider' range investment. At least one-quarter of a charity's investments (excluding so-called 'special' range investments) must be invested in narrower range securities such as government stocks, National Savings Certificates, building society investments, mortgages of freehold property or fixed interest stocks issued by public authorities. A maximum of 75% can be invested in wider range investments such as unit trusts or equities of companies which have an issued and paid-up share capital of not less than £1m, and have paid a dividend on all issued shares in each of the last five years.

Trustee Bill 2000

71.5 When the *Trustee Bill* becomes law, which at the time of writing is likely to be towards the end of 2000, charitable trusts that do not currently have wide powers of investment in their governing document, and that are therefore currently constrained by the *Trustee Investments Act 1961*, will be given wider statutory powers of investment. Trustees will be allowed to make any kind of investment, apart from land (see Chapter 74), that they could make if they were absolutely entitled to the assets of the trust.

71.6 Trustees will still have to comply with 'standard investment criteria'. They must take account of:

- the suitability of the type of investment proposed for the trust;
- the suitability of that particular investment;
- the need to diversify the investments of the trust.

71.7 Suitability will include considerations such as size, risk, ethical considerations and the need to produce the balance between capital growth and income that is required to meet the needs of present and future beneficiaries.

71.8 Trustees will also be required to review the charity's investments from time to time and consider whether, taking the standard investment criteria into account, they should be varied.

71.9 Before investing *s 5* of the *Trustee Bill 2000* requires trustees to obtain and consider advice from a person or body reasonably believed by the trustees to be qualified to give investment advice, unless in the particular circumstances it would be unnecessary or inappropriate to do so, for example if the cost of obtaining advice would be disproportionate to the benefit to be gained from the investment.

71.10 Charities that already had wider powers of investment than those contained in the *Trustee Investment Act 1961* are, ironically, likely to find that their powers are now narrower than those now proposed in the *Trustee Bill*. They may need to consider applying to the Charity Commission for the conferral of 'the general power of investment' if they are not to be disadvantaged.

Charities Act 1993

71.11 Unless forbidden by their governing document, trustees in England and Wales also have power under the *Charities Act 1993 s 24(7)* to invest in 'special' range investments which include common investment funds and common deposit funds. The Charity Commission considers that charities currently subject to the *Trustee Investments Act 1961* should aim to hold no more than 20% of their capital in common investment funds that invest solely in overseas equities.

Governing document

71.12 The governing document of a long-established charity may contain a power allowing trustees 'to invest in any investment authorised by law'. This in fact gives the charity only narrow powers of investment because at the time of writing the trustees are limited to the powers of investment conferred by the *Trustee Investments Act 1961* (as amended) or to investing in Common Investment and Deposit Funds (not Scottish charities) established under the *Charities Act 1993* and earlier legislation. More modern constitutions are likely to include wider powers of investments, avoiding the requirement for a division into narrower and wider range investments. However, as mentioned in paragraph 71.10 above, once the *Trustee Bill 2000* is enacted charities that presently have wider powers of investment than those permitted by statute may need to amend their governing document.

Widening investment powers

71.13 At present trustees wishing to widen their powers of investment may amend their governing document, providing it contains a power of amendment and they obtain written consent from the Charity Commission (Inland Revenue Charities (Scotland) (formerly FICO) in Scotland). If the governing document does not contain a power of amendment the Court may grant or vary powers of investment. Normally, this will not be given for charities with investments of less than £750,000. Where the Court does allow a charity with a very large fund almost complete freedom to invest it may well insist on the need to take professional advice.

Investment duties

71.14 Charity trustees have a duty of care to the charity's beneficiaries when investing the charity's funds. They must act with the same degree of care that a prudent business person would exercise when investing on behalf of someone for whom they had a moral obligation to provide.

71.15 Trustees also have a duty to invest the charity's funds in ways that are likely to produce the highest level of return consistent with minimising the charity's exposure to risk. This duty means that trustees who do not invest surplus income or, for example, merely put it in a bank account which earns a comparatively low rate of interest, are acting in breach of duty and could be personally liable to compensate the charity for lost investment income.

Ethical investment

71.16 The duty to maximise financial return must also override the trustees' personal code of ethics or their preferred types of investments and has implications for the extent to which a charity can adopt an ethical investment policy. The circumstances in which a charity can adopt an ethical investment policy were defined in 1993 by the judge in a case brought against the Commissioners of the Church of England by the Bishop of Oxford, Richard Harries. The Bishop argued that the Church's policy of investing in arms companies and companies that perpetuated apartheid in South Africa was against the ethical principles of the church and was therefore in breach of trust and should cease. Although the Bishop lost this particular case, the judgement clarified the circumstances in which trustees should take ethical considerations into account when defining their investment policy (*Harries v Church Commissioners for England [1993] 2 All ER 300*). The Charity Commission's advice, CC14 'Investment of Charitable Funds' takes account of the judgement in the *Harries* case and states that if trustees are considering establishing an ethical investment policy they should bear in mind the following.

- Any ethical criteria adopted must reflect the needs of the beneficiaries of the charity, not the trustees' personal views.
- Trustees should avoid investments that directly impede the furtherance of the charity's objectives, e.g. a cancer charity should exclude investments in tobacco companies and a charity for the relief of alcoholics should exclude investments in breweries or pubs.
- Trustees should avoid investments that might be to the charity's financial detriment, e.g. investments that would result in a loss of financial support from donors or members.
- Trustees should avoid investing in companies that potential beneficiaries regard as acting against their interests, and which could deter potential beneficiaries from accepting help from the charity.
- While in most instances it should be possible to identify investments with at least a similar potential return to those excluded on ethical grounds, where this is not

possible it may be necessary for the trustees to take a less principled approach. In order to avoid having a portfolio that is not sufficiently diverse to ensure good enough financial returns, the trustees may have to exclude investments in companies with more than a certain proportion of their turnover linked to the unacceptable product, rather than impose an absolute ban.

The need for an investment strategy

71.17 If a charity has surplus assets that the trustees believe would be prudent to set aside, they will need to develop an investment strategy. As the latest guidance from the Charity Commission on reserves makes clear, charities should set aside funds to protect the charity from fluctuations in income, to fund future commitments they have made to beneficiaries, or to fund repairs or a planned development (CC19 'Charities' Reserves'). However, the Commission warns that trustees should not allow excessive reserves to accumulate without good reason. If they do, the Inland Revenue could require tax to be paid on the investment income, as it would not be being spent on charitable purposes.

71.18 The investment strategy should facilitate the achievement of the charity's objects by creating sufficient income to enable the charity to carry out its purposes consistently year by year, while maintaining and, if possible, enhancing the value of invested funds. The strategy should be set out in writing together with any policy constraints. These could include for example:

- liquidity — the need for a certain proportion of funds to be kept readily accessible;
- ethical constraints — no investments in companies that impede the achievement of the charity's objects or that deter supporters;
- diversification — no more than x% of funds invested in any single company;
- restrictions — limitations on the charity's powers of investment;
- risk — the level of acceptable risk;
- monitoring — trustees to receive written reports on investment at specified intervals.

Professional advice

71.19 Investment advice should be written, impartial and given by someone with sufficient experience of charities and the types of investments they are permitted to use. This could be an accountant, bank manager, stock broker, investment manager, a member of the charity's staff or one of the trustees. However, if trustees give investment advice they should consider the extent of any professional negligence liability which they may incur by so doing. If the trustees decide to disregard professional advice they have received, they should minute their reasons for taking an alternative course of action.

71.20 Once a charity's investments have reached a size where they could benefit from specialist attention, the trustees may wish to appoint investment managers and delegate day-to-day investment management to them, providing their governing document contains a power to do so, or consent is obtained from the Charity Commission. The Charity Commission's guidance, CC14 'Investment of Charitable

Funds' suggests that trustees with sums of £100,000 or more to invest should consider appointing an independent investment manager to advise them in drawing up their investment strategy and on the selection of suitable investments.

Power to appoint an investment manager

71.21 If the trustees wish to appoint investment managers the charity's governing document must include powers permitting the trustees to delegate decisions or responsibilities to third parties. If it does not, the relevant powers should be obtained by amending the governing document. If there is no power of amendment in the governing document the Charity Commission can be approached to authorise the change.

71.22 Where the trustees have the power to appoint an investment manager it does not mean that they can abdicate responsibility. They must always retain control of investment policy, ensuring that there are adequate controls in place to check that the investment managers' powers are being exercised prudently, within the law and the powers in the charity's governing document, and that their performance is reviewed regularly.

71.23 Any investment manager appointed must:

- have at least five years experience of investment and financial management;
- be authorised to conduct investment business by the *Financial Services Act 1986* (i.e. a member of the Financial Services Authority);
- make regular reports (every three months) on the performance of the investment portfolio; and
- report all transactions to trustees within fourteen days of their happening.

71.24 Trustees should inform investment managers of their investment powers, lay down a detailed investment policy, ensure that the terms of delegated authority are clearly set out in writing and endeavour to ensure that these are observed. The delegation should also be reviewed every 24 months. Only if these steps are followed will trustees avoid liability for the acts or defaults of the investment manager. Further details on delegation to investment managers can be obtained from the Charity Commission, in their leaflet CC14 'Investment of Charitable Funds'.

Endowed charities

71.25 At the time of writing the Charity Commission are conducting a consultation exercise seeking views about whether or not endowed charities should be allowed to be more flexible in their treatment of investment returns. The Commission is undertaking this exercise as it is aware that the rules for the treatment of investment returns on capital funds are now so out of date that they can work against the interests of present and future beneficiaries.

71.26 At present trustees have to credit endowment funds with capital returns, whilst the income return is available for the general purposes for which the fund was established. The Charity Commission has recognised that changes in taxation and reward schemes have resulted in investment returns arising in a growing variety of ways that are no longer in line with trust law. The Commission is considering three ways forward:

- the continuation of the current arrangements for the treatment of investment returns from capital funds;

- complete liberalisation so that charities are free to spend or save any of their capital or income;
- a middle way called 'total return' that lumps together all forms of return on investments to produce a 'total return'. Some of this can be used to meet the needs of present beneficiaries while the remainder is added to capital to help meet the needs of future beneficiaries.

72 IT Planning

IT strategy must support the business plan

72.1 An IT strategy should support an organisation's overall business strategy and work towards its long-term goals and plans. As a charity evolves, so should the IT strategy to ensure that the supporting systems are extended and remain appropriate. The strategy therefore needs to be continually updated and revised to take account of changing circumstances, both internal and external. Only in this way can an organisation rise to new IT challenges in a well-considered, forward-looking and, thus, cost-effective way. The alternative, 'reactive' approach inevitably leads to compromises, unanticipated shortcomings and, at worst, project failures and wasted resources.

72.2 For a number of reasons, an organisation's IT systems can become out of date or no longer fully support the charity's objectives, for example:

- organisational growth, both size and complexity, may place strains upon the capacity of existing systems. For example, changes in methods of fund-raising activities, the introduction of new charitable activities or the establishment of a trading arm may mean that existing systems can no longer cope with current organisational needs;
- external factors can force the replacement of outdated systems, such as new accounting regulations, phasing out of supplier support for bespoke and obsolete systems or the introduction of the Euro;
- inefficiencies and shortcomings of systems become increasingly apparent as the volume of work increases. Users can find it difficult to work around problems when operational activities are no longer served well by the systems that were designed to support them.

72.3 Unlike the commercial sector where the cost of IT projects can often be written off over the life of a profitable venture, charities are expected to be business-like and accountable with public scrutiny over administration costs. As a result, there is often a tendency to stretch the life of a system, avoiding the cost of significant enhancement or replacement until it becomes unavoidable. This can lead to operational inefficiency and increased manual effort and work-arounds to cope with changing operational needs. In terms of management and staff time, this can be expensive. These costs can be hidden as the resulting inefficiencies are spread across the organisation and not easily isolated.

72.4 Those charged with making investment decisions often feel vulnerable when presented with bids for IT funding. They do not always consider themselves to be computer literate and can be nervous of the jargon and the way in which computer systems are often described and presented. However, the decision to change or upgrade systems is, irrespective of the type of organisation, primarily a business decision. If the costs and benefits cannot be explained in a language understandable by those who will use, ultimately benefit from or who are to authorise the project, approval should not be given.

Practical steps

Justification — getting approval

72.5 In justifying the time and resources required to prepare an IT plan, the following should be borne in mind.

- Organisations that have no means of measuring the success of their fundraising initiatives and performance indicators on financial performance, income and costs will fall behind those that are able to interpret results and make changes that result in improvements.
- Planning encourages creativity and fresh ideas that simply reacting to problems as they arise can never accomplish. Leaving IT decisions to the last minute leads to compromises that could have been avoided with careful planning.
- Holding on to systems that are burdensome and no longer support the business objectives can result in greater staff and management time, opportunity costs and reduced efficiency and effectiveness. Anticipating future needs and planning ahead provides an opportunity to compare the costs and benefits of available courses of action whilst there remains time to select the best stratagem.
- Recent attention to matters of corporate governance and accountability coupled with public scepticism emphasises the importance of budgeting and transparency of reporting.
- Trends and current supplier offerings should always be monitored to ensure that existing systems continue to provide good value for money against current products. It is essential to future-proof current and planned investment as far as practically possible, but equally important to recognise when it is time to move on.

Preparing an IT plan

72.6 The preparation of an IT plan need not be a costly exercise. It can often develop through an evolutionary process. The starting point could be to summarise the current computer equipment and systems in each department and propose changes in hardware and software supported by an argued business case as to the associated costs and benefits of the investment.

72.7 Once the proposed new systems and equipment have been approved, their introduction can be planned. It is often helpful to start by asking the questions 'What has got to be done, by whom and when?' It is usually useful to show the answer to this diagrammatically, for example using Gantt charts showing time along the horizontal axis and the various tasks to be performed along the vertical axis. Each task can then be shown by a horizontal line between the start and end dates of each. In this way, a view of the project can be shown including those tasks that are dependent on the completion of earlier steps or tasks. The chart can than be regularly updated with actual progress.

Involving the people — needs analysis and resistance to change

72.8 Resistance to and fear of change are enemies of successful IT projects. A participative approach promotes ownership. Ideally, no-one should be made to feel left out and it is important that those who will work most closely with the new system should feel committed to its success and comfortable when using it. Everyone should be regularly appraised of progress and expectations managed.

72.9 IT Planning

72.9 It is a good policy to welcome and listen to the views of staff in advance of the imposition of change. The extent to which staff and volunteers should become involved in selecting the new system will vary according to their duties, roles and responsibilities. They may not have a role in making the final investment decisions but those who feel involved and share a sense of commitment and ownership of a plan are most likely to support it.

72.10 Therefore, it is always useful to seek staff input in identifying:

- the strengths, shortcomings and inadequacies of present systems, as a basis for agreeing the essential needs of the new system;
- areas where workloads and tasks can be tackled more efficiently and productively by better use of IT or by streamlining processes;
- the strengths and weaknesses of candidate systems under consideration, for example in demonstrations, workshops or pilot studies as appropriate; and
- alternative systems of which they may have experience that may be suitable candidates to meet the needs of the organisation.

72.11 Where small numbers of staff and volunteers are involved, an appraisal of system requirements can be obtained through focused meetings and workshops. In a larger organisation, detailed questionnaires may be prepared to obtain information according to particular areas of individual staff expertise. One to one interviews with individual staff members or workshop sessions for groups of users can be arranged to discuss views and needs according to circumstances. The deliverable from this process should be to have a clear idea of what the new system should do and a list of key areas of required functionality, especially those that are non-routine or unique to the organisation. It would be useful for the next tasks if those needs were prioritised between the essential and those considered nice-to-have.

72.12 Finally, unless senior management take an active interest in the project and champion its success, staff may reflect the perceived view of management and assign the project a low priority. Experience suggests that successful IT projects are those where the chief executive and/or other influential senior persons take a personal interest in its success and champion the process. It is for this reason that a board 'sponsor' should be appointed. This will allow the board to make known its views to the team at project review meetings and also to feed back project status and progress to senior management.

Research — information sources and issues

72.13 There is no shortage of information on all aspects of IT. The difficulties lie in distinguishing fact from fiction, optimism from reality and promises from working solutions. To help keep abreast of IT matters, it is wise to choose one or two regular information sources of which the independence can be assured, such as publications by the IT Faculty of the Institute of Chartered Accountants of England and Wales. For information on popular matters, such as the Internet, the weekly technology supplements of some newspapers can be more relevant than magazines aimed at home users or the technically minded.

72.14 The software market is constantly changing through consolidation, innovation and development. Up to date, comprehensive, information on specific, specialist software products for charities can be more difficult to obtain, and time can be wasted investigating unsuitable products. Magazine articles and reference publications may be helpful, but can be out of date or incomplete. They are often misleading and poorly researched. Charity sector exhibitions and conferences are often useful sources, both for the information they provide and as a means of linking up with other similarly interested parties keen to exchange experiences and ideas. However, system implementations are only as good as the effort and planning that went into them and one person's unconfirmed adverse testimony may have nothing to do with the capability of the software but the way they went about installing and using it.

Economic use of external expertise

72.15 The decision whether to manage an implementation project in house or employ external consultants can be a difficult one. Many organisations, particularly charities, believe that they do not have sufficient in-house skill and resources for the staffing of IT projects. The most common argument is that other duties will inevitably result in an inability to provide sufficient time to the project resulting in loss of control, mistakes and time delays. Conversely, external consultants should have practical experience of systems implementation but any additional knowledge and experience they gain will depart with them at the end of the project.

72.16 As a possible solution to this problem, and recognising the need to keep costs to a minimum, it is possible to retain overall control of the project whilst using focused external consultancy expertise. It may be cost-effective to engage a consultant's services for some aspects of the selection process, either to supplement a known shortfall in expertise or as a sounding board or mentor in making sure that all matters have been given adequate prominence in the selection and implementation process. Thus, the external consultant may complement the skills of internal staff, give guidance and confidence and fill specific gaps in knowledge and experience, but on an as-needed basis rather than a full time basis.

Software and hardware

For not-for-profit organisations

72.17 It is important to bear in mind the diversity of the specialist software now available. It can range in price, from a few hundred to many thousands of pounds, and in after-sales support arrangements, which range from virtually none, or on-line support by modem to permanent on-site presence. The mainstream accounting software industry does not look upon the not-for-profit sector as a significant target and has traditionally made little effort to cater for its specialist needs, but there are a number of smaller suppliers offering specific solutions that do not always have the backup of resources or client base to guarantee continued support or investment in the product. There is, however, a variety of specialist software available to cater for the needs of the charity sector in the recording, analysis and administration of revenue. Requirements specific to the trading arms of charities are generally available within the commercial sector. Great care must be taken in assessing the viability of less well-known software products as their continued ability to meet needs unique to the not-for-profit sector, for example the SORP requirement for fund analysis, may be limited.

Accounting software

72.18 Given the shortcomings described above, organisations are often forced to overlay their particular requirements on the features and functionality present within mainstream accounting software applications designed for the commercial sector. As a general rule, if no charity-specific solution can be found, look towards a market-leading accounting software product with backup of resources and a number of customers operating in circumstances similar to your own.

72.19 The functionality of the nominal ledger is usually the primary consideration for charities choosing accounting software because of the need to analyse transactions according to the fund to which they are to be applied. The leading accounting products differ significantly in their ability to meet this need; SunAccount and Blackbaud are examples of packages that are known to meet this requirement, others can be made to do so and some cannot. The number of levels or dimensions over which they are capable of analysing transactions is often a key indicator of their ability to meet fund reporting requirements, both on the balance sheet and within the revenue and expenditure statement.

Fund-raising software

72.20 There is a variety of fund-raising software products available. The marketplace is constantly changing and consolidating, such that there are now only a handful of major players at the top end of the market offering products essentially similar in functionality. The differentiating factors tend to be price, specialist add-on modules and the style and quality of implementation, training and support. Single-user prices for the most sophisticated products range from £4,500 to £6,000.

72.21 At the lower end of the market, there is a wider variety of products and much greater disparity in functionality, price, operating system and quality of support. Some entry level and medium-priced products are still available only in DOS, with no plans to migrate to the Windows environment. Single-user prices range from £150 at the entry-level, up to a specialist module of £1,500. Generally speaking, the level of functionality is directly reflected in the price of software at this level. Great care should be taken in assessing the suitability of these products and whether they meet an organisation's particular needs.

72.22 Some or all of the following areas of activity are catered for in specialist charity systems:

- contacts, relationships and donor database;
- diary facilities;
- receipt administration;
- receipts analysis to nominal ledger interface;
- receipt analysis (by fund, project, appeal, etc.);
- covenant and tax claim management;
- grant-making and applications management;
- membership and subscription management;
- event management;
- volunteer management;
- office automation software.

72.23 Word processing, spreadsheet, database and presentation software applications can be most economically purchased in integrated suites. Practical advantages of integration include the ability to cut and paste between applications in the same suite incorporating, for example, a graph produced in a spreadsheet into a report in the word processing application. Ideally, the spreadsheet should integrate seamlessly with the fundraising and accounting systems to allow the transfer of information for further manipulation and analysis.

72.24 A variety of Human Resource systems specifically designed to assist in the administration and management of personnel is available. As a general guide, systems become cost-effective from about 50 employees upwards, although some are designed to cater for 500 employees or more. For further information the best sources may be to contact the Institute of Personnel and Development or visit the exhibitions at which the market-leading suppliers exhibit.

Selecting software — general guidance

72.25 It is important to have a clear understanding of the organisation's needs, which of these are important, and thus, which are not. One way to express this is to list the organisation's *functional* requirements distinguishing between those needs that are essential and those that are desirable or of little interest. This document is often called a '*Statement of Requirements*'.

72.26 The level of detail provided in a Statement of Requirements will vary according to the type of application and the complexity of the function it will be required to support. It could act as a discussion document for use within the organisation, can be used as the basis of an invitation to tender, a checklist to ensure that the requirements have been met, form a schedule to the contract as to what is to be supplied and may later form the basis of an implementation plan. Provided it is unambiguous and concise, it can ensure that there is no misunderstanding between users and the supplier as to what is required. It is clearly an important document and essential to get it right.

72.27 The extent to which the essential needs can be met at a reasonable price and without major modifications to the packaged system will be a key factor in the selection process. It is not uncommon for users to declare initially that most of their needs are 'essential'. This means that the selection exercise could become bogged down in making sure these 'essential' requirements have been met when some of the work could have been avoided by being more rigorous with the prioritisation of needs. It is interesting to note that essential needs are often no longer considered quite so 'essential' when faced with a large bill for changing the system to meet them.

Selecting hardware

72.28 The selection of hardware is often dependent upon the choice of software as sometimes there are restrictions as to the platforms upon which it can run. It is wise to seek advice from the software supplier on the minimum hardware and communications specification required to ensure that the performance of the software will not be inhibited, and to select a hardware manufacturer that will be reliable, enhanceable and maintainable.

72.29 Software resellers are usually happy to advise on and supply hardware suitable for the software they distribute but increasingly do not wish to become involved in the supply and maintenance of hardware where the profit margin is comparatively low. It is now common for the purchaser to obtain PCs from other, less expensive sources.

72.30 However, whilst there is no obligation to buy hardware from the software supplier, and assuming that they are willing to supply it, it may be convenient to arrange a single-source agreement such that one party takes responsibility for the supply and maintenance of all facets of the system. This avoids the problem of disagreement between the various suppliers for each component of the system over responsibility for fixing a fault, especially where it cannot be determined initially where the problem has arisen. For example faults could arise as a result of software, hardware, the communications system or operating system failure. The circumstances under which a single source agreement is appropriate depends on a number of factors, not least of which is size and sophistication of the system and the extent of in-house expertise to handle and manage the relationship with all the parties that may be involved.

Implementation guidelines

72.31 The most important element of implementation planning is to fully consider and agree what has to be done by whom, and this means establishing what both the supplier *and* the purchaser is going to do and when. An implementation plan is a collaborative effort involving all parties with the output of agreed tasks, resources and milestones together with a realistic timetable embracing installation, set up, testing and acceptance of the system. This will include the physical delivery, assembly and configuration of the system so that it can be be seen to be functioning throughout. Where there is a network, cabling will have been laid, connected and tested to all workstations and equipment.

72.32 The applications software is usually loaded before delivery, unless this is being supplied by another supplier or where specialist staff are required to install it. Pre-installed software is usually only tested in so far as its facilities or modules can be accessed and not that it has been set up to meet any predetermined requirements. For example, someone will need to clean up data from the old system before it is transferred to the new one, and someone will need to decide upon and set up all the reference information within the new system. The set up of accounting systems requires user input, for example, defining the chart of accounts and report layouts. Once everything is set up, it will need to be checked not only to ensure that it is correct and operates correctly within each area but that it also works correctly across the system as a whole.

Project management

72.33 In any implementation, there will be certain tasks which cannot be carried out unless certain other tasks have already been completed. Success of the project will require people and resources to be available to carry out their tasks at the right time as envisaged in the project plan. It is this vital stage of the planning process that requires someone to take overall responsibility for the implementation. Project management is required therefore from the time of drafting and agreeing the implementation plan through to ensuring achievement of the agreed milestones, ensuring that all resources are made available at the right level of priority through all stages up to the system going live. This individual is known as the Project Manager or Project Co-ordinator.

72.34 It is normal for the software supplier to provide a Project Manager. This person will often be very useful to the organisation and drive the project forward. However, the primary role is to manage the project from the supplier's perspective and the supplier's manager may not necessarily have an interest in ensuring that all the customer's obligations and tasks have been conducted, especially where they have no impact on what the supplier has to deliver. It is important, therefore, for there to be a Project Manager representing the customer. This is usually an internal role as this reinforces the sense of commitment and ownership although an external consultant may also have a role to play. This may include, for example, assuming a mentoring role or attending project review meetings to ensure that progress is being made and independently confirm that the correct course of action is being taken, particularly where in-house there is a lack of project management experience.

73 Joint Ventures

73.1 Where several organisations work together in partnership it may be advisable to set up a formal joint venture. Charities typically enter into joint ventures to carry out joint trading enterprises, or to work together on a particular initiative to promote a mutual charitable interest, for example, relief of Third World debt. Although many joint working arrangements do not need a separate legal identity it is often advisable to set up a joint venture company, or at least a formal agreement, in order to minimise the risk of disputes should things go wrong, particularly if losses are incurred.

Joint Venture Agreement

73.2 All the parties to a joint venture should be clear about their rights and obligations. Therefore, a joint venture agreement is drawn up setting these out, including the purpose of the venture, who owns it, how profits are to be shared, how it is to be governed, restrictions on competitive behaviour and arrangements for terminating the agreement. Other provisions will cover problem areas such as dispute resolution, inquorate meetings and partners who want or need to withdraw.

73.3 Joint ventures are relatively unusual in the voluntary sector. The issues to be considered before entering into one are much the same whether the venture is charitable or commercial. The charity should consider its legal capacity to enter into such an arrangement, the financial commitment and risk involved and whether or not the joint venture is in line with the objects of the charity and its strategic plan. As with sponsorship and commercial participation, charities may need to consider the extent to which a relationship with the other venturers is compatible with the good name of the charity and the degree of control they will have over the future direction of the venture.

Accounts

73.4 The financial statements will need to take account of the joint venture, although the precise accounting will depend on the charity's stake in the joint venture company and whether that company is a subsidiary or an associated company. Joint venture accounting is governed by FRS 9 and the accounts of subsidiary companies should be consolidated as required by the SORP. If a charity has a participating interest (within the meaning of *Companies Act 1985 s 260*) in an undertaking which is not a subsidiary and exercises significant influence over its operating and financial policy (usually presumed if one holds beneficially 20% or more of the voting rights), then it is probably an associate undertaking.

73.5 The accounting treatment will depend on the exact nature of the relationship:

- associates should be included on the net equity method i.e. just the net results and assets are included in the accounts;
- joint ventures should be included in the accounts on a line by line basis, reflecting the charity's share. This does not form part of 'gross incoming resources' and should be shown separately;
- less formal joint arrangements should be treated like a branch, with the charity showing its share of income and expenditure.

74 Land and Buildings

74.1 Dealings in property are frequently complex and often carry underlying risks which may not be immediately apparent. Although this chapter can indicate some general principles, in most instances it will be necessary to take specialist legal advice. Reasons for this include the topic's history, reaching back to the middle ages, and the variety and breadth of issues to which this chapter can do no more than allude. The principles set out below are of general application to all charities, including industrial and provident societies although most of the sections of the *Charities Act 1993* relating to land do not apply to industrial and provident societies.

74.2 The *Charities Act 1993* set out a new statutory regime for the disposals of charity land and relieved the Charity Commission of the need to give consent to most charity land transactions, placing increased responsibility on charity trustees.

General duties of trustees

74.3 The Charity Commission has set out trustees' duties regarding land in a number of leaflets, i.e. CC3 *Responsibility of Charity Trustees*, CC28 *Disposing of Charity Land*, and CC33 *Acquiring Land*. In this context land is taken to mean land in England or Wales with or without buildings and includes any estate or interest in land, such as a lease or right of way. The main duties are as follows:

- Trustees are individually and jointly responsible for the protection, management and supervision of the land.
- In managing the land trustees must act only in the interests of the charity and its beneficiaries, which means, for example, obtaining the best price on a disposal.
- Trustees must act honestly and must use the same degree of care as they would prudently exercise in dealing with their own business affairs, which means, for instance, that they must maintain overall control of the management of their land and ensure that the charity can afford a prospective purchase.
- Trustees must seek professional advice when purchasing or disposing of land.
- Any decision to dispose of, or mortgage, land must be taken by the trustees acting together.
- A disposal or mortgage of land is always a matter which should be undertaken and controlled by the trustees as a whole.
- Trustees must always have the necessary power or authority for the transaction.

Reasons for holding land

74.4 The reasons that charities hold land will have bearing on some of the processes involved in relevant transactions.

Functional property

74.5 Functional property is property, such as an almshouse, which is held on trusts which stipulate that it is to be used for the purposes of the charity. This is not the same as the charity simply allowing the asset to be used for charitable purposes. Confusingly whenever property is used for charitable purposes its related costs and depreciation or amortisation may be charged as a functional cost within the SOFA.

Permanent endowment

74.6 Land will form permanent endowment if the capital cannot be expended. The charity may or may not be allowed to dispose of the land, but in either case it will not be able to dispose of the proceeds, which may require reinvestment in line with the original terms of trust.

Investment property

74.7 A charity can invest in land if the governing document contains a power to do so, or if the trustees have obtained an Order of the Charity Commission authorising them to do so. An Order will be granted if the Charity Commissioners are satisfied that it is in the best interests of the charity to invest in property and will be dependent upon reports from solicitors and surveyors. Investment property may also be endowed.

Who can hold land

74.8 Incorporated bodies, such as limited companies, Industrial and Provident Societies and incorporated trustees can hold land in their own name since they are recognised legal persons. Unincorporated bodies such as associations and trusts cannot hold land or rent property in the same way; they must therefore vest title in the asset in a small group of holding trustees or a custodian trustee or the Official Custodian for Charities. Where a charity has several properties, it will often establish its own trust company for this purpose. The company never trades, it simply is a vehicle for holding title. In all these cases the person who holds the legal title is not the beneficial owner. They have no rights over the asset, but merely hold it on behalf of the charity. Vesting charity land in the Official Custodian does not change any of the powers the charity trustees have to dispose of it.

Acquiring land

74.9 Apart from where a mortgage is required, or where the purchase is subject to an Order of the Charity Commission, the acquisition of land by a charity is essentially the same process as that undertaken by a commercial organisation or an individual. However, the degree to which the governing document can be relied upon before a transaction is contemplated needs consideration. At the time of writing unless there is a clear express power for the charity to acquire the land for the purpose intended, the trustees may find that they are acting *ultra vires*. For instance, it may not always be correct to assume that a charity has an implied power to lease property for administrative purposes. This situation will change when the *Trustee Bill 2000* is enacted.

Trustee Bill 2000

74.10 When the *Trustee Bill 2000* is enacted (probably towards the end of 2000) it will give trustees of charitable trusts a specific power to purchase land in the UK, freehold or leasehold, as an investment, for the occupation by a beneficiary, or for any other purpose. Trustees will have all the powers of an absolute owner to manage the land. While the Act only authorises trustees to purchase land in the UK, it would be possible for a non-charitable trading subsidiary owned by a charity to purchase or own land outside the UK.

74.11 Land and Buildings

Disposing of land

Legal power

74.11 CC28 'Disposing of Charity Land' sets out the Charity Commission's latest advice on this subject. Before commencing a disposal charities must ensure that they have a legal power to dispose of land. This will need reference not only to the governing document, but also to the terms relating to the original acquisition of the property and to *s 36* of the *Charities Act 1993* (this does not apply to exempt charities). Where the relevant power does not exist, or where it is unclear as to what the original terms were, then the Charity Commission should be contacted. A Scheme may be necessary. The statutory procedures on a disposal do not necessarily apply in relation to a disposal to another charity, if the trusts do not prohibit such a disposal and the disposal is a means of furthering the charity's purposes. Similar conditions apply on the granting of a lease to another charity.

Charity Commission consent

74.12 Since the introduction of procedures under *ss 36–40* of the *Charities Act 1993* it is not normally necessary for a charity to seek the Charity Commission's consent for the sale of property. The detailed procedures differ depending on the transaction.

Granting leases for seven years or less where no premium is paid to the charity

74.13 No consent is required to the granting of such a lease if:

- trustees obtain and consider the advice of a person they reasonably believe to have the ability and experience to advise them competently on the granting of the lease;
- trustees satisfy themselves, taking into account the views of their adviser, that the terms they are receiving for the lease are the best that can reasonably be obtained in the circumstances; and
- the land is to be leased to someone who is not a 'connected person' (see 74.23).

Other transactions, including the granting of leases for more than seven years, leases for premiums, freehold sales, grants of easements, rights and options, exchanges of land

74.14 No consent is required for the above transactions if:

- trustees obtain and consider written advice on the proposed disposal from a qualified surveyor instructed by the trustees and acting exclusively for the charity;
- trustees advertise the property in accordance with the surveyor's advice, unless the trustees are advised not to advertise the property;
- based on the surveyor's report, the trustees are satisfied that the terms of the disposal are the best that they can reasonably achieve; and
- the disposal is not to a 'connected person'.

74.15 The surveyor's report is governed by regulations issued under the *Charities Act 1993*. The surveyor must be a fellow or professional associate of the Royal Institution of Chartered Surveyors or the Incorporated Society of Valuers and Auctioneers, and must have experience relevant to the type of property he is being asked to advise upon. The regulations themselves are available from HMSO, although trustees are encouraged by the Charity Commission not to rely upon the regulations alone, but to ensure that the report takes into account any other factors which may have specific bearing on this particular transaction.

Functional land

74.16 Trustees must advertise the fact that a disposal of functional land is intended, unless it is to be replaced on the same trusts, or the trustees are granting a lease for only two years or less, receiving only a rent and levying no premium, or the Charity Commission have issued a direction that these rules need not apply.

Mortgages

74.17 Special rules apply where a charity wishes to acquire property using mortgage finance, or indeed even if a mortgage is taken out on property already owned by a charity. A mortgage in this instance includes a charge over the property. These rules do not apply to exempt charities.

74.18 As with disposals, there is no need for a charity to obtain the consent of the Charity Commission to take out a mortgage as long as certain procedures are properly followed, although even the procedures set out below are unnecessary where a higher authority (e.g. a scheme) already exists. Usually the trustees must obtain and consider the advice of someone who is reasonably believed to have sufficient ability in, and practical experience of, financial matters to give them sound advice. This person can be an officer or employee of the charity, but must have no financial interest in the loan. The adviser must provide the trustees with advice in writing on whether or not the loan is necessary in order for the trustees to be able to pursue the particular course of action in connection with which the loan is sought, whether or not the loan's terms are reasonable (in view of the charity's own credit status), and the charity's ability to repay the loan on the proposed terms.

74.19 These requirements are set out in *s 38* of the Act, but occasionally prospective lenders require charities to obtain the advice set out above from an independent adviser, such as the auditor, as though confusing the requirements on disposal and mortgaging. Where a charity is asked to obtain such a report, it should ensure that the lender is fully aware of the exact requirements of *s 38* before incurring what may be otherwise unnecessary professional costs.

74.20 The Charity Commission has also made it clear that if a charity takes out an unsecured loan, and its assets comprise mainly land, then they will not necessarily grant their consent to any subsequent sale of land to repay the loan unless the borrowing had originally been authorised by the Charity Commission.

Register of charges

74.21 Limited companies have to maintain a register of charges as part of their statutory books. As a mortgage is a charge it should be recorded in the register, setting out the date of the charge, the name of the lender, details of the property concerned, and the amount. Notice of the creation of a charge must be given to Companies House within 21 days. Similarly an industrial and provident society must notify the Registrar of Friendly Societies about the creation of charge or mortgage within the same period.

Additional statements

74.22 Whenever a registered charity makes a disposal of land, including taking a mortgage, the trustees are required under *s 37* of the *Charities Act 1993* to make certain statements and issue certain certificates, some of which have prescribed wording and some of which will be drafted by solicitors. These statements are designed to demonstrate that the charity is acting within its powers in the transaction, and has complied with relevant statutory requirements. If the statements are wrong, and the charity has not complied in the appropriate way, then the purchaser's title will still be good, but the trustees may be liable for any loss arising from their actions.

Connected persons

74.23 These are defined in *Sch 5* of the *Charities Act 1993* as follows:

(*a*) a charity trustee, or trustee for the charity (e.g. a custodian trustee);

(*b*) a person who is the donor of any land to the charity (whether the gift was made on or after the establishment of the charity);

(*c*) a child, parent, grandchild, grandparent, brother or sister of any such trustee or donor;

(*d*) an officer, agent or employee of the charity;

(*e*) the spouse of any person falling within any of (*a*) to (*d*) above;

(*f*) an institution which is controlled

(i) by any person falling within (*a*) to (*d*) above, or

(ii) by two or more such persons taken together; or

(*g*) a body corporate in which

(i) any connected persons falling within (*a*) to (*f*) above has a substantial interest (that is, more than 20% of either the share capital or the voting power in general meeting), or

(ii) two or more such persons, taken together, have a substantial interest.

74.24 For the purposes of this definition, 'child' includes a stepchild and an illegitimate child, a 'spouse' includes someone living with another as that person's husband or wife, and a person controls an institution if he is able to secure that the affairs of the institution are conducted in accordance with his wishes.

74.25 The definition of connected persons for Scottish charities is given in FRS 8, which applies to the whole of the UK.

Special cases

74.26 There are a number of situations where a land transaction will be complicated by specific circumstances, some of which are unique to charities or certain types of charity. These cases will need expert legal advice, and may include the following.

Rentcharges

74.27 Not the same as a rent, a rentcharge is a regular payment in relation to property which the land owner makes to another person, often a charity. Rentcharges will be extinguished by 2037, and are therefore often released in exchange for a lump sum payment. The Charity Commission's consent may be required for this release. [*Charities Act 1993 s 40*].

Auctions

74.28 Although a charity may sell property through auction, it cannot control who will purchase it. If it subsequently transpires that the purchaser is a connected person, then the consent of the Charity Commission will be required. This should be made clear in advance.

Reverter

74.29 Under such legislation as the *Literary and Scientific Institutions Act 1854*, individuals were encouraged to pass property to relevant charitable institutions on condition that the property would revert back to the donor, or his successors, if the property ceased to be used for the purpose for which it was given. Other types of property affected include libraries, schools, burial grounds, places of worship and clergy houses. Charities holding such properties might not benefit from any sale proceeds on disposal of such a property.

Church halls

74.30 The Charity Commission have issued specific guidance on the use of church halls for other charitable purposes, including as village halls. Broadly this follows guidance in other parts of this section concerning the need for the trustees to take due note of their own particular terms of trust. It also points out that if a church hall is no longer needed at all for church purposes, then the trusts of the charity can be said to have failed and the property should be sold. Other legislation will need consulting, such as the *Parochial Church Council (Powers) Measure 1956*.

Churches

74.31 There are further specific provisions relating to churches, related properties and cathedrals. For instance the definition of charity in the context of the *Charities Act 1993* does not apply to some ecclesiastical corporations (that is, in the Church of England in respect of certain corporate property, nor to diocesan glebe land) nor to any trust of property for purposes for which the property has been consecrated. Cathedral land transactions are governed by other legislation, as are transactions relating to redundant churches (*s 96(2)*).

Taxation

74.32 Property transactions, whether on disposal and acquisition, or as rental or lease payment may all be subject to tax. Income tax or corporation tax may be due on amounts received, VAT may be charged on rent, gains may be subject to capital gains tax (for instance on a reversion), and council tax and business rates may apply. These taxes are addressed in their relevant chapters. Charities are exempt from stamp duty on conveyances, transfers of securities, assignments of existing leases or grants of new leases to the charity. [*Finance Act 1982 s 129(1)*].

Accounting for property

74.33 Property owned by a charity will normally be classified as a fixed asset and shown on the face of the balance sheet. Property donated to a charity will appear as an incoming resource in the year when it is receivable in accruals accounts. Expenditure on the acquisition of a property is capital, and may include enhancement and installation costs. It is often a matter of fine judgement whether certain costs on a property constitute repairs and maintenance, or some sort of capital expenditure improving the property. FRS 15, which governs all fixed assets accounting and depreciation, draws a distinction between expenditure which enhances performance and expenditure which maintains performance of a fixed asset. All fixed assets except land, but including buildings, should be subject to depreciation unless it is immaterial or unless the property is inalienable: both these exemptions are narrowly drawn and if a charity wishes not to depreciate buildings and associated works it should consult the SORP and FRS 15 for more detailed guidance.

74.34 The accounting value attributed to a property will depend on its purpose and nature of title:

- Freehold land and buildings held for charity's own use: at cost or valuation, less depreciation on the buildings.
- Leasehold property held for charity's own use: at cost or valuation, less amortisation, usually over the unexpired term of the lease.
- Investment property: at market value.
- Rented property: no value will appear in the accounts, as the charity has no legal interest in the land.
- Historic/inalienable buildings: in limited circumstances no value may appear in the accounts, but information on such uncapitalised items should be given in the notes, including the insured value.

74.35 FRS 15 requires revalued assets, usually land and buildings, to be professionally revalued every five years. For charities (but not their subsidiary companies) this valuation may be based on any reasonable approach, thus avoiding the cost of professional fees, subject to gaining advice as to the possibility of material movements in value. Investment properties should be accounted for at market value each year, and property brought into the accounts as a result of a gift at market value will not be treated as having been revalued, so the five year rule does not apply.

74.36 Property donated in the past can be a problem, but generally only where the SORP is being implemented for the first time or when there is a change in accounting policy. The value to the charity at the time of the donation (probably equivalent to cost at that time) is often neither known nor relevant. Revaluing may be an expensive option, but is often the only option. Once all property has been identified a register should be established to control future transactions. Anglican parishes are required to maintain this as a terrier (register of property), subject to inspection by the Archdeacon every three years.

74.37 Revaluation movements will be shown in the accounts within the statement of recognised gains and losses, except for depreciation and permanent diminutions in value which will form part of outgoing resources.

74.38 As with other fixed assets, trustees should be alert to property values being overstated in their accounts. Where this is the case the charity should conduct an impairment review under FRS 11 and amend the values accordingly. The application of impairment reviews to charities is usually straightforward, except for specialised properties such as hospices and historic assets such as monuments. In such cases the SORP asks charities to consider using alternatives to net realisable value, such as the intrinsic worth of the property, or the depreciated replacement cost.

75 Legacies

75.1 Legacies are an important source of income for many charities, although their future significance is less certain. The fall in house prices in the 1990s, after the rise in the early 1980s, and the increasing trend for individuals to pay for their own long-term care in old age, led commentators to suggest that income from this source would decline. This, however, is not proving to be the case, due in part to strong equity markets in the last half of the 1990s and the more recent upturn in the housing market.

Taxation

75.2 The tax status of legacies is discussed elsewhere (see Chapter 63). To ensure that charitable bequests are not subject to inheritance tax the bequest should be clearly and exclusively charitable, and the charity recipient should ensure that any receipts have not been inadvertently subjected to tax either on the capital sum, or on any income arising in the period pending distribution. For instance, the sale by an executor of an asset forming part of an estate will be subject to capital gains tax unless the executor is acting as bare trustee for a charity.

75.3 Charities may also wish to confirm the basis of any allocation of inheritance tax. It is normal practice for charities to receive their share of any residuary legacy before any deduction of inheritance tax, with that burden falling on the non-exempt beneficiaries. This practice was reversed in *Re Benham's Will Trusts, Lockhart v Harker [1995] STC 210*, but the Inland Revenue have subsequently confirmed that this was not a precedent to be applied generally in future, but was specific to the rather unusual wording used in the will concerned.

75.4 Not all apparently charitable bequests escape inheritance tax. In *Chichester Diocesan Fund and Board of Finance (incorporated) v Simpson (Re Diplock) [1944] AC 341, [1944] 2 All ER 60* the wording of the will was judged to be too wide in its purposes, i.e. 'charitable or benevolent', to be a charitable bequest. Although many charities would like to become involved with the drafting of wills to prevent this sort of thing occurring, the Charity Commission has repeatedly warned charities not to get too involved in drafting legacies or codicils for individuals. If a charity is involved in drafting a will in which it is a beneficiary, the will may be subsequently challenged on the grounds that it was drafted under undue influence.

75.5 These factors suggest that charities must take care in advising potential donors, and should investigate legacy receipts to ensure that no unnecessary tax has been borne by the charity.

Control

75.6 As with other sources of voluntary income, it is important to ensure that records of income are not only accurate, but also complete. Where it is unusual for a charity to receive legacies, then only normal controls are expected over non-contractual income: dual opening of post, cash receipt registers and maintenance of correspondence files all being important.

75.7 Where legacies are received fairly frequently, other controls can be implemented. A register of legacies should be maintained, which should record a legacy as soon as any notification of its existence is received. The income received can then be cross-referenced to this register, and the entry only closed when it is confirmed that all sums due have been received. Some organisations also keep records of legacies written in their favour, so that they can judge the effect of any legacy campaign, and ensure that legacies do not get diverted when due.

75.8 Specialist agencies exist which record details of charitable legacies, either specific or general. Charities may subscribe to these services as a way of identifying potential legacy income. As a control mechanism this can only work as a means of reviewing events afterwards, and only if the individual charity maintains adequate internal records.

75.9 It is possible to budget for legacy income. Legacy income is broadly predictable when measured as a four-year moving average, though it can fluctuate widely on an annual basis and just one legacy can have a substantial effect on the annual performance of a small charity. According to the NGO Finance 100 Index, legacy income has shown modest growth since 1992, growing at a faster rate than the Retail Prices Index, but at a lower rate than other income streams such as trading, investment income or fees. Where a charity has an established pattern of legacy income, then external information, such as the index, can give useful guidance to the organisation in determining whether an unexpected change in the pattern can be explained satisfactorily, or whether a control breakdown has occurred.

Accounting

75.10 In the past charities operated legacy equalisation accounts, which released legacy income over a number of years. These had usually been initiated by prudent treasurers wishing to avoid wild fluctuations in legacy income. However, the SORP requires all legacy income to be recognised as income when receivable unless it is incapable of financial measurement. This means that it is incorrect to defer the recognition of income simply because it is a large and apparently distorting figure. This position was underlined in the case of an incorporated charity which was in insolvent liquidation when the testator died. The liquidator was able to enforce collection of the bequest and use it towards paying the creditors (*Re ARMS (Multiple Sclerosis Research) Ltd 1996*).

75.11 The SORP requirement means that charities should not only recognise legacies already received, but also those notified. In other words it would be correct to treat as income a pecuniary legacy to which a charity is entitled, where probate has been granted, and where there is no doubt about the amount or certainty of receipt. An example of this would be where the charity has received notification from the personal representatives of the estate that a payment will be made. Administrators may take the view that this situation can only truly occur where the bequeathed amount is actually received after the year end but before the accounts are signed off. Residuary legacies are often difficult to value, but if they are likely to have a major impact on the charity's financial position it is good practice to refer to them in the notes.

75.12 This accountancy requirement applies only to where the legacy is capable of financial measurement. Very often a residuary legacy will fall outside this definition. Where this happens, the notes to the accounts should give an indication of the estimated amount receivable (where material).

75.13 For charities that are still uneasy about incorporating too much income into their day to day operations, placing legacies over a certain size in a designated fund may be a sensible option. Sometimes legacies will be restricted funds in their own right, but otherwise there is nothing to stop trustees regarding legacies as being in some way special, and setting them on one side for particular purposes. As long as this does not represent an unauthorised accumulation of funds, then representing such funds as part of designated funds would seem reasonable.

76 Liability

76.1 Liability means being held responsible for actions taken, or actions which should have been taken but were not (defaults). Some liabilities will fall on the organisation if it is a corporate body, some on the governing body, some on the members, some on the staff, volunteers and others acting on behalf of the organisation, and some on those claiming to act on behalf of the organisation when they are not in fact authorised to do so.

76.2 Questions of liability tend to arise when something goes wrong, such as the organisation running into financial difficulties, being taken to court for breach of contract, being fined, e.g. for failing to file accounts, or when it faces a loss that is not insured. Most people are unclear about who is liable in these situations and can become extremely worried in case they are personally liable.

Factors giving rise to a liability

76.3 Liabilities most commonly arise from organisations or people acting on their behalf committing:

- breaches of criminal law e.g. corporate manslaughter;
- breaches of statutory duty e.g. failing to put charity's registered status on certain documents;
- breaches of covenants or other property rights or duties e.g. selling alcohol on premises despite the existence of a covenant forbidding this;
- breaches of trust e.g. spending money on activities outside the charity's objects;
- breaches of contract e.g. failing to meet specified standards of service delivery;
- breaches of duty when facing insolvency e.g. continuing to trade when there is no realistic hope of financial survival; or
- tort (a civil wrong) e.g. libel.

Where does liability rest?

76.4 Who is liable in any particular instance depends on:

- whether the organisation is incorporated or unincorporated;
- who authorised the action, and whether or not they were authorised to do so;
- who carried out the action and whether or not they were authorised to do so; or
- who omitted to do something which they had a duty to do.

76.5 If a member of the charity's governing body or someone else associated with the charity is held personally liable for an action, or for omitting to carry out some action, they will have to use their own money to:

- meet the organisation's obligations;
- make good losses suffered by the organisation as a result of their actions;

- repay to the organisation any personal profit they have made as a result of their action; and
- pay fines or penalties arising as a result of their action.

In certain circumstances they could be imprisoned, though the number of instances in which this has happened is very small.

76.6 In some instances someone held personally liable may be entitled to be reimbursed by the organisation, or their fellow members of the governing body or by the charity's members. The court has power to relieve directors of charitable companies, company secretaries or senior employees from personal liability arising from negligence, default or breach of duty (*Companies Act 1985 s 727*) and any charity trustee from personal liability arising from a breach of trust if the person concerned was judged to have acted honestly and reasonably and 'ought fairly to be excused'. [*Trustee Act 1925 s 61*].

76.7 Where the members of a charity's governing body are held liable, the liability is joint and several. That means that each member could be held liable for all or any part of the obligation. If only some members of a governing body are sued for tort or breach of contract they are entitled to recover a contribution from the other members. The court decides what each person's contribution will be depending on their degree of culpability for the loss or damage. [*Civil Liability (Contribution) Act 1978 ss 1 and 2*].

76.8 The general rule of liability is that people are liable for their own acts, however there are many circumstances in which others may be held liable as well as, or instead of, the person who committed the act. For example, employers can be liable for unlawful race, sex or disability discrimination carried out by their employees, even if it was carried out without their knowledge, unless the employer can show they took all reasonable steps to prevent such discrimination from occurring.

Vicarious liability

76.9 Employers have vicarious liability for breaches of duty by employees and in certain circumstances could have vicarious liability for criminal offences committed by employees in the course of their employment. For example, following a disaster in which four teenagers were drowned during an activity holiday, the company operating the holiday was fined £60,000 and the managing director imprisoned.

76.10 Vicarious liability does not depend upon the employer being at fault in any way. All that must be proved for an employer to be found vicariously liable is that the person who committed the act is an employee of the employer, that the act occurred during the course of the employee's employment and the act committed is one which entitles the person who has been injured to bring court proceedings. Vicarious liability normally extends only to employees but in some instances courts have found employers vicariously liable for the acts of volunteers, either because they judge that the 'volunteer' is in law an employee or because in their view the relationship between the employer and the volunteer was such that it justified a liability being imposed. Volunteers working regularly in charity shops could come into this category. Even if the employer was not found vicariously liable the charity might still face a claim for its own liability in not properly training and supervising the volunteers.

77 Light Touch Regime

77.1 The light touch regime applies to 75% of registered charities i.e. those that are unincorporated and that have neither income nor expenditure above £10,000 a year. It simplifies their accounting and reporting requirements and the way in which their accounts must be scrutinised, in order to balance the need for public accountability with the burden and cost of compliance on the trustees of small charities.

77.2 Unless their governing documents set out more stringent requirements light touch regime charities must:

- maintain proper accounting records showing and explaining all sums of money received and paid out, the date, and what it was received for or spent on, and a record of the charity's assets and liabilities, and keep them together with copies of the annual accounts, for at least six years;
- prepare annual accounts on either a receipts and payments basis or an accruals basis, together with a statement of assets and liabilities;
- prepare a simple annual report describing the main activities and achievements;
- make a simple annual return so the Commission can keep its Register up to date; and
- make copies of the accounts available to the public on written request.

77.3 Unless specifically requested a light touch regime charity does not have to send its accounts or annual report to the Charity Commission each year.

77.4 Charities in the light touch regime do not have to have the accounts independently examined or audited unless their governing document requires this.

77.5 If trustees elect to prepare their accounts on an accruals basis they must be prepared in accordance with the Regulations, though they can take advantage of certain concessions permitted in the regulations, of which the most useful is the exemption from presenting a functional analysis of costs.

77.6 As with other variations in the accounting regime, no formal election is required for trustees to operate within the light touch regime.

77.7 The light touch regime is defined by reference to any one particular year, and takes precedence over other thresholds. This means that, should a charity have a large legacy in one year of, say, £250,000, but two years later their income has fallen to below £10,000, then no audit would be required. If, however, the income had only fallen to £20,000, an external scrutiny would be required, and because income had exceeded £250,000 in the relevant period, an audit would still be necessary.

78 Local Authorities

78.1 A local authority is defined as a county council, a district council, a London borough, a parish council, a community council (Wales), the Council of the Isles of Scilly, or the Common Council of the City of London. [*Local Government Act 1988 2 Sch*].

78.2 Charities and local authorities work together in a number of ways. Services that local authorities have a statutory duty to provide are often funded by local authorities but run by charities under contract agreements. Charities have to apply to local authorities for permits or licences to run certain fund-raising events (see Chapter 50) and for exemption from business rate relief (see Chapter 90). Local authorities sometimes act as a charity trustee or as a custodian trustees and they sometimes have powers to appoint charity trustees.

Local authority as trustee

78.3 Local authorities can hold or accept gifts of land or other property for the benefit of people living in the whole of, or part of, their area (*Local Government Act 1972 s 139*) although they cannot be the trustee of an ecclesiastical charity or a charity for the relief of poverty. Having the local authority as trustee has the advantage over a trustee body made up of a group of individuals that, as a body corporate, it has perpetual succession so there is no need for legal expense vesting property each time there is a change of trustees. More importantly, it has the advantage that the local authority may be willing to subsidise the charitable work if it can see that it is of benefit to the local community. It may do this through grants, or by providing premises or professional services free of charge.

78.4 However, there are also disadvantages in having a local authority as trustee. For example, the local authority may not appreciate that it cannot deal with charitable property in the same way that it would its own corporate property and end up in breech of the charitable trusts. Conflicts of interest can arise between a local authority's responsibilities to its council tax and rate payers and its duty, as charity trustee, to act in the best interests of its beneficiaries. The management of the charitable activities may not be given the same priority by the local authority that they would receive if managed by a group of trustees focused solely on the charity. Finally, if the local authority is restructured or reorganised a successor authority may not be aware that certain property is held on trust and is not part of the local authority's corporate property.

78.5 When the Charity Commission considers a proposal for a local authority to be appointed as trustee it will only consent if it is sure that the proposal is the best arrangement that could be made after taking into account the possibility of conflicts of interest and the need to safeguard both the charity's property and the beneficiaries' interests.

78.6 When dealing with a charity where the local authority is trustee the Commission will sometimes suggest that other arrangements might be more appropriate. For example, they might suggest that the local authority stands down as trustee and is replaced by a new, independent group of individuals. If the local authority wishes to retain some influence then they might retain the right to appoint some of the trustees. However, trustees appointed by local authorities must act in the best interests of the charity's beneficiaries even when this is in conflict with the interests of the local authority that appointed them.

78.7 In some instances a charity's governing document gives a local authority the power to appoint some or all of the trustees. *Section 79* of the *Charities Act 1993* gives some local authorities the power to appoint trustees of parochial charities that are not ecclesiastical charities and that were founded more than forty years ago. Where this is the case appointments are usually for a period of four years.

Local authority as custodian trustee

78.8 Local authorities can act as custodian trustee for unincorporated charities that are for the benefit of people in the local authority's area. This saves the charity from the expense of transferring title to property every time there is a change of trustee. As custodian trustee the scope for a conflict of interest between the charity and the local authority is less as the custodian trustee takes no part in the management of the charity.

Property

78.9 There is limited scope for some charities to transfer property to local authorities, with the consent of both the Charity Commission and the authority concerned. The property in question must not belong to an ecclesiastical charity, and must comprise either a public recreation ground or allotments, or be held for other charitable purposes connected with a parish or community council. A local authority also has powers to create enforceable bye-laws for recreation grounds of which it is a trustee or custodian trustee, or to which it has given money, or supplied goods or services such as grass cutting.

Rates

78.10 Charities are given 80% relief on non-domestic rates charged on properties if:

- the property is occupied by a charity and used wholly or mainly for charitable purposes; or
- the property is used wholly or mainly for selling goods donated to the charity and the net proceeds are spent on charitable purposes.

78.11 Local authorities have power to extend rate relief further, even up to 100%.

78.12 Non-domestic property exempt from local rating includes agricultural land and buildings, places of religious worship including church halls, and property used for the people with disabilities.

Fund-raising

78.13 House-to-house collections, street collections and some lotteries may need the permission of the local authority. 'House-to-house' collections include collections in offices, factories and pubs. Similarly, 'street' collections include collections in any public place. A licence will be needed for a house-to-house collection and many local authorities have regulations covering street collections. For more detail see Chapter 88.

Contracting

78.14 With the growth of the contract culture, charities increasingly find themselves entering into relationships with local authorities under a variety of documentation variously termed 'grants', 'service level agreements', 'contracts' and so on. Contracts and service agreements are described in Chapter 26.

78.15 NCVO has issued guidance on relations between charities and government, in particular drawing attention to the need for charities to avoid becoming too dependent on one source of finance, or having their own objectives unduly influenced by the availability of funds.

78.16 Before seeking funding, whether by contract or by grant, from a local authority, a charity should establish how the authority in question approaches the matter. Local authorities have widely differing structures to deal with charities, and also will have widely varying priorities as to the services which they feel they should provide or purchase. Local authorities provide services which fall into defined categories, but they also have powers under the *Local Government Act 1972 s 137* to give limited grants to charities where that will be of benefit to the local population.

78.17 The variety of services which a local authority may provide is so extensive as to permit most charities to be able to find at least one category within which it can validly seek to obtain funds either under grant or contract. For instance, local authorities are variously required to provide accommodation for a wide range of people in need and to provide child care services. They can enjoin charities in an even wider range of activities including historic building conservation, the provision of country parks, contributing towards the costs of maintaining recreational amenities such as swimming pools and playing fields, and the provision of premises for the arts. This great diversity of activity indicates that a charity ought at least to explore the potential for either obtaining assistance from the local authority, or for assessing its own plans in the light of the authority's own priorities. It may be that resources have already been committed to the same issue elsewhere, or that a changed approach by the charity to the same problem could better complement existing provision.

Best value

78.18 From 1 April 2000 all local authorities are required under the *Local Government Act 1999* to seek continuous improvement to services and functions through regular reviews of their economy, efficiency and effectiveness. Services provided by charities under contracts or service level agreements will be subject to review. The reviews will use performance indicators and if charities have not already developed indicators for their own internal use they may find it advantageous to do so now. Otherwise they will find that their services are assessed exclusively by indicators developed by the local authority.

Local authority controlled or influenced companies

78.19 A local authority may control a company in much the same way as any entity may do so, that is by shareholding or controlling the composition of board of directors. Local authority controlled (or influenced) companies, have additional requirements relating to disclosure and financing arrangements. This situation may become relevant to a charity particularly where the local authority has the power to appoint, or control the appointment of, trustees.

78.20 Local Authorities

Local authorities' powers in relation to local charities

78.20 *Section 76* of the *Charities Act 1993* permits local authorities to maintain an index of local charities, which is open to public inspection. *Section 77* empowers the authority to review the working of any group of local charities with the same or similar purposes within the council's area and to make recommendations to the Charity Commission. This review must be with the individual charity trustees' approval, and cannot extend to ecclesiastical charities. Charity trustees are specifically permitted to co-operate in such procedures under *s 78*. One of the purposes of these sections is to aid the efficiency of the sector by facilitating the merger of similar organisations, or the closure of dormant ones.

79 Lotteries

79.1 Charities raise over £125m a year from lotteries registered with the Gaming Board and an unknown amount from 'unofficial' lotteries. Lotteries offer charities a way to reach supporters who are not regular donors and people who would not normally give to charities. Lotteries can be as cost-effective as many other types of fund-raising. Returns from charity lotteries registered with the Gaming Board average about £1.69 for every £1 invested by the charity.

What constitutes a lottery?

79.2 *Section 1* of the *Lotteries and Amusements Act 1976*, as amended by the *National Lottery Act 1993*, states that 'All lotteries which do not constitute gaming are unlawful, except as provided by this Act and Section 2(1) of the National Lottery Act 1993'. Therefore there is a general rule of illegality which the Act goes on to vary by setting out exceptions that allow for the lawful conduct of small lotteries incidental to exempt entertainments, private lotteries, and society lotteries. Charities should make every effort to ensure that their raffles, tombolas, and prize draws are within the law or those involved could be subject to a fine of up to £5,000 or a term of imprisonment of up to two years.

79.3 There is no statutory definition of a lottery. The meaning of the term has been established by case law with the accepted definition being that given by Lord Widgery, CJ, in *Reader's Digest v Williams* [*1976*] *1 WLR 1109*: 'A lottery is a distribution of prizes by chance where the persons taking part in the operation, or a substantial number of them, make a payment or consideration in return for obtaining their chance of a prize'. Lord Widgery went on to say that three elements have to be in place for a lottery to exist:

- There must be a distribution of prizes.
- Prizes must be distributed entirely by means of chance.
- Participants must make some financial contribution in return for their obtaining a chance to take part in the lottery.

Prizes

79.4 Lottery prizes must be of some value. Many charities appeal for donated prizes such as holidays, flights, cars, restaurant meals, theatre tickets, electrical equipment, toys or bottles of alcoholic drink. If alcoholic drink is offered as a prize it constitutes the sale or supply of intoxicating liquor and therefore requires a Justice's licence. Donated prizes do not need specific accounting as they are treated as donated assets whose value is accounted for upon realisation — that is, when they are sold or won.

Financial contribution

79.5 Participators have to pay in order to have a chance of winning a prize. The payment does not have to be specifically for the chance to enter the draw. It could be included in the price of an admission ticket for an event or the price of a programme.

79.6 Lotteries

Distribution of prizes depends on chance

79.6 Prizes must be distributed solely according to chance. If any skill, however slight, is required the distribution will not be a lottery. A competition to guess the correct number of buttons in a jar was held to involve skill and was therefore a prize competition and not a lottery (*R v Jamieson* [*1884*] *7 OR 149*). However, competitions in which the 'correct' answer is determined by the entrants themselves, such as placing different brands of dog food in order of merit, are lotteries (*Hobbs v Ward* [*1929*] *45 TLR 373*).

Small lotteries incidental to exempt entertainments

79.7 *Section 3* of the amended *Lotteries and Amusements Act 1976* permits small lotteries that are incidental to an exempt entertainment. The Act defines an exempt entertainment as a 'bazaar, sale of work, fête, dinner dance, sporting or athletic event or other entertainment of a similar character, whether limited to one day or extending over two or more days. [*Lotteries and Amusements Act 1976 3(1)*]. The following conditions apply.

- The whole proceeds of the entertainment must be for the charity or, in the words of the Act, 'purposes other than private gain', with the exception of the expenses of the entertainment (other than those incurred in connection with the lottery), the cost of printing the lottery tickets, and the cost of prizes purchased.
- No more than a certain amount of the ticket proceeds can be spent on prizes (currently £250 [*SI 1993 No 3222*]). There are no restrictions on the value of donated prizes.
- No money prizes can be given i.e. bank notes, cheques, postal orders or money orders. Gift vouchers are not considered to be money prizes and therefore can be given.
- Tickets must be sold only on the premises of the entertainment and the result must be declared on the premises during the entertainment.
- The lottery must not be the only, or the only substantial, inducement for people to attend the entertainment.
- No one connected with the lottery can be paid a commission or a fee.

79.8 The income from small lotteries is exempt from tax under statutory provision *ICTA 1988 s 505(1)(f)*.

Private lotteries

79.9 Private lotteries are relevant to employees who work on the same premises, or people who reside on the same premises e.g. students in a hall of residence. They are not usually of interest to charities, with the exception of some membership organisations that run regular social events.

Private lotteries come under *s 4* of the *Lotteries and Amusements Act 1976*. They must comply with the following.

- Tickets may only be sold to members of the charity or others on its premises.
- The trustees must authorise a promoter, in writing, to conduct the lottery.
- Only the costs of printing and stationery can be deducted from the proceeds. The remainder must be spent on prizes and/or donated to the charity.

- Tickets for the lottery cannot be sent through the post.
- The lottery can only be advertised on the charity's premises.
- All tickets must be the same price.
- All tickets must show:
  - — the name and address of the promoter;
  - — a statement indicating that the sale of tickets is restricted to the relevant group;
  - — a statement that no prize won in the lottery shall be paid or delivered by the promoter to any person other than the ticket holder;
  - — the prize of the lottery ticket.

Society lotteries

79.10 Society lotteries are defined by the *Lotteries and Amusements Act 1976 s 5* as:

> 'a lottery promoted on behalf of a society which is established and conducted wholly or mainly for one or more of the following purposes, that is to say—
>
> (*a*) charitable purposes
>
> (*b*) participation in or support of athletic sports or games or cultural activities
>
> (*c*) purposes which are not described in (a) or (b) above but are neither purposes of private gain nor purposes of any commercial undertaking'.

79.11 Society lotteries run by charities must be registered with the Gaming Board under *ss 3(b)* and *(c)* of the Act if the total value of tickets to be sold exceeds £20,000 or if the value, when added to the sales of tickets sold in the charity's lotteries that have already taken place in the same calendar year, exceeds £250,000. If the value is lower they must be registered with the local authority and comply with its regulations.

79.12 Some charities prefer to operate large-scale lotteries through their trading subsidiaries to minimise risk to the charity and avoid tax. At first sight this would appear to be excluded by the Act under *s 5(1)(c)*, as the charity's trading company will be established for commercial purposes. However, the Gaming Board permits a charity's trading company to register with the Gaming Board, provided that the trading company covenants all its taxable profits to the charity.

79.13 Even if the lottery is run by the charity no tax is payable because an amendment to the *Finance Act 1995* resulted in *ICTA 1988 s 505(1)(f)* exempting charities from tax on society lotteries provided the income is applied solely for the charity's charitable purpose.

79.14 Society lotteries are potentially large income generators for charities. They are allowed to sell up to five million tickets, at a maximum price of £1 each, per calendar year, splitting the proceeds as follows: 50% on prizes, 30% on expenses, 20% going to the charity, thus generating an income of up to £1 million. The Charity Commission has no objection to charities running society lotteries provided that the trustees adopt a prudent approach and that the running of the lottery does not become an end in itself.

Rapid draw/online lotteries

79.15 Rapid draw lotteries and online lotteries are lawful provided that they are structured on a parimutuel (i.e. a proportion of the cost of the tickets goes into a pool to provide the prizes) rather than a fixed odds basis.

Gaming Board rules

79.16 The following rules apply.

- The trustees must nominate, in writing, one of their members (in charitable companies this means a member in terms of company law) to act as promoter.
- Each ticket must state:
  - the name of the society promoting the lottery;
  - that the charity is registered with the Charity Commission if its gross income is over £10,000;
  - the name and address of the promoter;
  - the date of the lottery;
  - the price of the ticket (maximum price allowed by the Act is £1); and
  - whether the lottery is registered with the local authority or the Gaming Board.
- Tickets must have a maximum price of £1 and the price of every ticket must be the same.
- The maximum prize is £25,000 or 10% of the total value of tickets or chances sold, whichever is greater.
- Proceeds must not exceed a total tickets value of £1m, or £5m annually.
- No more than 55% of the proceeds can be spent on prizes.
- Expenses are limited to 35% of the proceeds, or if these exceed £20,000 the maximum permitted is reduced to 15%, unless the Gaming Board gives consent to a higher level of expenses.
- The total of expenses and prizes must not exceed 80% of the proceeds, ensuring that at least 20% of the proceeds are available to the charity, unless the Gaming Board consents to a higher level of expenses.
- No ticket can be sold to a person under the age of 16.
- No ticket can be sold in the street or by a machine.
- No prize can depend on the purchase of more than one ticket.

Accounting requirements

Records

79.17 Records must be kept of each point of sale, details of tickets sold, returned unsold and not returned, together with brief reasons why unsold tickets have not been returned.

79.18 Records of all expenses should be kept and recorded, including: (a) those met directly from the proceeds; (b) those met by the charity; and (c) those met by a third party.

79.19 Where a society promotes a number of separate lotteries, periodic expenses should by apportioned between the lotteries and depreciation on start up and capital costs should be accounted for.

79.20 Records of each lottery should be kept for at least two years.

Returns

79.21 If the lottery is registered with the Gaming Board it will have to complete a Lottery Return (form GBL12) for the Board showing details of the proceeds, expenses and amount spent on prizes and how the proceeds were distributed within three months of the date of the lottery.

79.22 If a charity sells more than £100,000 worth of tickets or chances in a single calendar year it must send audited accounts for the lotteries to the Gaming Board. These should reach the Board within ten months of the end of the year in question. Where possible this should include a reconciliation of where tickets were sold and those returned.

79.23 If the lottery is registered with the local authority, the promoter must send the registration authority a return, certified by two other members of the charity appointed by the board, no later than the end of the third month after the date of the lottery showing:

- a copy of the scheme under which the lottery was promoted;
- the proceeds;
- sums spent on prizes and expenses;
- the charity's objects; and
- the date of the lottery.

External lottery managers

79.24 Society lotteries can be such large-scale operations that *s 9A* of the *Lotteries and Amusements Act 1976* allows the charity to appoint an external lottery manager (ELM) certified under *Sch 2A* of the Act to manage the lottery.

80 Memorandum and Articles of Association

80.1 The memorandum and articles of association (often referred to as the 'mem and arts') are the governing documents of a limited company, which need to be filed with the Registrar of Companies before any company can be issued with a certificate of incorporation. The memorandum sets out the organisation's purpose and powers and the articles its internal rules and procedures. Sections of the memorandum are known as 'clauses', sections of the articles are known as 'articles'.

Memorandum

80.2 The memorandum of association is the document that formally records that one or more legal persons (i.e. individuals or limited companies themselves) have formed the company. For a charitable company, the memorandum sets out:

- the charity's name;
- the address of its registered office;
- the charitable objects;
- the powers of the trustees to pursue the objects;
- the beneficiary group;
- the names of the members; and
- the size of their guarantee or share holding.

[*Companies Act 1985 s 35*].

80.3 The objects of a charitable company are usually stated in broad terms i.e. 'to relieve poverty, distress and suffering amongst refugees', though they are often supplemented by a more detailed list of the types of activities or services the charity will provide to achieve its objects, e.g. 'by the provision of a helpline'. This gives a charity the flexibility to develop its work in the future without the need to get the Charity Commission's consent to broaden the objects, as would be the case if they were defined more precisely.

80.4 The objects of a charitable company must be charitable within the law. Powers will be restricted to prevent transfers of funds to members or to third parties except in the pursuit of the objects or to organisations bound by similar restrictions.

80.5 A company is limited to carrying out those activities which fall within its objects, although transactions undertaken outside them cannot be declared void in order to avoid contractual liability. Although directors of commercial companies can subsequently ratify an *ultra vires* transaction, directors of charitable companies do not have the same power to ratify such transactions after the event. A commercial company's object can be all-embracing, e.g. 'to carry on business as a general commercial company'. Charitable companies cannot use such a phrase, however, as it would not be a charitable object.

80.6 The objects of a company can be changed by special resolution, though in the case of a charitable company registered in England and Wales, Charity Commission consent will be required. Changing the objects will be necessary if they have become too restrictive or out of date.

Articles

80.7 The articles of association give the rules and regulations that govern the internal proceedings of a company. They usually include:

- the membership of the company;
- details of directors/trustees including procedures for election, length of term that can be served, restrictions on eligibility, powers, expenses, etc.;
- procedures for calling and holding meetings, the annual general meeting and extraordinary general meetings;
- voting procedures;
- financial procedures;
- procedures for the appointment of auditors;
- use of the Seal;
- winding up procedures.

80.8 Many charitable companies' articles contain potentially restrictive clauses that serve no useful purpose. For example, there may be an article requiring the annual accounts to be audited, even though the charity is small and an audit would not be mandatory if this article had not been included. Trustees should periodically review their memorandum and articles of association to identify any such clauses and seek to amend or delete them and to ensure that corporate governance is in practice is complying with the articles.

80.9 In addition companies limited by share will include rules concerning the share capital and membership. In the case of a guarantee company this section will be much reduced and will cover the terms and rights of members.

80.10 In practice many companies do not create their own rules, but follow models published with the *Companies Act 1985* known as Tables A to F. Table A is the most commonly adopted format, being applicable to private companies limited by shares as many subsidiary trading companies are constituted. Table C relates to companies limited by guarantee. The Charity Commission, the Charity Law Association and the National Council for Voluntary Organisations have all published model memorandum and articles of association for charitable companies. There is less of a need for tailored models for subsidiary trading companies as they have even more standard formats. Companies can either be formed from scratch or bought 'off the shelf', already incorporated from incorporation agents. If this is the case the memorandum and articles of association will need to be reviewed and a number of changes will usually need to be made, not least the company name.

80.11 The memorandum and articles of association can be altered, but only by a formal process of a general meeting of the members and the passing of a special resolution. The meeting will usually require 21 days notice, setting out the proposal. It is possible to waive this notice period if 90–95% of the membership so agree. The exact percentage will depend on whether the company has made the relevant elective resolution. It is also possible for a special resolution to be passed not by an actual meeting, but by the circulation of the resolution in writing, and its signature by or on behalf of all members. [*Companies Act 1985 s 381*]. As mentioned above, however, certain changes including alterations to the charity's objects or powers, or to any clause relating to how the charity's income or property is to be used, will need the consent of the Charity Commission.

81 Mergers

Reasons for mergers

81.1 Mergers used only to be associated with the commercial sector but the growing number of registered charities chasing reduced funding has meant that charities, especially small ones, are now considering merger to increase their chances of survival. Merging can do away with the duplication of effort that charities are sometimes criticised for, providing economies of scale and greater efficiency. *Sections 74 and 75* of the *Charities Act 1993* introduced powers for small charities that facilitate and encourage merger.

81.2 There are two main forms of merger.

- A true merger, sometimes known as an *amalgamation* when a new organisation is formed and the merging charities are both wound up.
- A consolidation, where one organisation is dissolved and its assets transferred to another (transfer of engagements).

Merger, however, is not always a viable solution. There are complex legal issues and some charities may not have powers in their governing document permitting a merger. Even if merger is legally possible, in some cases diversity of effort is seen to be advantageous and there are emotive and cultural reasons why a merger may not work. Trustees of the charities involved must be satisfied that merger is in the best interest of the charity and its present and future beneficiaries.

Is merger legally possible?

81.3 Whether or not a merger is legally possible is determined by a charity's legal structure, the powers in its governing document and its objects.

Trusts

81.4 Modern charitable trusts will usually have the power to dissolve or transfer property to other charities or amalgamate with other charities. Problems can arise with older trusts which may not have the power to spend capital. In this case, the property of the charity may be regarded as a permanent endowment and can only be transferred if the small charities provisions of the *Charities Act 1993* apply (or in Scotland *LRMPSA 1990*). Should the trust have no power to amalgamate or dissolve, a Charity Commission Scheme is required.

Unincorporated associations

81.5 Most modern unincorporated associations will have powers in their constitutions to dissolve the charity and transfer remaining assets to another charity. Certainly the Charity Commission model constitution provides powers for dissolution if it is 'necessary or desirable' and powers for the transfer of assets. Again, it is with older associations that Charity Commission help may be required.

Charitable companies

81.6 It is usually relatively straightforward for charitable companies to merge as most memoranda of association will contain powers to merge with other charities with similar purposes.

Compatible objects

81.7 Whatever the legal structure, and even if a charity's governing document holds powers that enable a merger, it will only be possible if the two charities involved have compatible objects. It will be usual for the acquiring charity to have broader objects. If the objects are not compatible then an approach will need to be made to the Charity Commission.

81.8 For an unincorporated charity, the approach will be a for a *cy-près* application under *s 13(1)(c)* of the *Charities Act 1993* on the basis that the property of the merging charity could be used more effectively in conjunction with the property of the acquiring charity with similar purposes. For a charitable company the Charity Commission will need to give written consent for a Special Resolution amending the objects under *s 64(2)* of the *Charities Act 1993*. Again the Commission will only give consent in line with *cy-près* principles.

Common trusteeship and joint venture agreements

81.9 If the possible options for full merger have been exhausted, the standard alternative is for a common trusteeship arrangement where one charity is appointed trustee of another. A corporate charity appointed as a trustee by the Charity Commission under *s 35* of the *Charities Act 1993* will be a trust corporation and can thus act as sole trustee. Under a common trusteeship arrangement the two charities remain separate and must keep their own funds and accounting records. There can be practical difficulties in maintaining such an arrangement.

81.10 Another possibility to consider is setting up a joint venture agreement which enables two charities whose objects are not wholly compatible, but who have some overlap in their activities, to establish a separate charitable venture that can utilise the resources of both the charities in that area of work.

Implementing the merger

81.11 If the merger is an amalgamation (as described above) then the new charity is starting afresh and as such it is easy to establish suitable constitutional and operational arrangements. This is the more desirable form of merger if a change of legal structure is required. However, the more common form of merger is consolidation and the successor charity will need to ensure that its constitution is suitable to meet the requirements of the charity which is being absorbed and the demands of the combined organisations.

81.12 The most important considerations are:

- the name of the merged charity;
- whether the new constitution will need to include additional powers to allow the merged charity to meet its charitable purposes;
- what governance structure should be established, for example, what should be the representation of trustees from the original charities; and
- whether new membership provisions need to be put in place.

81.13 Mergers

Funds held on special trusts

81.13 A problem that can arise with merger is where the merging charity holds funds on special trusts. If the amount of the funds are small, it may be possible to use the small charities provisions in *ss 74* and *75* of the *Charities Acts 1993* to wind up the trusts and transfer them to another charity or to spend the permanent endowment. The small charities provisions cover those with gross income in the last financial year not exceeding £5,000 and not holding land on trusts which stipulate that the land is to be used for the purposes, or any particular purpose, of the charity.

81.14 If the funds are too great for these provisions to be applied or if the land is held on trust, then it may be necessary to amend the trust deed if there is an express power to do so, or to obtain a scheme from the Charity Commission.

Transfer of assets or undertaking

81.15 There are a number of other legal matters that need to be addressed aside from the constitutional issues raised by merger. There are two forms that the merger can take: either there is a simple transfer of assets or, as is more common, a transfer of the whole undertaking to the acquiring organisation. In this instance the acquiring organisation will need to investigate fully the assets, liabilities and risks being taken on including funding, contractual agreements, VAT and property. This process is often referred to as 'due diligence'. There will normally be a transfer agreement between the two charities covering the transfer of assets, liabilities and any indemnities.

81.16 A major consideration for service providing charities will be contractual relations and funding arrangements with third parties. The usual arrangement is for the existing contracts to be taken over by the successor charity. The consent of third parties will be needed for the transfer of contractual obligations and there may need to be a novation (substitution of new contract for former one) of existing contracts.

81.17 The merging organisation will need to protect its position, and its trustees' with regard to any future liability. There will be a potential personal liability for the charity trustees in an unincorporated charity. A charitable company will normally be wound up using the striking off procedure, which will then render the company directors (the trustees) personally liable for any debts arising after the company has been struck off. The transfer agreement will need to include indemnities to protect the trustees of the merging charity against this.

Employees

81.18 Charities should be aware that the *Transfer of Undertakings (Protection of Employment) Regulations 1981* (*TUPE*) (*SI 1981 No 1794 as amended by SI 1987 No 1442*) apply to mergers. This means that all the employees of the merged charity are taken on by the successor charity. Dismissal of an employee could be considered as unfair, and therefore lead to an unfair dismissal case being brought against the charity, unless evidence can be shown of an economic, technical or organisational motive for an employee's dismissal. A change in terms and conditions of employment is not recognised as an economic, technical or organisational motive.

Winding up of merging charity

81.19 Once the transfer of assets or undertakings has been completed, it is usual for the merging charity to be wound up. For an incorporated charity, the normal procedure is to make an application to be struck off the Register of Companies and to then send closing accounts to the Charity Commission so that the charity can be removed from the register. For an unincorporated charity, a copy of the Resolution winding up the charity and the closing accounts should be sent to the Commission.

Post-merger legacies

81.20 It is highly possible that, no matter how well publicised the merger is, the merged charity will receive legacies for several years after it has ceased to exist. Whether the legacy lapses depends on the construction of the gift. In the past gifts have been saved on the grounds that they are for a charitable purpose rather than a named charity. If substantial legacy income for the merging charity is expected it may be desirable to retain the merging charity as a shell or a dormant organisation. If the shell is retained then the acquiring charity can be appointed as trustee, though necessary amendments may have to be made to the governing instrument.

82 National Lottery

82.1 The National Lottery was established by the *National Lottery Act 1993* and has become an important, if controversial, source of funding for the voluntary sector. In less than six years awards worth £5 billion have been made. The awards range from £500 to assist local charities to multi-million pound grants for various large scale landmark schemes. Over half the grants allocated have been for less than £25,000. Around £1.5 billion a year (28% of total lottery proceeds) is currently distributed between the six 'good causes' or distributing bodies.

82.2 The distributing bodies are:

- The Sports Council of England, Scotland, Wales and Northern Ireland (16.66%)
- The Arts Council of England, Scotland, Wales and Northern Ireland (16.66%)
- National Lottery Charities Board (16.66%)
- Heritage Lottery Fund (16.66%)
- The Millennium Commission (20%)
- The New Opportunities Fund (13.33%)

82.3 All the bodies distribute funds throughout the UK, apart form the Sports and Arts Councils. These operate in their respective home counties, allocating their share of funding to each Council in proportion to the size of the population.

82.4 The Millennium Commission is due to be wound up on 31 December 2000 and its share will be reallocated to the New Opportunities Fund.

82.5 At the time of writing there is some uncertainty over the future of the Lottery as the licence to operate it is due for renewal. Two bodies have been shortlisted, the existing operator, Camelot, and a consortium known as the People's Lottery, led by Sir Richard Branson, that intends to run the lottery on a non-profit making basis. The final selection procedure has already led to Court hearings and may turn out to be protracted.

Policy directions

82.6 Before the start of the National Lottery in 1994, the government issued Policy Directions for consideration by the distributing bodies when determining their policies and assessing applications. These advised that all schemes should promote the public good. Originally, all distributing bodies except the NLCB were instructed to make awards only for capital projects, but this was amended in 1996 and revenue-only funding is currently available from the Arts and Sports Councils and the Heritage Fund as well as the NLCB. This means that funds can be used to pay people to start projects and the Sports and Arts Councils can invest in people as well as buildings. Other criteria that the distributing bodies were asked to consider included the needs of the disadvantaged, especially the disabled, a fair spread of funding on a regional basis and that awards made by all bodies except the NLCB should be matched by some partnership funding.

82.7 The White Paper (July 1997) proposed that distributors analyse the needs of their sectors, draw up strategic plans and work together to encourage applications amid growing criticism of the regional bias of successful applications and fears that many smaller organisations are missing out on much needed funding.

The National Lottery Charities Board

82.8 Established by *s 37* of the *National Lottery Act 1993* the National Lottery Charities Board (NLCB) currently allocates grants totalling about £250 million a year and by August 2000 had awarded £1.4 billion to 19,000 UK charities since the first awards were made in October 1996. The NLCB has 17 Board members including the Chair. There are five country grant making committees made up of Board members covering England, Wales, Scotland, Northern Ireland and the UK. There are also nine England Regional Awards Committees.

82.9 The stated aim of the Board is to 'help meet the needs of those at greatest disadvantage in society, and to improve the quality of life in the community'. It can make grants for any charitable purpose to any independently established charitable, benevolent or philanthropic organisation (of which there are around 500,000) and therefore not just to registered charities. It seeks to support both large and small organisations, at national, local, rural and urban levels. The NLCB does not expect to make grants for sports, arts or heritage projects as these are more appropriate for other lottery distribution bodies.

82.10 Until the end of 1997, grants were allocated under themed rounds which targeted poverty, youth issues and low income, health, disability and care, new opportunities and choices, improving people's living environment and community involvement and voluntary sector development. There are now two Main Grants Programmes (Poverty and Disadvantage and Community Involvement), an International Grants Programme, a Small Grants for Small Groups Programme and a Research Programme. These are outlined briefly below.

Main Grants Programmes

82.11 These two programmes are continuous. There are no closing dates for applications so organisations may apply at any time to suit their requirements. It should be noted, however, that it can take up to five months between submitting a completed application to receiving notification of the Board's decision.

Poverty and disadvantage

82.12 This programme aims to improve the quality of life for those people and communities who are at a disadvantage because of poverty or who are at a risk of poverty. This programme concentrates on the needs of particular groups including minority ethnic groups, women and children, and people with disabilities. It aims to fund projects that help people on low incomes, projects that help those living in disadvantaged areas and projects that prevent or reduce poverty.

Community involvement

82.13 This programme aims to fund projects that help people to become involved in activities that improve the whole community's quality of life, where community means either a grouping of people who live near to each other or a group of people with the same interests. This includes projects that support community initiatives and services, encourage people's involvement in, and responsibility for, the community and projects run by organisations that help community and voluntary groups become more efficient.

International Grants Programme

82.14 The International grants programme awards grants to fund development projects that tackle poverty and inequality, and improve the quality of life for some of the most disadvantaged people in Africa, Asia, the Middle East, Central and South America, the Caribbean and Central and Eastern Europe. Applications are accepted from voluntary organisations based in the UK that work with partner organisations abroad and organisations involved in development education in the UK. Grants are announced once a year and applications are accepted during specified periods (the fifth programme will run from 30 October 2000 until 16 March 2001). The previous four programmes have awarded £82.6m to 423 UK-based voluntary organisations working abroad.

Small Grants for Small Groups

82.15 There are two Small Grants Schemes, one for England and Scotland and one for Wales and Northern Ireland. Awards for All (England & Scotland) makes grants of between £500 and £5,000 to small groups in England and Scotland involved in arts, sports, heritage and voluntary and community activities. In England priority is given to groups with an annual income of less than £15,000 a year and in Scotland grants will only be awarded to organisations in this category. Groups must spend the money and complete any activities within one year of receiving the grant.

82.16 The Small Grants Scheme (Wales and Northern Ireland) makes grants of between £500 and £5,000 to small local groups with an income of less than £15,000 a year. Groups must spend the money and complete their activities within six months of receiving the grant.

Health and Social Research Programme

82.17 The programme funded medical research and social research into health, disability and social care. The programme has now closed but details of a new programme to fund research are due to be published in November 2000.

Applications to the NLCB

82.18 Applications for grants can be for funding of one, two or three years, for partial or sole funding, capital costs, revenue costs, a combination of revenue and capital costs, and for matching funds for European Structural Funds or European Union grants. It is the Board's policy not to give grants to replace statutory funding. The minimum grant is £500 and there is no upper limit. An organisation applying for funding must have a constitution or a set of rules outlining its aims, objectives and operational procedures, a bank or building society account with at least two joint signatories and must be able to provide an approved copy of its most recent signed accounts, or, if it is a new organisation, income and expenditure projections for the whole organisation for the period of the grant. Grants cannot be given to individuals. Branches of charities that have their own constitutions and meet the other requirements can apply in their own right.

82.19 The first stage of the application process is to obtain copies of policy documents and application forms from the NLCB and to check the eligibility of the proposed project against the NLCB's published policies.

82.20 For an application to be successful it should score highly against each of the specific criteria that are set by the Board. The form should provide clear evidence supported in detail that the criteria are met. The criteria that the assessors mark against vary but as a rule successful applications have showed evidence of the following:

- well thought out objectives;
- credible scale and nature of demand;
- innovation;
- evidence of user involvement or consultation;
- clear budgeting plans;
- appropriate management structure in place to carry out project;
- benefits to the whole community;
- community support; and
- evidence of how the project will be funded when the lottery grant is exhausted if there is no time limit on the project.

82.21 Successful applicants have been able to show themselves as being well organised and managed, financially sound, and with equal opportunities policies in place. The first stage of assessment is by a Grants Officer who checks that the application is complete, from an eligible organisation and falls inside the published policies of the round. It is then sent to an assessor who scores the application by deciding on a yes/no basis whether different criteria have been met. The assessments are reviewed by Grants Officers and Regional Managers, and a numerical listing of scores received by applications is created for each region or country. To ensure both a fair geographical spread and a range of types of activity, weightings are applied.

82.22 For applications covering the whole of the UK, the whole of England, Wales, Northern Ireland, or Scotland the Country Director makes recommendations to the appropriate country committee based on the assessment of the application. Applications relating to just one English region are submitted by the Regional Manager to the regional advisory committee (RAC). The members of the RAC are volunteers who use their knowledge of local needs to advise the Director of England about the types of grants that will benefit their area. The Director then puts forward final recommendations to the England Committee.

82.23 Decisions about applications made for funding from the International Grants Programme are made by the UK committee following recommendations of an advisory panel. Special research advisory panels advise and make recommendations to the UK Committee about medical and social research projects.

Other distributing bodies

82.24 Although the NLCB is seen as the main source of lottery funding for charities about 40% of the funds distributed by the other distributing bodies are given to charities or non-charitable voluntary organisations.

82.25 National Lottery

Arts

82.25 The Arts Councils aim to promote access, education and excellence in the arts through partnership by bringing the arts to a wider audience encouraging individuality and experimentation, nurturing creativity across the generations, embracing the diversity of our culture and exploring new forms of expression. Funding from the Arts Councils comes under the following categories.

Capital projects under £100,000

82.26 Organisations requiring support of less than £100,000 for capital projects (building work or purchase of equipment, instruments or vehicles) should apply to the Regional Arts Lottery Programme.

Capital projects over £100,000

82.27 The Arts Capital Programme runs alongside the Arts Councils' grant-in-aid and other lottery-funded programmes. Together these programmes provide a balanced package of support for the arts. The Arts Capital Programme has £176m to spend on arts buildings, equipment purchase and public art commissions, with awards from a minimum of £100,000 to a maximum of £5 million. There will be two spending rounds, of about £88m each, between 2000 and 2005. The first round opens for applications on Friday 29 September 2000 and closes at 5pm on Monday 22 January 2001.

82.28 Nine priorities have been set for the Arts Capital Programme and preliminary applications will have to meet at least one priority in order to be invited to make a subsequent full application for funds.

National Touring Programme

82.29 The National Touring Programme uses lottery funds to support the distribution of work from across a broad range of arts disciplines to audiences across England. The programme makes awards of over £5,000 towards time-limited touring projects, and may also contribute towards associated research or commissioning, and preparation. Before making an application applicants are advised to seek advice from Arts Council officers concerning an appropriate level for their application.

Other programmes

82.30 Funding is available from other programmes for recovery, stabilisation, film production and development of a wide range of arts.

Heritage

82.31 The Heritage Lottery Fund allocates money to safeguard and enhance the heritage of buildings, objects, collections and the environment, to assist people to appreciate and enjoy their heritage and to allow them to hand it on to future generations. Funding is given for projects related to natural habitats and countryside, urban green spaces including parks, historic buildings and sites, historic library collections and archives, museum collections, archaeological projects and industrial, transport and maritime heritage that are of outstanding interest and importance at a local, regional or national level. By August 2000 5,627 grants worth £1.5billion had been made from this fund.

82.32 Any organisation or individual can apply for a grant, although at present grants are not made for projects concerning privately or commercially owned sites or buildings. Consideration will be given to projects put forward by a public or other not-for-profit organisation that includes privately owned property as part of a wider area or umbrella scheme.

82.33 There are two ways in which the Heritage Lottery Fund allocates grants. The main grants programme funds projects where the main income requirement is for capital spending on work, or buying items, aimed at preserving and improving access to things that are of importance to the heritage. Applicants are expected to contribute some of the costs of the project and grants are not normally given for projects costing less than £5,000. The revenue grants programme supports projects aimed at widening understanding and enjoyment of the heritage, and widening access to heritage information, where the main costs are spending not related to capital. Projects should last up to three years. Again, applicants must contribute some of the costs of the project and grants are not normally given for projects costing over £100,000.

82.34 Applications under the main grants programme are assessed against seven published criteria including importance of the project to the heritage, access benefits and quality of design. Applications under the revenue grants programme are also assessed against seven criteria including in this instance developing new audiences for heritage, commitment to equal opportunies and evaluation strategies.

Sports

82.35 The Sports Councils operate lottery programmes that provide funding for both capital projects and revenue schemes to increase active participation in sport and recreation. Applicants can apply under the capital programme for building and construction, the purchase of land and/or the purchase of capital equipment. Projects must meet defined standards of good design, quality and technical requirements for the relevant sport or sports. Buildings must provide access for people with disabilities. Projects will only be considered for funding from the Lottery Sports Fund if they involve a sport or sports recognised by the Sports Councils.

82.36 Capital projects must be of demonstrable benefit to the local community and command a good level of support from the public. Applicants must have attracted significant partnership funding to ensure that the project can be completed and sustained.

82.37 Revenue programmes run by the Sports Councils can fund individual athletes and their governing body's performance plans. Revenue funding is also used to support major sporting events.

Millennium Fund

82.38 The Millennium Commission allocated funding for projects to assist communities in marking the year 2000 and the beginning of the third millennium. The Commission has now stopped taking applications for capital projects. It continues to fund the Millennium Award scheme which distributes grants of around £2,000 to individuals involved in community activities. The Millennium Commission will be wound up on 31 December 2000 and its allocation of funding will be redistributed to the New Opportunities Fund.

82.39 National Lottery

New opportunities fund

82.39 The New Opportunities Fund works with national, regional and local partners from the public, private and voluntary sectors to fund, fairly and efficiently, specified health, education and environmental initiatives across the UK with particular focus upon the needs of those who are most disadvantaged in society.

82.40 The New Opportunities Fund was created by the *National Lottery Act 1998* and made its first grants in 1999. The fund, which is a UK-wide non-departmental public body sponsored by the Department of Culture, Media and Sport, is responsible for distributing grants for health, education and environment initiatives determined by the Government. The New Opportunities Fund will deliver its specified initiatives by working in partnership with other organisations, including other lottery distributors.

82.41 Current health initiatives include Healthy Living Centres and Living with Cancer. Educational initiatives include Community Access to Lifelong Learning, Out of School Hours Learning, Out of School Hours Childcare and ICT Training for Teachers, School Librarians and Public Librarians. An environmental initiative is Green Spaces and Sustainable Communities.

Further information

82.42 For further information on any of the Lottery funding programmes please contact the relevant distribution body. Contact details are listed below.

Addresses

National Lottery Charities Board (NLCB)	St Vincent House Suffolk Street London SW1Y 4NL Tel: 020 7747 5300 www.nlcb.org.uk
Millennium Commission	Portland House Stag Place London SW1E 5EZ Tel: 020 7880 2030 www.culture.gov.uk
Heritage Lottery Fund	7 Holbein Place London SW1W 8NR Tel: 020 7591 6000 www.hlf.org.uk
English Sports Council	PO Box 649 London WC1H 0QP Tel: 0345 649649 www.english.sports.gov.uk

Sports Council of Northern Ireland	House of Sport 2a Upper Malone Road Belfast BT9 5LA Tel: 028 90381 222
Scottish Sports Council	Caledonia House South Gyle Edinburgh EH12 9DQ Tel: 0131 339 9000
Sports Council for Wales	Sophia Gardens Cardiff CF1 9SW Tel: 028 20300 500 www.sports-council-wales.co.uk
Arts Council of England	14 Great Peter Street London SW1P 3NQ Tel: 020 7312 0123 www.artscouncil.org.uk
Arts Council of Northern Ireland	77 Malone Road Belfast BT9 6AQ Tel: 028 90667 000 www.artscouncil-ni.org
Scottish Arts Council	12 Manor Place Edinburgh EH3 7DD Tel: 0131 240 2443 www.sac.org.uk
Arts Council of Wales	Holst House 9 Museum Place Cardiff CF1 3NX Tel: 029 20376 500
New Opportunities Fund	Heron House 322 High Holborn London WC1V 7PW Tel: 0845 0000 121 www.nof.org.uk

83 Non-departmental Public Bodies

83.1 A non-departmental public body (NDPB) is: 'an entity which has a role in the process of government but is not a government department nor forms part of a department. It is established at arms length from departments and may carry out executive, regulatory, administrative or commercial functions. Typically it carries out functions within a framework set by the responsible minister, but its degree of operational independence varies. It can incur expenditure on its own account and is usually financed at least in part from public funds. The use to which a body puts these funds is governed by a financial memorandum issued by the sponsoring department'. (APB Practice Note: Audit of Central Government Financial Statements in the United Kingdom).

83.2 NDPBs are similar to quangos, but often exist to deliver a charitable service, and may be registered charities in their own right. A number of museums for instance fall into this category.

83.3 Of the 223 registered charities with annual income in excess of £10m, 31 are NDPBs or quangos. NDPBs and quangos, including the British Council, the British Museum, and the Arts Council, are estimated to have a combined annual income of over £1.5 billion (UK Voluntary Sector Statistical Almanac 1998/99). In Scotland NDPBs include the 15 regional health boards, 22 local enterprise companies as well as organisations such as Scottish Homes and UVAF (Unemployed Voluntary Action Fund).

Gongos

83.4 Where an organisation becomes dependent on government funding to such an extent that it is to all intents and purposes controlled by that funder, much of the organisation's independence is lost. Its range of activity is determined by negotiating its annual grant terms, and trying to obtain as much flexibility within budget heads as possible. These charities, often referred to as Government Owned Non-Governmental Organisations (GONGOs), may not be NDPBs, but may be required to comply with terms under the financial memorandum which effectively put them under the same regime.

Structure

83.5 Charities that are NDPBs (or gongos) are often established as limited companies. They will use terminology and systems that would be more at home in the public sector and often have to operate under an even wider range of regulation than other similar charities.

83.6 The funding of a typical NDPB is provided, at least in part, by parliament via a sponsoring department. The terms of the funding will be governed by a financial memorandum, and the financial reporting requirements will be set out in an accounts direction, both issued by the sponsoring department. Annual accounts for all NDPBs are prepared on an accruals basis, and charitable NDPBs usually adopt the Charities SORP, although sometimes in a slightly modified format depending on the nature of their activities.

83.7 An NDPB has an accounting officer, who is formally responsible for the performance and stewardship of the charity, and for accounting to parliament each year. Normally the Chief Executive is the accounting officer, assisted by the Finance Director. The accounting officer is responsible for the propriety and regularity of the financial activity, keeping proper accounts, prudent and economical administration, and the efficient and effective use of resources. The finance director (sometimes referred to as the principal finance officer) is responsible for ensuring the charity's effective financial management and for the production of the annual accounts. The duties of the accounting officer, and the accounting requirements generally of NDPBs are set out in 'Government Accounting' (the manual published by the Stationery Office setting out the accounting rules and requirements in the central government sector).

83.8 Where a charity receives any form of government funding, it should clarify whether the terms of the funding are such as to impose these additional requirements. For instance the trustees may be required to take account of compliance with relevant authority, known as regularity. Regularity is defined as the requirement that a financial transaction should be in accordance with the legislation authorising it, regulations issued by a body with the power to do so under the governing legislation, parliamentary authority, and treasury authority. The financial memorandum may require the auditors to report not only on the accounts as prepared under the accounts direction, but also to report on non-financial measurements of performance which may or may not be specified.

Management

83.9 The management of an NDPB is also expected to meet a requirement of propriety, which is the behavioural aspect of regularity. It is concerned with standards of behaviour and corporate governance. Matters that would fall under this definition include open and fair competition in letting contracts, the avoidance of unnecessary extravagance, avoiding conflicts of interest or making a personal profit from public money. Propriety is not subject to any formal report, but auditors are expected to have regard to matters of propriety and to report any shortcomings to the relevant body. Their assessment of the appropriate standard will be based on any specific guidance issued by the sponsoring government departments, as well as whatever is considered to be acceptable practice in the public sector, which is likely to be informed by the findings of the Committee on Standards in Public Life.

83.10 In dealing with charitable NDPBs, or organisations which are required to account in similar terms, charities may therefore find themselves dealing with unfamiliar terms and procedures. Apart from these areas though, the ability of such an organisation to operate generally, or to enter into contracts, is governed by general applicable legislation, such as tax law and the *Companies Acts* and should not cause difficulties in a normal business relationship.

84 Overseas Activities

84.1 Charities may be involved in overseas activities in a variety of ways. In some cases they may simply send money or goods overseas, in others they may have overseas branches or projects and finally some may be part of an international organisation overseas grouping with funds and facilities being shared around the international organisation. There are a number of issues common to all these scenarios, and some specific to individual cases.

84.2 Just as the Charity Commission has no power to prevent a charity from setting up in England and Wales because there are already others addressing the same purpose, there is no international regulatory body that can regulate the number of agencies responding to overseas needs. Sudden emergencies can lead to a spate of new relief organisations seeking to help in an overseas area, often where other UK charities, or local or international agencies from other countries, are already established. Where a charity wishes to act in such circumstances it should first make enquiries through the overseas country's embassy, and through other organisations, in order to co-ordinate activities and maximise effectiveness.

Constitution

84.3 A charity may be registered to carry out charitable purposes abroad. In their first published 'Decisions of the Charity Commissioners', the Commission set out its position i.e. that the first three heads of charity (see Chapter 15) are charitable wherever the purpose is fulfilled. International charities set up for the relief of poverty, and the advancement of education or religion, are assumed to be for public benefit. Fourth head charities, 'purposes beneficial to the community', have a wide range of activities within them, from preserving old buildings to preventing cruelty to animals. A charity working overseas will qualify under the fourth head if the Commission considers that its activities overseas would so qualify if undertaken in the UK, and as long as its activity is not contrary to public policy. A charity cannot be registered with objects that are unlawful in the country or countries in which it intends to carry out its charitable activities.

Regulation

84.4 Regulating a charity's overseas activities is more difficult than regulating its affairs in this country. In its annual report for 1996, the Charity Commission, in relation to its investigation of the Palestinians Relief and Development Fund (Interpal), commented that, 'Where a charity's beneficiaries are overseas our powers of investigation in the locations where funds are distributed are often limited'. Interpal was registered in 1994 with the principal aim of providing aid to the poor and needy, including sick children and widows suffering as a result of civil or military action or national disasters. The charity confines its activities to Palestine and Palestinian refugees. Articles had appeared in the press alleging that there was a connection between Interpal and the alleged terrorist wing of Hamas and that Interpal part-funded Hamas. The Commission reported that it had carried out a detailed scrutiny of the charity's controls and records. It found them to be well-organised and there was no evidence of any donations being made for political purposes or that could not be accounted for. Scrutiny of the charity's publicity and documentation provided no evidence of pro-terrorist propaganda and interviews with staff and trustees showed they were 'motivated by faith and altruism rather than fanaticism'. The Commission recognised that Hamas would have supporters in the areas where Interpal was distributing aid but agreed that aid could not be denied to such people because of that support. On the basis of its work, the Commission was able to conclude that there was no evidence linking Interpal with support for terrorism and that funds were not being given solely because of an individual's support for Hamas but on the basis of their poverty and need. The trustees had taken all reasonable steps to ensure that the funds were being used within the objects of the charity and within the law.

84.5 The law permits trustees of UK based charities to be based overseas, although the Charity Commission has expressed unwillingness to permit this where it applies to a majority of the trustees, arguing that in order to discharge their responsibilities effectively trustees need to be able to meet on a regular basis. Some charities use telephone or video conferencing facilities to conduct some of their meetings, or use them to allow overseas based trustees to participate in meetings held in the UK. The Charity Commission has permitted some international organisations whose funding and support is international to have the majority of their trustees based overseas.

Trust obligations

84.6 The fact that money or other resources of a charity are to be applied abroad in no way diminishes the trustees' duty of good stewardship, or their responsibility to ensure that funds are applied only in furtherance of the objects of the charity. It is still surprisingly common to find organisations that treat any activity overseas as automatically not under the control of the trustees, as though once the goods have left the UK, there the responsibility ends. This is not true — the trustees are responsible for ensuring that the resources are applied for the relevant charitable objective, wherever that application may be carried out.

Tax

84.7 Charities working overseas have to be registered in the UK to qualify for UK tax reliefs (*Camille and Henry Dreyfus Foundation Inc v Inland Revenue Commissioners [1954] 2 All ER 466*). They need to take particular care that expenditure incurred represents only 'qualifying expenditure'. Where this is not the case, then an element of tax relief available under *ICTA 1988 s 505* may be withdrawn.

Grants to overseas organisations

84.8 A payment made, or accrued, to a body situated outside the United Kingdom is not qualifying expenditure unless the charity has taken reasonable steps to ensure that the payment will be applied for charitable purposes. To ensure that this is so the UK charity needs to be quite clear that the payment is within its own charitable objects, and also that the application of the funds in the foreign country will meet the criteria set out above i.e. would the activity be charitable if it was carried out within the UK? This is undoubtedly a fraught area — some of the issues in which UK charities become involved are naturally influenced by our own society's values, and would not necessarily be part of any internationally accepted protocol. This can also lead to charities being perceived as acting politically, as many international charities may focus their activities on campaigning for change in the policy or practices of an overseas country or international institutions such as the IMF or World Bank.

84.9 Within the UK charities can ensure that their expenditure is 'qualifying expenditure' by operating within the terms of their trust and rigorously checking the use to which funds will be put if they are donated to another organisation or charity.

84.10 Overseas Activities

84.10 Equal rigour should be applied when making donations to overseas organisations. An English charity, for instance, will often be regulated by the Charity Commission and its trustees' behaviour is governed by various legislation. In an overseas context the relevant legislation may be much less developed, there may be no regulatory body, and so the chances of error or corruption may also be greater. These factors should be considered, and, if necessary, appropriate controls and accountability introduced to ensure that payments are properly applied.

84.11 Note that *s 505* of *ICTA 1988* refers to accrued payments. Under the SORP they would only be accrued in the accounts if there existed a claim against the charity which arose from 'a duty or responsibility which obligates the entity either legally, or practically, because it would be financially or otherwise operationally damaging to the entity not to discharge the duty or responsibility. A moral obligation — such as results from the making of a non-contractual promise — does not create a liability unless it meets the definition [of a liability] (SORP Appendix I, para 15). Where trustees enter into long-term commitments, then they should be clear as to how the funding sent overseas will continue to meet the qualifying expenditure criteria, not just concentrate on the application of funds despatched during the accounting period.

Overseas expenditure incurred by the charity

84.12 When an organisation is operating overseas it is often true that the level of accountability to the head office in the UK is less stringent than applies in the UK itself. There are a number of reasons for this, and it will often depend on whether the structure of the charity is project or branch based and whether it is run by local staff and volunteers, or by employees recruited in the UK. Whatever the situation, it is equally important that expenditure incurred overseas is properly accounted for and controlled to ensure that no breach of trust occurs and no tax liability is generated.

Overseas income

84.13 Income paid to UK charities from abroad, such as rents and bank interest, is generally exempt from tax. A UK charity that receives income from which foreign taxes have been deducted may be able to recover the tax from the relevant tax authorities.

VAT

84.14 VAT is an indirect tax which operates, under different names, throughout Europe. Charities may incur similar indirect taxes in other countries. These taxes are not recoverable in the UK.

84.15 Charities often give goods and equipment away to a country outside the European Community. As exports these can be treated as a zero-rated business activity, allowing the charity to register and reclaim the VAT on the purchase. Customs strongly advise charities to retain documentary evidence that the relevant items have indeed been exported. A donation of goods to a charity for export can be zero-rated by the person making the gift.

84.16 Where goods are bought in a different EU Member State by a charity which is not VAT registered, then VAT will be charged in the Member State of supply and this tax will not be recoverable. Where goods are brought in from another Member State by a VAT registered charity the supplier can usually zero-rate his supply on being provided with the charity's VAT registration number and evidence of the removal of goods to the UK. The charity will then be liable to account for UK VAT on the purchase — declaring this as 'acquisition' VAT in box 2 of its next VAT return. The extent to which the charity can make a deduction of this VAT will be determined by the usage of the goods, e.g. if the goods will be used to make only exempt sales no recovery is allowed.

84.17 Eligible goods may be zero-rated when supplied to charities in other Member States, that are not registered for VAT in their own state, provided that evidence is produced to show that all the conditions of the appropriate relief are met.

84.18 Wherever overseas activities are involved, and especially where supplies involve different Member States, then a charity may need to take specialist advice. A number of special schemes exist to reduce diversity in the tax treatment, covering a wide variety of topics, including the tour operators margin scheme, triangulation and place of supply.

Accounting

84.19 The accounting requirements for overseas activities are the same as for activities carried out within the UK. There are, however, real practical difficulties in attempting to account centrally for overseas work as though it were a project based at headquarters. Before embarking on these activities therefore the trustees should consider and establish an appropriate level of accountability which recognises certain factors. Issues to consider may include the extent to which it is necessary or practicable for financial reports to be regularly conveyed to headquarters. For established projects, or branches, with their own bank accounts this is certainly feasible, but it is impracticable where projects are carried out in remote locations or where much of the financial activity is based on barter. In these cases the trustees may have to accept that project accounts cannot always be submitted on a regular basis. Also, exchange risks will affect the amount of funding to be placed in the relevant country. The risk may not only be adverse fluctuations in the exchange rate, but also restrictions on the accessibility of funds for withdrawal. Where the risk is material, these sorts of problems can sometimes be addressed by hedging, or by partnerships with other charities operating in the same country.

84.20 Assuming that overseas activities are to be brought into the annual accounts, then more planning will be needed in the accounts production process. An extended timetable is needed for the consolidation of branch activities within the UK, and so even more time may be required to consolidate overseas activities, especially if they are sufficiently material to merit the attention of the auditors. In some cases it will be necessary for auditors to visit the overseas operation. Usually it will be more efficient and cost effective for the charity to retain a firm of auditors with international representation in the relevant countries.

84.21 Information submitted by local branches will need conversion to sterling. This can be done either by the main charity informing the local operation of a standard conversion rate to apply, or by the headquarters converting all the returns on receipt. Exchange gains and losses would normally be regarded simply as part of the cost of the project — but good treasury management should reduce exchange risk. Although the position will vary from country to country, it is sensible to minimise holdings in unstable currencies, or use a locally acceptable stable equivalent such as US dollars.

84.22 If the UK charity is buying or supplying equipment, goods or services overseas, then exchange differences are likely to arise on transactions. These are treated as part of the relevant income or expenditure. Where assets held overseas are converted to sterling they may also give rise to an exchange gain or loss, which should be recognised through the SOFA in the statement of recognised gains and losses.

84.23 Overseas Activities

Overseas charities operating in the UK

84.23 Charities based overseas that operate or fund-raise in the UK may suffer the following tax disadvantages:

- tax on UK income such as interest will be deducted at source and will be irrecoverable;
- tax efficient giving incentives such as Gift Aid or payroll deduction schemes cannot be used to recover income tax paid by donors;
- they will not be able to take advantage of tax exemptions available only to charities registered in the UK.

84.24 The exact impact of tax legislation on an overseas charity operating within the UK will also depend on the tax regime of the country in which the charity is based and the status of the UK tax treaties. International tax advice may be necessary.

84.25 An overseas charity can overcome these tax disadvantages by registering its UK activities as a UK registered charity with the Charity Commission England and Wales or the Inland Revenue (Scotland). The Charity Commission is likely to insist that a majority of the trustees are UK citizens or at least UK based.

UK charities fund-raising overseas

84.26 A UK charity that fund-raises overseas may have to register in the countries in which it is fund-raising in order to qualify for any tax exemptions or tax-effective giving concessions operated by those countries.

85 PAYE Administration

85.1 Every employer has a duty to operate PAYE in respect of payments made to employees. It is the employer's responsibility to ensure that all persons who are employees are treated as such for tax purposes and that the PAYE regulations are then operated properly. Failure to operate PAYE results in the employer being responsible for any tax which should have been deducted from the employees' pay. Penalties are levied for failing to deduct tax as well as for failing to complete and submit the necessary forms correctly or on time.

PAYE audits

85.2 The Inland Revenue and the Contributions Agency send their officers to check that employers are operating PAYE correctly. These inspections check that proper procedures are being followed, that calculations are carried out in accordance with the regulations, that PAYE is applied to all persons who should be treated as employees and that, where benefits are provided to employees, they are correctly recorded on the appropriate end of year returns. These inspections will typically cover a period of up to three years but may extend to six years or even longer if the employer is seriously in default. The Inland Revenue will seek to collect tax for any errors discovered in the period under review.

Operating PAYE

85.3 PAYE operates by recording the weekly or monthly pay of each employee and calculating the tax thereon. This is done using PAYE code numbers, which are provided by the Inland Revenue for each employee and which represent the allowances or tax-free pay to which an employee is entitled. In some cases where taxable benefits or other income exceed allowances the employee is given a negative PAYE code. The PAYE code to be used first depends upon the employee's circumstances when he joins. Every employee should be asked to complete form P46 on which the employee certifies whether or not it is his main employment. These forms should normally be retained by the employer as long as the person remains an employee, as evidence of their status, unless the employer is instructed to send them to the Inland Revenue. Pay is calculated using working sheets and tax tables, supplied by the Inland Revenue, or a computerised payroll system, of which a number are commercially available. National insurance contributions, statutory sick pay and statutory maternity pay are calculated in a similar fashion. The amount due to the Inland Revenue for each month must be paid over by the nineteenth of the following month, covering both tax and national insurance contributions.

End of year procedures

85.4 At the end of the year, an employer is required to complete a form P35 showing each employee's yearly tax and national insurance and reconciling this with payments made. The form also contains a declaration to be signed by the employer certifying that all employees are included and that PAYE has been properly operated. At the same time, individual certificates of pay and tax deducted are provided to each employee (P60) and copies sent to the Inland Revenue. These forms must be submitted to the Inland Revenue by 19 May following the end of the tax year and forms P60 must be given to employees by 31 May.

85.5 PAYE Administration

Employees leaving

85.5 When an employee leaves during a tax year, he should be given a form P45, which certifies his pay and tax deducted for the year to date. This is then given to his new employer who operates PAYE based on the figures shown. In these circumstances, a P46 is unnecessary.

Taxable pay

85.6 The amount of tax and national insurance to be deducted is calculated by reference to an employee's pay. The definition of pay is not always the same for both tax and national insurance purposes. Pay includes all salaries, wages, overtime, bonuses, pensions, commissions etc. and includes holiday pay, Christmas boxes and any other cash payments. It also includes any liabilities of the employee that have been met directly by the employer unless these are genuine business expenses. The cost of meals and travel from home to normal place of work are not business expenses.

Termination payments

85.7 There are some payments on termination of an employment which are not taxable. Where an employee is entitled to a period of notice, which is not given but the employment contract does not provide for an alternative payment, the employee is nevertheless entitled to compensation in lieu of his notice period. This is not pay under the terms of the contract but compensation for breach of the contract and is not taxable up to a maximum of £30,000. Similarly, a compensation payment for a material alteration to a person's contract may also be non-taxable. Employers should, however, beware of making payments to persons who have reached or are near to retirement age as there are circumstances when the Inland Revenue can treat these as retirement benefits, in which case they are taxable. Sometimes, the position regarding such payments is not clear and it is as well for employers to seek professional advice rather than leave themselves open to a liability for failure to deduct PAYE.

Pension contributions

85.8 There are certain deductions which an employer may make from a person's pay before it is subject to tax. These are pension contributions to an approved scheme where the employer is the contributor and payments to charity under the payroll deduction scheme. Such deductions are, however, only allowable for tax purposes and not for national insurance. National insurance contributions are therefore calculated on the person's salary before such deductions.

Students

85.9 There are special rules and procedures for students working during their vacations, who will not earn sufficient to be liable to tax. The PAYE system assumes that a person will be paid at regular intervals throughout the year so that the allowances and rates of tax are apportioned on a monthly basis according to a person's earnings in the tax year to date of payment. This method of calculation can mean that persons who only work during part of a tax year may have too much tax deducted, which they can reclaim at a later date. This problem can be avoided for students by completing form P38(S) as soon as they start working and, if already employed, at the beginning of each tax year.

Benefits

85.10 Many employers provide staff with benefits as well as salary. While benefits cannot be subject to PAYE they must be declared to the Inland Revenue at the end of each tax year so any tax liability can be assessed. For employees who are not directors and who earn less than £8,500 a form P9D is used. For directors and employees earning more than £8,500 per annum the rules on taxable benefits are more complex and a form P11D must be completed. There is a special exemption for directors of charities or non-profit making concerns who earn less than £8,500 per annum but a director of a trading subsidiary of a charity would not qualify for this exemption unless they are also a full-time working director of that company earning less than £8,500 per annum.

85.11 The form P11D should show all benefits, whether taxable or not, including all reimbursed expenses. This includes reimbursed travel and entertaining expenses even if incurred entirely on the business of the employer. It is then up to each individual to make a separate claim for these items not to be taxed. In completing the form, the employer is required to calculate the cash equivalent of the benefit. In the case of a company car or mobile telephone, this will be the scale charge and in the case of a beneficial loan the amount based on the reduced interest rates applicable. The Inland Revenue publish a detailed guide to expenses and benefits (Booklet 480, 'Expenses and Benefits — A Tax Guide') and how they are calculated for tax purposes. Once completed, the forms P9D and P11D should be sent to the Revenue and a copy given to the employee by 6 July following the end of the tax year. The forms are designed to enable the employees to enter the necessary figures on their self-assessment tax returns, without themselves having to make complex calculations. The employer can, of course, be liable for penalties if a form P11D is incorrectly completed although in the case of a minor innocent error it is unlikely that the Inland Revenue would take any action.

Dispensations

85.12 Where an employer pays any expenses or provides any benefits which will not result in tax payable by the employee, the employer can apply to the Inland Revenue for a Dispensation. If granted, those items need not be included on form P11D. This avoids the submission of details of routine expenses, such as travelling and subsistence expenses which are properly controlled and are genuine business expenses.

P11D errors

85.13 When carrying out inspections, the Inland Revenue often discover that employers have omitted certain benefits from the forms P11D, often because they were not aware that they should be included. This typically happens with such expenses as staff Christmas parties and social events paid for by the employer which exceed the limit of £75 per head. In such cases, the employer will often not wish the employee to incur a further tax charge, particularly where the mistake may have happened for a number of years. In these circumstances, the Inland Revenue will treat the value of the employee's benefit as being the benefit received by the employee after tax has been deducted and will collect the tax from the employer.

Employers paying tax

85.14 If an employer wishes to provide such benefits and does not wish the employee to be taxed on them, arrangements have been introduced known as PAYE Settlement Agreements. These are formal arrangements whereby the employer agrees to settle tax on certain classes of benefit, which the employer settles on a global basis. This does not give rise to any tax liability for the employees. These arrangements can be made in respect of minor expenses such as taxi fares, small gifts etc., items paid on an irregular basis such as a holiday under an incentive award scheme or where it is impracticable to operate PAYE or to identify the precise benefit for each employee such as staff entertainment or the provision of company transport. The employer must apply to the Inland Revenue for such an arrangement, by 6 July following the end of the tax year and any tax payable becomes due on the following 19 October.

Inland Revenue guides

85.15 When starting a PAYE scheme each employer is provided with detailed guides explaining how the scheme should be operated. These are updated by the Inland Revenue each year and a new supply of forms is distributed. Employers should be familiar with these guides because not knowing what is in them is not considered an acceptable excuse by the Inland Revenue for failing to operate PAYE properly.

86 Pensions

State pension schemes

86.1 The legislation covering State, occupational, personal and stakeholder pensions for employees in a voluntary sector organisation is exactly the same as for any organisation. People of State pension age, which is currently 65 for men and 60 for women (changing to 65 progressively between 2010–2020), are entitled to a basic state pension if they (or their husband for married women) have paid national insurance contributions for the required amount of years. The amount of this pension is fixed and bears no relation to the amount earned.

86.2 In addition to this, a State Earnings Related Pension Scheme (SERPS) is available for employees who have paid full rate national insurance contributions for some or all of the period since April 1978. The amount received depends on the earnings on which national insurance contributions were paid.

86.3 Employees can also join an occupational scheme run by their employer or a personal pension scheme, to top up their State pension. From October 2001 all employers will have to offer stakeholder pensions to any employees who are not eligible to join the organisation's own pension scheme.

Occupational pension schemes

86.4 Though there is no legal requirement for them to do so, some charities set up occupational pension schemes to provide pensions for their employees. Occupational pension schemes are regulated by the Occupational Pensions Regulatory Authority. There are two types of occupational pension scheme. A final salary scheme is salary related and provides a pension based on the employee's salary at retirement and length of service. The other, a money purchase scheme, provides a pension which is bought with contributions made to the scheme that have been invested. Money purchase schemes commit employers to a fixed contribution, with the employee's ultimate pension dependent on how well the scheme's investments have performed. For salary related schemes, however, the commitment is open ended. Employers guarantee the benefit levels, irrespective of what it costs them. As different retirement ages for men and women contravenes *Article 119* of the *Treaty of Rome*, both sexes must be allowed to take their pension at the same age.

86.5 Whether or not an employee remains within SERPS whilst also a member of an occupational scheme depends on whether the scheme is contracted out or not. If contracted out, an employee is excluded from SERPS. Both the employee and the employer pay a reduced national insurance contribution. The rebate for those in final salary related schemes is 4.6% of earnings between the lower and upper earnings limits. Rebates for money purchase schemes depend upon the age of the employee. At least the total amount of rebate for money purchase schemes must be paid into the occupational scheme. Part of the rebate is deducted by the employer and the remainder is paid by the DSS at the end of the tax year.

86.6 The level of contribution made by the employee to an occupational scheme is set by the employer. In non-contributory schemes, employees make no contribution. Final salary schemes are subject to triennial actuarial review and contributions must meet the Minimum Funding Requirement levels, as calculated by the scheme actuary, for triennial valuations conducted after 6 April 1997. Employees may make additional voluntary contributions (AVCs) to top up the amount of contribution set by the employer. Employees can also take out free standing AVC (FSAVC) plans with an insurance company.

86.7 Tax relief is available on contributions made to an occupational scheme up to 15% of salary. For schemes set up after 1 June 1989, or for people joining after that date there is an earnings cap of £91,800 (2000/2001) on which tax relief can be claimed. There are limits on the benefits which can be taken from an exempt approved scheme.

86.8 An employer should seek independent advice before setting up an occupational scheme. They can be expensive to run and are generally only suitable if the scheme has at least 100 members. For smaller organisations, an industry-wide scheme run by an umbrella body (e.g. National Housing Federation) or schemes run by the Pensions Trust or the London Pensions Fund Authority, may be more appropriate. Certain insurance companies may also offer suitable schemes.

86.9 Employees in occupational pension schemes who change job can leave their contributions in the scheme or take a transfer value to another occupational scheme or personal pension plan. If the employee has been in the scheme for less than two years it is possible to get a refund of their own contributions less tax and administrative costs.

Part-time employees

86.10 One area of particular concern to voluntary sector organisations is that in the past it has been possible to exclude part-time workers from occupational pension schemes. Under the equal treatment rule set out in the *Pensions Act 1995*, part-time workers now have the same right as full-time employees to join pension schemes, on the grounds that as a majority of part-time workers in the UK are female, exclusion of part-time workers from pensions schemes amounts to indirect sex discrimination.

86.11 If a part-time worker can satisfy an industrial tribunal that the equal treatment rule has been breached, he/she will be granted admission to the scheme. Backdated membership can be awarded and the employer is expected to meet much of the cost. The only defence to such a claim is if the trustees or managers of the pension scheme (the defendant) can show that the exclusion is not related to gender but to a material factor. The employer will be treated as a party to the proceedings and will be entitled to appear and be heard at the tribunal.

Personal pension plans

86.12 Personal pension plans can be taken out by any employee who is not a member of an occupational pension scheme. Personal pensions are all of the money purchase variety (as described at 86.4). Some employers that do not operate their own pension scheme are willing to contribute a fixed percentage of an employee's salary to the employee's personal pension plan. However, if the employee moves to an employer with an occupational scheme, they may find that their new employer is not willing to offer them the choice of having the employer's contributions paid into either the employer's scheme or the employee's personal pension plan.

86.13 Unlike occupational schemes, direct tax relief on contributions to personal plans is unavailable, but if the plan is Inland Revenue approved, the provider of the plan can recover the basic rate tax paid on the contribution and apply them to the pension fund. Higher rate tax, if paid, can be recovered from the employee's tax office.

86.14 Personal pension plans approved by the DSS are contracted out of SERPS but, unlike occupational schemes, employees continue to pay full national insurance contributions. The difference between the full and contracted out rate is refunded by the DSS to the employee's pension plan at the end of the tax year.

86.15 An employer may arrange a pension plan for a group of employees. This is known as a group personal pension plan. The advantage of a number of staff joining the same scheme is that administration costs are minimised, and the employer does not incur the costs of running an occupational scheme. In addition, pension providers often charge lower commission for a group arrangement.

Stakeholder Pensions

86.16 The *Welfare and Reform Pension Act 1999* sets out the general principles for Stakeholder Pension Schemes, so that in future all employees will have access to a simple, flexible and cost-effective method of pension provision. As only an estimated 14% of the 28,000 charities that employ paid staff have occupational pension schemes at present, this legislation will result in drastic changes to pension provision in the voluntary sector.

86.17 Registered stakeholder pensions will be available from April 2001 and from October 2001 all employers will be obliged to offer membership of a stakeholder scheme to any employees who are not eligible to join an occupational scheme or group pension plan that their organisation operates. It will not be compulsory for employees to join a stakeholder pension scheme.

86.18 At present even those charities that operate occupational pension schemes or group pension plans often exclude certain individuals from their scheme. Therefore even charities with pension arrangements in place will have to decide whether to open the existing scheme to all employees or to introduce stakeholder pension schemes for some employees.

86.19 Individuals will be able to contribute up to £3,600 per year into a stakeholder pension scheme. Contributions will be paid net of basic rate tax, as with personal pension plans, and higher rate taxpayers will be able to claim extra tax relief. In some circumstances it will be possible to pay more than £3,600 a year into the scheme but this will depend on age and earnings (in line with personal pension plans).

86.20 Exemptions from having to offer stakeholder pension schemes are available for:

- employers with fewer than five employees (to be reviewed in three years time);
- employees who earn less than the National Insurance lower earnings limit (currently £67 per week);
- employers offering an occupational scheme open to all employees within one year of joining;
- employees within five years of Normal Retirement Date (NRD), over NRD and below 18;
- employers offering Group Personal Pension schemes to all employees within three months of joining and to which employees contribute at least 3% of salary.

86.21 The stakeholder access requirement does not mean that employers have to set up and administer their own schemes. Charities are obliged, however, to provide employees with information about a chosen scheme and provide information for the employee to get in touch with the scheme administrator. The employer will not be required to contribute to the scheme but will be able to do so if they wish. Charity trustees will not be liable for the performance of the scheme they choose.

86.22 There will be a cost for employers as they will have to deduct stakeholder contributions from employee pay and transfer them to the scheme on either a flat rate or percentage basis. It is estimated that it could cost between £10 and £25 per annum per employee to pass on contributions, £20 to £1,000 to set up changes to payroll systems and between £25 and £2,000 to nominate a scheme and consult employees.

87 Political Activities

87.1 A commonly held misconception is that charities are forbidden from engaging in any form of political activity. This is not the case, though there are some restrictions. Charities have a long history of legitimately using the political process to further their aims. From the campaign of the Anti-Slavery Society in the nineteenth century to more recent work on community care and environmental legislation charities have played an important role in shaping social policy.

87.2 In their annual report for 1991 the Charity Commissioners wrote: 'It is not the intention of the law, nor the business of the Courts and the Charity Commission to staunch the contribution of charities to public life. Charities operate for the public benefit. Charity trustees may bring their experience to bear where it is relevant, to reflect the interests of their beneficiaries wherever those interests may be affected. The nation would be impoverished if charities were to be cut off from public debate and the opportunity to inform decision makers. They have a wealth of knowledge and experience to bring to bear on the solution of problems and not solely on their treatment'.

New Charity Commission guidelines

87.3 The law makes a distinction between political purposes and political activities. Charities are not permitted to have directly political objects, so an organisation set up to achieve a political purpose, e.g. to further the interests of a political party or to change the law, policy or decisions of central or local government in this country or abroad, cannot be registered as a charity. However, an organisation set up to achieve a charitable purpose may engage in political activities, including lobbying for changes in the law, provided that they are carried out in furtherance of their charitable objects and within the Charity Commission's guidelines (either CC9 'Political Activities and Campaigning by Charities' or CC9a 'Political Activities and Campaigning by Local Community Charities').

87.4 The law on campaigning and political activities is based on case law, rather than statute, and as relatively few cases have come before the Courts it is not always easy to determine whether or not a particular action would be regarded as coming within the law. The Charity Commission's inquiry into Oxfam's campaigning activities in 1991 highlighted just how difficult it can be to draw the line between acceptable campaigning activity and unacceptable political action. Largely as a result of this inquiry, in April 1994 the Commission issued clearer, revised draft guidelines on political activities and campaigning with the aim of helping trustees to decide:

- whether or not any political or campaigning activities they were considering fell within the law;
- to clarify how the Commission would respond to allegations or evidence of charities carrying out unlawful political activities; and
- to give trustees reassurance that if they followed the new guidelines they would be regarded as acting properly.

Duty to take political action

87.5 Despite the clarification of the legal position, some charities continue to come under criticism, even from their own supporters, when they take political action. As

87.6 Political Activities

Brazilian Archbishop Dom Helder Camara so aptly put it: 'When I give food to the poor, they call me a saint. When I ask why the poor have no food, they call me a communist'. Sometimes this criticism of charities is regrettable, particularly given that the law not only permits charities to take action directed at securing, or opposing, changes in the law or in government policy in some circumstances, but also the law could find trustees guilty of acting in breach of their duties if they failed to take political action when this would be both within the law and the most effective way of meeting the needs of their beneficiaries.

Ancillary to objects

87.6 Any political activities a charity engages in must be directly related to its work and designed to further its aims. Political activities must be ancillary to the charity's stated objects, and not become the dominant part of them. They must be permitted by the charity's governing document and within its powers. When deciding whether or not to spend the charity's money on campaigning or political activities, the Commission's guidelines require trustees to satisfy themselves that there is a reasonable chance the activity will be successful in furthering the charity's purpose and so help those the charity exists to benefit to an extent that justifies the expenditure.

Public must be given information

87.7 If these requirements are met, charities can put their views to the government, and publish the advice or views they express to ministers. They can seek to inform and educate the general public, and advocate solutions to the problems they are trying to tackle, providing this campaigning and education work is based on a well-founded, reasoned argument based on research or direct experience. Charities must present their case in a way that enables people to make up their own mind, avoiding the use of data which the charity knows, or ought to know, is inaccurate or distorted by selection to illustrate a preconceived position.

87.8 Charities should provide the public with sufficient, accurate information to support the case they are promoting. Where the medium used makes this impractical (e.g. billboard advertising or a brief TV advertisement) the charity should be able to set out its full position if requested to do so.

87.9 Campaigning material may have an emotional content, but charities should not seek to persuade the public or the government on the basis of material that is merely emotive.

Voting records

87.10 Charities are permitted to publish individual MP's or political parties' voting records on relevant issues provided that they do so in a way that is designed to enable their supporters or the public to encourage those MP's or parties to alter their position as a result of reasoned argument, rather than merely in response to public pressure.

Research

87.11 Charities can conduct and publish properly constituted research studies or surveys that use a methodology appropriate to the subject. If research is undertaken to test a hypothesis, it must be designed to test that hypothesis objectively and not merely to look for evidence to support that hypothesis. The aim of publishing research must be to inform and educate the public. Charities must not publish research which they know, or ought to know, is flawed and must not undertake research for another organisation in the knowledge that the other organisation intends to use the results for party political or propagandist purposes.

Presenting views to government

87.12 The Commission's guidelines allow charities to provide their supporters, or members of the public, with material to send to MPs or the government, provided that the material is sufficient to enable supporters to put forward a well-founded, reasoned argument. They are also allowed to provide and publish comments on proposed changes in the law or government policy contained in Green or White Papers, or other documents, to respond to invitations to comment on proposed legislation, to supply Members of either House with material for use in debate which would further the charity's purpose, and to advocate a change in the law or public policy by presenting the government with a reasoned memorandum setting out the charity's case.

Petitions

87.13 Charities are permitted to organise petitions to be presented to either House of Parliament or to national or local government. It is good practice to state the purpose of the petition on each page the public is asked to sign.

What the guidelines prohibit

87.14 Charities must avoid all party political activities and must not take part in party political demonstrations. They must not seek to persuade members of the public to vote for or against a candidate or a political party which advocates or opposes a particular policy supported or opposed by the charity. When a charity advocates a particular solution to a problem, and that solution is also advocated by a political party, the charity must make it clear that its views are independent of those of the political party.

87.15 Charities must not attempt to influence public opinion or put pressure on government using data they know, or ought to know, is inaccurate or misleadingly selective.

87.16 Charities must not claim public support for their position on a political issue unless they can substantiate their claim.

87.17 Charities whose objects include the advancement of education must not overstep the boundary between education and propaganda. Material supplied should be sufficient to enable a person to form their own judgement about an issue and not merely restricted to presenting one set of arguments designed to promote a particular point of view.

Acting with other bodies

87.18 Charities are often invited to take part in joint action on political issues by other organisations working in the same field. Charities are not prohibited from joining alliances which contain non-charitable organisations provided that certain conditions are met. They may join only if the alliance can be reasonably expected to further the charity's own charitable objects. They may only take part in alliance activities that would be permissible for a charity to engage in and must dissociate themselves from any activities of the alliance that are not charitable and must not allow their name to be associated with such activities or their funds to contribute towards them.

87.19 Political Activities

Elections

87.19 Charities may comment on proposals put forward at local, national or European elections provided they relate to the charity's work and any comments are consistent with the Charity Commission's guidelines on campaigning and political activities and the requirements of electoral law. Charities may bring issues relating to their work to the attention of prospective candidates and raise public awareness about them provided that they do so in a way which is reasoned, well-founded, educational and informative.

Demonstrations

87.20 Care must be taken if charities are considering taking part in some form of demonstration or direct action that goes beyond handing out informative leaflets in a public place. Such events can involve significant risk and may alienate supporters of the charity or damage public support for it or even for the charitable sector generally. Public rallies and demonstrations can easily get out of control and the charity, or its officers, or those taking part may find themselves charged with committing an offence and face potential civil or criminal liability. If a demonstration is likely to interfere with the rights of others it becomes increasingly unlikely that the trustees could justify exposing the charity's assets to risk. Should the trustees decide to proceed with a demonstration that in the event gets out of hand because they have failed to exercise sufficient prudence in its organisation and control, the trustees could face a claim for want of prudence in their administration of the charity. In these circumstances the trustees could find themselves having personally to make good any financial loss the charity suffers as a result of the demonstration.

87.21 Charities should also exercise caution before requiring their staff to take part in a demonstration, as employers must not require employees to do any unlawful act. Where staff or trustees of charities take part in demonstrations in a private capacity they should take care to ensure that they are not perceived as being official representatives of the charity, for example by carrying placards or wearing badges carrying the charity's name.

Penalties

87.22 In addition to the risk of damaging a charity's good name and losing public support, tax relief can be lost on funds applied for non-charitable purposes. Trustees may be required to repay to the charity money judged to have been mis-spent on improper campaigning or political activities plus any additional tax liability incurred as a result.

Controls and advice

87.23 Any charity engaged in campaigning or political activities must have in place adequate arrangements for the commissioning, control and evaluation of such activities by its trustees.

87.24 Charities that are uncertain about the legality of any proposed campaigning or political activities should seek advice from their legal advisers or from the Charity Commission or SCVO.

88 Public Charitable Collections

88.1 *Part III* of the *Charities Act 1992* contains controls for public charitable collections. Although it is now eight years since the Act was passed, the accompanying regulations are still subject to consultation and are therefore not yet in force. No date has been set for the new regulations. At present collections held in the street, on public roads, pavements or footpaths are covered by *s 5* of the *Police, Factories etc (Miscellaneous Provisions) Act 1916* and house-to-house collections by the *House to House Collections Act 1939* and the *House to House Collections Regulations 1947* and *1963*.

Street collections

88.2 Street collections usually require a permit or a licence. There is no obligation, however, for local authorities to license street collections and there are no national regulations controlling the collection on the streets of money, or the sale of articles, for the benefit of charities. The *Charitable Collections (Transitional Provisions) Order 1974 (SI 1974 No 140)* contains a model licence that can be used by a local licensing authority that chooses to licence street collections, but its use is not obligatory. The relevant local authority should be contacted before a charity attempts to hold a street collection.

House to house collections

88.3 House to house collections must be licensed or have an exemption. An application must be made at least a month in advance of the month in which the collection is due to start. The application must specify the purpose of the collection and the area in which the collection will be made. Licensing authorities are:

- in the Metropolitan Police District, the Commissioner for the Metropolitan Police;
- in the City of London, The Common Council of the City of London; and
- elsewhere, the local authority.

[*House to House Collections Regulations 1947 (SI 1947 No 2662)*].

88.4 Large charities planning to hold a nation-wide collection, or a collection over a substantial part of England and Wales, can apply to the Home Office for exemption from having to apply to each local authority. Local police can give exemption from the need to obtain a licence for a local collection to be completed within a short time period.

88.5 A 'house' in terms of the *House to House Collections Act 1939* includes certain business premises including public houses and places of business, so fund-raising pub crawls come within this legislation. The Act also covers the collection of goods and the house to house sale of goods or services where at least part of the proceeds will be used for charitable purposes.

88.6 The licence is granted to the 'promoter' who is responsible for ensuring that the collection is carried out in accordance with the law. The promoter must keep a record of the name and address of each collector along with the numbers of the collecting tins or receipt book given to them. Collectors must be over 16 and carry a certificate of authority and wear an official badge, both of which they must sign. The certificate and badge must be returned to the promoter after the event and the promoter must then destroy them.

88.7 Money may only be collected in:

- a sealed tin or box which can only be opened by breaking the seal, and which shows the purpose of the collection and a distinguishing number;
- envelopes sealed by the donor, if authorisation has been obtained from the Secretary of State;
- any other way if the donor is given a receipt from a duplicate or counterfoil receipt book.

[*House to House Collections Regulations 1947 Reg 6(1)(13)*].

88.8 Money must be counted in the presence of the promoter and another responsible person unless the sealed tins are delivered unopened to a bank. The amount of money collected in each tin must be noted by the person counting the money. A return must be made to the licensing authority listing all donations and expenses incurred in connection with the collection within one month of the expiry of the licence.

88.9 When *Part III* of the *Charities Act 1992* is implemented the existing legislation covering public collections for charities will be repealed. Changes envisaged include:

- extending regulation to collections on private land intended for use by the public e.g. stations, airports, shopping malls;
- collections will be authorised by permit rather than licence and the permits will be issued by the relevant local authority;
- new regulations regarding the conduct of collections, certificates of authority, badges, minimum age of collectors etc.;
- grounds under which local authorities can refuse to grant a permit; and
- referring to both street collections and house to house collections as 'public charitable collections' and including both in the same legislation.

89 Quality Initiatives

Introduction

89.1 Many voluntary sector organisations are introducing quality systems as a way to maximise their effectiveness. Three of the most common models and systems used in the voluntary sector are described here together with a brief commentary about their use and value. The three quality initiatives are:

- BS EN ISO 9000;
- Investors in People (IIP);
- EFQM Excellence Model.

Each of these quality initiatives has a distinctive contribution to make. They are complementary and can be used alongside each other. The 'best' quality model(s) to use are the ones that best meet an organisation's particular needs.

BS EN ISO 9000

89.2 BS EN ISO 9000 is an international standard for quality management systems, developed from the British Standard BS 5750. Known as ISO 9000 for short, its full title reflects the fact that it is a British, European and International Standard. It is therefore well regarded as a 'badge of quality' world-wide and has been adopted by over 50,000 companies in the UK and over 127,000 world-wide.

89.3 The Standard is written in a generic form that fits any type of organisation, for example, manufacturing, service industries, voluntary organisations and further education. ISO 9000 is based on the premise that in order to do things consistently well, everyone needs to know what to do and how to do it. The best way to do this is to have documented procedures, as knowledge can more easily be shared in this way and there is less chance of misunderstandings, especially over time.

89.4 Defining and documenting your procedures and practices can provide a powerful starting point for quality improvement. Besides encouraging consistent practice across the organisation and subsequent customer satisfaction, the actual process of documenting procedures encourages organisations to review current practice and to question whether things can be done any better. Gaps in people's knowledge of how things should be carried out can be identified and rectified and staff understand what is expected of them.

89.5 However, one of the many criticisms levelled at ISO 9000 is that too much of the focus is on documenting all procedures, and not enough on how effective they actually are. This is not quite fair for two reasons. Firstly, the Standard provides fairly prescriptive guidelines on how to manage quality throughout the life cycle of a product or service and documented procedures must be in accordance with the requirements of the standard. Secondly, another fundamental principle of ISO 9000 is the notion of continual improvement, through both internal review and external assessment. In other words, as well as undergoing an external assessment, organisations are obliged to internally review procedures and systems for both compliance and effectiveness.

89.6 This notion of continual improvement is reinforced within the latest revision of the standard (ISO 9000:2000) when organisations will be required to have specific measures of improvement. The new standard will also introduce increasing emphasis on relationships with, and understanding of, the customer, his/her needs and satisfaction as well as staff training. In this way, the revisions will move the standard nearer to Investors in People and the EFQM Model.

89.7 Once the quality system is in place and established, an independent assessment by a certified body is carried out to check conformity with the requirements of the standard and to ensure that declared procedures are working in practice. If certification is awarded, the organisation must continue to be regularly audited by an independent certification body.

89.8 There have been many debates about whether self-assessment or validation by a certification body is best for voluntary organisations. Improved public perception of the organisation's image may well result from external validation, but the downfall is that there is a temptation to view obtaining ISO 9000 certification as an end in itself. If this is the approach, then organisations will try to get there as quickly and as cheaply as possible and quality will suffer because important corners are cut. ISO 9000 is a good quality badge to have, but it is much more powerful as a tool to help you set up and run a quality management system. Even if you do not choose to seek certification, the principles are sound and worth checking out.

Investors in People

89.9 Investors in People (IIP) is a national Standard for effective investment in the training and development of people in order to achieve organisational goals. It is a UK government business initiative, developed by the National Training Task Force and endorsed by the CBI and TUC. IIP is open to any organisation of any size from any sector and is now being introduced in a number of countries outside the UK.

89.10 IIP offers an invaluable alternative focus that other quality models (which tend to be more process driven) often gloss over, in other words, that effective quality management requires emphasis on the training and development of employees. While being about people, it is clearly directed at improving performance by linking training and development to the needs of the business.

89.11 The standard provides a set of criteria by which organisations can be assessed in terms of their effectiveness in using training and development to meet organisational targets and improve performance. These criteria are based on four key principles:

- a commitment, from the top, to develop all employees;
- a regular review of the training and development needs of employees and a plan to meet those needs;
- action to train and develop individuals throughout their employment;
- the measurement of the organisation's success in using its investment in training and development effectively.

89.12 The benefits of IIP can be seen both for the organisation and the individuals within it. The organisation benefits from a more systematic approach to training, improved employee communications and a more skilled and motivated workforce. Individuals often benefit from greater recognition, structured development and increased job satisfaction.

89.13 Local Training and Enterprise Councils (TECs) in England and Wales, Local Enterprise Companies (LECs) in Scotland and Employment Agency (TEA) in

Northern Ireland provide help and support to organisations implementing IIP. Should a charity wish to pursue the IIP award, it must first write to its local TEC or LEC stating the intention to commit to work towards the Standard. TECs, LECs and TEAs can also provide training and an initial assessment, the purpose of which is to identify how your organisation measures up to the national Standard and identify action to close any gaps.

89.14 Following the assessment visit, if the charity meets the Standard it will be formally recognised as an 'Investor in People' organisation and can publicise this through use of the IIP logo. Further re-assessments will either take place after three years or every 12–15 months in order to ensure that continuous improvement becomes an integral part of organisational management.

EFQM Excellence Model

89.15 The EFQM Excellence Model was first introduced in 1991 and was developed by the European Foundation for Quality Management (EFQM), a body of 14 'leading' European companies. The EFQM was formed in order to promote business improvement through the use of Total Quality Management (TQM), and the group developed the model using considerable expertise developed from the Malcolm Baldrige (USA) and Deming (Japan) Award Models.

89.16 The EFQM Excellence Model was designed as a generic framework for assessing and then continuously improving the performance of an organisation across all its activities. The Model is applicable as much to 'non-business' orientated organisations, such as non-profit organisations, as to private sector organisations. However, a public and voluntary sector version has been published that recognises the richness of differences that exist between these different types of organisations and draws out some small differences. It is this Model that is keenly promoted to the voluntary sector by the National Council for Voluntary Organisations (NCVO).

89.17 The EFQM Excellence Model is not a standard (such as ISO 9000 and IIP). The Model is a non-prescriptive framework that recognises that there are many approaches to achieving sustainable organisational excellence. The Excellence Model is a self-assessment tool, although it can also be used to obtain external validation through participation in the European Quality Award (or a national equivalent) which uses the model as the assessment criteria.

89.18 The Excellence Model's key distinction, when compared with the other 'quality' models, is that it attempts to link organisational processes with actual results. Unlike ISO 9000, for example, this Model places as much emphasis on the necessity to measure outputs, outcomes and impacts as it does on the processes available to enable these.

89.19 The model has nine elements, which have been identified as the key components of business excellence. There are five 'enabler' and four 'result' criteria. The 'enabler' criteria are concerned with what is done to run the organisation and how it is operated, how it manages its staff and resources, how it plans its strategy and how it reviews and monitors key processes.

89.20 The 'result' criteria are concerned with what the organisation has achieved and is achieving as seen by those who have an interest in the organisation, for example, its customers, employees, the community and funders. These cover the level of satisfaction among the organisation's employees and customers, and its impact on the wider community. The framework places percentage weightings on each of the nine criteria, representing a consensus view of their relative importance, but these are only of direct relevance to applicants for quality awards.

The EFQM Excellence Model

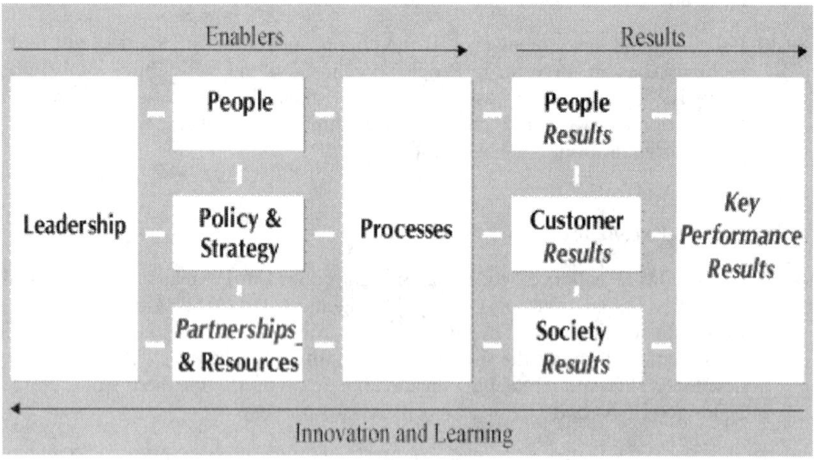

89.21 The starting point for most organisations is to conduct a self-assessment against the Model, which can range from a quick assessment to a fully evidenced and externally validated report. A key part of the detailed 'health check' is that it highlights those areas where an organisation is performing well, as well as those where it is performing poorly. The typical outputs are a score profile against the Model, and much more importantly a prioritised improvement action plan that can provide a valuable input to the annual organisational planning process.

89.22 The EFQM Excellence Model is a non-prescriptive framework that recognises there are many approaches to achieving sustainable excellence in organisations. This lack of prescription for specific controls and procedures allows organisations to build their own underlying tools and procedures. However, the Model's flexibility and non-prescriptive style may frustrate organisations if their priority is to determine clear standards and measure achievement against them.

89.23 It is for this reason that many organisations may find value in referring to more prescriptive standards, such as IIP and ISO 9000, as compliments to the Excellence Model. There is no duplication or complication and each of them can contribute to improving the performance of an organisation within one or more of the nine boxes of the Excellence Model.

89.24 The relationship between the Excellence Model and IIP/ISO 9000 is diagrammatically expressed below.

Conclusion

89.25 All three quality initiatives described above have their own specific characteristics. The quality path chosen for a particular organisation will depend on its particular circumstances. While the Business Excellence Model provides an overall look at

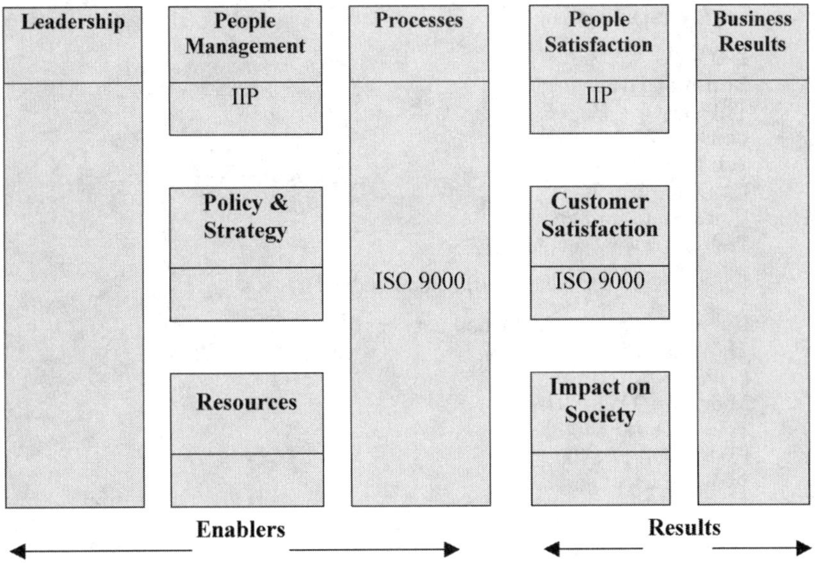

performance, Investors in People looks at developing staff and ISO 9000 helps improve the way processes are managed.

89.26 In summary the Business Excellence Model helps trustees and managers to ask the right questions, and the other two initiatives help them to find solutions. Collectively they can help improve all aspects of organisational performance, encouraging the constant review and improvement of performance.

Further information

EFQM

The British Quality Foundation
32–34 Great Peter St
London SW1P 2QX
Tel: 020 7654 5000
Fax: 020 7654 5001
E-mail: mail@quality-foundation.co.uk
Website: www.quality-foundation.co.uk

Investors in People

Investors in People UK
4th Floor
7–10 Chandos Street
London W1M 9DE
Tel: 020 7467 1900
Fax: 020 7636 2386
E-mail: information@IIPuk.co.uk
Website: www.IIPuk.co.uk

89.26 Quality Initiatives

BS EN ISO 9000

ISO 9000
British Standards Institution
389 Chiswick High Road
London W4 AL
Tel: 020 8996 7327
Fax: 020 8996 7400
E-mail: info@bsi.org.uk
Website: www.bsi.org.uk

For details of accredited certification bodies

United Kingdom Accreditation Service
21–47 High Street
Feltham
Middlesex TW13 4UN
Tel: 020 8917 8400
Fax: 020 8917 8500
Website: www.ukas.com

90 Rates and Council Tax

Business rates

90.1 Uniform business rates apply to non-domestic property. Other property used solely for residential purposes is subject to council tax. Rates are due from the owner as long as the property is occupied. No rates are payable in respect of voids of between six weeks and three months, and most empty premises attract half rates thereafter. Properties used for a mixture of purposes are assessed on a case by case basis.

Exemptions

90.2 Certain churches enjoy full relief from rates. These are the Church of England, the Church in Wales, and those certified under the *Places of Worship Registration Act 1855*. The relief extends to their administrative buildings, church halls and similar buildings used in connection with a place of worship. This phrase encompasses a range of other buildings operated in connection with the church. Where property is used for the day care of those who are ill or disabled, or the provision of welfare or workshops for people with disabilities, then full rate relief is available under the *Rating (Disabled Persons) Act 1978*.

90.3 Apart from these specific exemptions, all charities are entitled to 80% rate relief under the *Local Government Finance Act 1988 ss 43* and *45*, as long as the property is used wholly or mainly for charitable purposes. Under *Local Government Finance Act 1988 ss 47* and *48* further discretionary relief is also available up to another 20%, thus allowing local authorities to grant charities complete exemption from rates. The relief is available to charities, or to not-for-profit organisations which use the property for educational, social welfare, philanthropic, religious, literary, artistic or scientific purposes, and not-for-profit clubs using the property for recreational purposes. This discretionary relief is less likely to be granted if the organisation does not make its facilities widely available. Under separate regulations the relevant authority has to give one year's notice of a reduction in these reliefs, and the change must take effect at the end of a financial year.

Mixed use

90.4 The reliefs almost exclusively operate where the property is 'wholly or mainly used' for the charitable or similar purposes referred to. 'Mainly used' is defined as more than half (*Fawcett Properties Ltd v Buckingham County Council* [*1960*] *3 All ER 503*). Charitable purposes normally exclude fund-raising but include the sale of donated goods. Premises used partly by a charity for its purposes and partly by a non-charitable subsidiary trading company will qualify for relief only in respect of the part actually occupied by the charity.

Charity shops

90.5 Charity shops selling donated goods are often operated as trading subsidiaries, in which case they are not automatically entitled to 80% relief, though some local authorities are prepared to grant it. Even where shops are operated by the charity itself, relief could still be restricted if all the proceeds, minus expenses, are not paid to the charity.

90.6 In some instances where donated goods are sold alongside ordinary trading goods the trading activity may be carried out by the charity acting as an agent for the trading company. The charity may claim that it is occupying the whole premises, for the sale of both donated and bought-in goods. The charity would therefore be occupying the shop partly for charitable purposes and partly for another purpose. However, the charity will not necessarily lose its rates relief because it may still be able to satisfy the local authority that the shop is occupied mainly for charitable purposes.

Future prospects

90.7 The Deakin report* criticised this regime because certain authorities fail to recognise some organisations, such as village halls, as charities qualifying for the 80% relief on the basis that they were neither registered, exempt or excepted. This imbalance is exacerbated by the variation in authorities granting the 80% or 100% relief. The report recommended making 100% rate relief mandatory for charities.

Council tax

90.8 Council tax relates to domestic property, defined as that used wholly for residential accommodation, and is payable by the occupier. Charities do not get any general relief from council tax. Therefore council tax has to be paid on some charitable property which, if it were not residential, would qualify for relief from uniform business rates, for instance hostels, nursing homes and almshouses.

90.9 Although the tax is usually payable by the occupier, there are specific cases relevant to charities where the owner, rather than the occupier, is liable. These are:

- nursing homes, residential care homes, student halls of residence, dwellings occupied solely by students, hostels, dwellings in multiple occupation;
- dwellings occupied by religious communities whose main activities are prayer, education, the relief of suffering, or contemplation;
- dwellings occupied by a minister of religion in connection with the performance of his or her duties; and
- dwellings occupied by staff who live there in order to carry out work for their employer.

90.10 Charities that are liable for council tax will need a clear policy on whether or not they wish to recover it, or part of it, from the occupiers, particularly where there is a chance that by not trying to recover it they could be argued to be replacing statutory provision.

90.11 Because council tax is assessed partly on the value of the property, and partly on the basis of occupancy, some charities will be able to obtain reliefs because of exemptions granted to classes of people with whom they work:

- full-time students;
- those in hospital or in care, or severely mentally impaired;
- those in hostels or night shelters;
- careworkers;
- members of religious communities;
- certain international visitors (soldiers); and
- prisoners.

*('Meeting the Challenge of Change: Voluntary Action into the 21st Century': The Report of the Commission on the Future of the Voluntary Sector).

Scotland

90.12 The new regime for business rates and council tax also operates in Scotland. Local authorities have often operated the reliefs in respect of water and sewerage charges, but Scottish charities now need to apply to the individual privatised water companies (who publicise their policies on the matter) for reliefs.

91 Receipts and Payments Accounting

Introduction

91.1 Accounts prepared on a receipts and payments basis summarise all the cash transactions that actually took place during the year and show the remaining cash and non-cash assets and liabilities. They do not purport to show a true and fair view of a charity's financial position. Unlike accruals accounts, receipts and payments accounting makes no adjustments to allow for expenditure made in one accounting period that relates to costs incurred in another.

91.2 Unincorporated charities with annual income and expenditure of £100,000 or less (or in Scotland gross receipts of £25,000 or less) are permitted to prepare receipts and payments accounts and a statement of assets and liabilities if they wish rather than accruals accounts, provided that they do not have another statutory obligation to produce accruals accounts. Larger unincorporated charities, charitable companies and industrial and provident societies do not have an option to produce accounts prepared on a receipts and payments basis. They must produce accruals accounts.

Principles

91.3 Although accounting on a receipts and payments basis is simpler than on an accruals basis it in no way lessens the trustees' responsibility for maintaining the accounting records and ensuring accountability. Consequently many of the fundamental principles set out in detail in the main SORP for Charities follow through into receipts and payments accounting. For instance, the year-end accounts should still distinguish between restricted, unrestricted and designated funds and indicate the existence of liabilities and certain assets that may be recoverable. To an extent these accounts are not pure receipts and payments, they are a hybrid format. The only substantial differences between these and accruals accounts are that:

- accruals, prepayments, depreciation of fixed assets and valuation movements can be ignored; and
- there is no need to present a traditional balance sheet—a statement of assets and liabilities is required instead (or in Scotland a statement of balances).

Income and expenditure

91.4 Many donations to charities are not in cash form and therefore will not feature in receipts and payments accounts. Therefore in some cases the choice of accounting presentation will determine the accounting presentation that must be adopted. For instance, accruals accounting requires donated assets for functional use and receivable items, such as pecuniary legacies, to be treated as income, whereas they are excluded from income in accounts prepared on a receipts and payments basis. Preparing a charity's accounts on an accruals basis could show the charity's income as being more than the £100,000 threshold, so the charity will have to produce accruals accounts, whereas preparing the accounts on a receipts and payments basis might record the income as being less than £100,000, giving the charity the option of preparing accounts on either a receipts and payments or on an accruals basis.

91.5 No formal guidance exists for organisations that find themselves in this position but there are some common sense guidelines. First, it is important that the accounts are at least internally consistent. Second, the accounts must be comparable from one year to another so that if a charity's income or expenditure is fluctuating around the £100,000 threshold, it would be advisable for it to adopt the higher requirement, i.e. accruals accounts, in order to avoid the expense of having to restate a previous year's figures. Where timing determines on which side of the threshold a charity falls, such as deferred legacy income recognition, then it will be particularly important to consider the impact of the transaction in the foreseeable future.

91.6 Charity accounts must include all the charity's activities including those carried out by, or otherwise relating to, branches. Receipts and payments accounts may only be prepared if the charity's gross income, including that of branches, is under the relevant threshold. Care must be taken to assess the effect of this amalgamation process in advance. If the combined results of the headquarters and branches exceed the threshold, then the accounts will need revision to an accruals basis and the information already obtained from the branches may need to be revised and supplemented.

Assets and liabilities

91.7 The statement of assets and liabilities is not a balance sheet. It is simply a list setting out the charity's assets and liabilities. Appropriate values may be added if available. The assets and liabilities will mainly comprise monetary items such as cash and bank deposits, debtors, loans and tax recovery claims. Other assets such as investments and stock can be included at cost. It is recommended, however, that their estimated value should be set out in a note to the accounts, but this is not a compulsory requirement. In some instances the insured value will be adequate.

91.8 Fixed assets should be included in the statement of assets and liabilities, whether owned or financed through lease or hire purchase, and even when the charity's governing document prohibits their resale. Where future lease payments (e.g. to finance an asset) do not constitute a liability, then the future commitment should be disclosed as related to the relevant asset. Other liabilities should be disclosed with any other commitments disclosed separately.

91.9 If possible, conditional liabilities (i.e. where a charity has agreed to make a grant of £2,000 to an organisation on condition that the organisation itself raises £1,000 from other sources) should be listed separately and guarantees and contingent liabilities should also be listed together with their estimated value wherever possible.

91.10 The Charity Commission has issued standard forms which can be used to submit receipts and payments accounts. They are not statutory filing documents. There is no obligation to use them; they are merely produced to assist smaller charities. To underline this point, the Commission's guidance leaflet (CC54) includes a specimen form of accounts prepared without using the standard forms. In practice the standard forms will be of most use to small charities with simple financial affairs, and where there is only limited demand from the public for information about their affairs.

92 Reclaiming Tax

92.1 Charities have a wide range of tax exemptions and generally have no liability to corporation tax or income tax as a result. Nevertheless, charities will have received income from which income tax will have been deducted at source. Where the charity has no liability or the liability is less than the income tax suffered, the charity can obtain a repayment of all or part of this tax.

92.2 In order to obtain a tax repayment, the charity must submit a claim to the Inland Revenue. Such claims must be sent to Inland Revenue Charities (repayments) at the office in Bootle or, for charities in Scotland, the Inland Revenue Charities office in Edinburgh. Before any such claim can be considered by the Revenue, they will need the appropriate forms and supporting documents. A charity can submit a repayment claim as often as it wishes but most charities find it convenient to make an annual claim at the end of each tax year. Larger charities, however, often make claims quarterly or monthly.

Form for claim

92.3 A repayment claim by a charity must be made on form R68. This is only obtainable from Inland Revenue Charities but a new form is usually issued each time a repayment claim is made. The form firstly requires details of certain dividends or other distributions where a tax repayment could be restricted because of anti-avoidance legislation. It then requires details to be shown of any payments made by the charity, which had to be paid under deduction of tax. As the charity must account to the Inland Revenue for the tax deducted, this will be taken into account when calculating the repayment due, unless the tax has already been paid to the collector in which case this is stated on the form. The form then requires the charity to list out all its income and chargeable gains, which would be subject to tax were it not for the specific exemptions applicable to charities. Tax credits and tax deducted at source from this income must also be shown. This includes income from Gift Aid, for which an additional form and schedules are needed.

Incorrect forms

92.4 The Inland Revenue will not accept the form unless the declaration has been completed and signed by an appropriate official of the charity, who will normally be the company secretary, treasurer or a trustee. In that declaration the person signing it states that to the best of their knowledge and belief the information given on the form is correct and complete and that the income and gains have been, or will be, applied only to charitable purposes. The form makes it clear that false statements can lead to prosecution and this could happen where there was a deliberate attempt to defraud or cheat the Inland Revenue. Prosecutions are, however, relatively rare. What is perhaps more common is that insufficient checks are carried out by the charity to ensure that the form is properly completed and that the charity is entitled to a full exemption from tax. If the Inland Revenue discover this situation after the repayment has been made they can, of course, assess the charity for the amount of tax overpaid. If they then consider that this resulted from negligent conduct on the part of the charity, interest and penalties can also be charged. The Inland Revenue provide a good deal of help and guidance to charities to ensure that their tax affairs are dealt with properly. They are not always sympathetic, therefore, when charities have not been following the correct procedures or have been careless in dealing with their tax affairs.

Additional documents

92.5 In addition to the form R68, the charity must submit a number of other forms and documents, depending on its income. For payments received under Gift Aid a list of all such donations must be submitted.

92.6 Where the charity has received dividends or interest on its investments, it should have received a tax voucher showing the amount of the tax credit and tax deducted. All original vouchers must be sent with the repayment claim form.

92.7 A charity has six years in which to make a repayment claim and the Inland Revenue normally have six years in which to make any assessment to collect tax. If, however, the Inspector discovers at a later date that a repayment claim is incorrect due to the fraudulent or negligent conduct of the charity, then the Inland Revenue have twenty years to make an assessment for the tax due. Full disclosure of all relevant facts is, therefore, extremely important if the charity is to avoid the risk of any later discovery by the Inland Revenue.

92.8 The Inland Revenue have stated that they no longer want charities to send their accounts with their repayment claims and even if they do they will not look at them. Instead the Inland Revenue will issue a self assessment tax return and then open an enquiry. If they require further information to see whether any tax is payable or if excessive repayments have been claimed, a charitable trust may be asked to submit their accounts. A company is required to submit its accounts with its tax return. If the Inland Revenue find something wrong they may well start an investigation into earlier years.

Inland Revenue procedures

92.9 The Inland Revenue have a statutory power to require a charity to produce its books and records for inspection by an Inland Revenue officer. This power extends to all books, documents and other records in the possession of, or under the control of, the charity, that contain information relating to the claim. Where a charity fails to produce the necessary documents, it can be liable to a penalty of £300 with an additional penalty of £60 per day until the documents are produced. The Inland Revenue now have a continuous programme of on-site visits to charities to examine their books and records.

92.10 If the repayment claim appears to be in order and is supported by the necessary tax certificates and vouchers, the Inland Revenue will normally make the repayment without delay. It is in the interest of the charity to ensure that all such documents are properly completed, if only to avoid unnecessary enquiries from the Inland Revenue, which can be time consuming and administratively expensive.

93 Recreational Charities

Enhancing social welfare

93.1 There are some 11,000 registered charities whose objects include recreation many of which are registered under the *Recreational Charities Act 1958*. The *Recreational Charities Act 1958* was passed to confirm the charitable status of a wide range of organisations previously recognised as charitable either under the 'fourth head' (other purposes beneficial to the community within the spirit and intent of the *Charitable Uses Act 1601*) or under the head of advancement of education, following a decision of the House of Lords in *Commissioners of the Inland Revenue v Baddeley*. The purpose of the *1958 Act* was not to extend charitable status to a wider range of recreational organisations, but to restore the position as it was understood before the *Baddeley* case.

93.2 The *Recreational Charities Act 1958* states that it is charitable 'to provide, or assist in the provision of, facilities for recreation or other leisure-time occupation, if the facilities are provided in the interests of social welfare'. The Act clarifies what it means by social welfare by requiring that the facilities are to be provided 'with the object of improving the conditions of life of the persons for whom the facilities are primarily intended; and either (i) those persons have need of such facilities as aforesaid by reason of their youth, age, infirmity, or disablement, poverty or social and economic circumstances; or (ii) the facilities are to be available to the members or female members of the public at large'. [*Recreational Charities Act 1958 s 1(2)*].

93.3 Therefore, a leisure facility run on a not-for-profit basis for the residents of a particular area could be granted charitable status, whereas a similar facility established as a commercial business would not. Similarly, rulings of the courts have judged that leisure facilities established purely for entertainment, or those which have a private membership, cannot be considered as charitable.

93.4 Many local authorities are transferring ownership of their leisure facilities to newly formed charities, many of which are established as industrial and provident societies, in order to gain the tax advantages which attach to charitable status. By using the local authority as a corporate trustee, or by drafting the governing document in such a way that the charity trustees must be council members or staff, the local authority effectively retains control.

Membership

93.5 Recreational charities may have members provided that membership is open to a wide group of the community or to some particular group in society e.g. the young, the elderly, those suffering from a particular type of social disadvantage, and they may charge fees for the use of their facilities or for providing training or coaching as they are trading in pursuit of their primary purpose.

Sport

93.6 The *Recreational Charities Act 1958* covers village halls, community centres, women's institutes and other centres for recreation. Care must be taken, however, to distinguish between recreation and sport as the law treats them differently. The promotion of a particular sport is not of itself regarded as a charitable activity, though the provision of sports facilities may be. The Charity Commission has granted charitable status to an ice rink in Oxford and a cricket ground at Hastings. However, amateur sports clubs are not normally awarded charitable status if they have a restricted membership or restrict the sports that can be pursued. Those connected with educational facilities such as schools or colleges are, however, eligible.

Charity Commission Review

93.7 As part of its review of the Register of Charities the Charity Commission issued a discussion document in 1999 on the *Recreational Charities Act 1958* for consultation, as they increasingly receive applications for the registration of recreational organisations of kinds that did not exist when the Act was passed. This document did not examine the question of whether or not amateur sports clubs should be entitled to charitable status, or the wider issue of whether or not the promotion of sport, or excellence in sport, can be a charitable purpose as these issues will be the subject of a further consultation.

93.8 Since the Act was passed there have been significant increases in the time and money available for leisure activities. There has been pressure on the Commission in recent years for charitable status to be granted to a wider range of leisure and sporting organisations than presently qualifies for it. However, public opinion polls commissioned by the Charity Commission do not suggest substantial public support for such an extension. Indeed they found that there was little public support for the principle of any sporting or other leisure or recreational organisation being granted charitable status. The public's view was that such organisations were for the benefit of the people who used them and who often paid for them. People who did not use them should not be asked to contribute towards them through tax and rate relief or in other ways.

93.9 The consultation paper sought views to help develop guidelines so it is clear how the Act is interpreted and how the Commission will decide which organisations are charitable under its provisions. At the time of writing no new guidelines have been issued.

94 Registration with the Charity Commission

The register

94.1 *Section 3(1)* of the *Charities Act 1993* requires the Charity Commissioners to keep a register of charities in England and Wales, unless they are excepted by *s 3(5)*. Scottish charities do not register with the Commission and are considered in Chapter 101. The Commission has a computerised Register which can be consulted by the public via the Internet or at the Charity Commission's offices.

Which charities have to register?

94.2 *Section 3(2)* of the *Charities Act 1993* states that all charities not excepted by *subsection (5)* must be registered. These exceptions include exempt and excepted charities, registered places of worship, and any charity which has neither (i) any permanent endowment, nor (ii) the use or occupation of land, and whose income does not amount to more than £1,000 per year. *Subsection 3(7)* requires the trustees of any charity that should be registered but is, in fact, not registered to apply for registration. It also requires trustees of a charity that is ceasing to operate or to exist to notify the Commission.

Charges

94.3 At present there is no charge for registration. However, charges may be introduced in the future to cover the cost of the service under *s 85(1)* of the *Charities Act 1993*.

The process

94.4 Information packs about starting a charity and applying for registration are available from the Charity Commission (in English and Welsh) and include a questionnaire and an application form. Apart from providing the Charity Commission with routine administrative information, the application form is intended to confirm that the activities of the proposed charity are indeed going to be in line with its declared objects. The questionnaire asks for information about the intended activities of the charity, about the proposed trustees and other relevant information. The Commissioners may request supporting material such as newspaper cuttings, accounts, minutes of meetings, publicity literature, bank statements, written pledges of funding, etc.

94.5 Once a governing document has been prepared it is submitted to the Charity Commission along with other documentation, including a declaration by the trustees that they are willing and able to undertake their role, and the application form.

94.6 The governing document should have been incorporated, executed or adopted as appropriate, and evidence provided that this has happened. This evidence will differ for each type of constitution. A limited company should provide a certified copy of the Certificate of Incorporation, the pages of the memorandum and articles listing the subscribers, and copies of any special resolutions. A trust should provide a certified copy of the executed trust deed after it has been signed, witnessed, dated and sent to the Inland Revenue Office of the Controller of Stamps in case it attracts stamp duty. The Commission recommends that the promoters of a trust should always refer to the nearest stamp office to check on the necessary procedure. An unincorporated association should provide a certified copy of the minutes of the general meeting at which the constitution was adopted and copies of the minutes of any subsequent meetings reflecting changes to the constitution. The Commission emphasises that the constitution, and any changes to it, must be approved by the members, not by the trustees alone.

94.7 Once the documentation is received by the Commission it will be checked, and may be referred elsewhere. For example, if the beneficiaries are vulnerable the Commission may carry out checks with other Government Departments and statutory bodies. If the application is novel or complex, then the Commission's legal staff may be involved, or the Revenue may be consulted. Subject to any issues arising from the application, and unless the name of the charity is not permitted under the *Charities (Misleading Names) Regulations 1992 (SI 1992 No 2355)* then the charity will be entered on the register and the promoter will be informed of the registration number.

94.8 This process can be as quick as a few days, as in the case of the Diana, Princess of Wales Memorial Trust, but typically takes several weeks or even months. In cases of dispute, for instance where an organisation is seeking charitable status in an area hitherto not considered as charitable, the process of arguing the point with the Charity Commission may take several months or even years before it is resolved. An initial rejection can be reviewed, then taken to the Board of Commissioners, and finally an appeal can be brought in the High Court. An appeal in the High Court can be brought not only by the promoters, but by any person, apart from the Attorney-General, who is, or may be, affected by the registration. If a charity's registration has gone to appeal in the High Court, then it will be suspended from the register pending the outcome of that appeal and will not be conclusively presumed to be a charity during this period. [*Charities Act 1993 s 4*]. Most appeals against registration are made by the Inland Revenue, as it stands to lose money if an organisation is granted charitable status.

94.9 When the charity is registered it receives its registration number and a certificate (form RE5) setting out the details of its entry on the register. Inclusion on the register is, for legal purposes, proof that the organisation is a charity. The registration may not be backdated, although the Inland Revenue may backdate tax exemption if the organisation can demonstrate that from an earlier point in time exclusively charitable activities were undertaken.

Removal from the register

94.10 If a charity no longer appears to the Charity Commissioners to be meeting the criteria for being a charity, *s 3(4)* of the *Charities Act 1993* requires the Commissioners to remove it from the register. This sub-section also gives the Commissioners power to remove from the register any charity that has ceased to exist or is not operating.

Declaration of registered charitable status

94.11 Registered charities with a gross income of over £10,000 in the previous financial year must state that they are registered charities on certain specified documents such as fund-raising literature, bills of exchange, cheques, receipts and invoices. [*Charities Act 1993 s 5*]. The Charity Commission has indicated that the following statements would satisfy the requirement.

- 'A Registered Charity'
- 'Registered Charity No'(followed by the charity's registration number)

94.12 Registration with the Charity Commission

- 'Registered as a Charity'
- 'Registered with the Charity Commissioners'

Penalties for non-compliance

94.12 Although the *Charities Act 1993* requires organisations that are charitable to register unless they are exempt or excepted from registration, it is not an offence not to register. However, an organisation that does not register is unlikely to get the tax benefits to which it is entitled. If the Charity Commission becomes aware of the organisation's existence and orders it to register, the trustees could be found in contempt of court if they continue to fail to register the organisation.

94.13 Failing to comply with the provisions of *s 5* of the *Charities Act 1993* which requires the organisation's charitable status to be declared on certain documents is a serious matter as it is a criminal offence punishable by a fine. Liability rests with the individual who issues, authorises or signs the document, regardless of whether they are a trustee or a member of staff.

95 Religious Charities

95.1 The advancement of religion is a charitable purpose. It has a wide meaning, extending to missionary work and the distribution of religious literature, in addition to the regular work of the church which includes the provision and upkeep of places of worship and burial grounds, conducting religious services, providing spirital guidance, paying and housing ministers and others employed by the church, religious orders and the caring for ministers and former ministers and their families.

95.2 The meaning of religion has been much discussed. It is presently accepted that in order to qualify for charitable status the religion in question must involve faith in a god or gods and worship of the god or gods. The charity must promote or advance that religion and benefit the public, not just the followers of the religion. The public benefit test means that religious cults can be registered if the public benefit is proved, whereas an enclosed order of nuns who spend their time in contemplation and prayer cannot be registered. This interpretation is not intended to cast doubt on the intercessory value of prayer, it simply means that charitable status requires the advancement and promotion of religion, not the practice of that religion. Similarly exorcism has been held to be charitable, whilst freemasonry was not.

95.3 Many religious charities are excepted from registration with the Charity Commission, including those associated with the Church of England and many non-conformist churches.

Places of worship

95.4 Individual local churches may be:

- excepted under regulation;
- designated religious bodies (Scotland);
- too small to register; or
- registered charities.

95.5 There is often a misconception amongst church groups, especially those which are not aligned to any particular denomination, that they do not have to register as charities. This is not so. If they qualify as charitable, then most are required to be registered under the *Charities Act 1993* as does any other charity. Exception under the *Places of Worship Registration Act 1855* does not relate to the activities of a group of people meeting together. The specific church organisations that are excepted from registration are set out in *Charities (Exemption from Registration) Regulations (SI 1996 No 180)*. (See Chapter 44.)

Roman Catholic Church

95.6 The Roman Catholic Church has a similar structure to the Anglican Church but there are several important differences. Both Anglican and Roman Catholic dioceses are registered charities, but Catholic parishes (unlike Anglican parishes) are not autonomous — their accounts are consolidated into the diocesan accounts. Canon law determines much of the Roman Catholic Church's activity but within the UK this does not have the same force of law as the Church of England's legal framework.

95.7 Religious Charities

Church of England

95.7 The Church of England has an extremely formalised structure within the State, with much of its powers and duties deriving from legislation. Its parish structure covers the whole of England, and many of its office bearers have powers which extend beyond the confines of the church context. At the top of the structure are the provinces of Canterbury and York, together comprising 43 dioceses, each of which is overseen by a bishop, about half of whom sit in the House of Lords. Anglican Dioceses are divided into archdeaconries, which are subdivided into rural deaneries. These are augmented by diocesan courts, provincial courts, and the court of ecclesiastical causes reserved. Between them these courts will deal with matters such as faculties and proceedings against priests including matters concerning doctrine, ritual or ceremony. A faculty is the legal granting of permission for altering a consecrated building or its contents, or other areas which may be determined by the bishop.

95.8 Synods, comprising elected lay and clerical members exist at different levels: deanery, diocesan and General. The General Synod has legislative powers.

95.9 The parish is led by the incumbent, who is priest in charge, vicar or rector. The terms vicar and rector are now almost synonymous, the original distinction dating back to the dissolution of the monasteries. Once instituted only the incumbent (apart from the bishop) has the duty and right to minister within the parish, and to receive a stipend. Since 1993 women may be ordained to the priesthood, although individual parishes still have the right to pass a resolution to the effect that they will not accept a female incumbent.

95.10 Churchwardens are responsible for the fabric of the church and have powers, along with the incumbent, which include the right to prevent people from entering the church. They may also remove people who cause a disturbance. The incumbent and wardens may be assisted by other lay officers, such as the verger (responsible for the internal fabric), readers (who assist with pastoral work), a sexton (usually responsible for the churchyard, grave digging and bell ringing) and side-persons.

95.11 The Parochial Church Council (PCC) (not the same as a parish council) is elected from the electoral roll of the parish at the annual general meeting, and functions like a board of trustees administering the church's affairs in, and sometimes beyond, the parish. Its chairman is the incumbent, but the treasurer will normally be a member, or co-opted member, of the PCC, which is a body corporate with perpetual succession. Its powers are derived from various pieces of legislation, principally the *Parochial Church Councils (Powers) Measure 1956* and the *Church Representation Rules* although much of its work is delegated to the standing committee, comprising the incumbent and wardens.

95.12 The annual meeting of the church must be held each year by 30 April. Amongst its business will be the receiving of the accounts and annual report, prepared and audited or examined under the *Charities Act 1993* and the *Church of England Accounting Regulations* requirements. Although these accounts and report do not need to be filed with the Charity Commission — the PCC is an excepted charity — they do need to be sent to the local Diocesan Board of Finance within 28 days of the AGM. Other business will include reports from various committees responsible for fabric and the electoral roll, and from the deanery synod. There is a publication produced by the Central Board of Finance of the Church of England on PCC accounting, 'The Charities Act 1993 and the PCC'.

Charities Act 1993 and ecclesiastical property

95.13 *Section 96(2)* of the *Charities Act 1993* states that the expression 'charity' is not applicable, in the Act, 'to any ecclesiastical corporation (that is to say, any corporation in the Church of England, whether sole or aggregate, which is established for spiritual purposes) in respect of the corporate property of the corporation, except to a corporation aggregate having some purposes which are not ecclesiastical in respect of its corporate property held for those purposes; or to any Diocesan Board of Finance within the meaning of the *Endowments and Glebe Measure 1976* for any diocese in respect of the diocesan glebe land of that diocese within the meaning of that Measure; or to any trust of property for purposes for which the property has been consecrated'.

Churches in Scotland

95.14 Certain religious charities in Scotland are treated similarly to excepted charities in England and Wales. A list of Scottish charities exempted from certain provisions of *LRMPSA 1990* is given in Chapter 101.

96 Reporting Accountants

96.1 Charitable companies in England, Wales and Scotland, but not Northern Ireland, are exempt from the requirement for audit if they fulfil the conditions set out in *s 249A* of the *Companies Act 1985*. The conditions for exemption are:

- the charity qualifies as a 'small company' for the purposes of *s 246* of the Act;
- it has gross income below £250,000; and
- its total assets do not exceed £1.4 million.

These conditions are different from those applying to non-charitable companies.

96.2 Charitable companies with gross income of between £90,000 and £250,000 are exempt from audit only if a report prepared by a reporting accountant is presented with the accounts.

96.3 'Gross income' is defined in *s 249A(7)* of the *Companies Act 1985* as 'the company's income from all sources, as shown in the company's income and expenditure account'. The income and expenditure account, if not prepared as a separate primary statement within the accounts, is the section of the statement of financial activities which precedes the total net incoming/(outgoing) resources for the year. This will equate to total incoming resources, with any non-charitable trading income shown net of expenditure restored to a gross figure, excluding movements on endowment funds which are not income for the purposes of company law.

96.4 Exemption from audit cannot be claimed where either:

- 10% of the members of the company deposit notice in writing no later than one month before the end of the financial year that they require an audit for that year;
- the company falls into one of the cases set out in *s 249B(1)* of the *Companies Act 1985*, which includes parent companies, except where the subsidiary company is dormant throughout the period; or
- the company's articles of association contain a requirement for audit.

96.5 The advantages of exemption from audit may be outweighed by other considerations. The trustees/directors of the charitable company may decide that the external assurance provided by an audit is desirable. It may also be a condition of funders, existing or potential, that audited accounts be supplied. Organisations qualifying for exemption are free to choose to have their accounts audited.

96.6 A reporting accountant must be suitably qualified, i.e. a member of one of the accountancy bodies specified in *s 249D(3)* of the Act or subject to the rules of such a body. A reporting accountant may be an individual, partnership or body corporate. A reporting accountant must also satisfy the same independence criteria as required for appointment as an auditor under *s 27* of the *Companies Act 1989*.

96.7 The role of a reporting accountant is limited compared to that of an auditor. The opinion expressed by a reporting accountant is limited to three areas.

- The accounts have been properly prepared from the accounting records that the charitable company is required to keep by *s 221* of the *Companies Act 1985*.
- The accounts have been prepared in accordance with the requirements of the Act.

- The charitable company satisfied the requirements for exemption from audit set out in the Act.

96.8 The latter two opinions are further limited in scope by the fact that they are given 'having regard only to, and on the basis of, the information contained in those accounting records'.

96.9 The function of a reporting accountant is confined therefore to giving limited assurance that the accounts have been 'properly prepared' and does not include consideration of the 'true and fair' view which company accounts are required to present. The procedures required to support a reporting accountant's report are limited to agreeing the correct extraction of the accounts from records maintained by the charitable company, a review of those accounts for compliance with the *Companies Act 1985*, and to ensuring that income is within the limit prescribed.

97 Research

Research not charitable per se

97.1 Carrying out research is not, of itself, a charitable objective. However, charities are permitted to carry out research, or to commission others to carry out research on their behalf, provided that research is included in the charity's objects, falls within its powers, and is for the public benefit. The research must be balanced and objective and the results must be made publicly available. Charities are under no obligation to publish their research, they are merely required to make the public broadly aware of the results and the conclusions that can be drawn from the results and make the results available to any interested party who wishes to scrutinies the results. Charities can charge a reasonable fee for access to the results of their research. Such trading would be regarded as primary purpose.

Intellectual property

97.2 In general charities should make the results of their research available reasonably promptly. However, the Charity Commission will sanction a delay if the results could be exploited commercially. In draft guidance on charity research issued in 1995 the Charity Commission advised charities to protect the valuable intellectual property arising from research under patent, or in other ways. The Commission stated that intellectual property should be used for the purposes of the charity or could be exploited commercially to raise funds for the charity.

97.3 In some instances it will be necessary for a charity's trading subsidiary rather than the charity to conduct research, for example if a third party sponsoring the research wishes to delay or restrict making the results publicly available for commercial reasons, or if a public body wishes to keep secret the results of research it wishes to commission a charity to conduct on its behalf. If this is the case the charity must not pass any intellectual property rights to its trading company free of charge. It must charge a fee or arrange for an annual royalty payment to be made. And, as with any other such arrangement, the trading company must pay the charity a fee which covers the cost to the charity of the use of any of the charity's assets.

Commissioning research

97.4 Charities commissioning others to undertake research on their behalf must either directly supervise and monitor the research themselves, or arrange for this to be done on their behalf, in order to ensure that the charity's funds are being properly applied. They should have a written contract that includes details of:

- how the research will be supervised;
- who will evaluate the results;
- who will own the results, and what share of the proceeds the charity will get if they are exploited commercially; and
- how the results will be published.

97.5 The trustees must be satisfied that the public benefit of the research will outweigh any potential benefit to the researchers.

VAT

97.6 Research that consists of original investigation is exempt from VAT if it is conducted by an eligible body (usually an educational charity) and supplied to an eligible body. Research that is routine analysis rather than original investigation is not VAT exempt.

Charity Commission Guidance

97.7 At the time of writing, the Commission is due to release updated guidance for trustees and staff of any charity that carries out or funds others to carry out research. It will apply both to charities whose main (or only) purpose is research, and to those that have research as a minor purpose.

98 Reserves

98.1 When individuals give money to charities they want it to be spent on charitable activities, not hoarded in a bank or used to purchase equities. Charity law requires that a charity's income is applied within a reasonable time of being received, unless the charity has specific, express powers in its governing document allowing it to hold income in reserve rather than spending it promptly. Failure to consider the matter and allow income to accumulate without good reason amounts to a breach of trust.

98.2 Charities, just like other businesses, need to hold reserves in order to protect their cash flow position, meet their liabilities and honour their commitments to users and beneficiaries. Trustees will at times face a conflict between their duty to act prudently, safeguarding the welfare of future beneficiaries, and their duty to apply income quickly. Some charities have been the subject of media criticism because of their high reserves, particularly those with reserves equivalent to between 5, 10 or even 20 years of their current annual expenditure. This type of publicity can bring a charity, or even charities in general, into disrepute, particularly if the charity is continuing to fund-raise.

98.3 Having too much or too little in reserve can deter funders. Grant making trusts and other funders scrutinise the amount a charity is holding in reserve and will be unwilling to fund projects if the charity clearly has sufficient reserves to fund the project itself, or where the charity has too little in reserve to ensure its medium to long-term survival. Holding too little in reserve can be costly, particularly when a blip in fund-raising means having to cut back on staff, with the associated redundancy costs, only to have the expense of recruiting new staff a few months later when funding has picked up.

98.4 The Charity Commission issued new guidance on reserves in 1999 (CC19 *Charities' Reserves*). The guidance is not prescriptive. Recognising the lack of homogeneity in the sector, it does not attempt to define what level of reserves a charity should have. Rather, it states that a charity should have a reserves policy and must be able to justify why it is holding a particular amount in reserve at a particular point in time. The level of reserves should be justified with reference to the charity's current position and future prospects. Where a charity holds income in reserve, the Commission in its role as regulator, will be seeking evidence that the trustees have given proper consideration to the level of reserve, can justify the position, and have included an explanation of their reserves policy in their annual report.

Guidance complements SORP

98.5 Paragraph 28 of the Statement of Recommended Practice: Accounting by Charities (SORP) already requires charities to include in their annual report 'a review of the transactions and financial position of the charity' which 'puts the accounts into an accurate perspective' enabling the reader to appreciate 'the purposes for which the charity's assets are being held' and 'the charity's financial position ... in the context of its future plans and commitments'. The latest Charity Commission guidance supplements this by requiring trustees to explain clearly in their annual reports:

- whether or not they hold reserves;
- the reasons why they do, or do not, hold reserves;

- if they hold reserves, the future needs, opportunities, contingencies and risks the reserves are intended to provide for or be a buffer against;
- the level of reserves at the end of the financial year to which the report relates.

98.6 The definitions of terms used in the Commission's guidance are the same as those used in the SORP. 'Reserves' are defined as 'the resources the charity has or can make available to spend, for any or all of the charity's purposes, once it has met its commitments and covered its other planned expenditure'. Reserves are therefore 'free' income which can be spent, at the trustees' discretion, to further any of the charity's objects, i.e. the work the charity is established to do as defined in its governing document. The definition of reserves therefore excludes:

- permanent endowment — capital, such as a building or sum of money, that has been given to the charity, on condition that it must be retained by the charity to be used or invested indefinitely and the income used to further the charity's objects;
- expendable endowment — capital that has been given to the charity, on terms that allow the trustees to convert part, or all of it, to income to be spent on charitable purposes if they wish;
- restricted funds — capital or income funds given to be used only for a specified charitable purpose;
- designated funds — unrestricted funds earmarked by the trustees for a particular purpose, such as future requirements of beneficiaries, or to fund repairs, but which the trustees are under no legal obligation to apply in the way they have designated, and which the trustees remain free to change the designation of should they so wish; and
- income funds — funds which could only be realised by disposing of fixed assets held for charity use.

98.7 Although designated funds are excluded from its definition of reserves, the latest guidance makes it clear that the Commission will frown upon trustees who set up designated funds principally in order to show a reduced level of free reserves.

Reserves policy

98.8 There is no legal rule about the proportion of its income that a charity may hold as a reserve. The Commission's latest guidance merely states that the level must be the result of a well-considered reserves policy, based upon the charity's current position and its future commitments and prospects.

98.9 Trustees holding income in reserve must have power to invest. Some will have an express power in their governing document allowing them to hold income in reserve, but others will have to rely on an implied power by which they can hold income in reserve if it is their considered view that this is necessary in the best interests of the charity. Trustees holding reserves without justification could be acting in breach of trust. A reserves policy should include:

- the reasons for holding reserves;
- the level, or range, of reserves that the trustees aim to hold, based on an assessment of their reserve needs;
- the trustees' strategy for maintaining, achieving or reducing reserves to that level or range; and

- details of how and when the reserves policy will be monitored and reviewed.

98.10 To determine the level of reserves needed trustees must take account of:

- forecasts of future income, including the risks to each income stream and possible new sources of income;
- forecasts of expenditure on planned activities;
- an analysis of future needs, possible opportunities and contingencies or risks where the cost could not be met out of income; and
- an assessment of the risk of not being able to fund future needs and the consequences of this for the charity.

98.11 In its guidance on reserves the Commission stresses that the amount of time spent preparing the reserves policy, and the detail in which it is set out, should be in proportion to the scale and complexity of the charity's affairs.

Re-invested income

98.12 The Commission's guidance recognises that many charities have not been spending income earned from their expendable or permanent endowment, but have been adding it to the principal. Reinvesting income generated from capital does not convert the income to capital. The Commission expects trustees to give, or at least estimate, the proportions of these retained funds that represent income and capital respectively. While the Commission does not expect the trustees to spend the income portion immediately, it does expect them to either make plans to spend it gradually or justify why they intend to retain the funds.

Donations and legacies to count as income

98.13 Many charities used to treat all large donations and legacies as expendable endowment, as they are difficult to predict. However, the latest guidance clarifies that, in the absence of specific instructions given by the donor or testator, large donations and legacies should normally be treated as income.

Tax

98.14 If income from investments is re-invested it could be liable for tax. The exemptions from tax on a charity's income contained in *s 505* of the *Income and Corporation Taxes Act 1988* relate only to income spent on charitable purposes. Investment does not qualify as a charitable purpose. However, in practice, the Inland Revenue normally exempts from tax investment income which is accumulated provided that the charity can show that the income is being accumulated for some specific future purpose, rather than merely to avoid tax.

Misrepresentation

98.15 The Commission's guidance reminds charities that when appealing for money they should not give the wrong impression about the extent or urgency of their need for funds.

Future action

98.16 Charities finding that their reserves are too high will have to reduce them gradually, either by expanding their existing work programme or by introducing new types of work. If necessary, they will have to apply to the Commission for permission to broaden their charitable objects.

98.17 If the Charity Commission comes across a charity that does not appear to have applied the principles set out in its latest guidance on reserves it will explore the reasons with the trustees and encourage compliance. As a last resort the Commission will use its statutory powers in cases where mismanagement or misconduct persist, where charity resources are at risk, or where the law continues to be breached.

99 Resolving Charity Disputes

Background

99.1 Traditionally, if disputes could not be settled by negotiation, they were dealt with through the litigation process. Litigation is time consuming, distracting and can be extremely costly. Moves towards the adoption of less adversarial and simpler means of resolving disputes were made in the early 1990s firstly by the Commercial Court and later by the Queen's Bench and Family Divisions. In the mid 1990s the Court of Appeal started to encourage what has become known as Alternative Dispute Resolution (ADR).

99.2 The Woolf Report into the Civil Justice System which was published in 1996 sought not only to simplify court procedures but also to encourage the settlement of disputes outside the Courts. The new Civil Procedure Rules which followed came into force on 26 April 1999. They introduced active case management, limitations on the requirement for disclosure of evidence and measures to support the efficient management of proceedings where litigation cannot be avoided. However, at the same time, it was made clear that the Courts would encourage parties to avoid litigation altogether by means of ADR.

99.3 ADR encompasses arbitration, expert determination, adjudication and mediation. There is also a process termed Early Neutral Valuation where, with the consent of the parties, a judge will assist in the resolution of the matters in dispute by providing a non-binding assessment of the strengths of the litigation. The most widely used procedures are Arbitration and Mediation.

Arbitration

99.4 It has long been the practice to incorporate arbitration clauses into legal contracts and these were in existence long before the wider development of ADR. Contracts will generally specify that, in case of dispute, the matter should be referred to a professional body who will nominate an arbitrator. Arbitration is governed by the *Arbitration Act 1996*.

99.5 The parties will make their cases to the arbitrator in a similar manner to a court hearing. On the basis of the evidence, the arbitrator will make an award which is binding on the parties. There is a process of appeal to the Courts but only in the case of 'serious irregularity'. Whilst a settlement under arbitration may be achieved more quickly, it can nevertheless be time consuming and costly where complex claims and counter claims need to be argued in front of the arbitrator. Charities are unlikely to favour arbitration as an alternative method of resolving disputes due to its cost.

Mediation

99.6 Mediation has been practised in the United Kingdom since the early 1990s, but its use has received a significant boost from the new Civil Procedure Rules. At case management conferences and pre-trial reviews the parties are required to state (a) whether they have discussed the question of ADR, (b) if not, why not and (c) if so, the result.

If ADR has not been discussed, the judge is likely to suggest that the parties should consider it.

99.7 An essential element of the process is its voluntary nature. Thus, disputes will only proceed to mediation where all the parties agree and, as a result, there will generally be a strong motivation to achieve a settlement. By contrast, Courts in the USA can mandate the parties to use mediation.

99.8 A mediator is an independent person whose function is to facilitate an agreement between the parties. The mediator does not pass judgement on the merits of the respective cases and, except on the rare occasions when he or she is asked to do so, will not give advice to the parties or suggest solutions.

99.9 There are a number of organisations which both train and accredit mediators and also provide mediation services. The parties, having agreed to mediate, will typically ask one of those organisations to put forward a name or names from those who are on their panel so that the parties can agree between them who the mediator should be. In larger cases there are sometimes two experienced mediators acting jointly as co-mediators and, in most cases, the mediator will have the assistance of a pupil who is training or gaining experience. The parties may be accompanied by legal advisers or experts and it is important that they have authority to agree a settlement.

99.10 Mediation is becoming widely used for commercial disputes, negligence and liability matters, matrimonial settlements, social and community disputes, employment problems and many other situations of conflict both national and international. Mediations are also used effectively to deal with internal disputes.

99.11 The London County Court is referring matters to mediation and the Independent Housing Ombudsman is also using mediation services. The National Council for Voluntary Organisations offers mediation services through a joint venture with the Centre for Dispute Resolution (CEDR). Experience shows that there is a high success rate from mediation proceedings.

99.12 If mediation is used to settle litigation in which case the proceedings will be stayed while the mediation takes place. The timing of the mediation can affect the likelihood of success and not all cases are suitable for mediation. Firstly, the parties must want a settlement, second they must have failed to negotiate a settlement informally and third, they need to have enough information to assess the strengths and weaknesses of their own and the other parties' cases. It is common, therefore, for mediation to take place when the litigation is at an advanced stage. There is, however, a trend towards earlier mediation to further minimise costs and the technique of 'preventative mediation' has been developed to guard against conflict in highly complex contract arrangements. In this case, a mediator may be briefed at the implementation of the contract in order to deal with problems before they escalate.

99.13 The format for a mediation is necessarily flexible and the mediator will tailor it depending upon the circumstances. The mediation will normally involve a series of joint meetings between the parties under the mediator's chairmanship and also separate private meetings with the parties individually. The process is designed to generate a better mutual understanding of the position of each of the parties and also to test the reality of their positions. The private sessions enable the parties to reveal matters to the mediator without the mediator necessarily passing that information on to the other party. Private sessions are confidential.

99.14 The mediator, or the organisation which has provided the mediator, will arrange a convenient venue, date and time ensuring that rooms are available for each of the parties and for the mediator. Each party will be asked to submit a case summary to brief the mediator on the issues. These case summaries will normally be provided also to the other parties.

99.15 Through the series of meetings, the mediator will attempt to bring each of the parties to the point where they gain a realistic appreciation of a basis for agreement. They may reveal to the mediator what their 'bottom line' would be in any settlement. In this way a mediator can assist the process of settlement by being an instrument of negotiation between the parties to the point where they can discuss together the basis of settlement.

99.16 Once agreement is reached the settlement will be committed to writing and considered binding upon the parties. The settlement is confidential unless the parties agree otherwise. Should they fail to reach agreement, then litigation may proceed. In these circumstances, nothing which has been revealed in mediation may be used in evidence, neither may the mediator be called as a witness.

99.17 Where settlement is not achieved at the time of the mediation, there can still be significant benefits. The issues in dispute may have been narrowed which may result in simplified litigation. Alternatively, the parties may decide to reinstate negotiations. In any event, the mediator will normally keep in touch with the parties and continue encouraging them to settle or reactivate the mediation.

99.18 A successful mediation will have facilitated communication between parties who are often estranged and enabled the resumption of negotiations in a calm atmosphere. (It is often important to the parties that they should have a continuing relationship.) It will often also have focussed on the causes of the conflict in a way which was not possible at arm's length or in court. As the process is non-binding until an agreement is reached and without prejudice, the parties are able to explore any possible avenue for compromise which would not be the case in court.

99.19 Mediations may be limited in smaller cases to a few hours but even large cases would not be expected to take more than a few days. The costs are therefore considerably less than those of a court hearing which additionally involves preparation time, an uncertain outcome and the risk of an adverse costs award.

99.20 As it is particularly important to charitable organisations that their funds should be maximised and their costs minimised, should they be involved in a dispute, mediation can be an effective and certainly less costly means of settlement than litigation. Above all, mediation offers a certainty of outcome should it be successful. Its confidential nature means that conflicts, particularly internal ones, can be resolved without funders and beneficiaries necessarily being aware of them and the loss of confidence that might ensue.

Charity Commission's powers to resolve disputes

99.21 The Charity Commission has a limited number of powers of intervention that it can use if someone is in dispute with the trustees of a charity. The Commission will use them if it regards its intervention as being an effective use of public resources and if it will protect the charity's assets from risk of loss.

99.22 The Commission will consider cases where:

- the way in which the charity is being run is putting significant assets or funds at risk;

- the charity's income is not being used for its charitable purposes;
- the trustees are not acting in accordance with the charity's governing document, or charity law or trust law;
- there is a real danger of the charity's name being brought into disrepute;
- the administration of the charity has broken down.

99.23 The Charity Commission will not become involved where the dispute is about how the trustees are managing the charity on a day-to-day basis as the trustees have broad discretion to manage the charity as they see fit. Therefore it will not become involved in cases where the dispute is:

- about a matter of policy or administration and the trustees are acting correctly;
- between trustees themselves, or between trustees and members;
- a contractual dispute or other dispute about property rights between the charity and a third party;
- about criminal matters unconnected with the running of the charity or furtherance of its objects;
- between charities or people or organisations that have entered into contracts with the charity;
- about matters that the Charity Commission has already considered or investigated unless circumstances have materially changed or significant new evidence has come to light.

99.24 The Charity Commission will ask the complainant to supply details of the dispute and details of efforts the complainant has already taken to resolve the dispute. If the Commission then decides the matter is something that they can deal with and their intervention would be in the public interest they will notify the complainant and invite the trustees and anyone else involved in the dispute to respond to the allegations.

99.25 Once the Commission has all the necessary information and is satisfied that the allegation is well-founded it will consider how to act. In less serious instances it will deal with it by providing information and advice to the trustees. If the issue is more serious the Commission will use its powers to intervene and put things right or prevent a reoccurrence. If necessary, it will use its powers to suspend or remove trustees or employees, appoint new trustees, freeze bank accounts, or if the matters are criminal refer them to the police or other appropriate authorities.

100 Schemes

100.1 Making a Scheme is the legal process used by the Charity Commission, under *s 16* of the *Charities Act 1993*, or the courts to amend, clarify or amplify a charity's governing document, when the trustees do not have a power to make the change themselves.

100.2 The *Charities Act 1993 s 16* gives the Charity Commission concurrent jurisdiction with that of the High Court to make Schemes for the administration of a charity. In practice most Schemes are made by the Charity Commission. However, *s 16(3)* excludes the Charity Commission from making Schemes that determine questions of title to property or the existence of a trust and *s 16(10)* forbids the Commission to act in circumstances where the matters would be better left to the court to decide, such as complex questions of law.

100.3 In most circumstances Schemes are made on the initiative of the charity, but the Charity Commission can instigate the making of a Scheme if there are reasons to believe that the charity trustees should have applied for one, but have failed to do so, either through neglect or because they cannot agree among themselves.

Using Schemes

100.4 Schemes are used for a wide variety of purposes including the following:

- To clarify the objects if they are imprecise or ambiguous e.g. if it is unclear whether the main purpose of a charity is to help children with a particular condition, or to support the parents of children with that condition, or to carry out research into the cause and treatment of the condition.
- To bring the objects up to date. A charity may have been established to provide a service which is no longer regarded as the most effective way of meeting the needs of the beneficiaries, such as the provision of orphanages, or for a class of people that no longer exists, such as slaves.
- To amend the objects if the cause or need for which the charity was established is now met in some other way or by some other body. Charities frequently pioneer new services or approaches to dealing with problems that are then adopted by statutory providers.
- To amend the objects if the service provided is no longer effective, for example if the grants made are too small to be of any significance.
- To amend the objects if the geographical limits specified in the charity's governing document need expanding, for example if a successful local service could be expanded into a national operation.
- To amend the trustees' powers in order to allow the charity to become more effective. For example, giving the trustees wider powers than those contained in the *Trustee Investment Act 1961* could increase investment income; including a power to use the charity's funds to provide trustee indemnity insurance might make trustee recruitment easier; removing a requirement to have the accounts audited could reduce costs for a charity with income below the statutory audit threshold; or including a power of amendment would allow charities to make further administrative changes without having to apply again for a Scheme.

- To appoint trustees where all the trustees have died or are refusing to act.
- To administer the charity if there has been incompetent or dishonest management.
- To apply the proceeds of a charitable appeal that has failed to reach its target, where the trustees have failed to specify in their governing document that funds raised could be used for another charitable purpose in this event and where the donors are either unidentifiable or where it would be impractical to attempt to trace the donors.

Changes to the objects clause

100.5 Although charities that are companies limited by guarantee or industrial and provident societies will have powers to amend their governing document under the *Companies Act 1989* or the *Industrial and Provident Societies Act 1965*, *s 64* of the *Charities Act 1993* requires any alterations to the objects clause of a charity to have the prior written consent of the Charity Commission in order to become effective.

Cy-près Schemes

100.6 *Section 13* of the *Charities Act 1993* permits changes to be made to the objects clauses of a charity only in limited circumstances i.e. when the original purpose has been fulfilled or when it would no longer be in keeping with the spirit of the original gift to continue limiting the charity's activities to the original purpose. Changes to the objects clauses must define a new purpose that is *cy-près* i.e. as close as possible to the original purpose. Schemes amending a charity's objects are therefore known as *cy-près* Schemes.

100.7 When considering an application for a *cy-près* Scheme for a charity originally formed by a single donor, the Charity Commission can take into account:

- the donor's religious beliefs;
- the donor's particular interests;
- what the donor believed to be worthy causes;
- the donor's interests in a particular locality; and
- any wishes the donor expressed outside their attested will.

100.8 A *cy-près* Scheme can also be used to amalgamate a charity that no longer wishes to remain in existence with another charity with similar objects.

Applying for a Scheme

100.9 The Charity Commission provides an application form for a Scheme. In most instances the form should be signed by all the trustees, or a person appointed by a quorate meeting of the trustees to sign on their behalf. This person does not need to be one of the trustees. Even if the charity cannot achieve a quorum, the Charity Commission may be willing to accept an application if they consider it to be appropriate. However, if a charity has an income of less than £500 a year, a Scheme can be applied for by one or more of the trustees, or by any person with an interest in the charity, such as a potential beneficiary, or, if the charity serves a local area, by two or more people resident in that area.

100.10 Schemes

100.10 The Charity Commission is ultimately responsible for making a Scheme and deciding the final wording. When it receives an application the Commission will usually discuss the broad outlines with the trustees. Once agreement has been achieved on these, the Commission will invite the trustees to submit a formal application. The Commission will then send a detailed draft Scheme to the trustees for their comments and final agreement.

Publicity

100.11 If the Charity Commission intends to make a Scheme *s 16(9)* of the *Charities Act 1993* requires them to notify the trustees of their intention, while *s 20(1)* requires them to give public notice at least a month before the Scheme is to be established. Once the Scheme has been established, *s 20(6)* requires a copy of the Scheme to be available for public inspection for not less than one month at the Charity Commission and within the local area in the case of local charities, in order to give the general public the opportunity to make representations to the Charity Commission about it. If the Commission wants to make further amendments as a result of representations received from the public, it will again allow the trustee an opportunity to comment upon them.

Sealing

100.12 The Scheme is sealed once the publication period has elapsed and the trustees have given the Charity Commission:

- an approved copy of the draft Scheme;
- a declaration confirming that the required notices have been published; and
- copies of pages of the newspapers or other publications showing the notices if this was required.

100.13 The sealed Scheme is a legal document and should be kept securely, preferably in a fireproof safe. Copies should be given to all current trustees and in the future to any new trustee together with a copy of the governing document.

Appeals

100.14 A Scheme comes into force on the date that instructions are given for the Commissioners' seal to be affixed to it. Notice has then to be given to the public that the Scheme has been made and the public then have three months in which they can appeal to the High Court against the Scheme.

Exceptions

100.15 Charities with a gross income of less than £5,000 in the last financial year, that do not hold any land and that are not charitable companies do not require a Scheme, but can use the procedures set out in *s 74* of the *Charities Act 1993* if they want to transfer their assets to another charity or charities, change the charity's objects or modify the trustees' powers.

100.16 If a charity has permanent endowment that does not comprise any land, and a gross income of less than £1,000 in the last financial year, and is not a charitable company, then it does not require a Scheme if it wishes to spend the permanent endowment as income, but can use the procedures set out in *s 75* of the *Charities Act 1993*. When all the endowment is spent the charity will cease to exist.

100.17 The Secretary of State for Education and Employment has statutory powers to implement Schemes for educational charities without reference to the Charity Commission. However, neither the Charity Commission nor the Secretary of State for Education have power to amend the objects clause of an educational charity within the first 40 years of its existence.

100.18 If a charitable school is unused or about to close the Secretary of State for Education has the power to make a Scheme in the form of a statutory instrument to allow any endowment to be used for a different purpose. The Charity Commission also has powers to make Schemes for ecclesiastical charities or ecclesiastical property held under trusts which do not qualify as charities according to the definitions used in the *Charities Act 1960*.

101 Scotland

The regulatory framework

101.1 The main legislation for the supervision and regulation of charities in Scotland is currently contained in *Part I* of the *Law Reform (Miscellaneous Provisions) (Scotland) Act 1990* (*LRMPSA*) and supporting regulations. However, in November 1999 the Scottish Parliament announced the establishment of an independent commission to review and reform charity law in Scotland. The commission is due to present its report early in 2001 and is likely to recommend wide ranging changes.

101.2 Scottish charities also have to comply with a wide range of legislation that applies to the whole of the UK, such as that relating to companies, employment, and equality rights issues. The Charity Commission for England and Wales has some powers under the *Charities Act 1993* to investigate charities operating in Scotland.

101.3 There is no Charity Commission for Scotland so any organisation wishing to represent itself as a charity must be recognised by the Inland Revenue as charitable for tax purposes. The Inland Revenue determines charitable status by referring to the English 'four heads' of charity (see Chapter 15). Recognition is given in a formal letter from the Inland Revenue and the charity is given a number starting with the letters 'SC'. This number appears on the Inland Revenue Index of Scottish Charities and should be used on all the charity's stationery.

101.4 Any body registered as a charity with the Charity Commission in England and Wales, or exempt from registering, is deemed to be a charity in Scotland.

Law Reform (Miscellaneous Provisions) (Scotland) Act

101.5 The main requirements of this are as follows:

- Only a body recognised by the Inland Revenue as a charity may represent itself as a charity.
- The Inland Revenue will maintain a public index of the names and addresses of bodies which are recognised as charitable.
- All charities must keep proper books of accounts and produce annual accounts. They must supply a copy of their accounts to the Lord Advocate within one month of receiving a request. Financial records must be kept for at least six years.
- All charities must provide a copy of their accounts, their accounting reference date, and their governing document to members of the public on request within one month. A reasonable fee can be charged to cover the cost of copying and postage.
- Where misconduct or mismanagement is alleged the Lord Advocate is empowered to investigate and where necessary seek remedies in the Court.

Supervision of charities

101.6 Supervision of Scottish charities is carried out on behalf of the Lord Advocate by the Scottish Charities Office, a division of the Crown Office. Supervisory powers include the power to carry out investigations into alleged misconduct or mismanagement and to bring actions before the Court of Session. The Lord Advocate can also investigate organisations which are not recognised bodies but which are holding themselves out as charities. During an investigation or inquiry the Scottish Charities Office may obtain a charity's records, and may suspend trustees for up to 28 days. Should the Lord Advocate identify actual mismanagement or misconduct, then a court order may be sought which may, either temporarily or permanently:

- suspend some or all of the trustees;
- freeze the organisation's funds;
- appoint a judicial factor (a court appointed administrator) to take care of the charity's affairs;
- prevent the organisation from holding itself out as a charity;
- if necessary, wind up the charity and approve the transfer of funds to another, similar, charity;
- seek expenses from existing trustees, personally.

Disqualification of trustees

101.7 A person who has been convicted of an offence involving dishonesty, or is an undischarged bankrupt, or has been removed under *s 7* of the *LRMPSA 1990* from being concerned in the management or control of any body, or who is subject to a disqualification order under the *Company Directors Disqualification Act 1986*, is disqualified from being concerned with the management or control of a Scottish charity. A person with a spent conviction under the *Rehabilitation of Offenders Act 1974* is not disqualified under *LRMPSA 1990*. Anyone acting when disqualified is guilty of a criminal offence, which carries a penalty of up to two years imprisonment. The Lord Advocate may grant a waiver from disqualifications.

Reorganisation of trusts

101.8 *Section 9* of *LRMPSA 1990* provides for a charity's governing document to be updated if its original purpose becomes out of date, or for the charity to merge with another, or for it to be wound up and its assets reallocated. Unincorporated charities with annual income of more than £5,000 do this by applying to the Court of Session.

101.9 Smaller trusts can reorganise through a simpler procedure. Those with an annual income of less than £5,000 do not need to apply to the Court but instead follow procedures laid down by regulation under *s 10* of *LRMPSA 1990*. A majority of the trustees have to agree that the purposes have to a large extent failed on similar grounds to that applying in *s 9*, and they may then determine that either a modification of the trust's purposes should be made, or the whole assets of the trust should be transferred to another public trust. This should be done 'to enable the resources of the trust to be applied to better effect consistently with the spirit of the trust deed'.

101.10 Trusts with annual income below £1,000, may spend their capital on the basis that this level is too low to permit the original trusts to be met out of income. Trustees must agree unanimously that this is the situation and must seek to apply *s 10* before relying on the power to spend capital granted in *s 11*. At least two months before spending the capital the trustees must advertise their intentions to do so in accordance with the relevant regulations, and must also notify the Lord Advocate.

101.11 Scotland

Dormant charities

101.11 Charitable funds lying in a dormant bank account (i.e. one in which there have been no transactions in the last ten years) can be accessed in a procedure contained within *LRMPSA 1990* if there are no persons remaining responsible for the charity. [*The Charities (Dormant Accounts)(Scotland) Regulations 1995 (SI 1995 No 2056)*].

Religious charities

101.12 *LRMPSA 1990* permits the Secretary of State for Scotland to identify some religious charities that are exempt from some of the Act's provisions, including the accounting provisions. These bodies must have as their principal purpose the promotion of a religious objective, their principal activity must be the regular holding of acts of public worship, they must have been established in Scotland for at least ten years with a membership of at least 3,000 people over fifteen years old, and must have their own internal authority which imposes a regime which is equivalent to the accounts and audit requirement of the *LRMPSA 1990*. The ten-year rule does not automatically apply in the case of mergers and demergers.

101.13 These exempt charities are listed in the *Charities (Designated Religious Bodies)(Scotland) Order 1993 (SI 1993 No 2774)*. They are the:

- Church of Scotland;
- Free Church of Scotland;
- Free Presbyterian Church of Scotland;
- Roman Catholic Archdiocese of St Andrews and Edinburgh;
- Roman Catholic Archdiocese of Glasgow;
- Roman Catholic Diocese of Argyll and the Isles;
- Roman Catholic Diocese of Dunkeld;
- Roman Catholic Diocese of Galloway;
- Roman Catholic Diocese of Paisley; and
- the Scottish Episcopal Church.

Accounts and audit

101.14 The presentation of accounts is regulated by the *Charities Accounts (Scotland) Regulations 1992 (SI 1992 No 2165)* and, where relevant, the *Companies Acts*. Annual accounts must be approved by the trustees, signed by at least one of them, and dated.

101.15 Where a charity fails to prepare accounts, or to provide copies of the accounts to the public, the Lord Advocate may apply to the Court for an order to prevent the charity, and any person engaged in its management and control, from carrying out further specified activities until the failure has been rectified. The Lord Advocate may also appoint a qualified person to prepare accounts at the expense of the persons involved in the management or control of the charity.

101.16 The accounts and audit requirements set out in *ss 4* and *5* of the *LRMPSA 1990* were never subject to the amendments generated by the deregulation task force in England and Wales. As a result the thresholds are considerably lower than those in operation in England and Wales. However, the governing document may stipulate a more stringent requirement.

101.17 Unincorporated charities with gross receipts of less than £25,000 per annum can elect to prepare receipts and payments accounts, supported by a statement of balances which reconciles opening and closing cash, shows changes in investments, lists estimated liabilities, and distinguishes the major funds in accordance with *Charities Accounts (Scotland) Regulations 1992*. Additional notes must disclose the purpose of the funds, i.e. restricted or unrestricted, details of grants to institutions where the total grants paid exceed 2% of gross receipts, trustees' benefits and any other useful information. The provisions of the SORP in respect of receipts and payments accounts should be followed.

101.18 Unincorporated charities with income over £25,000 and all charitable companies should follow the Scottish Regulations and prepare an Income and Expenditure Account and a balance sheet, together with a report on the activities of the charity.

101.19 The legislation, supported by the *Charities Accounts (Scotland) Regulations 1992 (SI 1992 No 2165)* requires all unincorporated charities with gross income or expenditure of over £100,000 in the current or preceding two years to have a full audit, or alternatively to have an independent examination if income is below £100,000 and the governing document does not require a full audit. The rights and duties of examiners under the Scottish regulations are very similar to those set out in the English regulations. The directions of the Charity Commission in respect of examinations cannot apply in Scotland, but the audit practice note 'The audit of charities' applies to auditors throughout the UK.

101.20 Under the *Charities (Exemption from Accounting Requirements)(Scotland) Regulations 1993 (SI 1993 No 1624)* there are further accounts and audit exemptions in respect of Scottish charitable statutory corporations, local authority trusts, and housing associations registered with Scottish Homes. None of the exemptions allows the charity to avoid making its accounts available to the public on request. As in England and Wales, Scottish incorporated charities require an audit if their income exceeds £250,000, otherwise a reporting accountant can certify the accounts of a charity with income between £90,000 and £250,000. No external review is required if the income is below £90,000 though it is recommended.

Audit of unincorporated charities

101.21 Because of the different regime for unincorporated charities in Scotland, some detailed audit procedures also differ from those applicable in England and Wales. Auditors or independent examiners have a right of access at all times to the records of the relevant charity and are entitled to require such information and explanations from the present or former trustees as they consider necessary.

101.22 There is no regulatory whistleblowing requirement in Scotland. Where an auditor or examiner resigns, then they must include in their notice of resignation a statement as to any circumstances connected with their resignation which they consider should be stated in the trustees' annual report. If the trustees fail to do this the auditor can then, as a member of the public, whistleblow.

101.23 Often the auditor will be the first to know that a charity cannot comply with a request to provide a copy of their accounts to a member of the public and therefore has a right to report such a matter.

101.24 Scotland

101.24 Under the *LRMPSA 1990* the Lord Advocate or his nominated officer may require any person, including the auditor or independent examiner, who he has reason to believe has relevant information to answer questions or otherwise furnish information with respect to any matter relevant to inquiries being made under *s 6*.

SORP

101.25 The charities SORP applies to all charities in the UK, regardless of size, complexity or constitution. Unincorporated Scottish charities should present the SOFA not as a primary statement but as a note, in a prominent form. A separate income and expenditure account is therefore always required, but the same treatment should be applied to items to be included in both statements. The income and expenditure should be analysed in enough detail so as to enable the reader to gain a proper appreciation of the charity, with supporting notes provided where appropriate. As covered in Chapter 107, movements in endowments cannot be dealt with in the income and expenditure account, but other funds may be presented using the columnar analysis of fund by type.

101.26 Grants payable should be disclosed as required by the Scottish regulations, and as set out above. In all other material respects the SORP and the regulations are sufficiently similar that compliance with the SORP will ensure compliance with the regulations, in respect of both the accounts and the annual report.

Fund-raising

101.27 The provisions of the *Charities Act 1992* in relation to fund-raising do not apply to charities in Scotland. Those provisions have, however, been accepted voluntarily in The Scottish Code of Fund-raising Practice developed by the Scottish Council for Voluntary Organisations and the Scottish arm of the Institute of Charity Fund-raising Managers.

101.28 House to house and street collections in Scotland require the permission of the local authority. [*Public Charitable Collections (Scotland) Regulations 1984 (SI 1984 No 565)*]. If the collection is to be carried out in 12 or more local authority areas throughout Scotland the charity can apply to the Secretary of State for an exemption from the need to seek permission from each individual authority.

Cross-border issues within the UK

101.29 Charities operating on both sides of the Anglo-Scottish border have to cope with the different legal systems in Scotland and England and Wales. To deal with this the relevant regulatory bodies have some power on the other side of their border. For instance *s 80* of the *Charities Act 1993* permits the Charity Commission to investigate charities operating mainly in or from Scotland and gives them power to remove and suspend trustees, staff, officers or agents if they find misconduct or mismanagement. Similarly *ss 6* and *7* of *LRMPSA 1990* give the Lord Advocate similar powers to investigate non-Scottish charities and charities managed wholly or mainly from outside Scotland.

Engaging with the Scottish Parliament

101.30 Scottish charities play a key role in Scottish society. The establishment of the Scottish Parliament in 1999 has led to many new opportunities for Scottish charities to voice their concerns and to take part in the development of policy. Parliamentary committees seek evidence from voluntary organisations on a regular basis and individual Scottish MPs seek briefings in preparation for debates.

The Compact

101.31 The Compact is an agreement between the Scottish Office and the voluntary sector on the principles of partnership that govern their relationship. As well as underpinning relationships between government and the voluntary sector it also extends to relationships with quangos and other public bodies, e.g. Scottish Enterprise.

101.32 In the Compact the Government commits to recognising and supporting the independence of the voluntary sector and to promoting understanding of the voluntary sector to all public sector agencies. Voluntary sector commitments include acknowledging the Government's public accountability for the resources it provides to voluntary organisations and recognising that Government, like all other agencies, acts within constraints. Both sides commit themselves to taking positive steps to involve groups who find it difficult to make their voices heard (e.g. minority ethnic groups and 'unpopular causes').

Further information

101.33 Further information can be obtained from the Scottish Council for Voluntary Organisations.

102 Secondment

102.1 One way in which charities can contain their costs is to persuade another organisation to lend it an employee for a period. This arrangement is commonly called 'seconding'. The first employer continues to pay the secondees' salary while the secondee is working for the charity. Most secondments are of staff working in the private sector. Until recently, the typical secondee was a manager approaching retirement age employed by a large company. For the company the cost was not significantly greater than giving the employee early retirement and was easily outweighed by the public relations benefits. Now companies are increasingly willing to second younger staff, seeing charities as a suitable training ground for up and coming young managers. After all, marketing a charity, developing its internal communications strategy, or upgrading its computer system are not fundamentally different from carrying out the same tasks for a commercial organisation.

102.2 Many companies will have a well thought out business case underpinning their corporate community involvement strategy, knowing that in order to thrive, business needs communities with income to spend and people who are not deterred from leaving their homes by the fear of crime. In almost every case a company willing to second an employee will be looking to gain something from the relationship. Charity trustees should take care to ensure that the arrangement is not weighted too heavily in favour of the company. There are tax and other legal considerations that companies and charities entering into secondment arrangements must take into account. Any company, sole trader or partnership seconding a member of their staff to a charity can deduct the relevant costs from their taxable profits. If the employer agrees to pay the secondee's expenses as well as their salary these are also deductible to the extent that they would have been allowed had the employee's services continued to be available to the employer. [*Income and Corporation Taxes Act 1988 s 86*].

102.3 Secondees, unlike volunteers, are employees. It is good practice for all parties to a seconding arrangement to have a written agreement clarifying which party is responsible for matters such as insurance, discipline, management control and legal liability. In some cases where disputes have arisen the courts have ruled that the secondee is employed by the original employer but in others, particularly those over where vicarious liability rests if a secondee has caused loss or injury, they have held the recipient organisation to be the employer, as they are generally the one with control over the actions of the secondee.

102.4 Business in the Community is an organisation that has done much to further partnerships between business and the voluntary sector including promoting the benefits of staff secondments, while Reach (Retired Executive Action Clearing House) acts as a brokerage placing retired business people with unpaid, part-time posts in charities. SCORE performs this function in Scotland.

Charity to charity

102.5 Charities too will sometimes second a member of their staff to another charity. This is permissible provided that the secondee is working on a project that is within the charitable objects of the first charity. When considering such an arrangement the trustees should be satisfied that seconding a member of their staff to another organisation is the most effective way of deploying their resources to meet their goals.

103 Self-assessment

103.1 Self-assessment of income tax for individuals and trusts was introduced in respect of the tax year 1996/97 and self-assessment of corporation tax was introduced for accounting periods ending after 30 June 1999. The previous rules for the assessment and collection of tax required taxpayers to supply information to the Inland Revenue so that it could issue an assessment, which was the legal charge to tax. The responsibility for arriving at the correct tax liability was split between the taxpayer and the Inland Revenue.

103.2 Self-assessment introduces a requirement to file tax returns by a fixed date and to pay all income tax and capital gains tax according to a fixed set of dates. There are penalties for late filing and late payment of tax, in addition to interest charges. While the new regime takes away the administrative burden of assessments from the Inland Revenue, it means that taxpayers are responsible for calculating the correct amount of tax due. Even where the Inland Revenue agree to carry out the necessary calculations for individuals and trusts, if the return is submitted by a certain date, this is little more than a numerical process. The Inland Revenue then carry out sample checks on tax returns, either where something appears to be incorrect or by random sample.

103.3 Most charities have no taxable income and therefore will not need to complete a self-assessment form. The new rules do not affect the tax repayment claims procedure. Charities should declare all income and gains on any repayment claim form.

103.4 Self-assessment for companies also has an impact on the trading subsidiaries of charities, as they are liable to pay corporation tax on their profits unless they donate them to the charity under Gift Aid.

103.5 The introduction of self-assessment has had an impact on charities as employers, as the PAYE administration rules have been changed to ensure that employees are given sufficient information to complete their own self-assessment tax returns. Employers are now required to supply all their employees with a P60 by 31 May and a copy of their P11D by 6 July.

104 Setting up a Charity

Is a new charity necessary?

104.1 The Charity commission is currently registering about 4,000 new charities each year. However, before deciding to start up a new charity there are a number of issues to be considered. Firstly, is there already a charity in the area doing similar work? If there is, it may well be more cost effective and efficient to work with them rather than set up another organisation. If the purpose of setting up the charity is to commemorate someone, it is possible to do this by setting up a restricted fund within an existing charity. Secondly, what are the prospects of raising funds? Charity fund-raising is a highly competitive marketplace and people may prefer to give to organisations with a proven track record. Thirdly, is it advantageous to have charitable status? Charitable status brings with it the opportunity to raise funds from certain sources, certain tax advantages, relief from business rates, access to advice from the Charity Commission and it gives reassurance to donors. On the other hand charitable status limits the objects of the organisation to being wholly and exclusively charitable, places limits on political and trading activities, and it usually prevents trustees from receiving benefits.

Purposes

104.2 If a decision is made to go ahead the next step is to consider:

- What will the purposes of the organisation be both in the short term and in the longer term, who will be the beneficiaries, what will be the geographical area of benefit, and what type of methods or activities will be used to achieve the purposes?

- Who will be the charity trustees, responsible for controlling the organisation, will there be members, and if so will the members be beneficiaries, or will there be supporters?

- Will there be a significant number of employees and will there be volunteers?

- How will the organisation be financed at the start and in the longer term, is there an endowment and if so what restrictions are there on how it can be used, how will funds be raised, will the organisation be entering into contracts, will land or buildings be acquired?

Legal structure

104.3 Once these issues have been decided the most suitable legal structure (i.e. trust, association, company, industrial and provident society, etc.) to use, bearing in mind how the charity is likely to develop over the next few years, will probably have become apparent. Before the governing document can be drawn up though a number of other issues will need to be decided.

104.4 If the charity is to have a national remit and will have local groups or branches some thought must be given at the outset as to whether to structure it as a single organisation or whether to adopt a federal structure with autonomous local branches.

Name

104.5 At this point there will still be a number of important issues to decide, including the charity's name. This must not be misleading, must not cause offence and must not be the same as an existing charity's name or so similar that it could give rise to confusion. The names of existing charities can be checked by viewing the Register on the Charity Commission's website or telephoning the Commission and asking for the Central Register. If a company wants to use the words 'charity', 'charitable', 'charities', 'charity's' or 'charities'' in its name it requires approval from the Secretary of State for Trade and Industry before a Certificate of Incorporation can be issued.

Trustees

104.6 The trustees must be over the age of 18 and not disqualified by law from acting as charity trustees (see Chapter 113). They must be willing and able to give the necessary time to take an active part in directing the charity. They should be selected for their relevant experience and skills, rather than their status or position in the community alone.

104.7 Decisions will need to be taken about how trustees will be appointed or elected. Will they be:

- appointed by the founder;
- appointed by the trustees;
- appointed by an outside body such as a local authority;
- elected by the membership;
- appointed by virtue of an office holder, such as the local vicar or mayor;
- appointed through trusteeship of another charity?

104.8 Will terms of office be fixed, and if so will there be a limit on the number of terms an individual can serve so the board will get a regular infusion of new blood? How often will the trustees meet and will the trustee board have sub-committees? What will be delegated to sub-committees and staff? What powers will trustees need, for example will they need wide powers of investment or a power to accumulate?

104.9 Once these issues have been decided the next steps will be to draw up a governing document, either with the help of a lawyer or using one of the available model governing documents, and apply to the Charity Commission for registration (see Chapter 94).

105 Shops

105.1 The first charity shop in the UK opened in Oxford in the 1940s and they are now a familiar sight on almost every high street, generating profits of over £70 million on a turnover of over £300 million. At first, most charity shops opened for short periods taking vacant premises rent free. Now the trend is for charities to take premises on a more permanent basis and budget for takings to cover the rent and other expenses. Costs are kept down by using volunteers to sort, price and sell donated goods, though many charity shop chains find it cost-effective to have at least one paid member of staff.

Fund-raising or trading?

105.2 Converting donated goods into cash is not regarded as trading, but merely as realising the value of the gift. Charity shops selling mainly donated goods can therefore be operated by charities and do not have to be run by trading subsidiaries. The gross proceeds can be accounted for as voluntary income and are exempt from corporation tax.

105.3 Charity shops that sell only bought-in goods are trading and therefore have to operate them through a trading subsidiary.

105.4 The sale of new goods that are made by a charity's beneficiaries, such as handicrafts made in a workshop for people with visual impairment, is regarded as primary purpose trading and therefore can be carried out by the charity.

105.5 Charity shops selling wholly or mainly donated goods, or goods produced by the beneficiaries, and operated by the charity also have the additional financial benefits of 80% mandatory relief on uniform business rates (this can be extended to 100% at the discretion of the local authority). Charity shops run by the charity can sell some 'bought-in' goods but must take care that these do not constitute the majority of their sales. Bought-in goods should normally be accounted for through the trading subsidiary. Direct costs of new goods are charged to the trading company and the charity must charge its trading subsidiary an amount to cover a proportion of the shop overheads e.g. rent, electricity, staff. Many charities use a method based on turnover e.g. if 30% of sales are of bought-in goods and 70% donated, then costs that cannot be directly attributed are split on a 30:70 ratio.

105.6 For VAT purposes, donated goods are zero-rated, others such as Christmas cards, candles and stationery will be standard-rated. Usually, input VAT relating to the shop should be recoverable since the shop will be selling zero-rated and mainly standard-rated goods via the trading company.

Regulations and controls

105.7 Charity shops have to abide by relevant consumer protection legislation and the food hygiene regulations when selling food or drink. Goods sold must conform to the *Sale of Goods Act 1979*, which stipulates that goods should be of merchantable quality and the General Product Safety Directive of the European Community. They must not sell electrical equipment unless it has been tested by a qualified electrician and carries a label to that effect. Other items they should not sell include:

- anoraks with drawstring hoods;

- safety equipment, such as children's car seats, cycle helmets, motorcycle helmets;
- firearms (unless pre 1850);
- certain knives;
- spectacles;
- alcohol, unless the shop has a licence;
- tobacco products; and
- videos that have not been classified by the British Board of Film Classification or that are not labelled according to the regulations.

105.8 Some items can only be sold if they conform to certain safety standards. These include:

- Toys
- Prams, pushchairs and cots
- Night wear
- Upholstered furniture
- Oil heaters
- Gas appliances

105.9 Many charities will have a policy of not selling certain items even though there is no legal reason to prohibit their sale. This is usually for reasons of hygiene or public health. Examples of items not sold by many charity shops include second hand children's shoes, underwear, and ear-rings for pierced ears.

105.10 Care needs to be taken whenever plastic bags are used for display and particularly when distributing unsolicited plastic sacks to homes in order to encourage people to donate goods, because of the potential suffocation hazard posed to young children. Sacks should be perforated or sealed in an outer envelope and labelled as to the dangers of suffocation.

Health and Safety

105.11 The *Workplace (Health, Safety and Welfare) Regulations 1992* apply to all workplaces. They cover a wide range of health and safety matters including ventilation, heating, lighting, seating and welfare facilities. If no employees work at the premises not all of the regulations apply, however it is good practice to follow them to ensure the safety of volunteers.

105.12 Equipment such as irons, steamers and kettles should be maintained in effective working order and volunteers and staff should be trained how to operate them safely. Floors should be kept clear of clutter and materials stored in such a way that they are unlikely to fall on anyone and cause injury. Fire exits must never be blocked. The use of step ladders should be avoided as much as possible and any step ladders provided should be suitable for use by elderly volunteers.

105.13 Staff and volunteers should be trained in the correct procedures for lifting goods in order to minimise the risk of back injury. They should also be trained in sorting techniques to minimise the risk of injury from broken glass, crockery or hypodermic syringes. Many charities provide their volunteers with protective overalls and disposable gloves to wear when sorting.

105.14 Staff and volunteers should be trained to deal with incidents, such as threats, abuse and assaults by customers, that could give rise to threats to their personal safety. Staff should be told to always put their safety and that of their fellow shop helpers first. If someone demands money from the till all staff, voluntary or paid, should hand it over rather than risk their safety. Where shop takings are high, money should be removed from the till several times a day and stored in a safe until it can be banked. Staff and volunteers should also be given training in how to deter shop lifting and what to do if they see or suspect someone of shop lifting.

105.15 Banking should be done frequently. The route to the bank, the times at which money is banked and the container in which money is taken to the bank should all be varied to minimise the risk of robbery.

105.16 Shops should have good internal control procedures including making sure that two people are present whenever takings are counted, a reconciliation is made between the takings and the till roll, till '*z*' readings are sequentially numbered, and there is a secure place for cash or valuables stored overnight on the premises.

105.17 Charity shop till receipts must state that the shop is a registered charity in order to comply with *s 5* of the *Charities Act 1993*. Failure to do this is a criminal offence punishable by a fine of up to £1,000.

Performance

105.18 The performance of charity shops is regularly monitored in an annual survey carried out by NGO Finance Magazine. In 1999 and 2000 the survey found evidence of declining profitability, as increases in sales were more than outweighed by increases in costs. The charity shops market may well have reached saturation with over 7,000 outlets. Profitability has also been hit by shifting patterns of consumer spending and the general downturn in high street retailing.

106 SOFA — Statement of Financial Activities

106.1 The Statement of Financial Activities (SOFA) was first introduced in the Statement of Recommended Practice on Accounting by Charities (SORP) issued in October 1995 and applies to all charities preparing accruals accounts under the SORP. In the majority of cases this statement replaces the traditional income and expenditure account in a set of annual accounts, although in certain cases, as discussed below, it will also be necessary to present a separate income and expenditure account. The traditional income and expenditure account was not thought to be the most suitable way of explaining a charity's activities, as the charity's primary purpose concerned the provision of benefits to its beneficiaries, rather than gain for share holders. Also, as many charities receive significant amounts of restricted income, their accounts must show this if the reader is to have a clear understanding of a charity's financial position.

106.2 The SOFA is a primary statement in a set of annual charity accounts. It analyses all amounts coming into the charity, the resources expended and contains a reconciliation of all movements of the charity's funds. It should be given equal prominence with other primary statements such as the balance sheet. For unincorporated charities registered in Scotland, the SOFA should be set out as a prominent note.

106.3 The SOFA comprises three broad elements: income and expenditure, investment gains and losses, and the reconciliation of opening funds to closing funds. All these figures are analysed over the three main types of fund: capital, restricted income, and unrestricted funds. A possible presentation of the SOFA is shown in Table 11.

Income

106.4 The following principles should be applied in the preparation of a SOFA, except in the case of immaterial items.

- All figures should be shown gross, not net. For instance, if a professional fund-raiser has been paid £90,000 to raise £100,000, then both of these figures should be shown, not just £10,000 as net income.
- Incoming resources should be recognised as soon as it is prudent and practicable to do so based on an assessment of entitlement, certainty, and measurement. In particular grants receivable should be accounted for when due, not on receipt. Similarly, legacies notified but not yet received should be brought into account when receipt is reasonably certain and they can be measured with some certainty.
- Incoming resources should all be accounted for irrespective of the source and analysed by source and nature into the following categories:
  - Donations, legacies and similar incoming resources;
  - Operating activities:

    — charitable

    — fund-raising;
  - Investment;
  - Other.

106.4 SOFA — Statement of Financial Activities

Table 11 Possible layout of a SOFA

Description	**Unrestricted funds**	**Restricted (income) funds**	**Endowment funds**	**Total funds in current year**	**Total funds in previous year**
Incoming resources (analysed)	–	–	–	–	–
Total incoming resources	A	A	A	A	A
Resources expended (analysed)	–	–	–	–	–
Total resources expended	B	B	B	B	B
Net incoming resources = (A – B)	C	C	C	C	C
Gross transfers between funds	D	D	D	Total = Nil	Total = Nil
Net incoming resources after transfers	E	E	E	E	E
Gains and losses on revaluations of fixed assets for charity's own use	F	F	F	F	F
Gains and losses on revaluation and on investment asset disposals	G	G	G	G	G
Net movement in funds = (E+F+G)	H	H	H	H	H
Total funds brought forward	I	I	I	I	I
Total funds carried forward = (H+I)	J	J	J	J	J

Note: Where necessary the detailed headings may be expanded or amended. The columnar analysis shown above is the minimum requirement where the relevant types of fund exist. Further analysis may be presented. In particular, some charities may wish to insert rows showing the cost of generating funds and a sub-total showing total charitable expenditure.

This means that any incoming resources, regardless of whether they are subject to specific terms of trust or form the capital of the charity, should be included as income on the face of the SOFA. This method of accounting for capital movements is contrary to normal, commercial, accounting principles, and means that company accounts with a SOFA including such items cannot present a 'true and fair view' of the charity's financial transactions and position unless a separate, summary income and expenditure account is also presented.

The SOFA should reflect resource movements, not just inflows and outflows represented by cash. This may require the recognition of income not captured in traditional accounting systems, such as donated items, facilities and services.

Expenditure

106.5 Expenditure should be analysed as follows:

- Costs of generating funds;
- Charitable expenditure:
  - — grants payable
  - — costs of charitable activities
  - — support costs
  - — management and administration.

Supporting notes should show the main components of each category.

106.6 Costs of generating funds may relate to more than just fund-raising expenditure. This category may also include costs of applying for or negotiating a contract, and some publicity expenditure, but only if that relates to fund-raising rather than promoting the mission of the charity.

106.7 Grants payable should include both legal and constructive obligations, and further analysis of institutional grants should be made in the notes. Although the precise amount of disclosure is a matter of judgement, the SORP requires all institutional grants to be disclosed where fewer than 50 have been made. Where more than 50 grants have been made the largest 50 should be disclosed.

106.8 Costs of charitable activities will comprise direct and allocated costs and may be expanded on the face of the SOFA or in a note. The headings should reflect income headings wherever possible. For instance, if one of the income headings is 'care services', then the related expenditure should be similarly labelled.

106.9 'Support costs' are an optional heading for material costs like office overheads where they are material and identifiable as an integral part of the charitable activities.

106.10 Management and administration costs are those costs which relate to the administration of the charity's assets, rather than to the running of the charitable activity itself. The specific examples quoted in the SORP include such items as the costs of compliance with constitutional and statutory requirements, investment management, and internal audit. However, these costs will include a proportion of management time and overheads.

106.11 It can often be difficult to establish where some types of expenditure should be allocated on the face of the SOFA. Any changes made in the underlying principles adopted year on year need to be carefully thought through and documented to ensure comparability from year to year.

106.12 Costs disclosed on the SOFA will often be an amalgam of nominal ledger cost items, allocated to the appropriate heading. For consistency and accuracy therefore, costs should always be allocated on a basis that is both consistent and reasonable. For instance, a childcare charity may spread the costs of its facilities between running playgroups and counselling, two functional cost categories which it may choose to disclose on the face of the SOFA or in a note.

Transfers

106.13 Transfers between funds will be comparatively rare as, generally, Charity Commission consent will be needed for the release of restricted funds and similarly for the formation of restricted funds by internal transfer. All transfers between different funds should be shown gross and not netted off. It is possible for the depreciation of restricted assets to be reflected through unrestricted funds and then a transfer made from the restricted fund balance to meet this cost.

Recognised gains and losses

106.14 This part of the SOFA should show realised and unrealised gains and losses on investments, as well as revaluation gains and losses on other fixed assets unless they represent impairment losses.

Limited companies

106.15 Limited companies are required to comply with the accounts formats under the Schedules to the *Companies Act 1985*. However, there is no fundamental conflict between the *Companies Act 1985* and the SORP although the SOFA may appear to alter the formats of the profit and loss account. As both accounts formats in the Act may be amended to use headings marked by Arabic numbers, the profit and loss account should be presented as a SOFA, subject to the clear identification of income and expenditure.

106.16 Where the Income and Expenditure account cannot be separately identified from within the SOFA, or there are such items as movements on the endowment fund or unrealised gains arising during the year, then a separate income and expenditure account is needed.

Industrial and provident societies

106.17 The layout of the SOFA does not conflict with the requirement for Industrial and Provident Societies to present a revenue account.

Small charities

106.18 Where full SORP accounts are prepared by charities with income below £250,000, certain minor disclosure exemptions are available. The most significant is probably in respect of the SOFA, where small charities can choose expenditure categories to suit their needs.

Notes

106.19 In all cases the SOFA requires a number of notes supporting the figures and providing more analysis. The more significant of these are notes explaining any trading subsidiary's performance, supporting analysis of costs, and specific disclosures in relation to such items as audit fees, trustees' expenses and employees' remuneration.

107 SORP — Statement of Recommended Practice

107.1 The Statement of Recommended Practice on Accounting by Charities — the Charities SORP — applies to all charities in the United Kingdom and the Republic of Ireland regardless of their size, constitution or complexity. This includes charities financed from permanent endowments, public appeals, regular subscriptions or Gift Aid, as well as from the proceeds of trading profits or from any other sources. However, where a Statement of Recommended Practice exists for a particular class of charities, such as housing associations or higher education institutes, charities in that class should adhere to that more specialised SORP. Like other accounting guidance, the SORP only applies to material items in the accounts. An item is material if its inclusion or exclusion makes a significant impact, either on the overall accounts or in the section of which the item forms a part. When in doubt, trustees should assume that an item is material. This materiality rule does not apply in respect of all disclosure requirements, for example the amount of trustees' benefits and the size of audit fees must be disclosed even if the amounts are not material.

General principles

107.2 The Charities SORP sets out the requirements in respect of the trustees' annual report (described in Chapter 115), the annual accounts, and summarised accounts (described in Chapter 3). It stresses that it is essential for a charity's accounts to be accompanied by an explanation of the basis on which they have been prepared. The accounting policies adopted for accrual accounts must be relevant, reliable, comparable, and understandable and be consistent with two fundamental accounting concepts:

- *The 'going concern' concept* i.e. the charity will continue in operational existence for the foreseeable future.
- *The 'accruals' concept* i.e. income is recognised when earned or receivable and expenditure when incurred, and not just when paid in or out.

107.3 In considering which accounting policies to apply trustees of charities are expected to apply the principals of the SORP.

107.4 Recognising the skill required to produce accruals accounts and the small size of the majority of charities, the SORP provides for the alternative 'receipts and payments' basis of accounting for charities with gross income below the applicable level, currently £100,000 in England and Wales (£25,000 in Scotland), in the relevant year.

107.5 'Income' is all resources which become available to the charity and which the trustees are legally required to apply in furtherance of its charitable purposes within a reasonable time of receipt. Income includes all trading and investment income, legacies (unless they are incapable of financial measurement) and all donations, fund-raising proceeds, grants, gifts in kind, gains from disposals of fixed assets and investments, and asset revaluation gains. All incoming resources should be reported gross as far as practicable.

107.6 Expenditure should include all outgoing payments, all losses on the disposal of fixed assets, provisions for depreciation and all claims against the charity when recognised as liabilities by the trustees.

107.7 The underlying objectives of the SORP are to improve the quality of charities' financial reporting and to enable charities to account in a more consistent manner making comparisons across the sector more meaningful. The accounts presentation has therefore moved away from the traditional income and expenditure format and adopted a different primary statement, the Statement of Financial Activities (SOFA) that shows the sources and application of all incoming and outgoing resources, analysed by fund. The detailed breakdown of the charity's activities by type of fund, and even by individual fund, is followed through in the balance sheet and in the notes to the accounts.

107.8 The SORP is a recommendation, not an accounting standard. However, the principles of the SORP are specifically referred to in the *Charities (Accounts and Reports) Regulations 2000*. For instance, *Regulation 6* states that the accounts shall be prepared in accordance with the methods and principles set out in the SORP. Within the overall framework of the SORP there is still considerable flexibility over how figures are presented and what additional information should be provided. This is because the aim of the SORP was to introduce greater consistency and comparability in charity accounting, rather than to set up a straightjacket.

107.9 The SORP specifies that where a charity is preparing accounts on an accruals basis, and not on a receipts and payments basis, then the charity's accounts should always comprise a SOFA (see Chapter 106), a balance sheet, and supporting notes. In certain cases two other statements will also be required, a cash flow statement and a separate summary income and expenditure account.

Balance sheet

107.10 The balance sheet shows the assets, liabilities and funds of the charity. Assets should be analysed between fixed assets and current assets. The balance sheet should show, or indicate in notes how the funds may be utilised, or must be utilised because of restrictions imposed by donors. The format adopted in the SORP is essentially the same as that in the *Companies Act 1985 4 Sch Part 1*. Investments held for long-term gain, which are therefore classified as fixed assets, should be carried at market value. Other fixed assets may be shown at either cost or valuation, less a provision for depreciation.

107.11 The balance sheet may be presented in one continuous vertical format or analysed by columns into various types of fund.

107.12 Some fixed assets can be excluded from the balance sheet. These are certain assets which are inalienable, historic or not susceptible to valuation. If they are excluded, then a note should indicate the extent to which such assets exist. Because much of the wealth of many charities, especially older ones, is represented by their fixed assets, it may be appropriate to create a fund which equates to the value of functional fixed assets, to make clear to the reader that much of the charity's apparent wealth is not readily available for immediate application.

107.13 Current assets and liabilities should be included in the accounts at their conventional valuations: cost, or net realisable value if lower, of current assets and the settlement value of liabilities. Liabilities should be analysed between current and long-term liabilities. Liabilities should only include genuine liabilities existing at the balance sheet date. Moral obligations and informal commitments are not liabilities. Where a charity has an enforceable commitment to funding, for instance a grant given for research over a period of several years, then this should be included as a liability, split between short term and long term. In exceptional circumstances it may be appropriate to exclude such liabilities on the basis that the charity is anticipating matching income to meet this cost. However, this cannot be done simply on the expectation that general fund income will be sufficient to meet the future liabilities. The anticipated income should relate specifically to the future expenditure, such as is the case when a child sponsorship programme is undertaken on the basis of continuing support pledges: the SORP equates this to reimbursement.

107.14 Liabilities will only include deferred income if the income is due to the charity in a future period or receivable when certain conditions are met. Current income relating to a specific purpose or geographical area should be treated as current year's income, within restricted funds if necessary. Income will only be deferred if the trustees are not entitled to draw upon it until the relevant period is reached. Effectively it is not theirs until that date.

107.15 The other side of the balance sheet is analysed by type of fund, distinguishing between unrestricted funds, designated, restricted and endowment funds. Where consolidated accounts are prepared the balance sheet also shows funds retained in subsidiaries.

107.16 Apart from other specific designated funds, the unrestricted funds may be split into separate reserves as necessary, including the following referred to in the SORP or accounting standards:

- Free reserves — effectively the charity's working capital;
- Functional fixed assets — funds held in fixed assets;
- Intentions — funds for commitments which are not liabilities;
- Pensions reserve — required for deferred benefit schemes;
- Contingent liabilities — setting aside funds for contingencies;
- Revaluation reserve — for limited companies' revalued assets.

Notes to the accounts

107.17 The supporting notes should explain the accounting policies, expand upon the information in the financial statements, and provide other useful information. The SORP sets out the following items for disclosure and expansion.

- Accounting policies: these should explain the policies applying to material items in the accounts, and may cover income streams, recognition of expenditure, asset valuations and recognition of gains, netting off, and the use of designated funds.
- An analysis of material funds by types of fund, showing the movement in the year and how the fund is represented: this analysis will show the opening balance, incoming resources, other movements and the closing balance. Where there are immaterial funds they can usefully be grouped together to save cluttering the notes with unnecessary detail. The only exception to this is any fund which is in deficit. This should always be disclosed separately and explained. If designated funds are shown on the face of the SOFA, then the note showing movements on these funds will usually show transfers only, not incoming and outgoing resources separately.

- A breakdown of fixed assets by cost and depreciation, the purposes for holding the relevant assets, and details of any revaluations: the basis of valuing assets and the depreciation policy will usually be set out in the accounting policies.
- An analysis of investments and investment income: both should be analysed out into their distinct types, such as properties, listed investments, investments in subsidiaries and connected persons, unlisted securities, and cash. All of these should be split between UK and overseas holdings. Further details of how the portfolio is structured should be set out as appropriate, showing for instance where any one investment represents more than 5% of the portfolio, or where there are significant restrictions on the realisation of any asset.
- An analysis of debtors and both short-term and long-term liabilities: where the charity's assets have been offered as security, details should be provided.
- Details of any loan made to a subsidiary.
- Transactions with trustees and connected persons: these should include expenses (a nil return must be made if there are no transactions).
- Staff costs: the total emoluments (i.e. remuneration and benefits-in-kind, as defined for taxation purposes) paid to the charity's employees should be shown and the average number of employees (full time equivalents) employed during the year. The note should also show the number of employees whose emoluments (including taxable benefits but not pension contributions made by the employer) for the year were £50,000 or more in bands of £10,000. Bands in which no employees' emoluments fell should not be listed.
- The total amount payable to the charity's auditor or independent examiner: this should distinguish between fees paid for the audit/examination itself, and fees paid for other services, such as tax advice.
- *Ex gratia* payments: these include any payments, non-monetary benefits, other expenditure or the waiver of rights to property to which the charity is entitled which is made not as an application of funds or property for charitable purposes but in fulfilment of a compelling moral obligation. Where the charity has obtained the consent of the court, the Attorney-General or the Charity Commissioners, then the nature and date of the authority should be disclosed. Payments that the trustees reasonably consider to be in the interests of the charity should not be treated as *ex gratia*.
- Details of indemnity insurance: the cost and the nature of any insurance purchased with the charity's funds to protect the charity from losses arising from the neglects of defaults of trustees, employees or agents, or to indemnify the trustees should be disclosed.
- Other commitments, guarantees and contingent liabilities: commitments which are legally binding should have been accounted for as liabilities, but charitable commitments payable by instalments to be funded out of future income should be described in the notes to the accounts. Other commitments may not be charitable, for instance operating leases. Particulars of all such material binding commitments should also be disclosed. Material guarantees, and the conditions under which they might result in liabilities need setting out, along with details of contingent liabilities. Where a contingent loss is material and probable it should be accrued in the accounts. Where loss is less certain, but not remote, then disclosure should be by way of note. This should set out the nature of each contingency, the uncertainties that are expected to affect the outcome, and a prudent estimate of the financial effect where an amount has

not been accrued. If such an estimate cannot be made a note in the accounts should show why it is not practicable to make such an estimate.

Other statements

Cash flow statement

107.18 The cash flow statement is a separate statement required only for larger charities i.e. those which breach two of the following three thresholds:

- gross income in the year in excess of £2.8 million;
- balance sheet total in excess of £1.4 million; or
- more than 50 employees.

The limits for Scottish unincorporated charities are set out in regulations under *LRMPSA 1990.*

107.19 Where an accounting period is not twelve months long, the figures should be pro-rated as appropriate. 'Balance sheet total' refers to the total balance sheet values of assets. Employee numbers means the average monthly number of persons employed. [*Companies Act 1985 s 247*]. The thresholds are applied to the current and two previous years and a cashflow statement must be produced if they were breached in any two of those years. The content of the cash flow statement is set out in Financial Reporting Statement (FRS) No 1 (revised).

Summary income and expenditure account

107.20 An income and expenditure account is required for limited companies if the SOFA includes movements on its endowment funds, that are regarded as capital, not revenue, transactions. This will be a summary income and expenditure account, derived from and cross-referenced to the corresponding figures in the SOFA. The summary need not distinguish between restricted and unrestricted funds, but should show income, expenditure and transfers separately in respect of continuing operations, acquisitions and discontinued operations.

108 Sponsorship

108.1 The term 'sponsorship' is used to describe many different types of funding arrangement. Charities can only engage directly in certain types of sponsorship and the tax treatment will depend upon the precise nature of each arrangement.

108.2 At one extreme some sponsorships are simply donations. For example, a runner in the London Marathon may ask for 'sponsorship', a swimmer taking part in a 'sponsored' charity swimming gala asks for 'sponsorship', or a company 'sponsors' a charity event or service in return for a simple acknowledgement of the company's support. What is being sought in all these examples is a donation to a charity, the amount of which may vary according to criteria such as the distance completed or time taken. Where this is the case, the sponsorship money can be accepted by a charity as a donation and will be free of both corporation tax and VAT. Because these types of sponsorship payments are genuine donations, companies and individuals can make them tax effectively by using Gift Aid.

108.3 At the other extreme, some types of 'sponsorship' are essentially business transactions in which the sponsor offers the charity money, or goods or services, but in return expects the charity to provide valuable advertising, publicity or entertainment for the sponsor. This type of sponsorship is essentially trading, as the charity is providing advertising, publicity or other services for the sponsor in return for the sponsorship payment. Such sponsorship arrangements will usually have to be structured through a charity's trading subsidiary, as the provision of advertising or publicity for commercial companies is not a charitable purpose and therefore cannot be carried out by a charity. When a sponsoring company receives a benefit in return for their sponsorship the payments will not normally be eligible for Gift Aid, but they can instead be deducted from the company's total income when calculating its taxable profits.

Tax implications

108.4 Sponsorship has VAT and tax implications. If the sponsorship is deemed to be a payment for services supplied, then the organisation supplying those services has to charge VAT on the amount of the sponsorship, unless the sponsorship is exempt, for example if it relates to a one-off fund-raising event such as an advertisement in a brochure. [*VATA 1994 9 Sch Group 12*].

108.5 If the sponsorship represents a trade, then the profits earned will be subject to corporation tax. [*ICTA 1988 s 18*]. This tax liability can be avoided if trading type sponsorship is handled by a subsidiary company that donates its profits to its parent charity under a profit-shedding deed of covenant or by Gift Aid. [*ICTA 1988 s 339*].

108.6 Sponsors will wish to be associated with the name of a charity, rather than its trading subsidiary. Therefore if a sponsorship agreement is made between the sponsor and a charity's wholly owned trading subsidiary, either because the legal restrictions on trading by charities prevents the charity from entering into a proposed sponsorship agreement, or because the charity needs to structure the agreement with its trading subsidiary in order to avoid paying corporation tax on profits arising from the sponsorship, then the charity should set up a licence agreement allowing the trading subsidiary to use its name.

108.7 Sponsorship

108.7 Many sponsorship agreements fall between the two extremes i.e. a pure donation or a purely commercial business transaction. Often the value received by the sponsor is worth significantly less than the amount of sponsorship they give or the services they supply. If this is the case, it is possible to split the sponsorship payment into two parts, though this must be done at the commencement of the agreement. The first part is regarded as the 'business' payment for the expected value of the anticipated benefits, attracting VAT and possibly some corporation tax, and the second is regarded as a voluntary donation which could be paid using Gift Aid tax to avoid any tax liability.

108.8 Where it is intended to apportion income for VAT purposes and the arrangement does not fall within clearly published guidelines (such as that given in VAT leaflet 701/1/95 in relation to affinity cards) it is sensible to obtain Customs' written agreement in advance.

Points to consider

108.9 Charity staff and trustees should remember that a charity's name is one of its most valuable assets, as it is the means by which the charity is known and by which its reputation will be judged. So before launching a sponsored event, or entering into a sponsorship agreement with a commercial company, there should be a minuted discussion showing that the relevant points on the following checklist have been taken into consideration.

- Could the sponsored event/association with the sponsoring company damage the charity's relationships with its beneficiaries, donors, funders, supporters or the general public?
- Is the type of activity to be sponsored in keeping with the charity's values?
- Does the charity's insurance cover give adequate protection against claims that might arise from the event/sponsorship?
- What risks does the charity face from this event/sponsorship?
- Is the sponsorship agreement generally to the benefit of the charity?
- Could the charity use its resources more effectively to raise money?
- Could the sponsorship agreement lead to the charity's name being exploited for non-charitable purposes?
- Does the agreement give the charity the right to terminate it if the commercial sponsor misuses or improperly exploits the charity's name?

108.10 If charities enter into sponsorship agreements with retailers, including banks, the sponsors are likely to come within the *Charities Act 1992 s 58(1)* definition of a commercial participator. This means that there will need to be a written agreement between the charity and the sponsoring company formulated in accordance with *s 59(1)* of the Act and the *Charitable Institutions (Fundraising) Regulations (SI 1994 No 3024)*.

109 Staff Recruitment and Development

109.1 One of the most important parts of any organisation is the people who work for and with it to achieve its aims and objectives. Attracting the right people and enabling them to work effectively and efficiently are key management tasks. A sure foundation is good and fair policies and working practices. Much of the work in charities is carried out by volunteers so it is necessary to decide how staff and volunteers are to be integrated into personnel policies. Key elements in the good management of staff and volunteers are:

- good practice in setting staff conditions, policies and procedures within the legal framework;
- effective recruitment; and
- staff appraisal, development and training.

Together they all help to attract, motivate and retain good staff.

Statutory obligations and the legal framework

109.2 Staff who are paid are in a contractual relationship with their employer, governed by employment law. Staff undertake to perform an agreed range of tasks and the organisation rewards them for doing so. These tasks must be legal and the person carrying them out must be controlled by the organisation. This element of control differentiates the employed from the self-employed and has implications for how income tax is deducted from payments made by the organisation.

109.3 Both sides in this relationship owe a duty of care to the other. The employer must ensure that the place of work meets health and safety regulations and the needs enshrined in common law i.e. to pay what has been agreed and not to make unreasonable demands; the employee must work safely and be loyal and conscientious in carrying out their side of the contract.

109.4 The trustees of a charity are obliged to use the charity's funds in the most effective way to achieve its aims and objectives. There are sometimes hard decisions to be made about the level of salaries and rewards that need to be paid to attract people of sufficient calibre to be effective and those that could lay the organisation open to charges about the misuse of funds.

109.5 Within eight weeks of starting work every employee must have the Statement of Particulars of Terms and Conditions of Employment. Usually it will have already been discussed with prospective employees probably at interview. The Statement sets out:

- the employer;
- the job title;
- date of start of employment in the post, and the date of start of continuous employment with the organisation;
- place of work;

- remuneration;
- working hours;
- holidays and special leave, including maternity leave;
- notice period;
- sickness and injury;
- pensions and retirement;
- disciplinary, grievance and capability procedures;
- any probationary period;
- collective agreements and determination of service conditions; and
- amendments to terms and conditions.

109.6 The requirement to issue the Statement prompts the need for policies on remuneration and all the items that follow it in this list. However, these are only the bare bones and the policies need to reflect the type of organisation (membership, philanthropic etc.) its culture, the staff's expectations, custom and practice to date, what can be afforded and what accords with the nature of the organisation's aims and objectives.

109.7 Many charities have found it convenient to tie their salaries to a relevant, nationally set scale e.g. universities, local government etc. However, this is not suitable for all organisations and many of the scales that were nationally agreed are breaking down, so more organisations are having to devise their own scales. Whichever approach is taken, it is still worth defining a pay policy for the organisation and this will include a system to reward extra individual effort or contribution to organisational success.

109.8 Salaries are not the only 'compensation' to be considered: holidays, hours of work, how sickness is dealt with, training, pensions and retirement all need policies, as well as other benefits that might be considered such as season ticket loans, cars, and even private health insurance.

109.9 The statutes that make up employment law are complicated. The essentials are: the *Equal Pay Act 1970* which enshrines the concept that people should be paid the same for doing the same job. This principle has been extended by EC directive to say that work of equal value must be paid at the same rate. The same principles of equality also apply to conditions such as hours of work and how pay is determined. The *Employment Protection Act 1975* introduced basic principles and established an employee's right to go to an industrial tribunal if they believed they had been dismissed unfairly or that 'constructive dismissal' had taken place. The way that the dismissal is handled is also important. The Act has subsequently been amended and a huge body of practice and case law has been amassed.

Anti-discrimination legislation

109.10 The *Sex Discrimination Act 1975* (since amended), the *Race Relations Act 1976* and the *Disability Discrimination Act 1995* are the main pieces of legislation. They make discrimination illegal on grounds of gender including gender reassignment, race and to some extent disability. There are exceptions, particularly in cases where a person's sex is a genuine occupational qualification for the job e.g. workers at a women's refuge. Indirect discrimination is also banned.

Employment conditions

109.11 The *Trade Union Reform and Employment Rights Act 1993* consolidated previous legislation and EU directives on employee rights. In May 1997 the incoming Labour government signed up to the European Social Chapter and made a commitment to a minimum wage.

109.12 The *Transfer of Undertakings (Protection of Employees) Regulations 1981 (SI 1986 No 1794)* protects conditions such as pay and other benefits when staff are transferred from one employer to another. This is a complicated area and expert guidance is advised.

Health and safety at work

109.13 Health and safety legislation imposes the same standard of care on all organisations regardless of their size and whether they are run by staff and/or volunteers. *The Management of Health and Safety at Work Regulations 1999* require employers to assess risks to employees, other workers, clients, members of the public and anyone who comes onto the organisation's premises or uses its services. Employers must draw up a health and safety scheme setting out a programme to reduce risks or minimise the negative impact of risks that cannot be avoided. Employers with more than four employees must put the risk assessment and health and safety scheme in writing.

109.14 Where employees are aged under 18 the Regulations require the employer to carry out a specific assessment taking into account the fact that young people may be inexperienced, immature and/or less aware of risks than adults.

109.15 The Health and Safety Executive has produced guidelines and a training video specially tailored for use by charities called 'Charities and Voluntary Workers: A Guide to Health and Safety at Work'.

Finding the right people

109.16 Recruiting new staff is often difficult. The whole future of the organisation hangs on finding and keeping the right people for the tasks to be undertaken and on those people working well together. The costs of changing staff are high, not only in terms of the funds actually spent on the recruitment process, but also the time that must be invested by colleagues while the new person grows to performing at the required level. Throughout, the process should be conducted in a fair and open manner and fit within the organisation's equal opportunities policy. Thinking in advance will reduce the likelihood of mistakes, though some things are very difficult to detect, no matter how good your process. Success depends upon being clear about several factors.

The job

109.17 The job description and person specification define the job to be done and the key skills, competencies, qualities and experience needed to do it.

Finding the right candidate

109.18 There are a number of options available. An organisation can:

- promote a member of staff;

- appoint someone from outside and exclude applications from members of staff; or
- consider internal and external candidates.

109.19 Unless a staff member is to be promoted, make the position known to the widest possible range of potential candidates in the most cost-effective way, and encourage applications from appropriately qualified and experienced candidates. Places to look for candidates other than amongst the existing staff might well include:

- the organisation's own networks;
- advertising in national and/or local newspapers;
- using confidential registers maintained by recruitment consultancies or agencies; and
- search, sometimes known as headhunting. This usually means finding and approaching candidates who are not actively looking for another post and persuading them to apply and is generally best left to professional consultants as potential candidates often feel more comfortable if approached by a third party.

109.20 Though many organisations in the sector would prefer not to use a proactive search agency to find candidates as doing so appears to conflict with their equal opportunities policy, it is becoming increasingly used to recruit chief executives and specialists in short supply.

Attracting the right applications

109.21 This depends upon writing the advertisement and job brief well. They should give an idea of the scope of the job and the flavour of the organisation, and state clearly any skills, competencies or experience that are *essential* for the post so that time is not wasted processing applications from unsuitable candidates.

109.22 Consider what benefits the job will offer to candidates in terms of career development, interest, public profile etc. It may be necessary to 'sell' the job to candidates if the post is hard to fill, the conditions are particularly onerous or the salary rather low.

The form of interview and other selection methods

109.23 Interviews always form part of the process, but are not the only way to select people. Increasingly, charities are using psychometric tests to assess critical numerical and verbal reasoning skills. Personality questionnaires and tests of management style, where appropriate, can provide useful information about how the applicant would fit into the organisation. The results can indicate areas to probe more deeply during the interview. Such tests should always be carried out by properly qualified people.

109.24 Interviews should be planned carefully so that by the end all the information needed has been gained. It is important to give candidates the opportunity to ask questions about the post and the organisation. Put candidates at ease so that they are able to think clearly and develop their replies to questions. Do not make assumptions — if something is important ask the candidates. As well as their skills, look for the special contribution a candidate could make to the organisation, which may come from their social networks rather than their professional or work experience.

Would an outside recruitment advisor help?

109.25 Outside help might come from an individual personnel consultant, from a recruitment consultancy or from an agency. Each makes a different contribution.

The individual consultant

109.26 A personnel consultant or an occupational psychologist brings an outside perspective to the process. This is particularly useful when making senior appointments and when a change of direction in management is required.

Recruitment consultancies

109.27 Sometimes called Search and Selection, recruitment consultants bring the same skills and expertise as an individual consultant and add expertise in finding and attracting the best candidates. They may have a confidential register of potential candidates and they will provide the administrative services involved in recruitment.

109.28 The consultant will expect to carry out preliminary interviews with perhaps two or three times the number of candidates that the organisation wishes to interview and will assist with producing the shortlist. They should also be able to help with planning the interview.

Agencies

109.29 An agency is primarily a source of candidates through a register. They do not offer search, though the agency staff will have experience in advertising. They will be able to undertake the administrative tasks involved in recruitment.

109.30 The services offered by consultancies and agencies often overlap and so it is advisable to contact several to find out exactly what they offer and for what fee.

Training and development

109.31 For any organisation to achieve its aims and objectives effectively and efficiently, its people need to be knowledgeable and skilful. This applies to all workers, whether paid staff or volunteers, including the trustees.

109.32 However well staff with the requisite skills are recruited, they still need training to keep up to date and develop so that they can move up the organisation. Changes in legislation, such as employment and data protection legislation, produce a need for staff training as do developments in technology, particularly database management systems.

109.33 Training in skills for a particular job is not enough. Staff need the opportunity to develop generic skills such as budgeting, report writing and presentation. They also need opportunities to practise their newly developed abilities so that they and the organisation get the best value from the training. Encouraging staff and volunteers to gain and practise new skills can be a powerful way to build loyalty to the organisation.

109.34 As well as developing individuals' skills, it is worth developing their ability to work as team members. Few jobs require people to work in isolation. Team working is the norm and often people need to learn how best to work as a member of a team — and as a member of a particular team. This does not apply only to staff. Many volunteers, including trustees, work in teams and would gain from training in team development.

109.35 Charities must reconcile meeting the individual's needs with spending the charity's funds wisely, so any training and development provided should contribute actively to the betterment of the organisation in fulfilling its aims and objectives.

Good management

109.36 Perhaps the most important factor in recruiting and retaining staff is good management, providing adequate resources to do the job, recognising an individual's contribution, keeping everyone informed and not allowing staff to burn themselves out. Management as a skill is frequently undervalued in charities and many make false economies by not providing adequate training to staff being promoted to managerial positions. Management training is an ongoing process and identifying training needs should be an integral part of any appraisal system. Training should be viewed as an investment, with an expected return for the charity that can be monitored. There is now a wide range of training tailored to the needs of the voluntary sector, including some excellent and highly cost-effective distance learning provided by the Open University Business School.

110 Tax Effective Giving

Gift Aid

110.1 The Gift Aid scheme for tax effective charitable giving was substantially changed in the *Finance Act 2000* and now applies to all donations large or small, regular or one off, except payroll donations. Previously the scheme only applied to donations of £250 or more (£100 in the case of Millennium Gift Aid). The changes took effect in April 2000.

110.2 This new legislation replaces the tax legislation relating to Deeds of Covenant. Payments made under Deeds of Covenant in existence on 5 April 2000 now qualify for relief for tax purposes under the Gift Aid scheme. Two quite separate pieces of legislation were amended by the *Finance Act 2000* (*Finance Act 1990 s 25* and *Income and Corporation Taxes Act 1988 s 339*) relating to gifts by individuals and gifts by companies. Some factors are common to both, but there are also notable differences. The legislation does not refer to the term Gift Aid as such, but to qualifying donations. Nevertheless, Gift Aid is a term which has been adopted by the Inland Revenue.

110.3 There is no limit to the number of Gift Aid donations an individual or company can make to a single charity, or to a number of charities, in the same tax year.

110.4 A qualifying donation must be a gift which satisfies the following conditions:

- It must be a payment of a sum of money. A promise to make a payment at some later date is not sufficient and any form of gift in kind or a gift of an asset will not qualify.
- It must not be subject to a condition that any part of it can be repaid.
- It must not be a payment from an individual under the payroll deduction scheme, since these payments qualify for tax relief in their own right.
- Neither the donor nor any connected person may receive a benefit above a certain limit in consequence of the gift.
- The payment must not be conditional on, or associated with, the acquisition of any form of property by the charity from the donor or a connected person. Therefore, a donor cannot make a qualifying donation to the charity, which then uses the money to purchase something from the donor. The fact that this extends to persons connected with the donor makes this restriction difficult to circumvent.

Gift Aid by companies

110.5 From 1 April 2000, companies (including companies owned by a charity) and unincorporated associations, such as clubs and societies, must make Gift Aid donations gross, rather than deducting tax from them. They also do not have to complete any forms or give the charity a Gift Aid declaration. The charity does not therefore have any tax to reclaim or have any administrative procedures to follow, other than entering the amount in its accounting records. These rules also apply to payments due under a Deed of Covenant, which was executed prior to 1 April 2000. Therefore tax should not be reclaimed on donations received from companies after

1 April 2000. These rules apply to all companies whether or not they are resident in the UK.

Gift Aid by individuals

110.6 Individuals still have to deduct tax from their Gift Aid donations and make a Gift Aid declaration. Therefore the amount paid by an individual is treated as a sum net of basic rate tax. An individual who is a higher rate taxpayer can obtain tax relief at the higher rate on the gross amount of the gift. The donor claims tax relief by giving details on their tax return or by writing to their tax office asking for an adjustment to be made to their PAYE code number or self-assessment tax calculation. The donor must have paid an amount of income tax or capital gains tax, at either the basic rate or some other rate, that is equal to or more than the tax deducted from their donation. This includes any tax suffered by deduction at source and tax credits on dividends.

The new legislation extends the range of people who can make Gift Aid donations from individuals who are resident in the UK to include:

- Crown servants and members of the UK armed forces serving overseas;
- Non-resident individuals, provided they have income or capital gains charged to UK tax that are at least equal to the gross amount of the donation.

Declaration

Format

110.7 Gift Aid certificates have been replaced by simpler and more flexible Gift Aid declarations. There is no specified format for Gift Aid declarations, provided that all the required information is shown (see below). The Inland Revenue has issued a model Gift Aid declaration form for guidance but charities are free to design their own if they prefer to do so. There is no requirement to ask the Revenue to approve a self-designed declaration form, but the Inland Revenue Charities are happy to advise or approve forms if requested.

110.8 Charities should ensure that their declaration forms comply with any other relevant legislation. If the charity intends to use the data provided by the donor for any purpose other than reclaiming tax, for example to build a mailing list, the form must comply with the *Data Protection Act 1998*. The *Charities Act 1993* requires registered charities to include a statement that they are a registered charity in fund-raising literature.

110.9 A charity must have received a Gift Aid declaration from the donor containing certain information and confirming that the donation is to be treated as a Gift Aid donation before it can be treated as a qualifying donation i.e. before the charity can reclaim tax. The details required on a Gift Aid declaration are:

- the donor's name and address;
- the charity's name;
- a description of the donations to which the declaration relates, e.g. 'the enclosed donation' or 'all donations I make on or after the date of this declaration' or 'all donations I make under the direct debit mandate below';
- a declaration that the donation is to be treated as Gift Aid donations;

- except where given orally, a note explaining the requirement that the donor must pay an amount of income tax or capital gains tax at least equal to the tax deducted from the donation, when the declaration is given orally;
- the date of the declaration.

110.10 The declaration can be written or oral, so donations can now be made tax effectively by telephone or over the Internet. However, if a charity receives an oral declaration, it will not be effective unless the charity sends the donor a written record showing:

- all the details provided by the donor in their oral declaration;
- a note explaining the donor's entitlement to cancel the declaration retrospectively;
- a note explaining the requirement that the donor must pay an amount of income tax or capital gains tax at least equal to the tax deducted from the donation, when the declaration is given orally;
- the date on which the donor gave the charity the declaration;
- the date on which the charity sent the written record to the donor.

Signature

110.11 There is no need for a Gift Aid declaration to be signed.

Declarations for gifts made by partnerships

110.12 A partnership is not a legal entity in England, Wales and Northern Ireland, so a donation by a partnership is treated as being made by the individual partners. However, one partner may make a Gift Aid declaration on behalf of all the other partners, provided that partner has the authority to do so. The declaration need only show the name and address of the partnership. Otherwise it will be necessary for each partner to make their own Gift Aid declaration. The partners can do this on a single declaration form provided it shows all their names and addresses. In Scotland, a partnership has a legal identity, so one of the partners can make a Gift Aid declaration on behalf of the partnership, and give just the name and address of the partnership.

110.13 The donation will normally be apportioned between the partners in accordance with the way they share profits. Each partner can claim higher rate tax relief by entering their share of the donation on their own Self Assessment tax returns.

Declarations on collection envelopes

110.14 A Gift Aid declaration can be included on envelopes used for collecting cash, such as those used for house-to-house collections or those used by many churches for regular giving, provided there is a means of identifying the donor. This could be done by asking donors to write their name and address on the envelope or to give a reference number that can be checked against a donor register. Gift Aid declarations can also be included on forms for sponsored events. However, it is the sponsor who is making the donation that must make the Gift Aid declaration, not the person participating in the event.

Cancellation

110.15 Gift Aid declarations can be cancelled at any time. Donors can do so by notifying the charity in any communications medium. Charities should keep records of cancelled declarations, including they date on which the charity received notification of cancellation. The cancellation takes effect either on the date the charity is notified or on a later date specified by the donor.

110.16 If a donor cancels an oral declaration within 30 days of the charity sending a written record, the cancellation has a retrospective effect so it will be as if the declaration had never been made.

Benefits

110.17 Charities may only provide a limited amount by way of thanks or benefit to its donors if their donations are to qualify as Gift Aid donations. A benefit is any item or service given to the donor, or to a person connected with him or her, in consequence of the donation and includes benefits provided under a membership scheme. However, a mere acknowledgement of the donation in the charity's literature will not amount to a benefit provided that it does not take the form of an advertisement. Newsletters and publications that have no face value, and are not normally sold to the public, and are produced for the purpose of describing the work of the charity, are considered to have no value.

Admission to heritage or wildlife sites

110.18 Certain heritage and wildlife charities provide free or reduced price admission to their members. The new legislation relaxes the rules on donor benefits for such charities, so free or reduced price admission is disregarded as a benefit when:

- it is to view property, the preservation of which is the charity's sole or main aim;
- it is to view wildlife, the preservation of which is the charity's sole or main aim;
- it is restricted to the donor and members of their family;
- it is available to any member of the public who makes a similar donation.

110.19 This relaxation of the donor benefit rule does not apply if the benefit extends beyond viewing the property or wildlife, for example to free right of admission to a stately home to attend a concert in the grounds.

Charity auctions

110.20 If a person buys an item at a charity auction and intentionally pays more than the market value of that item in order to support the charity, the amount paid over and above the market value can be treated as a Gift Aid donation, provided any necessary declaration is made and the limits on donor benefits (see 110.22 below) are not exceeded. For example if someone pays £10,000 at a charity auction for two tickets to a gala concert performance that sell at the box office for £150 then as the market value of the tickets does not exceed the limits of the relevant value test (i.e. £150 is less than 2.5% of £10,000) and the total benefit received by the donor in that year does not exceed the aggregate benefits test (i.e. the benefit of £150 is less than the permitted limit of £250) the payment of £10,000 can qualify as a Gift Aid donation.

110.21 Other payments for goods and services can also be split between the amount required to purchase the item and the amount that is really a donation. There are, however, many instances in which valuation of the benefit will be extremely difficult and a charity should seek professional advice in such a situation.

Donor benefit rules

110.22 The donor benefit rules contain two limits on the value that a donor, or someone connected with them, may receive as a consequence of making a donation. First, the maximum value of the total benefits that a donor may receive from the same charity in the same tax year is £250 (the aggregate value test). Second, the value of benefits received must not exceed the limits set out in Table 12 below (the relevant value test).

Table 12 Benefit limits

Amount of Donation £	Maximum Value of Benefits that can be received
£0–100	25% of donation
£101–1,000	£25
£1,001 +	2.5% of donation

110.23 These limits in Table 12 apply separately to each donation. However, special rules are used to 'annualise' the amount of certain donations and the value of certain benefits for the purposes of applying the limits. In order to assess whether the benefit exceeds the relevant limits, the total value of the benefits due over a 12 month period must be taken. This must then be compared with the total value of donations made in connection with those benefits over a 12 month period. The limits are then applied according to the 'annual value' of the benefits and the 'annualised' donations. These will usually apply where a donor makes a single donation but receives free of charge a monthly periodical, which has a face value. Alternatively, a charity may make a single gift to a donor who has agreed to make regular monthly donations.

Keeping records

110.24 A charity has to keep records to show that its tax reclaims are accurate. As far as Gift Aid from individuals is concerned, these records must show an audit trail linking each donation to an identifiable donor who has provided a valid Gift Aid declaration. In addition to accounting records, therefore, the charity will need to keep copies of all Gift Aid declarations. Where declarations cover donations the donor intends to make in the future it is important to keep those declarations for as long as they are needed to support tax reclaims.

110.25 If a charity fails to keep adequate records it may be required to repay to the Inland Revenue the tax it has reclaimed, plus interest and may also be liable to a penalty.

110.26 Records need not be kept on paper. They can be held on the hard drive of a computer, floppy disc or CD ROM.

110.27 Charitable companies should keep records a minimum of six years after the end of the accounting period to which a tax claim relates. There is, however, a shorter period for charitable trusts, which is the normal time limit for keeping records in respect of an income tax return. If, however, a tax reclaim is made late, the records need to be kept until the end of the quarter following the first anniversary of making the reclaim. The normal date for income tax returns is the first anniversary of the 31 January filing date following the end of the tax year. Clearly, if an Inland Revenue audit is in progress then the records must be retained until it is completed.

Donations from joint accounts, etc.

110.28 Charities often receive donations drawn on joint bank accounts and need to decide if the donation has been given by someone who has already given the charity a Gift Aid declaration. It is reasonable to assume that the donation is from the person who has signed the cheque, debit card slip, standing order mandate, or direct debit mandate. Credit card donations can similarly be made from accounts that have more than one authorised signatory and it is reasonable to assume that the person signing the slip or authorising a telephone donation is the donor. Where donations are made by telephone or through the Internet it is reasonable to assume that the donation is from the person who authorises the transaction. Where there is doubt the charity should ask the person who signed the documentation or authorised the transaction to confirm that the donation is from them.

Deeds of Covenant

110.29 From April 2000 there is no longer separate tax relief for payments made under Deed of Covenant as all future tax relief for such payments will be under the new Gift Aid arrangements. As a transitional measure a Gift Aid declaration is not needed for payments already in existence under Deed of Covenant before 6 April 2000. However, any donations made outside the terms for the Deed or after it expires must be covered by a Gift Aid declaration as should payments under a Deed of Covenant executed on or after 6 April 2000. Although there is no longer any tax advantage to setting up payments under a Deed of Covenant, it may be a way for a charity to ensure committed giving from a donor.

Gifts of shares and securities

110.30 From April 2000, individuals and companies, whether resident or non-resident in the UK, are able to get tax relief for gifts of certain shares and securities to charity when calculating their income or profits for tax purposes. This new tax relief will be in addition to the existing relief for gifts of shares, securities and other assets to charity when calculating capital gains. The new tax relief will apply to disposals by:

- individuals on or after 6 April 2000, and
- companies on or after 1 April 2000.

110.31 The tax relief will apply where an individual or a company disposes of the whole of the beneficial interest in any qualifying shares or securities to a charity either by way of gift or by way of a sale at undervalue.

110.32 Donors will be able to claim a deduction in calculating in the case of an individual, his or her income for the tax year in which the disposal takes place, and in the case of a company, its profits for the accounting period in which the disposal takes place.

110.33 The amount that donors can deduct will be the market value of the shares or securities at the date of disposal plus any incidental costs of disposing of the shares (broker's fees, etc.) less any consideration given in return for disposing of the shares, and the value of any other benefits received by the donor, or a person connected with the donor, in consequence of disposing of the shares.

110.34 Donors will claim the tax relief, at their top rate of tax, on their Self Assessment or Corporation Tax return. You should not reclaim tax on gifts of shares and securities.

Qualifying shares and securities

110.35 The following categories of shares and securities can be donated under the new tax relief:

- shares and securities listed or dealt in on a recognised stock exchange, whether in the UK or elsewhere;
- units in an authorised unit trust;
- shares in a UK open-ended investment company;
- holdings in certain foreign collective investment schemes.

110.36 Shares and securities listed or dealt in on a recognised stock exchange include shares traded on the Alternative Investment Market.

Payroll Deduction Scheme

110.37 The payroll deduction scheme came into effect in April 1987 as a method of encouraging giving. Employees can make donations from their own gross pay, before tax has been deducted. Therefore employees automatically get tax relief at their highest rate of tax. Such schemes can therefore only be used by those in employment or those receiving a company pension from which tax is deducted under PAYE. The total payment an employee may make under this scheme has been increased from time to time since it was introduced but from 6 April 2000 the limit was abolished. The rules are governed by both statute and regulations.

110.38 If an employer operates a payroll deduction scheme it must be approved by the Inland Revenue. It is up to the employees to decide whether or not they wish to join the scheme (which cannot be compulsory), the amount they wish to donate and the charity or charities that will benefit.

110.39 The employer deducts the amount authorised by each employee from their salary and this is paid monthly to a charity who has agreed to act as agent and been approved by the Inland Revenue. The best known agency is Give as You Earn (GAYE) operated by the Charities Aid Foundation. The agency distributes the payments to the charities nominated by the employees. The regulations lay down conditions with which the agency must comply, which include having a contract with each employer, providing receipts to the employer and certificates to the employees if requested, maintaining records for three years, which must be available to the Inland Revenue for inspection and the agency must neither retain money nor repay it to the employer or employees. The agency is, however, allowed to deduct charges from amounts paid to the nominated charities. Any charges made to the employer, or administrative expenses incurred by the employer, are deductible in arriving at the taxable profits of the employer's business.

110.40 Employees do not pay tax on the payments they make by deduction from their salaries, however, national insurance remains payable on their full salary. [*Income and Corporation Taxes Act 1988 s 202*].

110.41 The Government will pay a 10% supplement on all donations under Payroll Giving Schemes from 6 April 2000 to 5 April 2003 as part of a campaign to promote this method of charitable giving. The supplement will be distributed to charities by the Payroll Giving agencies along with Payroll Giving donations. Agencies are not allowed to deduct any administration fee from the supplement.

110.42 Payroll deduction schemes are administratively simpler than Gift Aid for both charities and the Inland Revenue, as the charity does not have to reclaim tax paid. However, they do place an administrative burden on employers and for this reason some employers are reluctant to take part in the scheme.

111 Taxation

111.1 It is a common misconception that charities do not pay tax. In fact charities are liable to pay most taxes unless they take care about the activities they undertake and the structures they use. This Chapter provides a brief overview of the main taxes and their bearing on charities, while specific taxes are dealt with in more detail in other chapters.

Income and corporation tax

111.2 Tax matters relating to charities and their subsidiary companies are all dealt with by one department of the Inland Revenue: the Inland Revenue Charities office based in Bootle for charities other than Scottish charities, whose affairs are administered from the Inland Revenue Charities (Scotland) office in Edinburgh.

111.3 Where charities receive voluntary income or operate only within the terms of the basic tax exemptions then they should not be subject to tax on their income. The Charity Commission has made it clear that they expect charities to adopt appropriate strategies to mitigate tax liabilities where it is appropriate and cost effective to do so, but that in some cases it may be appropriate for the charity to accept a small tax charge rather than set up expensive and cumbersome structures to avoid a liability.

Capital gains tax

111.4 *Section 256* of *Taxation of Capital Gains Act 1992* exempts charities from capital gains tax, as long as the gain in question is applied for charitable purposes. Normally, an individual who disposes of a chargeable asset at less than its value (i.e. gives it away) would be charged tax as though the disposal was at full value. Because there is an annual exemption (£7,200 in 2000/01) this could otherwise be used as a way of arranging a sale through someone to whom the asset was gifted just prior to sale, and who had not already used their exemption. These rules do not apply to a gift to a charity and so chargeable assets may be transferred tax free. Where an asset is likely to create a gain of an amount within the donor's exemptions, it may be worthwhile instead asking the donor to sell the asset personally, and for the proceeds then to be donated (net) by Gift Aid to the charity. Assuming that the donor has enough relevant taxable income, this not only avoids any charge to capital gains tax, but also increases the value of the gift as the charity can reclaim the basic rate tax paid on the donation.

Inheritance tax

111.5 No inheritance tax is payable on transfers to charities, whether made as lifetime gifts or on death. A gift which is conditional, and where the condition is not met within twelve months, will then cease to be exempt. Similarly, a gift which can be retracted, or which is dependent on a period of time elapsing, will also not be exempt.

111.6 Taxation

National Insurance

111.6 As an employer no special rules operate for charities in respect of National Insurance.

Stamp duty

111.7 Stamp duty is payable by the purchaser on a range of 'stamped' transactions. A series of *Finance Acts* has ensured that charities are exempt from stamp duty on stock and share transfers, land transactions and deeds of covenant, although land transactions require to be adjudicated as not liable to tax. Non-charitable subsidiary companies are subject to stamp duty.

VAT

111.8 VAT is an indirect tax operated by Customs and Excise and the existence of reliefs for charities for income or corporation tax should not be taken to indicate that there is relief from VAT. Any entity making 'taxable' business supplies (i.e. supplies liable to the standard or zero rate of VAT) above the registration limit (£52,000 in 2000/01) must be registered and submit a quarterly return to Customs, with the tax due. The general rules for charities and VAT are set out in VAT Notice 701/1/95.

111.9 There is no general relief for charities from VAT. Charities may therefore suffer VAT by having to pay VAT on purchases, i.e. input tax, without being able to reclaim that VAT as most businesses can. Certain specific reliefs operate for charities which permit them either not to charge VAT on certain supplies made by the charity, or which allow them to recover VAT on certain types of purchase. These reliefs are discussed more fully in Chapter 117.

111.10 There are a number of special schemes which operate for certain types of business e.g. the tour operator's margin scheme. Where a charity's activities come within one of these areas the charity will need to comply not only with the general VAT rules, but also the specific rules for charities and those for the special scheme.

Other taxes

111.11 Charities have no general exemption from other forms of taxation, such as insurance premium tax, air passenger duty, council tax and excise duties. Mandatory relief of 80% exists for business rates and a further 20% relief is at the discretion of the levying council. The non-charitable subsidiary trading company of a charity is not entitled to business rate relief.

112 Trading Subsidiaries

112.1 Many charities wish to undertake regular trading activity as a means of raising income. Where this extends much beyond a primary purpose of the charity, however, the exemption the charity has from paying corporation tax (or if the charity is a trust, income tax) will be lost. The charity is also at risk of committing a breach of trust if it carries on such a trade as it does not constitute a charitable activity. A charity should therefore consider setting up a separate non-charitable trading company that donates its profits to the charity. The trading company can be either a wholly owned subsidiary of the charity or can be jointly owned by a number of charities. A wholly owned subsidiary company is generally preferable in that it does not cause problems in dividing up and distributing the profits as would be the case when a number of charities are shareholders.

112.2 From April 2000, there is a new tax exemption for the profits of certain small trading and other fund-raising activities carried on by a charity. The Charity Commission has confirmed that if the charity is governed by one of its model governing documents, which contain prohibitions on 'any substantial trading activity', the charity may lawfully carry on activities falling within the new tax exemption, without having to set up a trading company.

112.3 The new exemption applies to the profits of all trading and most other incidental fund-raising activities, provided that the total turnover from all of the activities does not exceed the annual turnover limit or, if it does, there was a reasonable expectation at the beginning of the period that it would not. The profits must also be used solely for the purposes of the charity. The annual turnover limit is £5,000 or, if greater, 25% of the charity's total income from all sources, subject to an overall turnover limit of £50,000.

Investing in a trading company

112.4 Forming a trading company must be considered by a charity as the making of an investment and must therefore be within the charity's investment powers and policy. Any funding from the charity which the subsidiary may require must also be similarly viewed. The Charity Commission will not normally object to a nominal subscription of share capital but prefers to see the initial funding coming from commercial sources, to minimise the risk to charitable assets. However, the trading company will find it difficult to raise a loan without a guarantee from the parent charity, so the charity's funds would still be at risk. A loan from a charity to its trading subsidiary may well be considered non-qualifying expenditure by the Inland Revenue, which could result in the charity losing tax exemptions.

Transferring profits

Profit-shedding covenant

112.5 The most tax efficient method of donating the profits of a subsidiary trading company to the parent charity is through Gift Aid. Until April 2000, a company could obtain tax relief for a payment under a deed of covenant but this relief has been replaced by Gift Aid. Companies that are wholly owned by one or more charities have nine months from the end of the company's accounting period to make the Gift Aid payment. This means that companies now have time to calculate their taxable profits and complete their accounts and corporation tax computations before the payment has to be made.

Dividends

112.6 A trading subsidiary can also pass its profits to its parent charity using a dividend. The payment of a dividend is not generally a tax efficient method because it still leaves the company with a corporation tax liability and the tax credit on dividends that charities can reclaim is gradually being withdrawn.

Financing the trading company

112.7 A trading subsidiary should be financed on a commercial basis. Any loan should bear interest at a reasonable rate and there should be a repayment schedule. Any payments of capital or interest should actually be made, rather than just recorded in the accounts. Because companies have working capital commitments, they often do not generate enough cash to repay loans without incurring tax liabilities. This problem is exacerbated by the interaction of the calculation of profit on an accounts and tax basis.

112.8 The taxable profits of a company often exceed the profits shown by the company's accounts, for example because the company has incurred expenses which are not allowable for tax purposes, such as entertaining its customers, or because the tax relief for capital expenditure is less than the depreciation charged in the accounts, which is not itself allowable. If a Gift Aid payment equals the whole of the company's taxable profits, the company will be unable to build up reserves and can actually become insolvent if it has insufficient capital to cover this deficit. The parent charity may well be unable to provide additional funding in these circumstances because to do so would breach its investment powers. Alternatively, the charity may lose its tax exemption because it is making a further non-qualifying payment. An investment is only a qualifying payment for tax purposes if it is made for charitable purposes i.e. for the benefit of the charity and not for the avoidance of tax. Unless it were in itself a commercially sound investment, ignoring the fact that the profits of the company were to be donated for charity, a loan or subscription for further shares by a charity would not fulfil those criteria. To resolve these problems, the charity should plan the setting up of a trading subsidiary carefully and prepare proper business plans, cash flow forecasts and profit projections.

112.9 To deal with such situations some charities decide that it is better to allow their trading companies to retain some of their profits each year so that the trading company has sufficient funds for working capital. This leaves part of the company's profits subject to corporation tax but may be preferable to the charity losing its tax exemptions or the trading company becoming insolvent. A Gift Aid payment can vary from year to year according to current needs.

112.10 The subsidiary company can, of course, seek external finance. Anyone considering making an external loan will, however, look at the trading company's ability to make the necessary interest and loan repayments and would be unwilling to lend money to a company which cannot build up any reserves because it donates all of its taxable profits to its parent charity. The trustees of the charity should regularly review its subsidiary company's performance and the viability of the charity's investment in the subsidiary. Once a trading company is established the Charity Commission expects funds to flow only in one direction, namely from the trading company to the charity. Trustees who continue to fund loss making trading companies could be judged to be acting in breach of trust or breach of their fiduciary duty.

Managing a trading company

The Directors

112.11 Trustees and staff of the charity are permitted to be directors of the trading company and staff, but not trustees, can be paid for their service as directors. However, in order to avoid conflicts of interest it is advisable to ensure that some trustees are not directors of the trading company and that some directors of the trading company are neither trustees nor staff of the charity.

Staffing

112.12 The trading company is legally a separate organisation from the charity, so care must be taken that the correct contracts of employment are in place. In some instances it may be appropriate to have joint contracts of employment.

Accounting and administration

112.13 Bank accounts and financial records must be kept separate and any paperwork and records should clearly indicate whether they relate to the charity or to its subsidiary trading company. The charity can make a management charge to cover the management of its trading company in addition to charging for providing premises or shared resources. Note that rate relief may not be available for the portion of a building used by a trading company. The loss of relief should be borne by the trading company.

Insurance

112.14 A charity's insurances will not cover its trading company unless the policies specifically state that they do.

VAT

112.15 The relationship between a charity and its trading subsidiary gives rise to a number of complex VAT issues. Chapter 117 touches on these but professional advice is usually called for.

113 Trustee Duties and Responsibilities

113.1 In their leaflet CC3 'Responsibilities of Charity Trustees', the Charity Commission defines charity trustees as 'the people responsible under the charity's governing document for controlling the management and administration of the charity, regardless of what they are called'. Many charities do not use the term 'trustee' but refer to the members of their governing body by some other term, for example 'the council', 'the management committee', 'the directors', 'the executive committee', or 'the governors'. However, no matter what they are called, those defined in the governing document as the charity's governing body are the charity's trustees. It is increasingly regarded as good practice for charities to include the word 'trustee' in the name of the body of people who bear the legal responsibilities of trusteeship. For example, many charities now refer to their governing body as 'The Trustees' or 'The Board of Trustees' or 'The Council of Trustees'.

113.2 Charity trustees have legal, financial and managerial duties i.e. legal obligations, and responsibilities. Although many of these are set out in guidance issued by the Charity Commission, the principles apply equally to trustees of Scottish charities.

Legal duties and responsibilities

113.3 Trustees are responsible for the proper administration of the charity in accordance with the law and its trusts, as set out in its governing document. As the governing body of a charity, the trustees have both ultimate power and ultimate responsibility for everything the charity does and how it does it. Their overriding duty is to pursue the objects of the charity as set out in its governing document. The trustees must apply the income and property of the charity exclusively for the charity's objects, applying it fairly between those qualified to benefit from it both now and in the future.

113.4 Charity trustees must not use the charity's resources to do what should be done by statutory services (unless their governing document explicitly permits this) though they can complement or supplement those services by providing additional benefits.

113.5 Trustees have a fiduciary duty to the charity as a whole. 'Fiduciary' means 'in good faith', so trustees must always act in good faith (i.e. in the belief that what they are doing is correct), and in the interests of the beneficiaries, setting aside their own interests, preferences and prejudices.

113.6 Trustees also have a duty of care. Therefore they must act reasonably and prudently, with the same degree of care that a prudent business person would exercise in managing their own affairs. Note that this is a higher duty of care than that required of company directors who merely have to act honestly and in good faith with a degree of skill commensurate with their knowledge and experience. When dealing with investments the standard of care which trustees must exercise is higher still. They must act with the degree of care that a prudent business person would exercise in managing the affairs of someone for whom they were responsible. In practice this means that trustees need to know about the legal, financial and managerial issues affecting the charity, though they are not expected to have expert knowledge. If they hold themselves out as having expertise in a given area, however, they will be expected to act with a higher duty of care, and this will be taken into account should any issue come to the attention of the courts or the Charity Commission.

113.7 The *Trustee Bill 2000* introduces a new 'duty of care' for the trustees of both charitable and non-charitable trusts to minimise the risk of loss or injury to the trust. It states that in exercising any of their powers trustees 'must exercise such care and skill as is reasonable in the circumstances, having regard in particular to any special knowledge or experience he has, or holds himself out as having'. In addition, if someone acts as trustee in the course of a business or profession, they must exercise such care and skill as is reasonable in the circumstances, having regard to any special knowledge or experience that it is reasonable to expect of a person acting in the course of that kind of business or profession. The duty of care applies to a trustee when they are:

- dealing with the trust's investments;
- acquiring land;
- entering into arrangements for others to act as agents, nominees or custodians;
- insuring the trust's property;
- dealing with reversionary interests, valuations and audit.

The duty of care does not apply if, or in so far as, it appears from the trust instrument that the duty is not meant to apply.

113.8 If trustees do not seek advice on matters on which they are not experts, be they legal, financial or managerial, they could be judged as having acted imprudently and could be personally liable for the consequences. The *Charities Act 1993* requires trustees to seek professional advice in some instances, for example, in relation to certain land transactions.

113.9 Trustees have a duty to avoid conflict of interest and should not take part in any discussion or decision where they have a conflict of interest. If ever a trustee's personal, business or professional interests are likely to conflict with those of the charity, the trustee should disclose that interest to their fellow trustees. As a matter of good practice many charities now keep a public register of their trustees' interests. In some instances trustees may face not a conflict, but a duality of interest. For example, they may be a trustee or staff member of another charity working in a similar field and owe a loyalty to both organisations. Where this is the case the trustee must act in the best interest of the charity whose affairs they are then considering.

113.10 Trustees also have a duty not to profit from their position as trustees, unless the charity's governing document specifically specifies otherwise or the Court or Charity Commission authorises a payment. Therefore they must carry out their duties without payment, either in the form of money or preferential access to services. Trustees of unincorporated charities have a statutory right to be reimbursed for any out of pocket expenses incurred in connection with their service as trustees. Trustees of charitable companies can be reimbursed if the governing document permits it.

113.11 Trustees must take their responsibilities seriously. The Charity Commission's leaflet CC3 'Responsibilities of Charity Trustees' states that, 'To be a charity trustee is not a position of honour without responsibility: it requires time, understanding and effort'. Trustees are required to act personally (i.e. to play an active role), meeting as often as is necessary for the proper administration of the charity, giving the time necessary to study board papers before the meetings, and keeping themselves informed about the charity's activities. They must also avoid conflicts of interest and must not profit from their position as trustees.

113.12 The time trustees need to devote to their trusteeship will vary considerably from one charity to another depending on a number of factors including:

- the size and complexity of the charity;
- whether or not the charity has volunteers and/or employs paid staff;
- the nature of the charity's work and whether the charity is operational or grant making;
- whether or not the governing body has to represent the views of its members; and
- the stage of its organisational development.

In some organisations the trustees will have both a governing and an operational role, whilst in others their role will be restricted to the charity's governance.

113.13 In their governing role, the trustees must ensure that the charity's mission is still relevant and that the charity has clear direction and purpose and a sense of urgency to get on with the work it is established to do. They should develop and agree the charity's strategic objectives and major policies and guard the charity's ethos and values. The board of trustees must set clear objectives, establish the charity's priorities, safeguard its assets (money, property, equipment, human resources, by ensuring that there are adequate financial controls (see Chapter 68) and that any land or buildings the charity owns are well maintained and insured, and use the assets efficiently, effectively and exclusively to benefit those the organisation exists to help. Trustees have a duty to protect all the assets belonging to the charity. Where day to day management and operations are delegated to staff, the board of trustees still remains ultimately responsible for all the charity's activities, so their key responsibility is to appoint the right chief executive, give that person clear direction regarding the charity's objectives, policies, values and ethos, clear guidance about the degree of authority the board of trustees is delegating to them, monitor their performance, offer support and assistance as required and take appropriate action if their performance falls below that expected.

The board of trustees' main responsibilities are to:

- act as the ultimate body to which staff and volunteers can appeal in relation to internal grievance and disciplinary matters; and
- periodically review its own performance and take any necessary steps to improve it.

Delegation

113.14 Trustees are required to act in person and any decisions affecting the charity must be made by the trustees acting together. However, the duty to act personally does not mean that the trustees have to do everything themselves. They can delegate a wide range of tasks to others but must give them clear instructions that define:

- the functions or tasks that are being delegated, and the results that the trustees expect;
- the limits of the authority which the delegate may exercise on the trustees' behalf;

- the types of decisions that can be made by delegates in the course of their work and the types that must be referred back to the trustees;

- how and at what intervals the delegates are to report progress to the trustees.

113.15 If the charity's governing document gives the trustees the power to delegate authority for a particular aspect of the charity's work to a subcommittee of the trustee board, or to delegate authority to a task group or committee whose members need not necessarily all be trustees, or to staff they may do so. However, any decisions made by such groups or staff remain the responsibility of the full board of trustees. The terms of reference and reporting-back procedures of any committees, subcommittees, task groups or staff should be laid down in writing and agreed by the board of trustees. Decisions about important matters must be reported to the board of trustees as quickly as possible.

113.16 Trustees of charitable companies must also comply with the legal requirements placed on company directors since that is their dual role. They must ensure that the charity keeps up to date with its company returns and record-keeping and must not continue trading as a company if they know, or should have known, that the company is insolvent. They must also avoid conflicts of financial interest between the charity and themselves or any person connected with them such as a partner, spouse, child or stepchild, or business partner of themselves, their partner, spouse or child.

Joint responsibility

113.17 Trustees are jointly responsible for the activities of the charity and must act together. No trustee acting alone can bind his or her fellow trustees, unless specifically authorised to do so. However, the board's decisions do not have to be unanimous, so the majority bind the minority. Trustees are bound by the decisions of their fellow trustees even if they were not present at a meeting where the decision was taken. Trustees may protect themselves to some extent by having their dissenting vote recorded in the minutes, but if the matter is serious, particularly if a decision constitutes a breach of trust, they should consider resigning

Joint and several liability

113.18 A board of trustees has joint and several liability. This means that if the board of trustees agrees to do something under a contract then the multiple parties that make up the board make one promise which binds all of them, and, in addition, each party also makes a separate promise binding him or herself to honour the contract. This does not entitle the person or corporate body to whom the board of trustees has made that promise to receive more in total than they were promised, but it does entitle them to obtain what they were promised either from the board of trustees or from any one or more members of the board.

Financial duties and responsibilities

113.19 The financial responsibilities of charity trustees are wide ranging and should not be left to the treasurer or finance committee alone. All the trustees have a duty to be aware of the charity's financial position and they can be personally liable for the misuse of charity funds. They must protect the charity's assets and make sure that the charity complies with the accounting and audit regulations contained in the *Charities Act 1993* and any relevant Statements of Recommended Practice (SORP) such as the SORP for charities or for housing associations, or the *Companies Act 1985* if the charity is a company.

113.20 Trustees are responsible for:

- approving and monitoring budgets;
- ensuring that the charity has adequate resources to meet its commitments;
- ensuring that proper control is exercised over both income and expenditure;
- fund-raising policy and activities;
- overseeing any trading activities;
- ensuring the tax affairs of the charity are managed effectively;
- establishing policies for reserves and investments;
- ensuring that any investments earn the best possible return without putting the capital at risk and are in accordance with both the charity's investment policy and its powers of investment as set out in its governing document; and
- making sure that the assets and income are used exclusively to pursue the charity's objects, adequately protected and managed efficiently and effectively.

113.21 In addition, trustees are responsible for ensuring that reasonable steps are taken to prevent and detect fraud and other irregularities. Trustees should make sure that the charity has adequate controls for operating the charity's bank account which cannot be abused by unscrupulous people. Cheques over a certain amount should normally be signed by at least two people, including one trustee, unless there are other controls which give a similar or greater degree of protection. If the charity is large enough to warrant having internal audit staff, these staff should report directly to the trustees.

113.22 Any money that a charity has should be placed on deposit if it is needed in the near future, or, if it is not needed in the immediate future, it should be invested in accordance with the investment powers in the charity's governing document, or failing this the *Trustee Investments Act 1961*. However, money must not be allowed to accumulate unless the trustees have decided to set it aside in a designated fund for a specific charitable purpose, or unless the governing document contains a power to accumulate.

113.23 Any funds, land, buildings or other assets which form part of the charity's permanent endowment (that is assets which have been given to the charity to keep in perpetuity but with the charity benefiting from the income that can be earned from the asset) should be preserved and invested to produce a good income while protecting the real value of the capital.

Managerial duties and responsibilities

113.24 Trustees have a number of important managerial responsibilities, which may include responsibilities in relation to:

- setting strategic objectives;
- strategic planning;
- policy making;

- employing, managing, appraising and rewarding staff;
- managing volunteers;
- giving account to statutory and regulatory bodies as required by law, to funders and to other stakeholders (beneficiaries, volunteers, staff, the general public etc.);
- monitoring the work of the charity;
- evaluating the impact and effectiveness of the charity's work;
- managing the charity's property and land;
- managing the charity's public relations; and
- representing the views of the charity.

113.25 In addition, depending on the work of the charity and whether or not it employs staff, the charity may have to comply with the legislation covering such matters as employment, health and safety, environmental matters, data protection, child protection and trading standards.

113.26 The Board of Trustees, or a sub-committee of it, may also have to act as the final internal group to which senior staff can appeal against decisions made in relation to disciplinary or grievance matters.

113.27 In seeking to carry out their responsibility to manage the charity's affairs effectively the trustees should periodically review their own performance and take any steps needed to improve it. If necessary trustees should review their governing structure, the size and composition of the board, its method of recruitment and ways of working and its need for training or other support.

Disqualification under the Charities Act 1993

113.28 *Section 72* of the *Charities Act 1993* disqualifies people from becoming trustees of a charity if they:

- have unspent convictions for offences involving deception or dishonesty;
- are undischarged bankrupts;
- have been at any time removed from trusteeship of a charity by the Charity Commission or the Court in England, Wales or Scotland, because of misconduct;
- are disqualified from being company directors under the *Company Directors Disqualification Act 1986*;
- have failed to make payments under county court administration orders; or
- have made compositions (i.e. come to an arrangement) with their creditors and have not been discharged.

114 Trustee Indemnity Insurance

114.1 Charity trustees have statutory and/or common law rights to be indemnified by the charity for their losses in some circumstances, for example losses to third parties arising from the charity's or their own breach of contract, negligence or breach of duty.

114.2 In their leaflet CC3 'Responsibilities of Charity Trustees', the Commissioners state that 'if trustees act prudently, lawfully and in accordance with their governing document then any liabilities they incur as trustees can be met from the charity's resources'. Trustees are fully protected by the general law of Trust's unless they have:

- acted contrary to professional advice;
- failed to act in accordance with the charity's governing document.

In addition, trustees cannot be held responsible for the wrongful actions of staff or agents provided that they exercise proper care in their appointment and supervision.

114.3 However, in situations where the trustees are liable to the charity, they cannot be indemnified by the charity. For example, if trustees committed a breach of trust by funding a project outside their charitable objects or breached their fiduciary duties by not seeking professional advice about their investments, the trustees would be liable to make good any loss the charity suffered as a result.

114.4 The Charity Commission has powers to take proceedings in court to recover from trustees personally any funds lost to the charity as a result of a breach of trust or breach of duty. Trustees' liabilities are joint and several which means that each trustee could be held liable for all or any part of the loss.

114.5 Similarly trustees cannot be indemnified against fines or penalties, such as fines for failing to submit accounts on time or breaching health and safety regulations, as this would be contrary to the public interest.

Trustee indemnity/liability insurance

114.6 Trustee indemnity insurance, or trustee liability insurance as it is sometimes known, offers trustees some protection against their personal liability as trustees and most policies also indemnify the charity against liabilities arising from the wrongful actions of trustees and sometimes of staff or other agents. Some policies offer a choice of protection: for the trustees, for the charity, or for both the trustees and the charity. Available policies do not normally cover contractual liability, redundancy payments made to the charity's employees, or liabilities under a lease.

114.7 The Charity Commission will give permission in some circumstances for charities to use charity funds to purchase insurance that protects trustees against liabilities arising from:

- acts properly undertaken in the administration of a charity; and
- acts undertaken in breach of trust, but due to an honest mistake.

114.8 Charities wishing to use the charity's funds to purchase this type of insurance must have the power to do so in their governing document or apply to the Charity

Commission for permission. If a charitable company does not have the power in its governing document it will need the Charity Commission's consent to amend its governing document. Charitable trusts and associations will need the Commission's consent by letter, by an Order made under *s 26* of the *Charities Act 1993* or by a Scheme made under *s 16* of the Act. If the Commission agrees, this will be given to amend the governing document. The Commission normally gives consent to applications made by charitable companies, but is less likely to give it to applications made by unincorporated charities. If a charitable industrial and provident society does not have power in its governing document it will have to apply to the Registrar of Friendly Societies for permission to amend its rules.

114.9 The Commission does not allow charities to protect their trustees from liabilities arising from acts which the trustees knew were wrong, or acts which the trustees took in reckless disregard of whether they were right or wrong. To this end the Commission requires trustee indemnity policies purchased by a charity to include an exclusion clause on the following lines: 'The insurers shall not be liable for loss arising from any act or omission which the trustee knew to be a breach of trust or breach of duty or which was committed by the trustee in reckless disregard of whether it was a breach of trust or breach of duty or not'.

114.10 This restriction lessens the value of the insurance if the reason for purchasing it is to protect the trustees. If trustees know an act is wrong, or if they behave recklessly, they cannot be indemnified against losses arising from it. If a loss results from a wrongful action which is either an honest mistake on the part of the trustees, or sanctioned by the trustees acting on appropriate legal or professional advice, the Charity Commission has stated that they will not require trustees to make good any losses arising as a result of that wrongful act. However, the policy could still represent good value for the charity, as it should indemnify the charity against losses arising from the trustees' wrongful acts, even when the Charity Commission recognises that these are due to honest mistakes and does not require the trustees personally to reimburse the charity. For example, if trustees did not seek advice about investments and as a result the charity's investment income was lower than could have been achieved, the Charity Commission would, in some circumstances, reprimand the trustees but not require them to make good the loss. However, the charity would have sustained a loss none the less and could make a claim against a trustee indemnity insurance policy.

114.11 Wrongful actions are of four main types.

- Breaches of trust or fiduciary duty: for example, doing something which is outside the charity's charitable objects, failing to show a proper duty of care or failing to take professional advice.
- Breaches of statutory duties: for example, failing to submit accounts on time, to deduct PAYE, to declare the organisation's charitable status on all its financial documents or to provide employees with a written contract of employment.
- Breaches of contract: for example, failing to pay utility bills, builders, suppliers or to repay debts.
- Tort or breaches of common law duty: for example, acting negligently, causing nuisance, libel.

114.12 All charity trustees could face personal liability for the first two types of wrongful actions listed above. Incorporation will protect some trustees from liabilities for breach of contract and tort. However, the trustees of charitable companies will have additional responsibilities as company directors. For example, they will have to comply with regulations regarding the proper recording of minutes of meetings, filing of returns etc and these can be protected by taking out directors and officers liability insurance.

What risks are covered?

114.13 Most trustee indemnity policies cover:

- poor investment decisions resulting in a loss to the charity;
- claims for wrongful advice or negligence in service delivery;
- industrial tribunal awards; and
- maladministration resulting in a loss to the charity.

Some policies will also cover:

- fraud or dishonesty by trustees, staff and/or agents;
- libel;
- negligence;
- legal costs;
- inadvertant breach of confidentiality or copyright/intellectual property rights; and
- contractual liabilities.

Risks not covered:

- fines or penalties; and
- claims arising out of death or injury on charity property.

114.14 Trustees could also be held vicariously liable for acts committed by employees in the course of their work and may be held liable for acts by other members of the board of trustees if it can be shown that they authorised the action and/or that they were negligent in allowing it to take place. For example, in 1994 a company was convicted of corporate manslaughter after four teenagers were drowned while on a canoeing trip organised by the company's activity centre. The company was fined and the managing director imprisoned for three years.

114.15 Charities may purchase insurance to indemnify trustees against the costs of a successful defence to a criminal prosecution brought against them in their capacity as charity trustees. However, charities may not purchase insurance against the costs of a defence regardless of whether or not there is a finding of guilt.

114.16 Charity trustees who seek and act upon advice from the Charity Commission under *s 29* of the *Charities Act 1993* are protected from liability if they are later judged to have committed a breach of trust.

Payment for insurance

114.17 Charity law does not generally permit charities to pay for insurance that indemnifies the trustees, as this would not be consistent with the principle that trustees must not benefit from their trust. However, if the Charity Commission believes that allowing the purchase of such insurance would be in the best interests of the charity, it will give consent in some circumstances. For the same reason the Commission has allowed the registration of charities whose governing document explicitly allows the purchase of trustee indemnity insurance.

114.18 There are no restrictions on charities taking out insurance to indemnify the charity from losses arising as a result of the trustees' actions. Similarly, there are no restrictions on trustees purchasing trustee liability insurance to indemnify themselves. Where they are willing to pay the premiums personally, trustees are not subject to the restrictions imposed by charity law and so they can obtain greater protection.

Disclosure

114.19 Details of trustee indemnity insurance paid for by an unincorporated charity must be disclosed in the charity's annual report in compliance with the *Charities Act 1993*. For limited companies the same disclosure will be made in the notes to the accounts in accordance with the SORP.

Charity Commission advice

114.20 In their leaflet CC49 'Charities and Insurance' the Charity Commission recognises that where a charity simply distributes income periodically, the risks (to the trustees) are likely to be negligible or non-existent. On the other hand, for the trustees of a charity which is a major provider of services, such as a school or hospital, the potential risks may be considerable. The Commission advises that when trustees are considering taking out trustee indemnity insurance they should take into account:

- the degree of risk to which they are exposed;
- the value of the indemnity required;
- the cost of the premiums; and
- whether the insurance is likely to be in the interests of the charity.

114.21 They require trustees who are considering using charity funds to purchase trustee indemnity insurance to consider whether other steps should be taken to reduce the risk of personal liability, such as:

- recruiting trustees with business and professional acumen;
- providing trustee induction and other training;
- having clear internal procedures;
- having clear management structures and controls; and
- having clear internal financial controls.

114.22 The Commission usually gives consent to charitable companies that can demonstrate that:

- the trustees have considered the issue thoroughly;
- the trustees have identified a risk against which the Commission allows a charity to purchase insurance and where insuring against this risk could be said to be prudent;
- the trustees are satisfied that the risks cannot be dealt with by other means;

- the cost of insurance is reasonable in relation to the income of the charity;
- the insurance which the charity intends to purchase has the required exclusion clause; and
- the insurance policy fulfils the requirements relating to indemnity of the costs of a defence to a criminal prosecution.

114.23 Most professional advisers see limited benefit in a well-run, professionally staffed charity taking out trustee indemnity insurance as protection for their trustees because:

- the risks faced by trustees can be minimised by good management and clear controls and procedures;
- the Charity Commission restricts the risks that may be covered by trustee indemnity insurance purchased with a charity's assets to those where trustees are at very low risk (see 114.7) either because they would be indemnified by the charity or because the Charity Commission would be most unlikely to require the trustees to make a payment to the charity; and
- trustees are more likely to become the subject of claims if it is known that they have insurance.

However, this type of insurance may still be well worth considering if it protects the charity from the wrongful actions of its trustees.

114.24 A decision about whether or not to take out trustee indemnity insurance should be made by the whole body of trustees. The case for taking out such insurance must depend upon what is in the best, overall interests of the charity. Trustee liability insurance is no panacea. It should be viewed as catastrophe insurance — most unlikely ever to be needed, but invaluable if it is. Trustees should be reminded that even if they have trustee indemnity insurance there remain some situations in which they could be personally liable.

115 Trustees' Annual Report

115.1 The requirement for registered charities to prepare an annual report for each financial year springs from the *Charities Act 1993 s 45*, although for many charities the production of a narrative document which describes the work of the organisation during the year has been a long-standing practice. Scottish charities are also required to produce an annual report under *s 5* of the *LRMPSA 1990*. The detailed contents of the annual report are, to some extent, up to the trustees, as long as they meet the minimum requirements stipulated in the *Charities (Accounts and Reports) Regulations 1995, SI 2000 No 2868* (for registered charities) and comply with the Charities SORP. There are special rules for smaller charities, limited companies and Industrial and Provident Societies, which are described later in this chapter.

The purpose of the annual report is to discharge the trustees' duty of accountability and demonstrate their good stewardship by describing what the charity has achieved during the financial year. Charities with a gross income of more than £10,000 are required by *s 45* of the Act to send an annual report to the Charity Commissioners within ten months of the end of the financial year, together with their accounts and the report of the auditor or independent examiner.

115.2 The annual report is a statutory document and should not be confused with other documents which a charity may produce, such as progress reports or an annual review published for publicity and marketing purposes. It should be signed and dated by at least one of the trustees who has been authorised to do so. Any annual report sent to the Charity Commission must be open to public inspection at all reasonable times. [*Charities Act 1993 s 47(1)*].

Contents of the annual report

115.3 The SORP requires the annual report to contain (i) legal and administrative information and (ii) narrative information explaining what the charity is trying to achieve and how it is going about it. Charities are not required to use these headings but the report must contain the information described under these headings.

Legal and administrative information

115.4 This is usually the driest part of the report, and it is often relegated to the back of the document or appended to it. Details to be included here are:

- the name of the charity as it appears in the register and any other name by which it is known;
- an indication of the nature of the governing document e.g. trust deed, Royal Charter etc. and how it is constituted e.g. if it is a limited company, an unincorporated association etc.;
- the registered charity number and registered company number if applicable;
- the names of all trustees who have acted at any time throughout the year, the method of appointment or election and membership of any subcommittees. Where there is a corporate trustee the names of the directors or other persons managing the corporate trustee;

- details of specific restrictions imposed by the governing document;
- the principal address of the charity and the address of the registered office if the charity is a company.

115.5 In exceptional circumstances where the disclosure of their names or any other information would endanger the trustees, these details may be omitted by agreement with the Charity Commission. However a note giving the reasons for the omission should be included in the Report. In the case of a charitable company, if the Trustees' Annual Report is also to serve as the statutory directors' report, the trustees do not have the option of withholding their names.

Narrative information

115.6 The aim of the narrative section is to explain what the charity is trying to do and how it is going about it. It should describe the charity's achievements, objectives and plans, and link the accounting information with the charity's activities. The revised SORP has a less prescriptive approach to what should be included in this part of the annual report than the original version. It states that the annual report should include:

- an explanation of the objects of the charity;
- the organisational structure and decision-making process;
- relationships with related parties;
- a review of activities, including developments, volunteering, fund-raising etc.;
- policies governing reserves, investments and grant making;
- funds in deficit;
- the trustees' approach to risk management.

115.7 Listing the objects of the charity as set out in the governing document may not be particularly informative, especially if the objects are very broad. What is required here is an informative statement about what the charity is trying to achieve (this could be the vision or mission statement) and how it goes about trying to achieve it.

115.8 The detail of how the charity is organised is often of much greater interest to those preparing the annual report than to the reader. Therefore a balance needs to be struck between useful information and simply reproducing internal systems information. Organograms showing the governance and senior management structures may be helpful.

115.9 The review of activities should cover the development, activities and achievements of the charity during the year, so that the reader can judge its effectiveness and appreciate the progress that has been made. This section should also describe any important events that have taken place during the year and how the charity has responded to them.

115.10 Increasingly charities are focusing on reporting not just their financial performance, or even their outputs, but on the outcomes and the impact of their work. This has been also been a source of comment by the judges, in the annual Charity Accounts and Annual Reports Awards and reflects the need for organisations to demonstrate their effectiveness in other than purely monetary terms. Hence this section of the annual report should support descriptions of achievement with statistical information. The 1995 SORP gave the following as examples: the number of beneficiaries reached, how many times the charity's services have been called upon, and the unit costs for services provided. In practice most charities would now want to look beyond providing this type of additional data and report, for instance, on the impact their work has had on the beneficiaries reached, the beneficiaries' views of the usefulness of the services provided, and the value for money they represent.

115.11 The review of activities should also contain details of the extent to which the charity is dependent on unpaid volunteers, or donations-in-kind, and other intangible sources of income, if not shown in the accounts. For charities where the involvement of volunteers is crucial to some or all of its operations, it is not unusual for a nominal value to be placed on the volunteer time donated in order to communicate its scale and worth.

115.12 There is no statutory or SORP based requirement for a treasurer's report. The 1995 SORP had a detailed requirement for a financial review but this is no longer specifically required. However, some sort of financial comment is an implied requirement since the SORP notes that the report should help readers understand how the numbers in the accounts relate to the structure and activities of the charity. Financial matters that are specifically referred to include:

- effectiveness of fund-raising activities;
- the policy on reserves, the rationale for the policy and the actual reserves level;
- grant making policies;
- funds in deficit.

115.13 It is common for a financial review to be illustrated by graphics. Many charities use imaginative ways of presenting some financial analysis to support the narrative: pie charts and bar charts are common, and histograms are also used. Whatever method is used, graphs should not simply be a way of saving words or breaking up the text: they should be considered as a means of effectively communicating complex ideas. Simply showing an analysis of expenditure in a pie chart may communicate little more than is obvious from the SOFA, whereas a graph depicting longer term trends and demonstrating good stewardship or greater financial needs may be more informative.

Smaller charities

115.14 The regulations permit small charities to prepare a simplified annual report, briefly summarising their main activities and achievements during the year in relation to the charity's objects. A small charity is defined in the SORP as one which is not a limited company and the amount of its gross income for the year does not exceed the threshold set by regulations (currently £250,000 for charities registered in England and Wales).

The pro forma for a trustees' annual report included in the Charity Commission's Receipts and Payments Accounts Pack CC57 asks for details of:

- the charity's name;
- other names the charity is known by;
- registered charity number;
- principal address;

- names of trustees who acted for any part of the period covered by the report, with dates;
- names of any person or body entitled to appoint trustees;
- details of the charity's governing document;
- a brief explanation of its objects;
- particulars of any special trusts;
- particulars of any other trusts which are united with the charity for accounting purposes; and
- the names of advisors e.g. lawyers, investment advisors, bankers;

together with a brief summary of the activities and achievements in support of its objects.

115.15 Theoretically a charity which prepares accruals accounts which comply with the SORP should still prepare a full annual report, since the SORP requirements specifically refer to both annual report and accounts, and the briefer annual report is only permitted under the accounting regulations. In practice smaller charities will often have less to report than larger ones, and even when preparing accounts under the SORP they are entitled to prepare briefer annual reports under the regulations. Where advantage is taken of this arrangement, the accounting policies can helpfully clarify that it is the accounts that comply with the SORP, and not the whole of the charity's reporting procedures.

Limited companies

115.16 Limited companies, whether incorporated with a share capital or by guarantee, have to prepare a director's report, the minimum content of which is laid down by the *Companies Act*. The content depends on whether or not the company is small, as defined by the *Companies Act 1985 s 247*. A small company is one which meets at least two of the following criteria:

- 50 or fewer employees
- turnover not more than £2.8 million
- balance sheet total not more than £1.4 million.

115.17 These criteria are applied to the current and two previous years; a company must fulfill two of the criteria in two of those years to qualify as small.

115.18 For a small company the directors' report need only include the names of all director's who served during the period, principal activities, directors' interests in shareholdings, political and charitable contributions over £200 each, and a statement that the company is taking advantage of the exemptions available to it in preparing the directors report. For larger companies further information is required as set out in *Sch 7* to the *Companies Act*, such as details of material differences between market value and book value of interests in land, liability insurance paid for by the company for its directors, and information about the health, safety and welfare at work of the company's employees.

115.19 Charitable companies have to prepare both a director's report and a trustees' annual report. These can be produced as two separate documents or they can be combined into one provided that it contains the information required by both company and charity law. Where the reports are combined the title page should clearly indicate this.

Industrial and provident societies

115.20 *Section 45* of the *Charities Act 1993* does not apply to exempt charities, so there is no mandatory requirement for Industrial and Provident Societies to produce an annual report unless they are required to do so by other legislation or their own rules, or unless they are specifically requested to do so by the Charity Commissioners under *s 46(5)*.

Public accountability

115.21 The trustees' annual report is a public document, in the same way that the accounts are. For registered charities outside the light touch regime this means that the annual report must be filed with the Charity Commission, along with the accounts, within ten months of the year end. Where the Charity Commission request an annual report from a charity which falls within the light touch regime, then if the request is made within seven months after the year end the ten-month filing rule applies, otherwise the charity has three further months in which to produce the report from the date of the request.

115.22 *Section 47* of the *Charities Act* requires the trustees to provide a copy of the charity's most recent accounts to any member of the public who requests a copy in writing within two months. (In Scotland accounts must be provided within one month.) The charity can charge a reasonable fee for a copy. This section does not specifically refer to annual reports as well, but the purpose of the annual report is to put the accounts in context, and therefore most charities would automatically provide the two together.

The audit of the trustees' annual report

115.23 The auditor of an unincorporated charity has a duty to review the trustees' Annual Report. When the annual report is being planned, if it is to be anything more than a routine statement attached to the main accounts, then the finance staff and auditor need to liaise carefully in advance of production.

115.24 Audits under the *Charities Act 1993* provisions for accounts prepared on an accruals basis require the auditor to consider whether any information contained in the accounts is inconsistent in any material respect with the information presented in the trustees' annual report. Similarly an independent examiner has the same duty, again only in respect of accruals accounts. No such requirement exists under receipts and payments accounting. However, auditors have a further duty, under the Auditors' Code, to prevent their reports from being included with other information which they may consider misleading. Therefore auditors will usually want to check such information to ensure that there are no inconsistencies which could confuse readers of the accounts, or cast doubt on the reliability of the audited information. A similar duty operates in the case of the audit of a limited company in respect of the directors' report and any other report issued alongside it.

116 Trusts

116.1 A trust is the traditional legal structure used by charities in England and Wales. The concept of trusts dates back at least as far as the Middle Ages. Three parties are involved in the setting up of a trust. The first is the donor or settlor who gives the second, the trustee, money or other assets to be used to benefit the third, the beneficiary, sometimes in a particular area, known as the area of benefit. The trustees become the nominal owners of the trust property but they may not benefit personally from it. They hold it in trust on behalf of the beneficiaries and have a duty to ensure that it is used exclusively for the purposes set out in the trust deed. The beneficiaries have a beneficial interest in the trust property.

Term 'trust' can be misleading

116.2 The term 'trust' is widely used with a number of different meanings. Most trusts are private trusts, set up to benefit an individual or a specific group of people, such as family members. Private trusts are not charitable as they do not benefit the public. Public trusts are established to benefit the public, or a relatively large section of the public, rather than identifiable individuals. Most public trusts are charitable. Charitable trusts are different in that they are established for the benefit of the public, or a substantial section of the public, and for purposes, or objects, that are recognised as being wholly and exclusively charitable (see Chapter 15). The governing document of a trust is usually a trust deed, or a declaration of trust, but charitable trusts can also be created under the terms of a will.

116.3 All charities are subject to trust law and all hold their assets on trust. However, not all are legally structured as trusts and even having the word 'Trust' in the name of an organisation does not necessarily imply that the organisation is legally structured as a trust. For example, the National Meningitis Trust is a company limited by guarantee.

Advantages

116.4 Trusts are relatively cheap and simple to set up. There are few statutory requirements governing trusts, so the formalities and expense of administering one are minimised. The number of trustees can be as small as two, though the Charity Commission usually insists on a minimum of three. Trustees are generally appointed by the existing trustees so it is easier to create a board with a balance of skills and experience than it is for organisations with democratically elected boards. Unless the governing document specifies otherwise, the *Trustee Act 1925* gives trustees the power to replace trustees when they retire or when:

- they are out of the UK for a continuous period of more than 12 months;
- they refuse to act as a trustee; or
- they are unfit or incapable of acting as a trustee.

116.5 Most trust deeds contain a power to amend the powers and administrative procedures so changes can be made quickly, easily and relatively cheaply by each trustee executing a supplemental deed. The Charity Commission has to be informed of any amendments.

Disadvantages

116.6 Trusts are unincorporated organisations so the trustees are personally liable for the trust's debts if the trust cannot meet them.

116.7 Charitable trusts may not amend their objects clauses without first obtaining the consent of the courts or the Charity Commission.

116.8 Trustees are appointed rather than elected and this lack of democracy may be regarded as a disadvantage. It certainly makes the trust structure unsuitable for many membership organisations.

116.9 A trust's assets are held by the trustees, rather than the trust, so if a trustee changes the new trustee must be appointed to hold the land or investments. However, this disadvantage can be overcome by incorporating the trustee body (see Chapter 61).

Using the trust structure

116.10 A trust is a suitable legal structure for an organisation such as a grant making foundation that has substantial assets but does not deliver services or employ a large number of staff. It may also be suitable for organisations that have very secure funding, or that do not have long-term financial commitments and so are extremely unlikely ever to be in a position where they cannot meet their financial obligations. Trusts are not suitable structures for organisations with an active membership because the governing body is not democratically elected.

Private charities

116.11 When individuals use their own money to set up charitable trusts to support causes they believe in, they sometimes make the mistake of thinking that these trusts are private and that their affairs should not be open to public scrutiny.

116.12 No such category is recognised either at law or indeed in the Charity Commission's administration of charities, which classifies charities into those established for local, national or overseas benefit, charities connected with the Armed Forces and charities administered by the National Health Service. A so-called private charity should therefore be registered with the Charity Commission unless it has neither permanent endowment, nor the use or occupation of any land, its income from all sources does not exceed £1,000 per annum, or unless it is exempt or expected from registration.

116.13 All registered charities are required to make their accounts available to the public both through the general filing requirement, and the requirement of the *Charities Act 1993 s 47*. The provision of accounts to interested members of the public applies equally to small registered charities operating under the light touch regime. *Charities Accounts (Scotland) Regulations 1992* (*SI 1992 No 2165*) similarly require accounts to be made available to any member of the public, and also for the accounting reference date to be provided on request.

117 VAT

VAT general administration

Introduction

117.1 VAT legislation contains no general relief for charities, and this aspect is often widely misunderstood. There are some specific reliefs contained within the *VAT Act 1994*, which are explored in greater detail at Chapter 121. As far as charities are concerned, their VAT accounting requirements and rules are probably more complicated than those imposed on any commercial business, despite their need to constrain administration costs. The nature of activities carried on by charities can cause problems, especially in the area of recovery of VAT on costs. Great care, therefore, needs to be taken to avoid pitfalls and to maximise VAT opportunities.

117.2 On a general basis, most charitable activities are either non-business activities from a VAT point of view or they are VAT exempt. In either case, this means that input tax on related costs is not recoverable and, indeed, many charities are unable to register for VAT as they do not have any taxable income. As a consequence, many charities have extremely significant irrecoverable VAT costs. These have grown since the introduction of VAT in 1973, with the ever increasing widening of the VAT net and increase in rates that at the time of writing stand at 17.5%.

VAT registration

117.3 Charities are required to register for VAT if their taxable activities exceed the current registration limit: at the time of writing, this is £52,000. In considering its turnover for registration, a charity must take into account its branch activities which are normally regarded as part of the same legal entity as the main charity. Therefore, branch income must be aggregated with the main charity's income to determine whether the registration limit has been exceeded. The registration limit is based on the value of taxable supplies in the previous 12 months or if a charity expects to exceed them within the next 30 days.

117.4 Voluntary registration may be applied for if there are taxable activities, but the value of these does not exceed the registration threshold. Charities should bear in mind that it may actually be to their advantage to register for VAT if the recipients of their supplies can recover VAT charged. This is likely to be particularly the case where supplies are made to local authority or public sector bodies. Similarly, registration may be beneficial if a charity's supplies are zero-rated for VAT.

Business and non-business activities

117.5 As already mentioned, charities that only have non-business activities may not register for VAT. The dividing line between business and non-business activities can often be a very fine one, particularly in the areas of sponsorship and other fund-raising activities. As a particular point, *VATA 1994 s 94* specifically states that a body that has objects which are in the public domain and are of a political, religious, philanthropic, philosophical or patriotic nature will not be treated as carrying on a business in relation to subscriptions paid by members. In return for this subscription, the member must receive no facility or advantage other than the right to participate in the body's management or to receive reports on its activities. However, with effect from 1 December 1999, many subscriptions became exempt, rather than outside the scope of VAT, because subscribers have the right to participate in the management of the body concerned and/or receive reports on its activities. Where a body offers subscribers benefits in addition to those described above, the subscriptions are taxable. The change to the legislation followed on from the judgment of the ECJ case of *Commission of the European Community v Italian Republic (Case C 45/95), [1997] BVC 536.*

117.6 There is no comprehensive definition of 'business' in *VATA 1994*. Nonetheless, it is much wider in scope than the definition associated with direct taxes, and a profit motive is not necessarily decisive. Therefore, although a charity may not be deemed to be in business for direct tax purposes, many activities in the course or furtherance of the charity's objectives are deemed to be business for VAT, even though they may be performed for the benefit of the community. It is therefore crucial for charities to recognise that, for VAT purposes, they are likely to engage in business activities. They therefore need to identify those activities to avoid the risk of exposure to assessments to tax, and possible penalties and interests. It is also important to recognise that VAT incurred on costs in connection with non-business activities is not recoverable. In determining whether a charity's activities are business or non-business, Customs set out the following tests by way of guidance:

- whether the activity is concerned with the making of supplies for a consideration;
- whether the activity has a degree of frequency or scale; and
- whether the activity is continued over a reasonable period of time.

117.7 It does not matter whether the amount charged for the supply equals or is greater than the cost to the charity of making that supply, nor indeed whether the charge is below cost, although special rules do apply for non-business supplies of welfare as dealt with in Chapter 46.

117.8 The following activities are generally considered as being non-business:

- The receipt of donations, bequests, grants etc. However, care needs to be taken in the area of grants, as they could be consideration for services rendered which would mean that they were business income. A donation must not generally give rights or benefits to the donor beyond a simple acknowledgement and mention in programmes etc.
- Voluntary services performed free of charge.
- Sale of shares and other investment activities.

117.9 The following activities are generally regarded as being business activities:

- The sale of donated goods.
- Sales of Christmas cards and other trading items.
- Receipt of sponsorship income.
- Provision of name and logo, for instance, under affinity credit card scheme arrangements.
- Admissions to premises for a charge (e.g. to concerts etc.).
- The provision of membership benefits by clubs, associations and similar bodies in return for a subscription or consideration.

117.10 VAT

Business activities

117.10 It should be remembered that these can be taxable at the standard rate or zero-rated, or can be exempt from VAT. Many charities will become involved with making exempt supplies, for instance in connection with welfare, education and the provision of healthcare. Further details on the making of exempt supplies are contained in Chapter 46.

Recovery of VAT on costs

117.11 This is a very complex issue for charities. It is complicated by their mixture of non-business, exempt and taxable income. VAT is only recoverable to the extent that it relates to taxable activities. Therefore, charities have a problem in calculating their recoverable input tax and the steps that usually need to be followed by a VAT registered charity are as follows.

- Step 1: classify all the activities of the charity into:
  - — non-business;
  - — taxable (i.e. standard and zero-rated);
  - — exempt.
- Step 2: identify all input tax incurred and attribute it as far as possible to the three areas of activities. This is known as direct attribution. VAT attributable to taxable supplies is fully recoverable. The VAT that is attributable to non-business and exempt supplies is generally not recoverable. VAT that cannot be attributed to the income areas, which will broadly be the charity's overhead costs, needs to be apportioned. This VAT is known as 'residual' input tax.
- Step 3: the residual input tax has to be apportioned on a basis to be agreed with Customs and Excise unless the 'standard method' of VAT recovery is used. This is an output based method of calculating the proportion of residual VAT recovery and focuses on the value of supplies. This method can often act to the detriment of charities and in many cases it may be better to seek approval from Customs and Excise to adopt an input tax based method taking the ratio of costs associated with the different activities, rather than comparing income.
- Step 4: under the partial exemption rules, VAT incurred on exempt supplies can be recovered if it falls below a certain limit (the de minimis limit). Currently, the limit is that the input tax must be less than £625 per month on average (£7,500 in the VAT year) and must be no greater than 50% of the total input tax ie the VAT incurred that relates to business activities. Applying this test to each period means that in some period a full recovery of VAT may arise but that the figures for a full year, carrying out the required annual adjustment, will not enable a full recovery. Where this occurs VAT previously claimed by applying the de minimis limit will be repayable to Customs. Conversely, where the de minimis limit has been exceeded in one or more periods such that no VAT recovery was achieved, the annual adjustment may allow recovery if the figures for the full year are de minimis. An annual adjustment must be carried out each year.

Charitable trading subsidiaries

117.12 The same rules apply to trading subsidiaries as apply to charities. However, trading subsidiaries are unlikely to have non-business activities, but may well be partially exempt. One easily overlooked area that needs to be watched is the aspect of supplies between charities and their trading subsidiaries. These may arise in particular on recharges for staff and overheads. Where the charity and the trading subsidiary are separately registered, these supplies will be subject to VAT at the standard rate, subject to the normal rules for turnover etc. It may be possible to include a charity and its trading subsidiary in a VAT group to avoid this problem but the charity must be a corporate body for this to be the case. A special concession applies where staff seconded by the trading subsidiary to a charity work purely on the charity's non-business activities. However, this is often not the case in the area of shared staff. It may be possible to put into place joint employment arrangements which avoid a VAT charge needing to be levied. However, this area is complicated and both tax and legal advice will need to be sought.

Charity Tax Review

117.13 The outcome of the much heralded review of Charity Taxation was disappointing for those concerned about the impact of VAT on charities. The regime is still complicated and there has been no lessening of the irrecoverable VAT burden that charities suffer. Changes to the rules for advertising and fund-raising events were welcomed and are described in Chapters 4 and 50 respectively. In addition, the threshold below which charities and other businesses do not have to account for VAT when they deregister was raised from £250 to £1,000.

118 Volunteers

118.1 About 80% of charities are run entirely by volunteers and many of the largest professionally staffed charities such as Oxfam and the Imperial Cancer Research Fund also rely heavily on volunteers, particularly for fund-raising. Without volunteers much charitable work could not be done and much social need would go unmet. Volunteers are not just a source of unpaid labour. They often bring particular commitment and dedication to their work and can lend legitimacy and credibility to an organisation. Potential major donors are more likely to listen to an appeal from people they regard as peers who themselves give willingly of their time to a particular charity, than to an appeal from one of the charity's paid fund-raisers.

118.2 The use of volunteers may give rise to a number of legal issues. These should be given serious consideration to protect both charities and volunteers. Charities have legal responsibilities for the health and safety of their volunteers and must ensure that these are discharged. They also need to be clear about whether or not their volunteer management practices could be interpreted as establishing a contractual relationship between the volunteers and the organisation or the trustees. Volunteers should not find themselves with unexpected tax or national insurance liabilities or find that their volunteering has an unwelcome impact on any state benefits they may be receiving.

Expenses

118.3 Volunteers are entitled to be reimbursed for any out of pocket expenses incurred as a result of their volunteering. These expenses are not subject to tax or national insurance and do not affect a person's entitlement to benefits. Reimbursement of genuine expenses does not turn a volunteer into an employee.

Remuneration

118.4 Some volunteers also receive remuneration, often in the form of an honorarium or benefit in kind. Unless the person is on an official employment training or return to work scheme which specifically allows payment tax free, any remuneration will be taken into account when assessing an individual's liability for tax and national insurance and may affect their entitlement to benefits. A benefit such as free or subsidised accommodation is generally regarded as remuneration, but perks such as discounts on the price of the charity's publications or events are generally not classed as remuneration for tax purposes.

118.5 Payment of remuneration does not of itself turn a volunteer into an employee for the purposes of employment law. It is legally possible to be a 'paid volunteer' i.e. an employee for the purposes of tax and national insurance but with no rights under employment law. It is the existence of a legally binding contractual relationship between the 'volunteer' and the organisation that gives the 'volunteer' rights under employment law. If there is a contractual relationship, and this does not need to be in the form of a written contract, then the 'volunteer' will no longer legally be a volunteer, but an employee or self-employed. For there to be a contractual relationship, there must be an agreement between the parties to the contract that some form of payment, or something else of material value, will be given in return for work, goods or services and the parties to the contract must intend there to be a legally binding relationship.

Employment law

118.6 Employment law was framed to protect employees and employers and does not always meet the needs of charities, particularly those charities that want to remunerate their volunteers but do not want to give them employment rights. Charities may wish to consider making it clear in all relevant discussions and documentation that their relationship with their volunteers is a voluntary one and is not intended to be legally binding. However, this may not be sufficient to protect the charity, as industrial tribunals generally assume that if one party agrees to pay another for work, the parties intend the relationship to be legally binding. In some circumstances, for example if payments are more than a token amount, it may not be advisable to state that the relationship is not intended to be legally binding, because such a statement could be interpreted as depriving an employee of their statutory employment rights. This would be an illegal act if done by an employer.

118.7 Applying employment law to volunteers is bound to give rise to decisions which appear contrary to common sense or to lack consistency. For example, in one instance a tribunal ruled that volunteers who were paid for their work were not held to have a contract of employment (*Milton and Another v Department of Transport [1944] COIT 5086/44*) because they were carrying out a voluntary public service and another volunteer was held to have a contract of employment, although she did not receive payment, because she had received training and was under an obligation to repay the charity if she ceased to be a volunteer without good reason before working for the charity for a specified number of hours. Also there was an expectation that, after working for a certain number of hours without payment, at some time in the future the volunteer might be paid for further work (*Maria De Lourdes Armitage v Relate and others [1994] COIT 43538/94*).

118.8 Many charities regard having some sort of written agreement or contract with their volunteers as good practice. However, since some aggrieved volunteers have successfully obtained damages from charities as a result of industrial tribunal hearings, much greater care has to be taken with the wording of such agreements. If a charity wants to ensure that its unpaid volunteers are engaged in voluntary work rather than employment, any volunteer agreement should make it clear that the relationship is binding in honour only and is not intended to be legally binding. It should refer to intentions, expectations and privileges rather than rights and obligations. Employment terms such as 'contract', 'leave', 'disciplinary and grievance procedures', 'promotion' and 'dismissal' should be avoided. For example, the volunteer agreement should include phrases such as 'Charity X expects its volunteers to turn up on the day they have agreed to work unless they are sick or have notified the charity in advance that they will be away on holiday' rather than phrases like 'Volunteer X's hours of work will be from 9.30 am to 12.30 every Monday. Volunteer X will be entitled to take 4 weeks annual leave'.

Benefits

118.9 The rules concerning the receipt of benefits by volunteers are complex and change frequently. It is good practice to check the position regularly with the National Centre for Volunteering (or Volunteer Development Scotland) or the relevant benefits agencies. Volunteers in receipt of benefits may be required to inform the relevant benefits agency that they are doing either paid or unpaid voluntary work. If this is the case, it is the volunteer's responsibility to inform the agency, not the charity's, though it is good practice for charities to remind volunteers that they may need to do so.

118.10 Volunteers

118.10 There are no restrictions on the number of hours volunteers in receipt of benefits can work for a charity with the exception of those receiving incapacity benefit or severe disablement allowance, who may not do more than 16 hours of voluntary work a week, and those in receipt of jobseeker's allowance, who must be available to work 40 hours a week and to attend for interview or start a job at 48 hours notice. Jobseeker's allowance is reduced if a volunteer is paid more than £5 a week, or £15 if they are entitled to the higher earnings disregard. State retirement pension, war disablement pension, war widow's pension and widow's benefits are not affected by paid or unpaid voluntary work. Housing benefit, council tax benefit and family credit are not affected by unpaid voluntary work but may be affected by paid voluntary work. Statutory maternity pay is not affected by volunteering, paid or unpaid. Maternity allowance is not affected by unpaid voluntary work but is not paid for any day on which paid voluntary work is done. Invalid care allowance is not affected by unpaid voluntary work unless it prevents the volunteer from caring for the invalid for at least 35 hours a week. Volunteers can receive up to £50 a week for paid voluntary work but above this level the allowance is stopped. Income support is not affected by unpaid voluntary work, but if the work is paid the volunteer will start to have their benefit reduced once they earn more than £5 a week, or £15 if they are entitled to the higher earnings disregard.

Health and safety

118.11 All charities have a common law duty of care to protect the health and safety of their volunteers and if they are employers they have a statutory duty to protect the health and safety of the public which includes their volunteers. It is good practice to treat volunteers in exactly the same way as employees regarding matters of health and safety, even though health and safety legislation may not apply to volunteers in exactly the same way as it does to employees. Volunteers should be trained to carry out their work safely, in ways which do not put them or the public at risk.

Insurance

118.12 There is no statutory duty for charities to extend their employer's liability insurance to cover volunteers, but it is good practice for them to do so. As employer's liability insurance only covers claims arising from the employer's negligence many charities also take out personal accident insurance to cover accidents or death that happen in the course of volunteering but which do not result from the charity's negligence.

118.13 Charities have vicarious liability for the acts of their employees but not for the acts of their volunteers. Therefore a member of the public could bring a claim against a volunteer, for example for damages resulting from being given incorrect advice by the volunteer. Charities should protect their volunteers by making sure that either their public liability insurance, or their professional indemnity insurance, or their product liability insurance indemnifies volunteers if any claim is brought against them.

Driving

118.14 Volunteers do not need to notify their insurer if they use their vehicle only between their home and their usual place of volunteering. However, if they use it during the course of their volunteering activity they must notify their insurer in writing. They are entitled to be reimbursed by the charity if their insurer increases the premium because the vehicle is used for voluntary work. If volunteers claim for mileage they must keep a record of all journeys made on behalf of the charity.

Discrimination

118.15 The *Race Relations Act 1976* and the *Sex Discrimination Act 1975* apply only to volunteers who have a contract with a charity. *The Disability Discrimination Act 1995* applies only to volunteers who have a contract with a charity which employs 15 or more people. However, as a matter of good practice, charities should recruit and treat their volunteers as if these Acts applied to them i.e. they should not discriminate against volunteers on the grounds of race, colour, ethnic origin, religion, gender, marital status or disability, unless such action is justified.

Age restrictions

118.16 There is no statutory minimum or maximum age for volunteering, but some insurance policies will include restrictions. Where this is the case volunteers should be informed. The common law duty of care a charity has to protect the health and safety of their volunteers will be higher where the volunteers are children or young people. The *House to House Collections Act 1939* requires children under the age of 16 to be accompanied by an adult if they take part in house to house fund-raising.

Volunteers from overseas

118.17 There are no restrictions on volunteers who are nationals of European Union countries or Iceland or Norway. Most nationals of other countries will need a work permit to take up employment, paid or unpaid. Those who do not need a work permit in order to do paid work face no restrictions on volunteering. Overseas students who volunteer are required to complete form OSS1, available from Job Centres. There are no restrictions on volunteering for refugees and people given exceptional leave to remain in the UK. Asylum seekers are allowed to do voluntary work, provided that they receive no payment, other than genuine reimbursement of expenses, and do not receive any benefits apart from the training necessary for them to do their volunteer assignment.

119 Wales

Regulation

119.1 Welsh charities are subject to the same charity legislation as English charities, apart from minor differences relating principally to the use of the Welsh language. Similarly UK-wide legislation, such as company law, employment law, tax law and the law on human rights also applies to Welsh charities.

Devolution

119.2 Devolution and the establishment of the Welsh Assembly have brought new opportunities for Welsh charities to engage in public debate and influence policy making. *Clause 114* of the *Government of Wales Act 1998* requires the Welsh Assembly 'to made a scheme setting out how it proposes, in the exercise of its functions, to promote the interests of relevant voluntary organisations'. It also states that the scheme should specify how the Assembly will provide assistance to relevant voluntary organisations, how this will be monitored, and how it will consult voluntary organisations on matters of concern to them.

Compact

119.3 The Welsh Office and the voluntary and community sector in Wales have agreed a Compact as a framework for future working relationships. The Compact highlights the main commitments and expectations of both parties with supporting papers that include policy statements on volunteering, community development and working in partnership and procedures for representation and funding administration.

Voluntary Sector Scheme

119.4 The Voluntary Sector Scheme will be based on the Compact and will set out the practical arrangements to enable voluntary and community organisations to engage with Assembly Secretaries and committees. These will include:

- A National Assembly-Voluntary Sector Forum made up of members of the Assembly and elected representatives of the sector to oversee the implementation of the Voluntary Sector Scheme;
- Meetings between each Assembly Secretary and Subject committee with relevant voluntary sector networks in order to plan co-operation;
- Panels of voluntary sector advisors who can be called on to serve on Assembly working groups and give advice to committees.

The Voluntary Sector Assembly Centre

119.5 The Wales Council for Voluntary Action (WCVA) has established a Voluntary Sector Assembly Centre in Cardiff near the Assembly building. It offers practical support and advice to help voluntary organisations make the most of the opportunities devolution has brought. The centre provides:

- An information service on the Welsh Assembly's work programme, documents and legislation and information to Assembly Members about the voluntary sector, relevant contacts, key issues and priorities;

- Briefings and advice on how the Assembly operates and how voluntary organisations can best take their issues through the system;
- 'Hot desks' for voluntary organisations to use when working at the Assembly;
- A meeting place for voluntary organisations to meet Members of the Assembly and hold press conferences and receptions.

Language

119.6 Special provisions exist recognising the right of Welsh organisations to use the Welsh language in their official documents. These apply separately to limited companies and registered charities.

Limited companies

119.7 Documents delivered to the Registrar of Companies under either the *Companies Act 1985* or the *Insolvency Act 1986*, which relate to a company whose registered office is in Wales, may be in Welsh as long as they are accompanied by a certified translation into English. This requirement is amplified in the legislation specifically to cover areas such as group accounting and filing, but also the annual accounts, directors' report and audit report filed with the Registrar, as well as subsidiary accounts which are not included in a group consolidation.

119.8 Under the *Companies Act 1985* Welsh companies are required to state that they are limited companies, even if they are incorporated under the Welsh equivalent 'cyfngedig' (shortened to cyf).

Registered charities

119.9 Registered charities with income of over £10,000 are required to disclose their charitable status on their official documents. The Charity Commission has clarified in their guide to the legislation that where a document is produced entirely in Welsh, then the equivalent (Elusen cofrestredig) is permissible.

119.10 A limited company whose name does not include the words 'charity' or 'charitable' must disclose its charitable status on all correspondence and similar material. This does not apply if the Welsh equivalents (elusen, elusennol) are used and the related documents are entirely in Welsh.

Further information

119.11 Further information can be obtained from the Wales Council for Voluntary Action.

120 Welfare to Work

120.1 People living on benefits are amongst the poorest in society. The government believes that the most effective way to tackle poverty, while at the same time keeping public spending down, is to help people off welfare dependency into employment. 'Welfare to work' is the generic term for a series of Government initiatives to help specific groups of people into work by giving them work experience and the chance to obtain qualifications. Welfare to Work impacts on the voluntary sector in three ways. Firstly, it will reduce the number of people needing to seek help from certain charities. Secondly, the initiatives allow some voluntary organisations to help their beneficiaries in a totally different way. Instead of 'giving them a fish to feed them for a day', employment training will be equivalent to 'teaching them to fish so they can feed themselves for life'. Thirdly, the funding provided for the Voluntary Sector Option provides a source of subsidised labour that should enable a charity to expand their work. However, the costs of training and managing those taking part in the scheme have to be offset against the reduced labour costs. The main New Deal initiatives are described below.

New Deal for Young Unemployed People

120.2 Young people aged 18 to 24 who have been unemployed for at least six months, and who are receiving Jobseeker's Allowance, qualify to take part in this initiative. It provides opportunities for work in a subsidised job with an employer, work in the voluntary sector, or with the Environmental Task Force, or full-time training and education to build on basic skills and obtain a recognised qualification.

New Deal for Long-term Unemployed People

120.3 This initiative will pay a subsidy of £75 a week for up to six months (or 1 year if the jobseeker is disabled) to employers taking on jobseekers aged 25 or over who have been unemployed for at least two years. The employer is expected to pay employees taken on under this scheme at the same rate as that paid to existing employees.

New Deal for Lone Parents

120.4 The government has recognised that one of the main barriers preventing lone parents from seeking employment is the lack of low-cost childcare provision. Therefore, this initiative, which focuses on helping lone parents living on Income Support to find work through personalised job search help, advice and training, will also provide resources for after-school childcare, much of which may be provided by voluntary organisations.

New Deal for Disabled People

120.5 The initiative aims to help people with disabilities and those who have experienced long-term illness to reduce their dependency on benefits. It is open to people who are claiming incapacity benefits, including Incapacity Benefit Severance Disablement Allowance and Income Support by virtue of incapacity and is entirely voluntary. Personal advisers offer tailored support in finding suitable jobs or training opportunities.

New Deal for the Over 50s

120.6 This scheme helps people aged over 50 to return to work where they or their partner have been on benefits for more than six months. It is a voluntary scheme available to people who are economically inactive as well as unemployed. As many workers aged over 50 have skills that have become rusty or superseded the scheme offers in-work training grants of up to £750 to help them acquire accredited training to take up and keep a new job in addition to personalised advice.

New Deal for Partners of Unemployed People

120.7 This initiative is targeted at the partners of people who have been unemployed for six months or more and offers them specialist advice to help them back to work.

New Deal for Communities

120.8 The New Deal for Communities provides funding for the intensive regeneration of some of the poorest neighbourhoods, by helping local people improve their areas by tackling worklessness, reducing crime, raising educational attainment and improving health.

Employment Zones

120.9 Employment Zones complement the New Deal for Communities, tackling problems faced by areas where unemployment is particularly high and persistent. Personal job accounts combine monies previously available for benefits, employment and career services to provide individually tailored packages designed to help people aged 25 and over to find and keep work.

Taxation of New Deal Payments

120.10 The full wages of New Deal participants in the Employment Option or who are in waged placements under the Voluntary Sector or Environmental Task Force Options are taxable in the same way as the wages of any other employee. The weekly subsidies paid to employers do not affect the amount of tax that is due on the wages.

Participating in the Voluntary Sector Option

120.11 The Voluntary Sector Option is usually delivered through a two-tier structure. Firstly, there is a single organisation or a consortium of organisations that contracts to provide all the Voluntary Sector Option places in an area. This organisation or consortium is known as the 'Lead Provider'. It takes overall responsibility for the provision of all aspects of this Option, including arranging training and help with jobsearch. Secondly, there are the organisations that actually provide placements to participants. They are sub-contracted by the Lead Provider and are known as 'Placement Providers'.

120.12 Placement Providers must provide high quality work experience for a minimum of 30 hours a week for six months. This must include a short period of induction. They are also expected to help participants with their search for a job and arrange for them to spend the equivalent of at least one day a week in good quality training or education that enables the participant to work towards a recognised, approved qualification such as a NVQ (or in Scotland a SVQ). Training can be provided on the placement or it can be sub-contracted to a local college, training provider or TEC and it can be delivered flexibly in a block or on day release. Participants can choose to work towards a qualification related to the work they are doing on their placement or one that gives them transferable skills to enable them to apply for other types of work.

120.13 At the end of the placement the Placement Provider gives participants a certificate and a work reference reflecting their achievements and progress against their personal New Deal Action Plan.

120.14 The total placement fee per participant varies according to the costs of each project and can be used as 'match funding' in bidding for other sources of funding such as the Single Regeneration Budget and the European Social Fund. The placement fee is made up as follows:

- 20% for planning and induction;
- 50% for supervision, materials, clothing, administrative costs, travel and jobsearch expenses;
- 20% value added fee to reward improvements in the participant's employability;
- 10% outcome fee payable on the participant finding sustainable employment or self-employment.

120.15 Placement providers also receive a training allowance of £750 per participant to go towards the cost of training.

120.16 Charities wanting to join the scheme should start by attending a briefing session held by the Employment Service New Deal Co-ordinator in their Region where all the necessary information is provided. Bids are assessed by Employment Service Regional Contracting Teams and Government Offices for the Regions using a nationally agreed scoring system. Contracts vary in length according to the nature of the project but can be for up to three years.

121 Zero Rates for VAT

121.1 Certain supplies of goods and services made to and by charities are zero-rated under UK law to assist them in their work. This relief is estimated to save charities about one-third of their potential VAT costs. The zero-rating provisions are found in the *Value Added Tax Act 1994 8 Sch* and reliefs that particularly assist charities are as follows.

- Group 3 — books, etc.
- Group 4 — talking books for the blind and handicapped and wireless sets for the blind
- Group 5 — construction of buildings, etc.
- Group 6 — protected buildings
- Group 8 — transport
- Group 12 — drugs, medicines, aids for the handicapped, etc.
- Group 15 — charities, etc.

121.2 A zero-rated supply is the most favourable for VAT purposes, for the supplier is entitled to recover input tax (i.e. VAT on costs) on the purchase of goods and services attributable to that supply but does not have to account for VAT on the supply which it makes.

121.3 If a charity makes only zero-rated supplies it may request exemption from registration. This may be granted at the discretion of Customs. Exemption saves the charity the trouble and expense of having to keep proper records and accounts for VAT purposes and render returns, but input tax on purchases of goods and services for the charity may then not be recovered.

121.4 A charity should take professional advice as to whether it is required to register for VAT and, if not, whether it would be beneficial to do so.

121.5 The Customs and Excise Notices mentioned in this chapter are available from your local VAT office. The information contained in these Notices and in this section is for general guidance only, and can never be a substitute for detailed professional advice which will take into account a charity's precise circumstances. The zero-rated supplies made by and to charities are considered in greater detail below.

Zero-rated supplies made to or by charities under *Group 15*

Sales of donated goods

121.6 The sale of donated goods by a charity, or a trading subsidiary of a charity that arranges to give all the profits of the sale to the charity, is zero-rated under the provisions of *VATA 1994 Group 15, item 1* provided:

- the goods have been donated to the charity or its trading subsidiary with the intention that they will be sold to raise funds;
- the sale takes place as a result of the goods having been made available to the general public for purchase e.g. in a shop, at a charity auction or elsewhere; and

- the sale does not take place as a result of any arrangements relating to the goods entered into by the parties to the sale before the goods were made available to the general public. In addition, with effect from 1 April 2000, zero rating applies to the sale of donated goods to disabled people and people receiving means tested benefits, and donated goods that are of too poor a quality to be sold to the public e.g. unsaleable clothing that is sold to rag merchants and similar businesses.

121.7 These provisions assist charity shops in particular as they do not have to add VAT to their sales. However, these shops often sell 'trade' goods that they buy in, as well as donated goods, and the zero-rate does not extend to the resale of purchased goods e.g. new T-shirts, gift items or confectionery.

121.8 Customs' view is that the sale of bequeathed land or buildings by a charity does not qualify for zero-rating under this provision. Their argument here is that, in most cases where dwellings or land are bequeathed to a charity, the property would not have been a business asset of the deceased person or the charity. Any supply of the property is thus normally outside the scope of VAT and the charity is not able to claim input tax deduction on expenses in connection with the sale. Any charities which have zero-rated land or property sales under this provision should review their position.

121.9 *Item 2* of *Group 15* zero-rates goods donated by businesses to charities for sale or export. Ordinarily a business donor would have to account for VAT on such goods. Property which is bequeathed to a charity does not qualify as donated for sale or export unless it is bequeathed specifically for that purpose. Also, goods donated for the charity's own use do not qualify.

Export of goods

121.10 *Item 3* zero-rates the export of any goods by a charity to a place outside the EC whether or not in return for consideration. This provision enables a charity to recover VAT on goods which have been donated or purchased by the charity for export. As such activities are zero-rated, charities are entitled to reclaim VAT incurred on the goods themselves and any handling, transport, storage or associated overheads, subject to the normal rules.

121.11 Charities must be able to satisfy Customs that the goods have been exported. They are required to keep records of exports and should be able to provide a clear and ready link between these records and the proof of export required. For example, the normal evidence of sea freight exports is a copy of the bill of lading or sea waybill or equivalent.

Donated medical and scientific equipment

121.12 Zero-rating applies under *item 4* of *Group 15* to the supply of 'relevant goods' for donation to a nominated 'eligible body' where the funds for the purchase (or letting on hire) are provided by a charity or from voluntary contributions. The goods must be supplied for donation; that is, the goods must be supplied to a nominated eligible body which will in turn donate them. Where the donee of the goods is not a charity it must not have contributed wholly or in part to the purchase of the goods.

121.13 The supply of 'relevant goods' to an 'eligible body' may be zero-rated under *item 5* if that body pays for them with funds provided by a charity or from voluntary contributions.

121.14 Zero-rating also applies under *item 5* to the supply of 'relevant goods' to an 'eligible body' which is itself a charitable institution providing care or medical or surgical treatment for 'handicapped' persons. 'Handicapped' means chronically sick or disabled. Where the 'eligible body' is a charitable institution, it is not regarded as providing care or medical or surgical treatment for handicapped persons unless the supply is made in a 'relevant establishment' and the majority of the recipients are 'handicapped' persons. A 'relevant establishment' is:

- a day centre other than a day centre which exists primarily as a place for activities that are social or recreational or both; or
- an institution which is approved, licensed or registered under the relevant social legislation or which is exempt from those obligations by that legislation.

121.15 Notwithstanding the above, a supply will qualify for zero-rating where an 'eligible body' provides medical care to handicapped persons in their own homes, and the 'relevant goods' are used in or in connection with the provision of that care.

121.16 By concession, where 'relevant goods' are supplied to a charity:

- whose sole purpose and function is to provide a range of care services to meet the needs of handicapped people (of which transport might form a part); or
- which provides transport services predominantly to handicapped people;

the supply of those goods will be zero-rated, as will the repair and maintenance of those goods and the supply of any further goods in connection with that repair or maintenance. This concession applies to supplies made on or after 26 November 1996. In order to be eligible for this concession, a charity must demonstrate that it meets the requirements of sub-paragraphs (i) or (ii) through its charitable aims and objectives, its publicity and advertising material, its day to day operations, any documents which it has issued for the purpose of obtaining funding from a third party such as a local authority and any other evidence that may be relevant.

121.17 The repair and maintenance of 'relevant goods' is zero-rated under *item 6* provided they are owned by an 'eligible body' and the services are paid for by a charity or from voluntary contributions. It does not matter how the goods themselves were bought in the first place. Spare parts etc. supplied in connection with the repairs and maintenance are also relieved. If the owner or hirer of the goods repaired or maintained is not a charity, it must not have contributed, wholly or in part, to the cost of the repairs or spares.

121.18 The goods and services can only be zero-rated if the supplier is registered for VAT and he is given a declaration in a prescribed form that the goods are either being purchased by an 'eligible body' or are to be donated to an 'eligible body'.

121.19 'Relevant goods' cover the following areas:

- medical equipment;
- scientific equipment;
- computer equipment;
- video equipment;
- sterilising equipment;

- laboratory or refrigeration equipment for use in medical or veterinary research, training, diagnosis or treatment;
- ambulances:
  - — vehicles designed or adapted for transporting the sick or handicapped, including minibuses adapted for the carriage of handicapped persons in wheelchairs
  - — unadapted motor vehicles with more than 7 and fewer than 50 seats used by an eligible body that provides care for blind, deaf, mentally handicapped or terminally ill people mainly for their transportation
  - — rescue equipment solely for the purpose of rescue or first aid services undertaken by a charity providing such services.

121.20 'Eligible body' covers all health authorities and NHS trusts in England and Wales and their equivalents in Scotland and Northern Ireland. It also covers hospitals whose activities are not carried on for a profit; research institutions not seeking to make profits; and charitable institutions providing care or medical or surgical treatment for handicapped persons.

Advertising

121.21 With effect from 1 April 2000 the range of charity advertising qualifying for zero-rating has been extended. Zero-rate relief was also extended to certain fund-raising products such as collection boxes, envelopes and label stickers. More details are given in Chapter 4.

Medicinal products

121.22 *Item 9* zero-rates the supply to a charity, providing care or medical or surgical treatment for human beings or any animals, or engaging in medical or veterinary research, of a medicinal product where the supply is solely for use by the charity in such care, treatment or research. This relief is restricted to charities that will be using the products or substances themselves; a charity which donates these items to another charity cannot obtain relief.

121.23 Customs are wary of attempts to obtain relief under *item 9* for 'equipment' which does not qualify under *items 4* and *5* above, on the grounds that it is a medicinal product. Such attempts will generally fail on the basis that an explanatory note to this item explicitly excludes from relief 'an instrument, apparatus or appliance'. Medicinal products which qualify for relief are those capable of being consumed or otherwise absorbed into the body. For example, a pill to be taken orally would fall within this description, whereas a syringe would fall outside it. Customs have provided the following guidance on *item 9* in their internal guidance to officers. Medical and veterinary research should be given its technical meaning i.e. it is restricted to activities which are directed towards opening up new areas of knowledge or understanding, or initial development of new techniques, rather than towards mere quantitative additions to human knowledge. Medical or veterinary treatment includes the administration of medicines, physiotherapy and surgery.

121.24 Imports by charities of medicinal products can be zero-rated provided the charity gives the supplier a certified declaration that the goods are to be used for the specified purpose. The appropriate declaration must be presented with the Customs entry form. This relief also applies to imports of talking books for the blind and handicapped and wireless sets for the blind (see 121.63 below) subject to the same condition.

121.25 *Item 10* zero-rates the supply to a charity of a substance directly used for synthesis or testing in the course of medical or veterinary research.

121.26 Further helpful guidance on this complex area of VAT reliefs is given in Customs and Excise Notice 701/6, printed in March 1997 and available from local VAT offices.

Construction of buildings, etc.: *Group 5*

121.27 It is important that planning advice is taken at an early stage in relation to any construction or property development to be carried out by a charity. This is an area where costs are high, but equally an area where high savings are potentially available. *VATA 1994 8 Sch Group 5* provides a number of reliefs for buildings (or parts of buildings) intended for use solely for a relevant residential or charitable purpose (referred to as 'qualifying buildings').

Construction services

121.28 The supply of services and related supplies of goods in the course of construction of the following attract zero rating:

- a building intended for use solely for a 'relevant residential purpose';
- a building intended for use solely for a 'relevant charitable purpose'; and
- the conversion by a housing association of a non-residential building into dwellings or a building intended solely for a relevant residential purpose.

121.29 Use for a relevant residential purpose is defined as use as:

(i) a home or other institution providing residential accommodation for children;

(ii) a home or other institution providing residential accommodation with personal care for persons in need of personal care by reason of old age, disablement, past or present dependence on alcohol or drugs or past or present mental disorder;

(iii) a hospice;

(iv) residential accommodation for students or school pupils;

(v) residential accommodation for members for any of the armed forces;

(vi) a monastery, nunnery or similar establishment; or

(vii) an institution which is the sole or main residence of at least 90% of its residents.

121.30 Note that the above do not include use as a hospital, prison or similar institution or a hotel, inn or similar establishment. However, where, for instance, relief is available under (ii), the fact that the building is licensed as a hospital does not preclude zero-rating.

121.31 Use for a relevant charitable purposes means use by a charity in either or both of the following ways, namely:

(*a*) otherwise than in the course or furtherance of a business;

(*b*) as a village hall or similarly in providing social or recreational facilities for a local community.

The relief under (*b*) applies to church halls and also following recent case law to buildings constructed for charitable playing field and recreation ground organisations (e.g. cricket pavilions and changing rooms), provided there is use by the local community.

121.32 The zero-rating provisions only relate to that part of the building intended solely for a qualifying purpose i.e. for a relevant residential or charitable purpose. Thus if a builder constructs a shop with a flat above it the construction work relating to the flat will be zero-rated, whilst that relating to the shop will be standard-rated.

121.33 In relation to a building intended to be used for a relevant residential purpose, Customs have indicated that the existence of an office is ignored. Similarly, where a building is to be used for a charitable purpose, Customs apply a concession whereby business use will be ignored provided that this is likely to constitute less than 10% of the total usage. However, there is no provision for apportionment if the qualifying use falls below 90%.

121.34 Non-business/business use was historically based on the time a building was available for use for charitable as opposed to business purposes. With effect from 1 June 2000 the use of a building can be measured by reference to:

- time (entire building);
- time (parts of a building only);
- floor space (entire building); or
- head count (entire building).

However, if a method other than a time based method applied to the entire building is used, prior written approval from Customs must be obtained.

121.35 The zero-rating relief is conditional on the charity providing the contractor carrying out the construction work with a certificate specifying that the building is intended to be used for a qualifying purpose before the supply is made. Zero-rating by certificate is only available to contractors or others making supplies direct to the customer. Certificates must not be given to sub-contractors.

121.36 The construction of a building does not include the conversion, reconstruction or alteration of an existing building. However, the construction of an annexe to an existing building is eligible for zero-rating if it is intended for use solely for a relevant charitable purpose and is capable of functioning independently of the existing building. Additionally, the main access to the annexe must not be via the existing building and the supply must be covered by a qualifying use certificate.

121.37 The contractor can also zero-rate the supplies of building materials used in the course of construction, with broad exceptions including carpets, built-in furniture (other than kitchen units and some basic bedroom wardrobes), and appliances such as cookers, fridges etc.

Design and build contracts

121.38 The services of an architect, surveyor or any person acting as a consultant or in a supervisory capacity are standard-rated regardless of whether zero-rating is available for the works. However, a charity may obtain relief from VAT on those services if they are subsumed in a design and build contract. Therefore, if under the terms of the contract between a charity and a contractor, the design, construction works and materials are supplied without any separate identification of the design element, the VAT liability of the design element follows that of the building. For example, it will be zero-rated if the supply by the contractor is zero-rated. Customs will need to be satisfied the supply is a composite one of zero-rated construction services.

Disposal of interests in qualifying buildings

121.39 Zero-rating relief is available where the developer of a building is either selling for the first time the freehold interest, or is granting, assigning or surrendering a lease of over 21 years in a building intended solely for a qualifying residential or charitable purpose.

121.40 Where only part of the building qualifies for zero-rating under these provisions, the consideration for the supply must be apportioned. Further, the supplier must obtain a certificate with regard to the intended use of the property before the supply takes place in order for the zero-rating provisions to apply. These conditions are consistent with the provisions relating to the construction of such buildings explained above.

121.41 In relation to a lease or tenancy zero-rating is restricted to the premium, if any, or if not to the first payment of rent due. This limits the recovery of VAT incurred to the construction of the building and not the ongoing upkeep and maintenance of the building which will be exempt from VAT if the building is a qualifying one. A zero-rating relief also applies to the first grant of a major interest of a 'converted' building. This applies where the developer has converted a building that was previously non-residential into a residential building or, alternatively, when the building was originally constructed for residential use but has not been lived in since 1 April 1973. The relief might arise, for instance, in the case of the conversion of an office block into a student hall of residence. Unfortunately, it does not assist in the conversion into an otherwise charitable building that is not residential.

121.42 In the above cases, the zero-rating does not extend to carpeting materials, soft furnishings, built in electrical appliances such as cookers etc. when the developer must disallow the VAT he incurs on the purchase.

Change of use

121.43 The zero-rating relief for the first grant or construction of qualifying use buildings is withdrawn if the building is used for non-qualifying purposes. [*VATA 1994 10 Sch para 1*]. A charge to VAT is triggered where within a ten-year period the person to whom the relevant zero-rated supply was made:

- grants an interest in, right over or licence to occupy all or any part of the building, after which the building (or part of it) is not intended to be used for a relevant residential or charitable purpose; or
- uses the building for a non-qualifying purpose.

121.44 The value of the self-supply is equal to the VAT that would have been chargeable had the original supply not qualified for zero-rating. There is no concession for the intermediate qualifying use and thus this is a tough claw back mechanism on which care should be taken.

Conversions of non-residential buildings — concessions for charities

121.45 Some charitable organisations are prevented by legal constraints from selling a converted property, even to an associated organisation. They are, therefore, unable to sell the freehold or grant a lease of over 21 years in order to qualify for zero-rate relief and recovery of their conversion costs. Nor do they qualify for a refund under the do-it-yourself scheme (see 121.53 below) if the conversion is carried out in the course or furtherance of business. However, the Commissioners will consider refunds of VAT on an extra-statutory basis (News Release 15/96 13 March 1996). A charitable organisation which considers that it qualifies is advised to write to its local VAT office.

Protected buildings: *Group 6*

Approved alterations

121.46 From 1 April 1989 the supply in the course of an 'approved alteration' to a 'protected building' may be zero-rated. Generally speaking, an approved alteration means a major alteration which affects the character of a 'protected building' for which listed building consent has been obtained. In the case of a church which is a 'protected building', any alterations rank as 'approved' for this purpose.

121.47 Approved alterations do not include any works of repair or maintenance or any incidental alteration to the fabric of a building which results from the carrying out of repairs or maintenance work. The construction of a building separate from, but in the curtilage of, a protected building does not qualify as an approved alteration, but may in itself qualify for zero-rating under the *Group 5* provisions.

121.48 The supply of building materials in connection with the construction services are also zero-rated. The services of an architect, surveyor or any person acting as consultant or in a supervisory capacity are standard-rated. However, if a charity negotiates a design and build contract (see 121.38), the VAT liability of the design element of the project follows that of the building and may be zero-rated. A 'protected building' is strictly defined as a building which is:

- a listed building or scheduled monument within the meaning of the relevant statutes; and
- designed to remain as or become a dwelling or number of dwellings after the reconstruction or alteration; or which
- intended for use for a 'relevant residential or charitable purpose' after the reconstruction or alteration.

121.49 Broadly speaking, a listed building is one which is included in a statutory list of buildings of special architectural or historic interest compiled by the Secretary of State for National Heritage in England and by the Secretaries of State for Scotland, Wales and Northern Ireland. A scheduled monument must be one that is included in a statutory schedule of monuments of national importance.

121.50 Where all or part of a 'protected building' is intended solely for use for a relevant residential or relevant charitable purpose, a supply of approved alterations to the building (or part of it) cannot be treated as such unless it is made to the person who intends to use the building for such a purpose and, before the supply is made, that person has given the supplier an appropriate certificate to that effect.

Substantial reconstructions

121.51 The sale of a long lease by a person 'substantially reconstructing' a 'protected building' is also zero-rated. The definition of 'protected building' covered in 121.48 above also applies for the purposes of this relief. A protected building is not regarded as 'substantially reconstructed' unless at least one of the following conditions is satisfied when the reconstruction is completed:

- at least 60% of the cost of the works carried out to effect the purported substantial reconstruction would, if carried out by a taxable person, be zero rated as attributable to approved alterations; and
- the reconstructed building incorporates no more of the original building than the external walls together with other external features of architectural or historic interest.

121.52 It should be appreciated that these reliefs are narrowly drawn and professional advice must be taken by a charity wishing to come within these provisions. Further details on these provisions are contained in Customs and Excise Notice 708 'Buildings and Construction'. The relevant certificates are also reproduced in this Notice.

Do-it-yourself construction — *VATA 1994 s 35*

121.53 A person (including a charity) carrying out certain works which are lawful and otherwise than in the course or furtherance of any business may claim a refund of VAT charged to him on the supply of any goods (and not services) used by him for the purposes of the works. The works covered by *s 35* are:

- the construction of a building designed as a dwelling or number of dwellings;
- the construction of a building for use solely for a relevant residential purpose or relevant charitable purpose (referred to as 'qualifying buildings'— see 121.27 above);
- a residential conversion, i.e. the conversion of a 'non-residential' building or the non-residential part of a building into either a building designed as a dwelling or number of dwellings or a building intended for use solely for a relevant residential purpose.

121.54 Projects must involve the construction of a new self-contained building which is to be used for specified activities. The construction of a building by a charity intended for use as a communal residential building, benefiting either the aged, sick, disabled, needy or young people, or for the social, cultural or artistic benefit of the community in general would qualify. There must be a self-help element in the total project but what constitutes a self-help element often requires careful discussion with the local VAT office.

121.55 A building intended for use by a charity for non-business purposes or constructed by a charity and intended for use as a village, community, church or similar hall providing social or recreational facilities for the good of the local community would also qualify.

121.56 Relief is available for materials, builders' hardware, sanitary wear and other articles ordinarily installed by builders as fixtures. Examples of the kind of goods covered are published by Customs in Notice 719. Refunds can be claimed on the building materials which would be zero-rated when supplied with zero-rated work but not on those which would be standard rated. Thus carpets and built in appliances such as cookers etc. are not eligible for refund. The intention of *s 35* is that a refund is available if the supply of the relevant materials would have been zero-rated had the project been constructed by a contract builder. In relation to qualifying buildings, goods relating to other works on the site such as paths, patios, drives, car parks, boundary walls and fences will also qualify provided that they are built at the same time.

121.57 Charities cannot claim for refunds on conversions unless the conversion creates non-business residential accommodation. Where it does, then VAT recovery can be obtained on both the goods and sub-contractor services associated with the conversion, other than services of professionals such as architects. A charity carrying out a conversion in the course or furtherance of a business will not qualify for a refund under the DIY scheme (see 121.53 above). However, the Commissioners will consider refunds on an extra-statutory basis.

121.58 Housing associations are regarded as being in business and cannot use the scheme.

121.59 Further details of the scheme may be found in Customs and Excise Notice 719 'VAT refunds for do-it-yourself builders and converters'.

Drugs, medicines, aids for the handicapped: *Group 12*

Reliefs for charities looking after the handicapped

121.60 Various items in this group zero-rate the supply to a charity making available to handicapped persons by sale or otherwise, for domestic or their personal use, of the following supplies.

- Medical or surgical appliances designed solely for the relief of a severe abnormality or severe injury. Also, certain other goods designed for invalids and handicapped persons including motor vehicles designed or adapted for the disabled, lifts, hoists, special beds etc.
- Services of adapting goods to suit a handicapped person's condition and subsequent repair and maintenance of the goods.
- Services of constructing ramps and widening doorways to facilitate access by a handicapped person.
- The provision, extension or adaptation of a washroom or lavatory for use by handicapped persons.
- Services necessarily performed in the installation of a lift for use by handicapped persons in a residential or day care centre.
- The supply to a charity for making available to a handicapped person, of an alarm system which will enable him to alert directly a specified person or control centre.
- The supply of services by a control centre in responding to calls from an alarm as specified above.

121.61 The goods and services above can only be zero-rated if the charity gives the supplier a certified declaration which the supplier keeps for production to Customs and Excise if requested. Without such a declaration, the supplier becomes liable for VAT.

121.62 Further description and explanation of these various statutory reliefs are included in Customs and Excise Notice 701/7/94 'VAT reliefs for people with disabilities'.

Talking books for the blind and handicapped and wireless sets for the blind: *Group 4*

121.63 'Talking books' for the blind and severely handicapped when supplied to the Royal National Institute for the Blind, the National Listening Library and other similar charities are zero-rated. Included is certain apparatus and tapes designed or specifically adapted for such use and non-specialist sound recording equipment. Also zero-rated are wireless receiving sets and non-specialist sound recording equipment supplied to a charity for free loan to the blind. Further details of the relief are contained in the Customs and Excise Notice 701/1/95 'Charities'.

Books, etc.: *Group 3*

121.64 This zero-rating group allows a charity to buy publications, books, leaflets etc. on a zero-rated basis. It also enables aspects of charity's supplies to be zero-rated e.g. the quarterly magazine supplied as part of a membership package. It is thus a very useful relief, particularly when used in conjunction with the zero-rating for advertisements.

Transport: *Group 8*

121.65 This is a broad general zero-rating provision for the commercial transportation of passengers. It also affords some specific reliefs from VAT for the supply to a charity providing rescue and assistance at sea (e.g. the RNLI) of lifeboats and associated equipment, together with their repair and maintenance. It also allows zero rating for slipways for handling of lifeboats.

Index

Index

Index

Index